Where Were We?

Other Works of Interest from St. Augustine's Press

Joseph Pearce, *Beauteous Truth: Faith, Reason, Literature and Culture*

James V. Schall, S.J., *The Regensburg Lecture*

James V. Schall, S.J., *Modern Age*

James V. Schall, S.J., *The Classical Moment*

James V. Schall, S.J., *The Sum Total of Human Happiness*

James V. Schall, S.J., *Remembering Belloc*

Marc D. Guerra, ed., *Jerusalem, Athens, and Rome:*
Essays in Honor of James V. Schall, S.J.

Kenneth Baker, S.J., *Jesus Christ – True God and True Man*

Ernest Fortin, A.A., *Christianity and Philosophical Culture*
in the Fifth Century

Servais Pinckaers, O.P., Morality: *The Catholic View*

Rémi Brague, *On the God of the Christians (and on one or two others)*

Richard Peddicord, O.P., *The Sacred Monster of Thomism:*
An Introduction to the Life and Legacy of Garrigou-Lagrange, O.P.

Josef Pieper and Heinz Raskop, *What Catholics Believe*

Josef Pieper, *Happiness and Contemplation*

Peter Geach, *God and the Soul*

Gabriel Marcel, *Man against Mass Society*

Dietrich von Hildebrand, *The Heart*

Robert Hugh Benson, *Lord of the World*

Peter Kreeft, *The Philosophy of Jesus*

Peter Kreeft, *Jesus-Shock*

Philippe Bénéton, *The Kingdom Sufferth Violence:*
The Machiavelli / Erasmus / More Correspondence

H.S. Gerdil, *The Anti-Emile: Reflections on the Theory and Practice*
of Education against the Principles of Rousseau

Where Were We?

The Conversation Continues

Frederic Raphael and Joseph Epstein

ST. AUGUSTINE'S PRESS
South Bend, Indiana

Manufactured in the United States of America.

1 2 3 4 5 6   23 22 21 20 19 18 17

Library of Congress Cataloging in Publication Data
Raphael, Frederic, 1931-
Where were we?: the conversation continues /
Frederic Raphael and Joseph Epstein.
pages cm
ISBN 978-1-58731-934-1 (hardback)
1. Raphael, Frederic, 1931—Correspondence.
2. Epstein, Joseph, 1937—Correspondence.
3. Electronic mail messages. I. Epstein, Joseph, 1937—II. Title.
PR6068.A6Z48 2015
823'.914—dc23
[B]   2015032127

∞ The paper used in this publication meets the minimum requirements of the American National Standard for Information Sciences - Permanence of Paper for Printed Materials, ANSI Z39.48-1984.

St. Augustine's Press
www.staugustine.net

I am delighted to think that if posterity takes any interest in us the tale will everywhere be told of the harmony, frankness, and loyalty of our . . . relationship. It will seem both rare and remarkable that two men of much the same age and position, and both enjoying a certain amount of literary reputation . . . should have encouraged each other's literary work.

Pliny the Younger to Tacitus

January 1, 2014
Dear Freddie,

Let *Where Were We?,* your title for our second volume of electronic correspondence, begin on this, the first day of the new year. We ended our first volume in 2009, which means that five years have gone by with the usual swoosh. As one grows older, the length of the minutes, hours, days, weeks, and months remains much the same; it's only the decades that seem to whiz by.

During these past five years, we still have yet to meet or to speak to each other over the phone. You have produced two books (your Josephus volume and *Ticks and Crosses,* the sixth volume of your journal entries) and I have done the same (a book on Gossip and a collection of essays). We have continued to send brief e-mails to each other, commenting on the passing scene, and sending along our various literary scribbles. Our friendship has, if anything, strengthened, or so I feel.

Vain in every other authorly way, I have never, somehow, been able to pester my various publishers about the commercial fate of my books. Instead I have always awaited my royalty—more usually peasantry—statements. So even today I don't know if our first volume of electronic correspondence, *Distant Intimacy*, sold in respectable numbers or not. The review press, which I don't think we need dwell on, was less than ecstatic, to put it gently. English reviews in prominent places tended to be crushing, with a nice aroma of envy and resentment clinging to what they, the reviewers, wrote, though Richard Davenport-Hines in the *Spectator* wrote generously about the book as did Robert Low, and a few others. In America the book tended to be overlooked, and went unreviewed in the *New York Times*, the *New York Review of Books*, and other prominent places. We've both had a handful of good letters and e-mails from readers, both friends and strangers, which has been a source of gratification. Nice to have both swell reviews and appreciative comments from sophisticated readers, but if I had to have one over the other, I should prefer the latter. Enough, though, of grapes, both sweet and sour. I don't wish to linger on what I think unjust reviews, for I have no desire to be diagnosed with Irish Alzheimer's, a condition in which one is said to have forgot everything but one's grudges. Irish Alzheimer's is of course to be distinguished from Jewish Alzheimer's where you remember everything but the people who have been kind to you.

Since last we corresponded regularly, the most momentous event in the quiet lives we live in Evanston is our acquiring a cat, a three-month-old, small-headed Calico named Hermione (after Miss Gingold). This cat will soon be three years old, and has provided us with much pleasure of a calming kind. She turns out to be highly social, and most evenings sits with us—more specifically, she sits in Barbara's lap—as we watch episodes from *A Touch of Frost*, DVD movies, and other television fare. This elegant creature brings much comfort (whatever happened to the once faddish term "creature-comforts?"), and no trouble whatsoever. Barbara, as Director of Feline Food Services, feeds her, and I, as Director of Streets and Sanitation, clean her litter box. (As you will note, we go in for fancy titles chez Epstein.) Since she is a house, or rather an apartment cat, Hermione knows no world outside our six-room, sixth-floor apartment; nor does she have any congress with her species, which is a touch sad. On the other hand, living with us she is guaranteed food, safety, and a longer life than if allowed to roam free. I not infrequently think, with the most mixed of feelings, that she is likely to outlive us, or, as the English say, or at least used to say, to see us out.

The chief thing I recall from J. F. Ackerley's *My Dog Tulip* is his remarking that, after years of homosexual cruising, often with bruising after-effects, he acquired Tulip, his Alsatian bitch-hound, who gave him what he claimed to be searching for from all the rough-trade characters he had picked up—namely, uncritical adoration. Hermione does not offer adoration, of any sort, critical or uncritical. Dogs tend to suck up, cats to tell you to bugger off. I wonder if the difference between people who favor dogs and those who favor cats isn't that the former wish to be adored and the latter recognize that adoration isn't in reality available?

I suspect that Mme B and you keep no livestock. This suspicion is based on the fact that you move between France and England with side trips to Greece and other mildly exotic places. You are a few years older than I but I believe I precede you on the march into old age. The first reason for this is you continue to have energy for travel, whereas I now look upon all travel as a form of mild but genuine torture. I have no interest in going anywhere, and will travel only if paid a preposterous fee to do so, and nobody, I'm not disappointed to report, is offering me such fees.

A further stride into old age is that I have decided no longer to give talks or lectures or appear on television or radio. The chief reason I have done so in the past has been to flog books, though I don't think my flogging made much difference. I now see no point in doing more of it; there's nothing in it for me in the way of glory, profit, or edification. Let other morons do it. This moron prefers to stay out of the dim limelight offered to those of us of the scribbling trade.

As for that trade, I'm pleased to report that it continues, with editors offering me books to descant upon and for the most part accepting the stories I send them. Just now I owe pieces on Erich Auerbach, Lord Charnwood's biography of Abraham Lincoln, and the Diaries of George F. Kennan. I am also to do an essay on Big D, not Dallas but Death, with Victor Brombert's recent book *Musing on Mortality* as the occasion, or excuse. All this comes under two headings: 1. Keeping busy, and 2. Continuing to get my education in public.

I write "keeping busy," but in fact I think of myself as a slothful fellow. My form of sloth entails doing lots of things that enable me to avoid the thing I should be doing. The thing I have been avoiding doing just now is the book I am supposed to be writing on the elusive subject of Charm. I have roughly half of it—some forty-odd thousand words—written. Yet halfway out to sea, I feel intellectually wobbly and rather lost generally. I am too far out to turn back, but am at that stage where I wish I hadn't set out in the first place. Who needs this book? I ask myself. Who above all needs me to write it? This would be immensely depressing if something similar hadn't occurred in almost every other book on a single topic that I have written in the past.

Reading as we both know is much to be preferred to writing. I have been reading Dante, in the Laurence Binyon translation, at the rate of a canto a day—a canto a day keeps the Italians, dare I say dagos, away. I'm also working my way through Erich Auerbach's *Mimesis*, which as you know is a work of impressive erudition. Not, as the dopes today say, "a real page-turner" or a "terrific read," but a work worthy of its difficulty.

Two days ago I finished *The Diary of Noel Coward*, which is filled with good things. I don't think we've ever mentioned Noel Coward, but I admire him a lot. He was a craftsman, and never had any doubt that he was put on earth to entertain in the most charming ways he could devise. He was excellent at sniffing out false gods in the theatre, and has properly rough things to say in his diary about Brecht, Arthur Miller, Beckett, Edward Albee, Harold Pinter, John Osborne, Arnold Wesker, and other would-be salvationists of our poor souls. I have been driving around Chicago in recent days listening to him sing his songs on my car CD player, and marvel how clever the best of them are: "Uncle Harry," "Mrs. Worthington," "I Wonder What Happened to Him," "Don't Let's Be Beastly to the Hun," "There Are Bad Times Just Around the Corner," and many more. He wrote popular songs without condescension of any kind. He had the absolute minimum of formal education, yet read with penetration and taught himself foreign languages. As a homosexual, he never played the victim. He knew the limitations of his talent and was not easily conned about it or much else. He gave much pleasure, as writer and performer and friend. He is my candidate for the most charming man of the twentieth century.

Yesterday the biography of your daughter Sarah arrived here. I've barely glimpsed the prose, but I was enraptured by the illustrations. As a visual artist, she was excellent in many different styles and manners. I cannot wait to show it to my granddaughter Annabelle, who is herself a painter and illustrator, as a stellar example of the fact that not all contemporary art need be junky.

Best, Joe

London S.W.7. 2.1.2014.
Dear Joe,

I suspect that the pleasure which we take in our correspondence is more irritating to our critics than our alleged erudition. Let us go on then, you and I, with our faces turned to the future, however brief the actuaries might assume it to be, in my case especially. I shall proceed somewhat in the spirit of Louis B. Mayer, who once advised an MGM producer engorged with rage at what someone had done to him (as opposed to the reverse, which never keeps anyone hot under the choler) that he should "do what I always do: turn the other cheek." "Really, L.B.?" "Sure. Turn the other cheek . . . and bide your time."

I will let one example stand for the cases when I ignore L.B.M.'s advice and take prompt epistolary offence. One D.J. Taylor decided, from way back, to constitute himself the gadfly, bugbear or rug-rat who finds a way of getting his gums into my work whenever he can work it. Since he is at once in evidence everywhere in the literary prints and without any discernible personality or wit, one senses the ambition of someone who has decided that if he can see his own name often enough it will signify that he exists. How come he was sanctioned by our good friend Robert Messenger to break our bones in the *Wall Street Journal?* I imagine that he solicited the gig; those not likely to be first choices tend to get to be good at making calls. My response to the initialed gentleman was as follows:

Dear Mr. Taylor,

You are quite wrong, for motives I shall not attempt to divine, about my propensity for writing angry or reproachful letters to other writers or kindred tradespeople. During almost sixty years as an author, I should be surprised to learn that I had done so, on an average, more than 1.74 times a year. I rather wish I had done it more often, in view of how many shits, false reputations, self-important pundits and other fat fish there are in the little English pond in which you like to dangle your worm. I am, in truth, a timid soul and lack Joe Epstein's happy pugnacity. That he makes me a little braver is, no doubt, one of the reasons that I like him. Our correspondence is not "factitious"; we have been writing to each other for more than ten years and the suggestion that we go public, if the letters merited it, came only after that. The Coetzee/thingummy number to which you allude was of a quite different order.

As for Roy Fuller, he began our brief correspondence (about forty years ago), if I remember rightly, by objecting to my review of a bad novel of his. My reply may or may not have been a "rigmarole," but it requires no remarkable wit to guess that the egregious Anthony Powell (who wrote more wearisomely pretentious prose, especially in his autobiographies, than anyone ever allows) said about me what he thought would please Mr. Fuller to hear about an arriviste of dubious provenance (Powell married a duke's daughter, I think, and so upped himself in his own estimation). It would be nice to pretend not to guess why you should choose to retrieve the rigmarole remark from some dusty heap, but I suspect I know very well: to attack me puts you in solid, as H. Bogart said in *The Maltese Falcon,* with the London in-group who are easiest defined as those who think that Schlink's *The Reader* is a fine piece of work. Other definitions are available.

Oh, it has come back to me! Roy Fuller had, I recall, with effort, used the word "micturate" in prose narrative and I found that absurd. Is it not? Such people, you may agree, if it doesn't endanger your standing, should piss off, even if they do combine the profession of letters with that of soliciting. As for saying that I dislike literary critics, can it be that you suppose yourself to be one? Otherwise you fabricate a foolishness. I do not despise them (I recur regularly to Kenneth Burke and René Girard); I do despise some reviewers, especially those who can't stick to the subject in hand and pursue vendettas in the pretense that their target has provoked widespread dislike and disgust by his reckless conduct.

Literary critics can be tiresome but they are not the same brand of people as the *partouzes littéraires* who fill the pages with their verbiage. I happen to be reading Sainte-Beuve (I hope that's all right with you) from whom, I realize, Proust learned enough, in terms of prose style, to be impelled to put him to the sword to avoid acknowledging his influence. Sainte-Beuve's essay on Molière alone shows how wrong Proust was to accuse him of insisting on matching a man's fictions against his life. Your review of Joe Epstein's and my volume suggests that Kraus and BHL are arcane characters; but are they? Or are you afraid that your readers may think so? As for talking about Josephus, I was writing a book about his life and work that took me more than two years to research and write. Imagine being so flash as to mention it to a friend!

You describe me as a "novelist and screenwriter." It requires little wit to hear the implied sneer. In truth, I am happy to stand on that little platform in the stream, but I have also written at least a dozen books of short stories, biography, essays, translation and allied merchandise, including five (soon to be six) volumes of extracts from my notebooks.

I do hope your imminent novel gets the reviews it deserves.

You may be utterly amazed to hear that I never heard back from him. He is probably taking L. B. Mayer's advice. I have not seen a single review, laudatory or just, of his latest fictional number, which seems, from the blurb, to have taken its inspiration from two loud sources, *Fatherland,* a what-if novel by Robert Harris, and *The Plot Against America,* Philip Roth's forty-third best recovery of *temps perdus.*

Your christening of your new feline friend "Hermione" precipitated an immediate attack of Madaleinitis, aka Proustipox, of which the symptoms include a recall, in protracted sentences, of some long-lost incident which brings in its train a host of revenants. The first paying job I had in the spring of 1955, after returning to England from a long continental trip, the fruit of a "studentship" from Cambridge, during which I wrote my first novel, was as a scriptwriter for a radio show starring, yes, now we're getting to it, Hermione Gingold. As an undergraduate, I had written skits, as they were called, for the Cambridge University Footlights, in those days an all-male, often camp, association of would be smart-asses. In 1954, our show—*Out of the Blue*—was brought to London, thanks mainly to the astute ambitions of the President of the Club, Leslie Bricusse. Jonathan Miller was our star, but I too twinkled somewhat (not least when impersonating Graham Greene). We were hot tickets for three weeks, during which we were feted by Ken Tynan and some of us became confident that we had already as good as rounded the corner to success.

I went along, but with reservations. While eager to go where the applause came loudest and fastest, I was set on the idea of being a novelist, alone (with Beetle), misunderstood and unalloyed by mercenary ambitions. On the other hand . . . we had no money. So, I was very happy when a BBC producer recruited me to supply weekly material for La Gingold. She was a somewhat rugged old mistress of the kind of clever comedy featured in "intimate review," a now extinct art-form of which Beatrice Lillie was another held-over mythical figure from pre-war theatre. Leslie Bricusse was in Bea's West End show, performing allegedly amusing monologues (which he and I had written) while she repaired her make-up and alcohol intake, and had made the first famous entries in his now bulging address book.

I concocted comic material for Hermione in tandem with my friend Tony Becher (later a Professor of Education). He came down from Cambridge, where he worked at the University Press, for the weekend, during which we devised household hints for Aunt Hermione's advice to young brides. Tony returned on Sunday afternoon and I typed out, revised, and again typed out our smart little squibs. I recall that I delivered the first set to Hermione's rather grand flat in Capeners Close and went home to our basement apartment on— or rather under—Chelsea Embankment (in the same block, though scarcely on the same level, as George Weidenfeld) and waited by the FLAxman-numbered telephone for her comments. The first words from the famous deep voice were, "I've read the script, darling, and it's all WRONG!" It was too. But we did improve with time and succeeded, at least once, in "corpsing" Hermione, who got the giggles while live on mike. It was hard to believe that she had been the love for whom Eric Maschwitz wrote "These Foolish Things," but she was, she was. Someone once sent me the words of the dirty version, but I can't find them and cannot remember who it was. Pass the Madeleines.

Tout a toi, Freddie.

Wednesday, January 8, 2014
Dear Freddie,

I never met Hermione Gingold but did see her once on stage, in a road company version of *A Little Night Music*. Jean Simmons had the female lead in the part of Desiree, but Gingold came near to stealing the show. Even now I can hear her, in the half-talky manner the Italians call *parlando*, do the song "Liaisons": "At the palace of the Duke of Ferrara,/ Who was prematurely deaf but a dear/At the palace of the Duke of Ferrara/I acquired some position plus a tiny Titian . . ." She was a knockout.

A Little Night Music was of course written, words and music, by Stephen Sondheim, now I suppose the doyen of American, and thereby probably world, musical theatre. This past week I watched on the cable channel HBO a ninety-minute documentary on Sondheim, who is eighty-three, that consisted chiefly of interviews with him at various times in his life. This gave one the opportunity of watching him go from a sleekly handsome young man to a solemnly bearded fat one. Sondheim hit the success gong early, having written the lyrics for Leonard Bernstein's *West Side Story* when he was twenty-six. Two years later he wrote the lyrics for *Gypsy*, music by Jule Styne. When he went off on his own, writing lyrics and music both, his successes were less commercially spectacular, but over a long career he has won all the prizes, Oscars and Tonys and Grammys and Pulitzers ("Gee, Dad, I'd rather it had been a Wurlitzer") something called the Laurence Olivier Award, everything but the Ben and Bessie Nourishkeit Medal for long-distance spitting. A pretty good run, I'd say, but has it made him happy? You guessed her, Chester, not quite, not really.

Sondheim writes often brilliant but somehow not memorable songs. The one exception is "Send in the Clowns," which is both brilliant and memorable. I have not seen all his shows, but my sense is that most do not quite satisfy. This has been my experience with those I have seen. I have heard old-line theater people say that he ruined American musical theater by bringing seriousness to it, and there may well be something to this. Seriousness is not what musicals are, or need to be, about. One doesn't go there to hear a disquisition about modern art, which much of the second half of his *Sunday in the Park with George* is about.

In one of his interviews during the HBO documentary Sondheim takes time out to report what a monster his mother was. His explanation is that, when his father left his mother for another woman, she took it out on him, Stephen, always berating him, putting him down, doing her best to squash him. He claims in the documentary that, some twenty-five years ago, before she went into the hospital where she would die, she sent him a letter telling him that her only regret in life was having him for a son. He did not attend her funeral.

Now why do you suppose that Stephen Sondheim, a man who through his adult life has garnered status, prestige, vast sums of money, the love (in his case) of beautiful men, and other of the world's gifts, has to announce to the world that his mother was a perfect bitch? What might be his motive in doing so? Retroactive vengeance? Giving his life, as we should say today, a narrative? Pure release? What it gave me was the willies. You'll remember the willies, cousins to the creeps, that sad sinking feeling that one would rather be elsewhere while something shaming was going on.

How do you suppose it came about that confession is the reigning mode serious conversation in our day takes, especially among the celebrated? Has the therapeutic truly triumphed, as I fear it has? Why did Stephen Sondheim have to drag his vile mother in on an occasion devoted to honoring him? Why does nearly every movie star, successful author, famous athlete, have to have an abusive father, an alcoholic mother, a suicide brother, something wretched and heartbreaking in his or her past that will be useful for the talk shows? I once wrote an essay called "The Crime of a Happy Childhood," underscoring the point that a childhood without tyrannical, neurotic, drunken, or otherwise crushing parents is coming to seem, if not quite a crime, empty, at a minimum drab. Meanwhile I nominate Stephen Sondheim for a Siggy, in the category of unwanted confession in a public place. The Siggy should look handsome up there on the mantelpiece with his Oscars, Tonys, Emmys, and Grammys.

Do you, like me, read books in your bathroom? Someone once told me about an eighteenth-century wit, whose name I cannot recall, remarking to an unpleasant author who had sent him his book that he was reading it in his "necessary room" and had it before him now but it would soon be behind him. Not that I spend so much time in that room, but I have become adept at reading a paragraph or two there even while afoot—old guys, you will have noticed, make water slowly—and these paragraphs, along with the reading I get done while seated in the same room, do add up.

I not long ago read in the bathroom a collection of essays called *Churchill's Black Dog, Kafka's Mice and other essays* by a reasonable English shrink named Anthony Storr. My current bathroom book is something called *How Literature Saved My Life* by a man named David Shields, who is fifty-seven and lives in Seattle. I had read an earlier book of his called *Reality Hunger*, about which I remember nothing but his certainty that fiction was now dead, a closed shop, the shutters sealed, a sign on the door reading Lost Our Lease. The reason Senor Shields knew it was dead, even though he once wrote it, is that he can no longer read it. He can't read fiction but he can write the following hideous sentence, which I can copy out but not really read: "Metafiction's existential questions recontextualized in a minimalist, i.e. factual, mode." He nowadays goes in for what he calls literary *collage*, a blurring of distinctions between autobiography, essay, and anything else you happen to have around the house. His writing is best read in the bathroom.

The new book, *How Literature Saved My Life*—by the way, I don't believe it did—is more distressing, because it doesn't so much argue for the death of fiction but for that of serious reading of any length. Shields writes: "Books, if they want to survive, need to figure out how to coexist with contemporary culture and catalyze the same energies for literary purposes. The cut-to-the-quick quality: *this is how to write and read now, or at least this is the only way I can write and read now.*" Shields quotes his daughter remarking: "Honestly, most people my age don't have the attention span to sit down and watch a two-hour movie, let alone read a book."

The blog, the e–mail, the text, the tweet, these are the reigning literary forms of the day, Shields contends, and, objectionable as I find all of them, and as unbeguiling as I find him, I don't think he is entirely wrong. All these forms feature extreme concision and informality, and, literarily, no interest whatsoever in delicious foreplay. Wham, bam, thank you, Ma'am is the literary order of the day. All of course are lashed to wireless and digital technologies, those most mixed of mixed blessings. Something there is about these technologies that incites impatience. I note this in myself. If I read something on a computer that runs to, say, more than twenty paragraphs, I find myself beginning to skim, itching to scroll down to the end, to get to the actual bloody bottom line. The computer and its auxiliaries seem to have set in unstoppable motion an international plague of attention deficit disorder.

Another literary victim of the new technology is style. One notes the witty remark in an e–mail, text, or tweet, but one doesn't, in any of these forms, linger over the delights of style, of words beautifully conjoined and deployed. I am a great style snob. I can scarcely bear to read anything that isn't well written. I read, the way I prefer to eat and make love, slowly, which is another way of saying that I love reading. I'm not sure that the hippest of the young any longer do; reading is for them akin to what food is for someone whose taste buds have gone out, fuel—or to drop the gustatory analogy—information purely.

My point here is to wonder if you and I, who are pleased to read and write books and hope to do more of it before departing the planet, aren't the literary equivalents of blacksmiths during the early decades of the twentieth century, when the automobile was coming into vogue in a big-time way, banging away on our anvils.

I have long considered myself fortunate in having a fair number of people write to me to say that my various scribblings have given them pleasure. When I receive such letters—increasingly of course they are e-mails—I feel a little like Holden Caulfield's older brother Buddy, whom people wanted to call on the phone after reading his books, and a good feeling it is. Yet, with very few exceptions, the people who do write to me, my sense is, are in their fifties or older, many of them much older.

Ought we, my dear fellow blacksmith, to sell our anvils for scrap iron? Are we, I ask, in danger of becoming, if we are not there already, dinosaurs? Consider, please, these questions from a writer happy enough lolling about in the late Pleistocene but a bit concerned about whether the leaves and grass are likely to hold out much longer.

Tomorrow is my birthday. I shall be seventy-seven. Hip, hip, oy veh! Hip, hip, oy veh! Please send neither roses nor champagne. I prefer no fuss over this unmomentous occasion, and my only observation upon it is to note that, touch wood, I'm pleased to be here; here, of course, being above the ground.

Best, Joe

London S.W.7. 9.1.14.
Dear Joe,

There's always more to be said once a limit is reached. Allow me to recur to memories of Hermione Gingold. She had a catchphrase "Out of your tiny Japanese mind," which was found quite unexceptionable in 1955. One of our recording dates for the radio series fell on July 13, 1955. I recall it as cold and mid-wintery. We had assembled to be funny on the morning on which a certain Ruth Ellis, a "good-time girl" in the jargon of the good old days, was hanged by the neck until she was dead for the murder, as it was judged and juried to be, of her demon lover, a racing driver who did her wrong (and often). She was the last female to be hanged, in rubber knickers, in England. Today, we may be sure that there would have been properly furious, feminist demonstrations and, no doubt, a reprieve which would not at all be influenced by the fear of lost female votes and similar mundane considerations.

In old England, the company rehearsed my and other people's silly jokes while borne down, Hermione no less than anyone else, by the callous execution of a woman who had committed a *crime passionel* which, across the Channel, might have made her a heroine. But our business was to make 'em laugh, on the dot of 7.30 p.m., and that is what Hermione did, not least by the drollery of her voice and intonation. Would you bank on a writer (not me) getting a laugh out of the line, "Tea, Gregory? Milk?" She prolonged Gregory until it sounded quite droll, but the big laugh was procured by when she proposed "*Milluk?*"

My Footlights chum, Leslie Bricusse, had—fans will recall—become translated to the West End on the coat-tails of Beatrice Lillie. As a result, he was soon a backstage familiar of Noel Coward, with whom Bea had performed before The War. Coward had been an early subject of suburban awe and eager emulation on my part. My parents' library—transported from N.Y.C.—included his *Play Parade,* published handsomely by the Literary Guild. At the age of thirteen or so, I read *Private Lives, Design for Living* and *Cavalcade,* often alone, sometimes reading the dialogue aloud with Dorothy Tutin, the single child of our neighbors in the same block of flats. Dotty was pretty, had a voice like a belle and an excellent forehand. I shared my first cigarette with her in the toilet of the tennis courts. She became a professional actress and, in due time, a star of the National Theatre. She and I acted with a sophistication that, as they say, belied our years. Madly grown-up as long as Noel supplied the means, we relapsed into dated gaucherie when the words ran out. We made out like crazy on the page, but I never kissed her for real.

Coward, like Willie Maugham, was reviled both for his levity and for his advertised determination to "travel through life first-class." He made enemies of some people, in the case of the Sitwells by refusing to take their pretensions seriously, but he entertained millions, not only by the wit of his lyrics but also by the clipped manner in which he performed his own words. Although discreetly and unashamedly queer, as they used to say, he always claimed that his greatest love was Gertie Lawrence, with whom he appeared in *Private Lives.* I never saw them in it, but I did see Alan Rickman and some nice lady do the same piece, several years ago, and lack-luster work they made of it.

Noel was very practical with regard to his profession and despised the Method. The great art in theatrical performance was, he said, to remember your lines and not bump into the furniture. The Master's attitude to his own texts was, however, on one occasion at least, rather solemn, not to say pompous. In the early 1950s, la Gingold and the other Hermione (Baddeley), who were not the best of friends off the boards, got together in a little played Coward piece entitled *Fallen Angels*. Perhaps we laughed more un-inhibitedly in those days, but I recall literally falling off my seat when an early girl friend and I went to see the play. When she remained unamused, I dumped her. I took Beetle to the same show and she loved it.

Hermione, our Hermione yours and mine, played one of two wives who, in the golfing absence of their husbands, went on the town. The morning after, they were still in evening dress, drinking champagne. One of La Gingold's feet hurt, so she took off that high heeled shoe and put it to cool in the ice-bucket, after which she limped, with—believe me—hilarious effect, around the stage. When her husband came home, she declared how much she had missed him and what a quiet night she had had. He said, more or less, "Then why are you still in full evening dress?" Her next line was: "Yes." She made the monosyllable into rather a long declaration of rueful unapology. The house came down, yet again.

The two Hermiones were no longer young and made no bones about displaying their mature shamelessness. If, like the male partners in Doc Simon's *The Sunshine Boys*, they had come to detest each other offstage, they played together, *mano a mano*, with flyting verve. The production was a smash. Its success must have enriched the author, but Noel was not amused. He took offense at the outrageous mugging of the two clowning ladies and allowed his displeasure to be known in public. It is the only occasion I know of on which he failed to have a sense of humor. When challenged by some Australians in an elevator to "say something funny," he retorted, "Kangaroo." Worked for him.

My initiation in showbiz was due to Leslie Bricusse, who recruited me to supply the dialogue which would go between his words and music in what he had already planned to be a lifetime of musical comedy hits. Leslie had all the qualities I lacked when it came to advancing boldly in theatrical society. Like Agag, he trod delicately but with mounting purpose. The London West End theatre was dominated, in those days, by "Tennants," a producing company led by "Binkie" Beaumont. Although homosexuality was literally a crime, it was very much the rule among theatricals. Binkie's country retreat was known, among cognoscenti, as "Pinching Bums." It was said that after one weekend, he told a young actor, "You're no good in bed, you're no good on stage and you're no fucking good to me." Exit, unpursued by anyone.

Leslie was not of that persuasion, but he was amusing enough to be a sort of sexual *shabbos goy*, as our mutual friend Sholem Aleichem might say: he was good to have around the house, even if he declined to be dragged upstairs in male company. I earned a useful six pounds a week in royalties from the

Bea Lillie Show during its longish London run. Six pounds was then the basic wage of a working man; it paid the rent, with something to spare, on our basement flat on Chelsea Embankment, while I worked on my second novel.

When la Lillie and Leslie went on tour, the money stopped coming in, even though the show drew big provincial audiences. After I asked where my usual check was, I was advised to look at the contract which I had barely scanned when I signed it. Sure enough, sub-section (c) of the payment clause stipulated that I should receive payment "as long as the show is running *in the West End of London."* So there I was, until I wasn't. As lessons go, it was cheap at the price. I still can't be bothered to read contracts fatter than I am, but I have people who do. The most enduring compliment the world can offer a writer is that people still want to steal his words and the fruits thereof. Only the other day, I noticed that some scribe had lifted chunks of a review of mine in the *TLS*, cf. stealing the tips from a coffee shop counter.

Do I read books in "the bathroom"? Doesn't everyone? I define an intellectual as one who cannot go to the loo until he has found his glasses. You mention reading Anthony Storr's essays while installed. I knew him slightly when we were both members of a London club. He had a theory that the very English, but also universal, addiction to detective stories, even though the solutions nearly always disappoint, derives from the necessarily frustrated human desire to be a witness of, yes, the Primal Scene. We are said to have an insatiable wish to witness the mysterious moment of our own conception. Do you buy it? I am with Edmund Wilson in not giving a damn who killed Roger Ackroyd. I re-read the best Raymond Chandler, but P. D. James, a venerated and very longwinded thrillerene in these parts, is never going to toodle to the loo with me.

Diarists are ideal stoolies: but Ken Tynan, with all his English vices (self-admiration not the least) has, after many a summer, worn thin. Duff Cooper is both grand and shameless; Greville, a nineteenth-century political hanger-on, perennially juicy. My most recent quick perusal guy is Greville's degenerate modern analogue, a Gordon Brown courtier called MacBride, who writes execrably and whose revelations show only what a fall there has been since Dizzy dazzled the Brits. I can tolerate a man behaving like a boor, but not his writing like one too. I think it was big Benjamin who made the remark you cited re "I have your book before me . . . etc." Certainly, he told some postulant who had sent him his latest volume, "I shall waste no time in reading it." My kind of Jewboy.

Tout a toi, Freddie.

January 16, 2014
Dear Freddie,

Thanks for the lowdown on Binkie Beaumont, who dances in and out of *The Noel Coward Diaries* with great frequency. (How do you suppose he acquired the nickname Binkie?) The only two people who come in for more frequent mention are Cole Leslie and Graham Payn, who were homosexual and both of whom lived with Coward for long stretches of time. Unlike W. H. Auden or Somerset Maugham, who had gay partners who put them through all the hoops in hell, Noel Coward seemed in good control of his sexual life. He never seemed, *à la* Auden and Maugham, hostage to his sexuality. As Churchill was said to have declared about alcohol, so Coward with sex: he got more out of it than it got out of him, or so one gathers from the diaries and letters.

I owe you thanks for arranging to have Fiona Hardcastle at the *Daily Telegraph* invite me to write a 1,400-word piece on the wintery weather that is being blamed on the polar vortex (a term that to me sounds like something to do with the female reproductive anatomy). She asked me for the piece on a Thursday, and needed it by Friday. I didn't answer straightaway, being a bit uncertain if I had 1,400 words on the weather in me and if so was uncertain I could disgorge them in so brief a time. So I wrote the piece first, and only then told Ms. Hardcastle that I would be pleased to write it, and then sent it off to her. Not having heard from me straightaway, the *Daily Telegraph* commissioned another writer, a slightly lower than middlebrow woman novelist, to write the piece. The novelist apparently did write the piece, though Ms. Hardcastle, who was exuberantly generous about my scribble, informed me that my piece had "trounced [Madame X] in levels of majesty" and that the paper would be running mine. About "levels of majesty" I do not know, but the news that my scribble would not go to waste was most pleasing.

What pleased me quite as much was my ability to turn out the 1,400 words in roughly four hours. I do not normally think of myself as, in Max Beerbohm's phrase, "a dash-off writer." Yet to write reasonably well and to do so quickly suggests that I may be beginning to know something about scribbling. Stand back, working press, that's me.

Because of time restrictions the *Daily Telegraph* sent no galleys, so I was unable to make some of those small changes that we boys down in *belles-lettres* love to do. The editing of the piece was light, but I was sorry to see a neologism of mine fall under the editing blade. ("Yours, sir," said Henry James to Bruce Richmond, then the editor of the *TLS*, "is the butcher's trade.") The neologism was the word *punafor*, which I invented to describe the use of a metaphor that is simultaneously an unconscious pun. An example, from the *Daily Telegraph* piece, was my description of learning about the results of cold weather on the homeless as "chilling." I should be delighted to see the word punafor catch on, which thus far, alas, it hasn't. A neologism of mine that has caught on, at least a bit, is the word *virtucrat*, which describes someone whose politics chiefly reinforce his sense of his own high virtue. Two other neologisms of mine that have not made the cut are "youth drag" to describe anyone who dresses much younger than his or her true age; and "Bayarrea" to designate too much talk about how elegant is life in the San Francisco Bay Area. The notion of inventing a useful word, and thereby depositing something new into the bank of language from which one has made such large withdrawals, is one that I much like.

This past week I finished reading *Thomas Mann's Diaries, 1918–1939*. Less the extensive scholarly apparatus, the book runs to 343 small-print large pages. Mann's is not among the world's great diaries, being much too given up to the mundanities of their author's life: what he ate, what he wore, what he smoked, the music he listened to, the day's weather. His opinions of other writers he is reading are mentioned only in a glancing way. He finds Chekhov "pleasant, but really unsatisfactory and pointless." Kafka he finds "certainly unusual, but otherwise rather tedious." Balzac and Tolstoy get higher marks. Ideas, mentioned in passing, go undeveloped. "Absolutely necessary that German literature needs the Jews" is an entry one should have liked to have enlarged upon; so, too: "The Jews are always more acute where truth is concerned; their brains are not befogged with myth." (Mann was of course married to a Jew, a Pringsheim.) His distaste for his four-years-older brother Heinrich's heavy-breathing writing comes up a fair amount. His own homosexual longings are mentioned in passing.

The main interest in the Mann diaries is political. He writes that "one is a fool to take politics seriously." But the problem is that politics took him seriously, ending by the Nazis making it impossible for him to live in Germany. He had Hitler's number straightaway, and he didn't let many chances pass to proclaim him for the lout that he was. "I have in the end stood up like a man," he tells himself. By 1939, Mann is 64 and sufficiently famous to be a touch surprised when people do not know who he is.

The *Diaries* make Thomas Mann seem deeply humorless, and one has to remember that he wrote *Confessions of Felix Krull*, one of the genuinely amusing books of the past century. Mann may well have been the twentieth century's greatest writer. He wrote four great novels: *Buddenbrooks, The Magic Mountain, Joseph and His Brothers,* and *Felix Krull*—and not many others can touch that for high-quality production. He took on the great themes, and worked them through in their full complexity. I find myself admiring him greatly without being especially nuts about him. His Germanness is probably what puts me off. I read the other day that when Thackeray met Goethe he compared the meeting to a visit to the dentist. Kafka, Robert Musil, Robert Walser, Thomas Bernhard, W. G. Sebald—so many dentists in German-language literature.

You are more reticent about your health than I. But, then, I suspect you are in better health—and therefore shape—than I. Even though you are a few years older, I know you swim fairly regularly and are still thwacking tennis balls around. My two sports are walking, at a gentle clip, and wielding a television remote. I also happen to be a Jewish Scientist, which is like a Christian Scientist, but without the religion part, which means I prefer to keep my distance from physicians.

Four or so months ago I found I could no longer do so when I began to have stomach troubles. The troubles brought on the usual intestinal inconveniences, which I prefer not to detail—Gibbon on this subject says of the always busy Julian the Apostate that "he yielded only with reluctance to the indispensable call of nature"—along with my having lost five or so pounds. I waited a few months hoping all this would go away, and when it didn't I finally took myself to what in the United States these days is called my primary physician. One's primary physician is a fellow who sits behind his computer and directs one to various medical specialists. Before seeing my primary physician, however, I had to take blood tests. I generally assume that my blood tests will reveal both shoes to have fallen—that I have three different cancers, the beginning of multiple sclerosis, and insipient signs of Alzheimer's. What my blood tests this time out did reveal was that I was low in calcium and B-12, signs that I wasn't properly absorbing the nutriment in my food. My primary-care physician suggested I go on a non-fat diet and made an appointment for me with a gastroenterologist.

The gastroenterologist, a American-Chinese in his early thirties, and hence a man likely to see me out, deduced that I have a mildish case of something called Celiac Disease, an auto-immune disorder of the small intestine that, like your Mum and Dad in Philip Larkin's poem, "fuck you up." The gastroenterologist put me on a gluten-free diet, which I have been on for the past month or so, and my return to my old mediocre state of health has been just about complete.

Gluten, as you may already know, is a protein found in wheat, rye, and barley, which means that I cannot eat bread, pastry, pasta, or anything else made with flour. Fortunately, gluten-free diets are rather faddish just now—Novak Djokovic is on one, and claims it does wonders for his game—so upscale supermarkets currently carry gluten-free breads, pastas, cookies, and more. The only slightly complicating factor is dining in restaurants, where I can order neither sandwiches nor pasta. But as deprivations go, not being able to eat foods containing gluten is very low on the scale.

Certainly Celiac is much to be preferred over those three cancers, multiple sclerosis, and Alzheimer's mentioned earlier. So I have been sighted going about our apartment singing—after the song "Born Free"—"Gluten free, as free as a gluten." I mention this only so that you will appreciate the kind of low humor my wife has to put up with. Talk about long-suffering wives, Barbara, I do believe, qualifies.

Finally, in the great Offers I Can Refuse Department, an east-Indian attorney, a woman practicing law in Florida, writes to tell me that she is much impressed by my piece on the demise of the WASPs in America. What I wrote reminded her of the WASPs, or the equivalent thereof, in India. She suggests that she and I write "about the WASPs of India. I can introduce you to the industrialist wasps as well as to the royal WASPs in Jaipur and Calcutta and ask them about their families and make inquiries as to how to get the new moneyed class to engage in civic activities!" I wrote back to tell her I was honored to have been asked but that my (gluten-free) plate was rather full just now and so would have to pass on her enticing invitation. Does it never cease raining in the old Republic of Letters?

Best, Joe

17.1.14. London S.W.7.
Dear Joe,

Boasts against the current is my preferred reading of (poor) Scott Fitzgerald's view of our process through life. Age offers frail opportunities for self-satisfaction, but there they are, as in: today Beetle and I have been married for 59 years, a lease of happiness for which there is no jeweled celebratory emblem. Neither of us is in a wheelchair or requires extra-mural care or fails frequently to forget the number we first thought of. I can even remember the names of people I was at school with, too many of them, and also the name of the man I had lunch with yesterday, Robert Skidelsky, economist and biographer (very, very good on Keynes, rather too encomiastic on Oswald Mosley) and a descendant, by a collateral route, of the great "Skid" Simon, alias Skidelsky, bridge player *sans pareil* and writer of not entirely forgotten entertainments such as *Don't, Mr. Disraeli* and *A Bullet in the Ballet*, which contained a footnote on the victim "Don't feel too sorry for him, his Petrushka was lousy." He could even make bridge books hilarious.

Robert and I have become friends in old age (though younger than I, he is a Lord, which confers illustrious wrinkles), but get along very well, since I always have questions for him (to which I am likely to supply answers as well, unless he gets in there smartly). We lunched in a big, brassy brasserie; chromatic is truer, but "brassy" is more fun; style is a great liar, and that's the kind of man I am, sometimes. Another of my professorial friends, the philosopher/biographer Ray Monk, said, tartly but not without justice, that he liked to say things that were true whereas I liked to say things that were brilliant. And? The trouble with what's "true," especially in biography, is that it is rarely, i.e., never, the whole truth. It is a petty amusement of mine to make note of things which I know about people which, nice or not, would certainly escape even the most diligent researcher into dusty boxes and antique memories: not all the whitewash of Arabia can efface my memory of Harold Pinter saying, in the *après-guerre* of 1967, "we (sic) gave the Arabs a bloody nose." I have more in the locker.

Skidelsky and I were in a booth, lapped in words and with *antipasti*, including "parmesan custard" ahead of us, when a white-haired, busy woman came over and reminded me who she was: the wife of a man who was the "floor-manager," and a very good one, on a TV series I wrote nearly forty years ago. I scrambled all cerebral forces to recapture her name,"Christine!" and, with antique courtesy indistinguishable from both vanity and irony, I stood up and embraced her and then introduced her to my host. She did not quite throw herself into a Persian grovel but her excitement was, as Ian McEwan would have observed, palpable; she did indeed palp him, nicely, and then delivered broadsides of effusiveness. By the time she had vented all of her superlative ammunition she had pretty well forgotten who I was. I remarked, while on the *escalier* where so much belated *esprit* is spilt, that Coleridge complained, while composing *Kubla*

Khan, about being interrupted by the person from Porlock—gratefully, as Stevie Smith had the wit to guess—but that he was at least spared the Porlock person's wife.

Robert and I then resumed discussing the similarities between philosophy and economics. Both are, I claimed, eliminatory: "discounting" a common specialty. Yes, it was that kind of a lunch, folks. The revenge of the *prox.acc.* is now and again to provoke that look in professorial eyes which betokens an uneasy fear that someone not of their fraternity, and wholly without post-graduate honors, just might have thought of something which they might/should have. I relish instruction, but such moments are as delicious as parmesan custard. The difficulty of those eminent persons who have what the cant calls "fields" is that they are so busy sowing and reaping that there is almost always something, just over the fence, which flowers unseen by eyes that have to be fixed on the relevant (not to mention the main chance, fat commissions, TV series and ever higher tables). The reward of not quite flying high enough is that one is the *rara avis* who tries harder. I am, in truth, more eager to amuse and dazzle than to disconcert or distress my—as our old friend H.J. would say—interlocutor. I confess, however, that you have to locute good to inter me.

Robert gave me a lift in the black sliding-doored vehicle which came to take him back to the House of Lords where he was due to put ermined endorsement on some government measure which would have gone through whether he and his lordly colleagues ayed or neighed. Being appointed fifth wheel on a fancy bandwagon is an honor few refuse. To avoid taking R.S. out of his noble course, I asked the driver to drop me a mile or two from our flat in South Kensington. It was raining very hard and I had no umbrella. Beetle hates walking in the rain, but I like the facile stoicism of allowing it to bounce on my now polished dome and walking past those huddled in doorways with just a spot of vintage British-style phlegm. I recall (do I ever, these days!) that it was said of the Tommies, in the Battle of the Somme in 1916, that they advanced through German fire so intense that they went forward bravely but with the sidelong slant typical of those walking, chins tucked down, against a wind-blown deluge.

One of the many forms of good fortune I have enjoyed is never to have been under fire nor even aware of the danger of instant death. Since we last corresponded, however, I have been mown down by a bicyclist in the Gloucester Road when I was crossing the tarmac of No-Person's Land, between appropriate markers and with the lights in my favor. The road was wide and there was no other traffic when I was struck and felled, with no

Robert Capa available to capture the moment for posterity, by a woman who had acres of spaces into which to pedal but contrived to ride smack into me. I fell like an old flower, weed even, reaped in a second, and lay there, stunned and unfractured, while she kept saying how sorry she was. Advised by Whiplash Willie (played by Walter Matthau in one of Billy Wilder's less triumphant numbers), I should have insisted on police and ambulance attention, demanded name and address and had my solicitor demand recompense for my writer's block and kindred direct consequences of the lady's want of due care and attention (blindness would not work as a defense). As it was, she said "sorry" so often that, in an unscripted outburst, I invited her to piss off, which she did, with—as the best-sellers have it—alacrity.

I enjoyed the brief are-you-sure-you're-all-right attentions of a young female passer-by to whom, as I stumbled realistically to the curb before the torrent of truly dangerous traffic was unleashed in our direction, I confessed that I was. A classier kind of accident victim might, as Frank Harris put it in his once forbidden *Life and Loves,* have "improved the occasion" by suggesting that the young person accompany me to a nearby hostelry, but I did no such thing and no biographer, however diligent, will find evidence to the contrary. I don't deny that I have taken a great deal of chaste pleasure in the embraces of actresses, of all ages, but I have never crossed lines, even when there weren't any.

You will remember that Dr. Johnson decided to refrain from visiting Garrick backstage because the sight of the actor-manager's young women, *en déshabillé,* "excited [his] amorous propensities." I am rather *pudique* in that regard. Invited to ride home with one particularly beautiful young leading lady, after she had shed all her clothes, very willingly, for a scene in which she lounged, in accordance with my script, like Velasquez's Rokeby Venus, I kissed her nicely and closed her cab door for her, from the outside. I had no sense of lost opportunity whatever. Unlike not a few in the Biz, I do not fear the constabulary knock, although England is being gripped, not to say groped, by a series of savory scandals in which TV personalities, several in their whitened eighties, are accused of taking sexual advantage, often [decades ago], of innocent young persons who frequented the TV studios in which culturally important programs of popular music were being confected. Legendary Names are being dragged through the streets on hurdles and crucified on billbawds.

The Monster who triggered the present surge of virtuous recrimination was one whose fame almost certainly did not cross the Atlantic (I hereby vow never again to refer to it as "the Pond"), Jimmy Savile by name. Even in the days of his first flushness, when he introduced *Top of the Pops,* a 1960s program which you need never have seen in order to turn it off, said Savile shone, as Sir Walter Raleigh said of the court (and the church), "like rotten wood." He made outrageousness his business suit: he wore lurid costumes, smoked big, big cigars, had dyed hair, in various hues, and—with a kind of horrible genius—tricked himself into the exception who deserved to ply the rule. The one-off of all time, he raised large sums for charity and even larger ones for himself and he could, because so revenue-rich for himself and others, do no wrong, even when he did. "Fame is the spurt" might serve as a working title for his story. Of course, none of the now penitent, once young girls who donned their mini-skirts ("pussy-pelmets" as the argot had it) and twisted and shouted on cue are held, even in retrospect, to have been, so to say, tickled by the attentions forced upon them.

For old movie-hands, now is the season of armchair discontent when we are deluged with DVDs despatched to Academy Members in the hustled hope that we will put crosses in the boxes which will lead to Oscar-winning speeches of wince-inducing gratitude. Last night, in the course of this honorus jury service, we watched a movie called "August: Osage County." Why do modern movies so often have unmemorable titles? For the same reason that you don't call hamburgers by their first names: all product, in the arts not least, tends—as we used to say in philosophy—to the fast food model. Everything must be tasty but apt for prompt excretion from memory's digestive tract.

August whatsit had a vintage performance from Our Great Living Actress, *La* Streep; it was superbly observed, every t dotted, every eye crossed. Julia Roberts renounced make-up to prove just what a trouperene she was and left her perfumed charm in the dressing room. If the setting was Oklahoma, it was without a beautiful morning or a serene evening, although the director could not resist shots of the sun sinking in luminous glory behind the long, flat horizon. This was American drama without humor and Hollywood cinema without images, but not entirely without voice-over, even though the movie was avowedly stagey. When the three sisters (geddit?) and their mother and aunt and who all else sat down to table, family secrets *façon* Tenn Williams were the *plat du jour.* Twisting and shouting proved that all the assembled thesps were at the tops of their voices.

Can that really be the time?

Tout à toi, Freddie.

January 23, 2014
Dear Freddie,

In the small-world department, I had a telephone conversation with your friend Robert Skidelsky's son William. Our subject was Roger Federer, upon whom William S. is attempting to write a book. He called thinking me, wrongly, an expert on the subject. We had a pleasant half-hour or so chat—on his dime—on things Federeristic. My main contribution was to inform him that I thought Roger Federer's only physical flaw was a perhaps slightly too-wide nose.

I didn't know that Robert Skidelsky was in the House of Lords. In this age of unlordly Englishmen the House of Lords must be a highly comic institution. I have always liked a remark made by a friend of Conrad Black upon his ascending to the House of Lords, that it would give Conrad, the son of a rich man, a chance at last to meet some ordinary people.

That yours and Robert Skidelsky's is a late-life friendship reminds me that three days ago I attended the funeral, at a nearby and elegant Catholic Church called St. Gertrude's, of a near-friendship made late in life of a nice man named Jon Anderson. Jon was a Canadian, fairly well born in Montreal, who went into newspaper journalism in that city. At an early age, he became head of *Time Magazine*'s Montreal bureau, after which he was sent to work in the magazine's Chicago bureau, with the promise, never made good upon, that he would next be sent to work in its Paris bureau. Jon quit *Time*, and worked for the two Chicago dailies.

The main event of Jon's life was that he married a woman named Abra Prentice, a great-granddaughter of the first John D. Rockefeller. The marriage lasted, I believe, roughly a decade, and produced three children. The couple lived in the best apartment in Chicago, the penthouse of the building on East Lake Shore Drive next to the Drake Hotel. I recall a story about their having a grand piano delivered to the apartment by helicopter. Jon not long ago told me that the marriage was a decent one until his wife's mother died, leaving her another thirty-five million, which put the kibosh on the marriage. The problem with marrying a rich woman is that, though the pay is good, the hours tend to be way too long. The couple had a pre-nuptial agreement, and Jon, I gather, left the marriage with only what he brought to it: tall good looks and a sweet temperament.

The funeral was a Latinless mass, conducted by a likeable Mickano (as I have taken to calling the Irish) priest who had married Jon and his second wife, a black journalist who worked with Jon on the *Chicago Tribune*. Roughly four hundred people attended, most of whom took communion toward the end of the service. (I know a woman who worked in the bakery of our local supermarket who loved everything politically incorrect and otherwise *outré*, who once called out to me, "Joe, you must try one of our new diet communion wafers. They're called, 'I can't believe it's not Jesus.'") The great moment in the funeral service for me was when Jon's second wife—I don't know if the Rockefeller wife was in attendance—sang, at adagio tempo and in a high voice, "This Little Light of Mine."

Less than a year ago Jon sent me an e-mail suggesting we meet in the late afternoon for coffee at a shop in his neighborhood. I was once on a local radio show with him on which we were flogging our books, mine a book on snobbery, his a collection of his newspaper columns. I don't believe he turned out another book. The ambition gene was not strong in Jon, which may account for the lovely absence of malice in him, even toward his ex-wife, of whom, in my presence, he never spoke damningly. From me he wanted only an audience for some of his best anecdotes, which usually weren't even about himself. He had rather a winning selflessness. So much was this so that he never mentioned having multiple myeloma, which was what killed him at age seventy-eight.

I admire anyone who, knowing he is about to depart the planet, can keep his illness to himself. Christopher Hitchens got a (not very good) book out of his death by cancer. Clive James, though well enough to continue giving interviews and to translate Dante, tends in these interviews to make it known that, owing to various diseases, he is not long for this world. Last week I read a memoir by a man named Daniel Menaker, a former editor at the *New Yorker* and editor-in-chief at Random House, who begins by telling his readers that he has lung cancer, as of the moment in remission, and ends on the same dour note. The problem in publicly announcing one's forthcoming death is one of plotting; in narrative foreshadowing must be done with a light touch. People cannot bear an interminable moribundity. After their reading of one's forthcoming death in an interview or article or book, readers become impatient for the promised event to take place. Best, I should say, not to bring the subject up and to depart the premises, going, against the boorish Dylan Thomas's advice, gently—and quietly—into that good night.

On the subject of impatience, that shiny new appliance, the Internet, has added greatly to the intensity with which we feel this emotion. The

Internet has speeded so many things up, and I wonder if, on balance, it is a good thing. Last week I sent you an e-mail and when I didn't get an answer for thirty or so hours, I was concerned that something had happened to you or someone in your family, so quick are you normally in responding to my e-mails.

On the literary front, in the good/bad old days, one sent off an essay or review or short story to a magazine and assumed at least a three-week wait for a decision: one week for it to get there, another week or so for it to be read, and a third week for the letter of response from the editor to arrive. If the manuscript was sent abroad, add a further two weeks for the wait. Nowadays, if I sent a manuscript off to an editor and do not hear from him or her after three days, I worry: 1) that it has been lost in cyber-space, 2) that he or she doesn't want it and is nervous about telling me that it didn't work out; or 3) that the editor was fired, is ill, or by now deceased. I have a few editors who respond to things I send them within the hour; and I adore them for their promptness, even when the news is bad. Promptness may be the greatest gift an editor can bestow upon an author. And yet. . . and yet . . .

The Internet is also responsible for a serious reduction of decorum in public life. I have fifteen or sixteen million Google hits, and hits, quite literally, many of them turn out to be. On the Internet I have been called, among other animadversions, an idiot, a fool, a loudmouth, a JAP (standing in my case for Jewish American Prick), and—the law of contradictions having long ago been suspended—both a homophobe and an old poof. A week or so ago, I received an e-mail with a @harvard.edu return address from a twenty-eight-year-old stranger that begins by addressing me as Joe, and then informs me that something I have recently written in the *Wall Street Journal* is "bunk." In a few following paragraphs this fellow jauntily demonstrates how much smarter, sounder, more sensible he is than I, and ends by writing: "Your piece represents a dangerously misleading way of thinking and talking. Give it up." I wrote back: "Forgive me if I do not answer your e-mail point for point, but it is so self-righteously unpleasant that I don't feel I owe you a detailed response," and I concluded, "May you, as the Jews said about the Tsar, live and be well, but not too close to me."

Which leads me to the third point in my tirade—rare to find enumerated points in a tirade, don't you think?—and this is that there is something about the Internet that does not encourage careful reading. I sometimes read the comments that follow a piece of mine that has appeared on the Internet and am stunned by how badly I have been misread. This gets back to my point about the Internet as an encouragement to impatience. Any composition that appears on a computer (iPad, smartphone) screen that runs to more than fifteen paragraphs somehow carries an enticement to scroll down, to get to the bottom, the actual bottom line, literally and figuratively, of what the fellow who wrote it means, goddammit anyhow. I feel this impatience myself, in a way I never do with magazines and books in my hands. No John Crowe Ransoms, no F. R. Leavises, no close readers on the Internet. Finally, I think that somehow style is not greatly valued on the Internet, style in the sense of well-chosen words nicely deployed in carefully constructed sentences. People on the Internet are too hot for information, the true gen, the straight poop, the real lowdown, to slow down to note a piquant phrase, an interesting syntactical turn, a lilting understatement.

This past week we watched on television the most recent movie version of *Anna Karenina*. Directed by Joe Wright, it has Keira Knightley and Jude Law in leading roles. I expected it to be shoddy and found it excellent. On screen it is staged as an operetta but without singing, though it is elegantly choreographed. Of the various previous movie versions of the novel I have seen—the Greta Garbo, the Vivien Leigh—this is perhaps the only movie version that gives the character Karenin a fair shake in recognizing him as a victim and less a self-righteous than a truly righteous man. Naturally it leaves out a great deal—impossible to get the details of a 600-page novel into a two-hour movie—but it is the only film version I can recall that tells the story of Levin and Kitty. If you've not yet seen it, I recommend it to you and Mme R. with my usual half-your-money-back guarantee. (What I do with the other half of the money is my business.)

The movie is one in which the credits are shown only at the film's conclusion, so it was only then that I learned that the screenplay was written by Tom Stoppard, which I suspect has a lot to do with its quality. Tom Stoppard is the only living playwright whose plays I care to attend. Not only is his intellect of a greater range and higher caliber than all other contemporary playwrights, but unlike almost every other playwright about whom I know he writes without approved ideological backing, baseless anger, resentment, delight at long last at being out of the closet. He is a talented man, and I admire him.

I neglected to salute you and Mme R. on your 59th wedding anniversary. From the promontory of this grand occasion, it begins to look as if this marriage will last.

Best, Joe

24.1.14. London S.W.7.
Dear Joe,

My friend Richard Davenport-Hines, a writer in the trim, stylish tradition of Harold Nicolson (whose *Some People* is a vivid prosopography of his life and times) has co-edited, and just sent to me, a generous clutch of Trevor-Roper's letters. It comes in the wake of his co-adjutor Adam Sisman's biography of my quondam external examiner (in the Classical Sixth at Charterhouse). H. T.-R. is renowned for being a historian who began several *magna opera* but brought none to term. Accused, not unjustly, of expending himself on an excess of ephemera, he was a dab hand at piquing the overblown: Lawrence Stone, A. L. Rowse and, not least, the complacent Arnold Toynbee, whose dreadnaught *Study of History* T.-R. torpedoed amidships in *Encounter*. That excellent mag, sponsored by the CIA in its halcyon days, was the finest use of a few bucks from Uncle Sam's treasure chest that anyone ever slipped into a brown envelope. It says something for the intellectual climate of the 1950s, before global moral downsizing, that Spender, Koestler and Co., *Encounter's* front and center men, were mortified, and vilified, because they had taken Uncle Sam's pennies and ran a literary forum that fought a good fight against Stalinism and its fellow-travailers.

Trevor-Roper has never, to my knowledge, been nicknamed Trevor-Ropey, but daunting scholar as he might be, he committed memorable gaffes, usually through biting bullet-points rather too quickly, especially when lucrative *Sunday Times* issues were involved. The public wreck of his reputation came when he gave his imprimatur to the crudely forged *Hitler Diaries,* although—he claimed later—little alarm bells were already ringing even as he did so. Earlier, however, he had scrambled to second Mark Lane's *Rush to Judgment* re the Warren Report re JFK's assassination. His superficial reading of the evidence laid him open to damaging pecks from Warden Sparrow of All Souls' College, the mecca of post-graduate Oxonian *morgue.*

T.-R.'s letters are written in a register which flatters his correspondents by presuming that they will pick up his references, not least in Homeric Greek, without needing a pony. Whoever pulls rank also promotes his reader. When we were fellow-guests at the floating—on a smart canal—retirement party of the literary editor of *The Sunday Times,* I asked Hughie (as I never dreamed of addressing him) about a Carthusian friend of mine called Robin Jordan to whom he had awarded a scholarship at Christ Church. He told me that my friend's selection was one of the greatest mistakes of his life: Robin had consorted with theatricals instead of getting on with his French and German. One can conclude that, in his own estimation, T.-R. had rarely pitched into any very deep bunker; except Hitler's, about whose last days he wrote the best-seller which led him to prefer the pleasures of being pelted with *Louis d'Or* rather than to honor Clio's call to greatness.

After Gibbon finished *The Decline and Fall of the Roman Empire,* you can't blame him for resting his case; but his output was exceeded by William Hickling Prescott, for whose Gibbonian stylishness I have a recurrent *faible.* Mr. P. went from his *History of Ferdinand and Isabella* (with size fourteen footnotes), in three voluminous volumes, to *The Conquest of Mexico* (three more). After polishing off Pizarro's gilded conquest of Peru, in two, he lit out for a lazybones trip to England. Oxford gave him a degree and Queen Victoria perhaps a smile (Prince Albert hadn't died yet) and then, before H.J. could say "*à l'oeuvre, mon bon,*" Prescott hastened back to his *History of the Reign of Philip the Second* (not many laughs there). Failing sight prevented him from completing more than three of the projected four volumes, before he died, aged sixty-three, in 1859. My sources suggest that he might have finished his literary Escorial palace, had he not broken off to do an appendix for his master, William Robertson's *History of the Reign of the Emperor Charles the Fifth.* Prescott's graciousness under pressure is rarely matched in our age of unacknowledged copy, a pittance-for-your-pains executives and the-Jim-Campbells-are-coming satirical journocrats.

Are there now any scribes as prolific as Prescott? Lift-with-both-hands books do get printed, but not a few—for instance, Orlando Figes's *The Whisperers*—are botoxed with archival material (not unusually such stuffing is culled by graduate student galley-slaves). To which of today's plethora of historians does a man turn for pleasure, rather than for downloaded info-infill? Niall Ferguson is the Henry Ford of his set, but where is the Macaulay—*pace* T. S. Eliot, Thomas Babington knew how to mint a phrase, whether or not it would wing true—or the Steven Runciman of today? Stephen of Blois remains in the ranks of my dusty mental *personae* thanks only to Runciman's delicious account of how he missed a key battle in the First Crusade and, like Henry IV's *brave Crillon,* for all his previous and subsequent exploits, never quite made up for it.

In a show of British mock-modesty, T.-R. proposed Runciman for the Regius Professorship of History which, he had already been tipped off, was coming to himself. Old Ropey deserved to be tagged with what Tacitus said about the Emperor Galba: *capax imperii* (capable of assuming the purple, which T.-R. did only in patches) *nisi imperasset* (if only he hadn't done it). Galba made a mess of being empurpled, largely because he tried to wish old republican virtues on his soldiers, instead of lashing out the sesterces to bribe them to stay on his side rather than connive with his usurping murderer. Whatever the old saw whines, style does not at all have to be the man. One can be quite a shit—A. J. P. Taylor is a contender—and still write like an angel; and be angelic without one's words having Homeric wings (Elie Wiesel?).

A question re style: in the case of three possibilities, Messrs (a), (b) and (c), say, what would you think of a writer, allegedly pearly beyond price, who indicated that he was opting for (c) by referring to him as "the latter"? Am I too fine for the modern world if I remark that "the last" is preferable, not to say *de rigueur*? Daniel Mendelsohn, on whose Cavafy's translations I have been working, and working, for the *TLS*'s shilling, chooses "the latter" (the duet of Keeley and Sherrard) of a trio of his predecessors on whom to bestow the compliment of "being instrumental in persuading a new and younger audience that Cavafy's 'unmistakable tone of voice,' as Auden memorably put it, was worth listening to." Unless a few ducats had been tucked in your top pocket, would you accept the author of that sentence as a guide to the Alexandrian's *erga*? How does "being instrumental in persuading" differ from "persuading" and who knows whether K. & S.'s readers were "younger"? Like, than whom? And while ". . . little children died in the streets" is certainly memorable, is Auden's phrase *supra* the kind of *mot* you'd want as your epitaph?

Mendelsohn's go-to-guy reputation in New York has gone to his shaven head, which I am damned if I will hoop with a halo. One of the drab consolations of being over eighty is the knowledge that reticence will get you nowhere; outspokenness *non plus,* but as final gasps go, why not? I have more than enough projects to keep me writing till the Great Examiner calls time. I shall not refuse any plausible commission, but I have an emulous colleagiality with the amateur who demands no shilling before entrenching himself in his library. My friend Mark Glanville, whom you entertained when he was in Chicago, writes that a local scholar in Puglia "has just told me he's completed his history of Oria from Minoan times to the present day, in 760 pages." What a moment when some village Casaubon comes to term and gives birth to what has gestated for so long and—hats off—for which no hot hands are waiting!

Oria is a small hill town, where—though this is not its only claim to attention—Beetle and I climbed, one Sunday morning, to the tiny ghetto, adjacent to the town-crowning church, where a community of Sephardim once eked out barely tolerated lives. The patchwork magic of Puglia—adjacent to Old Calabria where Norman Douglas did his famous rambling—owes much to its mongrel population. Mark, who read Greats at Oxford, has found his happy home in a *masseria* down there. Trained as an opera singer, he has taught himself to play the folk instruments which accompany the "Griko" words which, now rubbed by time and peasant usage, were imported from Byzantium. Mark hopes to be commissioned to do a book about the region. If he can match N. Douglas on Calabria or Claudio Magris on the Danube (and trump Neal Ascherson on the Black Sea), it will be quite something.

Trevor-Roper was a pronounced fan of Douglas (as against the "mean" D. H. Lawrence). One of the things they had in common—on the side—was a penchant for travels in the company of comely young men, not to say, which is true in Norman Douglas's case, young boys. His unacknowledged companion in Old Calabria was twelve years old. T.-R. was, no doubt, chaste in his admiration of, for instance, the undergraduate Alan Clark, later a famous cocksman, historian, and admirer of the *Wehrmacht* and pretty much all it did for the late lamented A. H. Esquire. Master Clark thought he was good at French because, while he was one of Mrs. Thatcher's minor ministers, someone at the Quai d'Orsay—home (*La Maison* indeed) of France's duplicitous *corps diplomatique*—told him so, with the result that his diaries are *bourrés* (what else?) with egregious errors which Clark was too smug and his portly editor, always seen in public in an M.C.C. tie, too obsequious and up on his luck to verify.

Christopher Hitchens, neither your favorite deutero-Orwell nor mine, despite the advertised bravery of his exit—was it Left or was it Right?—from his publicized life, was guilty of similar haughty misusage. Such people lack the wit or the modesty to solicit the marginal advice which wise friends are so often willing to supply. Paul Cartledge recently saved me from saying that E. R. Dodds's *The Greeks and the Irrational* was published in 1950, rather than in 1951. Literary chess is a game of perpetual checking. While my old friend Peter Green is translating the *Iliad* in his late eighties, with the intention of proceeding to the much more (in his opinion) "grown-up" *Odyssey,* that best of scholars always finds time, as Prescott did, and you do, to mark a friend's copy with a gentle red pencil.

Tout à toi, Freddie.

January 28, 2014
Dear Freddie,

Oxford University Press sent me a copy of *One Hundred Letters from Hugh Trevor-Roper*. Owing to the press of other work, I haven't yet begun reading it. In good vain writerly style, though, I did check the index to see if my name appears, which—what a sad setback!—it does not. (Your really vain writer checks the index for his name in books written long before he was born and undergoes a similar disappointment. Didn't they see me coming?) I never knew Trevor-Roper, but, having long admired his prose, I was able to persuade him to write a few things for *The American Scholar* during my days as that magazine's editor. He also wrote me a pleasing letter about an essay I wrote on Edward Shils not long after Edward's death.

Edward and Trevor-Roper were in league at Peterhouse against Maurice Cowling and a clutch of mad-dog conservatives who wished to return the college to its proud place in the seventeenth century. Edward would on occasion show me amusing letters, composed in longhand, from Trevor-Roper, documents of purest animadversion, studded with pledges to "crush the snakes at Peterhouse crawling at my feet."

I've written about the Adam Sissman biography of Trevor-Roper, but I'd quite forgot that HT-R aligned himself with Mark Lane during the Kennedy assassination conspiracy-fest. My guess is that his mistake about the false Hitler diaries was in good part owing to his need for money. His mid-life marriage to the high-maintenance Xandra, seven years older than he and daughter of Field Marshall Haig, put him on a track much more skittish than most academics—excluding perhaps Isaiah Berlin, who married the wealthy de Gunzburg woman—could easily manage.

Trevor-Roper's generation of English historians was a remarkable one, including, along with him, A. J. P. Taylor, E. H. Carr, C. V. Wedgwood, and Lewis Namier (the last, as you know, born a Polish Jew). They represent, even more I think than the analytical philosophers of the same generation, English intellectual life's last hurrah. That Trevor-Roper—Evelyn Waugh, in an act of de-hyphenation regularly addressed him as Roper—produced no single great book is a fate he shared with Arnaldo Momigliano, Isaiah Berlin, and Edward Shils. (I once saw a table of contents for a sociological *magnum opus* Edward never got round to writing; it ran to 250 pages, double-spaced, to be sure.) Perhaps all these men knew too much to succeed at the beblinkered concentration required to write a single great book.

I well remember Trevor-Roper's splendid attacks on Toynbee, Taylor, Carr, and Lawrence Stone. None of these historians ever quite recovered from them. He chose not to go after Namier, though in a letter to Bernard Berenson he wrote that Namier was "in my opinion, the greatest living historian writing in English," and then warns Berenson against allowing Namier to visit him, for "he is also without doubt, the greatest living bore. And for that distinction the competition, I'm afraid, is even hotter."

Encounter, in which I believe all Trevor-Roper's attacks appeared, was the best intellectual journal of my adult life. I was too young to read Cyril Connolly's *Horizon* (1940–49), its main competitor for this laurel, though I long afterward obtained a full run of the magazine, which I've since turned over to Robert Messenger. My guess is that Stephen Spender didn't have all that much to do with the day-to-day running of *Encounter* and that the presiding editorial genius was Irving Kristol, Spender's co-editor. Spender was useful chiefly for his social-intellectual connections. He has always seemed to me a man along for the ride. He later claimed not to know that the CIA was helping to finance *Encounter*, which is not easily believed. Frank Kermode, who took over the English co-editorship of the magazine, also bleated whiningly when the CIA funding of *Encounter* was revealed, picking up his skirts and nether garments, running from the room crying, "My integrity, my reputation, my good name!" Dante, you will recall, reserved a place in Limbo for those who refuse to take a stand, that vast multitude of the pusillanimous and the cowardly, who are forced to run noisily in circles while being bitten by insects; and there, surely, Kermode must through eternity reside. What I gather the CIA asked of the editors of *Encounter* was that, in a Cold War atmosphere, they hold their fire on criticism of the United States but otherwise publish whatever they wished. My only regret here is the CIA didn't underwrite the magazine even more handsomely.

I wrote for *Encounter* when Melvin Lasky was its editor, a bit after its glory days. I suppose if I had written for it earlier I would no longer look upon those either as the glory days. I find that I have only to publish in a magazine—the *New Yorker, Commentary,* the *TLS, Commentaire, Merkur*—to discover its prestige automatically diminished. The old Groucho standard is at play here: How good, after all, can a magazine be that would have me as a contributor?

At the end of this past year I wrote a check for $99 to renew my subscription to the *TLS*. I also subscribe to four or five other magazines, but I find the *TLS* the most indispensable of the journals of the current day. Only from it do I feel that I regularly continue partially to fill in the wide gaps in my knowledge. The contributors to its pages never talk down to me, nor do they seem merely good students grown older. Above all it is not a salvationist journal. I not long ago came upon the word "salvationist" to describe magazines used by Wolcott Gibbs, the long-deceased *New Yorker* writer, to describe *PM,* a New York leftist daily of the 1940s. Salvationist newspapers and magazines, be they of the left or the right, are out to save our souls; they have thick and uncrossable political lines. Their readers are the chorus to whom they preach. Their editors are Salvation Army officers without uniforms or the support of drums and bugles. That the *TLS* has no political line, that it continues to take serious things seriously, that it is still able to find people to write intelligently—and for lay readers intelligibly— on what might seem arcane subjects (a recent issue has a review of a book on the history of whistling) is what makes it in our day so extraordinary. I don't want to know how low is its circulation—my guess is that it falls between 25,000 and 30,000 subscribers—for, were I to find out, I would know how sadly small is the number of serious readers left in the Anglophone world.

Despite their decline in so many other ways, the English continue to perform well at intellectual journalism and television theatre. Chez Epstein we watch lots of English-made detective stories, *The Last Detective, Poirot, Miss Marple,* and, most recently *A Touch of Frost.* (Like you, I do not give a rat's rump who killed Roger Ackroyd, and do not read detective stories, though I don't mind watching them in movies or on television.) Do you know this last-named show, which I gather was a great hit in England? The eponymous (as we boys who write for the quarterlies like to say) hero, played superbly by an actor named David Jason, is Jack Frost, a late-middle-aged detective with a penchant for unhealthy food and a disorderly life who works for a public-relations-minded superior called Superintendent Mullet in a provincial town in Yorkshire called Denton. Some of the scripts were written by Malcolm Bradbury, a decent critic one of whose novels (*The History Man*) I read millennia ago. The stories are perfect in their way, obeying the first law of fiction: be unpredictable yet plausible. To give you some notion of the general tone of the series, in an episode we recently watched, Detective Inspector Frost is in a police lineup in which a good-looking woman is attempting to point out a man who has been impersonating him. She stops in front of Frost, and says that he resembles the impersonator a little, but the latter is better looking and dresses more smartly.

The one troubling aspect of English detective stories on television, though it is not a serious detraction from *A Touch of Frost*, is the violence, the lengthy displays of purplish corpses (often in autopsy settings), the lingering views of blood-soaked surgical operations. Barbara turns away at the spectacle; I look down at the book or magazine in my lap. (Riddle: What do you call a Jewish boy who cannot stand the sight of blood? Answer: A psychiatrist.) Is all this bloodiness meant to stand in for realism? Are there immensities of viewers who relish such displays of flesh tortured and destroyed? Do millions of middle-class people, English and American both, sitting primly in their living rooms, groove on it? What do you suppose all this gore means?

Which reminds me that the new received opinion—about to be stepped up to the august level of conventional wisdom—is that the best writing nowadays is being done for television. The idea here is that now that cable television has arrived, providing shows that, broken up into episodes, go on for six or eight hours—and, if successful, much longer—writers have room to stretch out, developing characters in nuanced ways, offering subtle twists in plot, even permitting amusing digressions. All this, the argument runs, all this freedom of a kind presumably not allowed poor movie scenarists, confined to their paltry two-hour scripts, gives television writers a crucial edge. Examples put forth on behalf of this argument are *The Sopranos, Wired, Deadwood, Boardwalk Empire, Breaking Bad*. Among these I've watched only *Boardwalk Empire* (from which I've dropped out, since the plot descended chiefly to fucking and shooting) and *The Sopranos*, which I found more amusing than moving. The best line in the thirty or forty hours of *The Sopranos*, surely, is given to the zonked out Tony Soprano, having nearly overdosed on anti-depressants and discovering his Mafia family fallen onto hard days, who exclaims, "Psychotherapy and cunnilingus got us into this."

This new bit of received opinion may be owing in good part to the fact—I believe it is a fact—that movies have been going through a long bad patch, so many of them presumably having been written for adolescent boys, who are said practically to take up residence in multiplex theatres, watching the same drivel over and over. I suspect that the money for writing for television is nowhere near so good as that writing for movies, which itself I'm told isn't as opulent as it once was, unless one is the chief honcho of a winning show, *a la* Dick Wolf, David Milch, or David Chase, in which case one becomes a simple zillionaire.

Returning to the *TLS,* I note that the man from clan Campbell has a note in the back of the January 17 issue on a forthcoming contest for the 2014

Hatchet Job of the Year Award. You are a candidate for your "mauling" (his word) of John Le Carre's *A Delicate Truth* and on the victim side of the ledger as the co-author of a tome yclept *A Distant Intimacy* hatcheted, not to say macheteed, by Craig Brown in the *Daily Mail*. You are thus in a unique position to decide, in this matter of hatchetry, whether it is better to give or to receive, though I am fairly certain I know your answer.

Best, Joe

London, S.W.7. 31.1.14.
Dear Joe,

What does the name Frank Harris mean to anyone these days? A shady editorial eminence in his *fin de siècle* heyday, he retained notoriety, at least until the 1950s, as the author of *My Life and Loves*, a scabrous autobrio, full of beans and bonks. Banned as obscene in old England, it was published, in three floppy volumes, printed on hairy grey paper, by some deutero-Girodias in Paris, that garlicky repository of un-English sports. In 1954, while on post-graduate travels funded by a studentship bequeathed to the management of my Cambridge college by a benign clergyman called Harper-Wood to encourage "creative writing," I purchased Harris's erotic *vade mecum*, for research purposes, and went with it back to the small hotel bedroom—Cyril Connolly's idea of an author's spiritual home, but never mine —in Juan-les-Pins. Its one window gave me an intermittently loud view of the main Marseille-Nice railway line. I averted regret at not having Beetle with me by beginning my first novel, on a marbled block of unlined very white paper. My hero, Frank Smith, was an English Johnny "Cry" Ray, whom I had seen and heard at the London Palladium, thanks to the spare complimentary ticket of the second-string drama critic of the *Daily Telegraph*, Guy Ramsey, an Oxford friend of my father's. Trip on any paving stone, nibble any *Madeleine* and the gush of *temps perdus* is hard to staunch.

It was said that Harris's franknesses owed as much to imagination as to active service of the ladies who, on the page at least, gave him so many openings. "Oh you little dear, you!" he would say before diving beneath the covers for lubricant preliminaries. Frank was a naughty worldling, but unlike his betters, he—alongside the gallant Reggie Turner—did a good deed in sticking by Oscar Wilde when the latter was defenestrated by smart

London. The English specialize in Rat Weeks, when they turn and rend the famous. R. Turner is remembered, by me at least, for saying "I don't know why people make so much fuss about first editions. It's my *second* editions that are rare." What does *"efsha"* mean and why did it come to mind?

Today's enlightened Britain has convinced itself that Wilde was ill-used in a way that can and must "never happen again." The cant says as much about anything likely to recur any minute. Arrested now, Oscar would almost certainly be treated with even more vindictive venom, orchestrated by high-minded journocrats, than in 1895 when he was sentenced to two years imprisonment. We may celebrate Gay Marriage, but pedophilia is regarded with greater horror today than when under-age rent boys were two-a-penny. Wilde's sentence was onerous with hard labor on the treadmill in Reading Gaol, but any twenty-first-century celebrity, convicted of paying underprivileged boys for pleasuring him, would be lucky to get away with double as long in chokey and, on his release, would find a righteous lynch-mob waiting with a rail to run him out of the neighborhood.

In Jolly Old today, three separate trials are going on of men who have been Household Showbiz Names. The charges—of assaulting or raping young women or under-age girls—mostly go back to the 1960s and 1970s. Not a few of the women who have now "come forward" to give evidence of how they were robbed of their innocence were teen-age fans of the then young actors or performers, two of the latter now in their early eighties, the other a stripling in his late sixties. All the accused are certain to be ruined, even if not convicted and, if they are, will be locked up for a long stretch, as the result of things done to girls whom they claim to know nothing about. But then, as we heard "Mandy Rice-Davis" say the other night in Andrew Lloyd-Webber's tune-free "musical" *Stephen Ward,* about a 1963 *cause célèbre,* "they would, wouldn't they?" Is it disgraceful to recall that one young female stripling of the period told me, in not particularly *sotto voce* Oz-speak, how she had five theatrical studs in a single week of the happy 1960s (and would have had added to her score, had she not had a bit of an off day on the Saturday)?

All this turning of old stones and exploring of overgrown avenues comes in the wake of a mega-major scandal, of which even the U.S. media may have caught the sour wind, concerning one Jimmy Savile, a man so odious at first sight, back in the 1960s, that it seemed that one could smell him through the TV. Nevertheless, for decades of high popularity, this grotesque, over-white "entertainer" fronted all manner of cue-applause type shows in which he arranged big-hearted treats for deprived and unloved kiddies. The least publicized of these chances of a lifetime was to be fondled, in greater or less depth, by Rolls-Royce-driving, Romeo y Julieta-smoking, lycra-upholstered "Jim."

Only after his death, by which time he had acquired a knighthood and adjacent honors, was it revealed that Savile had, from Dawn to dewy Eve, rummaged among handicapped and mentally disabled persons, often very young indeed, in order to sate his appetites with unresisting meat. He acted with impunity thanks to the indulgence of a BBC entourage whose salaries depended on his success and who, on that account, kept mum (and dad, no doubt, not to mention who all else). Now, like Oliver Cromwell's corpse when Charles II was restored to the throne, the scoundrel's reputation has been dug up and dragged around the streets on a hurdle.

And so back to Frank Harris who once boasted to the prelapsarian Oscar Wilde that he had been bidden to dine by yet another of *fin-de-siècle*'s titled hostesses. To which Wilde responded, "Yes, Frank you've been in all the great houses of London: *once!*" I still have *Life and Loves* on a high shelf alongside a copy, bought in New York, I think, of *My Secret Life* by "Alfred," a priapic Victorian gentleman whose erotic adventures and purchases he chronicled with some nice period detail. Literally twice over in the case of a comely prostitute who took him back to her rooms, put a match to a coal fire in the grate and, primed with a sovereign, rendered herself, as goggling Google would put it, "topless." She then confessed that it was her time of the month. Alfred says that the girl then stooped to conquer him in a gracious and satisfactory way.

In the ancient of days, when we were friends, Jonathan Miller suggested that we make a film based on Alfred's confessions. Jonathan assumed that said gent had time for nothing but eating, drinking and, as the patois used to have it, a spot of "how's your father?" I preferred to imagine that, to friends and colleagues, he was a man above suspicion, renowned for his terse chairmanship of worthy committees, social *disponibilité* and getting up when ladies came into the room. He could (and can) be seen as Mr. Hyde to William Gladstone's Dr. Jekyll. Mr. G. himself may well have had more to hide than toff-struck biographers—Roy Jenkins *supra pares*—have chosen to investigate. An addicted redeemer of fallen women, Gladstone would accost ladies of the night with salvationary injunctions when on the way home from Prime Ministering to see his dull, polyphiloprogenitive wife. Disraeli, who had, in his youth, swung both ways with shameless ostentation, returned directly to 10 Downing Street to find a hot meal prepared by the not very handsome Mary-Anne. He admitted that he had married for her money but told her that if he had to do it again, he would marry her for love. She was scatty, but even Gladstone liked her.

Observing whores is no rare activity among authors: Dostoyevsky, Baudelaire, Flaubert were world-class spectators of women who offered *plaisirs tarifiés.* On a happy occasion when he passed *aux actes,* Big Gustave was infected venereally by that Egyptian *poule de luxe* who taught him a memorable thing or three. In the process of adding post-graduate cosmopolitan color to my palette, *moi aussi* did a Flaubert when the *trottoirs* of the now dismantled Parisian *Les Halles* were decorated with *putes de tout bord.* Like British tourists who read the London newspapers without detaching them from their foreign racks and divvying up, I gazed with interest at the erotic buffet which insular morals deterred me from sampling.

At the far end of the long gallery of my mind's eye, I can still see a French officer, in full fig, with *képi* and swagger stick, which he taps against his tall, brown boot, as he negotiates at length with a woman who looks to be worth every centime. Are today's porn-on-the-cob audiences delivered from hypocrisy, sore feet and what Rousseau called books to be read with one hand, by easy access to what remained at once delectable and invisible to me, Flaubert and, for egregious instance, Henry James, whom Max Beerbohm portrayed sniffing the shoes left for polishing in a hotel corridor in the hope of divining what went on behind the bedroom doors?

Among the films sent this year to every member of the Academy is *Blue is the Warmest Color*, winner of the Grand Prix at Cannes last year. It features a very long episode in bed in which two naked actresses, said to be "straight" off-screen, enact a woman-on-woman *passade* in which furtive imagination need play only a small part, even though what a character in last night's episode of TV's *Grey's Anatomy* was tricked into calling "Jenny Taylia" are not openly involved in the prizewinning four-hander. Yet the most piquant moment in the French movie was when the heroine (because a victim of hypocrisy and unlikely dialogue) was deceived by a fellow female student's kiss into supposing that it Meant Something and so discovered what she Really Was. That was indeed a (fully dressed) dramatic revelation, whereas giving us what we were presumed to have come for was like a treble scoop, with speckled topping, that disposed one not to, all right, come again.

I was about to tell you more about the star-pitted *trottoir* on which you have lingered but never got busy, viz. *le showbiz*. Time requires that the decline of Cinema, and its stars' rise to the stratosphere in *Gravity*, be a topic to which we—as academics say when they mean "I"—"will return in due course." Meantime, one more thing re friend Frank: Old Willie Maugham, whose house, in Harris style, I visited just once, told me that the rogue had written two or three surprisingly good short stories. "Indeed so good that p-p-people doubted whether he had written them himself." Never true of the Old Party's pieces.

Tout à toi, Freddie.

February 6, 2014
Dear Freddie,

All I can remember of Frank Harris's autobiography is the phrase "I lifted her skirts," or was it "I raised her skirts," which appeared with boring repetition. Harris was a small and ugly man, for whom many women of his day were apparently prepared to abandon their skirts. In Max Beerbohm's caricature of him Harris looks like nothing so much as a chesty duck sporting a Nietzschean mustache. Beerbohm claimed to take all of Harris's stories with "a stalactite of salt," and remarked of his prowess with women that "women like men to be confident, and Frank did not lack confidence."

Another homely man for whom women of the day seemed to develop a distinct roundness of the heels was H. G. Wells, one more less than obviously attractive man who also was richly confident. People reported an aphrodisiacal musk-like smell about Wells. Among his other achievements, Wells bestowed an illegitimate child on Rebecca West, a boy, Anthony West, who went on to loath his mother. Is there a book here, I wonder, on the subject of great homely seducers of the western world? If so, I feel relieved not to be writing it.

You speak of whores—of *putes de tout bord*, actually—and it reminds me that your own experience of them might have been more extensive had you remained to grow up in Chicago, the city of your birth, rather than in London, that of your youthful upbringing. Whore-mongering was part of the early education of boys of my generation in Chicago: not *poules de luxe* but *poules des pauvre*. Visiting if not frequenting whorehouses—more commonly called cathouses, never brothels or bordellos—was an initiation rite in my balmy (in every sense of the word) adolescence.

Five or six of us, in the cars of one or another of our parents, would drive out to the nearby working-class towns of Braidwood or Kankakee, Illinois, to such establishments. The cost in those days was $3 and $5 for what was known, in the state-of-the art term, as half-and-half. Something called "around the world," which was beyond my pocket and imaginings both, cost $10. An old joke I still enjoy has a young man walking up the stairs to a bordello who discovers his father descending those same stairs. "Dad, you, here?" he asks, in astonishment. "For three dollars," his father responds, "why should I disturb your mother."

Once inside the usually one-story motel-like buildings of these establishments, one chose a woman—most of them youngish—and went to her small room. I recall going off with a girl whose name, written on her mirror in lipstick in fancy cursive, was Rusty. There one was checked for venereal disease, handed over one's shekels, and was then instructed not to bother removing one's shirt or socks. Henry Ford, inventor of the assembly line, and Frederick Taylor, the industrial time-study man, had nothing on these girls. As for the sex itself, Edward Dahlberg, author of an autobiographical volume called *Because I Was Flesh*, once ranked the quickness of his own adolescent sex slightly above the flash-like arrival of sundown in Quito—a most accurate simile, I should say, judging by my own experience, of adolescent sex, not of the sunsets of Quito.

On other occasions, we picked up streetwalkers on the west and south sides of the city. The same fees, the same procedures, the same Quito-like alacrity prevailed. The only memorable adventure of this kind that sticks in my memory took place at the apartment of a woman named Iona Satterfield, alleged to have been the ex-wife of a light-heavyweight with a glass jaw named Bob Satterfield. Iona was what in the bad old days was called a mulatto—the approved word today of course is bi-racial—and most attractive, though I found her more than a touch less so when, washing up in her bathroom after my Quitoesque bonk, I discovered a burnt-spoon and syringe atop the toilet tank. Years later I saw her driving around Chicago in a maroon Lincoln convertible, top down. I hope she lived to a calm old age.

But enough of my mildly misspent youth on the streets of Chicago and its far banlieus. The main point is that owing to your parents removing you from Chicago to London you wound up at Charterhouse and I at Whorehouse.

Yesterday I finished a 3,200-word piece on Erich Auerbach, written for *The Weekly Standard*. The occasion for the piece is a recent translation of a dozen or so of Auerbach's essays called, with a Krautishly light touch, *Time, History, and Literature*. In preparation for the piece I also read Auerbach's book on Dante and I reread his masterwork *Mimesis*. I came away much impressed by *Mimesis* and in my piece called it the best work of literary scholarship-criticism published during the past century. (If you can think of a better, please do not hesitate to say so.)

German scholarship, when genuine, remains impressive. I rather doubt that the world will ever again see its like for pure density of erudition. In Erich Auerbach Germanic heaviness is nicely leavened by his Jewish *heimishness* and common sense. In the books of his that I read there is no element of intellectual display or heavy-breathing polemic, though I gather Auerbach and E. R. Curtius, rivalrous contemporaries, didn't think all that well of each other. Instead one gets a winning earnestness and the pleasure of watching a well-stocked mind with a critical edge at work.

Auerbach called himself a philologist, a word one doesn't hear much these days. The work of philology ranges widely, but what united the old-line philologists was their polyglottism. Auerbach walked the streets with eight languages in his head: Latin, Greek, German, French, Italian, English, Spanish, and Portuguese. In *Mimesis* he half apologizes for not taking up the subject of Russian realism in any extensive way because "this is impossible where one cannot read the works in their original language." For the philologists to have read a work in any but the language in which it was written is not quite, not really, to have read it at all. I won't say where this leaves me, who read Auerbach's *Mimesis* and other works I mentioned all in English translations.

I have also been reading Schopenhauer. "My nights were sour," Ira Gershwin wrote, "spent with Schopenhauer." I, unlike the poor fellow in the song, never read him at night, for he is too dark to read before sleep. Yet he is the only German metaphysician I can read without incurring migraine.

Schopenhauer, too, I read in translation, in which he appears to come through with great clarity and force. His famous pessimism is heartfelt, and when you are in his grip fairly persuasive. "No man is happy but strives his whole life long after a supposed happiness which he seldom attains, and even if he does it is only to be disappointed with it; as a rule, however, he finally enters harbor shipwrecked and dismasted." And, from the same cheery essay, called "The Vanity of Existence," there is this: "We shall do best to think of life as a *desengaño*, as a process of disillusionment: since this is, clearly enough, what everything that happens to us is calculated to produce." Then again: "Man is at bottom a dreadful wild animal." Schopenhauer thought freedom of the press a permit to poison men's hearts and minds, man a dreadful wild animal, suicide on balance a pretty good idea. A fun guy, Arthur Schopenhauer.

Apart from the pessimism, there are of course many brilliant bits in Schopenhauer. "Thoughts come not when *we* but when *they* want," he writes, which strikes me as having a high truth quotient. He is also up to the moment in scientific research when he remarks of the brain that "anatomy can describe it but physiology cannot understand it," which is still so. (I have a friend, a neurologist, who informs me that anyone who tells you he knows how the mind works is a liar.) And how's this for cutting close to the bone, my bone at least: "Talent works for money and fame . . .," while genius goes after higher things.

Behind my real crush on Schopenhauer, though, is his power as an aphorist. The aphoristic philosophers—Nietzsche, Santayana, Wittgenstein—are the boys who light my fire. What I suppose I am exposing here is my snobbery about style. I realize that Kant, Schelling, Hegel, Fichte were great philosophers, but I'd rather admire them than have to read them.

This past week Barbara and I watched, over what in the United States is called Public Television, a two-hour documentary about J. D. Salinger, who was famous for hiding from his fame. He allowed no interviews, ceased writing for publication in 1965, and permitted no movies to be made from any of his stories. His one novel, *Catcher in the Rye*, has sold more than sixty-five million copies in I'm not sure how many languages. (The line of people who have wanted to make a movie of it winds around several blocks.) In America bright children now read it in grammar school, if not in preschool. The book's message is that the world is a crock, filled with phonies and built on hypocrisy and lies. Maybe not such a good thing for the very young to read, but they have for generations now, gobbling it up.

Salinger's own narrative, as we should say nowadays instead of his life, centers around his experience in World War Two and all the brutal things he saw while an enlisted man in it. He suffered a breakdown after the war. He also married a woman with Nazi connections, though the documentary does not specify what, precisely, these connections were. He seems all his life to have taken up with girls in their late adolescence, a few of whom, now not very fetching women in their sixties, appear on camera to talk about their relationship with him. No one quite said so, but his fancying girls much younger than he is, in the documentary, implicitly connected with Salinger's wanting to recapture life before World War Two killed his innocence. He had a second marriage, which produced a son and a daughter; and broke with the daughter when she wrote a memoir about him. One respects his right to his privacy, which came down to that of wishing to ward off the various kooks who felt that he wrote for them and the publicity machine that is American cultural reporting. Yet he, Jerry (as friends called him), does not come off in this documentary as very likeable.

The great question, which the documentary touches on, is what has Salinger been writing all these years since 1965? At its close the documentary mentions the existence of four completed novels and a work of non-fiction. These, if I remember rightly, won't begin to be published until 2020. I, for one, can wait. Toward the close of his publishing days, Salinger was becoming more mystical; interested in Buddhism and all that. My suspicion is that these works will be suffused with more such gassy mists.

Although when in my late adolescence and early twenties I was much taken by Salinger's stories about the Glass family, I now realize that what I took away from them was reinforcement of my own superior sensitivity. Salinger was, like E. M. Forster, a sensitivity specialist. You will recall that the only aristocracy Forster claimed to believe in was "the aristocracy of the sensitive, the considerate, and the plucky." Reading such writers made one feel oneself sensitive, considerate, and plucky, when one was in reality merely touchy, conceited, and lucky. One also neglected the fact that Forster and Salinger's sensitivity was based on contempt for all who did not think as they did. Sensitivity is itself a fine thing, but I say beware all who claim sensitivity for themselves. There is an excellent chance they will turn out to be brutes, if not rapists.

Best, Joe

7.2.2014. London S.W.7 5RF.
Dear Joe,

January wasn't the poet's idea of "the cruelest month" but I don't know why. Tax collectors circle and buzz; New Year resolutions perish as the Alexandrine days drag their slow tails along. One fills the coming year's diary as if having dates guarantees that one will be alive to honor that wedding or grace that forum. When will the bracket close, with a terminal year, on our names in those damn reference books it was once so grand to be alphabetically ordered in? They all go into the dark, old Tom said, and you don't have to cross London Bridge or figure in the *Almanach de Gotha* to blow your fuse. Meanwhile the synapses are overloaded, and memories of old friends become encased in black. Yes, one is sorry; yes, we shall remember them, possibly; but how little one turns out to know about other people, once we are left with nothing but retrospection, just a few references in the index of our lives! I have often (well, once or twice) thought of doing an autobiography in index form, as is done in the one volume concordance of Proust which I have on my shelves.

As day succeeds to day, it is borne in upon octogenarians that death comes not only to archbishops. What then shall be done? Keep working, watch your step and avoid knocking up against actuarial tables. When Jean Racine was told that nothing could be done to save him, he threw an unfinished play into the fire, and to hell with posterity's laurels.

Our keen-eared son Stephen went, last week, with his latest lady, to the much trumpeted production of *King Lear* at the National Theatre, directed by the can-do-no-wrong man of the extended moment, Sam Mendes. Stephen was unable, for the first two hours, of however many there were, to decrypt a single word of the text which was being delivered into post-modernity by our latest very great actor indeed, whose name means nothing to me. The text was, it seems, subordinated to the vanity of the director who suspected that Lear was suffering from Alzheimer's. Mendes, whom I have never met, directed the James Bond number, *Skyfall*, an unthrilling, unamusing mega-hit which has garnered a billion bucks and made him a chevroned *Schlockmeister*.

In artistic mode, he earlier directed *Revolutionary Road* which pretty well begins with a scene in which husband (De Caprio, L.) and wife (Winslett, K., the ex Mrs. S.) have a row driving home, in Richard Yates's 1950s novel, after she has starred in some amateur theatricals. Now if you begin a movie about a couple with them having a row, it says in my book that you cannot then make the whole movie about how their marriage is a shame and a sham and like that. But if you are an artist of Sammy's run, that's precisely what you do. Fellini said that a movie was "like a circus: you don't follow a dog act with a dog act." But Master Mendes hasn't had time to listen to back numbers such as Maestro Federico and so his movie was a dog act followed by a bitch act and then another dog act and Ravel's *bolero* was a masterpiece of richly varied melodies in comparison. Compare this year's low budget black-und-white *Nebraska* which is full of clever *péripéties*, but whose director's shoes are not unlatched by fawning followers of fashion.

But then again, to be honest, as the sports commentators say on a, yes, regular basis, how enviable it would be to achieve the cultural status of what logicians call "a necessary proposition"! In the arts, this involves becoming someone on whom a given society prides itself, even if the said pagod (Byron's term for his idol Napoleon) is as unreadable as Doris Lessing's science fiction or as merely colorful as David Hockney, whose vast show last year at the Royal Academy looked as if it were the result of a painting-by-numbers competition. Must we grant that Lucian Freud was a master? *De mortuis nil nisi gush.* A nifty gloss on that point: I read in a reliable source that when the Arcadians made a peace deal with the third-century B.C. Spartans, a key clause read: "No one shall be made good for rendering aid to the Spartan party at Tegea"; which, being translated meant that no one was to be put to death for being pro-Spartan. My mind's storerooms are filled with that kind of bric-à-brac.

I share your admiration for Auerbach (not many laughs there, however), as the note on page 106 in my Josephus is there to prove. However, I cannot claim that friend Erich's work is something to which I turn when filled with *Weltschmerz* and kindred symptoms. Mimesis is also one of the recurrent topics of René Girard, whose works I read, back in the 1980s, quite as if I believed, as I suspect he did, that he had the key to turn the world's lock. As soon as any critic or philosopher thinks he has the moral, critical, analytic equivalent of E=mc squared, he don't. Girard remains appetizing because he writes the clear French which flatters one's competence and is, if no Yorick, entertainingly combative. A writer without a touch of paranoia is likely to be a dull dog.

Talking of which, a showbiz "friend" of mine died the other day; call him Peter. I remembered, with no loud sigh, how he came to a "meeting" at our London flat with his sniffy dog in literal tow. I greeted him with a few extra degrees of warmth because I had heard that he had a serious cancer. His dog, Brandy, was some kind of a terrier, rather too inquisitive when it came to the detritus on my study floor, and of a certain pungency. P. and I talked over "our" project and I noticed with what touching affection he lowered a hand to the black and whiteness of his unleashed pooch when it sniffed in his proximity. P. smiled a lot and said "yes" when he meant "almost certainly not," but never "no," in case one suddenly grew bankable and he found that he had closed the door on his hot, if dying, hopes.

Despite my lack of conviction that our conclave would ever come to anything I could put in the bank, I was as courteous as T.E. Hulme's "creeping Turk" (not a breed that I have ever encountered, since Turks, in my experience, are quite upstanding and, unless vexed, quite grandly courteous), but I was pretty sure that *ex nihilo nihil* was likely to come. After pooch and master had departed, I asked a friend of the latter whether he always went everywhere with his terrier. "Only since he was told that he had this cancer." I said: "Do I see the connection?" "How about when Peter looks at you, or me, he can see that we know what he knows: his lease is pretty well up. Brandy doesn't. With Brandy, he's still the same man he was before. He doesn't see death reflected in his eye." Did J.R. Ackerley dote on Tulip because he (she? Surely not!) didn't know that he was, as a gay actor once ad-libbed in a piece of mine, a "home-owner"?

Life tends to collapse into quite a slim volume as one is obliged to consider it from the nervous eminence of accumulated years. I notice that quite a few of your stories refer back to the schooldays of their protagonists. (I am prim enough to think that each of them can have only one protagonist, since the etymology . . . OK, that's enough of that; the time is gone when fancy folk, such as Hugh Trevor-Roper, just might have labeled one of nature's many number twos "a deuteragonist," the subsidiary figure introduced to the tragic stage by Aeschylus and now Oscarized as [Best] Supporting Actor). However keenly you, Joe, can recall your high school days, no institution, I am pretty sure, stocks a man's mind with as many adhesive memories as the English public school, with its monastic boarding houses and, until recently, its beatings and betrayals. For Cyril Connolly, those were indeed the days: "At Eton with Orwell, At Oxford with Waugh,/ He was nothing much after, and nothing before." Not that Cyril meant a word of it; he was delightedly indignant when "Cyrillism" became a Leavisite term of abuse for Sunday literary journalese.

You mentioned that dumpy H. G. Wells had a surprising number of female admirers. To one, I seem to remember—can it possibly have been the virginal Enid Bagnold?—he gave lunch at the Café Royal and then proposed that they "go upstairs and do funny things with our bodies." Perhaps it played better than it reads. Connolly, not greatly given to washing or changing his socks, also seems to have succeeded in enrolling some fancy ladies (sha-sha-sha went the wind in the rich first wife's hair). Subsequent *mesdames* kissed and, by God, they told (Elaine Dundy fictionally, Barbara Skelton frictionally). Might it be that the whiff of a place in an eventual biography is almost as attractive to the *donne* as H.G.'s scent of honey?

A proposito, in the index of my phantom autobiography, there would be: "West, Rebecca,

   F.R.'s two days' work in Paris with, page x;
   Appreciation of coconut ice cream at Jamin with, p.y.
   warm and revealing correspondence with, pp. z et seqq.,
   excommunication, F.R.'s by, p.d.q."

Rebecca told me, and not only me, I'm sure, that she had no idea why her son Anthony West turned so venomously against her. The shadow of the domineering scold was invisible to her. Not much of a novelist, though copious, she did write the once derided and then she-was-right-after-all 1,000 plus pages of *Black Lamb and Grey Falcon*. The moral was shorter: stay out of the Balkans.

Back to school. Is there any stronger evidence of the persistence of human character (in the face of smart allegations that "I" is a composite figure, with no necessary connection between the person who writes this letter and the one who crossed the ocean to become, as it turned out, some kind of a pissy Englishedman) than the vividness with which some of us—we few, we unhappy few—recall episodes from four pubescent years in what my friend Brian Glanville (his father was *né* Goldberg) once called, with unusual hyperbole, but no lack of painful recall, "Auschwitz without the chimneys"? He became a good writer, very good when it came to short stories, before spending his life, and making his living, by reporting and writing on football, which we both had, he more bitingly than I, in the *Carthusian*.

What was I like at school? Early in January I had a letter out of the dark grey of the English winter in a handwritten envelope (quite rare now) from someone whose (sur)name, Luke, meant nothing to me. I read on with apprehension and then with surprise. His screed was a thank-you letter, in manuscript, for having been so kind to him when he was bullied in my "house," Lockites, back in 1947 or 1948. His letter informed me that he had been victimized to the point of having his wrist broken and I, holding no formal position of authority, had been alone in coming to his rescue. I believed him, of course. Stained glass window coming up! But wait! Imagine that his letter or another such, once opened, had accused me of crushing the writer with my sarcasm (I don't do wrist-breaking) and leaving him in a state of self-doubt so incurable that he had achieved nothing more in life than writing a column, on the back page of a literary mag, in which he was incapable of speaking well of anyone. "Pull down thy vanity," said Ole Ez, who never did. I can do it easily, by remembering borrowing a pen from a poor student, losing it and not buying him another until his father wrote me a threatening letter.

Despite my gallant intervention, Luke was withdrawn from Charterhouse and sent to another very expensive "public" (i.e., private) school where he benefited from close supervision and attentive teachers and, in time, became a successful barrister who could afford to send his three sons to Eton and keep five horses in the grounds of his country house. I was gratified by the prospect of beatification supplied by the gospel according to this particular Luke and thanked him cordially, and sincerely, for taking the trouble, after sixty-six years, to write as he did. I did not express surprise that a successful retired barrister should write "delishious" where, as philologists say, "delicious is preferred"; but then it is, we are promised, only in Victorian times that English spelling was formalized into "right" and "wrong"; shades of the pretentious modern Greeks who confected *katharevousa,* a meta-language uncorrupted by creeping Turkisms as the current demotic was. Official Greek was piped with an elaborate grammar which served to faze (as in phase out) provincial oiks, as we used to call the haitchless, when they applied for jobs in the higher bureaucracy.

Byron's quondam mistress, Jane Harley, Lady Oxford, the delishious wife of the fifth earl and mother of the "Harleian miscellany," on account of the various fathers of her husband's putative offspring, was renowned for her idiosyncratic spelling. Googling to check which earl she was attached to (the fifth), I see that "Slapperdating.com" promises contact with Oxford women of today who are goers, and no doubt, have the appetite, if not the quality, of Byron's lady. Which prompts another autobiographical index entry: "Kubrick, Stanley, Tells F.R. re opportunities for sex-to-go, 'we were born too soon'." *Le pauvre.*

Tout à toi, Freddie.

February 12, 2014
Dear Freddie,

Your story about the man who always traveled with his dog because the dog didn't know he had cancer is oddly touching. I don't know if the phenomenon has yet arrived in England, but in America we have had for some while now something called Service Dogs, whom people with various disabilities, physical and emotional, are allowed to bring into places where dogs are not usually allowed. A subset of Service Dogs is Emotional Support Dogs, who attend those suffering from anxiety, depression, bipolarity, panic attacks, and other psychological disorders. These dogs are fitted out with jackets with Service Dog written on them.

Avant la lettre J. R. Ackerley, it strikes me, used poor old Tulip as a Service Dog of sorts. Ackerley claimed that the acquisition of Tulip allowed him to cease his homosexual cruising, which not infrequently ended up with him, Ackerley, duct-taped to a chair while some denizen of the world of rough trade went through his drawers extracting such valuables as were over-looked by the depredations of the previous guardsman, navvy, or bus driver Ackerley brought home. Ackerley claimed that he got from Tulip what he had been hoping all along to get from these young men, which was uncritical adoration.

I used to tell this anecdote to students in a course in prose writing that I taught. At the close of it, I asked if they had any questions. No one ever did. "You call yourself writers," I would say, "and yet none of you is interested in whether Ackerley had sex with the dog?" I then calmly told them that so far as one knows he didn't, but the question, for writers, is not insignificant.

How different with cat owners, or at least this cat owner, whose cat, the beautiful and resourceful Hermione, does not give but demands uncritical adoration. When she has had a sufficiency of such adoration doled out by me, she walks away, with a "sod off, Schmuckowitz" look over her shoulder as she seeks out more interesting activity than my pitiful ministrations; this more interesting activity generally means her eleventh or twelfth nap of the day.

Might it be that dog owners require uncritical adoration and cat owners, not feeling themselves deserving of such adoration, are sad masochists, the pet-owning equivalent of Somerset Maugham's Philip Carey in *Of Human Bondage*? Does this, as I fear, fall under the rubric of risky but not very in-teresting generalizations?

The other part of your anecdote that interested me was your noting that "I treated him [the man you call Peter] with a few extra degrees of warmth because I had heard he had a serious cancer." Maurice Bowra once remarked of a man noted for being unduly congenial that when he last saw him this man gave Bowra "the warm [as opposed to the cold] shoulder." Are people who make it widely known that they have cancer looking for the warm shoulder wherever they go? A very successful, by which I mean of course stratospherically well paid, American speakerine, as I'm told the French call news readers, named Tom Brokaw just the other day "revealed" that he has cancer—multiple myeloma, in his case. "I am very grateful for the interest in my condition," he remarked (at a press conference perhaps?), "but I hope everyone understands that I wish to keep this a private matter." Then why, Tom, dear boychik, did you reveal it in the first place, and on television of all places? Is Tom Brokaw, perhaps, a man in search of a national warm shoulder?

When my friend Edward Shils had colon cancer, from which he died at eighty-five, and people asked him how he was, he usually answered, "Apart from dying, very well, thank you." I hope that when whatever deadly dart fate has in store for me finally hits, I shall have the now uncommon decency to be able to keep the news strictly within my family.

Unless death hits young—nowadays this means under sixty—I'm not sure but that one's sympathy shouldn't be concentrated not on the dying man or woman (whom in any case we shall be joining presently) but on his or her family. They will be the ones left behind to suffer the consequences. Sorry to dwell so on this cheery subject, but I am just now attempting to write an essay on death, one that has the tentative title "Big D," and just yesterday read Montaigne's "To Philosophize Is to Know How to Die." Montaigne's message is that it is best to accustom oneself to death, for it will of course pay one a visit sooner or later, and often in the most unexpected way. (Montaigne wished to die while planting his cabbages, but died instead painfully of quinsy at the age of 59.) Of the surprise element in death, he writes:

> Leaving aside fevers and pleurisies who would ever have thought that a Duke of Brittany was to be crushed to death in a crowd, as one was during the state entry into Lyons of Pope Clement . . . Have you not seen one of our kings killed at sport? And was not one of his ancestors killed by a bump from a pig? Aeschylus was warned against a falling house; he was always on the alert, but in vain; he was killed by the shell of a tortoise which slipped from the talons of an eagle in flight. Another choked to death on a pip from a grape; an Emperor died from a scratch when combing his hair; Aemilius Lepidus, from knocking his foot on his own doorstep; Aufidius from bumping into a door of his Council chamber. Those who died between a woman's thighs include Cornelius Gallus, a praetor; Tigillinus, a captain of the Roman Guard; Ludovico, the son of Guy di Gonzaga, the Marquis of Mabtuya; and—providing even worse examples—Speucippus the Platonic philosopher, and one of our Popes.

Who was it called the orgasm "little death?" To go from little death to the real thing, big death, was once thought to be an exit devoutly to be wished. The actor John Garfield was long rumored to have checked out in this way. I know a longish joke—vastly redacted here—about one Yankel Dombrovsky of the shtetl of Frampol who comes shamefacedly to his rabbi to admit that his wife died while they were making love, at least he was fairly certain she was dead, but he completed the act anyway. The rabbi, outraged, calls a meeting of all the Jews in the shtetl, at which he roundly condemns Yankel D. for this beastly act, and then looks up to the synagogue's women's gallery to exclaim, "And you, women of Frampol, to prevent such a heinous act ever occurring again in our village, in future, I beseech you, in future move a little!"

Earlier this week I finished reading my bedtime book of the last few months, John O'Hara's collection of stories *The Horse Knows the Way*. The book is slightly more than 400 pages long, and very readable. The reason it took me more than two months to read it is that, contra the cliché about "cuddling up in bed with a good book at night," I find I cannot so cuddle for longer than fifteen or so minutes before falling asleep.

I know you are an admirer of John O'Hara, and so am I. What I admired about him was his professionalism, a part of which was his industry; he was most productive. He was also highly skilled, not least at writing dialogue; a few of the stories in *The Horse Knows the Way* are written entirely in dialogue. He prided himself on this skill, and I recall reading him remarking that if one were going to have characters speak in stories one had to be aware that no American woman who had graduated high school would ever use the term "half-a-buck."

O'Hara's high spirit was also pleasing. He thought he was a contender for the Nobel Prize, and vowed that if he won it he would use part of the money to buy a Rolls-Royce. When it became evident that a large wad of the dynamite inventor's money wasn't coming his way, he bought the Rolls anyway. Before doing so he wanted everyone to know that he wasn't going for any understated Bentley either, but would only be satisfied with the real thing, the car with the "broad in her nightgown on the hood and on the radiator the initials R & R, which don't stand for Rock 'n' Roll."

I have to report that the great majority of stories in *The Horse Knows the Way* didn't work for me. By "didn't work" I mean didn't stick in the mind afterwards, left no residue. Part of the problem is that O'Hara's subjects are beginning to feel more than a little dated; one of the chief among these subjects was adultery among the small-town country-club set. The little touches of snobbery that were in force in O'Hara's day are now no longer in force in ours. Irish Americans of social aspirations in O'Hara's generation—among them F. Scott Fitzgerald, Edwin O'Connor, Joseph Kennedy—felt the sting of WASP snobbery through exclusion and never quite got over it. Never having gone to Yale is said to have been the great deprivation of O'Hara's life. Fitzgerald may have mocked Tom Buchanan, husband of

Daisy, but his envy of Tom's confident social status was surely partially behind the mockery.

Two months from now, if you were to read me the titles of the stories in *The Horse Knows the Way*, I am fairly certain I shall not be able to tell you what stories fell under which titles. Part of the problem is one that O'Hara shares with lots of short-story writers—and I think he was probably a better short-story writer than novelist—of not being able to provide a satisfactory ending for his stories. He offers a fine flight but doesn't quite know how to land the plane. The commonest story of our day is the epiphany-ending story. "David gazed at the half moon over hovering over the Bosphorus and realized that life, somehow, would never again be quite the same." How too fucking sad, David, but please do try to carry on.

What does it mean to say that John O'Hara's stories leave no residue? I have half explained it by saying that his subject matter feels dated, or that he does not often supply satisfactory endings to his stories, but something deeper is entailed. Chekhov's subject matter is much more dated than O'Hara's, and his endings, too, often have up-in-the-air feelings about them. But there is something universal about Chekhov's characters that doesn't get into O'Hara's. This quality of the universal is, I suspect, what makes a story memorable. How one acquires a knack for the universal I haven't the least hint of a clue, but I should say that it is what separates the great from the good writers.

I seem to have written here chiefly about cancer, death, and mystery. Gloomy stuff. I attribute this gloom to the nearly unrelieved gloom of the Chicago winter. Gloomy is, I guess, as gloomy does, or something.

Best, Joe

14.2.14.London, SW7 5RF.
Dear Joe,

The meta-version of the story of my friend with the pooch is that he (Brandy) *did* know that his master was a dying man, but was too sweet-eyed to give any sign of it. Here Brandy doubles for the Duc de Guermantes who waved aside Swann's dignified indications that he was a dying man because the duke and his lady were on their way to a ball and didn't care to have distracting news about mortality. The ducal response was,

"You'll outlive us all." But only *le petit Marcel* did that, the artist as society's embalmer.

The poet Horace, not quite the nicest man in the ancient world (which didn't do "nice" all that much), did nothing to offend his patrons—Maecenas, when he was still princely, or Augustus himself—but his line about creating verses, *"aere perennius,"* more durable than bronze, had a tincture of sly triumphalism: whatever Mr. *Primus Inter Pares* might be doing to make Rome gleam like marble, by plating its public buildings with thinnish sheets of the best Carrara, Q. Horatius Flaccus's paperwork would outlast the ages and so it has, due—not least at least—to the skill with which he decked his verses with sweetly aligned self-deprecation. What modern writer has made candid comedy of a sexual fiasco such as happened to Horace on his travels to Brindisi to kiss the emperor's ass? Ian McEwan, in *On Chesil Beach,* turned *ejaculatio praecox* into a subject for fiction, and then made nothing of it except too much. I said my piece *là-dessus* in a high-minded journal whose editor, the unflinching Michael Schmidt, allowed me to remark on the ineptitudes which go to compose what witless critics proclaimed a masterpiece. Countercurrential is the way to go; it can be tough, but it's never crowded.

So what's good? I thought *Stoner* a fine slow-burner, but then John Williams published it back in 1965. My monumental tome of the week is a translation of Leopardi's *Zibaldone*, a work of polyvalent genius of which I was utterly ignorant. Leopardi's *mezzogiorno* father had a fine library and the lonely, phthisicky scholar, like Montaigne, had the means and the vanity not to worry whether "they" got it or even read it. Our "proposal" culture has not yet quite embargoed anything of quality from reaching the punters, but the publishing scoundrels (composed, *pace* Henry James, of executives, not writers) make sure that not much other than preconceived canned goods gets on the booksellers' rented tables. In today's England, torn between shame and regret at vanished supremacy, we are being dosed with pre-digested, TV-linked books commemorating the outbreak of the Great War.

No one much has remarked, even at this late stage, that Britain's greatness was ruined by the misguided notion, held dear by a genuine, liberal gentleman, Sir Edward Grey, that to go to war was a moral obligation, not a political decision. The German irruption into "gallant little Belgium" was made into an undeniable *casus belli* even though Belgian gallantry had been expressed, most recently, by King Leopold in granting license to his emissaries to murder several million inhabitants of the "Belgian" Congo. Grey did what seemed to him to be the right thing and it was (as Hermione Gingold said of my early radio script) "all wrong." Grey's quintessential *vecchio*-conservative predecessor, Lord Palmerston (one of Beetle's pagods, when she was a historian) got it righter when he said: "Countries don't have friends, they have interests." But then again, if Neville Chamberlain had been Palmerstonian, he would not have guaranteed the sovereignty of Poland when he knew that his promise was unredeemable, in which case . . . well, who knows. In other words, sports fans, it is—as my great uncle Maurice used to say—"all worked out to beat you." All the same, he added lamely, to celebrate the outbreak of the Great War is curious, but may—covers it, with flags even!—prove profitable.

That "added lamely" leads me, with admiration aforethought, to our John O'Hara, yours and mine, if no one much else's in today's ideologically rigged *bourse littéraire* (George Steiner's term). "Lamely" is the kind of adverbial qualifier which O'H. never attached to dialogue. He used "he said" "she said" almost exclusively, which allows the reader to act the words as he "hears" them. It is a good rule in fiction, although not unbreakable, *never* to say "he retorted" "she responded" or "he added lamely." It's a matter of courtesy (i.e. art) to enroll the reader's imagination by what is left to him or her to supply. D. H. Lawrence pointed out that Cézanne's apples were more succulent because the artist had, so to say, taken a bite out of them. What we omit stays in there, as Hemingway proved when, under prudish pressure, he removed all mention of abortion in *Hills Like White Elephants* and then discovered that what he had left out was all still there, in the silent spaces, for the reader to infer for himself.

The word is that Robert Benchley once said to O'Hara, "John, even your friends think you're a son-of-bitch." Have I got that right? Would it be better if the John had come at the end of sentence? That is just the kind of thing that O'Hara was careful to get right, and rightly. The mind's eye visualizes what is no longer to be seen; but the mind's ear is an equally vital element in the fictioneer's shifty anatomy. O'Hara's capacity to eavesdrop, even on people whom we need not believe he had ever met, is compelling and convincing, but it is, as your accurate appreciation implies, also fugitive. His ear is so keen that, like the hearing aid which I am reluctant to sport in public, it is also indiscriminate, though it does favor what classicists used to call "the dirty bits," as long as they are straight or—as in *Lovey Childs*—Lesbian. He never did guy-gay, did he? And what does that tell us? Not much.

O'Hara was hot when it came to titles, such as *The Hat on the Bed*, another bunch of stories which were fun to read, hard to recall; mainly, I suspect, because the dazzle of the chat made him lazy about the anecdote itself.

The only one that stays with me is "Natalie Jackson"; if not the title, the leading lady's name. She's a beautiful, happily married woman, who—having discovered that her husband was two-timing her—goes out in a motor boat and, like a latter day Medea, drowns the two children she had had by him. I think that she may have drowned herself too, but I don't get any response from my cerebral service. I wouldn't claim that the *reason,* in any guaranteed causal sense, that I can dust off Natalie Jackson is that, at whatever remove, it appears to merit the archetypal tag I just attached to it. Mix myth too obviously into your work and you risk looking as wilfully impressive as Updike's *Centaur.* Odd, and a little unnerving, that Natalie Wood was drowned, somewhat mysteriously, after leaving her husband and Chris Walken to carouse on the latter's yacht.

I learned a lot from O'Hara, especially how dialogue can (must?) incite the reader to sing along, in a way that prose, however subtle or euphonious, cannot do on its own. Even Proust, who appears to be the delivery man for prolonged prosology, comes alive because one recalls not only his characters' words but their silences too. *La* Verdurin's crushing of the Baron de Charlus into "uncharacteristic" inability to respond speaks louder than any prosaic account of his stricken appearance. What he cannot say enlists readers in the scene and pulls us to his side. How else should we find ourselves ashamed by the humiliation of an odious, absurd snob, with singular tastes? The switch of sympathies within a fiction is a trick which trumps expectation and, in doing so, honors the hope that our author can tell us something unexpected, but also *right.* Herman Wouk achieves it in *The Caine Mutiny* when the "good" Lieutenant, a mutation of Fletcher Christian in *Mutiny on the Bounty,* has been cleared of the charges against him when Captain Queeg goes, as the Brits say, doo-lally in the witness chair. Wouk has someone puncture the Lieutenant's exultation with the awkward truth that old salts such as Queeg had, while the U.S. slept, saved the sum of things for not much pay. Queeg had his revenge, of a kind, when played by Jack Nicholson in *A Few Good Men,* a manifest remake of Wouk's work.

O'Hara has modest but important lessons for writers, not least his economy. His later novels—*From The Terrace* in particular—have spasms of dialogorrhea, but *Appointment in Samarra* has durably terse qualities, not least in the bedroom scene in which the woman asks Julian English whether he has a "thing" and for the attention-gaining way in which he rolls up her sweater to gain access to her breasts; but—unlike a thousand titty-laters—O'Hara doesn't mention them, or any other anatomical feature. As a result, the reader's imagination collaborates with the writer. What did Julian

English look like? Does the author tell us? He *wishes* us to recognize ourselves in the self-destructive weak/strong man who does what we dare not do, wisely.

It was typical of literary milieus that that smart-ass apparatchik (Gill, was it?) on the *New Yorker* reviewed the novel under the rubric "Disappointment in O'Hara." Julian English would have thrown his drink in his face, rocks and all, and good for him, if disastrous for his long-term prospects. O'Hara's hope of Swedish honors gives us a glimpse of the naiveté which drink could not quite drown. It's not all *that* comic that he had such dreams. Imagine if he had survived to see Alice Munro laurelled! I sought improvement from her volume of short stories called *Dear Life*. In an early one I read, "He was going to go to England; but he died instead." Instead? Why? "He was going to go to England; but he died," does the work without ramming the "irony" up our noses. Later, I read: "Her mouth felt like a tundra." Was she crossing the desert at the time? No. This just comes out of a paragraph of banalities. How can anyone's mouth feel like a tundra and why would she choose to say so?

Henry de Montherlant (who got shirty with anyone who spelled his first name Henri, just as I do when postulants put a "k" on my Frederic) said that when he opened letters or requests for donations from strangers he continued until he came on a *faute d'orthographe,* at which point: *au pannier!* Montherlant was a *fascisant collabo,* whose *Le Solstice de Juin,* a Pétainiste salute to the *Wehrmacht*, has been airbrushed out of his Wiki bibliography. I still relish the strutty little swine's command of his language, especially in his *Carnets.* Henry would never admit to wishing that he had been enNobelled. The little *tauromane* had too much pride; but . . . both ears and the tail? Now you're talking.

French grammar supplies a thorny stick with which to repel the *étranger.* People from *outre-mer* do have a tendency to rush where frogs have never trod. Cf. Hemingway and his *copains* who imagined that, when that *garagiste* in Aix-en-Provence said *"C'est une génération perdue,"* she was referring to the company in the fancy motor, which—I'll bet—to her eyes didn't look *perdue du tout.* What she saying was, "We've lost a whole generation" (which France pretty well had and which somewhat explains the 1940 defeat which Henry de M., in *Le Solstice de Juin,* wanted to treat as a return sporting event, after which the combatants should shake hands and then, no doubt, combine to beat on the Jews and wallop *les Anglo-Saxons*). Ernest and Co. were buying gas, for Christ's sake, so why would a woman—who might well have lost a husband or sons in the *Grande*

Guerre—choose to label as "lost" a buncha kids making hay while the pre-1929 dollar shone?

On the Websterian topic which seems somewhat to possess us, I used to take comfort from Wittgenstein's "Death is not an event of life; it is not lived through"; but that's not quite how it is, is it, except for solipsists? Then again, W. did also say "What the solipsist means is true." And to that *madame la garagiste* might have said, had she stayed to listen, "*Et ta soeur!*" French for piss off.

Bien à toi, Freddie.

February 21, 2014
Dear Freddie,

Brandy you say was the dog's name. I have met girls in America named Brandy, though none so far named Tequila, Bourbon, or Amaretto, though, who knows, they might be out there. The United States over the past few decades has been on a goofy-naming binge, a spree of piss-elegance. God knows how many Brittanys, Tiffanys, and Kimberleys are today walking the nation's streets. The only bit I remember from Nora Ephron's novel *Heartburn* is the claim by the philandering male character—in real life based on the exposé journalist Carl Bernstein, in the movie played by Jack Nicholson—that he "dated the first Jewish Kimberley."

Our middle-class co-religionists seem to have gone in for this nutty naming in a big way. There are Kevin Footlicks, Hillary Slotniks, Kelly Rabinovitzes gamboling today in gardens not belonging to the Finzi-Continis. Without the aid of a few major metropolitan telephone directories, I'm sure I could find Hunter Hochbergs, Madison Mutchniks, Porter Potashskys, Cooper Kolatches. What is behind all this, of course, is a misplaced yearning for elegance, WASP version.

I blame it on F. Scott Fitzgerald, who, as an under-confident Irishman, also yearned for WASP elegance and might have achieved it if booze hadn't been placed in his way. For most people in the United States who have gone to college, Fitzgerald stands, or at least once stood, for *elegance par excellence*. I have no doubt that there are today as many Americans named Scott as once there were Georges, Roberts, and Davids. I remember once standing with Edward Shils in front of the Princeton Club, on West 44th Street in New

York when a boy in a yarmulke emerged from the club's revolving door. "Ah," said Edward, "F. Scott Feldman."

American blacks are even wilder in the crazy-naming department. In the bad old days, viciously mischievous medical interns used to advise illiterate black mothers to name their daughters Placenta or Clitoris, their sons Cervix or Gonad. Other blacks adapted the last names of presidents for their own first names, so that one had Washington Jones, Jefferson Smith, Roosevelt Greer. Now black naming has become much more exotic, featuring such first names as Rasheed, Jabari, Kinisha, and La Shanda (a *shanda* in Yiddish meaning of course a disgrace). Sometimes, at no extra charge, they will throw in a free-floating apostrophe, giving us Rau'Shee or L'Heureux or Mich'el. Piss elegance once more rules.

Hemingway may have preceded John O'Hara in being the first to insist on the straight *he said, she said* accompanying dialogue in fiction. Traditionally, the rankest of amateurs go in for such elevated locutions as "he opined," "she riposted." Years ago something called Swifties were devised that featured adverbial puns inserted into dialogue. "'I have epilepsy,' he retorted, convulsively," is an example. In *Sister Carrie*, Theodore Dreiser, a novelist of no style but great power, writes: "'Uh huh,' he returned pleasantly." Ring Lardner put paid to this nuttiness, or so one would have thought, when in one of his stories he included the sentence: "'Shut up,' he explained."

I had not noticed that John O'Hara did not go in for elaborating the physical details of his characters, including the most central ones. You must be right about his not bothering to describe Julian English in *Appointment in Samarra*. If he did, I missed it, and haven't the least recollection of how he may have looked. I know that in *Pride and Prejudice* Jane Austen does not describe Elizabeth Bennett, a brilliant touch which allows every young female reader of the novel to believe Miss Bennett looks like her.

How far to go in describing characters in fiction can be a fairly subtle question. A recent story of mine, which is to appear in the April issue of *Commentary*, offers minimal descriptions of some characters and none whatsoever of others. One can of course over-describe, another mistake of the amateur, going on about jaw-lines, eyebrows, knuckles, and trouser inseam, not to speak of the question of "which side." The rule of thumb and of the other four fingers is that one describes characters only insofar as physical characteristics influence their conduct or the plot of the story. For myself, the decision when to describe and when not is almost instinctual; usually I don't really have to think much about it.

A more interesting matter in the realm of description is that of sex, the tussle, the rolling about, the two-backed beasty going at the actual low and dastardly deed. In the fifty or so stories I have published, I have never been able to bring myself to do it, to get down, that is, to the nitty-gritty of the dirty details—the naming of parts, as the Henry Reed poem has it, and their engagement in fancy fornication.

I find I cannot bring myself to write, "He unbuttoned her blouse and gazed upon . . . She felt his manliness against her and unzipped his trousers and took . . . At the end, both breathing heavily now, he felt . . . while she stroked . . . " And so forth and Charles Swann. I can't do it, that is, without giggling. I have tossed various of my characters into bed with one another, but what they do once there I leave to my readers to imagine. A story of mine called "Bartlestein's First Fling" begins post-coitally, if you like—and I don't for a moment believe you would like such a phrase—with my hero and one of his employees on the floor of his office after a vigorous bonk. In another called "Kaplan's Big Deal," my eponymous hero compares the sexual expectations of a female French deconstructionist and the kind of woman who enjoys a weekend in Las Vegas. In a story called "The Count and the Prince," I have an émigré, low-echelon academic falling asleep to dream of making love to an adult student. When I finally arrange for the two of them to hop into the sack, I write, "They embraced and she took him by the hand into the bedroom, where they did things together that the Count hadn't even dared to dream." The Greenwich Village poet Kenneth Patchen wrote a book called *Memoirs of a Shy Pornographer*. I prefer to think of myself as the Sly Pornographer.

I'm with you on the reputation of the tundra-mouthed Ms. Munro. She is one of those lucky scribblers who has gone from being not all that interesting to becoming a master, with no stops in between for being merely not at all bad. I've read perhaps thirty of her stories, and remember very little of any of them, apart from their dour settings in the province of Ontario where artistic and other aspirations go to die. Some adultery, never very joyous, usually occurs. Humor never obtrudes, at least as far as I can recall. None of the characters in her stories ends happier, wiser, or with deepened understanding. They are chiefly there to illustrate the less than dazzlingly original point that life isn't much fun.

That Alice Munro has won the Nobel Prize doubtless has as much to do with her being a Canadian and a woman as with the amplitude of her talent. Apart from the big money it carries with it, the Nobel Prize has become among the most dubious of prizes. So many dud-writers have won it; too often it has been given for political and other extra-literary reasons. The Nobel Prize has also had the odd side effect of making many of its recipients posthumous, even as they continue to trod the earth. The prize seems to have had that effect on V. S. Naipaul, to have drained him of his energy and venom both. I am not sorry Alice Munro has won it; she is not an immodest or in any other way I know an egregious person. As for her posthumy, I note that she has announced her retirement from the literary trade, beating the prize's side effect to it. She should only, as a certain ethnic people say, live and be well.

Arthur Schopenhauer, the Jimmy Durante of German philosophy—he's got a million of 'em, a million of 'em—has a paragraph on not reading bad books. The secret "consists," he writes, "in not taking an interest in whatever may be engaging the attention of the general public at any particular time. When some political or ecclesiastical pamphlet, or novel, or poem is making a great commotion, you should remember that he who writes for fools always finds a large public."

Once upon a time that sentiment—the more popular a book, the more foolish it is likely to be—would have been self-evident to writers who thought themselves, and wished to be taken as, serious. No longer. Most of us in the scribbler's trade now prefer to have it both ways—to be thought intellectually serious and have the dough, too. In the United States, I think this changed in 1963 and '64, when two certified intellectuals, Mary McCarthy, with *The Group* (1963), and Saul Bellow, with *Herzog* (1964), had gong-ringing bestsellers. After this serious writers were no longer content to be, in Arnold Bennett's phrase, "small-public writers."

The large public, of course, isn't all that real. Bellow once told me that he thought himself a lucky fellow. "I publish a novel," he said, "and 50,000 people buy it, 5,000 read it, and 500 care about it." Those figures feel fairly solid to me. Yet today if one publishes a book, no matter how good, and it doesn't sell well one feels oneself somehow a flop. When I write a book, in the act of composition I honestly don't think—perhaps *fantasize* is the more precise word here—about its potential commercial success. I write it for the aesthetic pleasure doing so gives, and I write it in the hope of honoring the complexity its subject presents. Yet if the book turns out to be commercially negligible I feel, somehow, disappointed. I am, in other pathetic words, no better than the other punters at the roulette table of contemporary literature. On which ambiguous note, I send along my

Best, Joe

22.2.14. London SW7 5RF.
Dear Joe,

I have spent much of my writing life turning and walking away, more or less slowly, from showbiz and always waiting, dawdling at least, on the corner lest its agents lose track of me. At the heel and toe of each old and new year, I am reminded of my cinematic sins by the arrival of a deck of DVDs from various studios and producers, soliciting my handsome X on the voting slips which may procure the Oscar for the enclosed. Each year, the making of the movie is more obviously geared to how it can be publicized: hype springs eternal.

What else is old? You're right; but I can date this premeditation back to the middish 1980s when I was in California at the behest (there's no behest like a six-figure behest) of a producer called Gene Taft who surprised me by meeting me in a full-length raccoon coat in the heat of the Los Angeles afternoon. Like poor old King David, Gene gat no heat, whatever he did; on account, I suspect, of what he had already done in order to contract one of the first cases of AIDS which I encountered in person. Gene was a loser who had to tell you of the famous people he knew. Many were kinder to him than Tinsel Town legend promises.

He had commissioned me to re-re-write *An Affair to Remember*, the one in which, in 1939, Charles Boyer arranged to meet Irene Dunne on top of the Empire State building and did it so well that Cary Grant promised to do the same thing with Deborah Kerr in 1957. The women fail to show, in both cases, because they have been crippled in the interim—not a good spot—and don't want to disappoint their lovers' dreams. A little-known radio version was written by my friends Frank Muir and Dennis Norden (the Goodmen Aces of the 1950s BBC). In their version, the narrator tells us that, as on screen, the male lead eventually goes to see his love and finds her in a chair by the window. "As he approaches, she looks as beautiful as ever, but then . . . the rug slips from her lap and reveals her crutch." This rather British joke sounded funnier than it reads, and I guess it had better.

Anyway, as the kids say, a lot, Gene Taft had raised some money, not least because Warren Beatty—hot as a pistol in them days—had allowed his name to be associated with the project. We went to see Warren in his big, big Beverly Hills mansion and he brought down a water-color sketch by my daughter Sarah which she had given him and which, he said, he had pinned on the wall in front of his desk. I recall Warren coming to Stanley Donen's apartment in London, soon after we had made *Two For the Road*. He went on his knees and said, "Who do I have to fuck to make a movie with you guys?" After poor Taft was toast, Warren did actually make a version, not mine, of *Affair to Remember*, with Annette Benning. It was forgotten before it was remembered.

Another of Gene's improbable benefactors was Bob Evans, then recently deposed as head of production at Paramount Pictures. At his peak, he had married Ali McGraw, star of *Love Story*, and had lost her to Steve McQueen, whose black British homonym is featured, as director of *12 Years a Slave*, in this year's Oscar hotshot list. Bob, like Broadway's Jed Harris, was a boy wonder whose zenith was high and who subsequently plummeted. Bob's house was the mausoleum of his fame. It had walnut-brown awnings on the windows. We watched Irene being Dunne on the viewing room screen and then Bob came in, brown as one of his awnings, and showed us the gag-reel which the crew had made on his recent production, *Marathon Man*, directed by my friend John Schlesinger and featuring Lawrence Olivier as a bald slice of ham, Dustin Hoffman as Trotty True, the good guy. The spoof reel was of members of the cast impersonating Bob Evans. Schlez was pretty funny, Roy Scheider was funnier, Dustin was beyond brilliant in mimicking Evans's swivel-eyed, hesitant volubility. Dustin capped the routine by revealing, in his crutch already, a rubber surrogate penis which erected itself as he did his number. The performance didn't, as they say, need it, but Dustin made it his own. He has now mutated into a run-of-the-mill director of old fashioned harmlessness.

Bob Evans later took us to the offices, on the Paramount lot, where he was planning his pay-off movie, *Cotton Club*, for which he did not yet have a director, cast or all the money (a Hollywood euphemism for having close to none of it). Nevertheless, he did have . . . the poster! And it promised a big hit. Bob was Narcissus with his bullshit before him. In the end, which was quite a while in coming, Francis Ford Coppola was rented to write and direct but, as happens, a lot, the god had deserted him (and has never come back). Did Titian paint some bad, bad pictures that no one ever saw or is movie-directing more a sport than an art and, when you've had your big season, you've had it? Then again, how can the same man have directed *Mean Streets* and *Goodfellas* and then come up with *Wolf on Wall Street*, which makes Oliver Stone's *Wall Street* seem pretty much like a masterpiece? But then the latter had a sequel which was dead in the same brackish water as Scorsese's number.

Is Leonardo de Caprio someone with whom you want to spend time in the dark? Include me out. It took a fortune to make *Wolf on Wall Street* in order (you think?) to denounce fortune-hunters who have nothing better to do than get high on coke and rent tan-all-over, low-down depilated hookers to take the tedium out of share-pushing. The movie was not consistent even within its maker's own gimcrack standards. Suddenly, two-thirds of the way through, Scorsese has a "false flashback," showing for the first time what didn't happen and then—why not?—a reprise showing what really did (when the stoned anti-hero wrecks a new white Ferrari, I think it was). The movie ends with a coda in which the fallen villain, stripped down to his last Rolex, is reduced to lecturing on salesmanship, in New Zealand already. We see him asking a trio of students to sell him the pen which he is holding out to them. The first two make a lousy pitch and we wait for the third to deliver what Mel Brooks would call the kicker. But he is just as witless as the first couple. Izzy Diamond would've said, "But wait . . ." And there would have had to be a pay-off. Like, the third guy could say "How about you turn around and bend over and I'll stick your stupid pen right up your ass? Because who needs one today? Loser!" Just a thought. I can think again, if I have to; and the money's there.

De Caprio is likely to be pipped for the Oscar by Chiwetel Ejiofar, the suffering servant in *12 Years*, although the latter's expression hardly ever changes and he is left, very often, alone with the camera on his unmoving face and nothing whatever in his head. Hey, you're not against black people winning Oscars, are you? Because we have a rail waiting to run you people out of town. How about Chiwetel is no Sidney Poitier, Harry Belafonte, or Denzel? So? Never mind, think of the cheers, think of the DVDends! (Where is slavery principally and widely practiced today? *Parlons pas.*)

And now for the ladies, the women, the majority gender. Cate Blanchett v. Sandra Bullock, it looks like. La Blanchett is favorite, if only because she does actually get some acting to do in Woody Allen's *Blue Jasmine*, which also shows signs of having been written rather than story-boarded. *Gravity*, in which *la* Bullock, encased in a white spacesuit most of the time, attempts—in 3D already—to avoid being marooned in space, is a circus number and a very monotonous one too. You say you cannot be "*very* monotonous"? Go see the picture, but don't say I sent you.

Great-looking at fifty, Sandra—already an Oscarene—does a lot of weightless head-over-heeling in order to get into and out of space ships while all kinds of shit flies in the faces of her ducking audience. George Clooney, costumed like a quarterback with elephantiasis, flirts briefly with what he can see of Bullock (even so he gets the color of her eyes wrong) before—with Captain Oatesy gallantry—the perfect gent leaves madame to take the one available chance of salvation while he goes off to play the wandering star. It's a far, far better thing that he does, but he has done better, I think, even though Clooney is now Cary Grant II, sans charisma. *Gravity* has no plot, no wit, no good guys, no bad guys, only this lady pressing buttons of all kinds in order to get herself rocketed back to earth where she falls into shallow water and . . . that's it. *Gravity* is a circus with only one number. Why is space the biggest bore that ever cost more than *Cleopatra*?

Have you heard the story about Cary going to the Hollywood charity fundraiser to which, the invitation warned, there was positively no entrance without having your ticket with you? Yes, Cary arrived without and went up to the usual table where the usual dreadnought ladies, in glasses joined at the back with a loop of thread, sat checking the list. Cary said, "Listen, I'm sorry, but . . ." The lady didn't look up. "No ticket, you can't come in. Period." Cary said, "I'm Cary Grant." She looked up and her expression stayed forbidding: "You don't look like Cary Grant." Cary said, "Nobody does." Now you've heard it.

La Blanchett is a shoo-in, truth to tell. She does a lot of face-acting, cries real gelatin, looks like hell when she doesn't need to, and comes out crushed and acquainted with more reality than you get in Park Avenue. She plays the part of a Mrs. Bernie Madoff feel-alike; pitched from the penthouse heights of multi-millionairedom and, as her tubby hubby goes to jail, she takes off, literally, for San Francisco to stay with her humdrum sister. *Blue Jasmine* begins in foist class on the plane in which the impoverished-but-she-ain't-noticed-it-yet Mrs. M. talks kinda normally, but too much, with her neighbor Mrs. Ordinary. OK. Then they get off the plane and they're at the luggage carousel. Cate approaches her neighbor and is so insistent about seeing her again that even dumpy Mrs. O. can read her some kind of a nut. So: we have a movie which begins with showing, twice, that Jasmine is in, as the movie buffs say, deep poop. After which . . . poop is what she's in.

Oh she does have one moment of coming off the bottom when, against all probability, she persuades a handsome young local upwardly-mobile and then some politician that she is an interior decorator qualified to beautify his at least $12M waterfront house and then move in. That a smart young well-connected politically ambitious S.F.-er would fall for an unknown out-of-town woman with no social connections is low on probability, but it's required in order that Jazz can, once again, crash und burn. I enjoyed the movie, but it's no good by any even semi-serious standards. It is a vehicle designed to have its wheels fall off and, once they have done so, it stops dead, with madame on a park bench. So what happened to the versatile wit who directed *Hannah and her Sisters* and *Mighty Aphrodite*? As they say when you serve an ace, or two, followed by a pair of double faults: "Same guy!"

Here's the envoi for today. I saw in this week's TLS a teaser line for a review which said "Great Literary Failures." I didn't hasten to check out the list of nominees (waiting to hear "And the Wooden Spoon goes to . . ."), but my recent, lingering virus led me to imagine (put it that way) a writer turning hopefully to the listed page of certified no-hopers and finding that, after a lifetime of failing to figure among the *gratin*, he hasn't made that list either.

Tout à toi, Freddie.

March 3, 2014
Dear Freddie,

I do not envy you your seeing all those crappy Oscar-nominated movies. Once again here at chez Epstein we shall invite no one over not to watch the gaudy Oscars extravaganza. In his recently published diary, the diplomatist George F. Kennan, on March 25, 2000, when he was ninety-six, wrote of the "annual mock ceremony for the 'Oscars,' a ceremony as empty, silly and decadent as the films and glamour of the moving picture industry they are trying to glamorize." I'd say that that pretty well nails it.

Barbara and I have not seen any of the movies up for this year's Oscars. Nor are we likely to see any soon. *Gravity* and *12 Years a Slave* are not movies we would see even for nothing. *Nebraska* is a possibility, though it sounds a bit of a downer. I am against unearned depression, a commodity in which lots of movies and television these days seem to specialize. I would never want to see, for example, a movie about the Holocaust, or one about a slow death by cancer, though Julie Christie a few years ago was excellent in a movie called *Away from Her* about Alzheimer's that was endurable— the movie, that is, not Alzheimer's, was endurable.

We don't go to the movies at all, but rather let them come to us, over television or on DVDs. Most American movie theatres are now multi- or cineplexes, which means, as you know, several small theatres under one roof. This arrangement does nothing to increase the intimacy of movie-going; it chiefly makes the sound more thunderous. Getting through what used to be called the "Coming Attractions" in a cine- or multiplex is a small but genuine ordeal: the sound booming, the digitally conceived spectacles roaring at one from the almost too close screen, the guy in front of you reading text messages on his smart-phone, no, none of this is my notion of a good time. Some people argue that truly to enjoy a movie one must see it on a big screen. They are saying, as our good friends the Houyhnhnms like to put it, the thing which is not. I shall be content going to my grave without seeing a 3-D movie. I would rather jump back a step and see movies in 1-D. I am approaching the condition of Esta Kramer, the wife of my late friend Hilton Kramer, who, emerging from a wretched contemporary movie, exclaimed, "I never want to see again a movie I haven't seen before."

When it goes into DVD or is bought by HBO, I shall probably condescend to watch *Blue Jasmine*, though with no great high expectation of the flick's changing my life. One of the main reasons I shall be able to see it at all is that Woody Allen isn't in it. I admire Allen's productivity as a director, but I can no longer bear his nervous, psychoanalysandic, self-deprecating blitherings. I recall some years ago seeing his movie *Celebrity* because not he but Kenneth Branagh starred in it. Damned if Branagh in the role didn't do a perfect imitation of Allen. Woody Allen, who has said some funny things ("How can a benevolent God allow the Ice Capades" is one I've long appreciated) and created some swell sight gags (playing the cello in a marching band), has now worked his way up to deserving the supposed Queen Victoria put-down: "We are not amused." Even when he isn't in his own movies, he reveals his want of depth. *Midnight in Paris*, for example, though supposed to be about the 1920s of Hemingway, Gertrude Stein & Co., shows how thin his literary culture really is, or isn't. My last word on Woody Allen is that I used to enjoy him before he became a genius.

But, then, there are lots of Hollywood actors I no longer wish to see. On the female side, I don't want to gaze again upon the tortured *punim* of Julia Roberts. No more Meg Ryan, thank you very much, and the same goes for Michelle Pfeiffer, and the three or four hot actresses named Kate, with either a K or C spelling. Al Pacino's yelling has been outlawed from this apartment. He can take Ben Stiller with him. Jack Nicholson—put a fork in him, he's done. Dustin Hoffman has become for me more Rusty than Dusty. I'm sorry, Mr. De Niro, you don't seem to have a reservation. Robert Redford, whaddya kiddin' me? Tom Hanks, no more, Mr. Nice Guy. Bruce Willis, Sylvester Stallone, Arnold Schwarzenegger, Robert Downey, Jr.— strictly *verboten*. Leonardo di Caprio? Get outta here! Warren Beatty, not a chance. Without too much trouble, I could extend the list, male and female actors, castigated he them both.

As for Warren Beatty, it was not enough that he was U.S. Singles Bonking Champion ten years running, he needed to establish himself as an artist and a highly intelligent dude into the bargain. I recall, many thousands of moons ago, an article in *Esquire* by Rex Reed—himself still alive but long forgotten—in which Beatty made the vain attempt to establish his brilliance. He talked literature, he talked philosophy, he brought out his own little pathetic poems—the more he argued for his depth the shallower he seemed. I never saw a man bury himself so efficiently with his own speech. I remember reading this with great pleasure; few things, I suppose, are more enjoyable for a plain man than to watch an offensively handsome one go up in smoke and down in flames.

Sid Caesar died a few weeks ago. I don't know if his was a great name in England, but for a long stretch in the 1950s no comedian in America was bigger. He had a Saturday night show so good that even the most gregarious people remained home to watch it. On this show, called *Your Show of Shows*, he did skit comedy, wildly anarchic bits (samurais who spoke Yiddish, out-of-it German professors, nutty cavemen), and scored heavily with them. He had a team of writers that included Neil Simon, Carl Reiner, Larry Gelbart, and a very young (pre-genius) Woody Allen.

In the middle of the show, Caesar would come out from behind the curtain, usually dressed in the costume from his last skit, to announce, with a stammer, that "We'll t-t-take a c-c-commercial break and be r-r-right back," though he never stammered during any of his many skits. He was a large man, somewhat overweight, and later it came out—I believe he announced it—that he had a drinking problem. At some point, he went into psychotherapy, conquered his drinking problem, lost his stammer, became whippet thin—and promptly ceased to be the least amusing. Can't have it both ways—hugely talented and still in control of your life—is, I guess, the moral of this little story.

I remember watching *Your Show of Shows* with my parents and younger brother. If I had grandparents alive and living nearby, I have no doubt they would have watched it with us. In the 1950s in the United States we still had a unified culture. By this I mean the country—and I suspect this is true of England and all western European countries, too—wasn't divided into mini-cultures: youth culture, black culture, gay culture, and the rest. So-called variety shows throve on television. *The Ed Sullivan Show*, an early evening Sunday show, might have on the same night the coloratura Roberta

Peters, the comedian Jackie Mason, Chinese acrobats, an animal act, Victor Borge, and a ventriloquist. Such a nutty but in retrospect rather sweet melange is unthinkable today, and the culture is poorer for the fact that it is so.

I know Frank Muir and Dennis Norden from a BBC program called *My Word* that ran on Sunday afternoons on American public radio. They were both very funny, especially Muir, who would say outrageously witty things in a high English accent with an accompanying lisp. Goodman Ace (née Aiskowitz) was a name I had long known about without quite knowing what was behind it. He was something of a Jewish Robert Benchley. With his wife Jane, he had a successful radio show called *Easy Aces*, in which his wife specialized in malapropisms and did a Gracie Allen to his more sophisticated version of George Burns. The show was before my time. The Goodman Ace of my time was known chiefly as a comedy writer, a man behind the scenes. I not long ago heard a story about him in which he and his wife are dining at an expensive French restaurant in Manhattan, where they wait an excruciatingly long while for their food. Exasperated, Goodman Ace holds up his hand and calls out, "*Gendarme, gendarme.*" His waiter arrives to correct him: "Monsieur, surely you don't mean gendarme. You mean garcon." "No," says Goodman Ace, "I mean gendarme. There's been a holdup in the kitchen."

Recent English figures seem to have flopped on American television. I have in mind Simon Cowell and Piers Morgan. Their failures are, I think, well deserved. Cowell was cruel at his devastating judgments of would-be performers; Morgan was prosecutorial in his treatment of guests on a one-on-one talk show. Both men are entirely charmless, and seem little more than a television extension of the English gutter press. We Americans prefer our English television performers to be higher toned, Oxbridgean aristocratic a la Alistair Cooke, whom I, in an Anglophobe pet, used to attempt to take the considerable wind out of by referring to him, if only to my wife, as Al Cooke. Today, alas, there aren't even any Alistair Cookes around for we Americans to import. A shame, really.

If my movie-going life has fallen off, my reading life is, at least for the moment, picking up. My current bathroom book is V. Nabokov's *Speak, Memory*, which may be his best work and is filled with beautiful small touches; I've just completed the sweet chapter about his mother. Nabokov, so detached from everyone else, loved his parents, which is a great advantage in life. My bed-table book is Robert Burton's *Anatomy of Melancholy*, in which I had a bookmark at page 108—placed exactly when I cannot say—

but which I have now begun again, not having remembered a word of thos⌐
first 108 pages. The book is some 1,200-odd pages long. I've owned it for
at least three decades, and if I don't finish it this time around I shall probably
never do so. I also fear it may be on the stiff entrance exam for literary men
composed by the Jewish version of Saint Peter, St. Peterstein, perhaps. Finally, my morning reading is a superior book called, simply, *Plato* by the
German classical philologist Paul Friedlander, another of Hitler's gifts to
American academic life. Friedlander is deep but lucid, and reading him one
is serenely deluded into the belief that one is becoming a touch smarter.

So don't worry, Mom, I'm reading good.

Best, Joe

4.3.14. London, S.W.7. 5RF.
Dear Joe,

Like the man said, but I cannot remember which one, "Old age is a
funny thing to happen to a little boy." I dreamed the other night that I was
fifty and felt that I had better get on with things before . . . I woke up. No,
I did not find that I was wearing the bottoms of my trousers rolled; but I
do wonder for how many more years Beetle and I will be able to do the
rather rugged climb to our cottage on the Greek island we went to first
more than fifty years ago. Yesterday a man came to see me because he
wanted me to agree to be filmed, for as many hours as I care to ramble on
in my apology *pro vita mea*. He furnished me with a list of those whom he
has already embalmed and I found it quite an impressive company in which
to be boxed.

The man's name is Christopher Sykes, but not *that* Christopher Sykes
(a man famous for nothing that I know of except a book about Evelyn
Waugh, but famous all the same, in a certain generation). The list of those
already canned, casketed even, included scientists—Jeremy Bernstein,
Michael Atiyah, Bernard Lovell, Edward Teller (already), James Watson,
E.O. Wilson—as well as Philip Roth, Jonathan Miller, Paula Rego, Peter
Hall *et ceteros*. Who am (was?) I not to enter that *galère*? Even as I feared
that I was going to spill my substance in the air (for 10% of nothing), I consented to take my last (say it ain't so, Joe) chance to address the world from
the electronic equivalent of that balcony overlooking the Piazza Venezia

from which Mussolini sang bellicose arias to the *brava gente d'Italia*. Will anyone click on me, and shall I feel the tingle?

It is better, I have to hope, to declare myself at length in my own terms than to receive a Lifetime Achievement Award (fat chance) from some branch of the self-advertising community of the so-called Arts. *A proposito*, this year is the fiftieth anniversary of my election to fellowship of the Royal Society of Literature. Our countryman, the voluminous Jeffrey Meyers is also a Fellow, so you need not remove your *chapeau*. However, when I signed my name in the *Livre d'Or* with Byron's pen, I did have a sense of being made a petty cardinal. I had just been asked to write a movie called *What Makes Tommy Run* (seventeen weeks of working with a director/producer called Norman Panama at £750 a week; nobbad). Then came the summons to Parnassus (the prosaic slope) and I was Laocoon writhing in serpentine shame. I extracted myself from Panamanian canalization and resolved to take the high road forever after. And did I? I was soon charmed by Stanley Donen into writing a movie called *Two For The Road*. I fear that my autobiography might well be called *Hullo and Goodbye to All That*.

Now, still a kid, I find that showbizzy men rarely beat a path to my e-mail. I am reduced and promoted to being pretty much what I always thought I should and would be, a writer on his own, doing his own stuff. Hence I have just given my agent a short novel called *Private Views* and have an uneasy feeling (of election of a kind) that it will shock more publishers than will reach for their soon to be obsolete checkbooks. Even so, I remember that one Miranda Seymour, self-publicist *par médiocrité,* deplored the modest, implied sex in the last volume of my *Glittering Prizes* trilogy. It was improper that someone of my then age etc. Well, I'm younger than that now, but all the same . . .

My little book, which Steve Wasserman considers far too Briddish to interest a U.S. house, has a very long fuse. When my first novel was published, in the halcyon—you remember the now endangered halcyon—days of 1956, before the Suez adventure, like man's first disobedience, brought all those woes in its train, Ken Tynan came to the party which we gave in our basement flat on Chelsea Embankment. He brought with him a long-haired, beautiful woman of 33, one Elizabeth Jane Howard, a novelist who was renowned for her affair with Arthur Koestler and would be for the novel, *After Julius,* in which she elevated him to the pillory. I knew nothing of Ken's now amply revealed sexual predilections (in those uptight days men did not list such things in the public prints) nor, of course, did I know anything of the lady and hers.

Almost twenty years later, we became friendly with Michael Ayrton, artist sculptor and autodidact, whose name may just mean something to you. He was sure, when he was young and prodigious, that it (his name) would be emblazoned among the stars, but he suffered from self-inflicted errors of judgment, not least that of agreeing to become the art critic of the Stalinoid Kingsley Martin's *New Statesman* in his early twenties. He had already designed sets for John Gielgud's *Macbeth,* at a time when that meant something (was not Bakst among the prophets?). Modesty was never his style. It's said that M. "drove Gielgud to distraction...by his savage resentment, ungraciousness of manner and lack of charm and generosity towards the work people in every department. The leading lady told him 'Don't go on being insufferable longer than you can help. It's a sort of defense against something, isn't it? But it only gets in your way'." Can you guess what Michael was hung up about? His aunt was married to Israel Zangwill. His father was called Gould; he was an alcoholic, but not a Jew, but his mother... well, she was what she was and, whatever Bishop Berkeley might say, also another thing: M.P. and Chairman of the Labour Party. Michael was a lifelong socialist, but there was only ever one member of his praesidium.

When Jack Lambert asked me to review a volume of Ayrton's essays and fancies, the weather-vane Literary Editor of *The Sunday Times* said, "Say what you like, no one much likes him." I do not care to have my card marked; when I found *Fabrications* much to my fancy taste (it included a little number in which a curator finds that some of the Giacometti statues in his care have *grown* a centimeter or more), I gave it a nice boost. The *Observer* critic's piece, *par contre,* was headlined "A Bit of a Borges" (geddit?). Not long afterwards, Michael invited us to lunch at his house, not far from ours in the unfashionable Essex countryside. By then he had the air and beard of a wounded veteran. He had no London gallery. As a critic, he had shot down too many of his now eminent contemporaries (he later had a go at Picasso in his, alas, leaden novel *The Midas Touch*).

George Steiner and his historian wife Zara were the other guests at table. Michael had been a great cocksman in his day (so Steiner told me later), but was now married to a cookery writer called Elizabeth, who burnt the chickens. (When did anyone ever have an edible meal in the house of a restaurant critic or recipe peddler?). Having become a sculptor, Michael had gone into the lists against "Old Henry" (Moore) who was as spiteful as he was unchallenged. It may be that M. liked Beetle, and me, because we bought quite a number of his bronzes, but I prefer to think that we were somewhat fellow spirits. He had no Greek, but was a convert to Hellenism;

warped by spondylitis, he saw himself as the Minotaur *redivivus*. In the Minotaur we have, his hunched bronze gazes with puzzlement at the explicit human hand on his foreleg. At lunch, Steiner asked me why I was so much more intelligent than my novels. Yes, we hit it off right away. He also spilt red wine on Beetle's white linen sleeve. He cured it, he said, trilingually, with the contents of the salt cellar.

Once a cocksman, always, if it can be managed: Michael was not displeased to tell us that Elizabeth punished his recurrent infidelities with implacable fidelity. One of his pre-marital loves had been—now we are coming to it—Elizabeth Jane Howard. In exercising his *droit de génie,* he expected women to be exalted by his virility. Jane was not interested in the ride 'em cowboy style. She shocked unshockable Michael by her very precise wishes and never mind the *meum-tuum* stuff. She was, in short, a demanding submissive. Michael was unflattered by the role of the man in the velvet mask and, as they will say, moved on. What he told me lodged in my mind. I went back to it for a short story, in 1975, after he had died following a solitary visit to our French house. He had been so reluctant to leave that, on the last morning, he took the failure of his hire car to start as an omen that we should have him as our permanent guest. I found the urgent strength to push the sullen vehicle fast enough for the engine to engage and the parting guest gathered speed and off he went, forever. Michael died of undiagnosed diabetes. Where was his Jewish mother when he needed her?

In 1966, Jane Howard and Kingsley Amis came ashore on Ios (our Greek island) from the yacht on which they were cruising with publisher Tom Maschler. I had just given Kingsley a generous review for *The Anti-Death League*. At least his latest novel was not as bad as most of his recent work, but I didn't put it that way. Jane pissed in the field below our house in manly style. She was, at that time, the witch-beauty who had cast her spell on the most famous writer of the day. How he was at night she never disclosed. In the end, which didn't come for fifteen years or so, she threw him out because he was an alcoholic slob. I was not fascinated by Jane, who much later became friendly with our daughter Sarah's then husband, a wannabe novelist. Jane wished herself on them when they went, with their daughters, for an Aegean holiday on Ios. Jane was crotchety and, no doubt, jealous. By the end, Sarah hated her for her selfish pettiness. Nick continued to sit at her feet, pupil-wise. Jane published many successful novels, the last a saga of Forsyte-like toffs, which I have no wish to read.

I realized, towards the end of last year, that I had absented myself too long from fiction and its non-commissioned freedom. So I set about renovating and expanding the little number I did in the Eighties. I did not base my painter heroine, Katya Lowell, on Jane in any other regard than that K. too has specific appetites. The trick was to out-Vlad Volodya and write a scandalous book without using any *gros mots* and without a single description of what the author of *Lolita* called "the porno grapple." I am pretty sure that I have brought it off with some originality, but I also fear, *et pour cause*, that it will never find a publisher; and if it does, he moaned, some vengeful lit. ed. will make sure that Madame Seymour gets to play the dominatrix.

Here's the kicker: the day after I wrote the last line of *Private Views*, E. J. Howard died. And yet they say there is no such thing as providence.

Tout à toi, Freddie.

March 8, 2014
Dear Freddie,

Your remark about the other, the non-filming Christopher Sykes reminded me of an Italian restaurant in Chicago that had a sign over the bar that read: "Febo's—Famous for Nothing." I shall always be in the older Christopher Sykes's debt, though, for his telling the following anecdote about Evelyn Waugh. He visited Waugh in the hospital after the latter's hemorrhoid surgery to find him complaining about the post-operative effects. "Well," said Sykes, "you'll be feeling better soon, I'm sure, and at least you will no long suffer the irritation of the hemorrhoids." Waugh replied: "The hemorrhoids never really bothered me that much." When Sykes asked him why, then, had he undergone the surgery to have them removed, Waugh responded: "Sheer perfectionism." When one considers how deeply imperfect Evelyn Waugh was—forty or fifty pounds overweight, red-faced, porcine, addicted to pills and alcoholic, easily the rudest man in the United Kingdom—the notion of his going for sheer perfectionism through the removal of his hemorrhoids is very amusing. I have myself used the anecdote to ward off physicians who wished to do elaborate tests on me that I feel are unnecessary.

I suppose the closest thing America has to the Royal Society of Literature is the American Institute of Arts and Letters, of which I am pleased not to be a member and, if luck and good sense hold out, never will be. All the honor societies in America, and the country's honors generally, are, or so it seems to me, no longer very honorific; this chiefly because the personnel isn't there to fill their rosters. Distinction is on the way out in my country. (*Bang*—that, I believe, was the door slamming behind it.) Much of what passed for distinction, sad truth to tell, was probably never all that distinguished to begin with. If one checks the past membership in the American Institute of Arts and Letters and past presidents of American PEN and other such groups, one finds no shortage of dullards, doofuses, and dorks, to be perfectly alliterative about it. The problem, I suspect, is too many bloomin' honors floating around out there and too few homos erecti worthy of them.

In the middle of this last paragraph—you will have to believe this—a handsome paperback edition of Montesquieu's *My Thoughts* arrived from United Parcel Service. A thick vol., a genuine tome at 779 pages, I opened it up to check the leding, and, lo, I found the following:

> [**628**] When you are prodigal with honors, you gain nothing, because all you do is ensure that a greater number of men are worthy of them, so that the more you reward people the more it happens that others deserve to be rewarded. Five or six other persons are worthy of an honor you have granted to two or three; five or six hundred are worthy of an honor you have granted to a hundred and so forth.

Montesquieu's dates, I would remind you, are 1689–1755, which is another way of saying that of the dispensing of honors there is no end, and not many of them mean anything, and it was ever thus.

My view is the crass one of being only interested in honors and prizes that bring gold with them. ("I can stand a lot of gold," said Henry James). And this because the prestige isn't genuinely prestigious. Look about and one discovers the people in the same club or honored a year or two before one are worthy chiefly of contempt. Groucho Marx, as everyone knows, said that he had no interest in joining a club whose standards were so low as to allow him membership. I feel differently: I have no wish to join any club that is already filled with so many *putzim* that to be among them would lower my own perhaps too good opinion of myself.

Congratulations on the other Christopher Sykes filming you for posterity, or is it posterior? I have little doubt you will come across charmingly. I have never myself been filmed in the manner you describe, but whenever I view myself—on YouTube or C-span—it gives me the willies. You will recall the willies. They bring on self-doubt and a strong feeling that the rather unattractive person on screen can't, surely can't possibly, be you. The willies are cringe-making.

I have no further interest in going on television or radio or being interviewed for the press, and have resolved to turn down all future invitations to do so. Not, let me hasten to add, that the Medes, as I think of the good people from the media, are lined up round the block asking me to do so. (The diplomatist George Kennan claimed that he received between 500 and 1,000 such invitations in the course of a year.) I have decided that my meager fame—if fame is even the right word for such minuscule recognition as I have been granted—is sufficient. I have no wish to be better known than I now am. Above all, I have no wish to be known as a writer, which only makes some people nervous and others foolishly adulatory.

On four different occasions I have been sent around the United States flogging new books of mine in bookstores, which shall soon be extinct, and on local radio and television shows. The cost to the publishers who sent me out on this fool's errand was probably close to a thousand dollars a day to keep me sheltered, watered, and fed. Escorts, workers for public-relations firms, were sometimes provided. (I recall one in San Francisco who between trips to radio stations and bookstores regaled me with the therapy she and her now separated lesbian partner were undergoing to regain their equilibrium.) I appeared on time, in cleaned up condition, did my little dance, signed twenty books here, fourteen there, and hobbled off into the night neither wiser nor much richer. The highlight of my radio appearances came at a radio show in Marin County, in California, where the "host" (I guess I was the parasite) asked me if there was anything I wished to do. I told him I should like to juggle on radio (I once saw Buster Keaton do this in a film), which he allowed me to do, with lemons. Occasionally on these tours, after my dance, a man or woman would come up to tell me that he or she really enjoyed my writing, and I was—and always will be—pleased by this. But, apart from this and the regard of a rapidly diminishing number of peers, I do not require a lot more in the way of attention.

I had a commercial success with my book *Snobbery,* which sold some 60,000 copies and had a good paperback sale. But I do not see hitting the bestseller gong again in my lifetime. Given the gunk that appears on bestseller lists, I am ready to say that I *would* be less than fully proud to do so. I recently reread S. N. Behrman's *Portrait of Max.* At one point Max Beerbohm asks his secretary, Miss Jungman, later his wife, to bring out his latest royalty statement from the firm of Alfred A. Knopf. With much pride, he demonstrates the unrelieved number of zeros on it, then adds, *"There's a* publisher's statement." Near the end of his life, Max Beerbohm claimed to have roughly 1,500 readers in England, and 1,000 in America. Today, nearly sixty years since his death, those numbers are probably down to 500 and 300. Still, I find them numbers of which to be proud.

Nor do I have any wish to be genuinely famous. You, through your movie connection, have known several greatly famous people. Those people I know who have had a bit of fame did not live easily with it. Saul Bellow was, I should say, mildly famous—just enough so to seem ever so slightly disappointed when no one in a restaurant recognized him. Barbara and I used occasionally to go to dinner with a Chicago politician and his wife, and the night was a bleak one if some stranger didn't come up to tell him how much he admired him. He wasn't, let me add, in the least admirable.

Only three ways to fame in our day, and none of them is called literature: being a big-time movie star or athlete, being on television regularly, and being a serial killer. Do you know the name George Will? He is a man in his early seventies who has written a syndicated political newspaper column in the United States for many decades, but his real fame derives from his being on Sunday morning political gab shows. George has taken me to dinner a few times when he's been in Chicago, and once he took me to a baseball game. At the end of the baseball game, as we were leaving the stadium, we did not pass more than ten or fifteen yards in the crowd without some stranger calling out, "Hey, it's George Will!" "Great column on Bush, George." "Yo, George, go Cubs!" He pretended it wasn't happening. I thought it was hell, and was glad it wasn't me that people recognized and yelled at. Such fame, making one the center of attention, greatly cuts down on one's freedom. Writers especially, I think, do well to avoid it.

On the working-press front, I had an invitation last week from Fiona Hardcastle at the *Daily Telegraph* to write a piece on why the English no longer seem to be succeeding so easily in America. What occasioned the notion for the piece was the firing from an American television show of a boorish gutter-press veteran named Piers Morgan. The request came late on a Wednesday and the piece was needed by Friday. I had earlier promised an editor that I would have a review of *The Kennan Diaries* to him on Friday, and so had to turn Fiona down. Someone named Max Davidson, who is described by the *Telegraph* as "a seasoned traveler, wit, raconteur, bon vivant, and cricket critic," did the piece instead. None of his wit, raconteur, or bon vivant qualities was in evidence in the piece he turned in, which had a very low truth quotient.

My Kennan piece, which I did manage to complete on time, turns out to have been sent down to the printer with a typo in the first sentence of its penultimate paragraph. I try not to cry over spilt ink—or split oink—but typos in my own scribbling do cause a little black flag to wave in my heart. My friend Edward Shils, after pointing out to me a typo in one of his own magazine pieces, remarked, "You know, Joseph, now that they no longer defrock priests, one can't get any decent proofreading." Alas, even today, when they have begun to defrock priests for foul play with God's chillin', apparently one still can't get any decent proofreading. Might it be, I ask you, that we are living in an imperfect world?

Keep the faith and power to the *pupik*.

Best, Joe

9.3.14. London, SW7 5RF.
Dear Joe,

I admire your claim to famelessness, and wish, slightly, that I could mount as convincing a show of proud indifference to the bitch goddess and her cult. I never imagined that I should be famous when I decided that I was going to be a novelist and I suspect, looking back (and what a long view there is now in that *rétroviseur*!), that it was an error to think that being published was prize enough. In order to be hailed as great, one must first imagine oneself to be so, and never, never smile in self-deprecation. Now and again and again, I see myself as a figure of fun (who should not, if we are thinking of juvenile ambitions?) on account of my misreadings of the nature of adult life and art as I looked longingly forward from my parents' suburban flat, in Putney, S.W.15, to that Parisian, if possible, garret and the sweet anguish of being an unappreciated genius; but— the adversative had to come—there was something earnest and serious in my wish to join the booked in print. I did think that there was a world, essentially Gentile, to which intelligence might gain access and where I might hope to shine.

As it turned out, I owe more to my native land, from which I was forcibly embarked in 1938, than to Great Britain for what Henry James could stand a lot of, essentially because of that ungolden icon (correct use now looks incorrect, does it not?) the Oscar. Thanks to the award of an emasculated quasi-phallic gewgaw, our forty years on from 1966 were more cushioned than any divan I ever hoped to recline on when, in our Chelsea basement, I was composing my second Sinclair Lewisish novel, not more than five thousand miles from *Main Street*. It was called *The Earlsdon Way* and when it was done, and then done again (after the only manuscript was stolen from my publisher's office, on account, I am sure, of the sumptuousness of the briefcase in which it lay unread), I was told by the publisher of my first and frivolous novel that I should "not make any friends," if I wrote that kind of Zolaesque Jack-Hughesie stuff. I told Macmillan and co. I did not become a writer to make friends and I meant it and off I went (to Cassell's, down the road). I had Beetle and that, I have found throughout my writing life, has been a durable reason for refusing all substitutes.

I have had some long and many short friendships but I have never had one which, when ruptured, left me bereft or lonely. I have wept at the deaths of a number of friends: Guy Ramsey (a journalist friend of my father who, though he never wrote his *Madame Bovary*, fancied playing Flaubert to my Guy de Maupassant), and Michael Ayrton, a disappointed genius, a renowned amorist with—in his day—a penchant towards friends' wives, but whose day was all but spent when we got to know him, and Kenneth McLeish, with whom I translated poetry and drama from Latin and Greek, and who died trying to get his shirt off, as Heracles did when he put on that double-cuffed number stained by Nessus.

Ken and I used to speak at length on the telephone (on my dime, quite rightly) on Sunday afternoons, at much the time that I am fingering this to you, and we talked with great facility, many laughs, some fancy allusions and yet with no true intimacy (but what is that? I sometimes wonder). He was a brilliant linguist—a translator of Ibsen already and better, I am willing to believe, than another transient "friend" of mine, Michael whose name eludes me, no it doesn't; Meyer—and a musician whose composition tutor (Rubbra?) at Oxford said that his notes were excellent but he was not good at the pauses in between. Harold Pinter later took a First in pauses, and much Swedish good it did him.

McLeish sort of loved me and I him, but I never quite trusted him, not least re *la chose juive*. Oddly enough, whether on the several occasions we arranged to meet in London or when he came, once, to visit us in France, I was never sure what he looked like and just slightly relied on him recognizing me. He was like a quotation you are never sure you've got right. I make no distinction in the matter of friends and their value to me between Jews and those other people. Few will not let you down if it comforts their vanity or fills their purses or a hotter ticket arrives.

I make it a rule, which I do not always have the nerve to keep, to do something a little like what your father did, when he sued the rich (and powerful) if they failed to pay up: I am naïve (and prickly) when people don't keep their word. I was brought up to believe that you had to do it. Time was the British did indeed do so. Even the 10% men of the William Morris Agency had an iron house rule that they always returned clients' calls within twenty-four hours, whatever the good or bad or no news. Now? Tell me about it. Cue some small comedy re the London lit. world. I suspect you may have noticed the frequency with which one A. N. Wilson does major reviews in the *TLS*. This does not insure him against being mauled, from time to time (he is nothing if not prolific) when his own books come to judgment. Sadie and Maisie are systole and diastole—Larry Durrell's pet pair—in the British game. I once turned down an invitation to write the script of a very poor novel of Mr. Wilson's, about an M.P. who was a flagellant crossdresser or something of that everyday kind, and suspect (paranoia being, as Mr. Kubrick said, "knowing what's going on") that word got back to the author. I cannot even remember whether he ever mauled me in print, but who, as they say, is counting? (Someone, betcha!) Anyway (it too had to come), I saw a review by Master Wilson (the A.N. always summons the name Angus Wilson, a sweet man, once the chouchou of the London literary gaiety and then, all of a sudden, an impoverished exile) of a v. fat biography of Penelope Fitzgerald, which Beetle happened to be reading.

Ms. Fitzgerald is just the kind of lady novelist who rises perennially, in one form or another (Barbara Pym, thou shouldst be living etc.), on the English horizon, often in post-menopausal majesticness, not at all the same thing as majesty. Handbag-carrying Anita Brookner was/is another: no dialogue, no good, in most (repetitive) cases. I rarely read more than a page or two, however thick the surrounding laurels. Such ladies, some with chins, some not, win prizes like one o'clock, or rather like seven fifteen in the evening. So, Beetle was reading on bravely and at great length about la Fitzgerald's sorry early and middle history and I copped a look. Academically enhanced biographeuse Hermione Lee was clearly not only taking her time, which was her right, but too much of everyone else's. I didn't read more than I wanted to, so I did not read a lot, but the impression of being sat on by a hefty lump was there. I read A. N. Wilson's review of said tome and, by God, he got it bang right, and with no nastiness whatever. Then I read him, in a quickly subsequent *TLS*, on the letters of Hugh Trevor-Roper, edited by my friend Richard Davenport-Hines and, once again, Wilson was right on the mark.

I have another friend, the historian Andrew Roberts, who told me, when he was a young man (we lunched after I had reviewed his *Eminent Churchillians con* due gush), that he spent the first two hours of his morning writing letters to famous persons. He did not flatter them necessarily, but depend upon it that he commended himself to them by the intelligence of his effusive inquiries. Why not, indeed? I recall walking down Jermyn St, W.1., with another historian, the now literally Lordly Hugh Thomas, and he looked through the window of the no-longer-there, once notoriously louche—now soullessly renovated—Cavendish Hotel (celebrated in my friend Simon Raven's novel sequence *Alms for Oblivion*, in which the hotel is run by one Tessie Buttock, I think) and saw an old gent having tea. "That's Lord Sandwich," he said, "let's go in and talk to him."

"I don't know him," I said.

"Nor do I. Come on."

I went in, more behind than with him, and Hugh approached the sand-wich man without more, as they used to say, ado. To my amazement, the old chap was delighted to be accosted and made all kinds of revelations about whatever it was in which he had once had a backroom hand. I learned nothing from this lesson in pushiness, so strongly had my father warned me against that kind of, I fear, Jewy conduct. When I see a famous person available for chat, I turn and walk away. Whatever its motive, the move is not foolish. Old Maugham said it was better to quiz a vet, or someone of that mundane order, than a politician or, as they say today, celebrities. The latter have public personalities which they tote with them and which they furnish with pre-digested patter as Mr. Bergen did Charlie McCarthy (was it).

Of course there is often something quite polished, varnished even, about such performances. A Hollywooden screenwriter who penned (you think?) a lot of episodes of *Moonlighting* for Bruce Willis and Cybill Shepherd told me that he had been walking down the street with Bruce, in plainclothes, as it were, when the actor saw a good-looking woman coming towards them. Willis's face and posture altered. His lights came on. The woman looked at him and, so Glenn (the scribe) told me, she reacted by caressing her breast as she walked on by. Willis immediately reverted to his mundane self. "I just wanted to be sure I could still do it." Fame is the spurt? Who said that?

Cut back to A. N. Wilson. His two reviews in a row, readers may recall, seemed to me, all right, spot on. So what did Quixote do, despite the sneers of his inner fancy Panza? Wrote a note of appreciation is what, from the ranks of Tuscany even. Master W. did not immediately flush grateful. Days passed and I rued (yes, I did too) my quick-sottishness. I recalled that Mr. W. had written once that Israel had no right to exist. I began to buff my armor, wash my spear. More days went by. It occurred to me that, in a week or so, I would write to him and say that I was glad that he had not replied because I had bet a friend of mine ten pounds that he would not have the grace to do so. That would show him. You're right, of course: a day later, came a courteous note of thanks, signed Andrew Wilson. You can't lose 'em all.

I was going to tell you another story of the lit. scene in Old England and how I sent that Cavafy review, which had taken me four weeks to write, because it involved comparing Daniel Mendelsohn's graceless Englishing (lauded to the skies by the *NYRB* in-group who, betcha, had no Greek between them) with the original, and how, after the piece had been acknowledged and I was promised that the ed. in charge would write to me "in a day or two," I didn't hear *tipota*, as we *Hellenikoi* say among ourselves when we have nothing better to say, for five weeks, during which I considered following Sappho over the cliff and other forms of splashy self-immolation. Then Beetle suggested I ask, icy/politely, if said ed. was sick or worse. He was better, he replied: he was fine, and always had been, but he was a bit busy. I could expect a proof next week. All this *angst und Weltschmerz* for £300 and a copy for you to keep of Mendelsohn's artless, self-important jumboburger. Know what? Makes me wish I was rich and famous.

Tout à toi, Freddie.

March 16, 2014
Dear Freddie,

I have been under the weather with a knock-down cold. Nothing for it but to sleep it off, which I did, majestically, much of yesterday and the day before. Enforced sloth may be the best sloth of all. My dear Barbara worries about my health more than I do, and she looks after me wonderfully when I go down. The joke *chez* Epstein is that we are in an assisted living arrangement - not, to be sure, in a retirement home, to which we are pledged never to repair, but one in which we assist each other in all realms, from remembering words or the titles of movies to helping each other in minor illnesses and much beyond. A good marriage remains the most sensible and happiest of living conditions.

Which brings me to the passages about friendship in your last e-mail. "I have had some long and many short friendships," you write, "but I have never had one which, when ruptured, left me bereft or lonely." The reason you have never felt profound emptiness when a friendship ended, my more than guess is, is that you have Beetle, the closest and best of all possible friends. A good marriage, in which one's wife or husband is also one's dearest friend, in some ways disqualifies one for other friendships. One does of course genuinely, greatly even mourn the death of dear friends, and miss them sorely, as I nearly twenty years after his death miss Edward Shils, whom at least weekly I wish were still alive for me to exchange jokes, gossip, and serious thoughts with. I feel something of the same for Hilton Kramer, who underwent the horror of dementia before his death. But this sense of loss would, I haven't much doubt, have been deeper still had I not the love and constant companionship of my wife, who in my life is and always will be the first among unequals (a phrase that requires the Latin I do not posessess.

I met A. N. (Andrew, is it not?) Wilson once, briefly and many moons ago, in New York. He seemed mild-mannered, in the then young fogey style of the day. I've never attempted an A. N. Wilson book, all of which seem too thick for me. (Can a volume be too voluminous? I believe it can.) Like most writers, I am a slow reader, always mentally editing what I read, at the same time looking for things to appropriate for my own scribbling. It has not occurred to me to read his novels, and the subjects of his biographies —on Tolstoy, Jesus, Milton, C. S. Lewis, and others—have already been better written about by others, or so it has seemed to me. I do read him in the TLS, and find him interesting at 1,500 to 2,000 words. But a gentleman of my age, the grave yawning and all that, cannot really be expected to spend two or three weeks of my reading life on one of his not quite necessary books.

In our correspondence we have steered clear, rightly I think, of what in my high school were called "current events," elsewhere known as the news. I know I have done so chiefly because the news seems so ephemeral, so fleeting, so much part of the contemporary noise, and in truth I, who study none of it in any real detail, have so little to add. But in the current crisis in Ukraine - how I miss that definite article - I cannot help recall that the major Ukrainian city of Kiev was the model for Sholem Aleichem's city of Yehupetz. In Sholem Aleichem's day Jews were not allowed to live there without special license. And it was in Kiev that he, Sholem Aleichem, from his hotel bedroom in 1905, watched a pogrom of such brutality that so greatly shook him that he never again returned to Eastern Europe. The Ukrainians are being pushed to the wall by that very perfect model of a KGB-man, Senor Putin. One ought to have sympathy for them, but when I see those cold slavic faces on television, and think of the tolerance for the killing of Jews on the part of their ancestors, much of what sympathy I might otherwise have departs. And so, for now, shall I.

Best, Joe

London SW7 5RF. 17.3.14.
Dear Joe,

In age, I await tranquility like an overdue plane, anxiously. I try to regard things *sub specie aeternitatis,* as Spinoza, that noblest of apostates, recommended, and find that that is a young man's solution. Although Baruch/Benedict died in his forties, his call for serenity is that of someone with plenty of time ahead of him. It may be ignoble to announce one's fears but they are sometimes thrust upon one. For specific instance, we were invited a month ago to come to some college in your very own city for me to take the Methuselah part in a panel of moviemakers during a May week devoted to the seventh art. I said nothing to you because no tickets were booked and because postponement, as we used to be told in certain manuals of sexual expertise, adds to the fun. Kingsley Amis, *dans ses oeuvres,* was kind enough to tell us that, to avoid premature sorry-about-that, he turned his mind to thoughts of mashed potato. Bang on, as they once said.

The past tense *supra* indicates why we have resigned ourselves to remaining in Europe, at least until the day when some major major company tells me that my presence in the U.S. is worth anything they have to pay, which means, in specific terms, something like $4,000 insurance against medical and hospital billings (why and when did bills become present participular?), even if we stayed for less than a week. "Fings," the English used to say, "ain't what they used to be." Worse than that: neither are we. Senility is getting to know what it is to be up shit creek and there goes the paddle. For the rest, we are well. We creak and we groan, but, yes, we have come through and, yes, yes, we damn well do intend to go further.

Saturday night, our son Stephen took us and his new young lady (tall, dark, very clever, with a champion forehand) to see the stage version of the eighties movie hit *Fatal Attraction,* expertly directed at the Theatre Royal, Haymarket, by an old theatrical hand called Trevor Nunn, one of those Englishmen who have done parochially well with stage shows (*Les Miz* is one, I think), but never made the transAt leap into the movies. Sam Mendes is the overrated counter-instance, a moveable object kept going by high-velocity lack of substance. In Nunn's production, *Fatal Attraction* was divided into brief scenes as if it were a 3-D movie, which may have been because . . . there was a famous scene in the movie, known as "the bunny-boiler" in which . . . yes, that's the one! You can leave a lot out these days and still be perfectly understandable.

The so-called star who played the temptress impersonated in the movie by Glenn Close was long and blonde, but failed to look like the fruit of that forbidden tree which etc. In fact, even though Close never came close to Marilyn, you realized how good she was by comparison. The promise of things-you-never-did-with-your-wife was there in Close's eyes. On stage, the guy who wasn't Michael Douglas just couldn't resist the potato chips on the bar. *Bref,* the whole thing depended on recalling what happened in the movie. The production served only to underline that all that falls must converge: as the arts yearn for the mythical hundred percent share of the public, film, TV and stage resume the worst elements of one another. Box on, as the referees used to say.

In this week's *Sunday Times*, the "Chief Reviewer" John Carey was interviewed by a man called Bryan Appleyard who is the paper's resident *intello-à-tout-faire.* In a Buñuel movie, he'd wear a vertically striped waistcoat and take the toffs' hats. He told us that Carey thought *Don Quixote* was a pile of crap because it mocked an old guy who had rocks in his head (Carey seems to have felt that Cervantes was mocking his, Carey's, poor sick brother, which is a little proleptic for the time of year). Well, *Don Quixote* just happens to have merited close, pretty much book-length, attention from two of the pans in my pantheon, viz. Vladimir Nabokov and René Girard, each of whom found rare, and distinct, qualities in it. Proving what? *Nada, señor, pero . . .* There was more (at two bucks a word, why cut anything?): Carey, an Oxford professor who doubles as a journocrat, was vaunted for claiming that there was no such thing as objective criticism. Crap, he implied, is in the eye of the beholder. No one can possibly know—Thus Spake Careythrusta—that any book is better than another.

There was a philosopher in old 1950s Oxford, J. L. Austin, who said that he had never met a determinist who genuinely believed, behaved as if, he had no choice in any matter whatever. Now it may be true that we cannot prove that *Pale Fire* is a better book than whatever tops today's breast-seller list, but we all know that it's a bishop to a bugger (this was defined as "even chances" by F. E. Smith, but let it pass) that Nabokov trumps, oh, Alice Munro. Seriously, team, how can a professor of Eng. Lit. (retd.) maintain something as fifth-formal as that one book cannot be said, objectively, comrade, to be better than another? How then does he review as if, like the Centurion in the gospel, he had the warrant to say to one go and to another come and be superlative behind the ears and places like that? In academic practice, did he prefer John Donne to Allen Ginsberg (I was having trouble remembering the Howler's moniker) and Charles Dickens to Jack Kerouac (you want to hit the road, pal? Don't let me detain you) only because that was where the Chair was placed?

Would some deutero-Carey claim that there is no "objective" way of knowing whether one pianist was better than another, one dancer ditto, one singer, one draftsman or draftswoman, one fiddler, one whistler, one juggler, one soufflé? I bet you get the idea. No, apparently it's only among the word-smiths that you cannot, as Mr. Coward said of a certain lady's eyes, get a pin between the good and the dreck. What is more typical of the dodgy-*oggi*-minded than being ashamed of liking what's better (or cleverer) than something else? Today's Mr. Puffs preserve their critical tenure by promising that their pastry carries no clever calories.

Carey is the post-modern instance of Benda's treasonous clerk: surely he knows that he doesn't mean what he says but he also knows that the public wants to believe that anyone who thinks that quality matters (or even exists) is a supercilious, privately educated prig. Carey has always been very civil to me personally, but that does not dispose me to chew his crud. What he's saying re objectivity is entirely trivial: there is, he means, no *absolute* and unarguable standard by which a book or poem can be judged. You remember what Nietzsche said? No, not all of it, just this bit: "You say there can be no argument about matters of taste? All life is an argument about matters of taste." The false cleric preaches bullshit from his paper pulpit. He once wrote that Ida was a Greek goddess when it is, as every other schoolboy used to know, a mountain in Crete.

I learned from this week's *TLS* that just around the corner from where we live is the flat which John Hayward shared with T. S. Eliot (and not far away in the opposite direction is an unerringly bourgeois block of flats bearing a blue memento that T.S.E. lived *there,* after he had set up with Valerie, his second wife and a dragon whose breath it was wise to avoid). The article was one of the first, after more than half a century of fawning, to agree with Eliot's own view of himself: he was indeed quite beastly to meet, and shifty too. Do you ever have delusions of proprietary rights over things you have written? I have a notion, perhaps pathetic, that I originated the term "heterosexual camp" (say it is so, Joe) and was, therefore, piqued and pleased to see it used, *sans attribution,* re the crowd that used to hang out and swing, verbally at least, in Bina Gardens, a red-brick enclave a tenth as old as time. Naughty verses are the spicy knickers of poets on their day off.

My vision of Eliot, to whom all due honor, is essentially of an immigrant eager to wear any old hat which might enable him to pass for an *indigène.* To think of anti-Semitism as a deeply embedded characteristic, bacillus or Serious Idea, is in almost all cases baloney: it is a way of deciding who you aren't and thus heeling yourself, like an alien plant, into the rose garden to which Mr. E. will gladly show you the door. Ten times out of eleven, anti-Semitism is a weakling's cottonwool muscle. C. Ricks, S. Spender, C. Raine and other on-the-makers have spent their splendor "proving" that Tom only did it because it teases and would have been appalled by the holocaust (Ricks doesn't think it merits a capital letter), if he'd ever got round to thinking about it or even registering that it happened. Steiner thought he was being career-damagingly bold in even mentioning "the jew is underneath the lot" back in 1970; maybe he was. I used it as an epigraph in my 1963 novel *Lindmann;* but who's counting?

What does Carey think? Not long ago he did an easy piece about the latest number on Primo Levi but showed no knowledge of a book, *Il Lungo Viaggio di Primo Levi,* recently published in Italy which gives a very convincing account of the days before Primo and his callow companions were picked up by the Fascist police. During that time, two young guys, eighteen and seventeen, joined their group and were then suspected of being traitors. Primo had nothing to do with the decision to kill them, nor was he present when they were executed, but Frediano Sessi makes a strong, quiet case for thinking that Levi's suicide, if that's what it was, in 1987, had at least something to do with his long, guilty memory of that brutal, pre-Auschwitz episode. Carey has taken the low road and claims that there is no objective reason, comrades, not to call it the high one. *Eppure . . .*

Tout à toi, Freddie.

March 21, 2014
Dear Freddie,

Ages of tranquility, also of senility, kick in at different times at different places. In this regard, I shall not forget—until my own senility kicks in—

Stuart Oken, the would-be producer at Warner Bros. of a movie he had asked me to write from one of my stories, who told me that the following day was his birthday. I wished him a happy birthday, to which he replied, "Nothing very happy about it. I shall be forty-one." What he meant was that to be forty-one and not come close to banging the gong of Hollywood success was a disaster. Stuart had produced two relatively decent flicks—*About Last Night*, made from a David Mamet play, and *Impromptu*, a movie about George Sand and Chopin—but that was far from good enough. In an ever more youthful Hollywood—this was in the 1990s—he, at forty-one, was in danger of being thought an old fart when only young farts were wanted.

Stuart Oken soon enough dropped out of the movie business, and went to work for Disney, where he helped turn former movies—*The Lion King* and its like—into stage plays. He currently works as the CEO of a Chicago theater company. He is a decent man, and though he was canned by Warner Bros. before anything serious happened with my less than ept screenplay, I enjoyed my conversations with him. He was always quick to respond to bits of screenplay that I sent him, and his praise was moderate and measured, even if not quite believable. He wasn't one of those creative producers, who suggest one speed up the plot by turning the dog in the story into a lesbian.

I thought about Stuart, whose job was to turn movies into stage plays when you mentioned that *Fatal Attraction*, with that famous *lapin en ebullition*, is now a play. All that remains is to turn the damn thing into a novel, or, as the term of art has it, a novelization. Stravinsky, one of the great heroes of the avant-garde, when presented with some new twist in art, used to say (do your own heavy Russian accent here) "Who need dis?"

As a confirmed non-play-goer, I have taken to wondering why people go to (mostly terrible) plays, where they are charged ample fees to be told that the world is, essentially, a dark and crappy place. I had a now dead friend named Sam Lipman, in his boyhood a piano prodigy and later a powerful music critic, who told me that he had just seen Philip Glass's new opera. When I asked him how it was, Sam said: "Its message is clear: Die! Die! Die, motherfucker, but first hand over $125 for the privilege of being told this."

My impression is that it is chiefly older people who continue going to plays, many of them our co-religionists. Why they drag themselves to deeply unenjoyable plays that inform them that they, their social class, their race, their country, are all rotten is less than clear. Sometimes I think they are simply inattentive to the message of these plays. Some school friends of Barbara's once told her she must see the musical version of E. L. Doctorow's novel *Ragtime*. These were all middle-class, mostly church-going, Republican-voting women, and they somehow missed Doctorow's point—that the world would be better without villainous wretched rabble like them in it.

Sometimes I think that attending the theater, and much of performing cultural generally, has become a substitute for religion. If so, a damn poor one it turns out to be. People now go to plays as they once went to *shul*, or synagogue. They go in reverence and in the belief that it is good for them to be there. Improving. Makes them smarter, more elegant, accomplished, deeper. Not true, none of it, not a word.

When I was growing up in Chicago, the height of culture for Jews of the merchant class, which was my family's class, was musical comedy. People with a bit of money might go to New York for a week and see six or seven musicals. (My parents were never so dopey, I am pleased to add.) When the road companies for these musicals appeared in Chicago, they saw them again, commenting on whether the shows were better in New York or Chicago. Men schooled in practical sense, some of whom were themselves immigrants who had witnessed pogroms and arrived in steerage, men who faced down labor union toughs and negotiated with Mafia thugs, would sit in theaters, enthralled, listening to *Pajama Game* or *Damn Yankees* or *Hello, Dolly*. Go, as these same people used to say, figure.

Pardon my Yiddish, but I have a *faiblesse* for soft English names, and that of Brian Appleyard, interviewer of John Carey whom you mention, qualifies. An American biographer—of Gertrude Stein and Leo Stein, among others—walks the streets of America with the name Brenda Wineapple. How I wish I could arrange to introduce Brian and Brenda, see them to the altar, hold up the *chuppa*, and make certain that, in the style of the current day, they part their names in the middle, as the Irish called hyphenated names, and become Brenda and Bryan Wineapple-Appleyard, or is it Appleyard-Wineapple.

Brian is an especially soft name, which has never fit the bulky and brutish-looking actor Brian Dennehy. I had a dear friend named Peter Jacobsohn, an émigré from Germany, whose father Siegfried Jacobsohn was in Weimar days a famous theater critic and editor of the *Weltbuhne*, an intellectual journal that achieved the honor of having been banned by the Nazis. Emigration was tough on Peter; he never really caught on to England, where he lived for a while, or America, where he spent much the greater part of his adult life. Although roughly twenty years older than I, he worked for me at *Encyclopedia Britannica*, and our understanding was that I would always protect him from the higher-ups, which I was easily and gladly able to do. If Peter were alive today, I don't think he would object to being described as a Europeanized nebbish. The reason I bring him up just now is that he once told me that if he had been an Englishman he would have preferred his name to have been Brian Catspaw.

The most lilting name in English criticism is surely that of Benedict Nightingale. So often English last names are verbs or common nouns or even adverbs. Checking the credits of English movies or BBC productions as they scroll down, I look for Ian Jump or Viveca Wedge or Nigel Gangreen, or Vivian Dunfore or Penelope Lively. The last is of course a real name, and my wife had as discouraging a time with one of her novels as your wife did with one of Penelope Fitzgerald's. Then there is poor Penelope Gilliatt, ill married to John Osborne, bonked by the equally if oppositely unattractive Mike Nichols and Edmund Wilson, caught out at plagiarism, and dead of alcoholism.

I've not read Penelope Fitzgerald's most famous novel, *Blue Flower*, about the life of Novalis, I gather, but I have read three of her other novels: *The Bookshop, Offshore*, and *At Freddie's* (Freddie's turns out in the novel to be an acting school). All gave what I should call an unheated but genuine, yes, you have it, Pymish pleasure. I much liked her family biography of her father, who was for a time the editor of *Punch*, and his three brothers, one of whom was a classical scholar and cryptographer, another an Anglican priest keen on social justice, and third, the best known today, Ronald Knox. I note that one of Penelope Fitzgerald's novels won a Booker Prize. England, it sometimes seems, has more Bookers than hookers, which cannot be a good thing.

Another name that I have always enjoyed for the sheer acoustical pleasure of it is Arnaldo Momigliano, the (I think it fair to say) great historian of historiography, whose full name, to which one can practically dance, was Arnaldo Dante Momigliano. I myself have just enough Italian to get on the slowest train from Ravenna to Milan, but no Italian is needed to recognize that words and names ending in vowels carry an automatically lovely lilt. I recall on an Alitalia flight reading aloud to myself the instructions on the plane's toilet seat and feeling that it was pure poetry. Genius on the part of the Italians to end all their names and words on vowels.

I was introduced to Arnaldo by Edward Shils, and never met, or expect ever again to meet, anyone like him. He must have been 5' 3," and always dressed in rumpled black suits with vest. (He sometimes wore a sweater under the vest, which make it look as if he were wearing two suits simultaneously.) He had airline tickets pinned to the inside of his suitcoat jackets.

He carried what looked to be two full pounds of keys; most of them to library carrels around the world. He wore a Borsalino hat, which I have seen him jam into the overhead carriers on planes. (He once told me about going into a Borsalino shop in Milan to acquire a new hat; and after having done so, he inquired of the whereabouts of his old Borsalino. "Not to worry, Doctore," a clerk told him, "we have taken care of it.") For all his scruffiness, he was attractive to women, or so Barbara tells me. He also had, in good Italian fashion, late life love affairs, usually with much younger female classicists.

None of this would be of much interest if Arnaldo wasn't the magnificent scholar that he was. I have seen him in the company of Peter Brown, Glen Bowersock, and Hugh Lloyd-Jones, and all showed an implicit deference to him. His knowledge went well beyond that of ancient history. He seemed in possession of all languages. I once noted him reading Dostoyevsky in Russian. At the Quadrangle Club, the faculty club of the University of Chicago, I was one morning having breakfast with Leon Edel, in town to give a lecture at the university, when Arnaldo, who lived at the Quadrangle Club when in residence at Chicago, joined us. Edel was writing a book—not so splendid a one, as it turned out—on Bloomsbury. Had you just arrived at our breakfast table and knew none of the players you would have assumed that Arnaldo had already written three books on Bloomsbury. "Of course," Arnaldo said, in his heavy Piedmontese accent, an accent resembling that of Bela Lugosi playing Dracula, "Duncan Grant is the lynchpin, the key to the understanding of Bloomsbury." Edel was the next stage up from impressed.

I have arranged to write a review of Tom Holland's new translation of Herodotus. I did so because I wanted an excuse to read through Herodotus one more time before I join those slain Persians on some field distinctly not Plataea. The Holland translation is slangier than I would like, but it takes a lot to ruin Herodotus, one of the great storytellers and in Greek (I'm told) stylists of his own and every other time. The history of Herodotus's reputation, as you doubtless already know, has been very zig-zag. Thucydides, Aristotle, Plutarch, Cicero in their respective days all spoke ill of him, accusing him of being, variously, a lightweight, a plagiarist, a naif, and a liar. Now there is a lineup of heavy hitters to come out against you.

Two days ago I read Arnaldo on the subject of Herodotus's reputation, in his *Studies in Historiography*, and all comes beautifully, richly, complexly clear. Arnaldo shows how the rise of ethnography and of antiquarianism have both enhanced Herodotus's reputation, arguing that, far from being a dupe and a liar, he was a pioneer. Arnaldo sets out the motives of his calumniators. In doing so, he tosses around centuries the way a drunken spendthrift tosses around ten-pound notes. In fifteen magisterial—also majestic—pages, he sets all to rights. A dazzling performance, and what dazzles is the sweep of his knowledge and the depth of his judgment.

Reading Arnaldo also reminds me that I shall never be able to write, in earnest, the name "Diodorus of Halicarnassas" or use the adjective "postexilic." In an otherwise lucky life, my two regrets are that I was not a classicist and that I cannot play jazz piano. Perhaps in the next life I shall be allowed to sing the odes of Pindar while accompanying myself on the piano. Surely this is not too much to ask.

Best, Joe

London SW7 5RF. 24.3.14.
Dear Joe,

Your very enjoyable piece "The Folly and the Ivy" about Wrigley Field and its incumbents made me realize that I can outdo Rimbaud in this at least: *je est des autres*. Anyone can be somebody else, but I have at least a dyad buttoned into whatever I happen to be wearing. I once wrote a movie, quite a good one, about Chicago, in which I busked my way into a show of expertise about your town, thanks partly to a *visite éclaire* at the expense of my producer, Burt Weissbord, whose father had a big spread in Evanston. You may well know the family, since Weissbord senior was a big developer (he employed Mies van der Rohe) and was, I daresay, politically joined at the seamy side with folks at City Hall. After driving around the wooden walls of Wrigley Field, I felt entitled to make it part of my fictional furniture, but made the mistake of having my characters walk past it, to thousands of unseen cheers, during a night game. I was then told that it was just about the only major league ground on which they had not installed floodlights.

The movie was called *A New Wife*; Diane Keaton and Al Pacino were both committed to star in it. The problem was finding a director who would agree to have those particular actors imposed on him. Sidney Lumet had been ninety-nine percent certain that he could get out of a commitment which he wished he hadn't had; but did he? I gave the public a taste of what they had missed by putting a love-bite of the script in a radio piece I did last year about a fictional director called Jake Liebowitz. It played pretty damn well, but no shark came sniffing.

My duality, trailed above, emerged when reading about your somewhat lapsed love for baseball. In games at least, I am no kind of a Yank. I recall the names of a few teams and I did go to a game or two in Kansas City in 1948 (not major league, I don't think) but my heart belongs between the wickets. For whatever genetico-educational reason, cricket commands my sentimental attention more than any other game. I owe my aptitude for conformity to its rules and practices. I was properly dismayed to read that Harold Pinter, who—like not a few domineering persons without great sporting ability—ran, selected and captained his own team, instructed his flannelled fools not to applaud incoming or outgoing opposition batsmen. Some people do rather give themselves away, don't you find, Carruthers? I am a bad loser, but I do not withhold applause where it is merited, dammit. The beauty of cricket is that it embodies British vanity and duplicity at the finest level.

Without hypocrisy, what are we but nasty, vindictive, spiteful on-the-makers? Cricket used to be a game in which a batsman would "walk," if his bat had tickled the ball and he knew it, when caught "on the full," as you people say, I believe. The fielders had, and have, a ritual way of crying, "How was that?" (aka "Howzat?"), to which the umpire responds, if he deems the batsman to have touched the ball, by raising a single finger, the nicest possible version of "up yours." Gentlemen, I am trying to tell you, walked before the moving finger wrote: if you were out, out you went. After biggish money came into the game (never in the quantities soccer players receive), it was regarded as a little precious—quick, sottish even—to do the right thing. Batsmen may now edge the ball with a click, audible to everyone without my auricular malfunction, and they will still stand there, defiance dressed as innocence, until driven from the crease by electronic verificatory procedures.

Footballers have long been prone to dive when slightly fouled or even when they might have *been*, but that too has become an art form, known across the Channel as *"cinéma"* (ah what distinction an acute accent lends a word, but for how much longer, messieurs, in the light of electronic here-todayism?). It is up to referees to distinguish the crookery from the hookery, but the more help they get, from linesmen who can prattle second-opinions into their earpieces, the less certain is the referees' control of things on the field. The *ne plus ultra* (until someone goes further) came yesterday in a Derby game between Chelsea—the team of choice for South West Londoners—and Arsenal, ditto for North Londoners, except for those who support Tottenham Hotspur, whose supporters have so often been abused as "the Yids" that they have taken the name as a *titre de noblesse,* and why not?

Yesterday's was the one thousandth match in which the Arsenal manager, a Frenchman baptized, with *prévoyance fatidique*, Arsène Wenger, supervised his team's performance. Wenger, who combines anguished and dignified personal *prestation* with an almost comic lack of humor or generosity, has officiated over "the Arsenal," as my father always called it, for fourteen years, longer by more than a decade than any other "Premiership" *jefe* now that Alex Ferguson, a ruddy, uniquely successful, unlovable Scot, has retired from being the main, if not the only, man at Manchester United. Yesterday at Stamford Bridge was slated to be the clash of the titans, and the tight 'uns, if you want to play the Joycean card, since neither Wenger nor the Chelsea head honcho, José Mourinho, gives anything away that he might conceivably want to use later. I admire Arsène, because under his baton his teams have always tried to play beautifully, and often succeed. I have, however, been going to Chelsea ever since 1943 or so, when my father and I used to stand, literally, braced if lucky against an iron barrier, and sway with the undulating masses.

At Lord's cricket ground, where my team, Middlesex, played ("Yiddlesex" chorused my schoolfellows, in their lovely way) there was Edrich and Compton (cf. Francis Thompson's "my Hornby and my Barlow long ago"), at Chelsea, Tommy Lawton, England's center forward in the days when they were invincible at home (those days ended in 1953 when Hungary beat us 6-3 at Wembley). Lawton played for England with the great Stanley Matthews, who—even when he was past fifty—mesmerized the opposition with his dribbling skills. Matthews was a winger who sent in pin-point crosses which Lawton, in the terminology of the day, "headed home past the helpless custodian." In those days, the balls were hard leather and had stitches over the wound where the inner bladder had been inserted. Legend has it that Lawton frowned, with a sore forehead, at Matthews after one such score. "Anything wrong, Tommy?" "Next time, Stan, make sure the ball arrives with the stitches on the other side."

Fast forward to yesterday (there's an old man's stage direction!). Such are the oddities of emotions and allegiances that, although I was, as they say, up for Chelsea, I did not want Arsenal and Arsène to lose. Our son Paul was invited to the match and I told him I hoped it would be a five-goal thriller. It was, in the event, a six-goal non-thriller: Chelsea scored all six. This lopsidedness was due, in part, to the fact that Arsenal had a defender sent off for handling the ball when standing on his own goal-line. It was an act of folly, not least because the shot was almost certainly going wide. The referee, one Marriner, was all at sea: the Arsenal man he sent off was not the one who had handled the ball (and so conceded the penalty which was converted into goal number three). The guy on the line was called Oxlade-Chamberlain, a large somewhat black man, quite unlike the man shown the red card, whose name is Gibbs, and who resembles O.-C. only in his complexion, although no commentator has so commentated.

O-C did something, if never quite his best, to own up, but referees are never wrong. So on his thousandth occasion in command, poor Arsène was humiliated, not least because the Portuguese Mourinho, who smiles but has no grace, had labeled him a master of failure, or something nice like that, since Arsène has not won a major trophy for ten years, although his teams are always "there or thereabouts" as the pundits have it (and can keep it). Chelsea won and I was sorry. I was sorry when Joe Louis was dumped on his ass (so ending my childhood). I felt bad when Sinatra overtook Bing, although I never much liked the latter. F.D.R. was president forever too; not that I think as well of him now as I did when he sent us (ah us!) those fifty clapped-out destroyers in 1940, if that's when he did it.

I envy you meeting Momigliano and am slightly amused that he was of diminutive stature (like "Little Tommy Harmer," a Tottenham footballing genius too small to resist the buffeting he got from the louts he danced around until they bit his legs). Italian intellectuals when they are good are very, very good. I noticed the other day that Leopardi's fat volume of thoughts can be broken into Zi Bald One, which doesn't merit mentioning, but there it is, J. Joyce rides again, again. If Peter Brown bent the knee to Arnaldo, who should not? (My favorite remark of A.D.M.'s is, "After fifty years' study, I still have no clear idea what the ancients expected of their gods or the latter of them.")

It is a feature of my unlamented marginality that I have read a lotta lotta more scholars than I have supped with. The few I have met have left no indelible traces. One, a historian whom I have got to like, accused me, on first meeting, of not having thoroughly read a book of his that I had reviewed. I responded, *coram publico,* "I'll send you my notes, if you like, Michael. But I warn you: they're nothing like as amiable as my article." Since then, he's been, as they used to say in Hollywood, a bunny (Alan Pakula said as much of an idea of mine, but we fell out just the same).

The movie mechanicals have frequent recourse to something known as "double-sided sticky"; a roll of black heavy duty tape which was, yes, sticky on both sides. I don't do black, but stickiness in British or American form is not beyond me. Yet during the close on ten hours in which, last week, I delivered my pensées and then some to the camera of the very nice

Christopher Sykes who solicited them, I became aware that, topped and tailed by memory and good manners, my public life story sounded like one of roses most of the way. Where were the thorns of yesteryear? I have a chaplet of them in my trophy cupboard, of course (you can't be king of the Jews without one), but my narrative—as the cant has it—was of one modest moment after another, of which only my Cambridge scholarship retains its luster *d'antan*.

Just as well, the sulky repressed self mutters, in view of how the Brits treat me now: fifty years this year a Fellow of the Royal Society of Literature and the nearest I have come to being invited as a feature speaker (alongside Antonia Byatt, say, not that there's too much room) was when I was asked to compile a list of questions to ask Nigella Lawson about her latest cookbook. As for the R.S.L. itself, it seemed a fine and noble body of persons when I was first elected, but then Jeffrey Meyers was clocked on, and somehow the shine went off the gingerbread. Rebecca West said to me, over lunch at Jamin in Paris, that when they gave Jack Priestley the O.M. (Order of Merit, a company of two dozen enrolled theoretically by the Sovereign's fiat), it removed the merit from it forever. Tough room to play was ex-Cecily Fairfield. I was her epistolary centerfold for a week or three, but it didn't last. That old Gautier got it right: *tout passe*.

Tout à toi, Freddie.

P.S. On the telephone today, my Hollywood producer, swearing that we're going to make the movie this year, signed off: "I love you, Freddie. (Beat) I'm one of the few." No Englishman, Jew, Gentile or Phlebas the ex-Phoenician, could say that.

March 30, 2014
Dear Freddie,

My condition in respect to understanding cricket is close to that of Arnaldo Momigliano in respect to the understanding what the ancients expected of their gods or the gods of them. I much like the look and feel of the game, but it remains a mystery to me. I like it for the clothes alone: all that white flannel, wool, linen. I loved tennis togs when they were all white or, in the case of a pair of Fred Perry shorts I owned, a creamy tan. I also admire what I take to be cricket's leisurely slowness. Sports, preferably fast and violent ones, are the ones most in favor in America just now, though a friend of mine recently described rugby as "a bar fight gone out of doors." Baseball, the closest thing to cricket, has been declared too slow, too boring, for many of the young. I find the older I get the more I like calm and slowness in the games I watch. But I had better stop here before I shift into crank.

What is entailed in shifting into crank is giving way, as older players tend to do, to glorifying the past at the expense of the present. Ah, how much better life was when I was young, the crank quickly makes plain. There was less crime, intellectual standards were higher, manners were more elegant, the young were more respectful, divorce was practically unheard of, food seemed fresher, art hadn't fallen onto sleazy days, New York was better, the *New Yorker* was better, and on and on into the night. When I find myself shifting into crank, I think of a minor comedian with a very Jewish face named (I believe) Phil Stone, who used to do a bit in which he recounted wild myths. After each portion of the myth he would strum his guitar dramatically; penultimately, he would strum his guitar and announce, "The people of my village believe this myth. They believe it because they are stupid." Pause. And after the final loudest strum, he would add: "I believe it, too."

Shifting into crank is all very well with friends who are contemporaries, but much less successful when among the young, where one is quickly taken for a crank. As it happens, I am a crank. I just don't wish to be taken for one. I happen to believe lots of things I set out in the previous paragraph. The crucial event of our lifetime, I believe, is the elimination of the concept of the grown-up, for which we may thank the decade of the 1960s.

You mention having written a screenplay set in Chicago in which your convincing expertise about the city was based on a flash visit. Those of us in the scribbling trades do tend to be quick studies. In my mid-twenties I published an article in *Harper's Magazine* on the subject of urban renewal. The article was roughly 6,000 words long; my total knowledge of the subject was perhaps 8,000 words. (Today it is down to perhaps 200 words.) After this article appeared, I briefly became one of the country's leading housing experts. I appeared on a panel on the subject of urban renewal at the University of Chicago Law School; I was offered a job on the Planning Commission of the City of Baltimore and another as a speechwriter for the then Secretary of Health, Education, and Welfare. Other invitations and offers I won't say poured but at least dribbled in. The result was to cure me forever of belief in the reality of expertise, except in the most highly technical subjects.

Joe Louis was knocked out, a TKO in the sixth round I believe, by Rocky Marciano in 1951. I have the most distinct memory of this because I, at fourteen, was sitting in the movies at the Nortown, my neighborhood movie theatre, when they actually stopped the film to announce Joe Louis's defeat. Something stoical and dignified there was about Joe Louis, and I much admired him. Like you, I felt sad at the inevitable ending of his career.

A heavyweight fight, especially a heavyweight championship fight, in those days attracted more interest than any other sporting event in America. (Neither Louis nor Marciano was champion when Marciano finished off Louis.) Today boxing isn't even watchable; it seems too barbaric. When while channel surfing I do pass a boxing match, I hurry on past, as if it were a show on the ghastliness of Bubonic Plague in the middle ages or a course in open-heart surgery and likely to disturb my dreams. *Autre temps*, like the man says, *autre moeurs*.

Two days ago I had an offer I could refuse. I received an e-mail from an earnest fellow telling me how much he has enjoyed my writing over the years, and now he was about to publish a novel of his own in the autumn with Penguin, and wondered would I be willing to supply him with a blurb. He is in his fifties, is a geo-physicist who has been teaching at major American universities, and his novel has the interesting (to me) title of *A Mathematician's Shiva*. I wrote back to say that "for reasons too elaborate and boring to go into, I do not give blurbs." Boring my reasons may be, but my reasoning is not too elaborate. I do not give blurbs because it would take two days out of my life to read this fellow's novel, and, quite as important, I have no wish to join the marketing arm of any publishing house.

I used to give (please note the verb, with its faint suggestion of oral sex) blurbs when young. But I found I had to quit when a local couple, whom I knew fairly well, asked me for a blurb for their not even odious book on marriage counseling. I hadn't the verbal skills to have supplied them with even the most ambiguous of blurbs and be able to return to my desk the next day unempurpled with shame. I told them I could not provide them with a blurb, and they made plain to me that, as a human being, I was grossly disappointing.

I have had blurbs on some of my own books, but these have chiefly come from reviews of the books in question or from reviews of earlier books of mine. I have a blurb from Philip Larkin, the result of a review he wrote in the *TLS* of one of my collections of essays. I have another from Tom Wolfe, acquired by my publisher of the time. John Gross, in a review, supplied a third. On the back of a book I wrote about American snobbery, I supplied my own blurbs, signed by Henry James, Oscar Wilde, Marcel Proust, and Noel Coward, and all were deflationary. To this day I'm not sure how many people got the joke.

My policy on blurbs now is that I do not supply them for living writers but will give them for neglected writers now deceased. I am fairly certain that my blurb on a book would not result in the sale of three extra copies. Nor do I believe that blurbs generally help to sell books. (Yesterday's mail brought a book called *The Humor Mode* that contains, on its first two inside pages, no fewer than seventeen blurbs—seventeen, count 'em—not one of which is from a person I know.) Are you able to think of any living writers whose enthusiastic blurb on a book would induce you to buy the book? I cannot think of one.

Last weekend we saw a movie I'm not embarrassed to recommend to you. *You Can Count on Me* is its title, it was sent out into the world in 2000, and was written and directed by Kenneth Lonergan, a name I had not known before now. The movie is about a sister-and-brother relationship, and features Laura Linney and Mark Ruffalo, with Matthew Broderick in a secondary role. I don't know how much of Laura Linney you've seen *chez* Raphael, but next to Meryl Streep she seems to me the best contemporary actor going. Linney plays a single mother raising an eight-year-old child in a small upstate New York town, Ruffalo her screw-up brother down on his luck returns for an extended visit, and much complicated nuttiness follows therefrom. The craperoo quotient in the movie seemed to me very low. A few bonking scenes are shown, betwixt Linney and Broderick, her boss at a branch bank, but these do not greatly distract from or diminish the main story. (Someone once said that the more helicopters there are in a movie the worse it is likely to be. I wonder if something similar mightn't be said about the more bonking in a movie the less winning it is likely to be.)

One of the things that occurred to me watching *You Can Count on Me* is how few movies are about the complexities of family relations apart from those between husbands and wives or their lovers. In my own attempts at fiction, I have come to think that the family alone offers sufficient richness to float a literary career. The family, after all, was at the center of Tolstoy's greatest writing. So many of the best novels have been family novels, from *Anna Karenina* through *Sons and Lovers* through *The Forsyte Saga* through J. D. Salinger's unfinished chronicles of the Glass Family. I wonder if perhaps the novel hasn't slipped a notch or two when its interests veered away from the family. As for the movies, family relations perhaps tend to be too subtle for contemporary movie audiences, who go to movies for coarser reasons. The perfect movie plot, it just now occurs to me, would feature a couple bonking in a helicopter.

In the ascetic department, I spent two days this past week without my computer. The reason is that a few months ago I lost, quite mysteriously, two chapters of the book I am supposed to be writing on Charm. I woke one morning, turned on my computer, and, *poof!,* they disappeared, six or so thousand words off into cyberspace. I have been having problems with this book generally, and for a bit I thought it might make sense to rewrite the two chapters, or even eliminate one of them. But then I decided to have someone more adept than I make a serious effort at recovering them.

So I disconnected my Mac desktop and took it over to a local computer fixit place called PC Solutions. To make an unhappy story short, after downloading and running various file recovery programs, the gent who was working on my computer, an amiable Moroccan who grew up in Montreal, was unable to find my errant six thousand words. (If you happen to see them flying past your apartment in England or house in France, do wave at them for me.) They may not have been noble but at least they were grammatical words, and I shall miss them. I have heard of people losing entire manuscripts in their computers, and so perhaps I shouldn't be demoralized by my relatively minor loss. "Man rides machine," Ralph Waldo Emerson said. After this experience, I say, yeah, sure, right, what did that schmuck Emerson know? *Bubkes* is what he knew.

Best, Joe

ST LAURENT-LA-VALLEE. 30.3.14.
Dear Joe,

Ah the sweet comedy of the literary life, so dignified, so serious provided it's seen from a distance, without binoculars and with a cocked eye! The consolations of age include a sense of perspective and, if you're wise and lucky, of the absurd. Where shall I start? Craig Raine is as good a *terminus de quo* as I can come up with or down on. Does the name mean anything to you? If not, pray that he does not hear as much. I have known him, at a distance, since he told my friend Brian Glanville that I was the only reviewer in town, in the days when I was a regular on *The Sunday Times*, then a serious newspaper, who put on a dinner jacket before doing my thousand words or so. There was a time, we are promised, during the solemn salad days of the B.B.C., when the man who read the radio news was expected to do so *en smoking*, as the French oddly have it. So, I took Craig's remarks as a compliment, and why not?

Soon after, he started a magazine entitled *Quarto*. He was, at the time, a starry young poet whose slim volume *A Martian Writes Home* delivered an innovatory set of conceits. For instance, he described the about-to-burst blossoms of the chestnut tree as looking like *petits fours*. So they did, and do. This form of hot rococoa was a relief from the mundane cups of tea which Amis, Larkin and who all else in The Movement chose to serve. Craig asked me to review six volumes of Chekhov's short stories, for which I received (and expected) nothing more than the volumes which I can see in my shelves from where I sit. It was in a season when George Steiner was posing the tough alternative *Tolstoy or Dostoyevsky?* (I'll go with Lev; unlike G.S., I have small appetite for gushing over anti-Semites.) I suggested that Anton was a third alternative and to hell with grammatical niceties. *Quarto* went on long enough to establish its editor's capacity to be a maker or breaker (and thus his claim to be done by as he might well do you). Craig was also the poetry editor of Faber *and* Faber, a chair in which T.S. Eliot had sat for quite a while, allowing some to call him Tom and others Mr. Eliot. Craig bid some come and others go, and then he went himself, to New College, Oxford, where he became a protégé of Alan Ryan, a voluminous "liberal" polemicist.

Craig now affects the little big man's tubby, bearded strut and sports the free-spiritedness of the safely anchored careerist. If he wears sandals, it will be with First Eleven socks. Established as an Oxford ornament, he contrived to find funds, from here and from the Arts Council of G.B., to start another literary mag, entitled *Areté,* from the Greek, you will remember, for virtue. See Werner Jaeger's *Paideia,* which James Joyce might entitle Pie Dire, once an obligatory *vade mecum* for masters of the subtle arts. Where *Quarto* had been rough and ready, in paper and matter, *Areté* was, as John Schlesinger used to say, often, "piss-elegant." It comes out quarterly, fat and nicely printed, with all manner of chic-by-jowl contributors. One of the older soldiers convoked early to its banner was Raphael. I appeared two or three times in the first six numbers, loyal as a man can be who is glad of nothing more than an editor's nod.

Areté has something of the egregious, combative allure of Connolly's *Horizon.* Craig instituted a section headed "Our Bold" in which he is audacious in lambasting various *bêtes noircies*, amongst whom, I was not entirely sorry to see, was the quasi-ubiquitous D. J. Taylor. As issue succeeded issue, in jackets of variously tasteful hues, I was requested to do numbers on Mary McCarthy (whom I anatomized at length) and the shorter prose of W. H. Auden. I went into unimpressed detail over his desire to please most of the editors most of the time. His journo-prattle yielded some excellent work and a crop of winsome and unctuous Christianizing. Later, I sent Craig a story or two and in they went.

Although I was some kind of a stalwart, I never figured in the list of the *renommés* who were boxed in the ads which appeared in various places. *En bon philosophe,* I leaned into my back seat and took it that I needed no bush, as the wine-bibbers used to say, before bushes were what porn stars (and others) now dispense with. I continued to receive complimentary copies of every issue and counted myself in the swim and the loop, if never the chips. Then one day I sent him a chunk of a story which he decided not to print. He signed off "Much Love," which you can't take to the bank, but was payment in kindness. When he did it again, in order to make space for a bad movie script by an in-group chum, I decided to offer him no more opportunities to condescend.

I bore no grudge, it sez 'ere, and I soonish had an opportunity to prove it: your friend and mine Daniel Johnson asked me to review the no longer young Craig's new, first novel. The poet had belatedly discovered Monsieur Jourdain's medium. I told Daniel that, while I should be happy to speak well of Craig's book, if it was good, I was not willing to speak ill of it, if it was not. Was this a disreputable instance of insider-dealing? I didn't, and don't, think so. Craig's thin novel was given a porter of its own and round it was buzzed; *venit, vidi* and, in short order, back it went. I had feared it might not be good, but I did not guess that it was going to be gross. Duchamp's urinal was at least unused.

Craig had already boasted of his marital infidelity in the way that tenured men of genius have not been slow to do in our *m'as-tu-vu?* era. His mistress, he advised us, and informed his wife, had a long black hair growing out of one of her nipples; proof that he had indeed caressed the details. The "novel," *Heartbreak,* was an Advertisement for Himself worthy of the Dorothy Parker Memorial Library: it did not deserve to be put aside lightly, but to be hurled, etc. So I bunged it back to D. Johnson, saying that I preferred to pass rather than to dump on my boon-bearing buddy. Please, I added, not to mention that I had allowed this *coupe merdeuse* to pass from me. I cannot be sure that Daniel let slip a word or two, but it would be no great surprise if, in a garrulous *galère*, something had—as bishops used to say to actresses—inadvertently slipped out.

Now Craig is nothing if not a man who can carry a grudge and run with it. This quarter, he has a BOLD go at Philip Hensher, a fancy novelist whose prime fancy is himself, because P.H. took a swing at Craig in some mag or other. Here's the *ridiculus mus* shambling to be borne towards you: whatever did or did not reach Craig's touchy ears or other parts, when he brought out a fat chrestomathy of items culled from the first decade of *Areté*, not a single of my more than very few contributions made the cut. Nevertheless, something—whether or not it was honor—impelled him to send me the many splendored proof that I was no kind of a contender for his A-list. I suspect that there was indeed a vain and vengeful reason for my *limogeage*, but there are plenty of effects in life without any wilful cause.

In the dun-colored days when the *TLS* reviews were anonymous, a classicist friend of mine was convinced that a hostile review of his recension of Sextus Propertius had been written by another friend of mine, to whom friend A never again spoke a civil word, even though, in fact, it was another colleague who had played Brutus. Today, who has to have a deep, malicious reason for behaving like a shit? I am no longer invited to review books for the London-*Sunday Times*, where I was for quite a while much solicited. Why? Because, betcha, I once had a telephonic *lapsus* and, when he was only assistant lit. ed., called the present incumbent "Anthony" instead of Andrew. The kicker is, I did literally write a letter to the editor (unacknowledged in the modern style) recommending Master Andrew for promotion. No good deed etc.

The immovable head of the *Sunday Times* corner is their Chief Reviewer, John Carey (don't call him Professor, but never forget he is one). He has problems, in the English way, over his social origins. It is a year-one irony that an Oxford professor should have sentiments of rejection and an inferiority complex, but there it is; often in a fawn mackintosh. I admired Carey's early books on Donne and Dickens, especially the former, but he has allowed himself to become filled with hot air and swept up, up and away by journalistic fame. He makes gadfly pronouncements against literary elitism, which would not be listened to if he were not a member of the elite. As I have mentioned, he has pronounced recently that Don Quixote is a bad book. The irony is that Carey himself is a kind of Don Q., issuing from his Oxford fastness with a mission to put the literary world right and tilting at bastions of intellectual paperwork without seeing that they are windmills of his own surly confection. He has written countless long *Sunday Times* articles and never once discovered a new work of any quality.

Like Craig Raine, he sits high on a sense of his own entitlement, the Mr. Knowall who affects to hold that nothing is more worth knowing or reading than anything else. However, if you want scholarship, he can short order that for you, *pizza/cato*. Just the other day, a clutch of cash-and-Carey-type scholars brought out a slim symposiastic volume in which, to look good, the word *telos* was used where "goal" would do as well. It was given a plural *"teloi"* which looked even better. Does it matter that *telos* is neuter and its plural is not in line with *hoi polloi* notions but, if it matters, *telê*? Where is that grammarian's funeral? I just may go along.

Tout à toi, Freddie.

April 6, 2014
Dear Freddie,

I don't know my *Dunciad* well enough to be specific, but the poem must contain six or seven Craig Raines. I suspect he may also do a cameo in Balzac's *Lost Illusions*. The type of the literary operator has always been with us: literary men on the make, with nothing whatever to say, which doesn't stop them from saying it, are never in short supply. Over the years I suspect I've read twenty or thirty Craig Raines poems, without their making the least impression or leaving any residue. I didn't know of his Faber & Faber connection; nor have I ever seen a copy of *Aréte*.

I was struck by all the scribbling you did *gratis* for Craig R.'s magazine. I don't think I would have gone and done likewise. I recently wrote a few hundred words for nothing for a journal called *Academic Questions*. I suppose I would write at great length without pay if the cause were a good one. All other things being equal, I go for the dough. I suppose that makes me a money writer, which is a touch silly, since I don't make all that much money with my writing. But I do continue to be pleased by the astonishing fact that people are willing to pay me anything at all for my various scribblings. Their doing so allows me to think myself a professional.

Fifty years ago, working in New York on a magazine called *The New Leader*, I wrote to Dwight Macdonald, whom in those days I much admired, soliciting a piece for the magazine. He wrote back that he only wrote for money, and for much larger sums than *The New Leader* was likely to pay. I inquired if there weren't anything I could do to change his mind. One thing, he said, fund-raise.

Does the notion of money-writer overlap with that of hack? I prefer to think the former a more dignified gent. I take a hack to be one who writes to order, and will write anything that will bring him money. The money-writer won't write without money, but he remains his own man in the way the hack isn't. The money-writer retains, or at least can retain, his integrity; there are things he won't write, things he believes in, including the need to get his work published in the way he wrote it. The hack is mainly interested in money; the money-writer feels that what he does is good enough to deserve money.

Not that the money writer won't write for the money solely, so long as it doesn't violate his sense of himself as a craftsman. Five or so years ago a posh American magazine called *Town & Country* offered me $2 a word to write about the meaning of luxury in our day. The only thing wrong with the offer is that the magazine wanted only 1,500 words. (Whenever I am told that I shall be paid by the word, I invariably think of the song, "Ten Cents a Dance": "All that you need is a ticket," the song ends, "come on big boy let's dance.") Easy money, thought I, forgetting, as I generally do, that whenever those two words—easy and money—are conjoined, things don't quite work out that way. The editors there put me through a few hoops of fire, fiddling with my prose while my temper burned. Their fiddling somehow reduced the piece by 300 words, and my check was for $600 less than I had hoped. Easy money, you and me is quits. I reread the piece a few moments ago, and it is not disgraceful, but I may have been the only person to read it, for I never heard a word about it after its publication.

The money-writer—I speak autobiographically of course—wants it every which way, the dough, the show, the praise, the thought that what he has written in some indefinable way matters. I have sometimes published in a less well-paying magazine because the better audience the magazine provided was worth it. The best of all worlds here, I suppose, is to publish in the place that both pays well and provides that good audience. In America, the *New Yorker* was once that magazine, and perhaps still is. In my eight or nine appearances there I would sometimes hear from those hidden Americans - the physician in Tarrytown, New York, who knows ancient Greek, the grammar-nutty high-school teacher in Tyler, Texas, who feels the need to correct one's grammar - who are, to my mind, among the readers most worth having; more so than most academics and intellectuals.

The problem with the magazine world today—apart from the general trouble that all so-called hard print media are in when up against the internet—is that so many of them have become what, as I mentioned earlier, are called "salvationist" magazines. They want to save your soul through their sweet politics. In the United States today almost all magazines with any claim to seriousness have a political line—including, sadly, the *New Yorker,* which was always liberal in spirit but not until recently hostage to a political party (in this instance, the Democrats under Obama). This limits one's magazine publication possibilities greatly, though I shouldn't complain, for four or five magazines, all paying respectable fees, continue to ask me to write for them regularly.

The most interesting non-salvationist magazine of my adult lifetime was *Esquire* between 1963 and 1973, when it was edited by a man named Harold T. P. Hayes. Lively was the word for the magazine under Hayes. Tom Wolfe broke in, or rather broke out, in *Esquire* with a piece on a southern race-car driver; Gay Talese wrote a niftily deflationary piece on Frank Sinatra, Norman Mailer did his usual overheated writing about John F. Kennedy. Nora Ephron wrote for the magazine about what it was like to live with small breasts. Dwight Macdonald wrote about movies; Malcolm Muggeridge, then at the top of his game before he turned pious Christian, had a column in which he wrote always amusingly about whatever he fancied. Something winningly *outré* there was about the magazine. Articles in its pages on pinball machines could capture one's interest. The ostensibly dullest of subjects came alive in *Esquire* in that brief glorious decade under Harold Hayes, who, alas, died at sixty-three.

Hayes ran a writer's magazine. He knew how to fit writers up with subjects that would show them at their best. He seems to have had little in the way of disruptive ego of his own, and so far as I know never wrote for the magazine (though he would later publish three books, none of which I've read). As there are writer's magazines, so are there editor's magazines—magazines in which not writing but the editorial package is what prevails. In its most recent incarnation, *Vanity Fair* is such a magazine. After many years, I have finally let my subscription to it run out, for it developed no younger writers nor featured any distinguished older ones. The contemporary version of *Esquire* is also such a magazine. The current month's issue features "84 Things a Man Should Do Before He Dies, The Life List." I would extend the number to 85, adding that one of the things he must do is cancel his subscription to *Esquire.* I acquired a one-year subscription to the magazine for the meager sum of $5, but feel I over-paid, and cannot wait for the damn thing to run out.

If the *Esquire* of Harold T. P. Hayes was the best general magazine of my day, *Encounter*, in England, under the editorship of Irving Kristol and Stephen Spender was the best intellectual journal. I have always assumed that Irving Kristol, who was very intelligent, did all the intellectual heavy lifting, and the wobbly Spender made the social connections. I first discovered *Encounter* in 1957, while an undergraduate at the University of Chicago. As we should say today, I was blown away by it; the magazine turned me into an intellectual anglophile. I read it, to adopt the greatest of all clichés about magazines, cover to cover. We now know that the magazine was in good part financed by the CIA. If *Encounter* was salvationist, it wished to save the world's soul from Communism, not at all a bad project.

I wrote a few pieces for *Encounter* in its less palmy days, when Melvin Lasky took over as editor. Mel Lasky was an immensely loquacious fellow. I was once in a Manhattan restaurant where at another table Norman Podhoretz was having lunch with Mel. Norman came to my table to inform me that he had to return to his office, and would I mind taking his seat at Mel's table, assuring me that Mel would never notice the difference. Mel Lasky also had the habit, as an editor, of inserting clichés in one's work. Suddenly in one's pieces people were found hoisting themselves on their own petards (or was it foulards?) or breaking eggs to make omelets. When one insisted on their removal, he gave no trouble.

Which reminds me that the first piece I ever wrote for *The New Republic*, when I was twenty-five, was a review of the poems of Max Beerbohm. The piece was accepted, then returned to me with vast swatches of it deleted with a soft pencil. When I called my editor, a man named Bob Evett, to report that I could not live with such slash-and-burn editing, he said, "Oh, don't worry about it. Since his wife died, Gilbert [Harrison, then the editor-in-chief and owner of the magazine] gets drunk at lunch, and returns to the office to do his editing. I'll just tell him that you wanted everything restored, and he'll be fine with that." And so it was.

I had a great triumph this week. Reading an attack, in *Commentary*, on the best-selling liberal biographer Doris Kearns Goodwin, the attacker called her a virtucrat. *Virtucrat* is a word describing someone whose politics are fueled by the sense of his or her own high virtue; and it also happens to be a word I invented. Not to put too fine, or actually any, point on it, *virtucrat* is my word. That this minor item constitutes a great triumph ought to give you a clear notion of how quiet a life is led by your electronic correspondent.

Best, Joe

LAGARDELLE, ST LAURENT-LA-VALLEE. 7.4.14.
Dear Joe,

Why do people do things? The fiction writer's easy and wise response is never to say why, only what. Your stories are rich in circumstance but rarely go inside the heads of the characters. In a style which I endorse, you allow the dialogue and external action to indicate what mental urges may (but never certainly) lead to this or that. Our common tendency to observe and caress the details of everyday behavior and speech (including what is not said) does something to conceal our differences. Your literally professional practice, in eschewing unpaying propositions, comes of a certain practicality you may have learned, if not inherited, from Epstein *père*, whose want of cant when demanding payment set a piercingly pragmatic example: it's not the principle, it's the money. I leave it to the professoriate to point out that my choice of adverb derives from the fact that C. S. Peirce was a noted pragmatist.

My father was not reluctant to make money, but the salaried man lives in a different world from the self-employed, be the latter business-person or penny-a-liner. My father liked being in America and might well never have returned to England, but *force majeure* gave him marching orders in 1938 and I marched with him, if only around the heaving deck of the *Queen Mary* while my mother did justice to the Cabin Class menu. As we paced, he told me (as I have mentioned in several elsewheres) that I now had the prospect of growing up as "an English gentleman, not an American Jew." It did not occur to him that he might have condemned me to cultural schizophrenia; just my luck!

Your stories often feature what critics might call "moral choices." A man does or doesn't call a woman, or a woman a man. *Hinc illae lacrimae* and, since you have a generous heart, whatever it looks like on your sleeve, *illi risus* (dem laffs) as well. Your first book, if I remember rightly (and I had a copy long before we met, even if we never have), was about Divorce. You made one mistake, and were not afraid to admit and make copy of it, after being luckier (and wiser?) *en deuxièmes noces,* a phrase beloved of my old literary mentor, a certain Guy Ramsey, who died in 1959, but remains alive in my heart. Guy was, in some regards, a *poseur*: a journalist who, his coat a cape about his shoulders, played the Hampstead artist although he only ever wrote one novel, a thriller with no durable thrills; but he had beautiful handwriting, a trim style and well-stocked mental library (not least of tags it was useful to tie to his reviews), although he lacked sufficient *haut du pavé* credentials to validate his *rôle affiché* as Flaubert to my Guy de Maupassant. Guy had that ability, rare among the English at least, to treat young persons, especially my young person, as if there was no age difference; he instructed but he never condescended. He loved his rather plain novelist wife, Celia, with romantic passion and fidelity. He set me more good examples than I knew, including the copious use of full stops and the need, if humanly possible, to please one's wife before—to keep things in 1950s terms—pleasing oneself. In a word or two, nice guys finished last.

A proposito, kinda, we have been watching the boxed set of the HBO series *Boardwalk Empire*, which is sumptuously upholstered in 1920s décor and cozzies (as U.K. theatricals call their wardrobe), and recalls to me that 1936 visit to Atlantic City with my seersuckered father and 26-year-old pageboy-coiffed mother. Here's the thing which doesn't bother me, but is worth asking: can it be that 1920 Americans, however ugly their mug-shots, regularly larded their dialogue with fucking this and fucking that, even among ladies, if of questionable morals? Did "motherfucker" and "cocksucker" really feature regularly in period gangsterspeak? I kinda doubt it, but the old line may well apply: no, I was not there, Charlie.

So, to answer the question you have not put, why I still do quite arduous things for nothing or its close neighbor, has at least something to do with my bipartisan psycho-set-up. Why I am so timid with English literary slow-payers and so lacking in reticence, when it comes to American or foreign showbizzy-bodies who don't come up with the moolah, can be researched under the same rubric (a word rare, I suspect, in today's U.S. usage). In England, I still wear some mental equivalent of the bowler hat, never brown, in which my father went to the City every salaried day of his London life. I am an observer of the proprieties about which I can ironize as well as any Sinclair Lewis you happen to have on you. Hence, with rage and shame, I endure the fact that when, at the age of 82 (as my silly passport says), I asked the deputy editor of the *TLS*, oh so nicely, to tell me when my piece on Cavafy is going to be in the paper, he did not have the antique courtesy to respond return. He has not done so in the following three weeks, and what do I do? I bite on the bullet, sit on the drawing pin, stiffen the upper lip and take it on the chin. I must excuse him for having no manners but he will, you may be sure, never excuse me for mentioning it. His denial to me of further bread and water will be along the worn lines of, "The trouble with you people, if you don't mind my saying so . . ."

Why then bother with doing demanding reviews for minimal what were once called spondulicks? Money, now the principal topic of conversation in England, was once as taboo as two-backed beastliness before the admission of Lady Chatterley to polite circles, in 1960 (a much truer *terminus post quem*—quim?—than Larkin's 1963). It was nice, and economical, which was nicer, to assume that gentlemen never did things for the money, although emoluments were exempt from anathema if measured in guineas, a guinea being the sum of one pound and one shilling, which had no equivalent coin of the realm. Members of "the Professions" used this arcane quantity when submitting their accounts. It suggested that they were gentlemen, not players who lowered themselves by playing for cash (see under "tradesmen" and there they were; the jew was underneath the lot, but never mind that).

There was, until 1962, a fixture in the cricketing calendar "Gentlemen versus Players"; the former had their initials printed, on the match-card, before their surnames, where the players wore them latterly, as Jews their tails in the mythology of the Spanish inquisition. The distinction was echoed, in the 1950s, by that between serious writers and scriptwriters or journalists. Novelists were not necessarily respectable, unless they achieved a certain eminence, even when—Virginia Woolf set the fancy tone—they were not doing it for the money, like Mr. Bennett. Novelists were unlikely to possess First Class Minds or the degrees that certified them. Evelyn Waugh was lucky to get a third at Oxford, G. Greene a second. Scribble, scribble, scribble, their common consequential fate.

One of my early publishers assumed that I must have a private income to supplement the merely complimentary advances which his company disbursed. I didn't, but I was lucky enough, almost from the beginning, to get work first on the radio, TV, and then in the movies. I became a lifelong transvestite Persephone: in the penitential pits for two seasons of the year in order to have the gold to play the novelist come the spring. My adamantine chains turned to gold when I was still in my mid-thirties, after I won the silly Oscar. As a result I had few money worries at least until the turn of the present century. Yet I never lost my ambition to be the kind of intellectual who appeared in fancy prints. So now you know why I have been a patsy for people such as Craig Raine and who all else. I have, for instance, just sent in a piece to the London *Literary Review* which pays roughly a hundred bucks for a 1,300 word review, but the lady is prompt to be pleased and does not ever mess the copy about. She is said to be *richissime*, but classy London literary folk do their stuff for her few quid, not least because they are glad to figure in each other's company without any risk of having to buy a round of drinks.

There are always a few illustrious persons above the *gratin,* those in particular who receive noughty checks from the *NYRB* and its derivative the London *R.B.* Of these, Julian Barnes is Monsieur *Trois Etoiles,* Flaubert specialist *par excellence,* and then some, master of award-winning brevities, niceties and hot cakes. *Bref,* Barnes is the English interpreter of choice of all things French. Who will dare to say that he speaks the language without panache, as he does English?

Our mutual friend Gershon Hepner, an addicted master of *coupures,* sent me the following nugget not long ago:

"RODOLPHE'S POST-COITAL CIGAR

Julian Barnes ('Writer's Writer and Writer's Writer's Writer,' LRB, 11/18/10) reviews a new translation of *Madame Bovary* by Lydia Davis:

"After Emma's seduction by Rodolphe, there is a paragraph describing her post-coital, semi-pantheistic experience of the forest surrounding her, with which she is for the moment in harmony. But with the last sentence, Flaubert cuts this mood brutally: '*Rodolphe, le cigare aux dents, raccommodait avec son canif une des deux brides cassée.*' This great anti-romantic moment has Rodolphe turning both to another physical pleasure (as Gurov will with his watermelon in Chekhov's 'The Lady with the Little Dog'), and to masculine, practical matters. All the versions cited here begin, unsurprisingly, with 'Rodolphe, a cigar between his teeth . . .'"

Before I come to the crux, it's worth noting that Barnes is now so immune from criticism, his own or any editor's, that he can peddle clichés as if we were lucky to get them. How is it "brutal" to cut from Emma's *états d'âme* to Rodolphe's doing-it-himselfery? Barnes proceeds to analyze previous translations of the cited passage with ultra-scholarly severity:

"Wall goes on: 'was mending one of the two broken reins with his little knife.' Steegmuller: 'was mending a broken bridle with his penknife.' Hopkins: 'was busy with his knife, mending a break in one of the bridles.' Davis: 'was mending with his penknife one of the bridles, which had broken.'

"Rein or bridle? Knife, little knife or penknife? The difference is slight; all the versions contain the same information. Flaubert's sentence does its business by not drawing attention to itself; its very downbeatness is the point, after the more rhapsodic prose that has preceded it. Wall, Steegmuller and Hopkins all get this. Davis doesn't. Instead, she 'faithfully' sticks to Flaubert's sentence structure. But English grammar is not French grammar, and so the quiet *cassée* (which for all its quietness also hints at Rodolphe's 'breaking' of Emma) has to be unpacked into a 'which had broken'— a phrase which now seems pretty redundant, as what would he mend that wasn't broken? The sentence has a clunkiness which is imported, rather than faithfully transmitted, and quite unFlaubertian."

Barnes *dans ses oeuvres* doesn't note that all his indicted translators render "*le cigare aux dents*" as "*a* cigar between his teeth." Is it worth noting that the French for "a" is "*un*"? Since we are incited to believe that big Gus was the *mot juste* specialist, I still think that a translator is entitled to read his choice of article as deliberate: "*le cigare aux dents*" suggests something Churchillian about the way Rodolphe sports his cigar. In English the point can be made without distortion by saying "the cigar" (i.e., his usual). Cf. "Julian Barnes, the French between his teeth," meaning that Barnes regularly trades, for figurative guineas, on the idea that it is miraculous that he can actually read French.

Tout à toi, Freddie.

April 12, 2014
Dear Freddie,

I wonder if our fathers would have found much to talk about. My guess is not. Your father went to university, mine left high school at 17 in Montreal to live in Chicago, with an uncle named Joe Rudy who was formerly a bootlegger and always a grand sport. This Uncle Joe was a large man who carried a pocketful of silver dollars that he gave away as tips and to his many grandnephews and nieces, I among them. Your father had an aptitude for leisure: from things you have written, I know he was a golfer, a good dancer, a bridge player. My father did none of these things, and on Sundays—he worked a mere six-hour day on Saturday—he was itching to get back to "the place," shorthand for his place of business.

The two men may have differed most decisively in their notions of how the world worked. My father would simply not have understood your father's working for a large corporation, in however high or well-paid a job. My father's first axiom—also the Eleventh Commandment—held that "Only a schmuck works for someone else." Behind this unqualified dictum was the sensible notion that if one works for someone else one is no longer in control of one's own destiny. This someone else may tyrannize over you, trifle with you, transfer you to Houston. My father had a cousin at the third or fourth remove who was a lieutenant colonel in the U. S. Army. Although he was patriotic, and disappointed that he was himself too old to serve in World War II, my father simply could not fathom why a Jewish man would wish to spend his entire life in an institution as impersonal, rigid, and unrewarding as the military. When I say he could not fathom it, I mean, most precisely, it was beyond his reckoning. He just didn't get it.

Lest I seem to be looking down upon him, let me jump in quickly to say that, in all my father's confident philistinity, I think he was correct—only a schmuck works for someone else, at least insofar as he can avoid doing so. I have been lucky in my life, and so have you in yours, by and large to have worked chiefly for myself. As scribblers, we are sometimes, briefly, under the reign of editors who are the reverse of helpful. In your job as screenwriter, you must have felt the sting of fatuity from temporary bosses (producers, directors). I have worked for magazines and at the *Encyclopedia Britannica* for men for whom I had no respect. Still, we are lucky mother-grabbers, you and I, to have spent our working lives with the freedom we have had.

Chez Epstein we watched two seasons of *Boardwalk Empire*, hopeful, ever hopeful, that it would get better. The third season it dipped down to get much worse. Whole episodes seemed to be devoted to murder and unpleasant copulation (I first encountered a new word, *snogging*, for this latter activity only the other night in the subtitles of a Danish political soap opera called *Borgen*. Do you suppose the subtitlist confused *snogging* with the British word *shagging*, itself not very felicitous.) As for the swearing in *Boardwalk Empire*, it is as abundant as you say. I think you are also correct about the anachronistic nature of its choice of swear words.

My father swore, but I never heard him use the great f-word, nor did he fall back upon the s-word, though he was wont to call a phony or what he sometimes called a "four-flusher" also "a bullshit artist." He never called anybody by one of the many dysphemic names for the genitals, male or female. He would say "god damn" from time to time; he would less frequently refer to someone as a "real bastard." My father's swearing was earnest in its irritation or anger and not in the least ornate.

In my high-school days I briefly worked with a great fat man—so fat was he that he placed a towel over his stomach when driving so that the steering wheel wouldn't wear out his pants—whose swearing was positively artistic. If in traffic someone honked his horn at him, he would quickly lower his car window—this in the days before electric windows—and shout back, "Blow it out your duffelbag, farthead." He once pulled up at midday at the curb before a less than Arabian Nights bordello in a Chicago neighborhood zoned light industrial to ask of a friend and me, "Well, boys, how'd you like to get your peergees tickled?" I've not before or since heard that word, *peergee* (pronounced with a hard g), for the male member.

Pause for a pronunciation joke: A Jewish man of the immigrant generation returns from a visit to his physician to report to his wife that the physician said that he has herpes. "Herbes?" his wife asks [supply your best greenhorn accent here]. "Nu? What's herbes." The man says that he doesn't know and was ashamed to ask. "I'll look up in the dictionary," his wife says. She returns a few moments later to report. "Nothing to worry about. Herpes, it turns out, is a disease of the gentiles." Pause. Rimshot.

Your mention of the old-fashioned, even corny word *moolah* reminds me that there must be more slang synonyms for money than for male and female gentiles, so to speak, both. As for talking about money, along with among the English it also has no place in politer American circles. Within our family, though, "How much?" never seemed an unfair question. My wife's family, being more refined, rarely mentioned money, or at least precise sums. Barbara's Aunt Phoebe might be complimented on a new dress, and she would respond that, thank you very much, she bought it on sale at Sachs, a genuine bargain, more than 50 percent off. But then she would fail to specify the final tab. I loved them too much to give way to my coarse instinct to ask, flat-out, "So what exactly did it cost?" Oscar the Wilde said that "a cynic is someone who knows the price of everything and the value of nothing." I remember a New York editor, who shall be nameless to go with his gracelessness, who once visited an apartment of ours, and before he had his coat off said: "This is nice. What do you pay for an apartment like this?" I was so astounded by the *gaucherie* of the question that I told him.

Unlike you, I don't mind asking editors their fees for my scribbles. I used to preface such requests by saying, "And now the vulgar question: what will you pay?" but no longer do so. When the checks fail to arrive a month or so after publication of a piece of mine, I have no hesitation in inquiring about their whereabouts. My view here is that they should be embarrassed not I. Which reminds me that my dear departed friend Hilton Kramer, then the first art critic of the *New York Times,* was once asked at a dinner party by Woody Allen if he were embarrassed when he encountered visual artists whom he had attacked in the *New York Times*, to which Hilton, without dropping a stitch, replied: "Embarrassed? Why should I be embarrassed? They should be embarrassed for creating such shitty art."

My very first publication, at the age of twenty-three, was at the humble *New Leader* magazine in New York. Among its contributors were Sidney Hook, Bertrand Russell, Lionel Trilling, and others. I was two stages up from delighted to find myself in print and in such company. But after four or so weeks, no check for my contribution had arrived. I wrote to the editor, a former Menshevik named S. M. Levitas, whom I later learned smoked two packs of cigarettes a day without buying any, asking about my fee for the article. He wrote back to say that I was a young man and perhaps unaware that "the truth has no price tag." In other words, the magazine did not pay its contributors but he was there to encourage me to do more writing. Sheer genius, that, in the elevated *schnorring*, or clever begging, department.

More on moolah: in the offers I can—and did—refuse department, I had an e-mail this morning from a man representing a documentary film maker named Len Goodman, who is doing a film for ITV on Fred Astaire. He asked if I would be free to have my views about Fred A. as part of the film. He then offered three filming dates: one in New York, one in Los Angeles, and one in London. (He noted that he had my "book on [Fred Astaire] currently on order.) I sent a return e-mail asking if he planned to pay a fee for my participation. He said that a fee could be arranged, but that most people do this kind of thing for nothing, out of their love and passion for the subject and of course all who participated would get a "With thanks credit." He added that since I, "having written a respected biography on Fred Astaire . . . would have a great knowledge of him and the subjects surrounding his life and therefore have a great many insightful things to say about Fred's life," so he was able to offer me a fee for my participation. No mention, you will notice, of what this fee might be. I quickly asked. $250 was the sad answer, which evoked from me the response: "I am afraid that you will have to proceed without my participation, but thank you for thinking of me in connection with this project." His final word was that if more money became available, he would get back to me about it. I hope he doesn't. Being a so-called talking head on a documentary about a man who talked best with his feet does not seem to me to offer sufficient *koven*, or public prestige as our co-religionists have it, to expend three days of my life, with two of these days given over to dismal air travel. So on this project, for me, it is lights, camera, no action.

I fear I may make myself sound savvier about money than I really am. The rather sad truth is that I cannot think about money and how to earn it in a concentrated way for more than three minutes at a time. I am entirely ignorant about the stock market, cannot define a mutual fund, and am unable to force my eyes through a financial document of more than a single page no matter how I press my temples or squint in false seriousness.

Many moons ago I invited you to write an essay on Hazlitt for a book I was asked to edit on the subject of literary genius among Anglophone writers. In my note of invitation I told you that all I could pay for such an essay was $1,350, which was what each of the contributors to the book was to be paid. You accepted the invitation with the proviso that if you discovered any other contributor to the book received $1,400 for his essay you would see that I was put to death. In that response you encapsulated my literary-financial views perfectly. My ambitions in the money realm begin and end with my desire not to be screwed.

As a monoglot with far from fluent reading knowledge of French I attended to your sentences about Julian Barnes and the translation of *Madame Bovary* with keen interest. Barnes is himself, if he is anything, a Flaubertian, which in my view is not a good thing to be. Flaubert was a mean prick, and his migraine-making concentration on style may well have been owing to his not having any ideas—his chief idea seems to have been hatred of the *bourgeoisie*—that were even close to humane.

For those of us mired in a single language, the translation question is always a slightly nervous-making one. The great German philologists, as I noted earlier, considered reading a book in translation not really reading it all. I am currently reading Tom Holland's translation of Herodotus, which is marred though not ruined by his inserting contemporary phrases in Herodotus's text: "lifestyle" pops up more than once, people are "partying" or "rustling up" pretexts to go to war, Croesus tells a visitor to "relax" and enjoy himself, while Cyrus is "eye-balling" Croesus from his camp. Not good, any of this, but not, as I say, ruinous.

The first bit of translation snobbery I can recall encountering came when, as a student, I was told what a mistake it was to read the Russian novelists (chiefly Dostoyevsky and Tolstoy, of course) in the Constance Garnett translations. Truth was that I was so enraptured by the story-telling power of the Russians that I scarcely noticed the quality of the translation. If one Russian greeted another in the Nevsky Prospect by asking "How are you, old chap?" I could live with that. One definition of greatness in a writer is to be so good, so powerful, as to be above destruction by translation.

Class dismissed.

Best, Joe

ST LAURENT-LA-VALLEE, FRANCE. 16.4.14.
Dear Joe,

First of all, a small reminder of the comedy of the paranoid condition. I was, as the merest New Critic could divine from earlier pages, pissed with Craig Raine for omitting me from his chrestomathy of *Areté*, a choice of title so brimming with hubris as to deserve a measure of Apolline nemesis (how clever of dem Greeks to arm the God of moderation with a punctual dagger!). I had circumstantial reason to think that good old Craigers had it in for me because I declined to rave printwise about, or even abuse, his elderly prodigy's proof of loss of his novelizing virginity. So: yesterday, I had a bright as a butt-in e-mail from Master C. saying that the next numero of the aforesaid journal would feature Franz Kafka and that he would like, with my permission, to reprint the brilliant piece I wrote about Frantzi boy in the second issue of aforesaid pedestal for the self-made *arbiter litterarum*. So this is what it feels like to be a makeweight who has been made to wait. What did I say? "My dear fellow, be my guest," or voids to that effect. One of my Cambridge friends, perhaps the only manifest genius I have ever met, one Gordon Pask, an inventor, was said (by himself) to have begun his Ph.D. thesis "As I have said before . . ." As I have in declaring that the uses of courtesy include the irony that chooses not to speak its name or bare its fangs. It has amused me all my life in England to ape, sometimes sincerely, the gentlemanliness which my father wished upon me when he launched me on the insular *cursus*.

Few things, in the trivial line, give me more pleasure than to deal with people I do not trust as if their word was indeed their bond, or even their word, and with false friends as if we had stayed together when all but we had fled. It continues to rile me, however, when those of whom I expect nothing deliver precisely that. It makes me wish I had made that famous "fuck you money," a term of which Gadge Kazan, I think, first apprised us. The truth is that if you are of a certain character, twenty bucks will do and if of another twenty million will not. The lure of money is the lure of money; the notion of a satisfactory bundle is absurd, a "category mistake" as Gilbert Ryle put it, in his once daring *Concept of Mind*. I used to feel a little bad about losing/ relinquishing/ditching friends, but J. Epstein, my brother-confessor, has somewhat purged me of the guilt. They come and go, sometimes at their volition, sometimes not.

Ray Monk, the professor of philosophy at Southampton, claims not to understand what "category mistake" is meant to convey. Can he be serious or is he being philosophical? It seems clear to me that thinking that you can make a fruit salad with sliced apples, pears, bananas and a 1953 Chevrolet, means that you have either misunderstood what a fruit salad is or you think that a Chevrolet is a suitable tropical ingredient in one. Need we go on? The quite a bit younger Ray and I met because we shared an agent and an interest in Wittgenstein, whose biography he had had the nerve to embark upon, although others had foundered or stalled in the same pursuit. He achieved that very difficult trick, when it comes to abstruse figures, of completing a full account of W. in a single volume without leaving out the difficult bits, i.e. the logical and mathematical underpinnings of W.'s eclectic, not to say rambling, later lucubrations. Fame and fortune properly followed.

Back in the 1990s, I suggested to Ray that we edit a volume of exemplary pieces about The Great Philosophers. This evolved into a series of 50 page monographs, in which distinguished philopersons were invited to choose a single crux in their chosen or allotted gent's works. Little books were doing big biz back then, so we found a prompt publisher and made quite a success of the enterprise. I had the belated fun of red-penciling professorial essays and found silly pleasure in discovering their docility under fire. Bea Lillie (unless it was *la* Parker) had a line about a party of which she said,"If all the guests had been laid end to end I shouldn't have been at all surprised." When our little *bouquins* were bound together in a single volume, it sold, as a Welshman called Jenkins once said in my hearing "like hot kikes." His first name was Dai. His beautiful wife was Norma. Hence one of my dead friends' remark, "See Norma, and Dai."

The Great Philosophers is now in its unenriching twelfth edition. Not only did I strut my adjudicatory stuff, I also contributed a little number on Karl Popper (on which Roger Scruton, a curmudgeonly right-whinger of rare acumen and generosity, made a few much needed marks). Offers of chairs did not come my way, but I squatted in quiet, brief conceit. Ray and I were not ever of the same genre but—as you have discovered often, I but rarely—working together, even at a distance, is itself a generator of friendship, of a kind, when it is. Our case is exceptional, yours and mine, since we have exchanged confidences, however edited, which elicit affection as well as interest; cf. Micheau and Etienne de la B., but not unless you really really want to.

So, getting to it, Ray and I knew each other for some twenty years. He came to our house and I did not go to his, which suited me. He arranged for me to have the fun of delivering a lecture in the Ashmolean in Oxford, a parody, as it turned out, of Aristotle if he had been able to write his Cinematics. My fee was paid in applause. Well, even Nunky Sam can't tax it. Then just about two years ago, Ray asked me to contribute to a symposium, a *klatsch* even, on Biography at Southampton. It would precede, by a short head, the publication of his fatty on J. Robert Oppenheimer. I was to get my (and Beetle's) travel expenses and the honor of, *more Britannico,* opening the batting, at 10 a.m., which required my leaving London at 6 a.m. I arrived, fragile but unbroken, to be hailed, in a very friendly tone, by one Miriam Gross, who is dear to many booky persons but not to me. In her hayday, she was adroitly adjacent to people who approximated to library steps: they supplied access to a higher literary/social shelf.

Miriam's modest proposal was that we should share a taxi. I did homage to the seven-second Pinter pause before agreeing immediately. I knew that as lit. ed. of the *Sunday Telegraph* she had inspired some second murderer to can *A Spoilt Boy,* my first volume of autobiography. I am sure she knew it too, although you can rely on a *mafiosa* to persuade herself that she is extending a clean hand. Since I was promised that my expenses would be met, it did not require Christian charity to open the taxi door for madame. I suspect that a male, in the same context with the same back-story, would have known better than to presume on my courtesy, but there we were.

I did my over-prepared stuff for a sad *minyan* of conference attendees and stayed, for courtesy's sake, to hear the spiel delivered by a blanched London publisher who had just rejected my Josephus book. It was, yes, that kind of a show, folks. Afterwards, I was almost openly scornful (try doing that expression for us, class) of Stuart Proffit, the celery stick whose idea of a university lecture had proved to be commenting on a flow chart already, and of Miriam's question-time affectations of journalistic probity: "I have never used my position . . ." she began, when I knew damn well she had (internal evidence, old man). *Bref,* I hated the whole thing and myself for falling for it.

After lunch, Ray stood with me for at least fifteen minutes as we waited for my taxi to the station. I did not say one reproachful word and we both gave the impression that our friendship was on-going when we both knew/suspected that this was a *terminus ad quem* if ever there was one. Here again, class, is a chance for a clever exercise in improvisation: what is said must not hint at the breach which is as wide as the one at Harfleur to which Harry summoned his men (yes, I fatten the allusion, as Clive James did his Dante, justifiably, to avoid losing the unlettered). Appearances were saved, but all else was gone, like Virgil's Eurydice *ceu fumus in auras*; if you've got it, flaunt it because some rented D. J. Taylor'll get you whether you do or not.

The kicker was yet to come, when my expenses did not. I had sent the list, smartish, to one Professor Smith, whose business business was, and heard nothing for three weeks. I then sent a fiercely polite e-mail indicating, with quite a stiff finger, that I had received no acknowledgement. He took the opening like a randy goat: he had not been aware, he faluted, that a claim for expenses required acknowledgement. Gotcha, babe! Yes? No. Because now I had the chance to say that if he had had the routine grace to send my expenses by return, as he should have to someone required to be early on parade, etc. The last twist of the knife and the tail and the tale is, of course, that what had nothing whatever, administratively, to do with Ray Monk nailed down the lid on our friendship.

The strange thing is on what small bearings these things turn, or turn out badly. There is a huge literature about breaches between lovers who should have known better than whatever makes us now read on, but since fractured friendships cannot, in the normal way of things, be repaired in bed (some marital rows, it requires no great wit to see, are contrived to lend vigor and rigor to the consequent two-backed reconciliation), what is broke between chums tends to stay broke. I suspect that writers in particular are ill-equipped to forgive and forget. I am prepared to do the first, but not, if I can help it, the second.

I am now—the news, the big news!—getting towards what will have to be the end of my second volume of autobiography, GOING UP, and find that I can retrieve large tracts of my past, in which people I have not thought about for decades come surging, if not gibbering, from the pit, without my even having to spill sacrificial blood. Many are indeed dead ("who would have thought etc." does not require one to cross Mr. Eliot's London Bridge) and I am often sorry, but I seldom wish, even with the generosity pedal pressed to the floor, that I could see them again or make things up (there's an ambiguity for Empson to chew on). Clive James, whom I took to be an incurable enemy, when he savaged my antique TV series *The Glittering*

Prizes, and with whom I was reconciled thanks to his passion for our daughter Sarah (she fended him off at the pass, a lot, but liked him well), wrote to me the other day to say, *mas o menos,* that literature/the literary life had uncashable dividends in mutual sympathy and interests which those not in the lettered loop could never match or even imagine. Ain't it de troot?

Tout à toi, Freddie.

April 20, 2014
Dear Freddie,

Two days ago I sent off the manuscript for a collection of essays and stories on sports to be called *Masters of the Game.* Some of the pieces in the book go back to the 1970s. Might it be that I have now reached that stage of authorship where one publishes more than one writes? Beginning to look as if it might.

The idea for the book was that of its editor, a man named Rick Rinehart, with whom I have never spoken a word, who is the acquisitions editor of a firm called Taylor Trade Publishers, which is a division of a firm called Rowman & Littlefield Publishing Group, which (so many whichs, so few warlocks) is located in Boulder, Colorado. My previous collection, *Essays in Biography,* was published, and published handsomely, by the less than famous Axios Press. Do big-name prestige publishers any longer much matter. I begin to doubt that they do.

I recently received a royalty statement from Axios, which has treated me with every kindly consideration, that showed *Essays in Biography* has sold 7,220 copies, 5,873 in hardbound, 1,349 in electric versions. No great shakes, this, but respectable. My royalties thus far—I warned you that we Epsteins, unlike my wife Barbara's family, deal in actual numbers—have been $15,327.83. Not a figure to write home about, but then you ain't home; yet not a trifling figure, either, for a collection of essays by a writer who pays his readers the compliment of assuming that they are at least as intelligent as he.

What is significant about this, I think, is that, in the Age of the Internet, having a prestige publisher has come to matter less and less. In what we may now call olden days, the assumption was that if one were published by Alfred A. Knopf or Farrar, Straus, Giroux or Random House or W. W. Norton or Houghton Mifflin, one had had one's quality certified—one had jumped a hurdle and passed a rigorous test by your work finding acceptance with a quality publisher. The prestige of your publishing house wore off on you, its author, at least in part. The other assumption was that such publishers could do a great deal for an author by promoting his books and making sure that they were placed prominently and in sufficient numbers in bookstores across the land. Neither assumption any longer holds up.

I do not know if this is true in England, but in America what used to be called the "independent bookshop" is just about finished. Of the two great bookstore chains, Borders and Barnes & Noble, the first went under a few years ago, and the second is reported to be on the ropes. My guess is that of the 7,000-odd copies sold of my *Essays in Biography*, more than 6,500 were bought through Amazon.com and other online establishments.

The Internet, to make a sad story stark, has just about finished off the American bookstore. My guess is that before long it will finish off the quality publisher. The Internet, that greatest of all mixed blessings, is a merciless monster, an unrepentant smasher of institutions and traditions. Its next victim will no doubt be all publishing in paper. Were they alive, Maxwell Perkins, Bennett Cerf, Alfred A. Knopf would, I daresay, cack their pants.

In a recent issue of the *TLS* I came across a remark of Degas to Whistler, who, as you know, dandified himself and did all else he could in the effort to promote himself, an American artist in London. The remark, which I've seen and been struck by before, runs: "Really Whistler you behave as though you have no talent." The question I put to you, and to myself, is how does a person with talent behave?

I like to think I am a person of talent, but I do not think it very often. I do not wake to say thank goodness, disheveled though I am, at least I am talented. I do not walk the streets thinking with pleasure of my talent. On occasion I will read something I wrote five, ten, twenty years ago, and say to myself, that ain't too bad, shows talent. Sometimes people have cultivated me because they like the notion of being around someone thought talented; it seems to enhance their own views of themselves; perhaps they hope a bit of the magic will rub off on them. Noel Coward has a few strong words on this phenomenon in his diary: "A little extra personality; a publicized name; a little entertainment value above the average; and there they [people] were, snatching and grabbing, clamorous in their demands, draining your strength to add a little fuel to their social bonfires."

Literary talent, it strikes me, is less God-given than musical or visual-arts talent. Literary talent comes into play later than these other two forms of artistic talent. (My artist granddaughter could draw and manipulate arts materials from roughly the age of three; and I strongly suspect the same was true of your daughter Sarah.) I suppose there is a God-given, or born-with, element in literary talent, but it develops more slowly and dies more easily. Conrad after all published his first novel at the age of thirty-eight or –nine. Our man Henry J. is good on this point: ". . . if you haven't, for fiction, the root of the matter in you, haven't the sense of life and the penetrating imagination, you are a fool in the presence of the revealed and assured, but if you are so armed you are not really helpless, not without your resource, even before mysteries abysmal."

Getting back to the question suggested by Degas, how does a talented person behave, my answer is very modestly, never pushing it, at no time insisting on privileged conditions or asking for special dispensations. A genius, on the other larger hand, can forget about all these restrictions, and most that I know (none personally) about have.

If I am so talented, why don't I sleep better? (I love a non-sequiturial question. I once heard about the Jewish mother of an acquaintance, ask of a physician of great reputation, "If he's so brilliant a doctor, how come he's bald?") V. Nabokov, I read in *Speak, Memory,* was never a good sleeper, not even as a child. He hated, it seems, to lose consciousness. "Sleep," he wrote, "is the most moronic fraternity in the world, with the heaviest dues and the crudest rituals." Maybe if I had so sparkling a consciousness as the Montreux magician, I, too, would have preferred never to close it down, even for a night, though a good soporific, it occurs to me, might be reading him on his lepidopteran adventures. Odd, is it not, that this dazzling writer's most boring writing was about his greatest passion?

Older gents of my acquaintance tend not to sleep well. Many of us are interrupted two, three, and more times a night by what in the U. S. Army used so delicately to be referred to as "piss call." Others find their minds racing, filled with guilts, terrors, remorse over opportunities lost, revenges still to be paid, sins committed and others regrettably omitted. So common, one might say endemic, among older players is want of sleep that there are sleep clinics and in medical practice a branch has come into being known as sleep medicine. Both do a brisk business.

As a young man one talked of sports and sex—and what better (mostly) indoor sport is there than sex? As a middle-aged man one talked about money and food. And now as an older man one talks about the past and sleep. Scarcely anyone I know among men roughly my age claims great prowess at sleeping. Sleep, the great desideratum, the ultimate luxury, who'd've thunk?

The Irish sporting pages is a description I've always liked for the newspaper obituary pages. I check them every day, online, in the *New York Times*. Three days ago an old, if not quite close, friend named Michael Janeway turned up in them. He was seventy-three and died of cancer.

Mike had the mixed advantage of having been born the son of a moderately famous man. His father, Eliot Janeway, was one of Franklin Delano Roosevelt's brain-trust team; more like the second team, my guess is. He later wrote an economic newsletter, and occasionally appeared on television as an expert economist. In that role he was always authoritative and confident, which is to say that he was a fairly high-level bullshitter. Mike once told me that when he was a boy of fifteen his mother asked him to clean out a closet in their Manhattan apartment. While doing so he made two discoveries: one that his father had been married before and two that he was Jewish. When he asked his mother why his father had never mentioned having been married before, she told him, "You know Dad, he hates to admit defeats." The more interesting, the Jewish, question, apparently, never arose.

Mike was himself the least Jewish of characters. He was handsome, in a WASPy sort of way. He had gone to Harvard, and made excellent connections there, connections that seemed to continue paying off through all his days. He had an unending series of sought-after jobs. He followed me as an associate editor of *The New Leader* in New York, then went on to work at *Newsweek,* thence to become executive editor of *The Atlantic*. From there it was only a short hop to the State Department (during the sad Jimmy Carter years), after which he took a high-ranking job on the *Boston Globe*, soon to become that paper's editor-in-chief, and from there he became the principal editor of the publishing firm of Little Brown. I became friendly with him on his next stop, Dean of the Medill School of Journalism at Northwestern, where he lasted six or seven years. He left Northwestern to become head of the arts journalism program at Columbia University, also working for the Pew Trust, and I gather remained there until his luck at last ran out and cancer sacked him.

Is all this what the Victorians used to call going from strength to strength? The point of Mike Janeway's career, though, is the absence of strength. Near as one could tell, he did nothing to change any of these institutions in which he held positions from which he might have done so. At Northwestern, upon departing, he claimed that his contribution was to increase the diversity—read: hired more blacks and women—of the Medill School, when the best thing he could have done was close down the joint. He was not so much as another face as another suit in the crowd, and sometimes seemed less a man than a resume.

And yet, as I say, I liked him. He was always respectful of me, even though he knew I knew he had friends I despised. (Toward the end of his days he ran round with such nationally famous Medes as Tom Brokaw.) We found things to laugh about. He arranged for me to become a member of a Chicago establishment club called The Wayfarers, which met the first Tuesday of every month to listen to balls-bluingly boring twenty-minute talks that felt as if they went on for at least three bad fiscal quarters. Although we hadn't been in touch for at least the past three years, I nonetheless regret his subtraction from the world. Had we run into each other on some social or quasi-professional occasion, I should have been glad he was in the room. Go, I ask you, figure?

I didn't know that Elia Kazan invented the phrase "fuck-you money." I love the phrase, even though I've never had the money—enough money, that is, to tell a boss, a publisher, or anyone else, "Fuck you, I'm out of here." Had I had serious fuck-you money, I would doubtless have achieved even less than I have. Had my father been a wealthy enough man to set up generous trust funds for his two sons, I should today be in Paris putting the finishing touches on *The Parched Parrot*, my first and only book of poems. Thank you, Dad, for neglecting to set up such a fund.

Best, Joe

LAGARDELLE. 23.4.14.
Dear Joe,

It must be very nearly Hitler's birthday, always a date to make the heart grow fonder of having survived the ludicrous psycho whom only Charlie Chaplin, with all faults, dared to find as ridiculous as he was (but never forget Jack Oakie's Mussolini). We tend to take people seriously in accordance with their capacity to do us good or evil, but that is an opportunist's measure, is it not? Nabokov, your friend and mine, got it right when he made the sinister Monsieur Pierre, the executioner in *Invitation to a Beheading,* into someone brought down by the laughter of his victim. Nice work if you can work it. The truth—that wiper of smiles off faces—promises that nothing is a sure specific against a tyrant and his minions. I continue to marvel at our Perigordine neighbor Etienne de la Boétie's acumen and nerve, during the age of pretty well absolute monarchy in France, in denouncing the toadyism (*servitude volontaire*) whose salaried servility is essential for keeping tyrannies in place. There was, I suspect, a great deal of local freedom in old France, even during the religious wars which Micheau derided when he said, *grosso modo,* that it required a great deal of confidence in one's own beliefs to roast other people to death for not sharing them (has any Islamic worthy or unworthy managed to say as much and stay alive?).

The principal license for La Boétie's outspokenness and his apparent impunity may well be that provincial French voices spoke out so far from the center of power that no one at Court actually heard or read them; at least, they did not have to say that they had (but always look carefully at any smile of denial). The internet may have enabled everyone to talk to everyone else in a virtual tower of babble, but no one is disposed, in an age of equal-opportunity foolishness, to take serious account of anything unless it accords with what he/she thinks already or provokes electronic custard piety (political rectitude). The notion that the tower of Babel might have reached the heavens (or as close to it as the Saudis now propose to mount), if all the people involved had spoken the same language and worked as one, is no longer convincing.

The comedy of what C.K. Ogden wished to believe, that he and chums could devise a simplified 500-word basic English which would allow everyone in the world to understand everyone else without ambiguity, is that to deprive mankind of double-talk, the counter-current of the undertone and the fun of the pun is to maim, not liberate the, oh, circumscribed. Paronomasia—why use a short word when a long one will do?—has been outlawed by posh persons not least because punning serves as the trap door under pretentiousness. How mere is the slip of the tongue that can tip "great writer" into "grey triter" (checklist available on demand)? Mass communication leads to mass banality. Why do we need to understand each other's meaning beyond a shadow of doubt? Stanley Kubrick's wife Christiane, a painter of whom I am not the first admirer, painted big sticky landscapes in shouting colors with no shadows in them; and hence nothing solid, credible or evocative. Shades of meaning are the best kinds: Flaubert's *mot juste* doubles with his appetite for uttering *maux justes*. As for *la* Kubrick, who has pursued me with unabated malice, it may safely be said of her that the peak of her powers is nothing compared to the power of her piques.

If completed by some modern consortium of people who understood each other perfectly, today's Tower of Babel would turn out to be a horizontal number with a series of identical compartments for identical people, none of whom would tolerate anyone living, literally or metaphorically, on a higher level than themselves. Such a tower would double for the longest bungalow in the world. The culture which requires that no one be left uncertain about its meaning or need to learn anything new, in order to get, as they say, the best out of it, is not a culture at all. It is a commodity whose purveyors have only one notion of what it would be to succeed: for everyone to pop its corn without needing to take a moment's thought and without being left any different (wiser, more independent-minded) than they were before. The measure of modern "cultural" success is that the consumer wants endless supplies of the same: satisfaction and dissatisfaction are squeezed, like striped toothpaste, from the same tube. More is less.

You make a nice distinction between people of talent and genius, to whose holder you grant the platinum license to play the fool or the pundit or whatever role enables him/her to keep working. I take it that without the production of worthwhile work, bad-assing around ceases to be legit. I don't know if poor old Scott F. (Hemingway's mud sure does stick) rates as a genius in your book, but *The Great Gatsby* seems great enough to qualify, even if I cannot raise any of his other fiction to the same pedestal. Scott could fashion and puncture illusion but the pie-eye could never see reality straight. Even allowing him his pantheon niche, he remains one of those unlovely figures who behaved worse at his peak than in sorry decline.

None of the many retrospectators of the good old bad old days in Juan-les-Pins has anything nice to say about Sarah and Gerald Murphy. The deaths of their two sons have been written up as if it served them right (for custom-tailoring their lives), but I cannot go back to their 1920s beachfront parties without seeing Scott throwing their precious—all right, in every sense—champagne glasses over the wall and onto the rocks beyond, in part, at least, because he was asked, very nicely, not to. I don't find kids lovable because they go and do the one thing you specifically requested them not to; genius *non plus*. Oh and another thing, when did you last still feel warmly about self-styled friends, talented or not, asking themselves to come and stay with you and then not writing a handwritten letter of thanks after, in Audrey Hepburn's words, being with you "month after month for three whole days"? Yes, I have specific people in mind.

Genius, in whatever measure, don't turn shit into sugar. How Scott came to write *Gatsby* I still find it difficult to understand; perhaps that disconnection, between the man and the work, is as good a warrant of genius as you can hope for. Old Willie Maugham was never accused of genius but you and I know that he was some kind of a *miglior fabbro* even if he did, from time to time, dredge his prosaic aggregate from a quarry of platitudes. Willie was the best kind of non-genius, a hard worker who did his best, knowing that Our Betters—typical that he should write a play with that deferentially scathing title!—quite often take less trouble than we do, not because they never blot a line but because when they hit the high notes there is no matching or denying them.

Bertie Russell always claimed that his first drafts were the best (cf. "that first fine careless rapture"), not least perhaps because he was something of a philo-journalist, forever up against deadlines and sometimes unable to get scribbling until panic primed the pen. That said and very often done, you do sometimes wonder how reliable canonical reputations are: Stendhal, for instance, doesn't bear re-reading, *à mon avis*: *Le Rouge et le Noir* was based, I seem to remember, on a *fait divers* (nothing wrong with that, old man) but it also reads as if it was. It belongs to the category of Classics which come across at least as well in translation. Once you know the plot, you know the lot.

A proposito, I was recalling in the current voluminous volume of my autobiography that I have not written anything much—other than my little Kubrick number—that was translated into other languages, perhaps because I have no great competence when it comes to plotting (my idea of fiction is to get hold of an interesting person and follow him, or preferably her, wherever I get led). I did, however, write a TV play, more than half a century ago, which was indeed plotted before the characters came aboard. *A Well-Dressed Man* told, in 48 minutes flat, the story of a lonely man who hears an appeal for a witness to come forward to save a man accused of murder from being hanged (that's how long ago it was composed). My Little Guy cannot resist being the Alibi Ike to whom, he imagines, an innocent man will be eternally grateful. Yes, you've got it: he commits generous perjury by vouching for the guilty man's presence far from the scene of crime, just for the grace of being Important to Someone. After giving evidence, the little guy goes home, to resume playing Chess by Correspondence (letter post) with a pen pal in Australia, when the doorbell goes and there is Mr. Tattooed, shaven-headed Beefy who says "Hullo, friend." End of Part One. It is unlikely that I can keep the tale twisty because, yes, in Part Two the little guy is so cruelly used by his parasitic tenant that he does him in.

Believe it, please, the piece was very funny. When I attended the first rehearsal, the two actors—one Peter Sallis, an old pro still at the receipt of custom, and big, bald Kenneth J. Warren, who died, literally, several years ago—were so hilarious in their straight-faced playing that their author literally (yes, literally literally) fell off his chair and took several seconds to, as they used to say, compose himself. In time, the piece was sold to a number of foreign countries. One day, I was telephoned by a French producer lady, who wanted to tell me how well it had played in frog. I asked her how long it had run in translation. "We did it in three half-hour episodes," she said. I said, "That's twice as long as when we did it." "We had a very imaginative translator," she said. I took that on the chin. "And tell me," I said, "did people laugh at all?" "Excuse me?" "Did it get some laughs, *quelques rires,* the play?" "*Rires?* Monsieur Raphael, you need not worry. We took your work as seriously as it deserves." "If not more so," I said. Comedy, as well as poetry, is often lost in translation.

I never saw the French version, but I wish I had if only because it was one of the earliest pieces in which the young Gérard Depardieu ever appeared, presumably as the beefy guy, though never as maxi-beefy as the double-decker Mr. D. now is. The great actor and pretty sad guy is, I believe, in tax exile in Belgium, *le pauvre,* unless he's bottled up (his now perennial condition) somewhere in Mr. Putin's Russia, which would render him more *pauvre* still; although, given big Gérard's capacity for the Rabelaisian, it might amuse him to be under the protection of *Monsieur Putain,* as French TV presenters have to call Vlad the Terrible and not break up when they do.

Tout à toi, Freddie.

April 28, 2014
Dear Freddie,

I never thought of Stanley Kubrick as married. Despite the mildly prestigious title, not an easy job, I should imagine, that of Mrs. Stanley Kubrick. Good to learn that, in the sweet-character department, the lady in question was no bargain either. You will recall Samuel Butler's remark about the marriage of Thomas and Jane Carlyle, that "it was very good of God to let Carlyle and Mrs. Carlyle marry, and so make only two people miserable and not four."

I like Audrey Hepburn's remark about house-guests "who stay month after month for three whole days." Ben Franklin had it that "guests, like fish, begin to smell after three days." Both Audrey and Ben—now there's an odd couple—agree on a three-day outer limit for house guests. My wife's and my policy is neither a guest nor an innkeeper be. We have an extra room in our three-bedroom apartment, but offer it to no one and use it generally for storage and a place to take naps. When people have asked us to stay with them, I say thanks, but no thanks, and then go on to explain—I hope they get the joke—that we have peculiar sex habits and they probably don't have the right electrical wiring to facilitate them.

That said I must go on to say that one of our loveliest European holidays was spent in the home of a former editor of mine at *Harper's Magazine*, who had moved to a Swiss village called Laconnex, twenty or so minutes outside Geneva. What made it so splendid was that he and his family weren't on the premises, but off visiting in the United States. After this I long ago decided that if anyone suggests we stay in his house or apartment, I shall say that we shall be delighted to do so, provided he and his family leave.

The notion of staying in hotels, even four or five star ones, holds no allure for me. One has to eat all one's meals in restaurants or through roomservice. (I once told friends of ours who, in their seventies, still go camping, that my idea of roughing it, is poor room-service.) Max Beerbohm wrote an essay called "Hosts and Guests," in which he concluded that he was strictly a guest. Barbara and I, it turns out, are pleased to be neither.

We are agreed that F. Scott Fitzgerald was no genius but that *The Great Gatsby* is a novel in which everything works. Fitzgerald published it when he was twenty-nine, and would live only fifteen years longer, pegging out at forty-four. May have been a good thing that he did not live much longer, filled with regret, as he doubtless should have been, that he could never again write a book anywhere near so good. The one-great-book writers are a literary phenomenon. Along with Fitzgerald, Ford Madox Ford qualifies, with *The Good Soldier* (I don't think *Parade's End,* which I attempted some years ago with no great luck, makes the cut), though the old boy wrote no fewer than sixty-one books. Proust and Joyce in some ways may be said to be one-book authors; in their cases the books were very great indeed. (On the Joyce ledger, I do not count as great *Finnegan's Wake*, which I think would have been more accurately titled *Pissing in the Wind*.) Montaigne could be said to be another one-book author, so, too, Cervantes. Must be a lovely feeling to know that one has written an imperishable book. I shall soon publish my twenty-fifth book, for which people have called me—most ambiguous of compliments—prolific. I reply thank you but I intend to keep trying until I get it right.

I wonder if the reason that you have been relatively seldom translated hasn't to do with the irony that is inseparable from your style. Irony, my guess is, doesn't translate well. I suspect that, of the great writers, the least translated must be Henry James, and for the same reason: the irony which he could never forego. Far and away the most translated book of mine is a short work called *Envy*, which has appeared in seven or eight languages. The reason for this has nothing to do with the intrinsic quality of the book but is that the book was part of a series on the Seven Deadly Sins, and Oxford U Press had a superior foreign-rights man who was able to sell, as they say in the trade, "the package" of all seven books in various lands. The money I received from these various translations was just a little bit more than nil.

Your idea of fiction, you write, "is to get hold of an interesting person and follow him, or preferably her, wherever I get led." I, too, need the interesting characters, but I also need a dramatic conflict in which to engage them. The finest conflicts, I find, are moral ones that, preferably, have unpredictable resolutions. The best, perhaps the only formula, for successful fiction I know is to make the unpredictable plausible. Do that, with a touch of seriousness and a dash of comedy added, and you have a decent chance of scoring a goal.

Where one finds the subject matter for fiction is another great question. My answer is, in the oddest goddamn places. The origin of a story of mine called "A Loss for Words," of which I am not utterly ashamed, came at a dinner party, when a woman I was sitting next to told me that she was out that afternoon buying heavier cutlery for her brother, a once nationally ranked tennis player named Seymour Greenberg, who had Parkinson's Disease. A vivid detail, that, I thought, calling up a man whose hands shook so badly that the heavier weight of his knives, spoons, and forks might give him sufficient ballast to reduce the shaking, if only a trifle, during meals. With that detail in mind I wrote a story about two men in a nursing home, one with Parkinson's, the other physically intact but sinking into dementia, who look out for each other. "I'd say we're one hell of a doubles team," the character with Parkinson's, himself a former tennis player, at one point says.

The other day, lunching with two friends from high-school days at a Jewish delicatessen called The Bagel, I noted two older gents, both with scraggly white-beards, eating without removing their caps, one of them in a heavy electronic wheelchair reading to each other. The man not in the wheelchair was reading what I took to be a poem, a quite poor poem of his own devising that had the phrase "climate change" in it; then later the two men read aloud to each other a script that one of them must have written; for a movie or a play I couldn't make out. What, as we say nowadays, were they thinking? What extravagant fantasies have they for their crappy poems and probably hopeless script? The two of them, whom I've decided to name Feigenbaum and Kizerman, refuse to leave my mind. The only way to rid myself of them, of course, is to write a story about them. All that remains now is to find the plot. (Isn't it the Aussies who say of a person gone mad that "He's lost the plot.") Upon what, I wonder, do people who haven't this grand sport of ours of scribbling expend their thoughts?

Etienne de la Boétie's confidence in writing against the inquisitions of tyranny in France and Spain reminds me of a fact that has long stayed in my mind about the Inquisitors of the Middle Ages: why they chose the method of executing people by fire. The reason, it turns out, that burning was the method of choice is that it was felt, in those days of tender conscience, that a priest shouldn't have blood on his hands. Makes a lot of sense, if you happen to be insane.

I've received a heavy dose of Vitamin P, as Thomas Mann called praise. Does Vitamin P, I wonder, come in pill, liquid, or injection form. I myself prefer the latter, which is to say mainlining it. Three days ago I was sent online an advance copy of *The New Criterion*, the magazine where *Distant Intimacy* was put down by a man whose name I cannot at this moment recall. Now there is a fine example of late onset dementia: not being able to remember the names of people against whom one is supposed to hold a grudge. The piece is called "On Joseph Epstein," a pleasing title. I have not before now had my name follow that particular preposition in a title. The author is a young novelist named William Girardi, and he has written chiefly about me in this piece as a literary critic. I shall spare you quotation, but suffice to say that in his general view western civilization would be in a lot worse shape had my parents not had the good sense to conceive me. If you believe that, there is some real estate in downtown Baghdad I should like to show you.

Is praise best laid on with an eye-dropper, a trowel, or with a crane and a bulldozer? Why is it that the tastiest puddings of praise often tend to turn up a cockroach at the bottom of the bowl in which it is served? In the *Hudson Review* several years ago my essays were compared to those of Montaigne, Pascal, Hazlitt, Orwell, and—wait for double pregnant pause—a glib reviewer for the *New York Times* named John Leonard. At the mention of the name John Leonard, Montaigne mounted up and road off, Pascal lifted his priestly vestments and scurried away, Hazlitt returned to attempting to seduce his chamber-maid, Orwell coughed up a rare guffaw. *Poof!* they were all gone, and so was any pleasure I might have taken in the praise. As a teacher I have had former students tell me how much my teaching meant to them, and go on to say that I and some other absolutely idiotic colleague— a raving feminist, a heavy-handed Marxist—were also his favorites among the faculty. I once had a young woman tell me how greatly she enjoyed my course in Henry James, and then add, "But then I've always been a romantic." I wanted to reply, before putting my hands on her throat, "And now you must die."

The cockroach in *The New Criterion* piece links me with a great gasbag of pomposity named Harold Bloom, a professor at Yale who achieved tenure just after the ejection of Adam and Eve from the Garden of the Eden, was it not? Bloom, an overweight Dionysian, admires Freud and Ralph Walnut Emerson and has memorized perhaps four-hundred yards of poetry, the only use for which, as far as I can see, is to invite him over to put an end to dull parties: "Oh, Harold, pray, do Wordsworth's *Prelude* for us. What fun!"

What is the moral of this story? Might it be that all praise is, somehow, insufficient? James Gould Cozzens, the too faintly praised American novelist, once wrote to his mother that "the reason I prefer to live as nearly like a recluse as possible is that I subconsciously know that people, the world, never would and never will greet my entrances into it with the reverent applause required for my pleasure and if I cannot have that I will not, in effect, play."

I am not in Cozzens's condition, but I recognize that the praise I want is no longer available to me. The (mostly) men who could dispense it have gone to their just reward, and in any case such praise as they might have for me, if any, would be too measured to give satisfaction. Nothing for it, then, but to try to gauge one's own true quality and thereby render oneself above both praise and censure. Not an easy trick, to be sure, but I can discover no other solution to the great silly praise problem. As things stand, I cannot get enough praise and none of it seems to do me any good. Last word—case closed.

Best, Joe

LAGARDELLE. 1.5.14.
Dear Joe,

I have to own up. It wasn't Audrey who coined that remark about people "staying month after month for three whole days"; she did say it, but it was—yes, folks—your 'umble, who had her say it in *Two for the Road*. I have always had a certain contempt for "speech-writers," whether the legendary Ted Sorensen (not that I buy the Kennedy legend with any more credulity than you do) or those workaday'n'night careerists who glaze malign masters with sugared phrases. The saddest of all are the scribes, and they must be many, whose words are read out, often as if in a foreign tongue, at press conferences by the victims of sudden horrors. There can be small comedy in the recitation of scripted texts. Years ago, when the English miners' leader Arthur Scargill was invited to give a formal radio lecture (nothing tranquillizes a revolutionary more surely than a quasi-academic podium), his text included the word "albeit," one of those dated locutions used only by faluters of a certain height. He pronounced it "all bite." Perhaps all good men with coal dust in their lungs say it so, but a moral comes with it: Avoid Smart Assing Unless You're a Smart Ass; and even then . . .

It used to be that people, however choked, declared their feelings because they felt them. What they said might be gauche or ungrammatical or—in the going cant—inappropriate, but there was an intimate relation between what was said and what was felt, or even faked. Humbug can be sincere too. Now, again and pretty well every time, your common man or woman (or detective) reads from a text in which "devastated" mourners are forever trying to "come to terms" with their loss and families are always going through "this difficult time." I still find it difficult to say anything in public about Sarah without the surge of tears and the overloading of the sinuses, but words which have, I presume, been furnished for the victims or the victimized are yet another element in their victimization: trite formulae allow us, the unaffected, to file the victims' particular anguish under a general rubric. Public officials are, no doubt, hedged by what is legally advisable, but the incapacity of the bereaved, in particular, to find words of their own testifies to the narcotization of the public by the media. It has become inappropriate, ungreen even, to employ any words which are not recycled to the point of having no tread left on their tracks.

You've read and written about a lotta lotta biographies and I note, with ticks for your margin, that you are rarely seduced by eulogistic formulae or the badges of merit attached to the mute, seldom inglorious subjects on whom biographers visit their funded attention. Their books are nearly always more orderly, more elegant and much tidier than any life one happens to have lived oneself. There are, at present, very few anti-biographies, of the kind that Robert Graves wrote about T.E. Lawrence. Length itself tends eventually to create a mausoleum festooned with reappraising praises and heavy with seconded thoughts. Harold Nicolson was probably the most candid of the guild of gilders when he confessed that, in the case of George VI,

I think it was, there was a certain difficulty in finding subtly varied terms to cover seventeen years during which that not wholly admirable monarch did nothing much except arrange the stamps, and swaps no doubt, in his then ducal collection.

Nicolson had in common with you the lightness of touch and neatness of phrase which spare us solemn sentiments in favour of the epitomized precision which promises that you have got the subject pinned. That inclusive brevity is not often found in those biographical numbers longer than any wise man first thought of. I have been reading Lucy Hughes-Hallett on Gabriele d'Annunzio; well some of her, some of it. It resembles, and so does Hermione Lee's life of Penelope Fitzgerald, one of those freight trains which I remember, from some life or other, watching as they went, quite slowly, clunk-clunkingly, across some Midwestern plain. The cars could be counted, like these authors' pages, in their hundreds, it seemed, and yet they came and threatened never to go, like those guests whom you so wisely never entertain.

I have no loud quarrel with the d'Annunzio volume, except that what I have read so far, with yawning admiration, gives me no urge to stay with the tour. This leads me to diverge from your view that one doesn't lose all that much by reading alien, prosaic writers in translation. What Hughes-Hallett cannot convey is the rodomontade which, in the Italian vernacular, allows its user to fling himself upon his horse and gallop off in all directions. If she could trust us to understand a quotation from his preposterously precious prose, we could be spared the spurious irony which she pipes aboard her fat cake. (Dr. Sir Jonathan Miller, when he was funny, had a Roman *alter ego* called Spurius Mucus, a joke not to be sniffed at.) The prize-winning lady's d'Annunzio is tracked but never quite caught because the lure of his incantatory style is never suffered to work directly on her reader.

I don't claim facility in reading foreign languages, apart from French, but there is a savor in original texts which no helpful accuracy, still less exegetic prolixity, can convey. I recently conned a Spanish novel, *Soldados de Salamina* by one Javier Cercas, before writing a deserved eulogy of Jeremy Treglown's *Franco's Crypt,* about the Spanish Civil war and its cruel aftermaths. I should never have looked at the Cercas except in the line of reviewing duty, but I took it at speed in my hit-and-miss Spanish and realized, very soon, that while it could, of course, be translated word for word, the surge and repetition of its phrasing would either be left behind or render it insufferable in English. There are wines and cheeses which can be enjoyed only *sur place*; books too.

The comedy, such as it is, of Christianity is that clerics of all cloths attribute divine originality to what Jesus said, regardless of the fact, as I understand it from Géza Vermès and others, that He had frequent recourse to the words and ideas of Hillel and kindred Talmud-slingers. He may have added some unique grace, but extraction from His background served to dress His translated words with a, for instance, Jacobean richness and rareness which they may not have had in Olde Palestine.

Two *personnes* from the Perigordine Porlock have just interrupted my sublime speculations by knock-knock-knocking at my mid-morning door. My neighbors Norbert (who is my age) and Bernard (who was a kid when we first came to this house) had an air of purpose. Peasants - *agriculteurs,* as political rectitude now calls them - come in pairs only when there is an Issue. I played a careful card, *de haut en bas,* by telling them that I had not heard the bell because I was elsewhere. "*Je suis écrivain. Et quand je travaille, je ferme les oreilles et je pars pour un pays lointain.*" If you want to stop a rustic frog in his tracks, come the fine phrases in as impeccable a style as you can muster, if possible with the air of citing the *franchise* of our friend M. de Montaigne.

What was the problem? Bernard, who has a field adjacent to our property, had managed, if not contrived, to drive his small van against a low wall of ours, not more than eight inches high, which projected from our outbuilding, a one-time communal oven, towards the paved road. Bernard (whose father was literally torn in half in front of his young eyes by a piece of farm machinery on which he snagged a button of his cardigan) rarely smiles, but today there was a kind of triumphant humor in what H.J. might call his "address." No truffle tastes better on a peasant's tongue than a legitimate grievance. He had come up to turn on the electric wire which, *en principe,* prevents his *bêtes* from trampling and consuming Beetle's vegetable garden (although there have been a few incursions) and, in setting off again, he had whacked his offside front wheel against our low, wicked wall.

Its wickedness is due to the fact that our gardener Laurent (a Muslim, allbite of Perigordine stock) had built the old wall out a few inches towards the road. If he had not done so, Bernard would have looked where he was going, but the (no doubt "unconscious," doctor) opportunity to damage his vehicle in a way which would Give Him A Right was irresistible, or merely not resisted. I will spare you the diagram, but it demanded skill to bash his wheel, from a standing start three meters away, with sufficient force to dent the hub. *Autres temps, autres murs,* as they don't say. But there we were and what was I going to do, or have done, about it? Nothing if not a metic for all seasons, I ironized subtextually in a way which defied translation and promised that the wall would come down as soon as Laurent came up; which he soon did, to do what local lore demanded. *Quel* fuss about *rien,* you may well say; but who can still wonder why that nice, moralizing Mr. Kerry has not made a lot of headway with reconciling Israelis and Palestinians and why, I fear, no one ever will? Sidney Smith remarked of two housewives yelling at each other from windows that faced each other across a narrow alley, "How can you expect them to agree when they're arguing from different premises?"

I make it a rule never to yell in French. It is their *pays, après tout.* How lucky to be able to play the *écrivain* and have it still mean a little something! Laurent told me just now that doctors used to provoke the same respect as writers, but not any longer: when the *agriculteurs* were *paysans* they took to their death beds with pious resignation and, after an *adieu* from the *curé,* departed zis life. Now, like all of us, they become incensed by doctors who cannot promise to exempt them from the mortal coil. De Gaulle remarked that old age was a *naufrage,* a shipwreck from which he did not expect anyone to rescue him. Today, the wreck must be rectified and made shipshape; that's what we pay taxes for, doc.

Had it not been for the rhubarbarians at my gate, I was going to treat you to a disquisition on the paradoxical differences between biography and autobio, of the kind on which I am embarked and still travelling, without prospect of imminent landfall, but that little number will now have to be adjourned, though not *sine die* nor yet *sans lendemain.* Can you wait?

Tout à toi, Freddie.

May 5, 2014
Dear Freddie,

I should have realized that Audrey Hepburn could never have made that clever remark about houseguests. I should have detected, instanter, the Raphaelian touch in it. But at least she made it in a movie. Our politicians make other people's remarks in so-called real life as opposed to reel-life. I wonder who was the last politician, American or English, who wrote his own speeches? The trend began with Nero, whose speeches were written by Seneca before he put him to his sloppy suicide. Today it is taken for granted, correctly, that none do. Every politician is now a ventriloquist's dummy, with the dummies, unlike in show business, accruing more fame and gold than the ventriloquists who put the words in their mouths. The advent of the professional speechwriter surely has a lot to do with the decline of great political oratory. Speechwriters can formulate slogans and snappy jingles— "ask not what your country can do for you, ask whom you can bonk upstairs in the White House"—but cannot supply either genuine feeling or true passion. Thank God neither Lincoln nor Disraeli had a Ted Sorensen on staff.

Arthur Scargill's "all bite" for "albeit" is amusing, though I suppose he could as easily have pronounced the word "abe it." *Amos 'n' Andy*, a famous radio show in the United States from the 1920s through the '50s, used to mock hi-falutin' Negro speech, in a way that political correctness will no longer tolerate. The show specialized not in mispronunciations but in charming malapropisms. The chief purveyor of these was a character called "The Kingfish." On one occasion, referring to his looks, he said, "Well, there Andy, I ain't no Jeff Chandelier, you know"; and on another said of his wife, "Sapphire's been galvanizing around town with this here John."

When students mispronounced words in my classes, I never corrected them, lest I embarrass the dear boobies. What I would do is bide my time, then repeat the mispronounced word in a correct pronunciation. The erring student might have said "bane-all" and I would later find a way to work the word "banal," properly pronounced, into the conversation.

On the third hand, I mustn't paint myself without fault in this realm. For years, I pronounced Cavafy's name as "Cav-a-fee," until a kind friend, the poet John Frederick Nims, gently corrected me, saying, "You know, Joe, I believe the name is pronounced 'Cav-aphee.' The mnemonic device, should you need one, is 'You're the kareem in my cav-aphee." I also for years mispronounced E. M. Cioran's name, calling him See-a-Ran, and only at his death, in a *New York Times* obituary, did I learn the Rumanian name is correctly pronounced Choran. Of the number of mispronunciations of foreign words I've doubtless committed, don't, as the Jews say, ask. I didn't know until my fifties that the name Maurice—pronounced in America as in France—in England is pronounced Morris. I reviewed E. M. Forster's posthumous novel *Maurice* in the *New York Times Book Review* when it was first published. Had I known that its eponymous hero's name is pronounced Morris I might have been more sympathetic to him.

Earlier this week I betook myself to the memorial service for a fellow teacher at Northwestern with whom, over thirty or so years, I rarely spoke. I went to her memorial because, so unpleasing did she seem to me, I could not imagine anything in the spirit of kindly or grand eulogy anyone might say about her. She was a large woman, at least six feet tall, with rather blubbery features, and a low hairline. She seemed nervous, at least in my presence she did, always wore trousers and reeked of the small brown cigars she smoked: George Sand without the wit or productivity. Behind her back the students, those cruel but not always imperceptive little bastards, called her Harpo, for she resembled that mute Marx brother, but in a brunette version. She and her husband, known to be a teacher of surpassing dullness, had no children, which was probably their chief service to humanity.

Perhaps eighty or a hundred people attended the memorial. Eight people spoke. I was able to endure only six of them. I have heard it said that if someone asks to speak at the memorial of someone you care about, don't let him. He only wants to speak about him- or herself. So it was at this memorial. Anything, I guess, to avoid speaking about the now dead honorand. A strange duck of a woman, a convert from Judaism to earnest Christianity—we Jews were pleased to let her go, with the promise of a return of a player to be named later—ended with a moderately lengthy poem that at no point touched on the life of her dead putative friend. Nothing of any personal interest was said about the deceased by anyone. The chief fact that emerged was that she was a rigid, rabid, and unrelenting academic feminist. (An academic feminist, as I'm sure you know, is no mere feminist. I am myself a mere feminist and so I suspect are you: someone, that is, who wants equality of opportunity and fairness for women in all realms of life.) An academic feminist operates under a pervasive paranoia, is phallomaniacal, touchy, humorless. (How many academic feminists does it take to change a light bulb? Answer: "That's not funny.") I left the proceedings, slipping out the back door, thinking how utterly misguided a life can be when one becomes, in Wallace Stevens's phrase, "a lunatic of one idea." Speak ill of the dead? Me? Now, there, I wouldn't say that, Mr. Gildersleeve.

I have not read Gabriele d'Annunzio, only read about him. From what I gather he is another of those writers, as Bertrand Russell said of D. H. Lawrence, "of a certain descriptive power whose ideas cannot be too soon forgot." Italian fascism, which is romanticism with leather and plumes added, is not my idea of a good time. I am sure you are correct that d'Annunzio is best read in the original. But then all Italian, with its lilting vowel endings, is best read in Italian. On my last plane flight to Milan I recall reading, in Italian, the instructions about using the vomit bag and thinking, *Bellissimo!*

I haven't read a book by Harold Nicolson in a long while. Years ago I read—and still have somewhere in this apartment—his *Some People*, which must be his best-known book. I also read his biography of Dwight Morrow.

He wrote in the age when one could write a biography without having to worry about its being definitive; its being excellent was sufficient. The biographer's style and point of view carried the book. Biographies did not then also serve as doorstops. (A recent biography of John Updike weighs in at a mere 576 pages.) I also read Harold Nicolson's diaries, chiefly for their gossip, which, as I recall, was fairly rich and lightly seasoned with anti-Semitism. Bit of a snob, our Harold.

His being married to Vita Sackville-West cannot have been an easy assignment. (Harold Nicolson is another candidate for the Nobel Prize for Marriage.) To be cuckolded is one thing; to be cuckolded by other women quite something else. Which would be harder to bear, I do not know and have no wish to discover. Of course, as a registered bisexual— where do you suppose one goes to register?—Nicolson himself did lots of business on the other side of the street. I know a man who used to date the movie actress Jodie Foster, just before she became a lesbian. I have never been able to work up the nerve to ask him what it was he did, exactly, that turned her permanently off men.

Returning to the eulogistic, what you say about speaking of the beloved dead strikes the gong. Even tougher than eulogy, though, is condolence. I am always nervous when making it; and the only thing worse than paying condolence is receiving it. The least note of the perfunctory, the merest touch of insincerity, and a screeching alarm goes off. Our good friends the politicians, when confronted with the need to say something about multiple deaths through disaster—fires, earthquakes, plane crashes—have come up with the automatic "our thoughts and prayers go out to the family." President Obama, who is called upon to say these words more than most people, does so in the same tone and tempo with which one might say, "I'm taking a leak, then going for a sandwich."

The best condolence letters I know were written by Henry James. When writing to the bereaved, he dropped his "mere gracious twaddle" and got to what was central about the dead person. He could even write with true feeling about the death of a dog, as in this letter to his friend the American writer Clare Benedict: "I send you . . . my tenderest condolences on the death of poor little gallant, romantic Tello. It must be the loss of the most intimate of friends, almost the nearest of relations, a brave little black, barking son and brother! This end of his career takes me back in memory to the other end—the melancholy days in Venice when he came to you for refuge and you covered him with your charity. You [and your mother] can at any rate both reflect that you filled to the brim for years the cup of his capacity for happiness, and that while he lived he was probably the most important and glorious dog in the two hemispheres." HJ was himself, as you probably know, a dog-owning man; he had a series of dachshunds, about whom he worried as others might about their children, which he of course did not have.

Earlier this morning I finished Tom Holland's translation of Herodotus. His version makes for a smooth run, though one is too often brought up by contemporary idiom or slang that lessens the gravity of the proceedings. Not good to have Xerxes call in the foremost noblemen of Persia "to pick their brains"; or to have him be "hugely impressed by Artemisia's take on things"; or to call an end to the "bad-mouthing" of his guest-friend Demaratus. The footnotes, supplied by your friend Paul Cartledge, are authoritative and impressive. Even though the book has a happy ending—as the reviewers now say, plot-spoiler alert: the Greeks defeated the Persians—I set it down with a feeling of sadness. The sadness derived from my sense that I shall probably not read through Herodotus, a most companionable author, again, at least not in this life. Pause here for deep sigh and an Alzheimer's joke.

A woman reports to her physician that her husband, a Christian Scientist, has been acting strangely lately. Since as a Christian Scientist he won't agree to see a physician, she has made a list of his symptoms, which she would like to read to him, to see what he can deduce from them. After she does so, the physician says: "Two possibilities here: your husband either has AIDS or Alzheimer's." The woman asks the physician what she ought to do. "Simple," he says. "Drive your husband thirty miles outside of town, and then leave him off. If he returns, don't fuck him."

I had an amusing indirect compliment the other day. A friend of mine named David Wolpe, via e-mail, sent me a—you should pardon the expression—tweet from a journalist named Jeffrey Goldberg in which Senor Goldberg describes the seventy-two-year-old singer Paul Simon, formerly of the team of Simon and Garfunkel, as "looking like a character in a Joseph Epstein story." I don't know Jeffrey Goldberg, who writes for *The Atlantic*, but it pleases me to think he knows my stories well enough to make a remark of this kind. Not at all by the way, it's a fairly accurate remark. A few characters who do look quite a bit like the aging Paul Simon may be found wandering around in my stories. Pardon my extreme vanity, but nice to think there is now something more than a few people understand to be "a Joseph Epstein story."

Best, Joe

LAGARDELLE, ST LAURENT-LA-VALLEE. 7.5.14.
Dear Joe,

It's widely believed that resort to autobiography coincides with slippered pantaloonery, to be indulged in only during the last of our seven ages (but the pharmaceuticals are working on an eighth). As against biography, writing about oneself is held to smack of the "self-centeredness" deplored by moralists, especially in the old England of the team spirit and, to offer an abstruse example, steady Buffs. "The Buffs," formally The Royal East Kent Regiment, was the outfit into which my father was drafted in 1918, just in time not to have to go to France for King and Country (just as my great-uncle Fritz—almost certainly Friedrich—did for the Kaiser, who then did for him, since he was killed in Flanders). "Steady the Buffs" no doubt referred to the cry "Play up and play the game," which rallied the ranks in some battle for a best-forgotten imperial cause.

After the epic showboating of which Achilles was the prototype, military tradition came to deplore individuality: a Spartan, who was on sick leave with an eye infection when the rest of his elite outfit fought to the death at Thermopylae, tried to redeem himself in his compatriots' eyes by rushing out of the line at the later battle of Plataea and flinging himself at the Persian ranks. He died, but without glory. The Greek hoplite (it sounds skippy, but denotes only "an armed infantryman") was supposed to stand firm so that his shield chimed with that of his neighbor and protected his flank. In prosaic post-Homeric times, rushes of egotism endangered your companions and never again procured hexametrical applause.

So: the biographer is the literary good soldier. He or—very often these days—she is rated according to the sobriety of her prose (which rarely has the flash and filigree of Lytton Strachey's unduly admired little numbers) and by the thoroughness of her research. Thanks, if that's the word, to the electronic machinery which enables us to correspond with such facility, whole chunks of stuff can be thrown, easily, into the compilation of those many high-hundred-paged numbers about anyone with enough fucks, killings or fame to excite a fat reward for bringing them to the sagging shelves, more dead than alive.

The Athenians were in such a hurry to build their long walls, before the Spartans found out about their construction, that pretty well anything served as in-fill, including the remaindered pseudo-Pheidian marbles which later decked any number of come-and-Getty-it museums. The modern biographer may be a scholar or an opportunist, but cumbrousness is a common badge. If there is written evidence of any relevance, then it deserves, if not requires, elephantine inclusion. Biographies of the Plod school grow obese on archives and "private information." Those of a fancier breed adopt the psycho-speculative mode. I greatly enjoyed, indeed gobbled, Leon Edel's Henry James when it first came out, but when I revisited it recently, second sighting sensed over-confidence that meta-Freudianism *à la* mod would pick the master's lock and enable the pattern in his carpet to be available for painters-by-numbers. Edel is still a pleasure to read, but is he still definitive? Certainly not on the lionized Bloomsberries. We shall never know what that "obscure hurt" was that H.J. experienced when, as an adolescent, he slid down (off?) a New England fence and was, we should be rejoiced to know, Never The Same Again.

Bernard Williams, a sententious philosopher whom the British are determined, in volume after volume of collected pieces and eulogies, to rank among the prophets, once told me, in a corrective tone, that "*nothing* is ever the same again" and that hence there was no virtue in my suggestion, over pre-prandial drinks, that the Holocaust was an event, series of events, so scandalous, in the old religious sense, that (so I was claiming) western civilization could never again be, or claim to be, the same as it was before 1940. You will, I hope, be smiling to see with what facility I can slip into a woolly sentence of Jamesian sub-clauses, deviations and conclusive eloquence.

If H.J. had ever given an account of exactly what happened That Day, Edel would, I suspect, have derived from it the "explanation" for the whole of the Master's *oeuvre,* its flaws, its beauties, its protractions, and its an-other-thingitis. What is likely to happen when a young man slides down a fence? There are two eminent possibilities: he damages his sexual equipment, or supposes that he has, or how about he experiences not what H.J. publicized, quietly, as an "obscure hurt" but an obscure *pleasure*? Suppose that hurt and pleasure *overlapped*, perhaps through the friction as he slid, perhaps (and here is what would be way out of line in principled, well-sourced biography) as something—a picket from the fence?—gave him, as it were, a kick in the pants.

What no biographer could ever divine, unless I told him, is that I learned the pleasure of masturbation, when I was eight years old, by rubbing myself, without knowing why it was so addictive, against a school bench to ease the anxiety of doing a timed Latin test. This doesn't merit going on with, but it is not mere smut: it suggests how much a biographer, however laurelled or even ermined, is likely not to know. I once asked David Garnett about Furbank's now classic life of E. M. Forster. "He got him all wrong," Garnett said. I bet (although I cannot promise) that Furbank didn't mention that, as Simon Raven promised me, Morgan served pushy ephebes on pilgrimage with bad sherry in chipped glasses. The low-down is not necessarily The Truth, but without a little dirt—the skid marks which not even the tightest ass can avoid—biography turns into cosmetic taxidermy.

Autobiography is always said to be unreliable. As Byron remarked, which of us dares look honestly into himself? And then who did self-inflation more cutely than his Lordship? He created his own myth, with the altered ego first of Childe Harold and then of Don Juan. Escaping the "tight little island," he ran away from himself in such a way that he never stopped bumping into himself at the other end. In Leslie A. Marchand (trust a plodder to have a middle initial), poor B. got the professorial bio-person he might have wished for, if only for the fun of laughing at his failure to achieve a living likeness. L.A.M. dogs his subject as closely as a plodder can and yet remains a mile away from George Gordon, Lord B. The autobiographical pages that John Murray and Tom Moore burned, for the sake of the poet's reputation, cannot surely have contained much in the way of erotic revelation that has not been reconstructed subsequently, one way and, of course, The Other, but what *fun* the incendiaries surely deprived us of!

Know thyself? Not an easy assignment. One of the rated philosophers of 1950s Cambridge wrote an essay, a *paper* even, about "the systematic elusiveness of 'I'." "I" escapes logic; it fits in no scheme, can be subsumed under no reliable rubric. The egotist can be put in his place, but rarely consents to stay there. Naïve philosophers sometimes used to begin with "I believe . . ." this or that, or both; to which the smart-ass 1950s response, quick as a flash and witty too, was "But this is mere autobiography!" The mereness derives from the unassimilable solus rexiness of any man who writes about himself. Flavius Josephus wrote the first prose autobio to, as they will say, come down to us (it omitted his childhood as Joseph ben Mattathias, but then all pseudonymous writers spring fully grown from their pages). F.J.'s selfie has made him few friends: his candor is read as camouflage, his reportage as fantasy, his self-deprecation, what there is of it, as shameless. It is the portrait of a man who has to make himself up as he goes along: life is fiction, whatever the facts.

Beetle sometimes says of my own present labors that I spend too much time "running myself down." I should leave that sort of thing to the hosts of

Media-land, who—like those ancient Midians—prowl and prowl around (and how we wonder what kept them when they fail to show!). I truly believe—see supra for ritual response—that I am less egotistical in the first person than when playing, as we do, when we do, the impersonal literary adjudicator who just happens to cut others down to size, because Justice Must Be Done. Which recalls a British lawyer called John Foster who said of a prominent luminary, much given to toffee biographical writing, that during her long hayday she was "Like Justice: not only done but seen to be done."

My current volume is fat with what I recall about the world and its citizens in the years between 1950 and 1962, although that is a *terminus ad quem* at which I have yet to dock. I see "myself among others" (a title too selfish to bear use, but not a bad *proxime accessit* to *Going Up*) more clearly than in any kind of a happy close-up. Wasn't it Oscar Levant who said to George Gershwin, "If you had your life all over again, George, would you still fall in love with yourself?" I feel no temptation to do so at all. The biographer is more likely to feel self-importance after he or she has wrestled some grand person to whatever prosaic level he can manage. Autobiography procures no chairs, no Major Awards, no Nobels (Sartre's *Les Mots* is, in the cant phrase, the exception that proves the rule, *and* disproves it, since he turned the Swedes down). One sees oneself, here and there, in various guises, and the novelist at least takes comfort in thinking that no one whose skin is a perfect fit is likely to create convincing characters or to grace them with contrariness. Despite himself, fortunately, Dostoyevsky was his own Grand Inquisitor.

What is more wearisome than "*états d'âme,*" in which scrupulously unselfish persons declare fine misgivings about the state of the world? I cannot recall which Medici said to Bernardo Strozzi, a Genoese painter of the first second rank, "*Prends garde à toi, tu commences à penser au bonheur de l'homme,*" but I'd be glad if he would make himself known to me. I have a friend who has spent much of the last fifty years worrying about the Bomb and kindred threats to the future of the future (not least, What's Happening Today In Ukraine). Now at seventy-one and a bit, A. is much, much older than I am. His latest encyclical cites People Who Know—they often parade three names—who claim that Washington's policy is likely, if not intended, to lead to nuclear conflagration.

My response is that if "the Americans" thought nuclear war was a way of making a buck (the Yanks' only credible motive in European eyes, especially the left ones), we should have had the big bang long, long ago.

Selfishness is/can/should be a way of avoiding the impersonal, often accusatory, overview *sub specie aeternitatis*. Our old friend Montaigne made an honest molehill of himself when he observed that a man can sit only on one pair of buttocks, no matter how elevated the throne. Obscure hurt, obscure pleasure, the man on his own can dare to say, if he chooses, what "we" would never have the nerve or knowledge to guess about him.

Tout à toi, Freddie.

May 12, 2014
Dear Freddie,

The Spartan who missed his chance for immortality at Thermopylae was—as I happen to know only because I've recently reread Herodotus—Aristodemus, the sole Spartiate survivor of the 300 engaged in the battle. Apparently there are conflicting stories about him: one has him passing out with his eye infection, the other that he was sent back to Sparta from Thermopylae with a message and could have returned to battle but chose not to do so. The Spartans, not big on forgiveness, afterwards called him Aristodemus the Trembler. Herodotus thought him the bravest man at Plataea, but the Spartans refused him honors for dying there. Your friend Paul Cartledge, in a footnote to the Tom Holland translation of Herodotus, claims that the reason for this "was not the fact that he had in effect committed suicide but rather the manner of his doing so—breaking ranks and losing self-control [in his rush to redeem himself by displaying his bravery] that decided the Spartans against rewarding him." For some reason the story reminds me of the old joke about the Japanese kamikaze pilot who flew twelve missions until he was dishonorably discharged for an insufficient death wish.

Writing one's autobiography poses the complicated negotiation between candor and tact. One must be candid yet one must not display oneself in too impressive a light. You know, I am sure, Orwell's discouraging two-liner about autobiography, which runs: "Autobiography is only to be trusted when it reveals something disgraceful. A man who gives a good account of himself is probably lying, since any life when viewed from the inside is simply a series of defeats." Every autobiographer, I take Orwell also to be saying, is guilty until proven innocent. You might cite the Orwell quotation to Mme R. when next she accuses you in your own autobiography of being too hard on yourself. On the other shaky hand, it's worth recalling that some of Orwell's own best writing has been autobiographical: the essays "Such, Such Were the Joys," "A Hanging," "Shooting an Elephant," the personal bits in *Homage to Catalonia* and *The Road to Wigan Pier*.

Not all that many great autobiographies have been written. I wonder if this isn't because the men who have had the great lives to write about hadn't the talent to get those lives down on paper, while those who have the talent usually haven't had lives all that worthy of recording. Which doesn't mean one can't write charmingly about one's own life. The last such (charming) autobiography I read was V. S. Pritchett's *A Cab at the Door*, which also gains from an excellent title. His family, owing to his father's inability to gain a financial foothold anywhere, was always moving. Pritchett also had his Christian Science upbringing to write about. One of the good guys, V. S. Pritchett, and it's a pity there is no one like him in England, or anywhere else that I know of, quite like him around today.

Of the great autobiographies, there is Benvenuto Cellini's, there is Rousseau's, there is Ben Franklin's, there is John Stuart Mill's, there is Vladimir Nabokov's, and I cannot think of many others. As it happens, I reread *Speak, Memory*—first published under the title *Conclusive Evidence*—this past week. (I'm to write about it for the *Wall Street Journal*.) Nabokov had an extraordinary story to tell—the story of deracination. He describes his life as resembling a spiral of circles, from the circle of his lavish boyhood in Russia before the Revolution, to the circle of impoverished years in exile in England, Germany, and France, to the circle of his settled but probably not altogether happy years in America, which he does not touch on in his autobiography. The Montreux years, too, you will recall, are left out.

Nabokov had exoticism going for him. The opulence of the aristocracy in Tsarist Russia was explicitly, wondrously exotic. His family had of course the traditional country estate and St. Petersburg mansion, and a battalion of servants. Nabokov sets all this out in what he calls "the careful reconstruction of my artificial but beautifully exact Russian past." The Nabokovs had not one but two chauffeurs and three cars—this in the first decade of the twentieth century. Footmen and kitchen help go without saying. Nabokov refers to a doorman—as distinguished, one assumes, from a butler—and another servant whose job it apparently was to answer the phone. In the country, gardeners and watchmen and other lackeys are in long supply. A stream of tutors for the five Nabokov children passes in and out. Four Great Danes are loosed at night to stand guard over Vyra, the country estate. And they say we Jews know how to live!

Speak, Memory, you may also recall, is not without its longueurs. The chapter devoted to its author's passion for collecting butterflies is one; another is the chapter on the elevated hobby of writing chess problems, whose achievement he compares to that of creating successful art. Nabokov is wise in never pumping himself up, never claiming virtue for himself. His portraits of his beloved parents; his character of "Mademoiselle" ("my enormous and morose Madame"), the tutor, whose native element was misery; his first loves, his Cambridge days—all these things are recounted without egotism obtruding. His tact is consummate. In a single paragraph toward the end of the book he hints, ever so gently, at his younger brother Sergey's homosexuality, which he claims to have discovered by reading a page, "in stupid wonder," out of the latter's diary, which "abruptly provided a retroactive clarification of certain oddities of behavior on his part." Sergey, as you know, died in a Nazi concentration camp that specialized in medical experimentation.

I have myself long ago put aside any thought about writing an autobiography. My life has been too quiet to produce an interesting one; nor have I known, or even met, a large number of famous or powerful people to remove the spotlight from my own all-too-calm days. I am not sufficiently soulful to write a book about the state of my soul. I was a much more interesting, if much less introspective, person when I was young. When I became, almost without conscious decision, a bookish and a scribbling man, the larger sense of adventure went out of my life, and I was henceforth almost entirely spectatorial in my interests, even in my passions.

Another disqualification I have for writing autobiography is that over the years I have been spending my autobiographical material in nickels and dimes in the couple of hundred personal essays I've written. I still have some loose autobiographical change in my pocket, enough to see me out, and I prefer to continue spending it the way I have my earlier autobiographical funds, slowly, a nickel and dime at a time.

"Biographical truth," claimed Sigmund the Freud, "was not to be had." Perhaps so. Biography is not mathematics but horseshoes: close counts. Like you, I am an admirer of Leon Edel's five-volume *Henry James*. I reviewed two of the volumes when they first appeared, and a blurb containing my mortal prose festoons the dust-jacket of the later vols. ("This monument to an artist is itself a great work of art—the single greatest work of biography produced in our century."—Joseph Epstein, *Washington Post*) I also read, when I began to teach a course in James, Edel's one-volume condensation of his five volumes, which is excellent, and probably would have been better to have had than the full five-gun battleship he produced first time round.

If only one could edit one's blurbs, I should now add to mine, the proviso: "Oh, and not at all by the way, skip the Freudian bits in Leon Edel's biography." I knew Leon Edel moderately well. He was a small man, with a carefully groomed white mustache, which made him look like Esky, the mascot who used to appear on the cover of *Esquire*. He called on me on some of his visits to Chicago. At least once he came to lecture at our town's very own otiose Institute for Psychoanalysis. Leon was a true believer in the doctrines of the Viennese Quack, as Nabokov never failed to call Herr Doktor Freud. ("Greek myths used to cover private parts," is the amusing way he characterized Freud's leading ideas.) Edel's Freudian disfigurement of James came, as you suggest, in the bloody "hidden injury" passages and also in his portrayal of the sibling rivalry between Henry and his brother William. I wonder, though, if even these blunderbuss psycho-go-go intrusions spoil the book. (Do you suppose Edel was looking for "the figure in the car-port?") For me they did not. For me it remains the best book I know at describing the life of a writer, his daily travail, his ambitions, his disappointments, his many setbacks, his achievements, his ultimate triumph. I found the story of Henry James's life in Edel's telling inspiring.

I have begun to read William James's *Varieties of Religious Experience*. This is part of my vague campaign to read for the first time some of the books I am supposed long ago to have read to certify my pretension to being a cultivated person. The book comprises the twenty Gifford Lectures that William James gave at the University of Edinburgh in 1901–02. At its very outset, James speaks of his feeling of humility at addressing a European audience when, in his experience, the traffic usually ran the other way: distinguished Europeans addressing scholars and students at Harvard. James's appearance at Edinburgh did not change the direction of this traffic. Currently the intellectual traffic, both ways, has slogged to a near halt.

One of the great intellectual changes in my lifetime is the admiration that Americans with intellectual and artistic interests had for almost all things European. As an undergraduate, I can recall feeling myself, as an American, an irremediable yokel, at least in the realm of culture. England, France, Italy were where the serious action was. These countries had the important writers and painters and musicians, the great museums and orchestras, the majestic buildings. All that seems left now are the buildings, the bricks. Americans of any cultural sophistication no longer look to Europe with yearning or high expectations of any kind. The players—the writers, the artists, the musicians, the intellectuals—have departed the premises. A mere half-century or so and, swoosh, they are gone. Not that they have been replaced by comparable American figures. They haven't. Some might think this the grumblings of an old gent claiming giants walked the earth when he was young and bemoaning that now only pygmies do. (You don't suppose, do you, the political correctness police will be after me for disparaging pygmies? Hope not.) But I do feel that something serious and important had disappeared from intellectual life, and I wish I could be reasonably optimistic about its return.

To end on a cheerier note, let's return to Byron's biographer Leslie A. Marchand's middle initial. Is it only Americans who insert middle initials betwixt their first and last names? I believe so. That single middle initial brings with it a high comic pomposity that passes unnoticed among my fellow gringos. Henry James does a funny bit on this in "Daisy Miller," where Daisy's little brother introduces himself to the story's narrator as Randolph C. Miller, notes that Daisy's real name is Anne P. Miller, and their father's name is Ezra B. Miller. I used to ask students if they saw any joke here. None ever did. Only then did I ask them how they would feel about Dante, Shakespeare, Beethoven, Proust, and Picasso if they were named Dante M. Alighieri, William L. Shakespeare, Ludwig J. Beethoven, Marcel C. Proust, and Pablo W. Picasso. Slowly, ah, ever so slowly it dawned on them. A million laughs, teaching.

Best, Joe

LAGARDELLE. 13.5.14.
Dear Joe,

Yes indeed; meaning that most, if not all, of the assessments in your last number seem just and even—excuse the abuse—mature. Edel made H.J. human and touching by careful attention to the man and the work, rather than by the audacity of the kind of contrariness and jargonized vocabulary which currently flash from select presses. If it weren't for Edel's five-volume solemnity, but never ponderousness, our old friend might have been abandoned to quickshotry, as N. Hawthorne somewhat has been, although he was in several respects much more original and less classy-conscious than H. James. Hawthorne deserves the floodlit niche he would certainly have if he had done more stuff, even if not all of it were as good as what he actually did do. Updike is an example of a reputation bolstered by a number of cod-pieces which no one is likely to "rediscover" (*The Coup*, for instance, and *Of The Farm* (yes, modest monosyllables too can be pretentious) even though the best—the first Rabbit and what else?—can be very good.

George Painter is one biographer neither of us has saluted so far; I ain't looked at his Proust in an aeon or two, but it had the sweet merit of being succinct and yet redolent of the pace and pose of the author in question. Painter didn't quite parody *le petit Marcel,* but he promised us that if you liked his foreplay, you would certainly have a good time with what followed. Proust seems to render anyone who writes about him the service of putting him/her on their best behavior. None of the many, many books I have read about him is manifestly unworthy of a letter of appreciation from that most eloquent of toadies. Even Julia Kristeva tempered her usual psychoanalytic show of omniscience with acute attention to the stuff; a nice contrast with the cases when you can't see the trees for the James Wood.

One of the curiosities of French life and culture is how close and yet distinct the two elements lie to each other. As Leopardi saw, the culture can falsify the life by the eloquence with which even the nastiest ideas are articulated, not least in fancy French prose. French writers seem much more grown up than their Anglo-Saxon cousins and rivals and hence appear persuasive, even when they are - as the cant used to say - spit-balling. The figure of Marshal Pétain retains a niche of a sort, even though condemned to national disgrace, not least because he said a few things which defy deletion. The first was involuntary, perhaps apocryphal, but still durable. One day, latish in the war, coming down in the elevator of the Hôtel du Parc, his headquarters in Vichy, during the Occupation, in full dress uniform, *mit* the képi already, he turned to his young aide-de-camp and said, *"Qui suis-je?"* As they reached the bottom, the young man responded: *"Vous êtes le Maréchal Pétain." "Ah oui!"* said the old soldier, and walked out, buttoning himself into who he was supposed to be, to meet the cheers which never quite failed to reach his ears. The Marshal's other collectible remark was when he said of someone, "He knows everything there is to know, and nothing else." How many of that kind of omniscient ignoramus now host and guest and blog *un peu partout* in the age of opinionators and journocrats?

Pétain's need of a prompt before he could go on playing the part of himself is pathetic only because his sidekick told the tale. In truth, who doesn't choose from a wardrobe of possibilities which personality to put on for this occasion or that? Hypocrisy (play-acting is at the root of it) is the essence of civility. Why do we write to each as we do? Your prose seems to flow as clean and sparkling as Horace's *fons Bandusiae splendidior vitro*. But why do I reach for that old line here when I am unlikely to use it elsewhere? It tells you something of which clothes I have chosen to put on today and it flatters as it challenges you, very mildly. Our game of literary tag makes me keen to amuse and to impress, not least because I know that, in other company, you are, as they say, a tough room to play. The style may be the man, but it changes, politely, according to the person to whom it is addressed. One does not put on a dinner jacket to eat a pizza. So? Follow this digression and it will come back, presently, as the English used to say, to clunk-click into the foregoing.

Here goes. About twenty years ago, when the word was out that I had been picked to play doubles with S. Kubrick, my stock was as high as it is ever likely to get. I was commissioned by a producer who had impressed me, some years earlier, by wanting to make a movie of a novel called *Somewhere Off The Coast of Maine* by Ann Hood. I expect you have read it, because I expect you to have read most everything. An odd choice for a Hollywood producer, so odd indeed that, back then, Mike Lobell couldn't raise a bean to commission me and, in them days, I never wrote movies for zip (my standard line, which never got a smile, was that I might as well write an epic poem). In Kubrick-time, Lobell got me a nice stack of $$ to write a modern love story (what else?) for which I had a few nifty ideas as well as the one he brought to me, about a marriage that breaks up after the death of a child. That's right, the kind of thing that, in those days, I assumed happened only to other people.

I wrote a script and it was pretty good and we had a penciled-in star, Meg Ryan no less (she got less later) and a director, the son of a Midwest crook-cum-conman. The director promised me that *This Man and This Woman* was going to be his next picture and he even played tennis with me and my son Stephen at the Queen's Club in London. So—I'll bet you saw it coming—Master Z. dumped us because Lobell wouldn't go pay or play (and because chummy had a hotter ticket). Sean Penn loved the script but the studio didn't love Sean Penn, not that day. So the thing dragged its slow length along and I was pretty sure the project was on its way to Morry Bund. But Lobell had more taste than his grey pigtail suggested and more persistence than most any producer: he was, is, determined to make the script, now so old that the original doesn't even have cell-phones in it (it will, it will). Lobell made his first money in the *schmatte* business and you're right, I don't mention the Fons Bandusiae to him all that often, but he likes quality projects, even if he did produce Demi Moore in *Striptease* or whatever the thing was called.

Two years ago, Mike came to London to produce a movie with Colin Firth, a supposed star with nice British manners (like so many, Firth came to public attention when playing Mr. D'Arcy). His presence on the screen is, in my experience, that of runner-up to the invisible man. This has not prevented him from winning an Oscar and being, supposedly, bankable. Lobell wanted to play tennis while he was in London, so I passed him to Stephen, now vice-chairman of Queen's, hoping that Mike would be a credit to his race, which indeed he proved. So now, we come all the way to the fact that, after all them years, Mike seemed a few months ago to have Richard Gere and Penelope Cruz and the (very little) money to make a version of TMTW but—today being today and almost certainly most of our tomorrows—not a bean for the scribe to do a rescript in order to accommodate a 60+ actor in a romantic roll. So I did this and that and all seemed as it wasn't, because a couple of weeks ago Mr. Gere (who had sworn that he loved Mike, more than a partner, a friend) got cold feet or whatever anatomical chill led him to unplug himself; not the money, I suspect, as he made out, but loss of nerve, if not yet of hair.

Now what indeed? The only v. good news is that Penelope is still with us, and she is, in my view, much more important than Master G., just as Audrey was, in the *bon vieux temps* when we were casting *Two for the Road* (Paul Newman passed).Last night, Lobell made his Canossa call to tell me where we stood, or where he would like me to think we stand, and—of course and what else?—to ask me to do the umpteenth rewrite, gratis, in order to remove the longer sleeves and easier waistband that I had tailored for Master Gere, also for nothing but a kiss. A call like last night's is as close as a modern producer comes to kneeling in the snow. Why would I do another pass, *à mon age,* when I could as well write that unwritten epic poem? Who could guess that what led me to lift Mike to his feet and embrace him, now without the pigtail, was not the prospect of fame or that elusive first-day-of-shooting bonus?

I told him the story, which he was kind enough to say he hadn't heard, about the guy who is waiting to cross the street next to a nun. As they stand there, she says to him "Would you like to come home with me?" He says, "Excuse me?" "Would you like to come home with me?" The man says, "You're supposed to be a nun." She says, "I *know*. But you just happened to catch me at the right moment." Copy that, pretty much, and you have what I said to Lobell when I agreed, yet again, to be what my mother (in restricted company only) used to call a *schtunk*. How come he got me at the right moment? No researcher, no Kristevan intuition or close reading could ever come up with it in the whole archive of my pollyvalent (parroting) wardrobe: I said I'd hang in "because" Stephen, who can be *dur comme fer* when crossed or displeased, had played tennis with Mike and really liked him. If Mike had done one little thing to embarrass Stephen, *chez lui,* made one dishonest line call, abused one of the club staff, I would have walked away without ever considering going anywhere with him.

Selena Hastings, for titled British instance, dug all the dirt on our old friend Willie Maugham she could for a pretty penny but never got the surface right, because she tried so hard to give the nudnik public the ugliness they like to pin to celebrities' hindquarters. What she never realized, I guess with some confidence, is that the Old Party would have portrayed her with more accuracy and brevity than she could ever muster by dredging available gutters. Alroy Kear (surely a transposition of Kir Royal?) is there in *Cakes and Ale* as Willie's recension of H.J.'s publishing scoundrel in *The Aspern Papers.* The Lady Selena can be glad that W.S.M. is too dead to nail her condescending ass. But why mention her among so many bio-parasites? Because I agreed to have lunch with her and told her of my experience at the Villa Mauresque and my theories about the stammering Maugham's garrulity in the secret theatre of his split personalities and she never even listed my little book about him in her bibliography nor, of course, thanked me for marking her card. When my Maugham book came out, I had a handwritten letter of congratulation from his (and Graham Greene's) friend John Sutro, in an envelope with a purple tissue-paper inner lining. Ergo, nuts to Selena Hastings.

Tout à toi, Freddie.

May 18, 2014
Dear Freddie,

I am a touch nervous about correcting your mother, of sainted memory, on the meaning of the word *schtunk*. In her usage, a *schtunk* was apparently someone easily preyed upon, a *schmoe*, a patsy, a sucker, a chump. My sense of a *schtunk* is that of someone unrefined, unpleasantly aggressive, a boor, a putz, a futz, a stinker, a schmuck to a very high power. When I was eight or nine years old, on a field behind the apartment building in which we lived, the Sullivan High School football team used to practice. The school's coach, a barrel-chested, bellicose man named Ralph Margolis, used to call his erring players *schtunks.*

The word appears in connection with your account of your recent movie dealings with Mike Lobell. I have a weakness for such Hollywood stories: the goofiness, the sheer unreality of them. One of my favorites has to do with a man named Daniel Fuchs. Fuchs was generally a defender of Hollywood, where he made his living for many decades. He had begun his career as a novelist, and in the 1930s wrote something called *The Williamsburg Trilogy*, later reprinted to good reviews during the brief Jewish renaissance in fiction. He cashed in his chips in his mid-twenties and went off to Los Angeles. He won an Oscar for writing a merely O.K Doris Day-Jimmy Cagney movie called *Love Me or Leave Me.*

The story Fuchs told was about some novel or play that no one had any luck turning into a screenplay. Finally, the "property" was turned over to him, and he was indeed able to find the way to do it. When his treatment was passed along to Louis B. Mayer or some other mogul of the day, the mogul was much impressed. "What do we pay this guy Fuchs?" he asked. When he was told that Fuchs was on the payroll for $650 a week, the mogul replied, "Let's get someone better than that to work on the actual screenplay."

In my single abortive experience with Hollywood, my producer kept responding that my screenplay would "make a swell little movie," or "an excellent little movie," or "a really fine little movie." Always that word "little." Then one day he told me that he thought it would make a "major" movie. When I asked him what made the difference between little and major, he said, "I can see Dustin Hoffman in the lead role in this movie, which would change it from a roughly $30 million to a $90 million movie." I asked him what the effect of that would be on the movie itself. "Well," he said, "you have a scene set in the Pump Room of the Ambassador East Hotel in Chicago in 1960. If it's a $30 million movie, we'll duplicate the banquettes in the Pump Room, so, too, the livery of the waiters, and we'll have a neon sign that says Pump Room. If it's a $90 million movie, we'll rebuild the fucking Pump Room." Now That's Entertainment.

You mention Mike Lobell having once worn a pigtail. What do you suppose is the difference between a pigtail and a ponytail? The latter, I guess, is longer. Matadors and mandarins used to wear pigtails. In America chiefly refugees from the 1960s wear ponytails. No man looks better for a ponytail. Pin a ponytail on Cary Grant, Gary Cooper, or Louis Jourdan, and they would instantly turn into three *schtunks.* The same, surely, is true of an earring, let alone two earrings, which some among the young—and now not so young—in America have taken to wearing. Inelegant, silly, not good.

John Simon's name comes up, twice, in *Distant Intimacy*, both times mentioned by you. I cannot resist reporting to you that a week or so ago he had a piece in *The Weekly Standard,* vaunting neither the poems of Gottfried Benn nor the not very readable last novels of Italo Calvino, but instead, *mirabile dictu*, a very low-grade television game show for housewives called *Wheel of Fortune.* John, that once immitigable, irredeemable, unrelenting highbrow turns out to be bonkers about the show, and regrets that it appears on television only five nights a week, apparently leaving him bereft on weekends. Famous savager of aging actresses that he always was, he now has a bit of a thing for the show's co-host, an aging Barbie Doll named Vanna White.

John will be ninety next year, and what is on display in his enchantment with this dopey game show is an old bull gone weak in the knees, a tiger who has lost his teeth. His ecstatic account of the show is comparable to you coming out to say that of course your favorite movie is *Lassie, Come Home* and my announcing that no book in the modern era could possibly hope to top *Jonathan Livingston Seagull.* Slashing attackers such as John Simon seem to have no language for praise, and whenever they do set out to praise something usually make a botch of it, in the attempt to show what pussycats they truly are, by going too far.

One of the small pleasures of growing older is being able to discern the trajectory of literary careers. John Simon's has been a remarkable, even oddly admirable, if scarcely enviable, one. For more than sixty years he has roughed up plays, movies, and books. (He's attempted to make up for it by occasionally writing admiringly about serious music, but his musical culture is not deep enough for this to leave any mark.) So far as I know all these years he has made a living writing only criticism, not an easy thing to do, even in the role of critic as Gestapo man.

I've been twice, maybe thrice, reviewed by John, in every case gently; in one instance, my book *Snobbery*, he praised me extravagantly on the front page of the now defunct *Los Angeles Times Book Review*, which doubtless helped my publisher move some merchandise. Always, at the end of his reviews, no matter how generous all that has gone before, he has to close on a paragraph or two noting small errors in the book under review. I don't know when he began doing so, but it soon developed into a tic. He could find a solecism in a sneeze, a misusage in a belch, our John. I once met a man who told me that John Simon corrected the toast he gave at a wedding. I pity the poor priest who provides him with last rites, if rites he requires; John is certain, before it is over, to correct his Latin.

Still on the subject of old bulls gone weak in the knees, I note that the current issue of the *New York Review of Books* hasn't a single contributor of any distinction. The paper's editor, Robert Silvers, the old Viceroy of India, as I have thought him since John Gross once told me that in their obeisance the intellectuals of England used to treat him thus when he showed up in the UK, is still at the helm, working away every day of the year, including Yom Kippur, marking up contributors' copy, asking penetrating questions, making crucial cuts. I wonder if he has any inkling that his game is over? The ponies, the mallets, the lush lawn are still there, but there are no longer any worthy riders, which is to say eminent contributors, to keep things interesting. I dropped my more than forty-years-long subscription to the paper three or so years ago. (As a one-time contributor, I am entitled, if I wish, to read it on-line.) I decided that it made no sense to continue supporting a paper whose politics I found so loathsome. I dropped my subscription to the *London Review of Books* even earlier. Why subscribe to such sheets? One might as well cut out the middleman and write a check directly to Hamas.

I note you slipped in a pleasing compliment suggesting that I am well read. I don't think of myself as such. I wonder if anyone is truly well read. Some people have read a lot more than others, but even they, I suspect, have great gaps in their reading. The two best-read men I have known have been Arnaldo Momigliano and Edward Shils. Edward had a personal library, here and in England of more than twenty thousand books, none of them trivial. I once saw him use a razor blade to cut an Alfred Kazin introduction out of a book—I cannot recall which it was—saying, "I don't want that Jew in my house." (Edward was himself Jewish.) Part of his intellectual power was that for extrapolation. He knew what he didn't have to read. The first time I met him, he asked me what I was reading. I told him a novel by Alison Lurie, a writer then in greater vogue than now. "Ah," he said, "about academic screwing, I take it." *Exactement!*

Among books I should like to have time to reread is *Anna Karenina*. Week before last Barbara and I, in nightly two-hour sessions, watched the ten-hour 1977 BBC version of the novel with an actress named Nicola Paget in the title role. I've seen the Greta Garbo version of *Anna Karenina* and the Vivien Leigh one, but neither lays a glove on Nicola Paget's. She had ten hours to build the character, as opposed to the roughly two hours movies allow, but she used the time well to layer the part with rich ambiguity and splendid complexity. The man who did the BBC adaption, a name I've not noted before, is Donald Wilson, who deserves much credit. Everything about the production feels right: the clothes, the décor of the rooms, the streets and estates (apparently it was filmed in Hungary). This version, too, of the great novel, gives due attention to Levin, the Tolstoy-like figure whose presence takes up, if memory serves, roughly a third of the novel.

How does it happen that the English are still so good at such work? I have more than once noted to you, and you seem to have concurred, the general cultural slippage in English. "It's Mick Jagger's country now," I have taken, regretfully, to saying. Theatrically, though, the English have kept the flag flying. I can only imagine what a botch Americans would have made of an adaptation of *Anna Karenina*. I wonder if you recall the American movie version of *War and Peace*, which came close to comedy. Audrey Hepburn was Natasha; now that elegant woman was a great many lovely things but Countess Natalya Illyinichna Rostova was not one of them. Her hopeless husband of the time—hopeless as an actor and, as you have told me, as a husband—Mel Ferrer was Prince Bolkonsky. ("In a pig's bristled ass he was," I can hear the rurally-raised father of an old friend say.) Most miscast of all was Henry Fonda as Pierre Bezhukov. (While they were at it they ought to have tried George Raft or, better, Jimmy Cagney, in the part.) Years went by before I could get the wretched memory of that adaptation out of mind.

The other night, round 3:00 a.m., arisen to make water, I fell in our bathroom on the way back to bed. Not only did I fall but I was unable to get up. (I must have been suffering dehydration.) So I crawled toward our bed, when Barbara awoke and helped me up. I'm fine now, but I did have a premonition while crawling along our bathroom floor. The premonition was that I would pass out, the screen would go black, there would be a brief pause, and the word *Fini* would appear on the screen, then dissolve into nothingness as would I. How's that for an upbeat ending.

Best, Lou (Morry's brother) Bund

LAGARDELLE. 22.5.14.
Dear Joe,

This week has been largely about *la France divisée en deux,* a frequent subject of lament for a condition without remedy. It is, in truth, no great scandal that French society is riven by fault-lines of various kinds; some of them at least resemble the articulations of the human body which enable us to crouch and reach at the same time (albeit with less elasticity, in my case, than a few years ago). The great division here is between Paris and the Provinces. The Jacobins forced France into a homogenizing brace and their tradition and politicians' ritual reiterations insist that the republic is identical with France. Yet, the *ancien régime* and the *douceur de vivre* which Talleyrand confessed, quite brazenly, to be missing, early in the brave new egalitarian world, continue to haunt the national ethos and, especially, French literature, where grammar, paradox and elegance, *à la* Chateaubriand, still have a place.

How do French intellectuals manage to contrive such elegant schemes for the modification, if not remodeling, of the entire world, read each other's texts with such punishing intuitions, perceive patterns of rare intricacy and general truths of rigorous subtlety and yet conduct themselves, in petty social practice, with vindictive heartlessness? Sartre biffed his chum Camus, but endorsed Stalin even as he knew him to be a mass murderer; Philippe Sollers, who imagines himself to be Poulou's *remplaçant,* just as his *compagne* Julia Kristeva supposes herself to be *la* Beauvoir and Susan Sontag rolled into one (which, the form suggests, was no sort of a physical or mental impossibility), aped the self-important viciousness of the Mao whose Cultural Revolution was a license for breaking any heads which nursed an idea that did not derive from the Chairman's addled vanity.

The ruin of the Western universities, which you have lamented with unanswerable clarity, is the more abject for being an act, many acts, of mimesis. Nothing is stranger than the voluntary servitude of the intellectuals unless it is the delight in dictatorship and doctrinal narrow-mindedness on the part of *maîtres-à-penser.* Every small pope is marked by the zeal with which his anathemas are pronounced (down on the east coast of Spain, at a place called Peñiscola, you can visit the offshore fiefdom of Papa Luna, aka the antipope Benedict XIII, who continued to denounce and sanctify long after he had been ejected from official recognition, and in the gateway is a metal cage in which the facsimile—I hope—of a heretic still dangles *pour encourager les autres*).It may be that no contemporary intellectual has as commanding a *mainmise* on the intellectual world as did Sartre, Althusser, Lévi-Strauss, not to mention (because why would I?) Chomsky, E. Wilson, or your *quondam* patron Mr. Silvers. The reason for the fracture of intellectual empires is the success of the journalistic pirates, of whom John Simon was an early jolly rogerer (sexual opportunism tends to go with intellectual boarding parties). Hitchens, Woods, Cockburn, Buruma, and that Canadian with the slick barber, the roughs and the smoothies, have achieved the division of the once serious world of scholarship and letters into opportunities for by-the-buckload fakery and flakery.

The misuse of foreign languages, which need never have been used anyway, is a small symptom of the element of bluff in the new professoriate and allied trades (C. Hitchens was your exemplary unpretty polyglot). A recent symposium, headed by a friend of mine of genuine scholarly competence and including a symposiast who is a remarkable Hellenist of very well-argued originality, was given to me by its convener and, politeness being my dated watchword, I sat down to be improved. And, yes, I was, to some degree, made aware of the helter and the skelter of humanity's Gadarene rush to whatever precipice will take care of over-population and civilization as we know it, unless . . . we are very, very careful. So far so unsurprising and, maybe, unarguable: so what answer do Our Betters supply? To place less faith in Mammon and more in . . . no, the G word cannot quite be advanced in high academic company, so "religion" was timidly uttered, like a sacrificial pawn, although "faith" (which may move mountains, but does nothing to budge our plague of molehills) might have served.

You mentioned in your last innings that John Simon was incapable of writing a review without pointing out some minute error, flaw, solecism (ancient artists always made sure there was one, to avoid the jealousy of the gods). I suspect that this allowed him to end up being the judge even in courts where he was not qualified to plead as a native: he might preside, but he can never be our President. I mention our nonagenarian friend because all of us scribes and Pharisees have a touch of Simony. Who can deny a quiver of relief when he spots the small error in the latest out-of-sight tome of, say, Jonathan Israel or Simon Schama or Niall Ferguson, the world heavyweight champion of lightweights?

Before we let go of the scruff of John Simon's neck (no one will deny that he has a lot of it), I have to say that I recall a symposium on The State of the Language in San Francisco, probably in late 1979 when someone said, for a reason to which oblivion has been kind, that there was no English word with the prefix "dis-" which was not, oh, disagreeable. This observation deserves to be filed under "lady-who-cares?," but Simon—you will not be dismayed to hear—came up with the goods, served with his usual caustic accentual molasses: "What about . . . disrobe?" Nobbad. Admiring crap telly is part of the new camp, is it not? When I denied ever having heard of some British TV daytime couch potatoes' show with hosts called Richard and

Judy, my female neighbor at an intellectual dinner table turned to me and said, "That's the most pretentious thing I've ever heard." Oh for the days when assuming fellow diners to understand untranslated Portuguese was what pretentious meant.

France and its divisions. In a new house just below our eye line but not more than a couple of hundred yards from our modest hilltop domain lives a nice young woman called Vanessa, who will come to the house and cut what little remains of my hair in fifteen minutes, at a euro a minute, before motoring on to the next customer. She is the daughter of our always cheerful twice-a-week help Véronique who reminded us that on Saturday afternoon Vanessa was celebrating her election to the *conseil* of our *commune* in the traditional fashion by raising a *Mai* and offering the company a *vin d'honneur* and her mother's *beignets*. I don't know about *noblesse* but the obligation had to be honored. Down we went in the heat and were greeted with the timid familiarity which old, alien residents receive in these parts, not least if they have a tincture of fame (in living memory, I was on a much-watched chat show to talk about voiking with Mr. Kubrick). Madame Raphael is more easily assimilated, since she is usually to be seen in the garden, doing what peasant ladies do in due season: *"Madame Raphael est travailleuse"* is the citation. And he? He is, yes, folks, an intellectual, hence not out of sight of Gallic respect, even though no one, I may be sure, between here and there has read a word I have written.

The dividedness of France is, I was always told, essentially between Parisians and others, but also, I learned on the weekend, when it comes to raising a stripped pine tree, tall enough to be the mast of the *Mayflower,* decked with hooped paper *couronnes,* budded with red, white and blue paper flowers, and flying the Tricolor a couple of times, from the prone position to the vertical, where it has to be attached to a thick, rooted *tuteur* in order to stand tall for the duration of Vanessa's elevation to high office, between Perigordins and other provincial *Français*. Only in our region, I discovered, after forty-five years of habitation, does this antique ceremony pull people together in a vestigial tribute to the raising of the Tree of Liberty in revolutionary Paris, even though there is no evidence of any reign of Terror or even of any savage *règlement de comptes* in the Virgilian landscape of our department: it lends itself less to great estates and social distinctions than to small-holding independence, gluttony, vinosity and venery. Peasant brides regularly went pregnant to the altar, having given promise of at least an even chance that they would come down with the desired son and heir. Today they often dispense with the altar.

The raising of the *Mai* needs many hands under a professional leader. Metal ladders are inserted as crutches when the handlers have to take a fresh purchase and then, up she goes, in a unison of applause. The villagers are, no doubt, of various political persuasions (not a few, I suspect, vote for the meta-fascist, anti-Muslim *Front National*), but they are united, however temporarily, in hand-shaking, *bisou*-exchanging politeness. Normally, the host has to climb and nail the sign calling for *"Honneur à Notre Elu,"* but Vanessa's husband was suffered to do the vertiginous honors.

The Perigord, it seems, has some kind of a gentle socialist heart, despite the aberrant votes of so many. Brittany, on the other hand, is militant in its assertion of individuality: its inhabitants refuse to pay the highway tax which is enforced in every other region. When *le fisc* installed wayside machinery for detecting cars which did not carry the necessary windshield ticket, they were burned down, again and again. Only the French, one realizes, a little late in the *jour*, could both acquiesce in the homogenization of Europe (under meta-Napoleonic schematic arrangements) and rebel against whatever the law-making bureaucracy in Brussels decrees, if/when it doesn't suit them. And *pourquoi pas?* you may say, but you don't have to.

By way of a kicker: that odd man John Bayley, Iris Murdoch's widower, toady, double-dealer (re Iris's decline) and winner of a wartime medal for gallantry, compiled a volume of criticism with the forever valuable title *The Uses of Division*. I am reminded of my friend George Axelrod who was asked, in the 1960s, whether he had been to see the play, directed by the absurdly high-minded, misguided Peter Brook, with the catchy title *The Persecution and Assassination of Jean-Paul Marat as Performed by the Inmates of the Asylum of Charenton Under the Direction of the Marquis de Sade,* and replied "No, but I've read the title."

Tout à toi, Freddie

May 29, 2014
Dear Freddie,

The other night *chez* Epstein we watched, on television, *The Big Sleep*. Three screenwriters share credit for it; one of them is William Faulkner. The dialogue, as you may remember, is dazzling; scarcely a line that isn't witty, funny, pungent, full of bounce. Whether this is owing to the screenwriters or to the Raymond Chandler novel, I cannot say, never having read the novel. In fact, I've not read any Chandler novel, though many moons ago I read a collection of his letters, which were very smart. Chandler must have been among the first Englishmen who sensed the gold rush in Hollywood. ("Millions are to be grabbed out here," Herman Mankiewicz wrote to Ben Hecht, "and your competition is idiots.") He was better educated than everyone he worked for, and it didn't take him long to develop that supreme contempt for his employers that only those who are deeply ashamed of their work can command, though he certainly had nothing to be ashamed of for writing the screenplay for *Double Indemnity*, which still holds up well.

In one scene in *The Big Sleep*, Lauren Bacall awaits Humphrey Bogart in his traditionally shabby private detective's office. When he arrives late, she asks him if he thinks he is Marcel Proust. Bogie needs a footnote. She explains that Proust was a French writer who stayed up all night and worked in bed. This does not come under the category of dazzling dialogue, but it is impressive as a cultural reference found in a popular movie. Difficult to imagine anyone today bringing Proust's name into a movie. *The Big Sleep* was made in 1946. In 1959 Ira Gershwin, for the song "Isn't It A Pity," wrote the line "My nights were sour, spent with Schopenhauer." Even more difficult to imagine anyone getting Schopenhauer's name into a song in the current day, and if they did, we couldn't hear it over the electric guitars. Were people smarter fifty or so years ago, or were producers less worried about bringing in the largest possible— which also means the dumbest possible—audience? The latter, I'm sure.

As for Proust, whose biographer George Painter you mentioned two electronic missives back, I like nearly everything about the old boy. I do not remember much about the Painter biography, except being impressed by it at the time—thirty years ago?—I first read it. (Someone once said that when a person of learning dies, it is as if a library burned down. Mine seems to be burning one wing at a time while I'm still alive.) I've cut my personal, that is my actual, library down drastically over the years, but I note that I've kept no fewer than twenty books about Proust along of course with his own books. No Proust scholar, a Proustolator is what I am. The only Proust biography published in English I've not yet read is Jean-Yves Tadie's 986-page toe-breaker, which carries the snappy title *Marcel Proust, A Life* and which is apparently thought the most definitive of all Proust biographies. A few years ago I read a splendid Proust biography, weighing in at a mere 936 pages, by an American named William C. Carter, a professor of French at the University of Alabama at Birmingham. Carter's is a no-nonsense work, without high-wire, backward somersault interpretations, elaborate *explicationes de texte* of Henri Bergson, and the rest of the high-toned *mishegoss* that Proust seems to bring out in fancy-footwork academics. Carter presents just the facts, ma'am, and lots, to me, of new ones.

Did you know, as I didn't, that Marcel Proust was a great spendthrift? This was so especially after his mother's death, when, according to Carter, his income was something like $16,000 a month—this, for a man with no children or family or lovers to support, was what our parents might have called a nice piece of change. He spent it lavishly, leaving tips, for example, of one or two hundred percent for the waiters at the Ritz. My favorite story of Proustian free spending, told by Carter and not hitherto known to me, was his hiring the Poulet Quartet to play a Cesar Franck quartet (the Quartet in D minor) he loved, but to play it past midnight for him alone in his apartment. Proust showed up late one night at Gaston Poulet's apartment to make this request. The amount of the fee was sufficiently large to attract Poulet's interest. A cab was waiting at the curb to pick up the other members of the quartet. In the cab, the violist noted that Proust was wrapped in an eiderdown coverlet and had a bowl of mashed potatoes beside him on a folding seat. To make a wild story short, after the assembled Poulet Quartet played the forty-five-minutes-long Franck quartet in his apartment, Proust, rising from his divan, asked if they would play it again, taking from a Chinese box a stack of fifty gold-franc notes, giving three notes to each member of the quartet. Each member of the quartet, according to Carter, was paid 45,000 ordinary francs for their night's work. Those French, half-Jewish, all homosexual novelists sure knew how to live.

I much like the notion of "the heavyweight champion of lightweights." Some of the lightest of these heavyweights do popular BBC and PBS documentaries. Simon Schama qualifies nicely here. I took a pass on his fifteen broadcasts about the history of Britain. But in the last month or so we watched Schama's mere five-hour—count 'em five—series, *The Story of the Jews*, which recently appeared on the American Public Broadcasting Station. Now in his middle sixties, Schama is a member of the final emigration of the British brain-drain. The drain clogged long ago and is now officially closed, but for a time an English accent, one with even the slightest aristocratic tinge, would bring an extra twenty to forty grand in academy salary in the United States. With that accent in tow, the greatest dullards had no trouble finding a job at American universities. I worked with such a man at Northwestern, who produced books about the contemporary theater that seemed, when I deigned to peek into one, to consist chiefly of lengthy summaries of uninteresting plays.

Simon Schama is, or has let himself become, known chiefly as a television performer. He is the Kenneth Clark *de nos jours*. Or perhaps, one cannot be certain, Kenneth Clark was the Simon Schama of his day. I didn't put myself through the full torture of Clark's very popular *Civilization* lectures when they ran on American television, but instead dropped in every now and then, distinctly not for laughs. I seem to remember his clicking up on the screen a Daumier drawing, and remarking, "The Bourgeois, there he stands, then as now, haughty, arrogant, smugly self-satisfied." I can't vouch for *then*, but *now* was 1969, the year of Clark's broadcasts, and the Bourgeois was not exactly enjoying leisurely days on the beach. With student protests ripping universities apart, with the smell of pot wafting in the air, and heady talk of LSD and other exotic trips constituting table talk in many once middle-class homes, our old pal the Bourgeois was more likely squirming as he watched his daughter lock the door of her room with a long-haired, head-banded, tie-dye shirted boychik within, his son declaring he hated him and wanted nothing (much) to do with his ill-got gain, and his wife under the spell of feminism contemplating running away with the maid. Haughty, arrogant, smugly self-satisfied, the Bourgeois, then as now, I don't think so, Sir Kenneth.

Simon Schama's Jew story is not so dopey, but neither does it cut very deep. As with all such television journalism, whenever you know a little something, it seems so thin as scarcely to exist. I thought of the complexity of your Josephus book when Schama lightly skated over Josephus in his commentary, characterizing him with the standard platitudes. The real problem with Schama's *The Story of The Jews* is that Simon Schama, who wrote and you might say stars in it, is on screen nearly full-time. Once bearded and begoggled with an ample Jewfro, he is now clean-shaven with wispy hair, no glasses, and looks like no one so much as a small-town jeweler from Duluth, Minnesota, you know, that fellow on Main Street who talks a lot with his hands.

Lots of wardrobe changes for Simon. Here the old boy is in Elephantine, there he is in Ukraine (the place has never been the same, for me, since it lost its definite article), isn't that him on the East Side of New York, scene of the *Ostjuden* migration to the new world? People of the Book, those Jews, you know, but wait here's the sacking of the Second Temple, Torah binds it all together, yo! expulsion from Spain, did he say Meyerbeer?, lots of pogroms, there's Simon in a yarmulke with a Torah pointer on the *bima*, nice suit but no necktie, what's he doing at Auschwitz?, Israel birth of a nation, pretty grand but not everything it could be, Palestinians an ethical problem no doubt about it, nice duffel coat, Simon, hands keep moving, 3,000 years of history, O.K. boys, that's a wrap.

Someone years ago must have told Simon Schama he was a terrific lecturer. Perhaps he is, with his gesticulating and rising voice emphases, but chiefly, I should guess, for less than penetrating undergraduates. Edmund Wilson says somewhere that teaching makes one dumber, because it entails spending too much time talking to children. Something to it. Students don't know as much as you; they are beholden to you for their grades, which is to say for their advancement through life, and thus cannot say, "Whoa, there, Bub, what you just said about the French Revolution, you have to know that's bullshit." After a while, all those youthful eyes gazing up at you, you begin to believe that you really are charming, brilliant, and wise. Were it only so.

Earlier this week I sent you an Op-ed piece I wrote for the *Wall Street Journal* on the latest American academic shenanigans, a phenomenon called "triggering," which calls for warning students, as the Surgeon General does on American cigarette packets, that certain books may not be good for their health. Are you ever called upon to write "Op-eds?" Not having read an English daily for decades, I wonder if Op-ed pages are as common in England as they have become in the United States. I have written perhaps twenty such pieces. They are sprints—800 to 1,000 words—and tend to be pure opinionation. (Any number of opinions, V. S. Naipaul says, does not constitute a point of view.) I haven't even a rough recollection of when the Op-ed page became a staple of American newspapers, but I think the idea was that having outsiders write what are essentially editorials—leaders to you, I believe—will freshen up a paper's editorial pages through diversification by way of outside voices. Whether they do or not, I haven't a notion.

When I lived in Little Rock, Arkansas, I had a friend named Jerry Neil who wrote editorials full-time for a brave newspaper called the *Arkansas Gazette*—brave because it took a principled stand against racial segregation at a time in the south when it took courage to do so and when it cost advertising and readers. This was in the late 1950s. I remember Jerry leaning back in his chair, typewriter before him, hands folded behind his head, remarking, "Who has it better than I? I arrive at the office around 9:00 a.m. and write an editorial telling Charles de Gaulle to shape up on the Common Market; after a coffee break I write another calling our racist governor a troglodyte. I return from lunch just sober enough to paste up the letters column. If there is time I might begin another editorial informing Konrad Adenauer that he is one *der alte* on the decline. At 5:00 Jackie [his wife] picks me up, we return home for drinks and dinner, sometimes passing on dinner, and the next day I start in all over again." I always took this to be a gentle satire on the hopelessness of the newspaper editorial, or leader. Jerry Neil died in his fifties, one of the good guys, who should have been in a better line of work.

Best, Joe

LAGARDELLE. 31.5.14.
Dear Joe,

Your story of Proust's profligate tipping turns me back nicely to the theme of the divided France. On the opposite political wing, that other magisterial figure Jean-Paul Sartre was equally disposed to overtipping, less—he would have it known—for the prompt attention it gained him *chez les garçons* than because he knew that waiters were always underpaid and relied on whatever was left on their saucers. Drawing attention to himself doubled with unselfishness. Sartre, although often late to bed, was—like *le petit Marcel*—also disposed to protracted self-analysis and that scrutiny of other people which reflected well on him for articulating their cause and effects. The more a man writes, in terms of wordage, the more likely is he to think well of himself, even if his topic is seemingly selfless. Sartre's notebooks are quasi-Proustian ruminations which allow no character to be of outstanding importance except the "invisible" author; Poulou and *le petit Marcel* are made garrulous, high-flying brothers by the French language and its subjunctive elasticity.

After the raising of our neighbor's May, which I described in my last innings, as the English say, I came back to our house and the telephone rang. That is now a rare event, partly because of my lapse from certain loops, but essentially (so I tell myself) because e-mail dispenses with time-wasting preliminaries and is never refused delivery, unless you put a comma wrong. I do not use a *portable* (cell), which gives Porlockian persons altogether too easy access. Our only undeterred terrestrial phone-callers are likely to begin "*Monsieur Raphael? Je me présente . . .*" after which, I cut them off at the net, knowing that they want to tell me that the termites are almost certainly undermining our foundations, the roof is in need of insulation and solar heating would save us a fortune in the long run. The small comfort of age is that long runs are not on the agenda. King of our modest castle, I sing along with Louis XIV: *après moi,* good luck and nuts to them all. I like to think that our sons will find a few life-easing goodies among what we leave behind, in whatever quasi-derelict state; as for the planet, it can take its chances.

The Cambridge University philosophy faculty sends me its rag, less to engage my attention or procure my participation than in the hope that I have enough ill-gotten gains to want the good opinions of those who can be bought by bequests. On the front of the current issue is the headline "Safeguarding the Future: the Centre for the Study of Existential Risk"; a little way on in the underlying text, we get ". . . how do we navigate these unknown waters when the stakes are so high?" The only navigable waters I know of with high stakes are in the channel between the Grand Canal and Venice airport. They have lanterns on them, which answers the philosophers' question.

For the rest, I do not feel that I have a penny piece at risk in the light of what may happen if the Chinese don't abate their CO_2 emissions or the Muslim world its pluto-barbarism. "Unprecedented risks" are imminent, they say, but not for me, old man, not today. Does the attached promise that philosophers are identifying new problems and then offering solutions raise the hope that they will give the future tense a longer lease? I recall Bertrand Russell's 1930s "solution" for the irrational behavior of so many people: they should become more rational. Think tanks are full of gulping fish, of all kinds of stripes, yelling inaudible and ignored answers to the urgent questions which the shameless and the powerful will neither bother to ask them nor stay to hear answered.

Now, as I was saying before I interrupted myself, my telephone was ringing. "'*allo, oui?*" sez I, speaking the language. No, it was not some selfless hustler to ask whether I could afford not to have immediate doubleglazing, it was a Parisian movie critic called Laurent Vachaud whose English drew all my French trumps and whose knowledgeable spiel was at once cosmopolitan and *typiquement français. Bref,* an *intello.* He had been commissioned by the French *Vanity Fair* (I didn't know there was one, *honnêtement*) to do a piece about Kubrick and did I have a moment? Dear God, I had about an hour and a half.

V. was one of those rare journos who had at least as much to tell me as I to tell him, not least about the Kubrick family seen in closer up than, for example, in a documentary, made several years after Stanley's death, in which the back story of happy patter-familiarities was sustained by a rather overweight and uncomely daughter and the dangerous, diminutive wife, for whom the sanctification of the late Stanley (who slept, and died, alone) is scarcely to be distinguished from her pension fund. The missing person at the happy table was Stanley's other daughter, his favorite, with whom, just before he started shooting *Eyes Wide Shut,* he had some kind of precipitous falling out. Quite suddenly, so Vachaud now revealed, she flew his fenced, rural coop and become a . . . scientologist. Stanley begged her to return, in a forty page handwritten letter, they say, but she didn't answer his appeals and he never saw her again. Poor guy; and poor girl possibly.

Jean-Luc Godard once said (when a man is said to have said something once, ten to one he bored people shitless with its repetition), "Film is truth at 24 frames a second." When a Swiss-frog Maoist cinéaste says something like that, try inserting a negative and you are likely to hit pay dirt. Film has so little to do with truth that it is almost an art form; the observation may not be catchy, but it's the truth. Now there aren't even any frames to the second necessarily. The posthumous film which I saw about S.K. and his lovable eccentricity was, of course, as much to do with truth as any advertising campaign. His loyal, but uncowed assistant Tony Frewin told me that a writer called Vincent Tilsley, who wrote a "classic" British series called *The Prisoner,* complained to him that he had written Stanley a many-paged, passionate letter, full of that accusatory deference which, addressed to famous strangers, claims a certain parity. He announced how much he admired S.K. and how shattered he was by having what he considered his masterpiece (about the late A.H., I think) hacked to small pieces by his TV masters and how he was sure that Stanley would understand.

Years later, he lamented that he had poured his heart out to a stone idol. My friend Tony asked him, "Did you send a stamped addressed envelope?" S.K. kept Tilsley's letter (he kept damn near everything, in labeled custombuilt boxes), filed under "cranks"; but he didn't have the decency to respond. Nor did one-book Michael Herr, who nevertheless wrote a couple, when I wrote to him after he told lies about my Kubrick book. You have to have a small mind to remember things like that.

Laurent Vachaud is a dedicated admirer of *Eyes Wide Shut,* into which he reads symbolic ingredients of the utmost ingenuity, linking the triangular imagery of Freemasonry with the Christmas trees so frequently to be seen in the décor (quite as if Christmas and birthdays did not come as frequently in American movies as leaves in Vallombrosa). Mordecai Richler's top of the range remark, that he was "world-famous in Canada," has some small-change relevance to my cinematic reputation. *Grosso modo,* the French know the work, the British count the Awards and the Americans count the gross. It's not the whole truth, and not worth framing, but it'll get you by. My only literary prize is the Prix Simonnet, for the best movie book (translated into French by my son Stephen) of the year 2000. So, Vachaud wanted to know all kinds of things, not least to what degree my script was in or behind what appeared on the screen.

I told V. that I didn't work with/for S.K. until I was in my sixties and, while already as naif as I am in my eighties (when I am pleased to be topping and tailoring a screenplay for Giuseppe *"Cinema Paradiso"* Tornatore), I was flattered to be enrolled by him, but did not imagine that he would allow me to leave much of a recognizable print on the final cut. I had absolutely no idea for how many decades he had been trying to make Schnitzler's *Traumnovelle*. Vachaud's conviction was that S.K.'s cardinal interest was in the notion of, as it were, the hidden hand. Tony Frewin (my deep throat during production and now my fellow veteran) told me S.K.'s watchword "Paranoia is knowing what's going on." Nice, a bit true, and a warrant for self-deception of the kind that detects the Hidden Hand in every glove (and allows conceit and a persecution complex to ride tandem).

Vachaud had an idea that *Eyes Wide Shut* was "really" all about the way in which the world is rigged by unseen forces (just as people, Professor Geoffrey Cocks their leader, read *The Shining* as a covert "tribute" to the Holocaust). What did I think? All I know is what I told *le bon* Laurent: although I didn't know it at the time, I was the umpteenth scribe in Bluebeard's—I will spare you the easy crudeness and say retinue—and for some reason, my translation of the Schnitzler hit the button with The Bearded One. Yet what I did was entirely without those consciously inserted symbols, left for clever critics to discover, like the toys Gerald and Sarah Murphy buried on the Juan-les-Pins beach for their spoiled, doomed sons to uncover. (I recall that Mary McCarthy had scathing things to say about writers who went back and sprinkled their work with symbols of the kind that would dignify it in the eyes of Maud Bodkin and allied literary tradespersons.)

I was given no specific brief whatever by S.K. I did a quasi-realistic job on Schnitzler's unhappily/happily married couple and avoided clever cut-aways to clocks with mean ticks and allied cinematic furniture. Why did S.K. pronounce himself "thrilled" with what I did, as against what those deep-sixed others did, if what he wanted was only a trellis on which his preconceived, prehensile fancy could get a hold? Vachaud remains unaggressively convinced that Stanley infiltrated some significant scheme between "Arthur" (Schnitzler)'s "beats" in order to signify the piece. My new *ami* is impressively bilingual and modest, but he has a talent for the clever parasitism which one might call *broderie française*.

This week's coda concerns one of those provincial literary figures in which the French specialize, Joseph Joubert (briefly saluted by Sainte-Beuve as one of Chateaubriand's entourage), who expressed himself, at some length, mostly in one-liners. His spirit is a distant neighbor of ours in Montignac, in the center of the Perigord. On the 13th of April 1802 he remarked to himself, "*La franchise à ceux qui en sont dignes. Mais on perd le droit d'être franc si on est brutal comme C-m-s.*" Frankness, he suggests, is proper to those who deliver it with grace. But one loses the right to be frank if one is "brutal like C-m-s." I cannot tell you who C-m-s is, nor does Joubert's editor tell us, but the line puts John Simon in his penny-a-lining place. Elsewhere, Joubert says that criticism "*sans aménité,*" without [a measure of] geniality, is no better than loutishness. One should, ideally, be provoked to smile at the same time as saying "*touché.*" Grace leaves room for grace; malice only for revenge.

Tout à toi, Freddie.

June 7, 2014
Dear Freddie,

Are you acquainted with the notion of the contrast gainer, so often useful in describing couples? I first heard it from Saul Bellow in connection with the publisher Jason Epstein and his wife, the late co-editor of the *New York Review*. "She's a contrast gainer," Bellow said, "next to him she looks good." The notion has no application whatsoever with that more famous couple, Jean-Paul Sartre and Simone de Beauvoir. A non-marriage made in hell, theirs, with each in different ways being equally repulsive.

She was stupid in the way only very bright women—Hannah Arendt, Mary McCarthy, Susan Sontag—sometimes are: exerting considerable intellectual ingenuity to arrive at all the wrong conclusions. Mlle de Beauvoir wrote a book, *L'Amérique au jour le jour* (1954), that might have had greater trenchancy had it been about the moon, so little did she get right about America. She was the very reverse of Henry James's man or woman on who nothing was lost—on her just about everything was. In her novel *Les Mandarins* she made a great thing about having had an affair with the Chicago novelist Nelson Algren, whom, in her obtuseness, she took for a proletarian writer. Whenever her name came up, Algren, no proletarian yet decidedly no gentleman either, always made it plain that she was a pain in the neck and other more tender places and, come to think of it, no great shakes in the sack either.

Supporting Communist revolutions well after the time when doing so could be counted an honest mistake, thus qualifying himself as one of Lenin's "useful idiots," Sartre's political foolishness requires no further chronicling from me. He is the very model of the man who never let particular facts interfere with the enticing generalizations, reality with the abstract. His contrast-gaining propensity was to make not Simone de Beauvoir but Albert Camus look great, when he was instead honorable and, as a novelist, merely good.

Not long ago I read—probably in a long review somewhere—that one of Simone de Beauvoir's late-life duties was pimping for Jean-Paul. She lined up young women for him to ravish, this prince of philosophers who never ceased to look like a frog. Power, fame, vast wealth, all are known to be powerful aphrodisiacs. Still, the thought of comely French girls slipping between the rumpled sheets of the bed of the wall-eyed J.-P. is a reminder that some women will do anything, absolutely anything.

I am pleased to learn of your "lapse from certain loops." I am in similar condition; days go by with no phone calls except from people who wish to clean our rugs, secure my credit cards, and sell me a device to wear around my neck enabling me to call the fire department from the floor when inevitably I go down for the count in our apartment. You are correct to say that part of the explanation for this is e-mail, which I much prefer over lengthy phone conversations. I am also very keen on the device known as "Caller ID," which lets one know who is calling and, in many cases, knowledge being power, not take the call. Unlike you I do carry a cell-phone—a flip, or dumb, phone, as opposed to a smart phone—but only two people are in possession of its number: my wife and my granddaughter. I may make three or four calls a month on it, usually of the most perfunctory kind. Were I to walk around with a smart phone, I should doubtless check it every five minutes to discover if any fresh prizes, ample inheritances, or offers of ambassadorships have come in for me. What *mishugoss*, as a formerly desert people say, or at least used to say!

Michael Herr's is name to conjure with, if these days one could find a reliable conjurer. I met him in the early 1960s in New York, but can scarcely be said to know him. He was modest, even shy, in those days, passing himself off as sensitive. (Beware the too obviously sensitive, I say; some among them are rapists.) His career, as you note, is that of a one-trick (or one-book) pony:

he wrote *Dispatches*, a series of articles on the Vietnam War for *Esquire*, later collected in what many reviewers lined up to say was a great book. With the grave yawning, I am not going to put myself through a rereading of a book about Vietnam, but I suspect that a lot of the praise had to do with the intense hatred of that war in the United States, and *Dispatches* played nicely into that hatred. So, too, did Joseph Heller's *Catch-22*, though his subject was ostensibly WW II, one of the greatly overrated books of its day.

Michael Herr hasn't done a lot of work since *Dispatches*: collaborating on a few movie scripts, writing a very poor pseudo-novel about Walter Winchell, and turning out his slender Stanley Kubrick book, which began life as a *Vanity Fair* article. I always wonder what people of such low productivity do to stay alive, which is to say, to earn a living. Perhaps Herr Herr (ah, if only one could find the occasion to say, "Hear, hear, Herr Herr!") has done a certain amount of reworking of movie scripts—"washes and rinses," as I believe Kubrick used to call it. Not infrequently it turns out that such people are married to successful physicians or crafty lawyers. Herr is now seventy-four, no sprung chicken, as a Russian émigré acquaintance of my mother used to say, and hence probably too old to have had a trust fund, for well-to-do Jews of our generation's parents didn't believe, correctly, in making things too easy for their sons.

I didn't know that there is a French *Vanity Fair*, but then why shouldn't there be? For all I know there may be a Taliban *Vanity Fair*. Success, they tell us, begets success. The American *Vanity Fair*, judging from its thickness, a heft supplied by ads for designer clothes of a kind one would not care to wear even if one could afford them, is a considerable commercial success. I subscribed to it for years, and only this past year let my subscription lapse. I subscribed because I thought I ought at least to glimpse it to see what the intellectual *demi-monde* was up to. Not much, it turns out, if *Vanity Fair* be any guide. The magazine has always been an editor's as opposed to a writers' magazine. No writers of any standing have ever been associated with it, that is, if one discounts the late Christopher Hitchens, who by now must know for certain whether his atheism was a good idea or not, and a fellow named James Wolcott who expends an artificially energetic style on low popular culture. The magazine still does celebrity profiles—everything you don't care to know about Brad Pitt, Julia Roberts, and George Clooney—and articles about exhausted royalty, which in America includes the Kennedy family. In short, not a magazine, *Vanity Fair*, for grown-ups.

I think you may be mistaken about your cinematic reputation. Whenever I mention to friends or acquaintances our connection, they are much impressed by the films you've written. True, wide fame outside the movie business may not be available to the screenwriter. I once saw David Mamet, during a television interview, responding to the question of how he felt about the movie *The Untouchables*, which he had written but not directed, say he felt "rather like an aunt" about it. "You know," Mamet said, when queried about what he meant, "it's not really my baby." I took this to be his way of saying that for it to have been his baby he would also have had to have directed it. But, then, I'm not sure these days how many directors are known outside the business.

As for certification of fame through prizes, I suspect that neither of us is in a good position to win prizes. One has to be with the show to win the standard prizes, and neither of us is. We're too odd, stand, like your man Cavafy, too aslant of the universe to qualify; we go our own way, and know no other way of going. A self-compliment is implied here, but let it stand.

My own prize garnering has been impressively minor. I once won something called The Heartland Prize ($5,000) from the *Chicago Tribune* for a book of essays. (When I told my mother about it, she said, "We get that junk in the mail all the time. I just throw it out.") I've won something called the Harold Washington Literary Award, named after the first black mayor of the city of Chicago; I've won a $3,000 prize for best Jewish book of fiction of the year (can't recall what year it was) from Hadassah, the Jewish women's charitable organization; I've been named, with several other undistinguished people, a distinguished alumnus of the University of Chicago; I've been awarded an honorary doctorate from a third-rate university on Long Island, whose president was fired soon afterward; and I turned down, because travel and a speech was required—this for a prize of $250—something called the Edward Lewis Wallant Prize for fiction. I have also been given something called the Presidential Medal for the Humanities, but all presidential medals of this kind turn out to have a heavy political taint: during Republic administrations they are given to people thought conservative; during Democratic administrations, to people acceptable to liberals. No prize finally can give serious satisfaction, if only because, once one sees the *schtunk*-laden list of people who have won it previously, all prestige, like a Christian evangelical audience at a Genet play, departs the hall.

This past week I read an excellent biography of Turgenev by Henri Troyat. The book is admirable not least for its want of avoirdupois; it weighs in at a slender 162 pages, and at its satisfying conclusion one does not feel the need for more. The book should be a model for all those beginning door-stopper 900-page biographies of politicians or writers of tertiary importance.

I don't know if you've read any of Troyat's books. (He was a Russian émigré to France whose dates are 1911–2007, and, speaking as I was a paragraph ago of prizes and awards, at his death the longest serving member of the *Académie française*.) He wrote novels, but I've only read his biographies of Russian writers: Gogol, Chekhov, Tolstoy, and now Turgenev. The Tolstoy biography reads as if written by Tolstoy; it's that good.

Troyat's *Turgenev* is not so magnificent as his *Tolstoy*, but Turgenev was neither so great a writer nor so interestingly contradictious a man as Tolstoy. He was, Turgenev, more than a bit of a masochist, suffering at the hands of women his specialty. He had a monstrous mother, whose idea of good time was ordering the flogging of serfs and the crushing of her two sons, who may have set this masochism in motion. You will know about his living for years among the family—including husband and children—of the opera singer Pauline Viardot. He was also a suffering liberal—a man who wanted change but was opposed to violence yet could not disown revolutionaries for whom violence posed no problem at all. Above all, he didn't wish to be on the wrong side of things. This is probably what made him so appealing to Isaiah Berlin. If one wants to understand the politics of Isaiah B. the key document is his essay—a work of purest self-identification—on Turgenev.

The hatred of Dostoyevsky for Turgenev, of the Slavophile for the westernizer, is well known, while Turgenev did not hate Dostoyevsky so much as he thought him an inept artist specializing in what he called "inverted platitudes," which entailed his always doing the predictably unexpected (and unreal) thing in his novels. Dostoyevsky's put-down portrait of the Turgenev as the effete scribbler Karmazinov in *The Possessed* is of course one of the great hatchet jobs in literature.

Turgenev late in life recognized Tolstoy as the great light of Russian literature, but in earlier days his opinion of his writing was off-kilter: he didn't think much, for example, of *Anna Karenina*, holding the subject of adultery in high places beneath Tolstoy and best treated not with high solemnity but with humor. Tolstoy never had a high opinion of Turgenev's writing. One evening when Turgenev was reading the manuscript version of *Fathers and Sons* to a roomful of friends, he noted that Tolstoy had fallen asleep.

The two men wanted to like each other, but whenever they were together they found grounds for strong disagreement. On one such occasion, at the home of friends, they argued so vehemently that Turgenev, a man of 6'5" or so, went against his cliché sobriquet of "gentle giant" and threatened to "smash" Tolstoy's face, and promptly left the table before doing so. He returned a few moments later to apologize. Back at Yasnaya Polyana, Tolstoy decided the apology was not good enough, and wrote a letter to Turgenev challenging him to a duel. Turgenev apologized more elaborately, and with time Tolstoy's temper cooled, though the two did not communicate with one another after this incident for seventeen years.

The reason I am going on about all this is that when I read the portion of Troyat's volume about Tolstoy's challenging Turgenev to a duel I couldn't help think what if the duel had actually taken place; and what if, moreover, the result was that both men fatally wounded each other. There, *poof!*, goes Russian Literature. If it doesn't disappear entirely—Pushkin, a man already dead from dueling, had already written his great works, Dostoyevsky remained, and Chekhov was waiting in the wings—it suddenly takes on a different, darker, less significant cast. What we have in this unaccepted challenge to a duel is, I think, one of the great what-ifs, or close calls, of literary history. But for Turgenev's unwillingness to duel, we might never have had *War and Peace*. Thank you, Ivan T., thank you, thank you.

Best, Joe

LAGARDELLE. 11.6.2014.
Dear Joe,

We are right, I think, to refrain from an excess of mutual appreciation, in public at least, but it is not indelicate to pay passing tribute to your—the phrase that trips from the keys—"clipped candor." The topiaristic dexterity is manifest in your shapely phrasing and in the pace it imparts. The candor is hedged (I recognize the box, as it were, because I am similarly cautious in being honest enough to offer ammunition to the enemy) by *pudeur*, which some may attach to a racial strain, but which I guess owes more than a little to the kind of marriage we both seem to have. You talked about Updike not long ago and we are promised that Philip Roth is now such an established master that he can afford to loll, pettishly, on his laurels. If in hostile corners (nothing more boring, in my view, than to look on literature as a contest, except against the clock), both made use of women, literally and then figuratively, in a way that I consider a little scoundrelly. While he does seem to have been led an unpretty dance by his first, nutty wife, Philip's depiction of Claire Bloom was particularly spiteful and, I think, unmerited. Claire was victimized by men, notoriously by one Hilly Elkins, a producer who once called me, to do a TV series about the Rothschilds (still not a bad idea), and she may indeed have been somewhat disposed to indulge men's dark desires, but she did have the rare kind of beauty which impels men of a certain stripe to punish her for possessing.

People seem to me very often to do whatever they can get away with, especially when it comes to the bedroom, if anyone ever gets that far these days. The English media are full of accusations brought against elderly showbizzy persons, often of small charisma, who are now arraigned for things wot they done back in the 1960s and 1970s, when their victims were too "innocent" or "ashamed" to tell the tales which now, we are promised, bring them relief (if not "closure") after decades of self-laceration. It used to be that ladies with a lurid past took the veil or devoted themselves to pious and penitential good works. Now they have become brave Amazonian tell-tales and are applauded for "speaking out," not least—in a famous current case—against a "publicist" who, for several decades, peddled their stories and paddled not a few of their canoes into richly rewarding waters.

I write with some bitterness (and lack of wide knowledge of the truth or falsehood of the English ladies' evidence) because of the particular case of our local doctor here in the Perigord, who has, I fear, now been definitively "struck off" (*radié* is the French term, if you ever need to show knowledge in that department) on the word of a woman who claims that he did things to her "down there" thirty years ago, when she worked, briefly, as his receptionist. No other female in this gossipy *coin* had chimed in, in the hope of relief from anguish or a few euros in her pocket, which is, *à mon avis*, very significant. Our neighbor, another patient of Michel's, is loud in her defense of him and, in tribute, puts out bags of beans for him to collect. Michel is one of the nicest, most generous men I have ever met—one of those who give the word *aimer* its full double, Platonic use (love and like, as Michael someone, a rated U.S. writer in the 1960s, once entitled a short story about a divorce: I'll bet you can supply his name)—and there isn't a damn thing I or anyone else can do to redeem him from the judgment of a distant panel of his alleged medical peers whose (female, nay feminist) chairperson declared that it was "about time" that a female victim was given credence. I could wish to be able to write an appendix to the Diary of a Country Doctor, but am blocked by an inability to infuse the story with distancing irony.

Funny folk the Frogs, as you were saying in your last. The disgust which you express for the Sartre-Beaver Famous Pair reminds me of what

Kingsley Amis, whom I shall never re-read, even if I am sentenced, unjustly, it would have to be, to spend the rest of my life alone with his works in a tight cell, once said about Vladimir Nabokov's Humbert Humbert in *Lolita*: "What the hell did the man think he was doing?" I suspect that V.N. did more thinking than doing in that department, but *Lolita* is, on second or third reading, a rather disgusting, brilliant book. Perhaps that is partly because it failed to entice me, in any unpublishable way whatever, to share H.H.'s appetites.

Recently I retrieved, for use in the *TLS*, a remark which I dredged from the slurry of remembered TV viewing "*J'adore la clandestinité*" uttered by a French novelist, who was boating against the currency of the (then) new "honesty" between spouses etc. You and I, *cher maître,* refrain from confessions (true or self-serving), but fiction licenses us in chaste excursions into the fanciful erotic, not that either of us does it, if he can avoid it, to breast-selling excess. An aeon or two ago, I was asked to do a movie (it used to happen a lot) about an English serial killer, who picked up young men, took them home and then, for fear that they would go and leave him alone, killed them and stored them, for conversational access, in various domestic apertures. In the usual problem-solving way of the eternal examinee, I suggested that the movie should look, with neo-realist care, at the man's mundane life as a trustworthy clerk in some insurance office (Kafka and Cavafy hid themselves in similar banality) and that the murders should always take place between chapters, as it were. Longish dark spaces would stand for the horrors which the audience would be incited to dream up for themselves, after which our guy would be seen again leaving for the office in the morning. The fun of the killer would lie in the ordinariness of his clerkly imposture.

In the end, one guesses, the killing is not what pleases the serial-criminal so much as the deception: the arch-scoundrel of modern England was one Jimmy Savile who covered his multiple rapes and gropes with the personality of a do-gooding Northern kidder devoted to good causes. I'll bet you he derived better-lasting pleasure from making fools of the BBC and the great British pub-lickers than from whatever he did to so many poor, sad, lonely, institutionalized no-hopers. There is always one more thing to be said, and it is rarely a nice one: the Savile case recalls the only Doris Lessing fiction I ever enjoyed, about a lonely woman on the South African veldt who is more or less raped by a fat, sweaty salesman. After he has gone, she cannot help wondering when he might come back. I am sure this story was not part of the Lessing oeuvre which appealed to the Nobel Prize committee. I wonder what did.

I share your admiration for Henri Troyat's *Tolstoy*. Unlike so many dressy pundits, he writes very clearly and does not obtrude his insights or "discoveries." I suppose that his first language was Russian, but he had that acquired clarity which quite often distinguishes non-native writers. Arthur Koestler wrote some slightly bonkers work (so did Isaac Newton and who all else), but his English is careful and, because it did not come easily, precisely weighted; so too is V.N.'s, of course, although immeasurably more fanciful.

As for Turgenev, he had the unhurried style of those who have never regarded writing as a job of work and can please themselves before they please others. Beetle and I read *Fathers and Sons* last summer with renewed delight. F.R. did, somewhat furtively, envy big Ivan the lasting renown which so slight a masterpiece procured, but his ironic good humor and, I guess, self-mockery keep the thing both light and fresh. Did being a very tall man have anything to do with his disinclination to overstate and overwrite?

Mr. T. has a signal place in my pantheon. I am pretty sure, although we shall never know, that I owe to him the one set of laurels on which I am unashamed to pride myself. In the Sixth (top) Form at Charterhouse, when preparing for the Oxbridge scholarship season, I checked through a lot of old exam papers and noticed that, in the Cambridge general (English essay) paper, there was always a question relating to "the Arts." I thought it wise, as well as congenial, to bone up in that department: names and dates, buildings and patrons, styles, subjects and biographical details were lodged in my cerebral filing cabinet.

When, in a cold hall in Emmanuel College, Cambridge, I turned over the general paper, on which I somewhat relied to distinguish me from the six hundred other candidates for two major classical scholarships, question 6 was: "The arts and their relation to life." I took a deep breath and wrote across the top of the first of my many pages: "Art is one of the four things which unite men—Ivan Turgenev." I knew, as I served that first ace, that I was going to win; and so I did, despite my less than perfect Greek prose and my rather too showy, if not "silver" verses (I suggested a three-syllable word, *madidas* at the end of a pentameter, which smacked of levity). Had there been a *viva,* as there always was at Oxford in those days, some snide don might have asked me to tell them more about this Mr. Turgenev. There was no *viva* and I got a major scholarship and I do care who knows it.

Which reminds me, for an *envoi,* of Tom Conti's story about the Pope which I just may have told you before, in which case the scissors can go in. So: the Pope is walking in the Vatican (presumably) when a little boy runs past and says "Fucka you" to the old guy. The Pope calls out to him, "Little boy, little boy, come back here. Do you know who I am?" "You're the Pope, innit?" "And do you know how I came to be the Pope. No? I will tell you. There are, in the whole world, more than a hundred thousand priests, and of those priests, five thousand can become bishops, and of the bishops about three hundred become cardinals, and out of those three hundred cardinals, one—just one—becomes the Pope. And I am that one. So, little boy, don'ta you ever say fucka you to me again, because—little boy—fucka YOU!"

Tout à toi, Freddie.

June 16, 2014
Dear Freddie,

I learned two days ago that my friend Dan Jacobson died, at 85, an easeful death his daughter reports, after a difficult few years in dementia. I call him my friend though we met on only three occasions: once at a three-day rather boring conference in San Francisco on international Jewish matters; once in London, where he stood me to a splendid lunch at his club, the Atheneum; and once in Chicago, where Barbara and I took him to dinner. All three occasions were filled with laughter and the feeling between us was one of instant camaraderie.

Dan's daughter married a Muslim accountant, and he attended her wedding in Detroit; and afterwards, visiting us in Chicago, did a wildly comical imitation of Muslim women glorying in his daughter's wedding gifts. In San Francisco, in a three-way conversation about Henry James's *The Portrait of a Lady* with me and a young writer named Allegra Goodman, I recall his remarking that Isabel Archer's rather sexually neutral cousin Ralph Touchett's problem was that he was afraid, precisely, to touch it. At the Atheneum he was highly amusing on his fellow club members.

I mention this because humor was not a high note in Dan's writing, neither in his novels and stories nor in his essays. Earnestness, intellectual seriousness, was his dominant note. Dan was smart, and talented, young. He published stories in *Commentary* and essays in *Encounter* in his early twenties. As you know, he was South African, born and brought up in Kimberley, diamond country, and the South Africans' treatment of blacks under apartheid being too much for him, he emigrated to England soon after university, at Witwatersrand in Johannesburg.

As a novelist and short-story writer, South Africa was Dan's great subject; my first acquaintance with his writing was a story in *Commentary* with the wonderful title of "The Zulu and the Zaide." But the further in time he was from his native country, the more he had to turn to writing historical fiction, in one case, *The Rape of Tamar*, using biblical characters for a novel. He did this at a very high level, but it must have been a strain for him. Because his writing didn't occupy him full-time, he taught literature at University College, London. I imagine him a splendid teacher, his seriousness working well on the young. In later years he found writing more and more arduous and did less and less of it. But everything he wrote was worth reading; nothing in a literary way that he did was shoddy or shabby; he was never without point.

We exchanged e-mails fairly regularly, and then, three or so years ago, it became clear that Dan's loss of memory made it impossible to keep up our correspondence. Word of this came by way of his wife Marg. Difficult to think of him utterly ga-ga, and I hope he never reached that state. I feel his death another subtraction of the kind fellows at our stage in life had better get used to, at least until such time as we ourselves constitute a subtraction from other people's lives.

On the subject of such subtractions, this past week I had my annual physical examination, never a trivial matter for this minor-league hypochondriac. I am, as I think I may have told you, a Jewish Scientist, which is to say that I prefer to steer clear of physicians, which may seem a contradiction in terms given this mild hypochondria, but I can live with the contradiction if you can. I steer clear of physicians because those bastards tend to find things wrong, things I, for one, a paid-up member of the Ostrich School of health and well-being, prefer not to know about. Every year at the time of my physical I feel that my blood tests will reveal me to have beri-beri, cholera, and hoof-and-mouth disease, not to mention seven different kinds of cancer. This time round, I am pleased to report, none of these or any other exotic diseases turned up. I was told that I was on the low-to-normal side in iron and calcium, and now have added these two pills to my pharmaceutical arsenal, and also a slight heart murmur. I'm O.K. with this; not to have a murmurous heart seems almost insensitive.

I share your attraction to Claire Bloom, whose elegant good looks I admired. (I felt similarly about Jean Simmons, but she, too, failed to give me a tumble.) Like Audrey Hepburn, Claire Bloom had no talent for marrying the right men. Rod Steiger, was it not, who preceded Philip Roth in pledging her his unreliable troth. As for Roth's troth, rhyming nicely though it does,

I gather it didn't quite exist. Wasn't part of Claire Bloom's complaint about the boy novelist that he was, in the cant phrase of the day, hitting on her adolescent daughter's girlfriends? Let us hope that at least he left the family dog in peace.

Roth, Updike, Norman Mailer, William Styron, that generation of American novelists were more than a bit sex-crazed. Sex in their youth was not the casual item it is today, or so - about today, that is - I'm told. Bonking, not socialism, was the name of their desire, and describing it afterwards in prose their notion of high literature. Saul Bellow, who was a bit older than they, even though a relentless skirt-chaser, at least had the modesty, in his fiction, to refrain from the naming of parts. For these other bozos the great bonk, with all its grisly details, was the central drama. I believe that because of their unseemly preoccupation with sex, the novels of Roth, Updike & Co. are, I strongly suspect, unlikely to be long-lived.

I've mentioned earlier that I have myself, in my stories, never been able to describe sex with a, so to say, straight face. I have had characters enter bedrooms, I have had two of them on an office floor awaiting post-coital tristesse (it never arrived), I have had one of them quickly compare academic to civilian sex, but I have never been able to recount, after I have them fall into the sack, what they did once there. Tolstoy felt no need to describe Anna and Vronsky bumping and humping away; Henry James describing Gilbert Osmond and Isabel Archer going at it is unthinkable. Yet both are much sexier, not to speak of many fathoms deeper, than those novelists of our time who have regularly limned the rather limited gymnastics of sex.

Still on the subject of sex, I cannot let pass your mention of Hugh Hefner, the great founder of *Playboy*, today walking about in his mansion in Los Angeles in silken pajamas, jacked up on Viagra, or some more high-powered compound, putting young women of misguided ambition to the torture of sharing his spinning round bed. Talk about the mating of beasts! Hefner must be one of the most unattractive, both mentally and physically, men in what used to be known as western civilization. The thought of the old boy once staging an orgy for Jonathan Miller is splendidly gigglesome. Did the polymathic Dr. Miller stammer a hesitant yes, or instead blithely and boisterously announce, "Let's do it, daddy?"

Years ago I heard a story about John Connolly, a pal of Lyndon Johnson and then governor of Texas, being given a tour of the Playboy mansion, at the time located in Chicago. The good governor was shown the elaborate kitchen, filled in on the extensive stereo system, taken down to view the swimming pool, paraded through the salons, Hefner himself serving as his cicerone for this tour. When the playboy of all playboys asked the Governor what he thought of all this magnificence, Connolly is supposed to have said, "Yeah, yeah, very nice, but when do I get laid?" An early instance, this, of what is now called cutting to the chase.

Unlike you, I've read *Lolita* only once, in my twenties, and probably shan't revisit the novel during this lifetime. I hadn't the intellectual courage in those days to declare the book high-class smut. I chiefly remember the dazzlingly ornate prose and the amusing details of what a traveler in America discovers in motels. I seem to recall a description of what one finds in the commodes in such establishments, a lengthy, amusing list ending with "human fetuses," though I may have made that up. That Nabokov did not entice you into a taste for nymphets—read, unpoetically, female children— is less than surprising; perverts, after all, are born not made. I've not read the posthumous novel, *Laura,* that Nabokov's son Dimitri brought out and which reviewers lined up to say is not as awful as I assume it really is. I gather the book is about a fat man who also has a jones for underage girls. My guess is that the novel probably shouldn't have been published, and wouldn't have been but for the greed of Nabokov's now dead son Dimitri, who, the Nabokovian acolyte Alfred Appel once told me, was strictly bad news.

Nabokov's career poses, at least for me, the question of how far style alone will take a writer. Fairly far, we know, but perhaps not quite to the finish line. Of Nabokov's books, the ones I admire are *Speak, Memory, Pnin,* and *The Defense,* all anchored, in some way, in his experience and not chiefly in his imagination. He of course would despise me for suggesting that he wasn't the very type of the pure artist. My dear friend Hilton Kramer, no Philistine, used to say that all writers can be divided between those who depend on irony and those who don't, and those who don't are better. Something to it, I, as a heavy-duty ironist, fear.

Saw a not charmless movie two nights ago that I feel I can recommend to you and Mme R., with my usual half-your-money back guarantee. *Mumford* is its title, and it was written and directed by Lawrence Kasdan and sent out into the world in 1999. The movie is about a psychologist in a small town who breaks many of the standard rules of therapy and is largely successful with his highly neurotic clients. The flick will not change your life, but I think it might keep the folks *chez* Raphael mildly amused for a few hours, which is all I ask from the movies.

One of the best things about *Mumford* is that, with the exception of Martin Short in a minor part, it does not have any actors I recognize. That in itself is often a great boost for a movie; and it surely is in this case. I wonder if Kasdan, whose previous successes in flickland would have attracted a namier (not Lewis) crew, planned this. The film probably paid for the obscurity of its cast at the box office, but it made it a much better movie than it would have been had, say, Tom Hanks played the psychologist and Julia Roberts one of his main patients.

Which brings me to an idea I have for a parlor game called Miscastings. In it players draw cards with the names of famous movies and their original casts, and have to recast the film as egregiously as possible. In the movie version of *Hamlet*, for example, you might want Mike Tyson in the lead role, with Bette Midler as Ophelia. A winning response to a miscasting of *High Noon* might be Danny DeVito in the Gary Cooper part and Whoopi Goldberg in Grace Kelly's. Joe Pesci as Forrest Gump. One need not restrict oneself to athletes and show-business people. One might want to miscast, say, Charles de Gaulle in the Zero Mostel part in *The Producers*, or Albert Einstein in *A Day at the Races*. The possibilities, I hope you agree, are endless.

Best, Joe

LAGARDELLE. 18.6.14.
Dear Joe,

Sometimes I have the impression that I have known very few people, particularly those whose names and numbers embellish the social and literary history of Our Times. Nevertheless, the indices of my notebooks have led me to be accused of name-dropping, quite as if I were the Ken Tynan or Woodrow Wyatt of my set, not that I have one. As I mention in the second chunk of my autobiography, which I shall consign—after the multiple revisions required to confer spontaneity—to my agent by the end of the current working week, when we were young and living in Paris (in the very unfavored 11th *arrondissement*), we met, during an uptown sortie, an American photographer called Jack Nisberg. He soon had us know that he was a friend of the aforesaid Ken Tynan, who was, from an early age, necklaced with and enriched by celebrity acquaintances as South Sea Islanders are/were with cowrie shells: while at Oxford, Ken gave a party for Orson Welles and charged guests a pound a head. Nisberg asked us who we knew in Paris; our answer was we didn't need other people."But don't you have a fun group? You have to have a fun group." We have never done fun fun; nor drugs, nor group sex, not even the bottoms-up-pishness of the Bacchic rout. I like to keep the table on a roar, if it can be worked, but I am not one for conferences, house-parties, festivals or think-tanking. I do not like alien beds, unless Beetle is in one with me.

You are saying, yes, yes, but who is this Woodrow Wyatt? He is (no, was) a very English figure, of the small, tubby, putting-himself-about order. A first-class second-rater, he had a good war, as the British say, actually very good; he was "mentioned in dispatches" during the Normandy campaign and, like many of his fighting bourgeois order, became a socialist, of the maverick variety: he rarely refused invitations which carried bibulous promise and upper-classy company (he called his son "Plantagenet" already). Lippy and contra-granular, he dared to disagree with the Labor Party about nationalizing the steel industry. Having proved that he had physical courage, he was not afraid to strut the moral version (which has never seemed to me to be very courageous, since I am, on a good day, in a good cause, nervously capable of it). Woodrow—not a common name at all in the U.K.—had a good opinion of himself and was not afflicted with reticence. The movie trade has a category of "dress extras"; those "*figurants*" near enough the camera to merit full costume and make-up. Woodrow was a *talking* extra—an extra *extraordinaire* even—at all the top tables *du monde*. Never a wit and never lost for a word, he talked in parliament, on the radio, on the TV, in front of the scenes and, so I now discover, behind them: he represented the British in negotiations with the Muslim League.

Woodrow's snobbery was rewarded with obloquy from unsmiling, party-lining Socialists and with goodies from upper-crusty insiders. In mid-life, he was awarded the chairmanship of the Tote (national betting syndicate), a sinecure worth signing up for in view of the stable doors it opened. Woodrow was one of those short men who can prance on the stilts of local fame with rare hauteur. He interviewed Bertrand Russell when it was possible to sell intelligence on television. His versatility also took him to the margins of showbiz. His equine interests meshed with those of Nat Cohen and Stuart Levy, who backed the production of, as cine-historians say, John Schlesinger's *Darling* (my title, my script, his achievement). When it was a big, big hit, people were in a hurry to get Julie Christie back under the hot lights. She never liked acting and, Albert Finney told me, she wasn't much good at the chat (but then how quicksilvery is he?).

The Oscar made Julie bankable and then some; we needed a quick vehicle and madame on board, before she decided that she wanted out of the biz. Woodrow came up with *Far From the Madding Crowd* and the rest, hurrah and alas, is a paragraph or so of film history. I wrote the script with serviceable diligence and John Schlesinger did a very much better job than contemporary critics allowed. Beetle and I were flown, foist cless, of course, to New York for the premiere, which was said to be all-important. We were shown into a suite at the Plaza with a living room large enough for, oh, try Mussolini, in his prime. The MGM guy looked around and said, "I'm embarrassed, Mr. Raphael, I am truly embarrassed." I said, "Don't worry: I've guessed: this is Schlesinger's." "Not at all, Mr. Raphael, not at all: this is you, of course it is, but where are the flowers?" The premiere was a flop (you Yanks didn't appreciate Dorset peasants' down-home chat). Life did not stay as suite as it was.

Woodrow had four wives; in our segment, she was Lady Moorea, the granddaughter of Luisa Casati, d'Annunzio's quondam mistress (quondam thing led to many others in his case). La Casati consented to eat only white meals. In time, she had to sell her jewels to fund her halibut habit and eventually went belly up. I was asked by Vincent Minnelli to write a movie script based on her life, which I did, but not to his satisfaction. Duly hacked by another hand, *A Matter of Time* was eventually made, with Liza of whom John Simon said, in his usual courtly way, that she should not appear in movies unless the director made sure she wrapped her legs around her face. Poor Vincent, as Stanley Donen calls him, never worked again. Stanley isn't convinced he ever worked all that well at the best of times. Stanley was an innovator in movie musicals, Vincent an interior decorator *de luxe* who, I am promised, once had a peacock stapled to the set by its claw because it would turn its argus-eyed tail on the action and wander off during a take. The two directors had Judy Garland in common. In that horizontal connection, Vincent wanted to fight Stanley, which might have been a hit, but the deal was never closed.

Woodrow was short-legged but some *coureur*; he ran all four legs of his own marital relay. By way of a finder's fee, he picked an affair, as one might a fight or a cherry, with the beautiful wife of a very dear, now dead, friend of mine. This might be known as the Tote Double, since said friend had anticipated the starter with a movie actress markedly less beautiful than his wife. "*Tournent, tournent, mes personnages!*" intoned Anton Walbrook in Max Ophuls's over-rated *La Ronde*, and did they not in 1960s London? Woodrow married onwards and upwards and—almost all pedestal and no statue—contrived to stand socially tall on famous shoulders including those of the Queen Mother, to whom he was especially devoted although, as he confided to the diary which he soon made available to everyone who would buy a copy, it was difficult to know what to give her for her birthday. This recurrent problem outlived Woodrow, since the old battler lasted five years longer than he, having completed her century.

I am a very sluggish climber. I never met Dan Jacobson, although I knew that he had come from South Africa and, if I remember rightly, married a woman who already had two children. I much admired his (as I see, 1956) novella *A Dance in the Sun,* but didn't follow his later work, perhaps because I associated him with Karl Miller, whose colleague he was at University College, London. I was, as you will see in *Going Up,* a contemporary at Cambridge of Miller's (Millers' indeed, since Jonathan and I were at St John's together). Karl was a clever constructor of a DIY ladder to highish places, editorial chairs in particular, and found people such as Noel Annan to supply the rungs. I tried a little early toadyism and went to see him at the *New Statesman,* after I had published half a dozen rather well-received novels. I had the vain hope that he might take me on as a reviewer. He asked, in his direct, charmless, Calvinesque way, what made me think that I was qualified to review fiction. Although he had never written any books at all at that stage, he had me there. By way of an envoi, he gave me a book of Erich Fromm's and asked me to validate my candidature by doing a specimen article about it. Know what? I dumped it.

A few weeks later, I was made a regular fiction reviewer for the London *Sunday Times.* As Holden Caulfield was heard to say, Big Fucking Deal, except for the fucking part. I heard that Dan was a good teacher, but I cannot believe that proximity to Professor Miller (who had done no teaching that I know of before Annan gave him that big leg up) made Jacobson's muse feel happily at home. Perhaps, like John Gross, he attained eminence, as did the Chief Eunuch in Joe Manckiewicz's *Cleopatra,* at the price of certain sacrifice: he became some kind of a courtier, but without Sir Walter Ralegh's daring. I became a fan of W.R.'s after being asked to write the screenplay of *Death of the Fox* by George Garrett. It was so clever a pastiche that it didn't contain a single scene that wasn't codded out with parodic period mushery and tushery.

Ralegh's "Go tell the court . . . Go tell the church" etc. is one of the masterpieces in English of reckless, lithe scorn (in which it is almost, but only almost, equaled by Chesterton's "Chuck it, Smith" number). Ralegh's last words deserve their fame: on the scaffold, rigged for him by the odious James I because he (W.R.) was, in Sellars and Yeatman's immortal phrase "left over from the previous reign," he bade goodbye to his friends, announcing that he was about to undertake a long, solitary voyage (the one to discover Eldorado had ended in disaster), and then knelt with his head on the block. The executioner appears to have hesitated before severing so eloquent a head. Ralegh said, "Strike, man, what do you fear?" Evidence enough that he kept his head till the last minute. His *adieu* deserves a place in the category of "Frame Us Last Words."

Poor Dan, his was not the way to go. Byron always dreaded ending like Swift, a staring specter. Webster was, we all recall, much possessed by death, but I don't know how death elected to possess him. I suppose the best death comes like a competent assassin, strikes when you're looking elsewhere, and there's an end on't. Suddenness is tough on the survivors, if they cared for you, but they get over it, usually; better anything than a drooling decline in the hands of rented carers. I finished the new volume of my autobiography with our purchase of a plot of land on the Cycladic island of Ios, which our daughter Sarah called "that place" and loved more than any other. I sat writing about the little house we still have and where Sarah's ashes are scattered and suddenly, after fourteen years, I quaked with solitary sobs, as if it was only yesterday that we were told of her death. If I don't stop this right here, I shall do the same thing again. That would never do.

Tout à toi, Freddie.

June 24, 2014
Dear Freddie,

Social climbing is not among my vices. Living most of my life in Chicago, I haven't the faintest notion where I might plant my crampons. London and New York have, or in former years have had, something resembling literary and intellectual societies. Chicago, I'm not a little pleased to report, does not. As for capital-S society, it vanished years ago; when the Society pages of local newspapers became the Style section the game for Society was up. Not that I should have been the least interested in traveling among the unlanded gentry of Chicago, most of whose forbears were in any case stockyards butchers and railroad men.

Barbara and I joke, happily, about the paucity of our social commitments. How many cocktail and dinner parties have we in store for the weekend? I will ask her of a Thursday evening. Same as last week, she will say, none. What do you suppose we are doing wrong? You must mean what do I suppose we are doing right? she replies. Just as I have known certain women for whom I should gladly pay a modest alimony fee not to be married to them, so are there cultural events and performances I would pay not to have to attend. Friends are all very well, and I have my share, but none can ever rival the intimacy of friendship with one's wife in a good marriage. Such a friendship makes the loss of other friends, though not trifling, much easier to take, as I said earlier.

Three or so years ago I lost a good friend owing to a falling out I had, years before, with his ex-wife. The ex-wife sent me an ugly e-mail after I published an op-ed in the *Wall Street Journal* in 2008 in which I said that, though I did not vote for him, I was pleased that Barack Obama won the presidential election - pleased because I thought it might get the race madness off the country's back. The woman in question is a child of the 1960s, a pure type of the virtucrat, whose politics are little more than an expression of her intrinsic goodness, took exception to my not voting for Obama to begin with. In her e-mail she made plain that I was not as good a person as she, and threw in some further insults at no extra charge. I resolved to have no more to do with her.

Pleasing to report, this didn't seem to affect my friendship with her ex-husband. Our friendship sailed on as before. Easy-going is the way I would characterize this friendship. We checked in with each other once or twice a week by phone, he sometimes dropped in at our apartment when in the neighborhood, occasionally we would go out to dinner *à trois*. We placed minuscule bets—from $2 to $5—on basketball games or Grand Slam tennis matches; and each comically gloated when he won. Neither asked anything of the other: not money nor therapy nor consolation. We were friends not because we needed each other but for the simpler, purer reason that we liked each other.

Then three or so years ago, his ex-wife, wanting to make things up, through e-mail invited Barbara and me to a Passover dinner. I, lying, wrote back to say that, thank you all the same, we already had another invitation. A week or so thereafter my friend called to say that if I couldn't be friends with his ex-wife, he found he couldn't be friends with me. The logic of this escaped me. I answered that I could understand this readily enough if she had been his wife, but she was after all his ex-wife. "But I love her, you see," he said. I pled with him to rethink this; we had after all been friends for nearly thirty years. If he did rethink it, he must have come to the same conclusion, for I've not heard from him since, and do not figure to do so in the days remaining to either of us on this planet. I was puzzled and saddened by this decision on his part, but, like you, finally neither bereft nor lonely.

I once wrote a book on friendship, though now, eight years after its publication, I have to conclude that it is not *the* book on friendship. I dedicated the book to a friend who gave me the idea for the book, and with whom I talked a fair amount about the general subject. He is a member of that peculiar religious sect called Freudians, and though I grew bored with his always finding peckers where cigars lay, I determined to overlook this. Then one day he asked me what my dear, deceased friend Edward Shils, after two failed marriages, did for sex. This fellow was not of sufficient stature even to pose so vulgar a question, and, not to put too fine a point on it, I told him that it was none of his (nor my) fucking business. I added that I would prefer no longer to receive his boring e-mails. The word "boring," of course, did it. Anyone of intellectual pretension would rather be called fascist than boring.

Hugh Kingsmill called friends "God's apology" for family. An amusing remark but in my experience one with a low truth quotient. I recently wrote an essay called "Big D," the title a near dysphemism for Death, at one point in which I tried to imagine the world with me no longer in it. Of course it would be much the same, and my death will be no more significant than the removal of a grain of sand from the beach. Only four people, I noted, would be affected, would be truly mournful, would feel a genuine subtraction in their lives at my death, I concluded, and all are family. Late in life, I begin to wonder if friendship, like nature, isn't a touch overrated.

But enough about me, said the solipsist, let's get back to my cold. Owing to this cold I've not shaved for the past three days, and have well underway a fairly grubby looking beard. What I have at present is the fashionable look called "double stubble," or "perma-stubble." This scruffy look came into being owing to the permanently unshaven look of a forgettable actor named Don Johnson on an American television show called *Miami Vice*. All sorts of youngish and not so youngish men now go about with the permanently unshaven look; a razor has even been invented to maintain perma-stubble. The look is part of the deshabillization of western culture. Soon we shall see—at the Oscars, like as not—men come up to receive their statue who are unshaven, shirt out, tiesless, in tuxedo jacket, jeans, and tennis sneakers.

Have you ever had, or have you ever contemplated, a beard? I haven't, having been impressed by the comment of George Balanchine that all beards since his father's generation were fakes. Since Balanchine was born in 1904, this would include just about all beards in the twentieth century excluding. perhaps only those of George Bernard Shaw and Vladimir Ilych Lenin.

Beards do yeoman service, I suppose, in hiding weak chins and camouflaging bad skin, but scarcely anyone looks better for wearing a beard. The gravest mistake is for a man in his fifties or sixties to grow a beard, for a white beard adds a quick ten years in age onto even those of the liveliest gait. Here I must confess that, a mere forty or so years ago one summer on holiday in Wisconsin, I attempted a mustache. The effect I was going for was early Errol Flynn or perhaps middle Douglas Fairbanks, Jr. The result turned out to be illegal Mexican immigrant sharecropper. The poor beast was eliminated after only a week's existence. I have ever since planned to meet my maker with my *punim* shorn.

Best, Joe

LAGARDELLE. 29.6.14.
Dear Joe,

Have you ever had a Julian English moment? Who was Julian English? I know and I am sure you know, even though the self-destructive hero of *Appointment in Samarra* does not figure in the top fifty among twentieth-century fiction's leading men (as for leading women, your list, please, if you can make one). J.E.'s durable place in my private rogue-heroes' gallery owes little to John O'Hara's overt description of him. He lives by virtue of two incidents: when he seduces a not unwilling female ("Have you got a thing?" she asked) and the money-shot when he throws his drink (plus rocks) in a local political boss's smug-ugly (Irish?) face: self-definition and self-destruction *d'un seul coup*. We are incited to imagine the silent applause as the cowards in the room admire the man whom they will now ostracize and whose suicide will relieve them of yellow shame.

Late last autumn, I asked the poetry editor of the *Times Literary Supplement* to find room for a review, brief if need be, of a Greek poetess, now in her mid-eighties, called Kiki Dimoula. She sounds as if she might have been a load of naughty fun in old Montparnasse, but she was/is, in truth, an Athenian wife and mother, now in her eighties, who makes her poems, as my Cambridge friend Dorothy Nimmo did hers, out of small domestic truths transformed, without inflation, into transcendent ironies and spiced with sly distinctions (for instance, between "yet" and "but"). Dorothy Nimmo was not prized by the British laurel distributors, nor ever, I suspect, so much as mentioned in the U.S., but one Craig Raine, who used to sign his letters to me "Much love," in the but-don't-try-cashing-me Oxford style, hailed her as a genius.

Kiki Dimoula's verses came to me, thanks to our friend Robert Baldock, in a handsome, Yale-sponsored *en regard* edition. Her elliptic Greek is well rendered by a pair of female translators, one of whom, presumably the spit and polisher, advertises having no Greek. It don't sound like a good system, but the result is admirable and, since the Greek is there, one can winkle out how the ladies got to the version they did. Where but the *TLS* might their achievement be saluted? The poetry editor, Alan Jenkins, was sympathetic to my suit, until he discovered that the book had been published more than a year before any review could appear. Who would have noticed or cared if the arbitrary date-line was transgressed? Not for a mere myrmidon to say or even murmur. My request did, however, have a quick sequel: Jenkins asked me to review Daniel Mendelsohn's *Complete Cavafy*. For all but a year, he had been unable to think of anyone qualified. A case of here am I, send it to me.

First, however, Raphael warned that he had had his published doubts re the versions of Cavafy's so-called "unfinished poems," which D.M. had been the first to translate, from Renata Lavagnini's fat variorum edition, published in Athens. Since the Knopf volume did not carry the Greek on the facing page, the average reader had to rely on Mendelsohn's accuracy. Checking his versions against the Greek text, I found that he did not always honor expectations and said as much, in *Parnassus,* a sort of paying *Areté,* edited by Herb Leibowitz, sidekicked by our friend Ben Downing: his own side being the one he kicks, you may recall.

Jenkins was keen for me to proceed with the complete number. The Mendelsohn volume was about to reach the annual barrier. For reasons which have at least something to do with honor, I set myself to be as scrupulous as could be. Working steadily for four weeks, I made line-by-line comparisons of more than a hundred of D.M.'s numbers with the original, as well as scanning whatever was left. In some silly sense, I was playing for England. With the generosity typical of classical scholars, professorial Hellenic friends scanned my finished piece and discovered neither crass fault nor silly bias.

The almost four-thousand-word piece appeared in print in late May. I might have guessed that D.M. would be press-button quick with an indignant letter to the editor. He did not deign to "quibble," as he put it, with my specific points (might it be that they were unanswerable?). A person of dignity might have dropped me a note thanking me, for instance, for my assiduous attention and promising that, among other howlers, in any future edition, the Greek for "eight" would not be translated "seven." That was not the way of the *N.Y.R.B.*'s *graeculus*. He chose to be lengthily outraged by my passing allegation that he had cut Cavafy out to be some kind of "poster-boy" for Gay Pride. He wanted everyone to know that other people (no names cited) had done that and that he was militantly opposed to their course. You could have fooled me; and he did. His tendentious recruitment of C.C. was declared in—for instance—the anachronistic suggestion that C.C. declaimed against "hypocrisy" and in the celebration of the "thrilling" nature of the Alexandrian's limp, reminiscential daydreaming.

My friend, the letters editor of the *TLS* took it upon himself to read only (and superficially) the introduction to D.M.'s chunky number before making the trenchant decision to ice my stiffly polite response. Said clerk knows no Greek, but he does spend the odd holiday in Corfu. He admits to envying us our house on the Cycladic island of Ios, which has not a noodle in common with the Italianate-Brits-on-the-lam flavor of *ci-devant* Calypso's island. Shortly after my restrained retort to Mendelsohn was adjourned *sine die*, I received a letter from one Gerald Messadié, a literary gentleman of my age, who lives in Paris but was born in Alexandria and spent the first twenty years of his life in that city and in Cairo. He began:

> "Allow me to deem it a lucky stroke that you were the one to comment on Cavafy's 'Complete Poems'—an ambitious assumption if ever—as translated by Daniel Mendelsohn. You were considerate, though circumspect and you are competent and informative. Dare I suspect, however, that the 'two cheers' you grant Mendelsohn may sound as less than one, which I am but half-inclined to bestow on him?
>
> ". . . He obviously knows nothing of the Alexandria nor of the Egypt of the epoch. . . . I can easily detect his misconceptions about attitudes and social conventions. Nothing could be more remote from the 'gay icon' he imagines than the rather obscure poet called Cavafy . . .
>
> . . . the sexual encounters which Mendelsohn refers to as 'deliciously illicit' . . . weren't illicit: they simply did not exist, since they weren't referred to.
>
> "Homosexuality there and in those times was no taboo, as Mendelsohn surmises. It flourished because neither the authorities nor the society acknowledged it. Not that it was embarrassing: it was considered a natural outlet for people with demanding appetites, men and women be they married, but better kept from public

sight . . . I remember the guffaws triggered in the late forties by the mention of one famous cruiser, the regent of an Arab country who rode by in a Rolls-Royce with his coat-of-arms in neon on the door.

"Whenever I read [Cavafy] I get the impression that he's sitting next to me, speaking in the subdued voice of a friend, never a bard, always a confident (confidant?). It isn't at all the one that Mendelsohn's prose (sic) conveys."

M. Messadié's English is nicely dated and fluent in the well-read Franco-Levantine style. The implication of his letter, of which the above extracts are no more than a third, is that D.M. is full of it. That is one thing; the other is that I have not thrown an even half-full glass at anyone's head and am branded, in my own eyes, as a coward for being, oh, discreet. ("And the sufferance badge goes to . . .") Does it matter whether or not I remain *persona grata* at the *TLS*? Should I be surprised that honor among showbiz thieves can be more reliable than the variety on show among the *fins esprits* of culture gulch?

How lucky I have been to have a world elsewhere than in literary London! Hollywood and adjoining neighborhoods may be artless, but—the fun of it aside—they armed me with the means to write as I wished, not as others commanded (I have been spared creative editing), during the months they literally afforded me. I could wish that I had the nerve to honor Julian English's example, but what point is there in flinging ice-cubes at cold fish? I console myself in the face of imminent ostracism (even what a man doesn't do can count against him) with the fact that I have argosies at sea in the form of three movie scripts, all of which seem to have some chance of being produced within the coming year. No, that does not entail or even promise that any of them will be, but it reminds me that, armed with a suitable spoon, supping with the devil can be preferable to waiting for the crumbs, let alone fair shares, to fall from eminent tables.

Tout à toi, Freddie.

June 30 2014
Dear Freddie,

If you were the House Un-American Activities Committee, I should swear before you that Barbara and I are not now, nor have we ever been, members of a "fun group." Part of the problem is that we may not be much fun ourselves and are thereby, *ipso facto*, disqualified from all such groups. Not, be it known, that we long to be in one. We are not boozers, we both took a pass on pot and, later, cocaine, and the idea of couple-swapping and other hijinx is for us four stages beyond unthinkable. We are squares, to the highest power, the very antithesis of the "fun couple," and no place could possibly be found for us in a John Updike novel.

I'm not sure when "fun" as an adjective came into goofy use. I think I may first have heard it in the phrase "fun time," or "fun place" (I have heard Italy described as such a place), or "fun shoes." I long ago heard a charming children's joke about the mushroom who returns home from school crying because he hasn't been invited to a party with the other vegetables in his class. Attempting to comfort him, his mother asks if these other vegetables are aware that he is a fungi.

I knew a higher than highbrow Englishman named Vernon Young—for Vernon, Ingmar Bergman was in constant danger of slipping into the frivolous—who went about in high Bertrand Russell-like collared shirts, and who once asked me, "What do you suppose Americans mean when, upon parting, they say, 'Have fun.'" Vernon was an X. Trapnel type, a literary bohemian with neither money nor scruples when it came to women, whom he lived off for most of his life. I was briefly his editor, and in my last dealing with him he was reachable "c/o Swerlow, Stockholm." I hope Ms. Swerlow has recovered by now. Vernon-like characters are no longer in play, and perhaps we ought to be grateful for that, though the literary landscape is poorer without them.

You are correct about my never having heard of Woodrow Wyatt. I am pleased, though, to be filled in on him. I love to hear and read about intellectual and artistic hustlers. A zillion or so years ago I wrote a story about one called "Marshal Wexler's Brilliant Career." The story was loosely based on a young man, an American then at Oxford, who wrote me a letter informing me that I was a towering figure in American culture. Without me . . . but thank God there need not be a world without me. At one point he wrote to inform me he was coming to Chicago, and asked if we might meet for lunch. Why not? thought I. At that lunch, a Chinese one during which he borrowed ten dollars from me, he told me that he was having dinner that evening with Saul Bellow. This fellow, I now realized, was doing intellectual tourism, and I was merely Siena. I also assume he wrote letters to other saviors of American culture, a few, who knew, even more towering than I. He turned out in later life to be a writer of high portentousness on foreign affairs and of exquisite moral snobbery on everything else. I have chosen not to provide his name, for I fear he would enjoy the publicity.

What to give the Queen Mother for her birthday? There indoubledeed is a puzzling question. One night on television I heard the comedian Joan Rivers refuting the bad feeling everyone seemed at the time to have about the Prince of Wales marrying Camilla Whatshername (I'm fairly certain it isn't Ginsberg). She thought the match rather touching; and although she wouldn't be able to attend the wedding, she did, she claimed, send along a gift: a George Foreman Grill for barbequing. A perfect touch, I thought.

Gift-giving is out of hand. Five or so years ago I gave a talk to a group of leading American divorce lawyers calling themselves, no doubt accurately, The Dirty Thirty. One of them happened to mention that she was going to a *bat mitzvah* of some extravagance that weekend. I ask what sort of gift she might be giving. She said she wasn't sure, but she did go on to tell me that she has a client, a Jewish woman with children twelve and ten years old, and as part of the divorce settlement she was asking ten thousand dollars be set aside to pay for *bar* and *bat mitzvah* gifts that the children would have to provide over the next three or so years. Now here is a point Maimonides failed to touch on in his *Guide for the Perplexed*.

The current (Summer) issue of *Standpoint* has an interesting article on Jonathan Miller—interesting for showing how a career such as Miller's stumps the journalist, in this case a fellow I've not before now heard of named David Herman. The story the article tells is that Jonathan Miller is a man disappointed in not getting the most out of his polymathic genius, though the author begs to disagree, arguing that, given all Miller has done on television, in directing for the stage and for opera, he really is a genius. True enough, he concedes, Miller has not yet attained the "national treasure" status of Alan Bennett—in our earlier volume you twice referred to Alan Bennett as a national treasure, but with a nice dollop of irony lavishly applied each time—but surely by now he has come to be so considered, all irony extracted. Miller's, the article ends, "has been an astonishing career, remarkable for its breadth and its quality. It is hard to think of anything else like it. The range of his achievements is breathtaking. Only now, as Miller approaches his 80th birthday, can we begin to take stock. If he is not a national treasure, that perhaps says something more about us than about Miller and his extraordinary creativity over almost 60 years." *Gesundheit.*

Accompanying the article is a photograph of Jonathan Miller, blotchy-faced, no discernible eyebrows, two-suiter bags under the eyes, a red chosen nose, thin white hair combed forward (ah, the Short Unhappy Life of Francis

Combover), the face framed by untrimmed sideburns, mouth pursed, rumbly clothes under a turned-up collared trench coat—the very picture of the failed genius. The caption, if one is to believe the article, might have read, "What might he have done if only he had concentrated?"

In the subtitle to the article Jonathan Miller is cited as a "remarkable polymath." The standard of polymathy has slipped badly. A polymath is now someone who knows two things. Anyone who has more than one language, can write on disparate subjects, understands both DNA and rugby, can smoke while chewing gum seems to qualify. One of the surest shortcuts to attaining to the status of polymath is to go to medical school and then not practice. (Did not Stephen Potter suggest that doing this was also a brilliant one-upman's ploy?) The possession of an M.D. combined with the ability to write a roughly grammatical English sentence rings the bell in America, where the effort entailed in getting into medical school precludes acquiring the barest modicum of culture. In the next life I suggest we both acquire M.D.s straightaway. A bit time-consuming, I realize, but it seems to pay off handsomely in the end.

I had an e-mail this week from a man who asked my permission to call to discuss a writer named Albert Goldman, whom I knew when I lived in New York in the early 1960s. The e-mail left the vague suggestion that its author was planning to write something—it wasn't clear what—about Al Goldman. I said sure, why not, and call he did. Albert Goldman wrote books on Lenny Bruce, Elvis Presley, and John Lennon; Norman Mailer and Pauline Kael praised his Lenny Bruce book extravagantly. Al died at 66; a good thing, perhaps, for had he lived longer logic would have compelled him to produce a book on Michael Jackson. In response to his John Lennon biography, Sir (you want to talk about deflation) I say Sir Elton John said: "Albert Goldman is human vermin." Had Sir Elton said that about me, I should proudly run it as a blurb atop all my books.

Al Goldman had a Ph.D. He wrote a dissertation on plagiary (from the Germans) on the part of Thomas De Quincey, which I helped him to edit for publication by some mildly obscure American university press. But his ambitions were always extra-academic. Show biz was the name of his desire. He wished to be a radical comedian on the model of Lenny Bruce; he was among those who egged Bruce on and convinced him he was a revolutionary figure, when he was merely a sometimes brilliant comedian. Al taught for many years at Columbia University, in the school of general studies, which he called "working the lounge at Columbia." He had a high, slightly piping voice, and his language was a combination of analysandic and hipster, jazz version. My guess is that he did not so much teach as do riffs, which his students loved. "I thought I told you to wait in the car," he might say to a student entering his classroom late.

Al was in psychoanalysis when I met him. So many intellectuals in New York in that day were; not least notable among them were the Trillings, who swallowed the Freudian Kool-Aid neat. (When apprised of her young son's fear of elevators, Mrs. Trilling remarked that what he actually feared was the dark embrace of the vagina. Good not to have had Diana Trilling as one's mother, no?) Al Goldman both believed in psychoanalysis and mocked it through humor. I remember him telling me that in a group therapy session he was in a young woman allowed how she slept with every man she went out with and then felt degraded afterwards. What, I asked, was his reaction? "I introduced her to Joel [a friend]," he said. Al was the music critic of *The New Leader* magazine, for which I then worked, and when he would come in to read his galleys, he would say, "Do you mind turning down the lights, playing some soft music, and bringing me a box of Kleenex." Once, to em-phasize his dependence on me as his editor, he asked me to take him to buy a typewriter. "Sick, huh?" he said after making the request. I didn't take him.

I have been saying for years that Freudian psychoanalysts ought to be made to pay reparations to their patients for so richly bollixing up their lives with sex-crazed notions. Al Goldman's psychoanalysis did give him a certain power of self-dramatization. Wherever he went he saw himself as lead char-acter in a play. When his books were attacked, they were out to get him— leave aside for now and forever who "they" were. He could be tough on women. Once when I was in his apartment I noted the picture of a woman to whom he was briefly engaged. I mentioned that she looked much younger than I had imagined. "The secret to looking young," he said, "is to be im-mature." On another occasion he told me a story of a woman staring at him on the New York subway and then, at the 14th Street stop, getting up and de-parting the train in tears. "Holy shit," he said to himself upon her departure, "that was my first wife."

Al was afflicted with the disease called "with-it-ness." He got on the rock 'n' roll train early but much too late in life for him, already near fifty. He published a heavy-breathing piece on a group called The Doors, in which he made them sound crucial to the modern movement in poetry and music, the Next Great Thing. I listened to The Doors sing a song with the refrain line "C'mon baby light my fire." My own fire remained unlit. When Al asked me what I thought of his essay, I answered that, after listening to The

Doors, I thought the groups would have done much better to have sung his essay. I must say he took the comment well.

Al Goldman is dead twenty years now. He left no children, but just those books on once with-it subjects nobody any longer wants to read. I am being hard on him here, but in truth I liked him. Whether he had it in him to write about more serious things, I do not know. I do know that there is no one to mourn him, read him, or give the least damn about him. Sad.

I assume you are wasting as much time as I watching Wimbledon. I shall be cheering on Roger the Lodger by God. I take it you will be rooting for that dashing obsessive-compulsive who goes by the name Rafa. If they meet in the finals, are you up for a $5 bet? I could use the tax write-off the loss would provide.

Best, Joe

LAGARDELLE, 24170 ST LAURENT-LA-VALLEE-FRANCE. 8.7.14.
Dear Joe,

The biographied Jonathan Miller whom you mention is, of course, in some ways the man, if not quite the superman, whom I have known for some sixty years (and not others, as it were). I do not doubt his rare qualities, but I do not recognise his genius, unless it is for his directorial-cum-doctoral bard-side manner. Nor does everything he touch turn to gold (if it did, would he would endure the Midas consequences without complaint?), although he has certainly touched all sorts of things, sometimes with fine results, for instance an excellent production of an operatic version of *Turn of the Screw*. His repeated tendency is to hold the mirror up to himself.

Jonathan and I overlapped at the same college at Cambridge and we both appeared in the university Footlights show which transferred to London in the innocent summer of 1954 and was a huge hit, thanks largely to his one-man, barefoot, bravura time on stage. With his red curls and readier mimicry, he was not only compared, as I am sure his biographer says, to Danny Kaye but compared by Danny Kaye to Danny Kaye, which is, as the frogs say, *le top du top*. That he was a medical student, and soon enough a Doctor, enhanced his lustre; "Let him through, he's a doctor" is a call which seems to work in social as well as accidental circumstances. Once in the public eye, Jonathan made a loud moral conundrum of the dilemma which theatrical fame cursed and blessed him with: should he pursue the bitch-goddess or vow himself to Hippocrates? He dithered importantly and then chose both.

I cannot say that we were ever close but we were close to it. Even before he went up to Cambridge he had done clever mimetic things on the radio, at a time when "being on the B.B.C." was a certificate of eminence or at least imminence. I was somewhat flattered ("chuffed" is the dated term) when he proposed that we write some comedy material together. He invited me to come to his parents' place, somewhere in West London, to confect something to wow the grockles. I recall a big, sunny, uncurtained room in which it quite soon became clear that we were not going to strike a plethora of sparks off each other.

In those days, the weather forecast on the radio, especially of the expected temperature, was posited on conditions on the Air Ministry roof. This must have been a hangover from the wartime days when if anyone had to get the weather right, it was the chaps who despatched other chaps, like my cousin Jimmy, to risk their lives over enemy-occupied Europe. Jonathan had the what-if idea that the Air ministry roof developed a sub-tropical climate of its own. The lofty meteorologists *in situ* would not be aware that only on that high Whitehall plateau were banana trees coming into flower and giant orchids opening white and hungry lips to succulent insects. I smiled and had no inspired idea how to whimsy on from there. I am not sure there was anywhere. I remember wondering, as I have with all sorts of people whom I should have admired, cleaved to, or taken advantage of, how soon I could get away. In some company (that of the very nice and able director Norman Jewison for instance) one crowded hour can feel like a month and half at the dentist.

Jonathan and I were clearly not to be Goodman Ace rolled into two, but we continued to get along very nicely, although he did find occasion, as embryo consultant, to warn Beetle that, if I continued to say the kind of abrasive things which I thought clever, I would end up having no friends. I was duly chastened, although in truth I have not been short of friends, however short I may have been with some of them.

It was Jonathan's style, in his comic heyday, to be principally a one-man-bandsman. His finest hours were, of course, in *Beyond The Fringe* and his finest minute in the show that everyone in New York or London had to see (and we never did because we were living in Spain and Italy) was in an exchange with the three other Oxbridge chaps after they challenged him on the rumour that he was, as they used to say, a member of the Chosen Race.

His up-there-with-the-best answer was, the stars will remember, "I'm Jew-ish. I don't go the whole hog."

That was, I think, the moment to sell one's Miller the Comic stock. He continued to be famous and televisually prominent for many subsequent moons but, like his admirer Mr Kaye, he ceased all of quite suddenly to be funny. He was sometimes droll, but I doubt if anyone laughed at his stuff after, oh, 1963. He wanted to be more than funny and became something just a little less: self-important. He was, I daresay, wise to refuse to con-tribute to a symposium about being good in bed, or something horizontal along those lines, but he let it be known that he had asked himself whether it was the sort of shilling that Isaiah Berlin would consent to take. Come orf it, the Brits used to say.

In his last year at Cambridge, after I had already gone down, Jonathan took leave from the dissectionist's bench to play the philosophical tourist (Wittgenstein's term for those who dropped by his rooms for a spot of pos-itivism but did not stretch to full communion). Wittgenstein was dead, but Jonathan had access to his disciples, who preserved the master's jargon and gestures. I recall that, at one of our chance meetings in the 1960s, J. an-nounced that he was thinking of writing a novel, but it would, of course, have to be *pas comme les autres*. That was as near as I can ever remember him coming to acknowledging that I had, at the time, written a novel or eight myself. He does have a number of publications cited in his wiki-C.V., but they are, as he might say himself, almost all meta-texts, based on Important Cultural Figures and, yes, Tropes.

In his Hullo-to-Berlin mode, J. did write one little book about Marshall McLuhan, in a modish series edited by Frank "Mr Choosy" Kermode (which is what made it modish). I do not have it permanently close at hand, but I did, at the time, accept its smart dismissal of all the glib stuff about the global village and the Medium being the Message, and the massage. Jonathan seemed, in 1971, to apply a corrective broom to all the exaggerated predictions which, in the event, have come truer than even the Canadian sage can have imagined. Every medium, including the Serious Novel, is now above all an advertisement for itself, and had better be a good one if you're hoping for Awards (and had better win them if you're hoping for an-other commission). I recall (one does, one does, with the years) Bob Evans, once the Irving Thalberg of Paramount Studios, showing me and a sad, sad man called Gene Taft, who wore a raccoon coat in the Californian sunshine, because he was dying of Aids, the poster for his new 1980 something movie about the Colony Club. The poster preceded production because it was the proof that the picture had to be a hit. It wasn't, in truth, but McLuhan had it right: what movie can now be made unless the advertising people say go, what book published even?

Jonathan's biographer has, I am sure, got it all right, some of it; but there is something about his subject which makes me wonder whether I am alone in ambiguous admiration for someone who has gone so dolefully from one institutionally sponsored success to another (he made just one commercial movie and it was not a hit, from a rotten book by Kingsley Amis). With more successes *au gratin* than other opera directors, TV presenters or neurologists might wish for, he has a flinching air of having been robbed. He was awarded a knighthood, despite declaring his contempt for English culture, and he will, if George Steiner is right, some day be the recipient of the Order of Merit, the top award for Exceptional Exceptions (Tom Stoppard is one), bestowed by the Sovereign herself, with a little help from her tipsters. So what makes Dr Sir J. sport that woeful countenance when there isn't a windmill he hasn't tilted in his direction? To tell you the truth, I am with Rhett Butler on that one. But there is a certain duty - don't you think? - on those who have been pelted with roses all down the track, to be gracious enough not to give the impression of having been cheated of the crown of thorns. Jonathan cannot be blamed for never getting quite what he hoped to be, but all the deserts he has crossed have been markedly well sprigged with luxurious oases.

I can finish with the kind of telling anecdote which no biographer could possibly discover in a month in the morgue. You may know, because Jonathan has talked about it quite a lot, and then some, that he once directed Laurence Olivier in *The Merchant of Venice*. When Larry wondered how Shylock should respond to the news that he had Antonio where he wanted him, Jonathan told him (that was the fun part) that he could do a little dance, like the one recorded on film of Adolf Hitler slapping his knees as he looked out over conquered Paris. We will not, as Jonathan's psychiatrist father, Manny Miller, would say, analyse that one; but to foist Hitlerian glee on a ghetto-dweller combines cute with…whatever, as no one will ever stop them saying.

Earlier this year, I recalled, I thought, that in that same production Shylock, on hearing that his daughter Jessica was marrying out, tore his clothes, or was it hers? I had not spoken to Jonathan for some time, for reasons We Need Not Go Into, but I had his unchanged number, so I dialled it with confidence that he would remember everything he ever did or had people do. It rang and rang and then I hung up, before the dreaded answering machine clicked in. A few seconds later my phone rang. And it was Jonathan. "Who is that?" said he. I declared myself and put my query, to which he gave instant accurate response (showing no interest in why I wanted to know) and we exchanged pleasantries, including my regret that we had not been friends and that was that. So what's my point? Just this: I have never bothered to use the facility which allows one to discover who the last caller was, because if he or she wants me that badly, he or she can try again. How interesting, because how petty, that Jonathan, the target of so many invitations, should need to know, that promptly, what it was that he was missing, the one thing, it might be to put a smile on his puss. And then, poor guy, it was only....

Tout à toi, Freddie.

July 10, 2014
Dear Freddie,

I finally acted upon your recommendation to see *Nebraska*, and was not disappointed. The movie has a relatively high truth—or if you prefer relatively low bullshit—quotient. For me the first hint that it might be an unusual flick is when David, the good son in the movie, is confronted by his overweight, in no-way-attractive girlfriend about his inability to make up his mind about their relationship. No regular movie would allow such an unprepossessing girlfriend, passing up the opportunity for a bit of T&A, as they say, or at least used to say, in the business. Making the movie in black-and-white was another artistically shrewd decision. Why bring color into what are essentially colorless lives? That so many utterly crappy movies are made these days is not in the least surprising; what does surprise is when a good one gets through the fine steel nets of the obtuse men and women with the power to say yes to movie projects.

The truth of *Nebraska* is in its rendering of the squalor of small-town American lives in the current day. These are the lives of people either left behind or who never had any wish to venture out. The want of the least style or good looks—with the possible quasi-exception of Will Forte in the good-son role—of the entire cast feels right. Who, after all, is one supposed to look attractive for in a Nebraska town of 1,200-odd people, or perhaps I do better to drop the hyphen and make it 1,200 odd, sadly odd, people? Nothing at all elevating about *Nebraska*, though it does have a mildly happy ending of sorts; the half-senile Bruce Dern character does get his truck and his compressor, whatever that is. The movie succeeds, I'd say, on its accuracy of portrayal: that ghastly wife, the dour picture of the family sitting around watching a pro football game, the sad scam of winning a million dollars that the Dern character can't get out of his head. The movie feels like nothing so much as Dreiser's character Hurstwood in *Sister Carrie*, down on his uppers but now dragged off to rural America to live out his years in senility.

I note *Nebraska* was nominated for six Oscars and won none. Other, less meaningful awards it did win. I also note that the author of the screenplay, a man with the impressively unexotic name of Bob Nelson, whose background is that he acted in a television comedy set in Washington State, comes out of nowhere. I thought the screenplay tonally just right, the casting perfect. Looking up the movie on Wikipedia, I discovered that the powerful thinkers at Paramount didn't want Bruce Dern for the main role, but thought instead of Gene Hackman, Robert De Niro, Jack Nicolson, Robert Duvall—in short, the usual suspects. For the son they had in mind Paul Rudd, Casey Affleck, or Matthew Modine, a mistake every one of them. Two-and-a-half cheers for the director, a man named Alexander Payne, for sticking to his original choices in the face of a bombardment from the ignoranti.

A new bookshop called Books and Beginnings has opened in Evanston. This item would not normally call for stopping the presses, but in the light of what is currently happening in the book business in America, it is noteworthy. I don't know if this is the case yet in England or in France, but in America the so-called independent bookstore is dying, and none too slowly. (In a note of reverse chauvinism, I assume that when an unpleasant trend shows up in America, it will soon enough raise its gargoylish head in Europe.) The alleged killer of the independent bookstore—or as they are now saying on the evening television news, "the person of interest"—is Amazon.com. But there is nothing "alleged" about, say I, with a nod toward Mrs. Malaprop, the alligator. As you know, Amazon.com offers books at heavily discounted prices, has an impressive inventory, and can usually get a book to its customers in a day or two. So dominant has Amazon.com become that those sentimentalists among us find ourselves now cheering for the giant corporation Barnes & Noble, the last remaining chain-store booksellers.

The import of this goes beyond the rather pathetic self-interest of us scribblers. Edward Shils used to say that there are four main sources of education in the contemporary world: the classroom, serious magazines and newspapers, the conversation of intelligent friends, and bookshops, new and especially used. Going into a bookshop, handling the stock, discovering books one hadn't known about nearby on the shelves, all this has traditionally been a form of education. For those among us who spent most of our classroom time stifling yawns, magazines and newspapers and bookstores have been the key source of education. They have, I know, for me. If bookshops go, and magazines and newspapers take another a step or two down on the ladder of seriousness, which so many of them seem to be doing, that leaves only the conversation of intelligent friends. Yet with all other supporting institutions on the wane, how are friends supposed to become intelligent in the first place?

The owners of the Evanston bookshop Books and Beginnings, a couple in their sixties now retired from other work, tell me people say that in opening a new bookshop they are in effect walking into a burning building. Their plan is to sell new books, remainder books, and serious used books. They are sufficiently savvy about books to cull the dreck from the wreck of contemporary publishing. I wish them well. When last in the shop I discovered a very clean copy of your *Some Talk of Alexander*; my own copy having somehow gone AWOL, I bought it for $10. I tell you this so that you know the book will have a good home.

I agree with you about John O'Hara, especially about his skill at dialogue. He prided himself on his good ear. I suspect that, *Appointment in Samarra* apart, his stories wear better than his novels. Rightly or wrongly, I never troubled myself with his triple-deckers: *A Rage to Live, From the Terrace, The Ewings* (first and second). Some of his novels—*Ten North Frederick, Butterfield 8* among them—made moderately successful movies, which may not be a compliment.

Earlier this year I read, as a bedside book, a collection of his stories called *The Horse Knows the Way*. I read them with a keener interest than I find in the stories of F. Scott Fitzgerald. O'Hara and Fitzgerald share Irishness, of course, which means that, as relatively genteel Irishmen—is Mickanos the politically correct term?—they also suffered greatly from snobbery. (So, too, did Joe Kennedy, the father of all those putatively great American politicians and certifiably great philanderers, founders and inhabitants of the mythical modern Camelot.) Snobbery plays through the writing of both men. I don't think the piquant touches of anti-Semitism that one finds in Fitzgerald are present in O'Hara, but I've never taken my anti-Defamation League fine-comb through his works. Lots of adultery in O'Hara, lots of country clubs, a fair amount of conflict between the generations. Over the course of a longish book of stories, which *The Horse Knows the Way* is, it all tends to wash together.

I'm surprised to learn that the *TLS* didn't allow you the chance to shoot back at Daniel Mendelsohn's reply to your review of his translation of Cavafy. D. Mendelsohn must have been in shock at your catching him out in various, some of them obvious, errors. He is the very type of the good student, Daniel M., and thus far in life has probably received only A's—not, mind you, the kind worn by Hester Prynne—and gentle pats on the head. Well, at least he didn't get yet another A in the tough Professor Raphael's course.

I have long supposed it journalistic etiquette to allow an author to respond to an insulting reaction to what he has written for a journal. I cannot recall ever having to fend off an unsatisfied author of a book I've reviewed, but I have had to deal with what the old shrinks—God love 'em, I don't—used to call free-floating hostility. If I sensed malice directed at me in a letter to the editor, I tended to transmogrify to instant rattlesnake, and bite its author in the back of the ankle, thereby making an enemy for life. William Dean Howells I think it was, said it's easy to make enemies but so difficult to keep them?

On one notable occasion a piece I wrote about a Chicago gossip columnist that attracted a letter from a writer named Studs Terkel, a man who made his living insisting how much he loved the huddling, shivering masses, in which he called me "a stuffed shirt." I informed the editor of the magazine that it was the etiquette in these matters to allow the author to respond, and that he was to return to Mr. Terkel to inform him that in my response I intended to call him a cracker-barrel Stalinist (which he was). Terkel withdrew the letter instanter. A troll-like little man, Studs Terkel will always live for me for a single comment he made about the 1960s, which runs: "What a time! Even guys like me are getting blown."

The failure of the letters-editor to allow you to respond to D. Mendelsohn is a reminder, which you don't need, that editors are not always helpful. A few years ago I read a piece in the *Sewanee Review* by a woman of a certain age named Merill Joan Gerber, who wrote a novel with the unpromising title of *The Hysterectomy Waltz*, stating that editors have finally driven her out of lit biz. She set out the Iliad of woes they've caused her over the years: asking for rewrites and then not publishing her; taking months to reply and then only to reject her submissions; carving up her compositions, and many other tortures. She couldn't, she claimed, take it any more, and had scribbled her last. Whether she has lived up to her promise I do not know, but there was nothing in her extended plaint that was in the least unbelievable.

The activity of foreign works having been co-translated by partners one of whom hadn't the language of the original poem was in vogue some years ago in connection with the then Soviet poets, Yevtushenko, Voznesensky, Akhmatova, and others whose names I cannot now recall. Robert Lowell was one of the participants; Anthony Hecht may have been another. Although a book of these translations may have come out of it, in the end it didn't come to much. The most interesting translation modus operandi I've heard of was that of Isaac Bashevis Singer, who used to sit in with his translators as they Englished his books. Singer, I gather, told them no, this isn't quite right, here is what I really had in mind, I don't think that's the word I want. Somehow it seems to have worked, for nearly all of Singer's fiction reads well in English. I gather that, at no extra payment, he also bonked some of these (preponderantly) middle-aged women translators.

I have been reading Ronald Syme's *Sallust*. I am reading it purely for pleasure. By this I do not mean merely that I have no plans to write about the book, but that I am not taking the least pains to sort out in my mind its complex narrative about the endless machinations of high-stakes Roman finaglers. I read it awaiting and delighting in Syme's magisterial sentences, which in their English show the effects of a life half-lived in Latin. Of Clodius's three sisters, all consigned to advantageous matrimony, Syme writes: "Absent husbands, pride of birth or the love of luxury and competition produced scandalous conduct in the Clodiae; while, on the other hand, wit and talent were far from being disdained." Then there was Sempronia: "A bold woman and well educated with a gift of affairs and taste for intrigue, Sempronia did not stop at crime; in her ardent pursuit of pleasure, no meaning attached to good fame and modesty; she seldom waited to be asked and courted." Quarrels among senators, in Syme's pages, are "enlivened by mutual charges of unnatural vice."

I remember many years ago being asked whether I should rather live in fifth-century Greece (with all its artistic grandeur and intellectual splendor) or in Rome at the outset of the empire (with all its vice, corruption, and murderousness). The correct answer of course is fifth century Greece—correct, of course, if one doesn't oneself happen to be a writer. For a writer—pass me that toga—there can no real choice, can there?

Best, Joe

LAGARDELLE. 13.7.14.
Dear Joe,

You're right to opt for the late republican/early imperial Rome rather than more or less Periclean Athens as a time in which to be an ancient scribbler. There were certain risks in the former period, as Cinna the poet discovered when he was taken for Cinna the ward-boss and done to death by those out to avenge Caesar's death and have a bit of fun in grab-it-and-run circumstances. The element of Bacchic pleasure in being brutal is almost always left out when crowds do revolutionary dances. Savagery needs no ideological warrant, but is energized by getting one. Even now (a needless sub-division), we in the English orbit—British TV is all too easily available even in our Virgilian rusticity—are being warned and threatened (rely on a measure of unadmitted masochism in Breaking News) that Islamic Jihadists, ISIS men, are all set to come back to the U.K. and continue the conversion of the world to Allah's overlordship, or else.

The threat is flagged by repeated broadcasts of young British Muslims, out in Syria, dressed up in amateur-dramatics cozzies and holding pillaged weaponry of all sorts, as they announce their merciless militancy and (by implication) their release from second-class citizenship, in glum enclaves, in English cities that no one in the executive echelons of society ever cares to visit. Videos of teen-age initiation and participation in massacres, crucifixions, torture and degradation (mere degradation) of alleged enemies of Islam (almost all of them other Muslims) are less often screened. It is feared that they will upset viewers and deter them from watching the ads which follow. The British are not all that bothered about what these teenage holidaymaking Halal butchers do to other Muslims, however much Foreign Office crocodiles weep for them, but they have a deep and understandable anxiety about their return to the U.K., inured to squeamishness and all set to enroll the U.K. (as their brothers somewhat seriously wish to include Spain and southern France) in the new Caliphate. You won't need to be mistaken for Cinna, poet or politico, to get your throat cut.

What then is to be done, old chum? Since prophylactic policing is not Our Style (yes, yes, of course it's just as well), we shall have to wait until an Outrage is, yes, Perpetrated back home, before . . . whatever has to be done gets done. I have no prescriptions and I retain, against much modern scholastic cynicism, a sentimental vision of the *convivencia* in which, under a genial Sultan, Jews, Muslims and Christian cohabited in old (pre Black Death) El-Andalus. The cohabitation was often nervous, but it had a compassionate, synthetic fineness in the higher reaches. The arrival of fanatical Muslims, who drove out Cordoba's amiable live-and-let-livers, precipitated the disintegration of what was, alas, never abidingly stuck together. Christians who insisted on abusing Islam, and refused to be spared martyrdom by promising not to bring pigs to market again, also made sure that either/or became the rule of the once civilized world.

Except for the malicious fun of it, no antique Roman was ever accused of atheism, still less of infringing dogmatic "beliefs," although the Greeks ordered these things somewhat differently: Socrates has been elevated as a proto-Christian martyr to (the sub-text suggests) democratic inquisitionism, although he could certainly have smiled and charmed his way into acquittal, or merely nominal chastisement, if he had not been such a showboating egotist. His fellow philosopher Empedocles threw himself into Etna to generate the rumor that he had never died; Socrates threw himself to the Athenian *demos* to procure similar *réclame*. Greek writers and artists did have to tread somewhat delicately. Talent of a rare order is always liable to excite righteous malice. Aeschylus and Euripides both ended in exile. Aeschylus, fueled for his very long haul by alcohol, went off to Sicily in a sulk after failing to get the Big One at the Great Dionysia for the whateverth time; but he had already sailed very close to the wind, in his treatment of the gods and their rude follies, and was spared arraignment, it seems, not least because he turned out the stuff, tragic and comic (none of his gags survives, thanks in good part to Christian flames) with such magniloquent fluency.

Euripides the so-called Rationalist was a rich crosspatch, who did most of his work, even when *persona* somewhat *grata*, in a cavernous study on the island of Salamis, but he—like so many—both scorned the values of your average Attic audience and also solicited its applause and, yes, awards. After he went into prudent exile, he wrote *Bacchae,* the most brilliant of his plays, in which the king who outlaws Dionysus and his Bacchic ravers is decapitated and has his head mounted on a pole borne by his high-as-a-kite mother. The limits of rationalism and the thrill of transgression were depicted, with derisive *superbe*, by a writer who had fled persecution for being so unsociably sensible.

Almost crossing the line into the territory of the unforgivable is a game played so often by writers and philo-persons (if you want to hear from the ladies, Hypatia of Alexandria is the charmer of choice) that we may guess that the road to fame is always likely to have precipitous edges. The trick of pretenders to greatness is to *seem* to be grappling with explosive topics but never to arm the detonator. William Styron is a recent up-there-with-the-best-of-them instance: all his "major" books treated of dangerous themes, but in no dangerous way. He was, if superficial memory serves, deeply wounded by the black reaction to his take on Nat Turner, since he had taken such trouble to whiten his principal player's character. How many black readers did he hope to have? Not a Pantherine lot, we may hazard; but he did expect brotherly pats on the back for the sensitive nature of his depiction of the hero of a story which, if I am right, has a dark underworld version in which the tag line was/is ". . . and then saddle up and go to town." Am I allowed to say this these days? And if not, by whose don't-say-so? Any good writer is wise to be an exile of a kind.

As for *Sophie's Choice,* Styron's "problem with Jews" was dealt with by making the lady of choice into a Polish woman. I recall the pride with which George Steiner produced Styron's number in order to show me that he, G.S., had been *ben citato* in the attendant Auschwitziana (there to show how serious and scholarly Styron was). The latter's best writing, to my mind, was *The Long March,* which lacked the clamorous overwriting of his big-band numbers. It owed just a little something to Herman Wouk, maybe, at least in the evidence *The Caine Mutiny* offered of how a nice liberal could be impersonated and pilloried in much the same woodwork.

I had a very friendly note this wet, wet Sunday morning (now melded, as they used to say, into an even wetter Sunday afternoon) from an English poet and translator called Elaine Feinstein, whom I have known, politely, and occasionally, for many years. She told me that she was looking forward to the "pitiless portraits" of 1950s Cambridge in the latest volume of my autobriography, as a vain misprint labeled it. Is pity a tone in which we are obliged to sketch those against whom life has thrown us? Did Goya do wrong, morally or artistically, in portraying the Spanish royal family as over-decorated noodles and Napoleon's French soldiers as, well, proto-Boches? Goya has always been my kind of artist, not least because he got better and more relentless as time went by. He began as a salon decorator and was educated by time, indignation and persistence into the unblinking, mold-breaking accountant of human cruelty and conceit. He died in Bordeaux, not all that far from our mutual friend Montaigne's Girondin retreat.

I am reading an interesting new text on Micheau and adjacent topics by Pierre Manent, a clever French higher educationalist who highlights the *mano-a-mano* between M. and Blaise Pascal. The latter appears much less lovable than Christian cant requires. Montaigne deals with himself as an object of interest and value and is, in some eyes, too much of an egotist. Pascal's egotism proves greater still: he needs to believe in God because only through Him can Monsieur P. be persuaded not to regard himself as, more or less, the supreme (human) being of his time (he did invent the wristwatch, I am told, and so always had it with him). The Christian idea of salvation, however cunningly dressed, is thoroughly self-involved: Christians can save themselves, severally, but they can't save anyone else, even by that famous charity which may give the charitable salutary marks, but does nothing to redeem the beneficiary.

If I write "pitilessly," which is not my purpose, it is for the sake of the only redemption in which I can well believe: truth-telling stylishness. I picked up Manent's book, and an armful of others, in a bookshop in Périgueux of a kind that doesn't exist in England, full of tough texts, classics and enough shelves of worthwhile reading to make one hope for a very late bus to eternity. The *librairie* is run, against the Amazonian current, by a retired couple who know and love their stuff. The proprietor added a piquant little number, *Mon Amitié avec Marcel Proust*, by Fernand Gregh, to my stack, for the sheer grace of it. I am touched to think you spent $10 on *Some Talk of Alexander*. I probably should have accepted a good, commercial editor and allowed the text to become diced vegetables in the modern Eat-Me style.

Elaine (b. 1930, in Bootle,) said something else: ". . . I have been much troubled by the Middle East: friends there, enemies here, and a sense of hellish pointlessness. A wish to abolish Israel altogether is making itself felt, particularly I think among nervous Jews." She is not necessarily one of the nervous Jews she cites, but there is something so craven and so widespread in the attitude she describes that it needs to be, oh sod it, *addressed*. Must we applaud Netanyahu's jingo-king-o'-Israelism? I do not think so. I could wish . . . all sorts of things without wishing Israel off the map. In truth, I was disappointed, back in 1967, that the Israelis did not keep their word (given to me personally—imagine!—by the third secretary in the London embassy) that they had no intention of extending their borders. David Ben-Gurion and I were of one mind there, I think. But he was who he was and I was no one at all and even he didn't affect the way it went.

Now is always too late, is it not? So I will not presume or hope to butt my way into influencing Israeli policy, conduct or diplomacy. I am not an Israeli, nor are those British Jews whose don't-make-waves-itis is a congenital condition, induced by their often happy experience of life under the tolerant (i.e., largely indifferent, if not nose-holding) aegis of Britannia. As a result, they feel that they are at risk more from gun-toting, drone-using so-called co-religionists out there in the Middle East than from any of the monomaniacs who have rallied to ISIS and will/may come back to haunt us. Harold Pinter's detestation of "Zionists" was principled enough to warrant his abuse of my old friend David Pryce-Jones, a civilized man if ever I knew one, as well as his (H.P.'s) merciless conviction that he had perfect moral pitch (Pascal got his from God, Pinter from Stockholm).

The rise of the counter-factual, not least in the fat work and not infrequent fat-headedness of Niall Fergusson, who doubles as TV's Monsieur Un

Peu Partout, has made the erasure of Israel a tempting subject for don't-blame-me English Jewish *bien-pensants*, led by Jacqueline Rose, the one who never blushes unseen, or at all, it seems. Their unspeakable, unspoken message is How much better it woulda been if all Europe's Jews had gone up the chimneys or sunk to the bottom of the Med or the Euxine. We (ah we!) would now have cheap gas and friendly Arabs all over the platz. Would we? Single Issuedom leads to false simplicities and arrogant assumptions. Am I among friends here? In any case, whether or not Israel is, as they said (on other topics) in *1066 And All That,* A Good Thing, there it bloody well is and will be, I hope.

The above doesn't in the least mean that squeamish Fred relishes the sight of Gaza being biffed or children blown to pieces, supposedly in the interests of peace; but I recommend the passage in my Josephus on the fate of the Jews of Scythopolis, in sunny first century C.E. Palestine, to anyone who supposes that Gentiles can be trusted to embrace Jews if only the latter would stop being so belligerent. A TV commentator has just said that the Gaza inhabitants are worse off than anyone being savaged in Iraq or Syria because they can't get away across any border. The same well-spoken, dead-lined face doesn't mention that the Palestinians are trapped (and have been for decades) because their Arab brethren won't give them passports or visas to get out.

Tout à toi, Freddie.

July 19, 2014
Dear Freddie,

You suggest that Socrates' relatively early death, at the hands of his fellow Athenians, was a good career move, and I think you are correct to do so. Impossible to think of him living much longer, and the form of his death, hemlock voluntarily drunk among friends, could not be improved upon. The same is true of Jesus. He departed the joint in the right way—tortured and betrayed—the right way for Jesus, that is. He might have been insufferable as an old coot.

One could put together an essay about people who had, so to say, timely deaths—deaths that helped their posthumous reputation. Orwell may have qualified here. Had he lived longer than his forty-six years, he, never much for humor, might have turned into a scold. F. Scott Fitzgerald, who gave every indication of running out of talent, dying at forty-four, definitely qualifies. The same may have been true for James Agee and Nathaniel West, but clearly not for John Keats. Pegging out at twenty-six is never a good idea, from the career or any other standpoint.

On the other side of the ledger, there are those who have lived too long. This group includes the macho-men writers. I wonder if Hemingway, in his depression, before he pulled the trigger of the shotgun that put *fini* to his Papa charade, didn't sense that his living any longer would be of no use to anyone and could only harm his reputation. Seeing Norman Mailer on television in old age, walking on two canes, hard of hearing beyond the help of hearing-aids, the very model of the sad old duffer, and thinking of the swashbuckler figure—the barroom brawling, head-butting, woman sodomizing, no-holds-barring, deep-sea-diving seeker of exclusively uncomfortable truths—he wished to project in his writing, one felt an earlier exit would have made a lot more sense. Instead Mailer departed the planet seeming like nothing so much as one's unsuccessful Uncle Benny, the guy who never made much of a living in the mail-order business.

As for William Styron, who made it to eighty-one and went out best known as the author of a book about his own depression, I agree with your character of him as the author of books on "dangerous themes" that were somehow not quite as dangerous as advertised. I read these books when they first appeared but do not now remember all that much about them. Styron's greatest gift, I do remember, was for writing landscape; a quality of which I am myself without an iota of skill. American Southerners tend to be good at landscape: they know the names of the flowers and the trees and what a hillock is and what a ridge isn't and get worked up describing deltas, rivers, Civil War battlefields, and what all else. Styron could write pages upon pages of landscape. I remember reading them with simultaneous admiration and extreme boredom. I once read a poem that began (roughly), "Women know 279 colors, men know 8." Southerners know 279 trees and flowers, it might be reworked to read, Northern urbanites know 6.

William Styron was a member of the Editorial Board of *The American Scholar* when I came on as editor. The previous editor was a man named Hiram Haydon, who, as a publisher's editor, discovered Styron and published his first novel, *Lie Down in Darkness*. The magazine's Editorial Board in those days was fairly namey: on it sat Jacques Barzun, Lillian Hellmann, Diana Trilling, Paul Freund, the physicist John Wheeler, the microbiologist Rene Dubos, and a few others. (Later Arnaldo Momigliano, Edward Shils, and Peter Brown came aboard.) Styron never missed any of our thrice-yearly meetings—two in New York, one in Washington—coming in from his Connecticut *estancia*. He married a wealthy woman, Jewish, named Rose, who was apparently an efficient hostess for Styronic parties for people like George Plimpton and the Kennedys, major and minor.

He behaved himself at meetings, though at drinks afterwards showed a touch too much enthusiasm for the hootch. On a few occasions he trysted, I do believe, with attractive women waiting in the wings. I remember his whispering conspiratorially with one such woman. He wore an inevitable blue blazer, Himalayas of dandruff on the shoulders. The only exchange I can now recall having with him was when I showed the board a mock-up of the new cover I wanted for the magazine, and he said that it seemed to him more appropriate for a Dutch philological journal. "Exactly what I had in mind," I replied. I have no wish to reread Bill Styron, and I wonder if many others do.

I'd not before now heard that Pascal invented the wristwatch. I am impressed by those who invent small but useful items that provide convenience or simple pleasures. The man or woman who invented the bacon-lettuce-tomato sandwich, for example, surely brought more happiness into the world than all the poetry written during the past fifty years. As for the convenience of wristwatches, when I think of them I am often reminded of the story that Max Beerbohm used to tell about his brother Herbert Beerbohm Tree, who one day noted a man coming off a mover's truck with a grandfather clock on his back. "I say, my good fellow," Beerbohm Tree remarked, "wouldn't it be simpler to wear a wristwatch."

"Never run away from business," my dear father, in one of his brief business homilies, counseled me. So when a man sent me an e-mail, opening with a paragraph or two of praise—as the quickest way to a man's heart was once thought to be through his stomach, the quickest way to a writer's is through his vanity—and then asking if I would like to contribute to a collection he was putting together under the title *The Good Book*, I naturally answered sure, why not? The book is to include various unlearned (I qualify here) scribblers turning in 3,000 or so words on Biblical books or passages they admired. The fee is $1,500, the deadline sometime in August. Not much but still easy money, no?

As it happened, I have been reading the Bible straight through in preparation for a final exam that I may be called upon to take in the perhaps not so distant future. I had read bits and pieces of the Bible over the years; I knew the big stories—Adam and Eve, Isaac and Abraham, Jacob and Esau,

Moses among the pharaohs on Sinai, the Kings Saul and David, the Joseph story from which Thomas Mann made much hay. Not quite the same as *davening*, I realize, but I now read ten or so pages every morning.

The Bible, I discovered, invented the *longueur*, of which it is more plentiful than the fields and flocks of the blessed of the Lord. Cole Porter gave us "Begin the Beguine," but the Bible gave us Begat the Begat. The book's many irrelevancies for our day are manifold. If Mme R. and you are ever thinking of sacrificing a ram, give me a call; I can fill you in on the details. I might even invite myself over for dinner, though with some trepidation that you might serve swan, which I learned is strictly *treyf*, or forbidden to Jews. Having said all that, there is of course much in the Bible that is sublime. Of *treyf*, or food forbidden to Jews, you must know the old anti-Semitic joke, about what constitutes the ultimate Jewish dilemma: the answer is, ham, on sale.

Before I had heard from the editor of *The Good Book*, I had taken a break from my Bible reading, at page 885 of the Norton Critical Edition of the King James Version, which is where "The Book of Job" begins. The invitation to write for *The Good Book* was incentive to return. I thought I might write about "The Book of Job," and jauntily walk, smiling, all the way to the bank with my small fee.

I don't know if you've read about poor Job and his boils in recent years, but as pure narrative I found his story disappointing. If I were writing it up in treatment style, it would go something like this: Satan puts God to the test of turning Job, a good, pious, and prosperous man, into a sponge for the gravest possible punishment, to see how deep his piety really runs. God visits physical ills (those boils), loss of family, dispossession of fortune on Job. Job, naturally enough, asks the age-old and still central question: Why me? Three guys show up to instruct him that he is wrong to complain, each taking up a slightly different position. Later a fourth arrives to correct the first three. Finally, God himself arrives with the whirlwind and does not in the least answer Job's complaints about the injustice of his treatment—never apologize, never explain being His motto—but instead reminds Job of His, God's, own astounding powers, as if to say to poor Job, "Do you realize with whom you are fucking, Buster?" Job catches his breath, replies, sorry, he was out of line. God restores him to his former position of high fortune— sheep, camels, oxen, the works—accompanied by a second family of seven sons and three daughters, and doubles his life span to a hundred and forty years. "So Job died, being old and full of days." Dissolve to credits. One loose thread ample enough for a man to hang himself is about the first family that God killed off, not a word. So my question is, if you were a studio executive, does this sound to you a workable script? I see your lips forming the words "Whaddya, kidding me?"

As for *The Good Book,* it turns out that another contributor has already signed up to write about "The Book of Job," which is probably a good thing. I thought I might do something from "The Book of Psalms," but three contributors have already latched on to various psalms. I shall move on to the book of Isaiah, which I've never read, in the hope of finding something there that I can write about without making a Balaam's ass of myself. Why is it that whenever I agree to write something that sounds to me like easy money, it rarely works out? I've not yet found the answer in the Bible.

What's in a name? A damn lot, as the balding fellow from Stratford on Avon rightly sensed. "The Book of Isaiah," for example, reminds me how fortunate Isaiah Berlin was in his first name. You will notice that in the Bible there is no Book of Freddie or Book of Joe. If Isaiah Berlin's first name were Sam or Lou or Phil—Irving was already taken—he'd never have attained to the same *réclame.* "I met an impressive fellow at All Souls last year," one imagines some frustrated name-dropper say, "named Sam something or other. Can't remember his last name. Helluva talker." Erich Heller, whom I much liked but who retained his Anglo-snobbery until the end of his days, used to pronounce the name Isaiah with the same reverence others reserved for the name Jehovah.

On the (for some people) vexed question of Israel, which is at the moment the lead story in the press, print and electronic, I am without complicated feelings. Unnuanced, chauvinistic, heartless though I may be taken for, I think Israel is right in its recent attacks on the thugs in Gaza. The world, or large parts of it, doesn't see any need for this gallant nation to defend itself from fanatics who in any case see only weakness in reasonableness. No group for whom I harbor more contempt than those fellow Jews who feel neutral on the subject of the survival of Israel, or insist they care not alone for Jews but for *all* people. The Jewish world needs a Dante to create a new range of circles in hell in which these Jews will undergo the most unrelentingly hideous torture.

I've just sent off an 1,100-word piece on William James's *Varieties of Religious Experience* to the *Wall Street Journal* for its "Masterpiece" section. I mention in it William James's "lambent lucidity," which he possessed in face-card spades. I suppose no one would say the same about his fifteen-months-younger brother Henry. (Did any family ever produce two such astonishingly yet differently talented sons?) Leon Edel, you will recall, attempted to make a Freudian sandwich out of the sibling rivalry between the two brothers. He based this on William's turning down membership in the American Academy of Arts and Letters, which extended membership to Henry first, and because William did not care much for Henry's later fiction, at one point suggesting he write "a $2 + 2 = 4$" novel, which was the last thing Henry wished to do. The sandwich, though, is inedible. The brothers loved and respected each other. What above all they had in common is that each in his different way was immensely impressed by the mysteries of life and did, each in his own way, what he could to elucidate them. In the realm of art and intellect, no other American family can lay a glove on them.

Best, Joe

LAGARDELLE, 24170 ST LAURENT-LA-VALLEE, FRANCE.
20.7.2014.
Dear Joe,

There used to be a sign on penny-in-the-slot machines on English piers which said "For Amusement Only." This promised that there were no prizes and that you were throwing your money away, just for the brief fun of it. In that spirit, I start with an appendage to the story of Daniel Mendelsohn's Cavafy translation. After the *TLS* had denied me the right to respond to his protracted self-glorification, I had a feeling of having been kicked into touch, if not oblivion, by those supposedly on my own side. I was redeemed by the letter from Gerald Messadié, of which I sent you a slice or three. He proved not only a prompt ally but a well-informed one, both on account of his 1931–1951 youth in pre-Nasser Alexandria, and also because he is the author of a considerable number of serious works on religion, literature and allied pursuits.

Since he gave me leave, I copied his letter and wrote one of my own to Master Mendelsohn, as well as enclosing my fifteen single-spaced pages of detailed notes taken, *au-jour-le-jour,* as I was conning his versions and comparing them with the Greek of which he claimed them to be reliable translations. I concluded by thrusting a little Ezra Pound up his ass in the form of "Pull down thy vanity, I say, pull down." Denied a private address, I mailed the packet to his London publishers, Harper/Collins, writing clearly on the front: "PLEASE forward unopened, Strictly Personal." For amusement only, guess what. You're right: the envelope was returned to me, with an unsigned note written in the first person, saying that it had been "opened in error and passed by mistake from office to office," before Mendelsohn instructed said person unknown to return it to me. For further amusement, count the number of unworthy acts in this base little tale. Mercantile publishers with no honor are matched by a "scholar" who cannot be wrong and for whom the evidence of someone else's careful attention to his work is assumed to be not worth a glance.

Shocked? A little. Surprised? Get out of here, as you people are known to say. What then was to be done? There is not a single publication in London where any interest could be shown in boating against the current or parading knowledge, however rudimentary, of modern Greek or of a great poet in that tongue. Then it occurred to me that I might have an ally in Oxford, where Craig Raine sits in the editorial chair of *Areté*. Craig told me that he had considered reviewing the chouchou of Master Silvers and the *NYRB* nocturnal council, but "decided against—not worth giving such a poor effort the oxygen of controversy. I thought (as I remember) that Mendelsohn was fustian, replete with archaisms, inversions, stale poeticisms . . ." He has kindly allowed me to quote him.

Now M. Messadié and Craig have been joined, under my tattered banner, by an e-pistle out of the blue from a ranking American critic, who prefers that I not name him in public: "You're enormously invigorating on Cavafy and Mendelsohn. I don't think anybody on this side of the Atlantic has the nerve to say even a word against Daniel Mendelsohn at this point; he's become a sort of sacred cow of the literati, some perfect blend of *NYRB* sanctimonious, homoerotic sentimental, and bestselling Holocaust memoirist. I think you were perfectly accurate and just. The air has been cleared. Many, many cheers!"

My son Stephen has just sent me a copy of a letter written by Stanley Kubrick in 1970 in which he warns the then head of MGM, James T. Aubrey Jr., not to proceed with a sequel to *2001, A Space Odyssey*, even though he does have the legal right to do so. Stanley goes on: "I own the tapir bone from 2001 . . . if you ever attempt to make the sequel I will cram that femur up your ass so far up it will take an as yet undiscovered alien super-intelligence to figure how to dislodge it. Seriously, don't fuck with me." This is followed by—what else?—"Best regards, ." It's worth going out to buy a hat just to take it off to Mr. K.'s ghost. Do you own a hat? I wore one, a Homburg already, to be married in; since then I never had one my size. I suspect that, in your editorial headgear, you would suggest deleting K.'s last sentence, which anyone might have written, though rarely to Massa Aubrey. Kubrick's little (possibly faked) diatribe reminds me of an ex-U.S. Navy remittance man with whom I played poker in southern Spain, round about the time that Ernest kept his promise and beat Gary Cooper to the barn. When (easily) provoked, Bill used an expression "Up yours with a hay-rake, Jack" which, in my anglicized ignorance I had never heard before. I ain't heard it since either; so tell me, y'all, is it a commonplace in Styron country?

Stanley K. was not always the most admirable of men, but there was a kind of intransigence in his self-involvement (not at all the same thing as selfishness or vanity) which few dare to match. I have said boo to a few geese (gooses are something else entirely), but I have a tendency to seek reconciliation even with those to whom I have, at first, reacted with cold rage. I had a long correspondence, years ago, with a Catholic priest, one Father Geary, who wrote to protest at my measured indictment of Pope Pius XII, whom Geary regarded as a savior of a rather precise number, in the high eight hundred thousands, of Jews. How then could I depict his Holiness (Hollowness?) as a villainous trimmer? How could I not, the class is asking, and I did indeed respond unapologetically; but with enough politeness to keep the dialogue going. The music, you will remember, goes round and round; and so it did, until I had filled a dossier with Father G.'s patient screeds and pro-Pius offprints. I then pulled the plug, conscious that nothing I had said, in really nice terms, had had the smallest impact on my correspondent.

Conan Doyle's *The Greek Interpreter* has a paradigmatic passage in which the said interpreter is put in a closed hansom cab and driven, it seems, quite a long way, before being taken to do whatever translation he has been rented to supply. Sherlock Holmes divines that the journey was long in time, but short in crow-flown distance, i.e., round in circles; don't ask me why it mattered a damn. So it was with Father G., as it had been with my late brother-in-law, while he was an unredeemed Communist, his shelves brown with floppy tracts from the Left Book Club and the even lefter Lawrence and Wishart's Works of Lenin and kindred page-turners. In discussion, one had the illusion that ground was being covered and that one was, as they will say, getting somewhere, whereas in truth . . . *yiro, yiro,* as Greeks say when they go round in circles. Yet I remain an unredeemed Man of Reason. Even though I am promised that Wittgenstein is now one more old hat, I cannot but seek to elicit what makes people think and say what they do, in the antique hope that they will come to see, of their own free will, that their views are addled.

I can find it in myself not to envy you your biblical gig. You had the fictioneer's instinct to select Job, on whom my once fervently admired, still admirable, René Girard wrote a voluminous gloss. It sits on my shelves with the rest of his stuff, but I could offer only the briefest synopsis unless granted revision time. If selected, I should choose to have some fun with Jonah's reluctance to go the whole way with the Lord's mission until the Big Guy splashed out and reminded him who was Boss. Jonah seems more likeable, and certainly human, for not doing the "Here am I, I send me" number as reported in a lyric selfie by Isaiah (there goes that song again).

Which leads me back to this book by Pierre Manent on Montaigne. His smart commentary prompts the guess that that Terentian slogan *Nihil Humanum A Me Alienum Puto,* inscribed on the *poutre* above Micheau's desk, is slyer than it seems. The emphasis, I suspect, should be on the *humanum*: the point being not only the obvious one that Montaigne does not regard any human emotion or desire, however gross or reprehensible, as beyond him. The unsaid corollary is: what *is* "alien"—because beyond sense—is the notion of a detachable, immortal (inhuman) soul which can be purified, as Pascal would wish, by repentance and believing on Jesus Christ. The more I read about Micheau, the more Hebraic his thinking—like that of Wittgenstein—becomes, if not 100% as W. confessed. This does not make M. any kind of crypto-Judaic "believer," but leaves him free to be honest. I like his trenchant tolerance and not least his acceptance of the consequences of age, amongst which he does not include "repentance" for youthful carnal indulgences. Our guy, I think.

Death and the archbishop never know when they are going to bump into each other. I have been transcribing my 1981 notebooks, for the upcoming—I hope—seventh volume and came across a passage about my translating partner, Kenneth McLeish's brush with mortality in Delphi in 1981. He collapsed at the end of a brilliant (and no doubt insistent) lecture by George Steiner, with whom he had spent some high quality time that afternoon. When asked by the Greeks whether he had had too much sun, the prostrate Ken could say only, "No, too much Steiner." Not bad last words, though he lived to say many more, thanks to the officer-like qualities of Geoffrey Kirk, a not very popular Professor of Greek at Cambridge, who played Paddy Leigh Fermor's commanding officer role and ordered up a helicopter to take Ken to Athens.

Tout à toi, Freddie.

July 26, 2014
Dear Freddie,

Your remarks about Daniel Mendelsohn, Craig Raine & Co. reminds me that I, in a distinctly un-Christian sense, love my enemies. Love may be a mite too strong; enamored of them won't quite do, either. Let me say that I am fond of them. One cannot, after all, correctly judge a man by who admires him. A better gauge is to be found in who hates him. My enemies— enemies too, is perhaps too imprecise a word, for these are not people I in the least fear, or even think much about—are none of them first-class people, merely people who think differently than I and tend to hold this difference against me. If in the last generation this list of people included Jacques Barzun, Hugh Trevor-Roper, Philip Larkin, William Barrett, and Sidney Hook, and a few others I should feel wretchedly, possibly even to the point of giving up the scribbling game. These men and others I admired have written, either in the public prints or in personal letters, about my writing in generous ways. (Barzun called me the William Hazlitt of our day; probably not true, but nice to hear all the same.) The people who have attacked me, on the other dirty finger-nailed hand, in print or spoken ill of me elsewhere, are not among those I would care to have as admirers. Their admiration could only bring on self-doubt. *Au contraire, mon frère*, they are perfectly right to despise me and I am not displeased they are around to remind me of my quality.

On this same subject, a review of *A Literary Education and Other Essays* that appears in the current issue of something called the *Los Angeles Review of Books*, written by a fellow named Sven Birkerts, suggests that I possess talent, wit, and style, yet goes on to assert that I really have nothing to say. I am, in this Birkerts's view, singing the same old songs, to none of which, it turns out, he can dance. The problem, he alleges, is that I am a man of the 1950s and he a man of the 1960s. The real problem, though, is that my opinions are not congruent with his greatly superior ones. I am pleased to report that S. Birkerts' review is not well written, nor is he, like many another Sven, big on humor. His criticism comes down to: we disagree, Epstein and I, therefore he is scum and hence must die. Ah me, oh well, and hey nonny nonny, in the supposed death-bed words of W. C. Fields, "On second thought, fuck 'im."

I don't claim to be impermeable to unpleasant criticism. As I grow older, though, the sting is considerably less. Perhaps I am sufficiently confident that what I write isn't entirely rubbishy. Perhaps I don't expect all that much from criticism to begin with. The whole praise-and-blame game may be near over for me. I have had more than my share of public—that is, printed—praise, but I cannot say that I have learned a lot from it. Mine is the paradoxical condition of wanting all the praise I can get, with the understanding that in the end none of it matters all that much. No one has told me anything essential about my writing that I didn't already know. No one who has attacked me in print has written anything close to crushing; nor has anyone caught me out at my genuine weaknesses. H. L. Mencken spoke wisely on the matter of being criticized when he said it is not injustice but justice that hurts. I have not yet been brought to justice.

You ask if I wear a hat. I own but do not too often wear hats. I not long ago bought a panama hat with a black ribbon, which I sometimes wear on excessively sunny, steamy summer Chicago days. In the winter I wear a cap—an eight-section cap, it is technically called. In America just now the great headgear is the baseball cap. Elderly men, young athletic women, infants, hermaphrodites all wear them. Their pervasiveness is such that I stay clear of them, lest I lose some of my cachet as a prominent reverse snob.

John F. Kennedy, it is said, helped kill the wearing of adult hats—fedoras, homburgs, porkpies—when he failed to wear a top hat to his inaugural. The hat would have spoiled his careful coif, I guess. From that point on men's hats became less and less *de rigueur*. My father wouldn't leave the house without his hat. A hatless man in public in our fathers' day was a less than fully dressed man. In rather better restaurants and in nightclubs there were "hat-check girls," with whom men left their hats. Today, if one wears an adult, or serious, hat, it is a considerable inconvenience. Hat racks rarely exist. Flying with a hat is impossible. The world is not organized for behatted gents.

I'm not sure why I find this a small but real subtraction. Wearing an adult hat lent a man a modicum of seriousness, marked him out as an adult. Adulthood these days is not every man's notion of a good time. When I began university teaching in my mid-thirties in 1973, not only hats but jackets and ties were abandoned by the younger professoriate. Jeans were the order of the day in classrooms. (Jeans and the Decline of Western Civilization—an essay waiting to be written.) With this fall, further slips came readily enough. Teachers began to call students by their first names in classrooms. ("What, precisely, did Nietzsche mean when he said that God was dead and man hovers on the edge of the abyss, Muffin?") Nor do they find any compunction in bonking these same students. Soon, the table nicely turned, students began addressing teachers by their first names. I recall a female student arrived in my office to complain about my putative severity in grading her papers, adding, as a clinching argument, that she had no such difficulty in the class she was taking with "Jerry," a teacher who, I had to assume, was, in the good earthy Yiddish word, probably *schtupping* her.

Because of this loosening of all the old formal bounds, when I began teaching in 1973, at the age of thirty-six, I had to make a wardrobe decision. I decided to stay with jackets and ties—bowties, as it happened—this chiefly because I wanted to put a bit of distance between the students and me. I also wanted to give the impression that, if pushkin came to shovekin, I might just be able to get a half-serious job outside the university, and had the wardrobe for it. I stuck with this costume through my thirty years, never removing my jacket in class, all the while addressing my students as Mr. and Miss, which they thought rather larky. My idea—and ideal—of the professor in those days, though I had no direct experience of them, was set by Lionel Trilling, Jacques Barzun, F. W. Dupee, all of them at Columbia, all possessed of what I thought the metropolitan spirit: one of urbanity, suavity, intellectual elegance. But the new academic standard in dress, carrying over to mental life, was one of high schlepperosity. The tone of the joint has been lowered considerably. Nor has it since then been raised. To this day in Evanston I sometimes sight former (you should pardon the expression) colleagues, in jeans, gym shoes, pea-caps in winter, baseball caps in summer, toting backpacks, and looking from behind no different than the students they teach. The only problem is that, from the frontal view, they show seventy-odd-year-old *punims*, creased and wrinkled in disappointment. They may live in a tower but there isn't anything ivory about it.

"Up yours with a hayrake, Jake" is entirely new to me, and a happy addition to my mental anthology of invective. Hayrake carries a nice rural flavor." In my high school one might announce as an exit line to someone with whom one has been arguing, "You know where it hangs, Tarzan, swing on it." In those same precincts, if someone mentioned that the fly of your trousers was open, the appropriate answer was, "There are only two kinds of people who'd notice that, and you're not a tailor." And for those who prefer a more stately meter, with rhyme added, there was always "Up your gigi with a lighted ciggy." This will give you only the merest sampling of what you missed by going to Charterhouse, wasting all that time on Greek and Latin, rather than to Chicago public schools, where such profane fundamentals were stressed.

You mention, with appropriate mockery, the phrase "page-turner," which one hears so often about current books, without your sensible mockery added. For myself I'd rather write a page-stopper, in which the reader pauses fairly often to consider an interesting point or striking metaphor or touch of style. The companion vogue word to page-turner is of course the phrase "good read," brought to us courtesy of the old trick of turning a verb into a noun, which puts the act of reading in the same league with a bonk or a bowel movement.

I was going to add that the only read used as a noun I care to contemplate is the proper noun Sir Herbert Read, whose own books, as I recall from youthful struggles with one or two of them, were distinctly neither page-turners nor good reads. Max Beerbohm certified this for me years ago when he wrote:

Honorable Doctor Dryasdust,
Look to your laurels, you really must.
You are so very moist indeed,
When one compares you with Herbert Read.

Sir Herbert was redeemed for me, though, by a story my friend Erich Heller used to tell about a young Colin Wilson—how many people still alive will remember that name?—then a nervous novice social climber, approaching Sir Herbert Read at a drinks party to tell him how very much he admired his book *The Nude*. "Actually," Sir Herbert replied, "I didn't quite write that one."

I'm seven or eight issues behind on my *TLS*s, but it strikes me that I've not seen a George Steiner piece there for a good while. I always read Steiner for comic relief. The pretentiousness beyond all possible pretentiousness, the exuberantly dark views, the polyglottery laid on not with a trowel but a bulldozer—Steiner provided lots of laughs of a kind no one else on earth can hope to provide. Should he pre-decease me, I shall miss him.

Not having met George Steiner, I do not have it in me to wish him ill. I wish him well, as the Jews in the Pale were said to remark of the Tsar, but not too close to me. I have had other writers, whom I have met, who I wished ill. Alfred Kazin was among them. A number of years ago I heard that he had a severe heart attack, and felt a touch of remorse. "I really loathe this man," I told Barbara, "but not enough to wish him dead." She paused, then said, "I understand. You merely wish him a great deal of stress." Exactly! I wanted his children to dislike him, I wished him complicated divorces—he had, I subsequently learned from his journals, both of these stress-inducers in ample supply—trouble with his feet, little things like that. I say, ain't malice grand?

I think I've noted that I keep a bedside book and a bathroom book along with books nearly everywhere else in our apartment. I say "nearly" because I recall reading that Harry Wolfson, the great figure in Jewish scholarship at Harvard and a lifelong bachelor, kept books in his oven and in his refrigerator. (One assumes he ate all his meals out.) I also keep a book, usually a novel, in my car, reading a paragraph or two at stoplights, a bit more than that in the occasional traffic jam I encounter. The last book I read in this fashion—and finished earlier in the week—has been V. Nabokov's *Transparent Things*. And very disappointing it was. Some years ago a rabbi named Harold Kushner wrote a hugely best-selling book titled *When Bad Things Happen to Good People*. I have a notion for a worst-selling book called *When Good Writers Write Bad Books*. *Transparent Things* qualifies. A novel without a plot, a satisfying ending, a single interesting character, it contains thirty or so amusing sentences and a fistful of exotic words. Did the consummate artist in Volodya fail to note this? Was there something strange in the water at Montreux? Something, clearly, went wrong. *Transparent Things* has now been replaced in the front seat of my car by Walker Percy's *Lancelot*.

We were invited to dinner this past weekend at the home of Gary Saul Morson and his wife Katie Porter. Both are sweet characters; he is a superior Slavicist, she a psychiatrist and the daughter of the painter Fairfield Porter. Before dinner, over drinks, I mentioned the parlor game I have decided to call Movie Miscasts, and Saul Morson said, instanter, Danny DeVito as Pierre Bezhukov in *War and Peace*. Untoppable. Game over.

Best, Joe

LAGARDELLE. 27.7.14.
Dear Joe,

Events in "the Middle East" have been somewhat loudly ignored in our exchanges, perhaps because there is nothing wise and eloquent or at all new to say about them. You were succinct in your support of Israel and I was/am happy to take the same line, that of what football fans call "a loyal supporter," the kind who continues to yell for our side in good times and in bad, as Babar the elephant puts it, despite any questionable tactics of players and management. Am I about to play the squeamish part and deplore what Israel has done, is doing and is prepared, it seems, to do again? I *am* squeamish and, no, I am not about to withdraw my support, as if it mattered except, perhaps, in the great phantom battle which, as usual, attends any evidence that Israel/the Jews (the distinction on which Jacqueline Rose and co insists serves only to underline the linkage) has/have done anything to defend themselves.

One has only to imagine what the BBC, CNN or Sky News reporter would have said if he or (more often now) she had been in Hamburg, Berlin, Leipzig or wherever else during The War, when allied bombers came in and dropped their loads on "innocent" civilians. Of course, attempts have been made, more or less eloquent, more or less in good faith, to accuse the Allies of being as bad as the Nazis in their "indiscriminate" bombing; but the ability of the media to play the part of venal Homeric gods, at once in the battle and above it, did not exist until the New Technology and the new vocabulary, in which fine feelings, of humane meta-Christian sentiments, are purveyed by journalists whose finesse rarely steps outside parameters acceptable to their paymasters.

The British have raised many memorials to their war dead, but were reluctant to do so in the case of Bomber Command; both its higher officers and the crews, of whom about a third, perhaps more, died on their very dangerous missions, were—until very recently—little honored. What they did seemed callous; the bombs fell alike on the just and the unjust. Few remarked that the allied raids, justified and effective or not (Albert Speer went against the *bien-pensant* script and confessed that the raids had been greatly disruptive of German production), were *preceded*, by quite a long period, by the German/Nazi raids on Warsaw, Rotterdam and other targets which, at the time, were not in "enemy" territory and were producing nothing to threaten the security of the Reich.

However denunciatory, it is noteworthy that none of the revisionists emphasized, or even mentioned, how many *children* died in the Allied raids. Whatever bully-boyishness was implied, the British and the Americans tend to be spared the suggestion that they particularly targeted children. It requires no very elaborate analysis of the not very sub text to see that, when it comes to Israel, the blood libel has been recycled, by nice journalists with humane consciences, to fit today's circumstances. I shall, as lecturers used to say, come back to this.

German indignation at the destruction of Berlin continued into the last days of the war and beyond. As I mention in my current autobiographical number, a clubman friend of mine, who was in Special Forces of some kind, told me in 1981 how . . .

"very late in the war, the R.A.F. had bombed two ships which were at anchor in a Baltic bay. They were, in fact, prison ships with 'Displaced Persons' on board. After the ships sank, the S.S. shot any prisoners who managed to swim ashore. Soon afterwards, British commandos captured Schleswig-Holstein; they found dozens of bodies washed up or left on the shore.

The German Field-Marshal Milch had surrendered to Tyldesley-Jones (then an acting brigadier) in order to avoid capture by the Russians. Arrogant and bombastic, he insisted that the British and the Germans should have united to destroy the 'Bolshevik savages.'

'Savages? What about your concentration camps?'

'For Slavs and such creatures,' Milch said.

'I want you to come for a walk with me.' The Brigadier led the Field-Marshal to the shore where the bodies had been heaped by the tide.

'Well?'

'Look closely,' Tyldesley-Jones said. 'Each of these men was murdered.'

Milch sniffed and bent to inspect the bodies. Each had a bullet wound in the temple. After he had looked at three or four, he burst into tears and sat on the wet beach."

This credible (*quia incredibile*) anecdote comes from a man—known as "Tiddly"—of no high intelligence but of a British order, of decency and truthfulness, of a kind which may still exist, in antique pockets, but has largely yielded to the fabricators of the shit-culture known as the media. Yes, the Medes did get through, the fanciful might say *fra parentesi*, just as Cavafy perceived; among them are those, such as Master Mendelsohn, who put a false construction on the very texts which they claim to translate. The triumph of whatever is said to be "appropriate," whether in conduct or in speech, has led to the meshing of news and comment and to the corruption of truth and honesty by columnists and solemnists, rough and smooth, whose business it is to moralize in whatever style will preserve their readership or lubricate their penny-a-lining facility. A recent example, re the present hostilities in the Muddle East, was sent to me by an ex-Leftist of amiable intentions and hopes. A *Guardian* journalist called Jonathan Freedland claims to be citing an old colleague:

"This conflict is the political equivalent of LSD—distorting the senses of all those who come into contact with it, and sending them crazy." He was speaking chiefly of those who debate the issue from afar: the passions that are stirred, the bitterness and loathing that spew forth, especially online, of a kind rarely glimpsed when faraway wars are discussed. While an acid trip usually comes in lurid colours, here it induces a tendency to monochrome: one side is pure good, the other pure evil–with not a shade of grey in sight.

But the LSD effect also seems to afflict the participants in the conflict. They too can act crazy, taking steps that harm not only their enemy but themselves. Again and again, their actions are self-defeating."

Good intentions are manifest here and so is the futility of their expression in falsely analogical terms. LSD, if I know anything about it, is a hallucinatory drug, taken voluntarily, sometimes (so Aldous Huxley claimed) enabling you to see the world in colors more lurid and exhilarating than normal—in Aldous's case sub-normal—sight can supply. Those who "drop" (as the word used to be) acid do occasionally suppose that they can fly, but seldom, if ever, delude themselves into thinking that they are, or possess, rockets with which to destroy their enemies.

The seeming even-handedness of Freedland's anonymous source is central to the Mercutio Complex, a chronic condition of today's Median Man: the plague he wishes on both sides makes him the only sane man with his brave head on the (cushioned) block. It is, generally speaking, more than his or her life or job is worth to come out clearly with an analysis which goes beyond the enumeration of typical horrors. Since, as Ed Luttwak has been forthright enough to say, the Israelis are better trained, have precise targets in their sights, and—unfair rather—better defenses for their civilian population, it is not surprising that (a) they suffer fewer casualties and that (b) they seem more, yes, callous than the enemies whose only ambition is to exterminate them. Hamas would like nothing better than to do to all Israelis (and all Jews) precisely what the media like to make out is what Israel is deliberately doing to schools, hospitals and, yes, that blameless organization known as "the U.N.," whose agencies perpetuate the myth that all that lies between mankind and happy days is the wicked doctrine of Zionism. Do I go too far? Is it far enough? I doubt it.

Among D.H. Lawrence's least read books (Frank Leavis's darling is now so thoroughly out of fashion that he must be worth another look) is *Fantasia of the Unconscious.* No one can be blamed if he or she is still waiting for the musical. It was difficult for even Leavis's Scrutineers to mount a reasoned defense of the crackpot text in which Lawrence imagined himself to come into clear about his vision of the human condition and reveal himself, *coram publico,* as a nutcase. If the grace of God doesn't hold, or better offers don't come along (oh that person from Porlock, how we do wonder what keeps him!), I can imagine being guilty of a similar self-certifying number. That of John Fowles was entitled *The Aristos* and paraded the self-esteem of a certain kind of writer, Henry Williamson another, whose conceit was best expressed, in the British style, by a cataloguer's knowledge of local flora and fauna: Tarka the otter and who and what all else. However wrongly or rightly, I have an unashamed feeling that The Greens are all, pretty well, officious *fascisants* under the po-faces, eager—like Pol-Pot—to send us into the fields and have us learn our lesson while picking pineapples with our bare hands.

My nutty book will begin with a recap of Raul Hilberg's strangely, perhaps wisely, callous-seeming study of the Destruction of the European Jews. I might be foolish enough to make mention of the indifference of the Walrus and Carpenter (as I have dared to call them), the British and the Americans, to the actual process of mass murder. How shall we (ah we!) account for the quantity of their tears and the failure to do anything practical to impede Hitler's, oh, crusade? Should we mention how F.D.R. gave the representatives of "the Jews" just one half-hour of his precious wartime time? Churchill did at least, and at most, instruct Anthony Eden, his right-hand manikin, to see to it that something was done; but was it? A happy logic, which required all Allied actions to be of military utility, entailed that the gas chambers were no proper target. Yes, yes, old ground.

My fantasia will go on to suggest that the discovery that some Jews had escaped extermination was not the best news that anyone on the victorious side got to hear. The crudest reaction was that of the new socialist British Foreign Secretary, handsome Anthony Eden's unhandsome replacement Ernest "give us a kiss, darling" Bevin, who—made aware of the desperate desire of survivors to reach Eretz Israel—said, "We're not 'avin' the Jews pushing to the front of the queue." The not all that repressed wish was, and is, that *all* Jews had disappeared.

Yes, yes, we all know, some of us, and others of us do wish we/you would stop "banging on about it." But here's where my fantasia kicks in. The Holocaust did, in the event, have a deeply alarming consequence: Hitler's crusade against the Jews whom Martin Luther had marked down for punitive/exterminatory treatment was so appalling in its reluctantly revealed cruelty that Christianity itself and its God, triune or whatever He/They were supposed to be, were hauled, if briefly, into question. There was an attempt to give Christianity some kind of a new look; it can be seen, for petty instance, in the poster-boy crucifixion which Graham Sutherland painted for the rebuilt Coventry Cathedral, which had been hit by the wicked

Huns almost certainly because it stood, through no fault of its own, in a heavily industrialized midland city. Christianity did take a toss in the 1940s. The assumption among post-war planners/hopers of almost all stripes, red or blue or in-between, was that religion was Not The Answer.

Karl Popper's advertisement for the Open Society scarcely mentioned religion or God, let alone Allah. Civilization was going, it seemed, to turn away from the God Whom Mr. Eliot did not find strange. Reason and institutional decency would prevail. History was now bound to be secular. Need I go on? What my old idol René Girard says in his *Job,* which your last letter prompted me to revisit, is the same old story about the same old story: "the scapegoat mechanism" lies (aha!) at the foundation of all societies, civilized or not.

The singular role of the deicide Jews is so important, so *reliable,* in the language of [western] morals (and of Judaeo-Christianity's parody, Islam) that not even the unabashed, unapologetic militancy of the Holocaust's survivors (any number of whom were, of course, denied access to the U.S. or to the U.K.) could be allowed for long to render obsolete the role of "the Jews," in the language of morals and the machinery of Christian self-importance. If Yeats's center is to hold, Jews have to be victims, as they deserve: it's in the Book. When they defend themselves, or strike at their enemies, Our Values are put in question and Islam's too. Long live the Yellow Star and the blood libel with it. We can all be one in Knowing Who Is To Blame. Facts and commentary, history and myth have their double and redoubled helices, twist round each other and provide readings which reinforce and confirm the governing principle.

Cut forward to a slice of contemporary, contemptible life, as conveyed to me by an intellectual/ex-academic close friend. He writes of a British media celebrity:

". . . talks loudly to be overheard, an utter show-off, with a raucous common laugh which he projects across the room in order to dominate his surroundings. A contemptible swank, as Carthusians & Paulines used to say. He sauntered out of the dining room once or twice, probably to smoke a fag, and glanced sideways with a smirk to judge the effect he made. He was at Dulwich with Paul Ettedjui, whom probably you know well from films. At Dulwich Ettedjui and his brother suffered from the last syllable of their surname rhyming with their race. Almost every day Master X would sidle up behind them and whisper in their ear, 'Gas the lot of them!'"

The Ettedjuises' father's name was Joseph, founder of the U.K. fashion house of the same name as his and yours. So it goes, on and on. My point being . . . Dear God, is that the bell for lunch? How fortunate for you and our readers that Raphael must now put away his mania and return to the middle of the road, in which position he can be put down by traffic coming in both directions!

Tout à toi, Freddie.

August 2, 2014
Dear Freddie,

I much like your attack upon the Medes, or media jerks, and could not agree with it more. Dante speaks of a circle in hell reserved for those who declare neutrality about things on which one cannot possibly be neutral. Of course the Medes only pretend to neutrality. Although the cumulative effect of their reporting from Gaza is clearly anti-Israeli, I'm not certain that they, Mede for Mede, necessarily line up in favor of the Palestinians in the current Israeli-Palestinian fight. Hot copy is their desideratum, and the copy is much hotter on the Gazan side of border.

Television Medes are great heroes in American culture. Every spring they are called up in disproportionate numbers to give commencement addresses; honorary degrees—long ago drained of all honor by having been given to plutocrats and politically correct dopes—are bestowed upon them. Some among them are considered our great American *chachem*, or wise men. Edward R. (always that R.) Morrow is a saint of journalism; Walter Cronkite was another Mede genius; a weightless fellow named Tom Brokaw, now in semi-retirement, is coming up fast on the outside. Diane Sawyer, wife of Mike Nichols, is about to retire from her Mede perch as anchorwoman on ABC, where her specialty has been extreme yet less than convincing feminine empathy.

On the major American television networks the salaries these characters draw are in the multi-millions. On local television stations in large cities the so-called "anchors," with a bit of seniority, make in the high six figures and possibly more. The qualifications for the job, for men, seem to be possession of a careful coif, an absence of any subtlety, and a tiresome cheerfulness; qualifications for women are roughly the same, with an ample bosom being no handicap and an age limit, I should guess, set at fifty or so. High-paid, well-groomed dolts is what they all chiefly are.

Among both the national and local television newscasters, I have noted a new trend. "If it bleeds it leads," was an old slogan in American journalism, which meant that stories of violence were featured. This still stands but now alongside it the Medes like to feature bits where people sob on camera. ("If they weep, it keeps.") So they send their myrmidons and myrmidonnas out to the scene of tornadoes, floods, wildfires, there to jam microphones into the faces of victims to ask how they feel now that their homes and sometimes their families have been wiped out. The victims—now twice victims for agreeing to talk to the Medes—naturally tear up and break down. That's a wrap—also a warp.

What makes the Gaza story so delightful to the Medes is that nearly every Palestinian, and Palestinian women especially, is a prince or princess of wail. Wail they do, emphatically—before Allah certainly, but before Median cameras most especially. "Tell it to Hamas," I rejoin from my chair before our television set when I hear Palestinian women exclaim their sad victimhood. After capturing these cameo performances, the Medes are happily off to photograph wounded children, families weeping over caskets, Palestinian lads throwing rocks at Israeli tanks. Wearing helmets and bullet-proof vests, the Medes comment portentously, before going back to the hotel for drinks, dinner, and a warm bed. It's a living.

I read Raul Hilberg's *The Destruction of The European Jews*, lo, fifty years ago, when, caught up in the controversy surrounding Hannah Arendt's *Eichmann in Jerusalem*, I sought to educate myself, at least a little, about the Holocaust. I read Hilberg in an edition with small print and double columns on each page. Read it is perhaps a euphemism; I staggered through it. Around the same time I also read Elie Wiesel, Emmanuel Ringleblum, Primo Levi, and everything else I could find on the subject. (Years later, in Lev Grossman's novel *Life and Fate*, I read the most stirring account in fiction I know of the Holocaust.) I did not become expert, but read enough to understand how hard-hearted and wrong-headed Arendt's book is.

I also read somewhere along the way that it was not uncommon for people who had probed too deeply in the literature of the Holocaust to attempt suicide. I believe it. No greater inducement to crunching depression is available than contemplating the mechanics of the Holocaust. I cannot to this day bear to look at those 1940s newsreel films that show the skeletal inhabitants of Auschwitz and other German-constructed hellholes freed by Allied troops, or the piles of corpses and bones and bits of booty shown in the background. Unspeakable, unthinkable, these words, on this subject, carry true weight.

I dragged myself to see the Holocaust movies: *Life is Beautiful* with Roberto Benigni and *The Pianist* with Adrien Brody and of course *Schindler's List*, the white ass upon which Steven Spielberg no doubt hopes one day to ride into Jerusalem dressed in the garments of a serious man. None quite succeeds, the Spielberg failing rather more dramatically than the other two. (The agent Sue Mengers is supposed to have entered the large living room of a Hollywood party, surveyed the occupants, and muttered, "Schindler's B List.") When in Israel, I walked round Yad Vashem, the Holocaust history center, in a half-dazed state. A Holocaust Museum and Education Center has gone up in Skokie, Illinois, fewer than five miles from our apartment, which I have no desire ever to visit. A character in an Isaac Bashevis Singer story remarks, "You can have too much, even of kreplach." The same applies, much more stringently, to the subject of the Holocaust.

The Holocaust is not a subject for pischers or bullshitters or George Steiner. Ultimately it may be a subject that qualifies for the "Vas ya dere, Sharlie?" question, though soon there will no longer be anyone left in the world who can answer the question positively. I cannot say that I walk the streets with the Holocaust even at the back of my mind. But Israel-Palestine brings it the forefront, for the Israelis, as has often enough been said, have only one war to lose; and God forfend they should lose it.

In keeping with the matter of subjects that ought to be out of bounds to pischers and bullshitters, there is a piece in the current (August 4, 2014) *New Yorker* about a poet named Edward Hirsch who has written a 75-page elegy on the death of his twenty-two-year-old adopted son through an overdose of drugs. Hirsch is the head of the grant-giving Guggenheim Foundation, and is himself the recipient of a MacArthur Fellowship, and other perfunctory prizes that poets, in careful alternation, give one another in these days that finds poetry at best an intramural sport.

Featured in the article is Edward Hirsch's grief at the death of his adopted son. The samples of the poem he has written that are printed in the piece are strikingly unimpressive. The sad fact is that nothing Hirsch says makes one believe in his grief. The reason one doesn't is that he is so open and public, so ready to rattle on and on, about it.

The real story, which seems to have passed over the head of the *New Yorker* writer, is that Hirsch and his wife in adopting acquired a sadly defective child, a not infrequent occurrence. Adoption is always a crap shoot; one never knows what one is getting, and in our day often the sad women who give up their children have serious problems of their own—drugs and alcoholism not least among them—that has left their children with mental problems of the most serious kind. The child Hirsch and his wife adopted turns out to have had what was at first diagnosed as Tourette's; then he had seizures, and epilepsy became one possibility, autism another. Every kind of school for the child was tried, all sorts of therapies undergone, but with no luck. The poor boy couldn't sit still. He grew into a wild kid, and began to experiment with drugs and run with the worst people. His father, in the fashion of our day, keeps telling him that he loves him, which of course doesn't much help. His mother, from whom our poet is now divorced, is very much a background figure in this article, as I am confident she wasn't in trying to raise this child against all the stacked odds of bringing him round to a normal life. Doubtless the manifold horrors of living with the child's problems helped to break up the marriage, though we are told that Hirsch now has "a partner." Early in the article the wife tells the author of the *New Yorker* article that the boy's life and death are too painful for her to discuss, and chooses not to be interviewed. She also "feels strongly that they are no one's business but hers and Hirsch's." She couldn't be righter. The poet, on the other hand, reports on his own emotional temperature: "slowly, I became stronger. I wasn't healing, but I was stronger." Edward Hirsch, clearly, is not the man his wife is.

Before the boy's death, we are told, Hirsch had written only two poems about him. Personal poet though he styles himself, he allows that "it didn't seem like a child was fair game [to write about] the way your parents are." He must have decided otherwise after the boy's death, and the poem, completed and sent off to the firm of Alfred A. Knopf, is to be published next month. One fellow poet calls it "a masterpiece of sorrow," another affirms that it deals with "material that is psychically dangerous."

An old joke has a middle-aged Jewish gent recount to a friend a prostitute's approaching him with the offer of inexpensive sex. Ten dollars is the price, but because it is so cheap they must do it in a nearby alley. In the alley, she takes the ten dollars from the man and instructs him to drop his trousers. When he does so, she runs off with his ten dollars. "What did you do then?" the friend to whom he is telling the story asks. "Shouldn't be a total loss," the man replies, "I urinated." I wonder if the phrase, "Shouldn't Be A Total Loss" might not make a good title for Edward Hirsch's poem. The real point of the poem, I feel fairly certain, is to exhibit its author's deep sensitivity.

Forgive me for going on so about all this, but I feel this poem and the *New Yorker* article about its author mark another substantial slippage in contemporary culture. That a major publishing house will be publishing such a work and that a magazine once known for setting a standard of urbanity promotes it cannot be a good thing.

Against my father's sound advice never to run away from business, I have decided not to write about a passage or book of the Bible for a collection of such pieces to be called *The Good Book*. I decided to drop the project altogether. I can do high-level schmooze as well as the next bozo, but I have decided I do best to stay away from schmoozing about the Bible, where my scholarship is nil and my ignorance genuinely impressive. I subsequently learned that the man chosen to write the introduction to the book is of such (to him) bearable lightness of being as to make me look a combination of Hegel, Kant, and Wilamowitz. Forgive me for disobeying, father, but this is a bit of business from which I must run away.

This morning I began a novel called *The Five* by, of all people, Vladimir Jabotinsky, the Zionist leader who, as you know, founded, among other Jewish defense organizations, the Irgun. I was put on to it through listening to an interview with Hillel Halkin, whose book on Yehuda Halevi you wrote about for *Commentary*. In this interview Halkin, whom I respect, calls *The Five* a masterpiece. The novel is set in Odessa in the early years of the last century before the Russian Revolution. Odessa was of course also the home of Isaac Babel, who set his Benya Krik stories there, and also of a rich stream of Jewish violinists. Of Moscow and St. Petersburg every amateur student of Russian literature is acquainted, but less is known about Odessa, where something like a Jewish middle class was allowed to flourish. The novel begins brilliantly. I shall read it over the next week with my morning tea and toast. Always splendid to have a good previously unknown novel going. Nice thing about the reading life, as you will have noticed, is that one is never out of business for long.

Best, Joe

LAGARDELLE, 24170 ST LAURENT-LA-VALLEE, FRANCE. 4.8.2014.
Dear Joe,

I mentioned last week that there is a nutty book to be written, somewhat in the Lawrencian manner. IN EARLIER EPISODES (working title, as they will say) would trace the low dishonesty of the post-war decades (lowness and dishonesty being by no means limited to Auden's 1930s) by joining up the dots re the fact of and responses to the Holocaust, the creation of the European Union and the "crusader" state of Israel. It will not claim to be a work of history but a psychic profile of what has not been said about the underlying, especially European sub-conscious and the return of the repressed and or the end of remission.

The Franco-German rapprochement, represented yesterday by François Hollande holding hands with the gentlemanly German President, presumably because *la* Merkel was too busy, is a vestige of the whole honourable, business-like attempt, inaugurated by the unimpeachable, impeccable Robert Schumann and Jean Monnet, to make sure that the Great War III would never take place between European powers. It seemed a small price to pay, and there might even be big dividends to be drawn, in fostering common interests and, incidentally, obliterating antique antagonisms. *"Enrichissez-vous,"* François Guizot said, back in the 19th century, when it was seen that, in his new electoral register, only a small, well-heeled number of people were eligible to vote. Post-1945 Europeans planned, consciously, to get rich after which all other things, moral lustre included, would be added unto them.

At the same time, but never admittedly, guilt re the Holocaust had to be found a place under the heavy, tightly woven carpet, which became the European Union. Nothing wrong with this noble endeavour, except that it insisted that the lion was not only going to lie down with the lamb, or the sheep, but also that there were no lions and no sheep, but some new animal altogether, the European goodybeest. Henceforth there would be neither north or south, neither east nor west (and we will never again mention Aryans, will we?). The treaty of Rome created a kind of secular Catholicism, in which we would not talk bawdy, as Robert Walpole recommended, so that all might join in, but rather make money, which doesn't smell, though a lotta humans seem to have a nose for it. Economics would create the homogenised, pacific Europe which neither nationality nor religion had ever generated. Even the 1968 students bought into altogether-boyishness by shouting *"Nous sommes tous des juifs allemands."* Meaning, no they weren't, but they'd like victim status and the attendant perks.

The replacement of "race" by allegiance, to an Ideal, of Unity, had a certain precedent among you people over there: whether or not Lincoln's war was legally justified or on the side of Progress, it had torn the U.S. in half and then put it together, with rough stitches, in a way which, whatever the scars and occasional rips, seemed to hold. Why remark that, under the star-spangled banner, all kinds of divisions remained, nicely occluded, race below all? The long humiliation of black Americans being beyond dispute, it is ignoble to argue about who had the worse deal, historically, Jews or Blacks. It is of the nature of such matters that, in the U.S., the two pariah groups should, at first, make some kind of common cause. To put things more truthfully than modern humbug finds "appropriate" (what else?), the Jews supplied the cutting edginess—Dorothy Parker's for instance, in those happy old days—and the legal savvy. This is not to say that there were no smart or fine black voices, Paul Robeson's not least, but Yankee Jews were able to claim, with justice, to be speaking for a principle, not for themselves, which was convenient as well as true.

What happened later—cue them glorious Sixties!—was that Black emancipation declared itself first by denouncing the most accessible, least dangerous of its enemies, i.e. its allies, the Jews. Blacks would not be mature, free-standing Men until, first off, they turned and rended their false "fathers." Poor Lenny Bernstein attempted to keep the alliance going, by paying those "reparations" which Tom Wolfe was there to ridicule in his radical chic number. The Wolfe in white clothing was on the money; and the money was soon on him, but that's another story. The "socialism" which came out of Lenny's drawing room, and did not quite dare speak its full name, began to be spelt out, at lengthy length, in the *NYRB.*, which—if I am right—grew in self-importance as the kids' "revolution" began to lose its dervishness, round about the same time that the draft was aborted. Within the Silvers' cabal, two strands emerged, not wholly unpredictable, old man: first snobbery, expressed in the recruitment of posh English academics to supply needed "bottom" (Isaiah B., Trevor-Roper and who all else, all the way down to Bernard Bergonzi) and to prove that "we" can hire and fire the best people; and then, *fra poco*, anti-Israelism, which became kosher, after the 1967 war, when de Gaulle said of the Jews (not the Israelis) that they were *"Un peuple d'élite, sûr de lui-même et dominateur."* The new anti-Semitism sprang, as anti-Israelism, from the horse's nose.

Comedy and tragedy go, as frogs have been known to say, *bras-dessus, bras-dessous* in this utterance, since, with the last two "accusations," that Jews were "sure of themselves and dominating," de Gaulle might as well have been speaking of himself (how he wished that all three allegations were still true of France!). Indeed, *le grand Charles* affected surprise when Raymond Aron, who had rallied to de Gaulle in London in 1940, broke with him on account of what he claimed had been a "compliment." He told the truth, he lied; de Gaulle was, in fact, outraged that the Israelis had made a pre-emptive attack on, in particular, Egyptian airfields against his specific advice. The Israelis' main weapon of attack during those decisive raids was, of course, the French Mirage fighters which de Gaulle then ceased, officially at least, to export to them. De Gaulle had an atavistic "fear" of *les Juifs* which went back, on narrow-gauge twin-tracks, to St Louis's Catholicism and Charles Maurras's *Action française*. The comedy was that de Gaulle complained, in 1940, that "more Jews than Frenchmen" rallied to his call from London.

Between 1948 (when the Arabs failed, despite British encouragement, to strangle the little Heracles in its small cradle) and 1967, Israel had been almost every European's gallant little power, surrounded by enemies who outnumbered and threatened at any moment to engulf it. The French and British, splendidly and ingloriously in character, saw nothing wrong in making use of Israel in 1956 in order to fabricate a righteous excuse for invading Egypt. That embarrassing (because futile) episode kept Israel in the traditional Jewboyish role of underlings who could sometimes be let usefully out of their box, as long as they could then be folded back into it again (smartass sidebar: the slaves who died at the battle of Marathon were buried in a separate heap from true-born Athenians, but thanks all the same).

Post the 1967 victory and, as the moralists will hasten to say, Israeli failure to return the "occupied territories" to their proper owners (who had been allocated them by, precisely, the French and the British after the so-called Arab uprising, fertilised such as it was with much gold), the typically stiff-necked Jews, aka Israel, became pariahs of a slightly different stripe; but it was a comfort of a kind to be able to say that they *hadn't changed*. The difficulty and the difference was that sufferance was not at all the Israelis' style of badge. Having no sense of shame, they did not yield the pavement, as Freud's father did, to the out-of-my-way Gentile.

The *NYRB*. evolved a meta-version of the schism which divided U.S.Jews and Blacks. To prove how emancipated, outspoken and unintimidated by dated loyalists they were, the editors and attendant (well paid) in-group demonstrated their fearlessness by becoming *de facto* anti-Semites. You can't get more emancipated, Jew-wise, than that, can you? In this way, the N.Y.R.B. crowd could be brave and not risk the slightest bloody nose, although scratched backs were not uncommon, among the chosen. Flash back and you'll find that there were Jews for Adolf, early on; and now there were New Yorkers for Edward Said and Yes, sir, Arafat.

First Zionism and then Israel had had certain uses for the European powers until 1967. In line with the classic recipe, during and after the Great

War, the British divided the Middle East—it was closer to Whitehall in those days and was known as "the Near East," until the Brits backed off—the better to rule it. The victorious Europeans also broke up the Ottoman Empire—with spiteful officiousness, according to Elie Kedourie—and turned most of the Fertile Crescent into "occupied territories" on a very big scale. Swathes of land were then divided by dotted lines and allotted to handsome fellows with big teeth and robed pedigrees who were posted as kings in more or less ungovernable territories with incompatible inhabitants.

The notion of a National Home for the Jews had been mooted, in 1917, by the first-class-minded A.J. Balfour, less out of Christian concern for persecuted Jews than for fear that "Jewish finance"—the usual, overrated, many-armed, Argus-eyed bogeyman of anti-Semitic fancy—would dish the Allies and put its *gelt* on Germany. Once the Central Powers were disempowered, Balfour's promise had to be kept, unfortunately; the British were still that honourable, if they really had to be. Some new Jews were admitted to Palestine. Fortunately, not all that many wanted to go. Thus the Arabs were rewarded, big time, and menaced very gently, in order to keep them glad to have the British there to blow officious whistles and pump oil at discount rates.

Mr Glib Synopsis now switches attention to Woodrow Wilson, the greatest political quack of Almost Our Time, and his recipe for European pacification: Self-Determination. What snake did he get that oil from? Its salesman assume that the world was composed of "peoples" who had been cruelly divided, by imperial conglomerates (the Austro-Hungarians in particular), and thus denied a natural right to self-expressive self-government. W. Wilson's good intentions issued licences to huff-and-puffers, greatish or petty, to lay claim to the "leadership" of "nations" which had previously, more or less sulkily or happily, co-existed. The Europe of racist ranters and raving revanchistes was not far to seek. The only people who were not allowed to be "self-determining" were, yes, The Jews. No one had liked them before, but now they were certified outsiders, for economico-political as well as the ongoing religious reasons; fuck 'em twice over time. Plus they were Bolsheviks; make that three times, for luck.

It is, of course, extra-curricular to blame anyone but the Germans for the Holocaust, and somewhat bad history, in terms of practical, murderous enterprise. All the bloody same, quite a number of willingly ancillary folk, Ukrainians not least, were implicated, even if they now want out of the index. Today's Ukraine, scanned as psycho-history, again illustrates the principle that the first enemy should be the weakest enemy: in the 1930s, the

Ukrainians were starved in large numbers by Stalin and that nice Mr Khrushchev (who put Joe in the dock as soon as the latter was dead), which gave them occasion, under the Nazi aegis, to get manly by massacring unarmed Jews. Now the "self-determination" number allows Russian-speakers to claim a right to, yes, dependent independence: they clamour for V. Putin esquire kindly to put his arm through theirs and his foot on their fellow-citizens' necks. The old schizo-number runs again: Ukrainians prove how Russian they are by willingness to shoot other Ukrainians.

A British general (name can be checked somewhere) told Golda Meir, in post-war Jerusalem, that "the Jews" must have done *something* to deserve (key word) the fate they suffered in the war. She got quite nasty, sources tell us, at the "innocent" suggestion that, as very usual, the Jews, deep down, surely had only themselves to blame. Refusal to accept responsibility, whether for Jesus' death or the Black Death or whatever else you have on the charge sheet, is part of what makes Israelis so embarrassing, not least to civilised, out-of-range Jews who, in the standard figure, prefer co-religionists who do not make waves.

The present condition of Europe is, in my never-to-be-published view, the consequence of post-1945 decades of false consciousness—remember that old number?—in which the illusion of a common culture, common purposes, common values even has been fostered in a grandiose attempt to make European history begin again *after* the Shoah. Statisticians and economists, our new masters of the world's game and gamble, are expert at deciding at which point the new analysis will begin and the figures made to conform with some preconceived scheme. The whitening of the European consciousness (like René Girard's "scapegoat mechanism") need not have been a conscious consideration *chez* Monnet and Schumann, but would the attempt at amalgamation ever have even somewhat succeeded if it had not supplied a great mantle of forgetfulness and self-forgiving?

The only trouble, some might say, is that an inconvenient number of Jews survived what "we" arranged in order to consign the bad old Europe to the oubliette. Here's the scarcely buried sub-text, team: whatever may be said about the folly or otherwise of her policies, Israel now stands as an irritant, an unapologetic assertion that the Jews will not do what's best for them and, oh, "us" and . . . go quietly. The European need is for the myth to be redeemed: let them—the Jews—do something *typically* unforgivable, especially kill children, and we will then be let off history's hook because the Holocaust will become retrospectively justified. What is being done in Gaza is indeed appalling, disgraceful and the rest. I dread the sight of it, let alone the journo-facts, however slanted, but that it is being done suits more books than will ever be written.

Oh! Two men in white coats have just come to the door, asking for me. What can they want?

Tout a toi, Freddie.
August 11, 2014

Dear Freddie,

Not long after reading your last e-mail, I reread my copy of your 1989 Parkes Lecture, "The Necessity of Anti-Semitism," to which it stands as a brilliant coda. Of Jew-hating there is no end, nor, I all too strongly suspect, will there ever be. "How odd of God to choose the Jews," as the English journalist William Norman Ewer wrote. "He did so," some unknown genius poet responded, "because the goyim annoy him." And these same goyim, in their turn, have never stopped also annoying the Jews, though "annoying" doesn't quite serve to describe inquisitions, blood-libel trials, pogroms, the Holocaust, and the current wave of European anti-Semitism that finds its excuse in Israel's defending itself against Hamas terrorists in Gaza.

Ten or so years ago, for a series of books on the Seven Deadly Sins, I wrote a little book called *Envy*, which contained a brief chapter titled "Our Good Friends, the Jews." In this chapter I attributed much of the motive behind anti-Semitism to envy. The hatred of Jews, I argued, is always admixed with envy. Certainly this is so in the modern era, where the Jews, given a bit of air to breathe and room to maneuver, have shone forth so impressively, and in such disproportionately high numbers, in science, the arts, finance, scholarship, you name it. But the greatest of all Jewish achievements has been the state of Israel, where a small band of men and women built on sand a modern nation where centuries of Arab lethargy and English colonial effort could produce nothing but aridity and tribal hatred. What could be more enviable, and thus more hateful, than Israel to the rest of the world as it lapses into discontent and decline?

That this anti-Semitism has shown itself in Europe is scarcely shocking. Who, after all, is there among Europeans to stop it? Anti-Semitism lay in wait, even, as you suggest, in the person of Charles de Gaulle And, as you also say, with increasing Muslim populations in the European countries, encouragement exists for politicians to skulk and lay low rather than stand up for Jews. The fact that, according to demographers, in fifty years Muslims will be the majority population in several European countries is as scarifying as any fact I know.

Not that anyone cares, but I have long ago given up on Europe as a body of nations likely to act admirably in any situation where even a modicum of courage or honorable sympathy is required. When I was eighteen or so and undergoing a cultural awakening, I felt as an American, as I suspect most of my countrymen then did, like a yokel next to all things European. Europe, in which I included England, had the great bricks filled with magnificent libraries and works of art; the great universities; the great artists and intellectuals and scholars. Now only the bricks and the visual art and books that reside within them remain. I cannot think of a single European intellectual or artist of the least moral force who might call his fellow Europeans to order on the matter of Anti-Semitism, reminding them that it has always been the ideology of scoundrels and death-worshippers.

Check that: I can think of Bernard-Henri Levy, Bernie Levy as I prefer to think of him, with his unbuttoned shirt-front and cuffs, a sad, even clownish reminder of the former grandeur of French intellectuals, from Emile Zola through Albert Camus. France also gave us the recently dead obscurantists, Derrida, Foucault, & Co. In England the generation of Orwell, Waugh, and Eliot has been replaced by Amis, Jr., McEwan, and Salami (as I prefer to think of him) Rushdie. In Germany there is Gesundheit Grass. Italy, which once had Silone and Primo Levi, now has only costly suits and elegant pasta dishes, Spain provides only tennis players. Americans no longer need feel themselves culturally and intellectually yokels, but there is no pleasure in slipping free of the feeling.

Ford Madox Ford originally intended to give *The Good Soldier* the title of *The Saddest Story*. That story was, in Ford's novel, the betrayals of friends within marriage. I'm not sure that such betrayals make the saddest story, but for anyone making a list of sad stories over the past half century or so the broken relations between blacks and Jews has to be in the top ten. When I was a boy of five or six I returned home from the playground one day to recite for my parents a poem that went "Eeny, meeny miny moe, catch a nigger by the toe, if he hollers let him go." This was the only occasion I can remember in all our days together that my father was genuinely enraged at something I had done. He slapped me—for the first and only time—then sat me down to a lecture about the strong affinities between blacks and Jews as pariah people throughout history. World War Two was well underway, and he knew about the fate of the Jews under Hitler. We were the last people to show prejudice against the blacks, he said, the very last. He himself had hired a black secretary, rather a forward thing to do in that day. He couldn't then know that before long many blacks wouldn't in the least mind showing prejudice against Jews.

I seem to be in a jolly decline-and-fall mood but the Civil Rights Movement in America, once led by such men as Martin Luther King, Jr., Roy Wilkins, Whitney Young, and a few others, was, in the 1950s and '60s, genuinely impressive. I lived in the south in the early 1960s, in Little Rock, Arkansas, where I was the director of the local anti-poverty program, and was in touch with many of the young people who put their lives on the line to repeal unequivocally immoral segregation laws. The only figure in the upper ranks of the Civil Rights movement with whom I had any contact was Bayard Rustin, an *éminence grise* of sorts, who was highly intelligent but had to maintain a background position in the movement owing to his having been picked up by the police for homosexual soliciting. During my single year as a publisher's editor for a firm called New York Times Quadrangle Books, I edited a book of Bayard's essays. He was intellectually sophisticated, and could be very amusing about Negro (as the word then was) pretensions.

One of the secondary leaders of the Civil Rights movement of that day was a man named Ralph Abernathy, known for bringing two mules to protest marches. "You know, Joe," Bayard said to me in his elegant Jamaican English, "some people in the movement are very good for going to jail, but beyond that they get in the way. Ralph's a case in point. When Martin [Luther King, Jr.] won the Nobel Prize, Ralph thought he won it, too, and went off with Martin to Stockholm. He kept getting into limousines meant for Martin and his wife, showing up at dinners to which he wasn't invited. I suppose Martin ought to have been thankful he didn't bring those fucking mules."

How did the old Civil Rights Movement roll off the track, to the point where today it is led by such clownish charlatans as Jesse Jackson and Al Sharpton, men who have made millions off what is known as "the race problem?" The slide doubtless began when then young civil rights workers declared for black power, and told Jews and others whites in the movement that their services—though still their money—were no longer required. The slogan "Black is Beautiful" came next; to be followed over time by ghetto-style defiance and rap music and ultra-sensitivity to anyone suggesting that there is anything wrong with black culture that the death of all whites couldn't cure. With the exception of a few black intellectuals—the economist

Thomas Sowell, the writer Shelby Steele—no one speaks honestly about black problems. To do so simply isn't allowed. In his *Diaries*, George Kennan, as long ago as 1975, after long being out of influence as a writer on foreign affairs, poses to himself the possibility of writing about, and becoming an influence on, domestic affairs. But then notes: "How can you write about domestic affairs when one of the very greatest of the problems is the deterioration of life in the great cities and when one of the major components of these this presents is the Negro problem, which is taboo." And which, forty years later, still is.

Like Woodrow Wilson, the Permanent President of the American Branch of the Good Intentions Paving Company, Americans really do want to do the right thing. Most people of equanimous temperament were, I think, pleased to see Barack Obama elected President of the United States, if only to get, at least partially, the race problem off the country's back. I know I was. That it didn't quite work, and that Obama has been a dud wasn't in the plan. In 2016, the country will doubtless elect Hillary Clinton, thus contributing, so many will think, to the end of the unfairness-to-women problem. This won't work, either, for Mrs. Clinton is clearly in business for herself; she is pure ambition, unfettered by anything resembling principles or true belief. Dwight Macdonald once described the Democratic Party and the Republican Party as Tweedledumb and Tweedledumber. I should prefer they now be called the Good Intentions Party and the Dullards Party. I am in the camp of the Dullards myself, though I don't attend many of their meetings and my hand would palsy instanter if ever it occurred to me to write a check in support of any of its candidates.

Back to our good friends, the Jews. This past week I read Vladimir Jabotinsky's *The Five*, his novel about Odessa in the first decade of the twentieth century, and found myself much impressed by it. The five of the title are the five children of an upper-middle-class Jewish family and their various fates. I learn from the novel that Odessa, a port and multi-national city, never had a Jewish ghetto, that its various ethnic tribes mocked one another but generally got along, that Jews there were not harassed by anti-Semitic laws as they were elsewhere in Russia. The novel itself, though not a masterpiece, is very good: penetrating about human nature, lyrical, alive on every page. You or I would be pleased to have written it.

That it was written by a man who devoted the greater part of his life to helping establish the state of Israel makes it all the more remarkable. I know of no precedent for this. Disraeli of course wrote novels, but, as I remember from having read them long ago, they felt rather tossed off, displaying talent, wit, a comic point of view, but never touching on profundity. *The Five* is profound. Among the various themes it takes up is that of talent. "But isn't talent a form of affection," asks one of the characters. "Perhaps it's even much more sacred and secret than affection." An unnamed minor character in the novel, "a major writer from the capital," is described by the narrator as having "sparks of true genius," but he is "not authentically talented," and so "all of his big books about Russian novelists and Italian painters, intensely meditative but leading nowhere, will be forgotten." The tragedy of another character in the novel is that he is "so richly endowed with semi-talent: piano, drawing, verse, wit, what have you," none sufficient to keep him from wasting his life in foolish adventures one of which brings him down. The novel is not perfect. (Wasn't it Randall Jarrell who defined the novel as "a prose narrative of some length that has something wrong with it?") But I recommend it to you, this time not with a half but with a full-money-back guarantee.

I have spent a fair amount of time this past week reading two books on grammar—*Gwynne's Grammar* by N. M. Gwynne and *The Sense of Style* by Steven Pinker—on which I am to write a review for Robert Messenger at the *Wall Street Journal*. The Gwynne book, which was a bestseller in England, is an old-fashioned, lay-down-the-law book on what is permissible and what is not in English composition, and has, for me at least, the charm of its author's unflinching rearguard crankiness. The other book is written by a psycholinguist and cognitive scientist (don't ask) who overrates his charm. Although only three hundred pages long, his book is a great slog up a mountain at the top of which I do not expect any refreshment, let alone treasure, waiting. The *WSJ* pays me a decent rate, but in the end my earnings for this piece will probably come to roughly $2.80 an hour. I also received this past week a royalty check for my book *Fabulous Small Jews*—I have taken to calling my royalties my peasantries—for $273. Like the man said, easy money.

Best, Joe

LAGARDELE. 12.8.2014.
Dear Joe,

I've read a lot about the uncompromisingly prescient Jabotinsky, but not his work. The novel you describe (and I will try to get hold of) seems to have the clearmindedness to be found, in a different pitch, in Arthur Schnitzler's *The Road to the Open*. We have visited Odessa and climbed the famous steps on which Eisenstein pitched the often-clipped scene of Tsarist soldiers firing on a crowd which included a woman wheeling, then losing control of that baby carriage which careers down towards the dock. The steps have now been abbreviated at the lower end by a new pavement. The city was indeed unique in Russia for the encouragement which its founder, Catherine the Great, offered to Jews to settle in it, on equal, toll-free terms with other pioneers.

Catherine was a predatory man-izer, as every schoolboy used to know. One of the earliest "dirty jokes" I ever heard was of how on musical evenings, the empress invited the comeliest of the palace guardees to join the dance. At a given moment, it was said, there was a race to see which of the young men could first insert himself in the empress's hot "gusset" (Edna O'Brien's smart notation), after which he had the privilege of kissing her hand. This reminiscence of the seamy side of my monastic English education is unworthy of a serious correspondent, but underlines the absurdity of seeking to degrade rulers or potentates, presidents or other, by virtue of their salaciousness. Catherine was both randy and practical in the satisfaction of her appetites, in a manner beyond the dreams or range of lesser women, and a visionary who was, *perhaps*, hoodwinked by Grigori Potemkin's prettying of the villagescape through which she was to travel. She certainly did create a great city by snapping her fingers (by the same means, she also instituted the Pale of Settlement).

Beetle's grandparents were said to have eloped from Odessa, she being of higher social standing than her lover. The girl's father cursed the fugitives and wished that their children would die. The first two did, but twelve survived. Her younger siblings were raised, in London's East End, by Rachel, Beetle's mother. In due time, they dispersed to more salubrious parts of the city and, as some people will, bettered themselves by head-down, hard work. Rachel (aka Ray and Ruchele) was married to a Polish Jew called Hyman Glatt, who went to work in a match factory when he was ten years old and came, alone, to England when he was fourteen. He later opened a clothing store in Marylebone High St., in the West End.

Ray took *Vogue* and became a stylish, if soon quite stout, lady. She was always cheerful, capable of making friends with all conditions of men and women in short time, and did not in the least wonder what Beetle and I were doing alone in the house when she went to the shop on Saturday afternoons. Tactful, generous and undemanding, she became a mother-in-law of whom

I have no adverse thing to say. Her polyphiloprogenitive mother, however, became something of a monster and borrowed a large sum of money from her young son-in-law, lost it in some business venture, and never repaid it. Who knows why people are as they are?

When we called in at Odessa, while on a freebie cultural cruise of the Black Sea, it seemed something of a deserted, yet busy, city (Schnitzler's vivid Vienna now has a similarly spectral air of grandiose destitution). If Odessa ever had a soul, it too had done a runner. We drove to a monastery and looked at a lot of impressive icons under the guidance of hirsute, dark-eyed Russian orthodox monks. I cannot remember any surge of spiritual revelation. There is something almost candidly bogus about the incense-thickened air of holiness to be found in renascent Russian religiosity. The revanchist appetite of Master Putin is, I fear, altogether more genuine. It led, not many weeks ago, to an oafish re-staging of Eisenstein's choreographed mayhem, when some fifty Odessans were done to death by a mob, though I cannot say whether the victims were goodies or baddies, dupes or dopes.

Oh, I have just remembered another Catherine the Great story, told by Sainte-Beuve, whose essays are delightful enough to make us understand why *le petit* Marcel felt that he had to write him off. It comes in his piece on the life of the Comte de Ségur. He had gone on a diplomatic mission, towards the end of the *Ancien Régime,* to St. Petersburg to secure a commercial treaty. *"On sait que la glorieuse impératrice n'avait pas seulement des pensées hautes, et qu'elle conserva jusq'au bout le don de caprices légers."* (We all know that the glorious empress did not have only grand ideas, she also kept to the end her gift for skittish foibles.) What more elegant way could there be to remind the reader of Catherine's sexual voracity? She was evidently taken with the young French count and invited him to one of her summer residences, possibly Tsarskoe Selo, where she allotted him a specific apartment (presumably easy of access). He wanted to succeed in his diplomatic mission but did not, so Sainte-Beuve says becomingly, want it attributed to "an ability outside the field of politics." How could he discourage the imperial *"fantaisie"* without giving offense to one who was used to getting what she wanted, fast?

As it happened, the empress took a regular afternoon walk in the grounds of the palace along two grassy walkways separated by a *"charmille,"* some kind of bower; she went in one side and back along the other. M. de Ségur arranged, one afternoon, to be in the second alleyway, and *"ne pas s'y trouver seul,"* so that he was observed by the empress, as if by mistake, engaged on a flirtation with one of the pretty ladies of the court, probably with her connivance. At dinner that night, the face of "Sémiramis" appeared heavy with clouds and "*silencieux.*" Towards the end, she made it clear to the young ambassador that she understood that his brilliant qualities required him to return at once to the capital, since he was obviously bored where he was. He made polite objections, but she insisted. He did as he was told and, when he saw her again, the empress abandoned her sulks: "*la souveraine et la personne supérieure avaient triomphé de la femme.*" Sainte-Beuve concludes that such pragmatic tolerance was more than the goddesses themselves would have displayed in heroic times.He then ties on a tag from the Aeneid: "*Spretaeque injuria formae,*" the resentment of beauty scorned. Where would you get such a quotation printed today, and who would recognize it, apart from the happy very, very few? But then again, that's precisely what makes us happy, some of us, isn't it, some of the time?

The coincidental fun of it is that the same tag was used by Sir Walter Ralegh in the Introduction to the History of the World which he wrote, most of it, while in the Tower awaiting sentence and then execution. The funny part being that, with less subtlety and more passion than the Comte de Ségur, he too had been somewhat fancied by his sovereign, the Virgin Queen Elizabeth I (when was a rapacious virgin a contradiction in terms?) and was disgraced when he crossed her by falling in love with, and secretly marrying, one of her ladies-in-waiting, Elizabeth Throckmorton. The Queen was less magnanimous than the Empress; Ralegh's career at court was permanently blighted, although he was later somewhat rehabilitated. There was a great scene of passion in some blossom-heavy royal orchard, in which *la* Throckmorton was reported, by John Aubrey, to have cried out "Sweet Sir Walter! Sir Walter!" At last, as the danger and the pleasure at the same time grew higher, "she cryed in the extasey, Swisser Swatter Swisser Swatter." This recalls the story of the virgin lady of quality who, in more recent times, was so rejoiced by her husband's amorous attentions on their wedding night that she asked him "Do the lower orders do this too?" When told they did, she said, "It's much too good for them!" The good old, bad old unreformed upper classes *dans ses oeuvres.*

I got to like Ralegh when researching a movie, back in the early 1970s, which was to be based on *Death of the Fox* by George Garrett, one of those academic occasional condescenders to fiction. Dick Zanuck and David Brown, who had run 20ᵗʰ Century Fox and produced *Two for the Road* (when no one else would, even after Audrey Hepburn had said "yes, please!"), took me to lunch at Les Ambassadeurs, then a smart London eatery, now submerged by a big new off-white hotel, and flattered me into taking on the assignment. They had set up their own outfit, after being sacked by Dick's father Darryl, and had bought the rights of *Death of the Fox* (a little too much obvious symbolism there, old man, some literary tutor might say) on the strength of good reviews in the usual places. When I read the text, it contained nothing but flummery; no scenes, no dialogue, and without even the maddening intelligence of, for instance, John Barth's *The Sot-Weed Factor*, which pastiched much the same period. The only Barth book I liked, not madly, was *The End of the Road*, an early work, with a memorable scene in which the bad guy is observed strutting around his living room in scoutmaster uniform, pleasuring himself, or so we are urged to imagine.

Garrett's confection was all wrapping and no candy; I had to do a lotta, lotta work to breathe life into it. I had just won the Oscar and could afford to be a little fancy, so the narrative was intercut with very brief scenes of carpentry, work on some structure which was not revealed for what it was until very late, when it was seen to be the scaffold on which he was to have his head cut off. The whole of his life was composed of acts of gallantry, gambling, gamboling and unwise insolence, not least to the dangerously influential Robert Cecil, whom Ralegh—a tall man by Elizabethan standards—was in the habit of calling "little man," with patronizing geniality. Try that with any small man and see how many favors it gets you. In time, Ralegh was literally shortened himself, by James I, on Cecil's prompting.

So: I did the script and mailed it to Dick and David. After not too long a wait, I received a three-page telegram (we did not yet have the telephone in our French house, where I am today "celebrating" my eighty-third birthday). Dick and David told me that it was the best screenplay that they had ever had pass through their hands and that they would not make any further comment until they had signed the best director in the world, who would be lucky to have access to it. Meanwhile, they loved me to death and beyond. I waited and waited and heard not another word.

A year or so later, they asked me to come to L.A. to talk about another project they wanted me to do, concerning a then famous heist in Nice. I flew out and the talks went well. A French director called Philippe Labro was attached and a new spate of research and recce was financed for a movie which, in the end, was never made. At the end of our huddles, and before I flew back to Europe foist-cless, I made bold to ask Dick and David what was happening to the best script they had ever seen. "Freddie, listen, it truly *was* the best screenplay ever, but you know what: who the fuck was Sir Walter Ralegh?"

Tout à toi, Freddie.

August 19, 2014
Dear Freddie,

I found your account of your wife's Odessan origins, on her maternal side, full of interest. Why the Russians, who under the czars or commissars, treated their people as a conquered nation, let up (relatively) on the Jews in Odessa remains another of those unsolved authoritarian-totalitarian mysteries.

My own European antecedents, on my father's side, are Bialystockian. My grandfather, avoiding conscription—a twenty-five-year term of service and near death sentence for Jews in the Czar's army—did a runner to the New World, shoring up with relatives in St. Paul, Minnesota. He did not succeed there, and moved on to Montreal, where he went into various dry-goods businesses, never quite making his nut in any of them. Along the way he acquired a wife and ten children, my father and his twin brother being the last of his progeny. Apart from what must have been the impressive expense of raising so large a family, my grandfather's mind was never really on business. He was a scholar, a Jewish erudit, and said to have been a leading figure in Hebrew education in Montreal. Being a leading figure in Hebrew education in Montreal in the early decades of the past century must have paid roughly the salary that is paid to pole-vaulters in old people's homes. My grandfather, whose first name, Raphael (pronounced Ra-foil) is your last, longed to write and to teach. One of his many sayings which my father, who loved his father, used to quote was, "One of the nice things about teaching is you don't have an inventory."

I was in my grandfather's company on perhaps a dozen or so occasions—when he came to Chicago for my brother's and for my bar mitzvahs, when we traveled to Montreal, which we did a fair amount in the 1940s—but cannot say I really knew him, which I much regret. Oddly for a learned man, he never acquired much English, and my father, who called him Pa, spoke to him chiefly in Yiddish. He was a dapper man; in the few photographs I have of him, he is in three-piece suits, and he had a mustache and well-tended goatee. He was *frum*, not merely keeping strictly kosher but laying tefillin every morning. I remember him, in vest and shirt sleeves, tefillin wrapped around his forearm and on his forehead, chanting morning prayers in the corner of the bedroom assigned him when he visited us in

Chicago. The visits were tough on my mother, for my grandfather feared that she couldn't keep to all the laws of *kashruth*, and he wasn't about to fall off the kosher wagon so late in his life. At my bar mitzvah, the rabbi, a cousin I later learned to George Burns (how's that for a tertiary name-drop?), made a very great to-do about my grandfather's scholarly distinction.

Retired at last from his wretched businesses, he was helped by a monthly stipend my father sent him. My father, the only solid financial success among his children, also paid for the publication of three books he wrote, in Yiddish and in Hebrew. I once inquired of my friend Ruth Wisse, a professor of Jewish studies at Harvard, if these books were worth seeking a translator for, and she candidly reported that they showed my grandfather to be a man of genuine learning, though not of great originality. Of my grandfather's eight sons, only one, Samuel, went to university (McGill); he later became a rabbi, but was too opinionated, I have been told, to hold a congregation.

The more I think of my father, the better man he seems. In *The Portrait of a Lady*, Ralph Touchett utters an aphorism that has stuck in my mind: "You are rich when you can meet the demands of your imagination." On this score my father was a billionaire. He dreamed of no villas in Tuscany, nor mistresses stored in Park Avenue penthouses. He was rich because he had enough money to give generously to (mostly) Jewish charities, even though he insisted on his own agnosticism, and to help his father and other members of his extended family in need. He was a good man, my father, and a better son than his own sons turned out to be.

"Skittish follies" to describe Catherine the Great's sexual voraciousness cannot be topped in the understatement department. No one would think to call that old girl "the virgin queen." Her skittish follies do, though, raise the question of nymphomania. The question, more precisely, is does it exist? Are there women who are truly insatiable? Adolescent boys, when I was growing up, would have liked to think so. In those dark days any girl who showed pleasure at sex qualified as a nymphomaniac, or, in the parlance of the time, a "nympho."

Today of course we have psychobabble in place of street slang. I suppose any woman who finds herself in lots of different beds might be termed a "sex addict," which seems to me the emptiest of terms. From the ages of fifteen to forty and a bit beyond just about every man I have known was a sex addict. The 42nd President of the United States, the Honorable William Jefferson Clinton, is said to suffer from this addiction, poor baby, even to this day, he should only live and be well. As opposed to sex addiction, I prefer the slightly awkward term "unseemly horniness." In these my silly sunset years, I have come more and more to view sex as a mostly comic subject, filed away under the rubric Much Ado about Not All That Much. Now that Freudianism has been justly pushed off into the broom closet, I wonder if we can't get back to viewing sex as an amusing, sometimes charming, (mostly) indoor sport? Not bloody likely, I hear you retort.

The mail—snail, not e—this week brought an impressive little hate note, which in its entirely reads: "Sir: Your cliché riddled essays and prickly ego remind me of my Father's failed intellectual pretentions. Mildly amusing but mediocre. Time to retire your pen." My correspondent signs his note "Best, A. Rothman," and includes his return address in Philadelphia on the envelope. He adds a postscript: "do not reply until after you die."

I have no intention of replying, neither in this life nor the next. Mencken used to answer such letters, in a previously printed-up postcard, "Dear Sir or Madame, You may or may not be right." I cannot complain about a bit of hate mail now and then, when I receive so many kindly and generous letters from readers. Still. I cannot help but wonder, at least a bit, about what brought out such bile in this unsatisfied customer. He does not say what it is, exactly, he loathes about me, apart from my mediocrity and (misspelled) pretentions. His note suggests he has a father problem. That he took the time to write his name, in fountain-pen, on a card that has the drawing of an owl on the outside, slip it into a envelope, attach a 45-cent stamp on it, then walk it down to a mail box, suggests his distaste for me is not fleeting. Are there other scribblers he contemns with equal venom? If so, I wish I could know who they are, so that we might form a club at which we could smoke, if the firm is still in business, Rothman cigarettes and reflect in therapeutic fashion where exactly we have all gone wrong.

As it happens, I published a story some years ago called "Postcards" in which a failed poet named Seymour Hefferman buys twenty postcards every month which he uses to send insults to various cultural figures, and which he signs with fake Jewish names and a false return address. My Hefferman means nothing more than a touch of free-floating malice. He hopes his insults will give his addressees pause, wing them in their confidence, slow them down a bit. One such postcard, addressed to a not-named novelist (meant to be Philip Roth) reads: "Dear Moral Leader, As a simple American, Midwest version, may I be permitted to apologize to you on behalf of all our countrymen for having let you down? Hard, I realize, to rise to your standard of moral equipoise as the self-acknowledged legislator of mankind. But does the world really need a pornographic Polonius? Don't believe it

}251{

does. As ever, Sherwin Skulnik." I don't suppose that Mr. A. Rothman has read my story, but his note does go to show that one can't invent anything.

Two big show biz deaths in the U. S. of A. this past week. First there was Robin Williams, followed a day or so afterwards by Lauren Bacall. Poor timing on Miss Bacall's part, for Robin Williams, having parted through suicide, swept the boards of publicity for more than a week. Timing is apparently everything not only in life but in death. John Dos Passos made the grievous error of dying on the same day as Colonel Gamal Adbel Nasser, and hence missed a front-page obituary in the *New York Times*. People were also not so secretly taken with the question of how a man so famous, so wealthy, as Robin Williams could be so unhappy as to kill himself. Something comforting in his offing himself to everyone not rich and famous that makes life a touch more bearable.

I never cared much for either Robin Williams or Lauren Bacall. Robin Williams's obviously manic, usually raucous humor was not my bowl of borscht. Manic comes from mania which itself comes from maniac. He could be wildly funny—a few days ago I passed along to you what I thought an amusing bit he did on a Scotsman's account of the origin of golf—but just as often he could begin quietly, then veer off into a slightly terrifying, much too energetic description of cunnilingus. Many people like a select few of his movies, most citing *The Dead Poets Society* and *Good Will Hunting,* but even these I felt overdone. Overstatement, everything done in bold-face italics, was poor Robin Williams' *modus operandi*; he resembled a tenor who could only do high C.

Like lots of men, I admired Lauren Bacall's velvety, high-maintenance good looks, her sexy gaze as in her characteristic move she put her head down and looked up. Her range, though, was fairly limited. Her appearance in those Humphrey Bogart movies—*To Have and Have Not, Key Largo, The Big Sleep*—were of course the making of her. In so-called real life she played the tough broad, the knowing New Yorker, guarded and absolutely bullshit-proof. Self-advertised bullshit-proof people, as you will have noticed, are generally themselves not utterly free of taurusal excrement, if you will allow a little elegant variation, not to mention wobbly spelling. From a few anecdotes I've heard about her, Miss Bacall was not without her snobbery, and, like all snobs, she could be coarsely unkind.

Lauren Bacall's life with Bogart has, I suspect, been much romanticized. They were married for twelve years, when he died of lung cancer at fifty-seven. The best lowdown, the true gen as Hemingway used to call it, on Bogart was supplied by Billy Wilder in a book of interviews with Cameron

Crowe. In those interviews Wilder claimed Bogart was an anti-Semite and a "shit," who wore a hairpiece and spat as he spoke, the spittle having had to be filtered out of his films. Lauren Bacall was later briefly married to Jason Robards and was, briefly, engaged to Frank Sinatra. Too bad that marriage never came off, for the two richly deserved each other. Few things more comforting, don't you think, than speaking ill of the recently dead. Clears the sinuses, they say.

I have been reading S. N. Behrman's mostly theatrical memoir, *People in a Diary*, which I first read thirty or so years ago. Sam Behrman had a successful career as a playwright in the thirties and forties, and made some profitable forages into Hollywood as a screenwriter. He had a *New Yorker* connection going back to Harold Ross days on the magazine, and published much of his books on Lord Duveen, the art con man, and on Max Beerbohm (*Portrait of Max*) there. His dates are 1893–1973. In *People in a Diary* he recounts that he had broken his connection with MGM and David Selznick, when Selznick insisted he remain another few weeks to patch up some scenes in a Greta Garbo movie. Going off to coffee at the studio commissary with Selznick, he and Selznick passed George S. Kaufman, who remarked of Berhman, "Forgotten but not yet gone." Today I suspect that Behrman's status is gone and forgotten both.

George S. Kaufman was a man who left a fine residue—all that is left, really, of the Algonquin Round Table—of anecdotes and amusing remarks. A relentless philanderer, who could make love to any woman but his wife, Kaufman is supposed to have told Irving Berlin that he much liked his song "Always," but would like it even more if he would change the title to "Thursdays." Neurotic as a flea, he tried his hand at psychoanalysis, but lasted only a few sessions. When asked why he dropped out, he answered that the shrink asked "too many personal questions."

I have always admired S. N. Behrman, not so much for his writing, which is never other than professional and graceful, as for his ability to see himself as a secondary character, a man on the sidelines. In *People in a Diary* he mentions, as if in passing, "I had married Elza, the youngest Heifetz daughter," and, quite rightly, we hear no more about his marriage. In all his stories and anecdotes in this book he never puts himself in the forefront. He refers to himself as among "those of us who were not geniuses but who have talent in various degrees."

The best anecdotes about Hollywood are those that feature men with an impressive deficiency of culture combined with a too heightened sense of commercial reality. Your ". . . who the fuck was Walter Raleigh?"

anecdote qualifies here perfectly. Sam Behrman's offering in these sweep-stakes is from Sol Wurtzel, an assistant to Winfield Sheehan at Fox, who, when Berhman asked about the release of a ridiculously updated version of Dante's *Inferno* he had worked on, replies: "You can't release Dante's *Inferno* in the summertime." Makes perfect sense, right? Irving Berlin nailed it: no business, absolutely none, like show business.

Best, Joe

LAGARDELLE. 20.8.2014.
Dear Joe,

Your story of A. Rothman (easily James Joyced into "wrath/man") and his Philadelphian malice is, I suspect, available in various versions in every writer's brotherly loving experience. I may have told you of a man also named too aptly to seem subtle, a certain Mr. Bor, who took it on himself to champion a woman whom he took me to have treated unkindly. In fact, I had known and quite liked the lady in question ever since we acted together in Cambridge. She was then involved with, and later married, one Jim Fer-man, an American graduate student—late of the U.S.A.A.F.—who soon be-came residentially British. In the early 1960s, we were frequent visitors to each other's homes. Jim became a TV director and I did my best to get him work on the pieces I used to do quite frequently on the box.

One such was an adaptation of my novella *The Trouble With England* (it was—I need hardly tell you—the weather). I delivered the shooting script to Associated Television just before we left England for one of our foreign stays. Hence I was deprived of the fun—the best you can have with your clothes on, as vulgar persons say—of being present at rehearsals. After transmission, I heard, from the producer, my friend Stella Richman, that all went very well. In other words, the ratings were OK. When we came back to London, in 1963, I happened to be walking to the (then) excellent Dillon's Bookshop adjacent to the London University Senate House when I saw Ian Bannen, quite a famous Scots actor in those days, coming towards me (he was most famous for being the anguished - because Catholic - lover of Samantha—aka "Big Sam"—Eggar, a red-headed transient movie star, later a producer who asked me to script Shirley Hazzard's *The Transit of Venus;* I passed). I stopped Bannen and said, "I'm Frederic Raphael and I hear that you were extremely good in my play on the box." He looked at me as if he expected to be asked to spare a dime. "*The Trouble with England*," I said, hoping to clear the cloud from his face, "I wrote it." The frown thickened. "Jim Ferman wrote that," he said.

Jim and I had been friends of a kind, not least (indeed mostly) because of proximity and also, maybe, because of the New York Jewish connection, although he was decidedly indifferent to the Jewish part of himself: since he had a freckled face and nice teeth and a straight, unremarkable nose, he could, as they used to say, pass. When I wrote a novel called *Lindmann,* about the Holocaust ("about" in the sense of being around the subject), I gave Jim and Monica a copy. Somewhat Georges Perecian *avant la lettre,* I took a certain pride in having written a long book on a then muted topic in which the word Jew never appears. Jim said that he had some critical thoughts about the book that he would like to communicate to me. I took the view that a bouquet of florid gratitude would be quite enough. He had never written any fiction, although he did have a master's degree in English. "Big deal," as Holden Caulfield woulda said.

My friend Harry Gordon, another American, whom we met when we lived in Fuengirola on the Costa del Sol on the hinge of the fifties and the sixties, told me that I had to confront Jim on the authorship of *T.T.W.E.*, if I wanted our friendship to continue. I preferred, possibly for sly reasons (who knows *exactly* what his motives are?), to be empowered by my secret knowledge, while continuing to be much as I was before to Jim. Coals of fire do warm the donor. I recommended Jim as a movie director to Jo Janni, for whom I wrote *Darling* and *Far From the Madding Crowd,* and who deserves a memoir to himself, and I was rewarded by Jim telling Jo that he didn't want to be a commercial hack like some people and that the only movie he was prepared to make was of David Storey's novel, *Flight Into Camden,* a doleful piece which may safely be said never to have taken off.

Storey's *This Sporting Life* was a pugnacious and eminently authentic debut from a student of the school of D. H. Lawrence (nothing wrong with that, old man). Storey was one of a regularly recurring set of provincial English writers held together by inoperable social resentments; when they become worldly and successful, they lose it. I had the sorry, unasked-for task of reviewing a late novel of his, *A Serious Man.* It gave me small pleasure to take it to the cleaners and leave it there. My review was as pitilessly fair as you might expect in the light of what Storey had said about my work ("sterile") some forty years before. I did have the residual decency to declare as much before proceeding to egregious justice re grammatical and other matters not of opinion. Between you and I, as Storey put it altogether too often, I ended up wishing that I could find something, *anything* to praise.

Jim Ferman's career, even as a TV director, languished not least, if not only, because he was a perfectionist; in other, practical words, he went way over budget and became that most imperiled of showbiz things, a luxury (and not a markedly amusing one). Just before Christmas 1970-something, he told me, in a rare moment of candor, that he and Monica could not afford to give their children any presents. So I sent him a check for £250, which was not a lot, although a lot more than it is now. His first reaction was, he told me in a rare handwritten letter, to be extremely angry. When he calmed down, he persuaded himself, with magnanimous benefit-of-the-doubtfulness, that I had meant well. He had decided, therefore, that he would not tear up my check but deposit it in the bank where it would earn two and a half percent interest (those were indeed the days!). In due course, he said, he would repay the money, which he hoped not to have to touch, plus the interest. Something for his long-nosed friend to look forward to; except that it never— you *guessed*?—happened. Does the cash remain in some corner of a foreign bank account that is forever Fred?

Not long afterwards, I was commissioned by the B.B.C. to do the TV series which I called *The Glittering Prizes*. No sooner was it was announced than Jim rang and asked me to allow him to direct at least some of the six 90-minute pieces. It was his last chance to redeem his career. I promised to mention his name to the producer, but I reminded him that I lacked the puissance to impose my casting on the Corporation. Soon afterwards, he was named as "Secretary" to the British Board of Film Censors and became the arbiter of decency (nipple-counter *extraordinaire*) for the English media. There is quite a lot more juice in them sour grapes, but I will cut back now to Mr. Bor, whom I had and have never met, reviewed or read. As the widow Ferman's champion, he took it on himself to ask me what it felt like to be a writer who would only ever be remembered for two things. I was floored, of course, and then, as I stumbled to a corner, feeling ropey, I had time to wonder whether all that many people, writers or no, were remembered at all, let alone for two things. Nobbad, as some people say.

Mr. Bor was, I need hardly tell close readers of the English scene (myopia is a national habit), a journalist on *The Guardian* which has a Jewish-sounding editor, a liberal conscience, worn on both sleeves, and implacable hostility to Israel, a small country of which you may have heard. I suppose one of Master Bor's two things was *The Glittering Prizes* but modesty forbids (a favorite phrase of Charlie Chaplin and Bertrand Russell) my guessing what number two might be. It was said of Anthony Eden, by my sometime chum Malcolm Muggeridge, that he "bored for England." Bor's aggression was so comically wide of the mark that, having no standard letter to hand, I made no effort to respond.

You mentioned Mencken's routine printed retort to critics. Woodrow Wyatt, whom I caricatured amiably in a recent letter, had a similarly prepared reply to captious constituents: "Dear Sir or Madam, I have received your letter. I hope you are now feeling better. Yrs etc. W.W." I recall that Edmund Wilson also had a printed response to solicitations, with boxes for him to tick in rejecting demands for interviews, invitations to lecture, etc. A smartass analyst might guess that to have a deck of such things readily at hand requires a certain expectation, if not wish, that opportunities to say "no" will not be lacking. Beatrice Lillie used to sing a little number, while seated at a table in the bar of a louche hotel, "I've come here to be insulted/ And I'm not going home until I am."

It is a strange thing, quite common with writers, to make enemies whom one has never met and of whom one cannot recall ever having written or said a single unkind word. George Orwell, known as "gloomy George" in the days when he and my *feu* friend Michael Ayrton used to hang out in the BBC canteen, hoping for subsidies, remarked how much easier it is to be ruthless about the work of those one has never met. He mentioned in particular Stephen Spender, whose account of his "experiences" (marginal was never so distant) in the Spanish Civil War excited Orwell's literally wounded scorn. When, by the usual kind of London chance, Orwell met Spender he found him so pleasant that he could never again charge his pen with bile.

I was once a speaker at the Byron Society and, at the reception afterwards, was approached by a very tall, white-haired man (since I am six feet one or so, I am rarely towered over, except metaphorically) who told me that he had found my little book on the poet very perceptive and amusing. I accepted the praise graciously while wondering who this presumably important, not to say patronizing, person might be and why he took it that he needed no introduction. If I were a cartoonist, I should long ago have done one showing a man in a big coat with astrakhan collar, a magnum cigar and a solemn homburg addressing the nurse sitting under the sign AMNESIA CLINIC with the words "Do you know who I am?"

Cut back to the very tall man and, yes, you've guessed: it was Stephen Spender. Even in his later days (though not as late as mine now are), he retained the air of an elongated *beau garçon,* a lifelong seducer left and right, straight and, oh, curved, whose charm was a reliable currency for all seasons and countries. His memoir *World Within World* has some delicious wartime Iberian details, not least of Sylvia Townsend Warner calling her lady-love "Comrade darling!" I also recall that Spender was sent to Spain by the British Communist leader, Harry Pollitt, with an invitation to get himself killed because "we need a Byron at this point." Aha indeed.

I had a recent experience of astonishing (to me) hostility when I was given the "privately printed" memoir of a film editor called Jim Clark, who cut both *Darling* and *Far From the Madding Crowd*. His French wife Laurence is Jewish. She told me that she spent two years of the war waiting for the knock on the door which would precede deportation and death. Her father, a law-abiding Frenchman, had been foolishly obedient enough to register as a *Juif* at the local police station. Thanks to some perhaps genial inefficiency, the family remained untouched. Jim had a very lucrative career (capped by an Oscar for, I think, *The Killing Fields*) and I had the unimportant notion that we agreed on most cinematic matters. He and Laurence visited us a few times; and we went to their big town house for dinner, once.

We might have gone twice, but the invitation was abruptly cancelled, on the morning of the feast, on account of some unspecified drama which Jim was tersely reluctant (can happen) to spell out. Was there anything I could do? There was not. Now I have not, to my not self-deluding knowledge, *ever* said anything disparaging, or anything much at all, about Jim or his adhesive lady; she used to call me regularly every summer, from her house in the Ile de Ré for a French chat about zis and zat. Jim was often working, but sometimes came on the line for a giggle or two. Chums but not friends, is what we were. Then, not long ago, Will Boyd, the very nice, very best-selling author, whom I first met when he came to interview me when he was on *Isis,* the Oxford magazine, sent me a copy of Jim Clark's movie memoir.

Will received properly flattering mention. I did not. The index led me to read that I was always banging on about anti-Semitism. *Moi?* Some might wonder what kept Jim so long from stating the obvious, but one or two might have been as surprised as I was that someone who had come literally out of his way—after inviting himself and his *épouse* to come and visit us in the Périgord—should decide, in the evening of our days, to piss on my gabardine. Why Will Boyd sent me the (privately-printed) text which I should never otherwise have seen, who can say? My guess is that he assumed, without checking the text, that I should be as nicely spoken about as he was.

Tout à toi, Freddie.

August 26, 2014
Dear Freddie,

One e-mail back you mentioned the name John Barth. I believe I read the novels of his called *The Floating Opera* and *Lost in the Fun House*; I write "I believe" because I remember nary a word of either. John Barth was born in 1930, and, as of 2012, was still pumping out novels, in the best postmodern and metafictional style, I assume. He was a winner of all the American prizes in the 1960s and '70s, and then reappeared as a prizewinner in the 1990s. I recall thinking I should but never did get round to reading his two door-stoppers, *The Sot-Weed Factor* and *Giles Goat Boy*. I am glad to have read neither, because I am fairly certain I would today remember nothing of these two book either; they would surely have been a great trudge through much literary muck and mire. ("Hiya, Muck." "Hiya, Meyer.") My taste does not run to *tours de force*, or any other sorts of tours, which is what I gather those two Barth tomes are, or at least set out to be.

Your calling up John Barth's name suggests the need for a new category of books: those one is pleased never to have read. What a lengthy list it would be! Titles rush to mind: Norman Mailer's *Harlot's Ghost*, Philip Roth's *The Breast* and *Our Gang*, a number of Updike vols., Sylvia Plath's *The Bell Jar*, the last four novels of Thomas Pynchon, the next four novels of Salman Rushdie, and oh, so many more. This could be followed by an accompanying list of books one regrets having read. Many of the same authors would of course appear on both lists. I believe I am one of the few people alive, or dead for that matter, who slogged through Mailer's *Ancient Evening*—surely Mailer himself couldn't have read it—and did so with eyeballs glazed like isinglass windows; I read it only because I was paid to write about it.

The Woodrow Wyatt response to unpleasant mail is excellent. Better than Edmund Wilson's postcard, which wasn't a response to insults but his form of turning down invitations to do conventionally authorly things. I have seen a copy of the postcard with its lengthy list of things he refused to do. He could have saved a bit of print, and instead of listing all the things he refused to do—sign books, supply photographs, etc.—simply had a postcard printed that read, Fuck Off. No one was more cantankerous than The Bunny, who beneath that cuddly sobriquet was a snarling porcupine. Earlier I mentioned an eighteen-century English aristocrat, who is supposed to have written in response to a mean letter something like the following: "I am reading your letter in the necessary room. It is before me now, but it shall soon be behind me." Might he, I wonder, be the same man who invited everyone he knew who stuttered to dinner, at table threw out a general question for the assembled company to discuss, then sat back, hand over his mouth, pretending to listen.

This is your first mention of having known Malcolm Muggeridge, the old Mugger, as I like to think of him. In his day he was a journalist whose appearance in a magazine was sufficient to compel me to buy it. That day was of course before he became an earnest Christian. Unlike the ample works of John Barth, I remember a good deal of what Muggeridge wrote. He was the first to call the bluff of the Kennedy Camelot Mafia, in a piece in the *New York Review* titled "The Loved One." I recall a piece he did about a book by the then Labor MP Wayland Young called something like "A History of Western Pornography." Muggeridge began by saying that contemporary profanity does not come easily to him; he is, he declares, "a man of the asterisk generation." Yet, he asserts, not to avail himself of certain key profane words would make discussing Wayland Young's "most earnest book" impossible; not to fear, he has hit upon what he thinks a solution. In place of that most common of profane words, he will supply the author's first name, Wayland, and for the male and female genitals he will substitute the author's last name, thus: m. Young and f. Young. After setting this up, his opening paragraph ends with a sentence that went something like, "There, now, that is much more comfortable for an old waylander like myself." Many lines also appeared about life surely being about more than people "gnashing their Youngs together." Another bit from that review I recall is the Mugger writing, "a prostitute of my acquaintance, whom I knew not for research but for waylanding purposes . . ." *Merveilleux!,* or so I thought, and think even now.

I gather the Mugger was in private life a lecher and DOM (Dirty Old Man) with oak leaf clusters. I recall reading a sad story somewhere about Kingsley Amis and Muggeridge, after a night on the town with sad Sonia Orwell, returning to her apartment and both doing ugly with her, in my old friend Joseph Mitchell's immortal phrase. Not a pretty scene to contemplate.

Then—bring in the cellos here—the Mugger got religion, and, like the song says, he got it bad, and that ain't (or 'tweren't, at least for his writing) good. His conversion seemed like nothing so much as the fat boy who cleans out the entire stock of the candy store and then pledges to go on a diet. More than a touch less than convincing, the picture of the Mugger as a sincere Christian, announcing that all is vanity and emptiness, and only the salvation of the soul matters. Let us hope his own conversion arrived in time for him to save his own soul, and, because of all the pleasure he gave me as that naughty fat boy and one of the great iconoclasts of our day, I also hope he resides happily in heaven.

Since I reported Mr. A. Roth(wrath)man's letter of a week or so ago to you, I now wish to put the world back in balance by reporting a charming letter I received this week from a retired CEO of a bank in Virginia City, Virginia. He reports that he just finished reading my *A Literary Education and Other Essays* "with pleasure and profit," adding that "it is always a joy to stumble into a sophisticated exposition of important ideas that correlate clearly with one's own." He is, it turns out, my contemporary, "of the same generation of the Fifties, sharing the same sensibilities and raised eyebrows over what came later." He closes by saying that now that he is retired he is "able to read much more widely than I used to, and I write merely to record how pleasant it was to encounter Joseph Epstein for the first time." What a lovely letter to receive; it put the sun in my sky and the splenetic Mr. Roth(wrath)man forever out of my mind.

Which brings me to the more general question of the reception of one's writing. Don't you suppose the instantaneous and spontaneous reaction to what one has written that the theater provides is one of the great, perhaps the greatest of, goads for writing plays? One sits at the back, or in the middle of the theatre, and watches people laughing, or crying, or worrying about the fate of the characters you have created. Sounds very grand. I rather doubt that writing for television or the movies works quite so directly, though you, who have done both, would know better than I. I suspect that immediate response is why Henry James attempted—sadly, misbegottenly—to write for the stage, though he shouldn't also have minded the rain of shekels he hoped would follow. "Do you know why Uncle Henry's plays don't succeed?" Henry James's nephew William James told Sam Behrman. "I'll tell you why. I've read them all. They're lousy, that's why they don't succeed." Sinclair Lewis also flopped as a playwright and so did Saul Bellow. John O'Hara wrote the book for the musical *Pal Joey*, based on some of his stories, but that isn't quite the same as having written a full-blown play. Your man Willie Maugham's having four plays on the London stage simultaneously is, come to think of it, an amazement, especially for the young man he then was, and more especially for a man whose true talent was writing fiction.

In some ways writing plays may be more difficult than writing novels and stories. No *longueurs* are permitted; digressions are similarly *verboten*. Time, by which I mean the audience's patience, is major factor; no one today would succeed with a play that lasted much more than two hours; the same is probably true of a movie. I've never thought much about the technical problems that playwriting entails. (Henry James claimed that writing for the stage gave him the idea of using what he called "the scenic" method, which he later made use of in his fiction.) Dealing with human complications of playwriting (actors, directors, producers, money-men, and the rest), seem to me at a minimum whelming, at a maximum staggering.

Added to this is that, in America at least, there is no strong theatrical tradition. All our putatively great playwrights—A. Miller, T. Williams, E. O'Neill—have been dolorous in the extreme. The genius of American theatre has been its musical comedies. I do not in the least gainsay these charming entertainments. But the fact is that no first-class mind in America has written for the so-called serious theatre. Among Englishmen the only serious person to write for the contemporary theatre is Tom Stoppard, and his cultivated intellect may well have detracted from the power, if not the cleverness, of his plays. In America people still go to the theater as they go to church. Santayana I think said that Protestants go to church to feel good about themselves and Catholics go to church to be reminded that they are bad. Americans theatergoers, whether they know it or not, are the cultural equivalent of Catholics; they pay top prices to be told they are bad, but without the comforts of confession.

Your mention of James Ferman having a master's degree reminded me what a sad racket the acquisition of diplomas and degrees has become. (Diplomas, I have heard it said, are the religion of the Jews.) You doubtless know the old saying about a B.S. standing for bull shit; an M.S. for more of the same; and a Ph.D. for piled higher and deeper. How trivial all these degrees, at least on the non-scientific side, have become, though those possessing them are still able to pull the wool over the toes of the uneducated. When I hear it said about someone that he has a Ph.D., I wonder where he went wrong? Why did he agree to put up with all the mental—I do not say intellectual—hazing that acquiring such a degree demands. When I edited *The American Scholar*, I used to get a fair amount of correspondence from people who placed the initials Ph.D. after their names. I was always tempted in answer to address them as Mr. Ph.D. Ah, the little niceties of intellectual status that aren't finally all that nice.

Great minds once again not only think alike but tell the same anecdotes. I have been telling your Orwell-Spender story for many years. I first picked it up in a collection of Orwell's letters. In my version, Orwell wrote to Spender that for years he was used to treating him in print as a (I seem to recall his actually writing) "a pansy poet" and a Communist sympathizer, but now that he has met him, and found him a fairly agreeable fellow, he can no longer treat him with "the same clean brutality." In my version, Orwell ends by adding that this is why he doesn't go out all that much.

For me the point of the story is that one really doesn't want to know that people whom one dislikes, even despises, for sound intellectual reasons, are likable, even charming, people. Worse is to learn that these same people live with wretched difficulties. Someone once told me that a literary critic I slammed in print has two autistic children. Jesus, Mary, and Joseph, I don't want to hear that. If one is to operate with something resembling Orwell's "clean brutality," at least where it is called for, best not to learn that the fraudulent poet or nutty critic or anti-Semitic novelist has a wife in a wheelchair or himself works with cerebral palsy children.

David Storey, Angry Young Man, I seem to recall. All those Angry Young Men—Storey, John Osborne, John Braine, and the rest—if still alive, would today be merely mildly Ticked Off (if not Completely Demented) *alte kakers*. Better, methinks, never to have been part of any literary group, whatever the immediate benefits in coarse publicity. Better to be in business for oneself, Joseph Epstein, or Frederic Raphael, Ink, or so I conclude.

Best, Joe

LAGARDELLE. 28.8.14.
Dear Joe,

I hope I didn't give the impression that the Mugg and I were hang-out buddies. The truth is, we met only when we coincided as "guests" (meaning you didn't get paid much, because you were pelted with kudos) on B.B.C. radio and television panels to discuss matters of moment. It required a certain agility of mind to give instant answers to the audience's questions. You might guess some of the questions from the evening's headlines, but panelists were not privy to them. My best innings was in quickquick, end-of-show response to a recurrent number: how much sex-education should be given in schools? I said, "You have to remember that a certain amount of instruction comes with the kit." It went down, as the innocent used to say, very well.

If I have a number of big names in my satchel, useful for dropping in order to prove that I am not closely related to Mr. Pooter (putative suburban author of *The Diary of a Nobody*), it is partly because of the intermittent frequency of such appearances. Malcolm—we were all Christian-namely in the greenroom before The Show—credited me, with flattering regularity, on something he was sure that I had said about Graham Greene, and may well have, viz.: "The thing about G.G. is that sin is all around where he is standing, but never quite includes him." I am not sure how smart that is, nor do I recall saying it; but I have done a lotta reviewing in my day and such phrases, perhaps more neatly compressed, come nicely at the end of a paragraph or a long day.

G. Greene was one of the literati whom I never even shared a crowded room with. I admired some of the early stuff (*England Made Me* is one hell of a title), but was doomed to review only the novels which seemed hurried and, very often, silly. One such was *The Human Factor* (no relation of the *Sot-Weed* guy) in which the anti-hero is said to undo his "fly-buttons." I made bold to say that G.G. had lived too long out of England (yes, I really did say that) to know that everyone sported zips nowadays ("thenadays" might be useful coinage). He responded tetchily, claiming that he never mentioned fly-buttons. Some remote reader rode to my rescue and said that Greene had evidently not read his own novel, on page x of which etc. Did the sporting grandee apologize to Raphael? He more probably muttered something about bloody deicides. My new good friend Gerard Messadié, who nailed Mendelsohn with a left and a right, is my age and is about to publish a book claiming that Jesus and Barabbas were the same guy and that he, or He, may have been crucified only in the sense of being roped to a cross, not nailed to it. Messadié is, if you Google him, a considerable scholar and knows his Aramaic. That will not, I guess, save him from being nailed by the *NYRB* people and their toadies in London.

Back to Muggeridge who always made a point of having something nice to say to the mechanicals without whom broadcasts could not take place in the remote places which the BBC's affectations of ubiquity had to serve. I recall him asking one of the female floor managers how her mother was. He was very sorry to hear that she had passed away. After which, next case. M.M. was scarcely an old fashioned gentleman (more an old-fashioned cad) but he had residual officer-like courtesy which required him to have a word with the other ranks before resuming the privileges of priority. Even I, cosmopolitan wanderer, perpetual metic (if you don't name it, someone else will), cannot sit easy until I have made sure that plumbers, gardeners, builders et al. have had a hot drink in cold weather or a cold one in hot. At my Public School, we were taught, as once-a-week military cadets, that the prudent duty of an officer is to be sure that his men eat before he does. It is the Right Thing and the prudence lies in lessening the chances of being shot in the back. I have alluded perhaps too often, *ici et là,* to Shelley's admiration for "antique courtesies," but I share them. They include, in my view, respect for the decent usages of grammar and syntax.

Muggeridge was all the lewd, dodgy and attitudinizing things we both know him to have been but he was also some kind of a timely tide-bucker when he was needed, not least—no, most actually—as Moscow correspondent of, I think, the then *Manchester Guardian* (it dropped the Mancunian tag some time in the 1970s and became *The Guardian*), in which posting he refused to honor the paper's limp liberal line and denounced Stalinism with rare insolence and nicely measured scorn. It may be that there was a measure of self-mortification in the boldness of his address. The title of his memoirs, *Chronicles of Wasted Time,* suggests that he imagined that he might have honored higher goals than Fleet Street deadlines, though it is hard to know what they might have been.

Hearing that Rebecca West was soliciting donations, Willie Maugham offered to pay the old, destitute Norman Douglas an annuity but on the condition that the old reprobate never knew its source. "Because," Willie said to *la* West (whom I also knew briefly), "you know what he read at Oxford, don't you? B-b-biting the hand that f-feeds him." Muggeridge went to Selwyn College, Cambridge, a somewhat remotely sited number for whose undergraduate population we unreformed snobs in the center had stupidly small regard. In Norman Douglas style, M.M. claimed to have learned nothing and met no one of significance to him while he was at Cambridge, but he did, nevertheless, go to Selwyn College. His judicious wince and wearily upward cast eyes offered an involuntary declaration of the provenance which allowed him to disdain it. I once read a volume entitled *Harvard Hates America,* an early number on the shelf of the new populism which has, it seems, pretty well succeeded in making the possession of any kind of high culture a good reason for deportation from the seats of power. "Correct me if I'm right," as someone must have said sometime.

If I have known any A-listers, he or she tends to have been of the same dethroned, *déclassé* order as Proust's ex-Queen of Portugal. By the time I met him, Muggeridge excited more pity than apprehension. He asked me to come down to his house in Robertsbridge, Sussex, in antique courteous terms: "Should you be anywhere near, do propose yourself for lunch." Truth to tell, I have never proposed myself anywhere. I will take almost any exam, and hope to shine, but I will never do what a number of our acquaintances, or even of people whom I have never met, have done and file for hospitality because they happen to be in our neck of the French woods and stuck for a bite or a bed.

With Vladimir Nabokov I missed improving chance meeting into something more substantial. After his death, as I may have told you, his wife, the formidable Véra, said that he and I had had rare rapport, on the one time we met. Now she tells me. My father gave me the worst piece of well-meant advice ever when he told me, as I first went up to Cambridge, that I should wait for the world to "beat a path to my door." It showed small signs of doing so, until . . . Well, I have some 137,000 words waiting publication of what happened when a certain unlikely person did eventually come, unbidden, to my door in "the Wedding Cake" of St. John's College.

Muggeridge ran himself down so often and so amusingly that he left quite a large, if flattish, mark on his times. He was right and wrong, here and there, left and right, *un peu partout*, in a parody of Pascal's image of the restless human condition. In that regard, he stood for the very type of the journalist: a man who makes the most amusing possible use of the confidences and friends he betrayed. In person, he had the appearance of one's favorite eraser: a polished and rounded rubbedness, shiny without being quite clean. His literally long-suffering spouse Kitty trumped all his ace remarks with one of her own, when she said of David Frost "He rose without trace." Malcolm realized that she was his one true wife when she was tubed up to give him her blood at a critical moment. I seem to remember a scoundrel in the absurdly overrated *Mad Men* having a similar moment of abject devotion, until he got better.

We have been enjoying one of my birthday presents from our son Paul, the mini-series *True Detective* in which Woody Harrelson and his colleague whose unmemorable, unspellable name cannot do his brilliant career a lot of good are so consistently, edgily inventive (and well supplied with clever, in-character words) that it is incredible—*quia credo*—that *Breaking Bad*, series 5, should have trumped it at the Emmys. The latter show was good for a while, but then became extended and distasteful like a naughty boy's chewing gum. I have proposed a French provincial spin-off, based on the inedible bread at one of our local *boulangeries*, entitled *Baking Bad*. Would you believe that so far there is no immediate word from the sixth floor or wherever it is that heads nod before they roll?

OK, you're still wondering what possessed me to read *Harvard Hates America*. As a true lit.biz detective you can guess: someone wanted me to write a movie and that might have supplied a primer to it. The someone was Herb (later Herbert) Ross, known to some as "the tiny dancer" (he was over six feet tall, what can I tell you?). He had suggested, when his suggestions could unleash development bucks, that I do a U.S. version of *The Glittering Prizes*. I tried, I did try, and—like the 1980s money—it wasn't all that bad. Herb liked it, but by the time of delivery he was not as bankable as before. The project went, as some said and still may, "pear-shaped." I have nothing against pears or their shape, but it never gets a good press. Can it be because that obsessional anatomic item the female breast is deemed uncomely when it assumes that form?

I think, by the way, that I have looked at Philip Roth's *The Breast* (it was both short and pear-shaped). As a fresh take, if not grope, on Kafka's *Metamorphosis* I never met a worse one. Why do top talents publish bad work? Can it be, Herr Doktor, because any man on a pedestal can have such hubristic vertigo that he needs to lower himself a little bit? You have to be a German, even a sorta nice one such as Thomas Mann, never to doubt your right to eminence. You know the story of the two German professors at the same university who became friends. In due time, one colleague proposed to the other that they address each other in less formal terms: "So please from now on, why don't we drop the Doktor/Doktor greeting? Call me Heinrich, do!" The other professor said, "You have one doctorate, Heinrich, but I have two. So: I will gladly call you Heinrich, and I too will drop one of my Doktors, so you can call me plain Doktor from now on . . ." You know it, you know it. Immanuel Kant probably knew it. I always preferred Schopenhauer, who is said to have hated women and may have been a life-long virgin. The things we know and the things we don't . . . And now, the things we never will: what's so great about Master de Lillo, for instance? I did attempt the thousand-page number which begins with some kid going to a baseball game, but I quit at the bottom of the seventh.

Tout à toi, Freddie.

September 1, 2014
Dear Freddie,

Your Doktor/Doktor joke reminds me of the old story of the boat about to arrive at Haifa from Berlin, filled with German-Jewish passengers. As the boat is pulling into harbor, a woman standing at the dock calls out, "Doktor, Doktor." At which point everyone on board rushes to one side of the boat, and it promptly sinks. Ah, those Germans, a laugh not a minute but perhaps every decade or two.

Graham Greene seems to me the very reverse of the writer who is Holden Caulfield's brother whom one wishes to telephone as soon as one completes one of his books. Four or so years ago I checked back in on Graham Greene by reading two of his novels, *The Heart of the Matter* and *The End of the Affair*, and found myself impressed by the craftsmanship but not much moved by the content of either. I suspect one has to feel oneself beset by sin, as only an old-line Catholic could, to sing along with these books. Years ago I read Greene's autobiography, in whose pages I marveled at its author's rare appearances and absence of introspection. Graham Greene isn't a strong candidate for the list of relatively recent writers likely still to be read fifty years from now. With the exception perhaps of *The Third Man*, a swell movie made from another of his novels, the pleasure element just isn't there, at least it's not there for me.

Wasn't Kitty Muggeridge a niece of Beatrice Webb? In her husband's writing she comes off as a smart and lovely woman. The David Frost remark is what I believe the Irish call a corker. In his writings, if perhaps not in his outdoor activities, the Mugger was always graciously mindful of his wife, or so I seem to remember, and he brought her into them fairly often. The one volume of Muggeridge's I have kept in my deliberately diminished library is *Things Past*, an anthology of his various writings. He had a style, left distinctive fingerprints on all he wrote; his signature device was the comma, which he used to good effect for pauses, pregnant and otherwise, and which enabled him to unfurl subordinate-clause-laden sentences of a hundred words or more, usually ending on a high and surprising note. Not many word-slingers around in the present day who can fire off such sentences.

Your public-school instruction to be good to underlings lest they shoot you in the back makes much sense. I've read that there was genuine concern during World War Two lest the men serving under Evelyn Waugh shoot him, so arrogantly and harshly did he treat them. I have never wanted anyone serving under me, in the military or in civilian life. As an enlisted man in the U.S. Army, this wasn't a problem. The few times in my life when I have had employees—in the anti-Poverty Program in Little Rock, Arkansas, at *The American Scholar* magazine in Washington, D.C.—I was made edgy about it: was I being fair to them?, were they doing all that was expected of them?, did they respect my leadership sufficiently?, did I give them every chance to show their skills? and so on into the insomniacal night. When I left *The American Scholar*, an acquaintance had a desk sign made for me that reads, "Responsible for My Prose Only," which is the way I prefer it. At various times in my life I have been guilty of wanting money, fame, and the love of beautiful women, but power I can live nicely without, thank you very much.

Nor have I ever yearned for servants, let alone full-time, live-in servants, nannies or cooks or even gardeners. A lovely woman named Jesse Waters used to clean our apartment every other week over a period of perhaps seven or eight years; and ever since she retired to live with family in Arkansas, roughly twelve or so years ago, Barbara has been sending her $500 every year for her birthday and another $500 at Christmas (I suspect she may be sending her still more on the sly). The preponderance of Americans, myself included, are of too democratic a temper, which means that we tend to feel more than a touch sorry for people in subservient positions—hence the impossibility of having servants.

We are at one on the subject of careful grammar and syntax. They are the basis of our trade, and as such require mastery. Correctness here, getting the little things right, is also the basis of elegance, or so I have come to believe. In writing I should rather be caught out making a factual than a grammatical error. In the realm of syntax there is theseadays (a play of course on your thenadays) some controversy about what does constitute an error. Our putatively most elevated magazines and journals split infinitives with the same happy gusto that the youthful Abraham Lincoln used to split logs. The question of whether or not to end sentences with prepositions is for most people no longer a question. Some are content to let *vox populi* set the rules; others of us, when a rule is broken or a word imprecisely used, reach not for our revolver but for our H. W. Fowler, who nicely sets out all the rules and many important linguistic distinctions, but also allowed that it is better to break any rule than write anything barbarous.

I recently sent off a review of two books on grammar—books that I mentioned to you earlier—to the *Wall Street Journal*. One was written by a deliberately charmless Englishman named N. M. Gwynne, an old Etonian who after a successful business career has become a professional pedagogue attached to no institution; the other by a Harvard psycholinguist named Steven Pinker (I sense a Pinsky in his past) who takes a more liberal view of grammatical lapses and swinginger syntax. Gwynne wants to remind us that the rules in these matters are crucial, Pinker to loose us from the bonds of schoolmarmish strictness. Pinker is on the side of the angels, yet I find myself lining up with Gwynne. I have no wish to be liberated from the age-old rules of language; I prefer to play the game with the net up and tautly stretched.

I have been reading with much pleasure *Sunset and Twilight*, the final diaries (1947–1958) of Bernard Berenson, kept between his 82nd and 93rd years. This is a book with which you and I, at our ages, can, as the kids say, identify. Thus far I've only read a hundred and seventy or so pages (of 543), but I find I am eager to get back to it. I read it with morning tea and at lunch. Many of the entries naturally enough touch on visual art. Berenson came to feel that, late in life, he could see, as an artist sees, which is to say he could see things in themselves as they really are, and not encrusted with concepts, theories, and history. Several are brief prose landscapes, for, as he notes in one entry, every view in Florence presents a different, generally majestic landscape. These to me are the most boring items in the book.

Like so much autobiographical writing, the best passages in *Sunset and Twilight* are those in which Berenson owns up to the worst things about himself. Why is it that the unpleasant qualities one features about oneself in writing turn out to be the most convincing? Berenson reports, for example, that he was unable to "stimulate" his wife mentally in the last years of her life, "and my two daily visits to her bedside during her last years bored her." This wife, Mary, you may recall, was the sister of Logan Pearsall Smith, whose other sister, Alys, married Bertie (not Wooster but) Russell. Exchanging the word literary for art, I wonder if this passage does not set off a gong for you as it did for me: ". . . philosophizing on art, as indeed all art criticism, bores me. Yet I continue to write it . . . I get so painfully constipated when my mind does not produce matter for print as when intestines do not function healthily." All his many guests, the famous as well as young students, get put through the strainer of his diary prose. "Somerset Maugham to lunch. Lined, wrinkled face, senile mouth, kindly expression (or is it of mere resignation?). Stammered. Utterly unaffected, and no trace of playing up to his reputation." He avers that, "few people wear well for more than a few encounters." He is less than certain how well he himself wears.

The most interesting entries are those in which he does a tentative summing up, questioning the value of what he has done, regretting all he has left undone, attempting to discover who he truly is and the meaning (if any) of his time on the planet. He is fairly certain that he will not be remembered, except in the hearts of those people who love him and will live (briefly) after him. He is pleased to have had no children, certain he would have been a poor father. Even though he is less than confident that what he writes will much matter, he cannot bring himself to cease continuing: " . . . to write, to write for print, [is] the only occupation I call work." He is against writing as a profession—writing, that is, to order, to please others; *others* include editors and the wider public; he will have no truck with "writing as a commercial product." This feeling, he suspects, "may go back to a Talmudic feeling against using one's higher functions for sordid ends." He is of course able to ignore all sordid ends because of the vast fortune he acquired as a professional connoisseur and attributer of Italian art at a time when people were insecure about the authenticity of the paintings they yearned to purchase.

Lots of lovely little touches in these diaries. Berenson has met everyone. Santayana and Bertie Russell, he tells us, were bad listeners. He admires Harry Truman for his naturalness. Arthur Koestler he describes as having un-Jewish features; "perhaps a touch of gypsy." His wife "rather washedout blonde, physically (to me) uninteresting." Italians seem unable to concentrate on music but treat it as "a condiment." Goethe is the German Samuel Johnson, only much greater. Croce he finds "even more uninterested in my approach to things than I to his. . ." Jews in his observation (and as a boy he was himself a Lithuanian Jewish immigrant in Boston) "are seldom at ease in society, seldom take themselves as a matter of course, seldom forget that are not 'in' or 'of.' That tends to make them either too polite to the point of cringing, or too amiable, too ready to be obliging; or on the other hand to keep gloomily, sulkily aloof until their superiority is amply recognized."

Perhaps most interesting of all, for us, are his feelings about aging, about being out of the running, a back number. "Age has little to look forward to, at most to getting no feebler, no less incapacitated for work and play, for work that is play . . ." He continues to write even though the sums his writing brings in are derisory, the satisfactions "generally spoiled by annoying misprints, distasteful ways of putting a book out, foolish or malignant reviews, etc., etc." He concludes that he writes because "I want to justify my claim to be still a useful member of society, and capable in some slight measure of influencing it—in short, that I am still able to pay passage on the ship of life which is carrying us all—whither?" Despite his age, his diminishing belief in his own importance, his anger at fraudulence in intellect and art does not diminish. He continues to get worked up at all the shoddy art he sees around him—to get some notion of his standard, he felt Henry Moore a lousy artist—yet asks, "why vex my soul, why fume with indignation, why denounce the age?" I believe him when he says that he feels no envy for the third-rate people, "the perverted artists and their verbal henchmen, lauded by the age, "and adds "I feel about it all as I do about Soviet doctrine and propaganda when it attracts adherents among the so-called intellectuals in our midst."

Hope I haven't bored you going on so long about old B.B., but I am finding so much that he has written in these diaries of his old age matches my own condition and sentiments and I thought you might also find it so.

To go from the splendid to the inane, I should like to nominate for a Racso, the reverse of an Oscar, one of the worst dogs of a movie I have seen in a few years, and when it comes to movies I have watched more dogs than the current president of the United States Kennel Club. The envelope, please . . . and the winner is . . . *Lost in Austen*, which was made in 2008 and I gather began life as a television mini-series. The movie is about a contemporary young woman, fixated on *Pride and Prejudice*, who finds a way— you don't want to know about it—into the household of Miss Austen's Bennett family. Casting, writing, direction, leading and supporting actors, Racso winners all. We watched it on DVD in astonishment. Could a movie really be this wretched? How did a group of men and women with a doubtless powerfully overestimated sense of their own street smarts agree to put money into such *dreck*? How, one wondered, might it end, or, better, when would it end? The case in which the DVD comes notes that its length is "approximately three hours," but in the actual viewing it felt just a little longer than the Thirty Years War. Karl Kraus defined a journalist as someone who, given time, writes worse. A good screenwriter, in my definition, is someone who doesn't need more than two hours to deliver the goods. Let us be thankful that Bernard Berenson wasn't alive to have watched *Lost in Austen*. He would, I daresay, have wet his pants in rage.

Best, Joe

LAGARDELLE. 2.9.2014.
Dear Joe,

I have always resisted paying attention to age. Thanks to a fairly robust physical inheritance and the absence of serious illnesses, I have loitered in protracted adolescence, the happy condition of a good many writers who have had the luck to feed themselves with their pens and kindred implements for the whole of their lives. I have been through most of the phases of innocence and vestiges of them remain with me, not least the sense of romantic election that comes from being, or deciding to be, an Artist. I made some remark on that topic to Stanley Kubrick, during one of our sometimes very long telephone conversations and he was provoked into saying "You don't think I'm an artist, do you?" I said, "Oh I don't know, Stanley; all I do know is that you need cameras and lights and actors and assistants and locations and caterers and several million dollars before you can practice your art and all I need is a pencil and a piece of paper." Kubrick said, "You sure know how to hurt a guy."

I suppose that the remedying of old hurts, and new cuts, by the sharpness of one's repartee plays some part in what keeps me at it. I suspect that you do not have the same quick sense of grievance, though you may merely be more tempered in concealing it. My thin-skinnedness goes along with my sharp tongue. There's a certain doubleness there: I have often imagined that I was amusing, or at least placating, possible enemies by the brightness of my memorable remarks. I made the father figure in my TV series *After the War* remind his Freddie-like son, "People seldom forgive what they fail to forget."

I am still amazed to be the target of sustained literary critical, journalistic barbs. A minor novelist but a pretty good one, William Cooper, the pseudonym of Harry Hoff, a civil servant friend of Charles Snow, told me that Anthony Burgess, a usually genial reviewer, had given him the shaft, as the English used to say, and then greeted him warmly at a party. When Harry was terse and distant, Burgess said, "Something wrong, Harry?" "Did you happen to read what you said about my last book?" Big Burgess clapped little Harry on the shoulder and said, "I was only having a little fun. I didn't mean it." "In that case," Harry said, "I hope I never see or speak to you again." The Jim Campbells are—you may depend upon it—always going to be coming.

An Oxford professor called Martin Goodman did my Josephus book no good at all (but then who knows how much harm reviews really do?) when he cudgeled it in the London *Literary Review* to which I am an intermittently regular contributor. The editor, Nancy Sladek, had either forgotten or did not know that I had reviewed his *Rome and Jerusalem,* a baggy academic monster on the ancient polarity, as he saw it, of the two cities. My review deferred to his professorship in matters of linguistic and historical detail, though I thought, rightly, that Alexandria was, so to say, always more polar, in Roman orientations, than Jerusalem, which scarcely figures in the historical "narrative" until the Jewish rebellion of 67.

As that great double act Antony and Cleopatra prove, Alexandria was Rome's hot, disgraceful Other, rather as, in the days of Empire, "Paris," that shame-free, bare-breasted fleshpottery, was to proper, Puritanical London. Alexandria was a place of Greeks, Jews and Levantines, in an immoral, temptation-filled *triple,* the name given to the three-decker specialty of the Buenos Aires sanwicherias when we were there in 1968. The local loaf, of rather moist consistency, was cut longways and the ingredients interleaved before the whole thing was rolled into the Porteño version of a Swiss roll and sliced. Alexandria probably had the eclectic food typical of harbor cities in its *popinae,* the Latin for fast-food joints you could pop into.

As usual, when reviewing professorial persons, I took it that Goodman was secure enough to take a little ribbing. So, when he chose to go *hors sujet* and claim that Romans, some Romans, were sentimental enough to care deeply for their pets and cited, as proof, Catullus's Lesbia and her eyes puffy from weeping for her dead sparrow (or, as some scholars have it, goldfinch), I dared to say that he was a better historian than reader of literary *loci.* The manifest truth was/is that Lesbia used her affectations of distress to frustrate her lover's ardor. Neither Gaius Valerius nor his posh lady was likely to cry over fallen finches. In *Darling,* there was a scene in which Julie Christie had just had an abortion and, when Dirk Bogarde came with the usual flowers, she asked about her goldfish (ah the deep critic, what he can find if he will!) and said, in a choked voice, "Look after the fishes, poor little things!" This after we had already seen her and her gay photographer friend Malcolm maltreating them. *"Beh le donne!"* said Alberto Moravia, not always wrongly.

Goodman had his specialty and it did not include literary criticism. The Romans reveled, literally, in exhibitions of cruelty to and by animals, although they did have moments of remorse, for instance when Pompey the Great (the Great *lobbus* in many respects) introduced elephants into the arena, as a special and expensive treat, and had them done to death for the pleasure of the electorate. As if unable to understand why they deserved such treatment, the elephants came to the edge of the arena and gazed with pleading anguish at the *populus Romanus* which then had a revulsion of feeling and pelted Magnus with abuse, too late to reprieve the sad, sagging beasts. Shows involving other, more easily transported animals continued for several centuries. Fine spirits such as Cicero preferred to absent themselves, but the circuses went on. One of his senatorial chums asked Tully, when he was governor of Bithynia, to send him some panthers for the arena, but the area had already been, as it were, fished out.

To tell the truth, I did not even glance at what Goodman said about my Josephus book. I feel no obligation to take notice of whatever medicine literary quacks of various kinds care to pour out for me. It is some kind of compliment, I try to tell myself, when doing my spiritual exercises, that I remain a target for darts from the same silly quarters that used to go for me when I was, as they say, unduly conspicuous on TV and elsewhere. I am no longer disposed to imagine that there is any dark motive for malice, aside from the pleasure people get from concocting it. The thing which is almost always missed out, when it comes to solemn consideration of "prejudice" and allied sports, is that there is a lot of fun in persecuting people, especially unjustly.

There is a clever scene in Louis Malle's film *Lacombe Lucien* (script by Patrick Modiano) in which the rustic lout, of no innately wicked disposition, having been recruited by the Milice (the Vichy French equivalent of the Gestapo), takes part in a raid on the bourgeois home of a family of *Résistants*. The rich boy, of pretty well Lucien's age, has been making a careful model of a torpedo boat, with every detail nicely painted and glued in place. He sees Lucien looking at it and makes some amiable remark, hoping for some kind of hobbyists' solidarity. Lucien sniffs and begins, slowly, sadistically, to pick the model to pieces. The artist is a fool if he doesn't recognize the spite which good work provokes and the need of those who all but admire it to tear it to bits.

The "who does he think he is?" motif runs through the whole history of art. When he "put men among the gods" on the Parthenon frieze, Pheidias had to run for his life from the Athens he had embellished; that prolific boozer Aeschylus only just escaped prosecution for blasphemy as did Euripides. Ovid, Voltaire, Thomas Mann all took to their heels. Even our old friend Michel de Montaigne, who dared to say that one had better be pretty sure of one's opinions before roasting people alive for failing to share them, had his mischievously tolerant books banned by a Church which never got round to excommunicating friend Adolf in case it "confused" the German faithful.

Your invention of the Racso award for the worst film of the season is, as they used to say, a lulu. The strange thing about the movies is that they can be both mediocre, art-wise, and have a powerful line to the emotions. A couple of nights ago, we watched one about Giorgio Perlasca, billed as "the

Italian Schindler," which our son Paul's very smart Italian lady sent me for my birthday. Charlie Chaplin was right, of course: no movie is ever good because it's technically flawless. Perlasca—played by an actor whom we have seen a dozen times as Inspector Montalbano in an artless, riveting series about a Sicilian cop—was a cattle merchant who happened to be in Budapest during Eichmann's murderous round-up in which he was eagerly assisted by the local fascists.

The film did not conceal (as Spielberg almost certainly would have) Perlasca's having previously volunteered, *en bon fasciste Italien,* to fight both in Abyssinia and in Spain. In Budapest, his "banality" does not prevent him from being outraged and then fearlessly bold in assuming the role of Spain's consul general, after the ambassador has fled, and filling the embassy premises with Jews, whom he then proclaims to be Sephardim and hence qualified for repatriation to Spain. It's true that Franco did offer sanctuary to Sephardic refugees, but his people also made lists of all the Jews resident in Spain in case Hitler won the war. "Belt and braces, old man," as the British used to say.

Perlasca saved a lot of people and managed to escape and live into old age in Padua, I think it was. Why was he good? Why was Eichmann evil? "Banal" the pair of them, although our Hannah had more fun turning paradoxical cartwheels over evil, while denigrating the low-grade Yidden for their sheepish lack of fight. And then, when she saw Martin Heidegger again, she didn't put her hands up but, according to some reports, her *jambes en air.* Cheap shot? Why not? By one of those strange coincidences, the director of *Perlasca* had the same name—Negrin—as the last leader of Republican Spain.

Like Arendt, the film depicted the majority of the Jews as despairing and lacking in fight, which may well have been the case, not least because they were taught that killing was contrary to God's law and that Jews should conform to the laws of the country in which they lived. I used to admire a book by a Jesuit called Cuddihy called *The Ordeal of Civility* in which, with some acuteness, he made a seemingly sympathetic study of the difficulties which those who had burst the bounds of the *shtetl* had in entering Christian societies. Civility and servility tended to go together. What Cuddihy never acknowledged was that within civilization itself all kinds of savageries, personal and institutional, were biding their time. Rough beasts shamble all over the place.

The key line in *Perlasca*—how often there is just one in any film that sticks in the mind!—comes from a minor character, a Hungarian Jewish lawyer who works for the Spanish embassy and relies on that for his immunity. Very late in the piece, he realizes that he has created a false persona for himself by being a *kibitzer*, never a participant in (Jewish) life and the hazards it entails. His vanity depends on an illusion of being *pas comme les autres*. Is there something of the *kibitzer* in all of us (including, for all I know, Phlebas the Phoenician) who look on life and describe it, with scorn or sympathy, from a distance, often in fiction, sometimes in think-pieces? Since you have been much more in the public world than I have, you may reject the "soft impeachment" (an Augustan phrase I learned from John Fowles, who wrote books which combined catchpenny motifs with a measure of the higher falute).

In bridge parlance, *kibitzers* are the onlookers who watch you make a mess of the hand and tell you, *après coup*, what the winning line would have been, as if you didn't know already. In today's English-speaking world, they are moralists and, very often, critics and opinionators, especially of the syndicated journalistic order, who affect to know who shall be saved and who should be damned, who crowned in one sense and who in quite the other. One of the fruits of age is a certain indifference about which list one is on, to starboard or to port. Grammar serves us both as a severe impersonal master; a man with any sense of pitch and rhythm needs no James Wood or his generic equivalent to put him in his place. I write as quickly as I may and correct and cut for as long as papa time will allow. What fun it is to be a carpenter! How foolish He was to play the Savior when he could have been sanding and polishing and blowing off the dust into philoprogenitive old age!

Tout à toi, Freddie.

September 6, 2014
Dear Freddie,

I have to complain about your lack of complaining about your health. The fact is that not once in what will soon be two books of e-mail correspondence have you mentioned a cold, a muscle strain, a visit to doctor or dentist. What kind of older Jewish gent are you, anyway? I go to lunch every week or so with three old high-school pals, and our illnesses, our minor afflictions, our *desolation générale*, is among our leading subjects. From you on the subject of physical deterioration, on the other unpalsied hand, not a peep. I do not mean to cast doubt on your birth, but are you certain that you are Jewish? Is it possible that you were adopted? Your conduct in the health realm doesn't, Hebraically speaking, compute.

Of the collection of grievances, like the writing of books, there is no end. So much is this so that the term grievance-collector has had to be brought into being. (The Yiddish word for grievance is *tiness*, as in "He has *tiness* against me.") Lapses in memory have allowed me to forget the names of most of the unimportant people who have spoken ill in the public prints of my various scribblings. (You will recall that Stendhal remarked that to write a book is to risk standing up in public to be shot; he failed to mention all the inconvenient places in which the bullets might land.) The difference between a collector and a connoisseur, I am told, is that the connoisseur wants only the best, while the collector wants everything. I prefer to think myself a grievance connoisseur (kind of sewer). My own collection of grievances is rather small but, I like to think, exquisite.

Allow me to set one out on display for you. I never passed it along to you, but a review of *Distant Intimacy*, our earlier collaborative volume, appeared in a local give-away paper called the *Chicago Reader*. The review was written by a former student of mine at Northwestern, a young woman I went out of my way to cultivate. A lumpish kid, she had been dealt a poor hand in being without physical allure. What seemed to me to make the matter worse is that she had a touch of imagination, just enough, I thought, to cause her to suffer from being unlikely to have the kind of romantic life of which she is likely to have dreamed. In a course I used to teach called Fundamentals of Prose Composition, she wrote a brief essay that had a scene with her as a child dancing with her dog in the rain. A homely child dancing with her dog in the rain—I found this moving. By cultivating her I mean that I took her seriously. On a number of occasions I met with her for coffee (hot chocolate for her) in a nearby bookstore café. Conversation wasn't always easy; there were occasions when I felt I was out on a blind date that wasn't working out. I persisted. I wanted her to know that I, a serious person, took her seriously.

Just before her graduation, she wrote to thank me for all that I had taught her in the classroom and for holding her up to high expectations, and to tell me how she was always ashamed to do less than her best for me because she didn't want to disappoint me. She also wrote: "And thanks also for the education you gave me all those afternoons at Borders [the bookstore-café] over those innumerable cups of hot chocolate. Those were some of the best times I've had in college and I am going to miss them. Thank you for being my teacher, also a friend, and, in some ways, the grandfather I always wished I had. I am really going to miss you." I wrote back to thank her for her letter, and instructed her never to forget that she is an extraordinary person and that, though it may take a bit of time, one day the world would recognize this.

Fast forward, as the recent transition has it, to the publication of *Distant Intimacy* in 2012. The title of her review was "Knowing When to Quit," and the punchline was that I clearly didn't, but should have done so many years ago. She wasn't political when an undergraduate, she avers, but had become so since that time, and finds that I write for what she calls right-wing magazines and papers (*Commentary, The Weekly Standard,* the *Wall Street Journal*) despicable. She thinks your and my correspondence petty and bitter, and wanders why Yale U. Press ever agreed to publish it. She wonders if the teacher she once admired wasn't in fact a fake, someone merely building up a pleasant persona. "Could anyone be that much of a fraud?" she asks. Her answer is, it sure looks like it. My "brilliance as a writer is to find depth and substance in things that most people assume are trivial. But instead he [and you with me] gives us crap like this, all surface and self-absorption for no purpose." What lends this grievance of mine its piquancy, speaking now you understand as a connoisseur, is the rich ingredient of ingratitude, which always lends zest to a grievance, *n'est-ce pas?*

I rather long one day to meet this now not so young woman, perhaps at a movie or concert, and re-introduce myself. I might mention that I read her review of our book with mounting interest, and ask if she has other such poison darts in her quiver. I should add that I hadn't realized she bore me such a deep grudge, and if there is anything I could do to make it up to her— a hot chocolate one afternoon perhaps—my phone number is in the book. If such a meeting were ever to come about, I hope I would have the *sang-froid* to make her squirm a good bit for being such an ungrateful jerk.

Which brings me to the distinction between a grievance and a grudge. I would say that a grudge is longer lasting and more deeply felt than a grievance. I would say that for a grudge to have any quality it must endure for no fewer than ten years. Norman Podhoretz tells a story about Wilfred Sheed, who wrote a wickedly damning review of Norman's book *Making It*, coming up to him twenty-five or so years later, and suggesting that they shake hands and banish all bad feeling between them. "Sorry," Norman said, "but the statute of limitations on that review has yet to run out." What makes this story all the better is that Sheed, when making this peace offering, was on crutches from the late-life effects of polio. Now this is what I call holding a grudge.

A. J. P. Taylor once said, apropos of his politics, that he had extreme views, weakly held. I would describe my grudges as merely dimly felt, but firmly held. One grudge I do hold I plan never to let go. The grudge is not against a person but against Phi Beta Kappa, the scholastic honorary society, membership of which is given to American university students who do well in school. Edward Shils used to say that Phi Beta Kappa's real function was to becalm, however briefly, neurotic Jewish mothers who nagged their children into hollow academic achievement. Phi Beta Kappa is the sponsoring organization of *The American Scholar*, and my grudge against it is that it did nothing to prevent my being fired from the magazine's editorship by a board composed of second-line angry black academics and third-line feminists and a nervous crew of liberals, who decided I was behind the times in not printing articles in the magazine about feminism, American slavery, and other topics from the rich buffet of victimology. (The liberals went along because the greatest fear of liberals, as Orwell noted, was to be outflanked from the left.) The fact is that, after twenty-odd years in the editorship I had had a good run, and was ready to depart the magazine. Still, but, yet, however, and nevertheless . . .

Eight or nine years ago, the current editor of *The American Scholar*, a decent enough fellow named Robert Wilson solicited a contribution to the magazine from me. I thanked him, but told him that I held a grudge against Phi Beta Kappa, not a heavy grudge, but my only active grudge, and would like to take it to my grave. He took this explanation in good part. I believe he understood.

I am nowhere near so efficient at repartee as you. I tend to be more of the Walter Mitty *esprit d'escalier* school of repartee. Years ago, at a University of Chicago Press party, I introduced my wife to a sweet character named Ned Rosenheim, a teacher at the university who specialized in eighteenth-century literature. "Swift's my guy," he said to Barbara. Only later did I regret not rejoining, "*Maupassant's mon Guy.*" The last time I taught a class in Henry James, when taking up *The Portrait of a Lady*, I asked a student named Jonathan Stern to describe Gilbert Osmond. "Well," he said, not pondering the question overlong, "he's an asshole." He said this without the least intent of *épate-ing* his teacher or shocking his fellow students. I told him that I couldn't allow such language in the classroom, but what I should have said, I realized half an hour or so later, was, "I'm glad, Mr. Stern, that I didn't ask you to describe Oedipus Rex."

You are right about the memorability, almost the imperishability, of single lines or bits from less than first-rate movies. From a *policier* called *The Laughing Policeman,* I have never forgotten Walter Matthau asking his assistant, played by Bruce Dern, what his week-or-so-long shadowing of a wealthy suspect in a murder case has uncovered. Not much, Dern reports of the suspect, who seems to spend lots of time at his gym: "He's playing all day," Dern says, "and farting in silk." In the movie called *City Slickers,* Jack Palance, playing his traditional role of the hoary-handed (is this the correct cliché) cowboy, says to Billy Crystal, "I have turds bigger than you." All I remember from a 1968 movie called *Interlude* is Oskar Werner's elegant raincoat, but, even now, nearly fifty years later, I haven't forgotten it. I wanted, still want, to own such a coat.

I don't think I ever told you about a friend of mine named Maury Rosenfield. Your mention of Stanley Kubrick requiring caterers, among other auxiliary troops, to perform his art, reminded me of him. Maury was a successful Chicago lawyer, and at one point forged a connection with Ben Hecht, who sought his help in freeing a black man in Alabama who was wrongly convicted of murder and awaiting execution on death row in Alabama. Hecht afterwards encouraged Maury and his wife Loie to get into the movie business, and they did, producing *Bang the Drum Slowly*, an early Robert De Niro movie—they paid De Niro $10,000—which in America has become a cult classic. They later produced a number of Broadway shows. "The toughest thing about producing a movie," Maury once told me, is the catering. On the set of *Bang the Drum Slowly*, the complaints about the food at lunch were apparently endless. At the time this movie was in production, across town they were making one of the *Godfather* movies. "I arranged to get the same caterer as was doing *The Godfather*," Maury told me. "If anyone henceforth complained about the food, I told them they were eating the same lunch as Marlon Brando, so shut up."

Maury lived in a plush Chicago suburb called Glencoe—known to the anti-Semites as Glen Cohen—and bought and later sold some radio stations that early put him out of the financial wars. Among his other movie ventures, he had an option on the Scott Fitzgerald story called "A Diamond as Big as The Ritz," a title much superior to the story that appears beneath it. He had acquired the services of an English writer named Adrian Mitchell to write a screenplay for it, and was unhappy with Mitchell's attempt. Maury, who had been reading me in *Commentary*, one day called to ask if I would read Mitchell's screenplay and let him know what I thought of it. I read it and reported that I thought it poor stuff. He asked me if I would care to try another version for him. After some hesitation, I decided not to do so, on the grounds that the story just wasn't there. But Maury and Loie and Barbara and I became and remained friends. He always went out of his way to do kind things for us, taking us to the ballet, or summer concerts at Ravinia, or to dinner at his posh country club.

Maury wanted to make a film of a story of mine called "Moe," and formed a production company to do so called Clotsworthy Skeffington Enterprises, after Lady Mary Wortley Montagu's first fiancé, a name he picked up and was charmed by in an essay I wrote called "Wise, Foolish, Enchanting Lady Mary." Maury was the reverse of everyone's idea of the vulgar movie producer. Nothing came of the movie "Moe"—talk about your non-sell titles—for soon after he formed the legal entity Clotsworthy Skeffington Enterprises, Loie Rosenfield died, and not long after Maury's own health began to fail. He had two knee replacement surgeries that put him in a wheelchair. He died, choking on a cookie at the home of his son Andy, in his early nineties. He was what we in Chicago call a good guy—by my lights, he was a great good guy.

After the grousing—and I do not mean grouse-hunting—of my earlier paragraphs, I have to report having had a letter from a man named William Hughes in Hutchison, Kansas, thanking me for the pleasure my books have given him, and wondering why I have never written on Epictetus. I thanked him, and told him that I have never read Epictetus, except in the most glancing way, though I hoped to get round to reading him seriously before too long. The following week's mail brought, as a gift, his personal copy of *Discourses of Epictetus*, a handsome and still clean edition, edited and translated by George Long, M.A. Oxon. This from Hutchison, Kansas, mind you. America, go figure, what an amazing country!

Best, Joe

LAGARDELLE 9.9.14.
Dear Joe,

One of the myths of British life is that of the Public School in which smaller boys were initiated in the game of snaking and laddering by being beaten, with rods of various caliber, by bigger ones, whose office it was to maintain discipline in the "boarding houses" to which members of the middle-class and above regularly committed their male offspring. The British penchant for incarcerating their young owed something to many parents' dutiful absence on imperial duty. It was sustained by a traditional coldness towards their children which probably had something to do with the rate of mortality, even among the well-heeled. There was a consequent reluctance to be heavily invested emotionally. I used to know which toff it was who met a young boy on the stairs of his grand house and, when the boy ventured to say "Good morning, sir," asked, "And who might you be?" "Please, sir, I'm your son William." Nth son, no doubt.

The routine of flogging smaller boys, not least for—in the case of Charterhouse—"festivity," the slang term for impertinence *de bas en haut*, was supposedly controlled by the Housemaster. He had to sanction the formal "execution" of miscreants, but the threat of official violence both cowed and excited the lower orders. At Charterhouse, the supreme chastisement was known as a "school beating," at which all the top echelons of the various Houses assembled to witness the rite. I gather that "hazing" in American universities can be of a sometimes savagely sadistic nature, but the British flagellatory system was a parody of justice and had to be conducted with due ceremony. There was a refinement, practiced in some school, whereby—after being given whatever number of strokes (a nicely ambiguous usage)—the victim, purged and restored to society, with a clean slate and a red behind, had formally to thank the "executioner" for his correction.

It was not quite gentlemanly ever to refer to such occasions in later life, although one Quintin Hogg, an irascible Tory politician and lawyer, took public pleasure in reminding Freddie Ayer, the festive, moderately leftish philosopher, that he, the Hogg, had beaten him at Eton. A crucial ingredient of this process was that the flogger should not take pleasure in what he "had" to do and that the victim should not cry out or ever indicate that he held a grudge. British justice, even in this puerile, parodic form, was not given, and was not supposed to be taken, personally.

The rewards of serving the unseen powers, by maintaining social discipline, included a graded series of privileges. Exemption from standing in line, the wearing of more or less fancy "haberdashery," chevroned and cable-stitched superiority prepared young men for the white man's burden in which the pleasure of domination and dominion was never mentioned and never wholly absent. Whether he was the young Leonard Woolf (granted summary powers over the "natives" of Edwardian Ceylon) or Eric Blair, aka George Orwell, playing the imperial cop in Burma, the ex-Public Schoolboy easily assumed the prefectorial role. It may well be that, with memories, very often, of what it was like to be chastised, such men exercised their powers with moderation and the justice which, so the white man's burden promised, was warranted by the British presence. Britannic majesty was at least secular: it did not enforce any fierce version of Christian doctrine, though its officers certainly sang Hymns Ancient and Modern in tropical churches and tin-roofed cathedrals of outlandish, often Gothic design.

The imperialist style included capital punishment, but it refrained, generally speaking, from massacres (one General Dyer was severely sanctioned, but not actually punished, for ordering his men to fire on an unarmed mob of Sikh demonstrators in Amritsar in 1919). In imperial India in particular, the Public School ethos allowed some two or three thousand often dedicated, rarely peculating "civil servants" to form a core and corps of "beaks" who promoted chosen Indians to run large parts of the sub-continent under their benign aegis. By respecting local dignitaries, princes and maharajahs at the top end, village "elders" towards the bottom, a wide-based "native" civilized service had an interest in the good opinion of the white men whose drearier burdens they were glad to carry. The sons of the best of the Brahmins went to English public schools. A few even played cricket, with marked style, for their adopted country. Even more were good at hockey.

This quick tour of antique horizons has relevance to some of the things you mentioned in your last letter, in which there were several *bribes*—in the French sense of "scraps"—that sprang memories of which you could have no knowledge. I knew Wilfrid Sheed, for instance, if briefly, after I had reviewed his *Transatlantic Blues* (1978), in some New York paper, in amiable terms. Sheed was an English-born writer who was transplanted, or transplanted himself, to America; I was/am the converse. Checking him out just now, I see that he was from a rather Brideshead-like family of Old Catholic aristocrats and that his godfather was G. K. Chesterton (of whom it may fairly be said, as the old Jewish tag has it, that his brother—a rank, witless anti-Semite—was worse).

Funnily enough, if not all that, I too reviewed Norman Podhoretz's *Making It*, also in a New York paper. My little number re Norman came out in 1967, the year after I won the Oscar and had brief rule of the roster. If I remember at all rightly, I somewhat underwrote Mr. P.'s then scandalous claim that it was nicer to be famous and well-paid than down there chained to some ignominious oar; but there was a tincture of big earnership in my attitude to a man who thought that getting $750 for a couple of thousand words elevated him to the big-time. The snideness must have been subtle, because when, a few years ago, our friend and patron John Podhoretz asked me to write for *Commentary*, he mentioned that Norman was still grateful for that old (*Herald-Trib*?) review of his coming out as a shameless success. You people used to have an expression "body English," which implied a certain elusive swoop and droop, perhaps on the football field. The literary equivalent allowed me, I suspect, at once to congratulate Norman on his readable candor and to drop the slyest wink to the wise that Hollywood, in those days, had mercenary lures beyond his sweet, greedy imagination. Ah the "development deals" of yesteryear!

Sheed was unlucky enough to contract polio, soon after, I think, Jonas Silk had turned it into an avoidable affliction, and—as the British used to expect—he endured crutched life without complaint. I was nice enough to his book (he wrote well) for him to call me when he came to London after being commissioned to do a piece about English football hooligans. I had a notion that the ruffians of the 1970s had been the salt of the empire, sprinkled far and wide, in the previous century and more. The soldiers of whom the Duke of Wellington said, *mas o menos,* "I don't know what effect they have on the enemy, but by God they frighten me" had become uncivil civilians. Once the world's policemen, all the way along the road to Mandalay, they were now repatriated, insular bully-boys with no natives, except a few West Indian immigrants, on whom to exercise their muscle. "Patriotism," so Dr. Johnson said, "is the last refuge of the scoundrel"; but he had never heard of Millwall Football Club and the parochial patriots who came to life on the weekend, when the enemy's scarfed partisans came to town to rumble. Sidebar: if our correspondence were to go viral, someone would be writing to tell us, *in case we didn't know,* that Johnson's much-quoted line referred not to genuine patriots but to a political faction of his time, higher hooligans as it were, who called themselves "patriots" the better to disguise their self-interest.

I introduced Sheed to my friend Brian Glanville, who has devoted most of his life and talent to writing about soccer. He wrote a number of excellent short stories and a 1958 novel, *The Bankrupts,* which anticipated even Philip Roth in its scathing depiction of a Jewish community, in North West London's Golder's Green, where—to his eternal chagrin—Evelyn Waugh was born. Some critics applauded Brian's accuracy (he said, for instance, that he had heard a lot about sensitive Jews, but never met one till he was twenty-five), others—in particular an actor called David Kossoff—accused him of doing dirt on His Own People for money. Brian sued Kossoff for libel. The British have no First Amendment to excuse lying. As it happened, sports fans, the judge in the Glanville case was Mr. Justice Hinchcliffe. Brian handled himself well in the witness box (matching the *superbe* of Kossoff's counsel with some Carthusian snap of his own) and, prompted by Hinchliffe's impartial partiality, the jury found for the plaintiff. Good old Hinchers!

At just that time, we rented a small house in London's Knightsbridge, not far from Harrod's. On the first day, since there was no space in front of number 14 for our small green Ford, I parked in front of our neighbor. Shortly afterwards, a card was put through our letter slot, FROM MR. JUSTICE HINCHCLIFFE. "Kindly do not park your car in front of number 12, since it keeps the light and air from the basement room and causes great inconvenience to all." Believe it or not, my educated docility was so well inculcated that I moved the car and never again dared to put it where no law of the land, or of the borough, had any right to forbid me. Did bad old Hinchers ever smile, say hullo or otherwise show symptoms of contingent humanity? Put it this old-fashioned way: no. No op-ed smartass can understand the busting-out-all-overness of London's swinging 60s unless he takes into account the social corsetry of decades of British decorum.

All of this relates to the attitude expected, under the Old Order, of a writer exposed to critics. A gentleman author endured without any overt wince or abiding grievance. If he could manage it, he might even affect, like Alroy Kear, in *Cakes and Ale,* to be grateful for his drubbing and so befriend and disarm his nemesis. As this letter set out to show, thenadays there was something unEnglish about anyone who challenged the judgment of the referee, sporting or literary, who—in the era of Harold Nicolson, Raymond Mortimer and Cyril Connolly—might be stern, but was assumed to be without personal animus. The history of literary feuds and furies reveals the absurdity of such blitheness, but the presumed neutrality of examiners allowed both the scholar and the literary novice to take pride (in modest tones) in his election. The critic's "can do better" was a compliment if you could swallow it without choking. My father used to greet every publication of mine with "I hope you have yet to write your best book."

Your mention of Oskar Werner's raincoat in *Interlude* was less obscure to me that you may well have thought. That (surely unmarketably titled) number was produced by a very nice man called David Deutsch. He was the producer of my first solo credit movie, *Nothing But the Best*, and launched me on a career which made me financially independent of Karl Miller and his centurion breed. Hollywood conferred a meed of the boldness which my education was calculated to scotch. David and his *Interlude* director, Kevin Billington, who later did nothing he had not done better earlier, came down to our house in rural Essex for a script conference with Master

Raphael. I am not sure that I administered any very enlivening medicine to the text they had rented. Fresh from his triumph in Truffaut's *Jules et Jim,* Oskar did *Interlude* because, *en bon Viennois,* he had always wanted to conduct a big band, Furtwängler-style. To call *Jules et Jim* "Truffaut's" pays too much tribute to the *Cahiers du Cinéma*'s auteur theory (Raphael has called this the *hauteur* theory, but who cares?). The piece adheres, as closely as makes no never mind, to the Henri-Pierre Roché novel, and demonstrates how often directors make their best mark on the back of some scribe's less than fully acknowledged earlier, often thicker work.

Your mention of Chicago's Glencoe (aka Glen Cohen) also fits into the creases of the lengthening tapestry of our distantly adjacent lives. For the English schoolboy of the 1940s, history was what the British did or, unfairly, had done to them. In an earlyish episode, in 1692, the guileless, hospitable Macdonalds of the aforesaid glen gave asylum to a bunch of Campbells who took food, drink and a couple of nights' shelter and then—altogether boys!—cut as many of their hosts to pieces as they could because they, the Macdonalds, had not come out strongly for the new English/British monarchical double act William'n'Mary. I am, of course, too well brought up to remark that the name Campbell has a place in our common bestiary. I was schooled to take Jim's brand of shit on the chin (not a pretty image, but we live in candid times) and even now I am just a little bit disposed to believe, like Josef K., that I must have done something wrong; but not as disposed as I once was. Joseph Epstein too now has his place in my education.

Tout à toi, Freddie.

September 11, 2014
Dear Freddie,

All those English public-school flogging stories always struck me, and strike me still, as litte more than sadism organized. Such, such, certainly weren't the joys. As a gringo, I'm pleased to have taken a pass on the flogging part of English public-school education, while sorry to have missed out on the Greek and Latin part. In the Chicago's (truly) public schools, corporeal punishment had long been outlawed before I came upon the scene. Bullying and fighting was restricted to the playgrounds and neighborhood parks, and teachers played no role in it.

The high school I went to on the far north side of Chicago was at that time perhaps sixty percent Jewish, forty percent Gentile. The Jews were from upward ascending families, the Gentiles mired in the working class, with parents who were policemen, laborers, lower-end white-collar workers. The social segregation between Jewish and Gentile kids was nearly complete; the only exception was athletic teams. A small segment of the Gentile boys formed clubs whose reigning spirit was thuggish: they wore heavily greased duck's ass hairdos, boxcar loafers or engineer boots, low slung jeans—Elvis Presleys and Marlon Brandos (of *The Wild One*) *avant la lettre.* "Hoods," we called them, short for hoodlums. They inspired a touch of fear, though little violence actually resulted. Once our basketball team traveled to play a school from a working-class neighborhood and afterwards hoods from the opposing school waited to beat up boys from our team, sending one of them to the hospital. At a football game I recall hoods from other working-class schools marching round to our side of the field, their fists wrapped round with bicycle chains, but the cops broke it up

Catholic kids, in that day when the Church had a much stronger hold over American families than it does now, went to so-called parochial schools, and did not much mix with public-school kids. Chicago was then an industrial city, with steel mills, stockyards, manufacturing everywhere dominant, and so much of the city was working class, which was also true of most Catholics in a very Catholic city. Chicago was a conglomeration of villages, each village dominated by an ethnic group. Religion and ethnicity, not race, were the main elements of division. Blacks in Chicago in those days were so deeply segregated in their own neighborhoods that one rarely encountered them, except in servile jobs as outer proles. But as a Jew one traveled in trepidation through Irish or Italian or Polish neighborhoods. I once wrote that I am old enough to remember being frightened by white guys, a line that today would have me in a political correctness version of Guantanamo. Rather like Borges's definition of the essential aesthetic experience as being on the brink of a truth that never quite arrives, the expectation of violence, mainly failing to arrive, was part of growing up in the Chicago of my youth. Better this, I think, than public flogging with headmasters and fellow students joining in the humiliation.

Your father's "I hope you have yet to write your best book" is a charming example of the inability of most of us, except perhaps through earning genuinely vast sums of money, to win our parents' approval. Your father, having gone to university, might have possessed an approval worth earning. My parents, though both were smart in the ways of the world, were so distant from artistic or intellectual culture that I never expected nor sought their approval for my modest achievements. With the exception of a single story based loosely on a zany customer of my father's, my mother, so far as I know, never read anything I had written. My father's standard response to an essay or story of mine was "Interesting." When he happened to read an approving review of one or another of my books in the *New York Times* or *Chicago Tribune*, he would say, "I see you got a nice send-off in yesterday's paper." I was never quite sure what a "send-off" was; better than a kiss-off, I gathered.

I once called my mother to inform her that I had just been offered a teaching post at Northwestern University, which pleased me not least because I have no advanced degrees. "That's nice," she said, "a job in the neighborhood" (I was living in Evanston at the time). On another occasion I told her that one of my books had won a $5,000 literary prize from the *Chicago Tribune*. "Oh, we get that junk in the mail all the time," she said. "I just throw it out." She wasn't being deliberately deflating, my mother; the small world of pathetic intellectual prestige simply had no meaning for her. In her unbookish way, she was of course right—it has no true meaning. And she was right, too, about my job at Northwestern, which turned out to be, lo for thirty years, little more than a job in the neighborhood.

Pleased to discover that you were among the few reviewers that treated Norman Podhoretz's *Making It* relatively kindly. I do not recall a book that was so roundly smashed by reviewers as it was. The problem wasn't the book, but Norman. Success had—or least had appeared to—come too easily to him. Although born working-class poor (his father delivered milk for a living), Norman was always the brightest boy in the class. At Columbia, Lionel Trilling took him up; at Cambridge, he became among the favorites of F. R. Leavis. At thirty he was made editor of *Commentary*. In Midge Decter, he married a smart and attractive woman (and took full responsibility in helping to raise her two daughters from a first marriage.) He was one of the few younger men granted full membership in the inner circle of the New York intellectuals. Modesty was not then Norman's long or short suit, and he could be intellectually very aggressive, never looking over his shoulder, not much caring about making enemies. Plenty, in short, were the reasons his contemporaries had to envy him. The axes had long been sharpened, and when *Making It* appeared, they fell. The review in *Esquire* carried the tag line, "Norman Podhoretz's Dirty Little Secret May Not Be Secret But It Sure Is Little." You and I, both discretely and now as a team, have been roughly handled by reviewers, but Norman was kicked in every tender place, boiled in oil, flayed, drawn and quartered, then nicely minced.

As for your remark about the size of Norman's ambition being relatively small, you are of course right. The intellectual world is a shrunken one, without sufficient power or fame to go round. Yet the other worlds, though the monetary rewards and the levels of fame may be greater, are scarcely more congenial. The world of politics or television journalism or high finance all offer impressive detractions sufficient to discourage, at least in my jaded view, any sapient homo.

I once wrote a book called *Ambition*, calling ambition the fuel of achievement. At my age, I find myself running out of this fuel, the fires of my own ambition having been banked by the passing years. I should still appreciate a great landfall of cash that would put me permanently out of the financial wars, but I require no legions of honor, memberships in putatively exclusive clubs, prizes that have previously been won by writers it wouldn't occur to me to read. I do not expect my writing to influence anyone, let alone change anything. I do not in any way see myself a major writer, nor do I long to be thought one. I want no larger fame and am content with the near obscurity in which I currently comfortably dwell. When someone recognizes me on the street, which doesn't happen very often, I am vaguely embarrassed, and sometimes say, "Ah, I see this disguise I have put on hasn't worked." I have decided to grant no more interviews, for I was brought up to believe that talking about oneself is bad manners; and I have never departed an interview without the stale taste of fraudulence in my mouth. My only remaining ambition is to write as well as I can for as long as possible, giving those who read me pleasure and perhaps a touch of painless instruction where I might know something they don't. "My gifts are small," Max Beerbohm wrote to his first biographer, a fellow named Bohun Lynch, asking him not to inflate his importance, "I've used them very well and discreetly, never straining them; and the result is that I've made a charming little reputation." I hope at the end of the game I am able to say, if only to myself, something similar.

We've never discussed memory, see loss thereof in older players. Bernard Berenson in his eighty-sixth year begins to complain seriously about the loss of his. "For instance," he writes, "the insurmountable difficulty in recalling who was here to lunch." His work as an art critic depended on his recall of the names of artists, and these begin more and more to escape him. Nor can he quite bring to mind precisely in which books he might find reference to them. Two years later, now eighty-eight, he notes: "memory of names gone, and for faces greatly diminished." Berenson didn't have the benefit of Google, that greatest of *aides-mémoires*. Yesterday at lunch with a friend I could not call up the name of Lord Charnwood, the English biographer of Abraham Lincoln. When I returned home, I googled (it's authentically a verb now) up Lincoln Biographers and there, bingo, the old boy was.

I find my memory fails me more in conversation than in writing. Thus far along the material I need for my writing is usually available to me. That Borges citation seven paragraphs back, for instance, was, as the psychobabblists say, there for me when I needed it. But not infrequently in conversations with friends the title of a book or play, the name of an author, will have disappeared, vanished, gone, I assume, where notes of music go, into the empyrean. One of the marks of great scholars is an unfailing memory. I cannot recall Edward Shils or Arnaldo Momigliano, even when in their eighties, mumbling, "What's the author's name, dammit?" or "The journal the article appeared in will come to me in a minute." We lesser mortals stumble over such matters. I also find, again in conversation, that I need to break into the flow of talk with an anecdote or joke, lest I forget it while awaiting my turn to talk. "Forgive me for breaking in," I will say, "but this reminds me of the story about the two old Jews in Crakow who . . ."

Some of this is owing to old age, but some, too, I like to think to an overload of information, brought on by television and by spending too much time online. Barbara and I watch a movie or an English or Italian detective story or drama nearly every night. We have done so for years now, so much so that on occasion one or the other of us is certain we have seen the thing before, the other quite as certain we haven't. I begin each morning after breakfast reading a few blogs, follow two people on twitter, check the headlines and obituaries in the *New York Times*, read an item or two from *Commentary Online* and *The New Republic Daily*, run quickly through something called *The Daily Beast*. Some mornings I also read things that people send me because they feel I would be interested in them. The result of all these mostly news items is to leave me less well informed than gently stupefied. My guess is that, in the information glut, mine is rather a delicate appetite. I have a friend, retired, who tells me that he spends roughly four hours every day passing his eyes over such gunk. What must the minds of those who walk the streets thumb-pumping their smartphones much of the day be like.

I also notice that when I read things on the Internet I do so differently than when I read things books, magazines, and newspapers. My patience is less. Presented with an item on the Internet of more than twenty-five paragraphs long, I find myself wanting to skim, to get down to, in the cant phrase, the bottom line. I note manifold errors and infelicities in what I read on the Internet, but I am not otherwise all that attentive to style. Style isn't what the Internet is about; nor is it about literature in even the most generous definition of the word. Information—just the facts, or, as often, the pseudo-facts, ma'am—is the name of its game. Small wonder that all this takes its toll on memory, since on the Internet soon enough everything washes into everything else, ending in blur, pure bloody blur.

I subscribe to a San Francisco literary quarterly called *Three Penny Review*. In its last issue it mentioned that it did not acquire its usual small grant from the National Endowment from the Arts because it was "too wedded to print." What I gather was meant is that the magazine didn't have a flashy website or was insufficiently *au courant* on webbish (rhymes with *nebbish*) activities and connections. Not a good sign, this. Too wedded to print—if it wouldn't offend Barbara, I shouldn't mind having the phrase on my grave-stone.

Cassandrally, Joe

LAGARDELLE. 12.9.14.
Dear Joe,

Our mutual friend Robert Messenger asked me recently to review the Hollywood diaries of Charlie Brackett. Who he? As you probably know, but few non film-buffs will, he was the early, long-time collaborator of Billy Wilder on, for famous instances, *Lost Weekend* and *Sunset Boulevard.* He was supplanted, around 1950, by I.A.L. "Izzy" Diamond. An archetypal Wasp, whose (alcoholic) wife claimed kinship with one of the passengers on the *Mayflower,* Brackett went on to win the last of three academy awards for scripting the 1953 *Titanic.* Did he ever wonder what would have happened if the *Mayflower* had struck an iceberg and foundered with all hands? Suppose a vessel carrying Semitic fugitives from Iberian inquisitions had included Izzy's ancestors and had been the first to hit Plymouth Rock . . . As Diamond used to say, after thought, if Billy had a particularly good idea, "Why not?"

When a youngish man, Brackett was also a novelist. Not even the London Library, the best-stocked literary reserve in London, holds any of his fiction. The only one listed on Amazon, *American Colony,* is a collectors' item costing several hundred bucks. So, I asked R.M. if he could locate and send me a couple of the handful of B.'s solo numbers. He did so with prompt resource. I found that Brackett had more in common, *qua* novelist, with Ronald Firbank than with, say, Scott Fitz. Robert appended a note in which he said how rare, how very rare, it was for a contributor to volunteer to read any book other than the one under review. Several writers consent to dress his pages only if sent short books on which to pass commissioned comment after a minimum of study. Are you surprised or shocked? I tick both those boxes; the measure of my innocence. I cannot believe that writing, of any kind, should not be done as well as possible; or that any reviewer, whatever his price, should not read around the given text before striving for Horatian *felicitas* in praising, or appraising, it well.

While on the Latinate beat, there is an old English story (oh the dust, the dust in memory's archive!) about a dinner party at which the *plat de résistance* was ox-tongue. When the dish slipped from its platter and fell to the floor, some zippy guest remarked "An unfortunate *lapsus linguae!*" The laughter of the diners impressed some outlier who did not share their schooling. Some weeks later, another waiter, bearing a sirloin of beef, tripped and allowed the joint to hit the deck. The outlier seized his cue to come out with "An unfortunate *lapsus linguae!*" and wondered why no one laughed. The snobbery of the anecdote is typical of the literary and social world to which I craved entry when I went, sixty years ago this Fall, to call on Somerset Maugham at the Villa Mauresque.

I sought no favors (and was asked for none); I wished only to tell the Old Party how much my ambitions owed to his example. I knew that Virginia Woolf and Frieda Lawrence despised Willie for being "professional," but I could see no disgrace in wanting to sell one's work, though my highest ambition was simply to be published. The important thing was that the work should be well done, after which—like the Henry James you cited a few weeks ago—one might enjoy whatever "gold" anyone might choose to pelt one with. *En passant,* do you ever want to read *To The Lighthouse* again?

The assumption was common, in the 1950s, that a novelist could survive only if in possession of a "private income." Though without pecuniary resource, I was more eager for fame than for fortune. My ideal lodging was a Chelsea garret (ours turned out to be a basement). As for lit. crit., why should one have any desire for that crusty pursuit? Easy: Mr. Eliot, the anti-Pope (and anti-Milton too), had proclaimed that we were living in an Age of Criticism. Had to be true then! This chimed with Frank Leavis's declaration that the Great Tradition of the English novel had reached term with Henry James. It remained only to expound and annotate what had been done as well as it ever could be. Meanwhile Frank's consort, Queenie, quizzed the paltry practitioners of the present, and their fans, in *Fiction and the Reading Public*. As for poets, Leavis, the man with perfect pitch, declared that Auden was out and Ronald Bottrall was in. (Like Pippa, he passed.) Being a philosopher, my knowledge of the manners and morals of the English school at Cambridge was, fortunately, all hearsay, but I did hear it. Leavis used to boast of his walks with Wittgenstein; Wittgenstein *non plus*.

The first issue of *Scrutiny*, the Leavisite house magazine, appeared in 1932 and the last in 1953; it no sooner came of age than it perished, as if too fine for the post-war world. I bought a complete set of the posthumous edition when it was issued in the early eighties. Thanks to Hollywood, I could afford to catch up backwards. I remember little more than the regular derision with which Leavis's *apparat* dealt with those outside its loopy loop. Maugham's *Don Fernando*, an essay on his passion for Spain, was the only one of his works to be noticed. It was, of course, deemed *regular*, in the Spanish sense of mediocre. Cyril Connolly was the epitome of the Sunday journalist and *flâneur* on whom the Doctor's eternally inflamed faction visited its heat. Eclectic and cosmopolitan, Eton 'n' Oxonian, lotus-eating Cyril was the antithesis of what Fenland Puritans were licensed to applaud. Yet it was Connolly whose little magazine, *Horizon*, published an early (if not the first) account, tersely composed by Arthur Koestler, of what came to be called the H/holocaust.

I cannot claim that *Scrutiny* deliberately ignored what was going on in Europe, but a rapid scan of the contents, between 1938 and 1946, has hit on no head-on treatment of All That, although Leavis himself did review Koestler's quasi-Zionist *Thieves in the Night*. The insularity of British "thought" and the conceits of "radical" attitudinizing have no better mausoleum than in those light-blue jacketed volumes. I don't, of course, mean to hint that *Scrutiny* was in any respect as anti-Semitic as the sainted Tom.

Wolf Mankowitz, later a literary re-visitor of Anglo-*shtetl*land in London's East End, from which he sprang, features once in the *Scrutiny* index, as the author of a scathing article about Dylan Thomas, an incontinent raver whose Welsh *hwyl* was not at all hwylcome in Downing College. We may be sure, sports fans, that had he not scathed the vatic bard, Master Mankowitz's little number would not have been printed. The party line was set by Leavis's own implacably humorless prose. He attracted clever, unamusing people, not the least of them, in my time, the John Knoxious Karl Miller, who dominated the London literary scene for decades. Leavis's diadochi adopted his stiff stringency and, since they rarely had any "creative" strain, were suited to "do the (literary) police," in a range of voices.

One of our middle-distant neighbors in the Périgord happens to be a Person of Importance in London circles. I will not identify him, to avoid any breach of confidence, but take my word that he is a high-ranking Insider. At least a dozen years younger than I, J. has the academic status to have been solicited, at some stage to review for the *NYRB*. As well as being very successful, in the cant sense of being egregiously loaded, with earned treasure and deserved honors, J. is a part-time, ex-academic of resource and erudition. He did not need the work from the *NYRB*, but he took the gig and sent the resulting essay to Master Silvers, who disagreed with its line and demanded radical revisions. J. declined to change a word. He was then paid the agreed fee and the said volume was dispatched to someone who could be relied on to know on which side his bread was bartered. J. has since regarded the *NYRB* with disdain. As for its London cousin, he notes with scorn its implacable anti-Israel line. He is not a Jew.

J. and I get along fluently on the basis of the Oxbridge connection, with no trace of One-Upmanship. Sometimes, as you and I prove, elective affinities declare themselves and one is well advised not to analyze why. J. had seen my *TLS* article about Mendelsohn's Cavafy and wondered, as he reached for another of Beetle's home-made walnut cookies, why I had denied the world the expected (and hoped for) caustic retort to Master M.'s letter. I explained that I had penned such a letter, but that it had been forbidden publication because it was deemed, by a letters-editor with small Latin and less Greek, to be unjustified. No one wanted any trouble with someone adjacent to the Golden Goose of Manhattan.

J. was generous enough to be amazed that my friends/colleagues had given me the "warm shoulder," in Bowra's famous phrase. I was gratified by his reaction and also shamed. Why, I now asked myself, had I, like the Baron de Charlus when abused by *la* Verdurin, been reduced to uncharacteristic silence? It cannot have had anything to do with money, and not all that much with prestige. Who but its own contributors are impressed by seeing their names figure on the *TLS* contents page? I chose to take Mendelsohn's refusal even to accept delivery of the fifteen pages of my specific notes on his text as evidence of his conceit and want of civility. His presumption that I had to have some "motivation" for not praising him signals the decline, the *lapsus linguae francae* even, of literary culture. All art is partisan and political now. My pen-friend Jed Perl has written ringingly on the same topic in a recent *New Republic*.

It requires an imaginative jump, but no record-breaking leap, to see how my experience is of a piece with your apprehension that Connolly's "closing time in the gardens of the West" is truly at hand; if "what lies beneath"—the political or psychic sponsor of a text—is the "real thing," then the common culture as we once liked to imagine it is doomed. Steiner likes to quote Paul Valéry's *"la profondeur de la surface"* and he is right: when quality is no longer the determinant of merit among decent people, we are left with pressure groups and single-issue "politics." The result is not the triumph of Good Opinion but rather of money, the ultimate, impartial measure of what anything is worth. What makes the grave and revered Silvers the panjandrum of contemporary letters is not the validity of his "line" but the size of his treasure chest. Capacity to rig the literary market has made him the Bernie Madoff of contemporary letters.

Mendelsohn and his kind cannot believe that anything can be said against the elect except for malign, "political" reasons. It had to be that my claim that he had, in effect, misrepresented Cavafy, in order to mount him in the Gay Hall of Fame, was "motivated" by unavowed but undeniable prejudice: in other words I was "homophobe," a term with small etymological validity, if anyone cares, but one which "explained" why I didn't agree that Master M.—Silvers's cardinal—was a genius. I am left feeling like Michael Douglas in a poor film with the necessary one memorable line, which he delivers with due incredulity: *"I'm the bad guy?"*

Jacques Prévert might have been talking about me when he said, in 1930, *"Il était aussi très douillet. Pour une coupure de presse, il gardait la chambre pendant huit jours."* I too am such a softy that on account of one press cutting I can shut myself in my room for a week. Is it that rare? Prévert was a street kind of a guy, *rue*ful in a very Parisian way. I shall have to make something Zolaesque out of my petty, pettish *affaire* or continue to suffer from mental indigestion. First, we'll take some time out beachside by the wine-dark Med; if far-sighted enough one might see Alexandria on the horizon . . .

Tout à toi, Freddie.

October 2, 2014
Dear Freddie,

Your notion of Robert Silvers as the Bernie Madoff of contemporary literature is hilarious. Yet Silvers is probably more to be pitied than poleaxed. The *New York Review of Books,* on which I'm told that at the age of eighty-five he continues to work seven days a week—you've doubtless heard of the orthodox Jewish detective who was on the case 24/6—is today an old bull gone weak in the knees. Silvers hasn't the guns, which is to say the contributors, left to put out an interesting journal. He is, for example, forced to call on Daniel Mendelsohn for reviews of classical material, when once he might have called on, among others, Arnaldo Momigliano or E. Badian or Hugh Lloyd-Jones. Mediocre American novelists and poets now review books of mediocre American novels and poems. Academic culture has run dry; the talent has dribbled away; the cup is empty.

I once described the contributors to the *New York Review* as mad dogs and Englishmen. The distinguished Englishmen—W. H. Auden, Hugh Trevor-Roper, Noel Annan, and others—have long ago bought the farm. The mad (left-wing political) dogs are less ferocious and even more boringly predictable now than once they were. After subscribing to it for more than half a century, a few years ago I canceled my subscription to *The New York Review*, and find I don't miss it in the least. Because I wrote a single piece for the paper in 1970, I have been given a password that allows me to read it online *gratis*. I don't often do so, though occasionally I will look in on it to see what I'm not missing. But, as the American disc jockeys used to say, the beat goes on. Bernie Madoff is at least enjoying the privacy of prison, while poor Robert Silvers, on what in America is known as a work-release program, is imprisoned in his own moribund paper. Moribund though it is, I note that Martin Scorsese has done a documentary about it, which sounds to me a certain winner of a little coveted Racso.

An old *New York Review* standby, chiefly in the mad dog division, was Joan Didion, who rarely appears there any longer. Ms. Didion's specialty has long been depression—years ago I wrote a piece about her and an equally depressed writer named Renata Adler to which I gave the title "The Sunshine Girls"—though in recent years Ms. Didion has put the pedal to the metal and sped up from depression to pure grief. She wrote a book about the death of her husband, John Gregory Dunn, a work called *The Year of Magical Thinking*, said by people who should know better to be a classical book about mourning. The book is most notable as a precursor to the new trend, and trend it has by now become, of writing about one's own illnesses and grief and death.

The more than prolific novelist Joyce Carol Oates followed Ms. Didion with a book about the death of her husband, though it did not hit the best-seller gong with anywhere the same resonance as Ms. Didion's. In her book, I learn from reviews, Ms. Oates reveals that she and her husband, a former academic and editor, had an agreement whereby he read her book reviews but not her fiction. (Now that's what I call a savvy pre-nup! He must have had a terrific lawyer.) Ms. Oates rather rapidly remarried, and has continued to churn out novels and stories with little regard for the forests her books are causing to be denuded. Ms. Didion, now eighty, has been more ecologically conscious, and hasn't published much since her commercially successful threnody over her dead husband.

In the grief line we have had Christopher Hitchens chronicling his own demise from esophageal cancer. This, too, has been published as a book, though not one you will find on the coffee table (which we don't possess) *chez* Epstein. The English writer Jenny Diski, who can be lively and amusing, has recently promised, in the *London Review of Books*, after having been diagnosed with cancer, a blow-by-blow account of the effect of the dread disease on her body and spirit. The bright side of this is that Ms. Diski's lengthy prose treatment of her cancer will allow fewer pages in the *London Review* for its regular fare of anti-Israel articles. Clive James, I note, has begun publishing poems whose subject is his own promised death from various maladies. An e-mail or two back I ranted on a good bit about a poet named Edward Hirsch who has written a long poem about his grief at the drug-overdose death of his adopted son. An age in decline and dissolution, Goethe told the faithful Eckermann, is one where subjectivity rules. Sounds right to me.

Joyce Carol Oates, I read somewhere, has by now published more than one hundred novels and books of short stories, and may have published more under different names. I've read none of these books, though I do occasionally glimpse a short story of hers when one appears in the *New Yorker*, and always depart disappointed by its unearned darkness and depression. The question her career poses for me, though, is why does one tend to distrust too great literary productivity. I know I do. Jeffrey Meyers, who by now must have published fifty or more books of biography and criticism, also falls into the too productive for their (career's) own good category. Peter Ackroyd, whose biography of Chaplin you economically dispatched in the current issue of *Commentary*, is another such relentless producer.

Behind the distrust of hyper-productivity is the belief—not altogether without basis—that something as complex as serious writing cannot come so easily and still be worthwhile. (We don't, by the by, show the same distrust of high productivity in music or the visual arts—consider Haydn, consider Picasso.) In literature, the response is how good can something be turned out with such alacrity and assembly-line regularity. We know the substantial dent that Trollope put in his own reputation when in his autobi-ography he wrote about taking up the job of novelist as if it were no different than any other. He mentions the number of pages he turned out (forty per week, with 250 words per page, though some weeks he managed as many as 112 pages). My favorite Trollope story is about his completing one of his novels midway in his regular morning working session, and, not one to waste time, he up and began another. Still, he was, after all, Anthony Trollope, which Oates, Meyers, Ackroyd & Co. cannot claim.

I shall soon bring out my twenty-fifth book, and hope I have not fallen into this pit of overproductivity, or prolificacy. Whenever anyone remarks that I have certainly published a lot of books, my standard response is that I intend to continue doing so until I finally get it right. I've not done a count, but I suspect you have published more books than I. My guess is that neither of us can help ourselves. We have the bug. By the bug I mean not grapho-mania—which I take to be the disease of having to write everything down— but the feeling that if one isn't writing one isn't quite living; or, to put it more theologically, one isn't doing what one was put on earth to do. I know that if three or so days go by without my inditing something of which I am not entirely ashamed I begin to feel delinquent, hopeless, quite worthless really. The only cure is to get one's bottom in the chair and begin tapping away. One would nonetheless, bug and all, like to avoid falling into the cat-egory of scribbler of whom readers say, What, him again?

On an aligned subject, Robert Messenger's remarking that not many re-viewers he deals with are up to reading more than the book they have been asked to review is another sad sign of what I call the Decline and Blumenthal state of literary culture. I always assumed that if one is writing about some-one one is under the obligation to read everything he or she has written. I long ago picked up this notion from Edmund Wilson. In *Shores of Light*, in his essay "The Literary Worker's Polonius," Wilson writes: "Such a reviewer should be more or less familiar, or be ready to familiarize himself with the past work of every important writer he deals with and be able to write about the author's new book in the light of his general development and intention."

In the early 1980s I was *Commentary's* critic of contemporary fiction, and felt under the obligation to read all the previous novels of every novelist about whom I wrote. Not all of them were worth the effort: John Irving, Norman Mailer, Robert Stone, John Updike would come under this rubric. That I am a slow, note-taking reader, especially of anything on which I am to write, made the task all the more onerous. My wage for many of these pieces must have come in at around thirty-five-cents an hour. When I appraised my then friend Saul Bellow of all this reading, he said that I resembled a detective who would go to the south of England to find evidence against a suspect. My true motive for doing so was that I wanted to be as well prepared as possible to write about my subject, and feared lapsing into error through omission. I, like you, believed, and believe still, that any kind of writing should be done as well as I could do it.

Which brings me to your question, Do I ever want to read *To The Lighthouse* again? Not in this life, I don't. In fact, I should like to blow Virginia Woolf's little boat out of the water. Surely no more vastly overrated writer is on the Big Board of Literary Reputations than she. I should say that she was a moderately talented essayist and reviewer, and a novelist not much above that. Her reputation is of course owing to feminism, specifically academic feminism: *A Room of One's Own* and all that. The female professors needed a twentieth-century writer of modernist cast, and came up with V. Woolf. (Edith Wharton was too upper-class, and Willa Cather too kind to religion and with too many middle-class readers, to qualify.) In Virginia W. they got, at no extra charge, a great snob, a part-time lesbian, and an anti-Semite into the bargain. I have long felt that, after Countess Tolstoy, Leonard Woolf deserved one of the early Nobel Prizes for Marriage.

To do the job properly, of course, would entail reading the seven volumes of Virginia Woolf's essays and the diaries and letters and those brittle novels. This would mean perhaps three months out of my reading life—a chunk of time I am no longer willing to spend with a writer I do not admire or feel has much to teach me. This is work for a younger man, or, better still, younger woman, though it is difficult to believe anyone is soon likely to take on the job. Everyone, in the current political climate, is—high marks to Edward Albee for prophesy—afraid of Virginia Woolf. Her inflated reputation will have to await the guillotine of Time, that toughest and fairest and most certain of all critics.

I wish to announce that the sly pornographer has struck again. I have a new story, one with the catchy title of "Kizerman and Feigenbaum," to be published in *Standpoint*, in which I conjoin a couple in carnal embrace. In the story, the male character is in bed in boxer shorts, awaiting the arrival from the bathroom of his paramour, and contemplating feeling, as he has been wont to do on similar occasions in his life, whether in the sex minuet, he is (mix metaphor, shake gently) the predator or the prey. I do not allow the woman an entrance, but instead have my hero, who owns a Jewish delicatessen in Chicago, say: "I'm not going to attempt to describe what Dinky and I did in her bed. I'm not that great at description. I'll only say that at the conclusion I didn't want my money back and leave it at that." Invitations for miscastings of this couple are cordially welcome. Just now I'm thinking Brad Pitt for the Jewish deli owner and Bette Midler as his inamorata.

Best, Joe

LONDON S.W.7. 5RF. 22.10.14.
Dear Joe,

There used to be a maneuver in British marching orders known as "breaking step." On hearing the command, the platoon ceased to march in left-right-left unison and, by some means I cannot recall, some then did "left" while others did "right" foot first. I believe that the order was given mainly, perhaps only, when marching troops were crossing old bridges (Chelsea one of them) on which, if booted unison continued, the whole structure was liable to get the shakes and might even disintegrate. Once the bridge had been crossed, there was a corrective yell, upon which well-disciplined infantrymen resumed their previous consistency. You will, with the close-reading skills of a literary veteran, divine the reason for this arcane allusion: having broken step to go off for that four-week holiday on our Greek island, I am a little out of synch. Your cue for me to resume came sweetly to my eyes, as did the sweet tactlessness of its content.

You have been very busy—Herodotus here, William James there—while Beetle and I slumped in sunny sloth without a ripple of reluctance. For more than fifty years, we have been going to Ios, one of the group of islands which encircle (hence Cyclades) the sacred island of Delos, where Leto gave birth, leaning on a maieutic palm—or was it olive? - tree, to those two not entirely amiable divinities, Apollo and Artemis. In March 1962, Ios was a depopulated, rockily beautiful island, without a single wheeled vehicle on its lava-laden tracks. Donkeys and mules were its taxis and its trucks. We were the only tourists to get off the boat, which took fourteen hours to come from Piraeus and arrived in the early hours of the morning. Since the undredged Ios harbor had no deep-water jetty, the *Despina*—a retired, renamed English Channel steamer—dropped anchor in the dark pool of the bay. We had to climb down (Beetle with baby Sarah, I with Paul) into small boats which bobbed under the rope ladder. It was not *very* hazardous, because helpful, competent hands were reaching up to us.

We rented a cottage with a rammed earth floor and a roof of bamboo matting covered with thick earth which sprouted flowers in the spring rain. We had to go across the field to the "earth closet" and literally kick shit when we were done. The "squire" of the island was a man called Artemis Denaxas, who admired the English and had dogs called Dick and Rover. He was known as "*ho plousios,*" Mr. Rich. We had been introduced to him, by chance, in Athens and he promised to help us find somewhere to live. He had presided, with a cavalry moustache and, very likely, with cavalier accountancy, over the distribution of Marshall Aid to the impoverished Greece (Greeks may be rich, very, some of them, but Greece never is) and could afford to lavish benefactions—running water, some electricity and a cheese factory, among other amenities—on his fairly grateful fellow-nesiots.

Denaxas was not in evidence when we landed. His first name was, unsurprisingly, unusual for a man (when I purloined it for the hero of my "Greek" novel *Like Men Betrayed*, Peter Green questioned the usage). Its mention procured no rare favors, but we were treated to the traditional *philoxenia* which greeted (the very few) foreigners with courteous attentions: we never met an islander without his giving us something, a red Easter egg, a biscuit, or the flower from behind his ear. I worked on my portable Olivetti sitting under the first buds of the vine which would grow across the trellis on which, in spring sunshine, I dangled our open, very British brolly as I two-fingered the keys in a fury of what it would not be silly to call inspiration.

On the last day of composing *Lindmann*, I hammered out more than thirty double-spaced pages. I had never before felt so free to express the outrage I felt about the Holocaust and the world's callousness. As I clattered on, I realized that our landlord, a certain Nikos, was standing nearby, on a wild surmise, like Keats's stout Cortez. He had never seen a typewriter before. When blazered, brass-buttoned Denaxas did show up, for Easter, he was unsurprised by the primitive cottage or the paucity of our diet. "We are," he told us, "in Polynesia."

That was then. Now, of course, the island has proper—E.U. funded—roads, taxis, buses, trucks and wi-fi. Everyone, it seems, carries a cellphone, except when swimming. Greeks use the Aegean in a domesticated way: those of a certain age in particular walk slowly into the water, and stand there, as if attending a reception in a spacious drawing room. They rarely stay close together, but carry on loud, intimate conversations at several dozen yards' distance from each other. Volume lends vitality. Only rarely do the talking heads go under water. No Greek has any idea that privacy might be precious. Only an idiot would elect to be alone. On a wide, almost empty beach, they will pitch their towels and their persons as close as may be, quite as if their intrusion were a favor.

On that first visit to Ios, I was keen to buy some deserted property, if only to leave a marker to return to where my muse was liberated from metropolitan calculation and our children happy to invent toys from rocks and roots and sand. The island was littered with abandoned, romantic-seeming, stone houses. Every time I asked for the price of some derelict *spiti* (the modern Greek for house is an abbreviation of the Latin *hospitium*), and accepted the figure named, it was promptly doubled, then redoubled. Only on the day before we had to leave (to rendezvous on Mykonos with my publisher friend Tom Maschler) did Flora, who came down from the village to help Beetle with the children's washing, ask me if I really wanted to buy a house. If so, I should come with her.

She led me up to the tall village and down the far side to a great golden scimitar of unoccupied beach. Her grandmother had left her a little *spiti* sitting at the top of several terraces of olive trees and cactus. Flora, who could not rely on her Bacchic husband, needed money to send her children to school in Santorini, the large volcanic island which exploded, around 1700 B.C., and put an end to the Minoan empire and, if the debunkers are right (they often are), caused the mini-tsunami which caused the Red Sea to recoil, on cue for Moses and our putative ancestors to cross with dry feet, before the waves returned to engulf their Pharaonic pursuers.

Flora's little house was, in truth, a derelict donkey stable, with a skeletal tree across the untrimmed bamboo-covered roof (like the one on Odysseus's "palace" on poor old Ithaca). I paid Flora her asking price, about $400, and it was ours. On the way back to the beach, we passed through a wide field directly adjacent to the sand. That too was hers; I could have it as well, if I wanted. It had a well and a lot of weeds. How much? *To idio*: the same. So I bought that too, more for her sake than ours; for fifty years, it remained an empty lot, although we did quite a bit of work up at our place on the hillside.

Slowly at first, and then with accelerating menace, houses and hotels grew up around our secret place. Word came, a few years ago, that the zoning rules were changing: if we did not build on the empty lot very soon, we would be interdicted forever. In the meanwhile, Ios had been a tourist resort, known for nudity, drink and drugs. In the wanton Eighties, it lost most of its summer charm, unless you wanted to see bands of wandering Teutons, long-yarded but of sorry aspect, as they cruised the beach, hoping for ephebes. Fortunately, the economic recession caused them to recede too. When my mother died, the family, led decisively by our businesslike, sentimental son Stephen, decided to use her legacy to build three modest houses, in her and Sarah's memory. This autumn, for the first time, Beetle and I did not climb the steep hill to the old *spiti* and its primitive plumbing and the cracked walls which Fred the amateur plasterer enjoyed caulking.

The new white houses have Cambridge blue shutters and are at once traditional in aspect and neatly luxurious within. Switching from our old place only hurt for a minute, as my American grandmother Fanny used to say. But I did find myself looking back as men may do, for all I know, at the first wife whom they have ditched but cannot forget. We had a very good, lazy time, but I was conscious, as I have not much been before, that the new premises doubled for a whited sepulcher, an investment for a future which Beetle and I, actuarially speaking, are unlikely to share for more than another, oh, decade or so. So, we swam, we walked, we ate, we slept. I did almost fill a neat little squared notebook with *obiter scripta*. Among the poems in the volume of the Greek Anthology which I happened to have with me was an anonymous distych which, being translated said, "To feed many slaves and erect many houses is the readiest road to poverty!" *Absit omen* indeed.

Speaking of distychs, there's a story, in Saint-Simon, I think, about the young French courtier/poet, trying to make a name for himself at court. Having composed a two-line poem, he thrust it into the hands of some ducal arbiter. The duke looked at it for a while and then handed it back, saying *"C'est très bien, mais il y a quelques longueurs!"* This reminds me, at a stretch in space and time, of how Barbra Streisand was seated next to Billy Wilder at an Academy lunch, soon after she had directed a movie called *Prince of Tides*. She was unwise enough to say to Billy "I hear that you were—," she dabbled her hand "—like that about my movie." Billy said, "No, Barbra, I wasn't like *that* about your movie. I hated it." This is in the tradition of the *nouveau riche* who asked his daughter's violin teacher, "Vot do you tink of my daughter's execution?" To which, yes, the answer was: "I'm in favor of it." Dateline? N.Y.C. 1937.

So, we did Greece and came brownly back to London to encounter, *contra rerum naturam,* no ugly news. It seems that I now have publishers for both the big and the little book I wrote earlier this waning year. I shall not grow rich on the proceeds, but I am happy not to be remaindered before printing. I also learned, with no more than a facsimile of regret, that in our absence Karl Miller, promptly obituarized as one of the Great Lit. Editors of All Time, had departed this life. He was one of the most sanctimonious people whom I ever tried to charm until I wearied of the exercise, about forty years ago. Didn't Auden write about some tyrant who, when he smiled, "little children died in the streets"? Karl never smiled. Beetle and I had him and his beautiful wife Jane to dinner in 1967 and have waited ever since for a return invitation. As you probably know, Karl edited the London lookalike of the *NYRB* and made it even more overtly anti-"Zionist" than Bob Madoff y Silver's little number. So Karl is gone and the world does not seem a duller place. As W.S. Gilbert so heartlessly wrote, in *The Mikado,* "I've got a little list/ and they'd none of them be missed". . .

There. I hope I am back in step.

Tout à toi, Freddie.

October 30, 2014
Dear Freddie,

Thanks for your paragraphs on your Greek (no longer-quite) hideaway. Until I read them I had only the foggiest notion of what your Greek holiday life was like. These paragraphs nicely put me in the picture. Somehow or other I am pleased that you have moved from your cruder house to the more modern setting of the newer houses. I do not, never have really, believed there is any virtue in roughing it. We have two friends, a bit younger than we, who still go camping, sleeping in tents, cooking on a hibachi, relieving themselves, for all I know, in the woods. I simply do not get it.

Your mention of the steamer *Despina* reminds me that Barbara and I recently sat through a three-and-a-half hour televised production of *Cosi fan tutti. I.* Despina is the name of the mischievous maid who turns the comic plot round at various points. (Despina, the good god Google informs me, is the name of one of the moons of Neptune, and also of a nymph who was a daughter of Poseidon.) Some splendid music in *Cosi fan tutti,* but three-and-a-half hours? Some might think this culturally roughing it. In fact, we didn't have the *sitzfleisch,* or bottom patience, for it, and, having it recorded it beforehand on our DVR, broke up the telecast of the opera into three separate sittings.

Opera of course remains the high point of the life of the *kulturny.* I seem to recall Sir Isaiah (not Schwartz) becoming a patron of the opera with his wealthy wife, the famous golfer and heiress, Aline de Gunzbourg. The height of Jonathan Miller's career, I gather, has been directing opera. People pay vast sums for opera tickets, await the great moment when a fat man or woman is stabbed and then begins singing loudly. As with camping out, I don't get it. A great deal of wondrous music was written for opera. I sometimes listen to operatic CDs—famous arias and all that—in my car; I not long ago discovered a splendid tenor named Joseph Schmidt, whose performances I can listen to over, over and over. But to go to the opera, to sit there among the ignorant rich and overweight women in fur coats whose dreams will never come true, is too much like punishment. Was it Lampedusa, author of *The Leopard*, who despaired of the future of the novel in Italy so long as Italians remained in thrall to opera with its not even ridiculous plots?

I also recently watched, over HBO, a Martin Scorsese documentary called *The Fifty Year Argument* on the *New York Review of Books*, which I mentioned (foreshadowed?) in my previous e-mail. Scorsese did another such documentary on a New York writer, famous for her writer's block—so long has it endured, she refers to it as a blockade—named Fran Lebowitz. Ms. Lebowitz is a no-bones-about-it lesbian who shows up at all Manhattan allrightnik parties in what look to be Anderson & Sheppard suits, Dunhill blazers, and Turnbull and Asser shirts ("Turncoat and Asshole," Saul Bellow, who wore them, used to call them). She is well known for saying the obviously overlooked, and thereby slightly outrageous, thing. In the Scorsese documentary, for example, she remarks that she doesn't in the least understand contemporary gay and lesbian culture. Being a lesbian, she avers, meant to her above all being free. Now, though, gays and lesbians wish to align themselves with the two most constricting institutions in the culture: marriage and the military. Like me on roughing it and going to the opera, Ms. Lebowitz does not get it.

I don't know why Scorsese bothers with these documentaries, for there is nothing especially artful about them. Perhaps he doesn't want his cameras to get rusty or his film to grow moldy. The *New York Review* documentary features interviews with the few still living members of its older stable of writers—Joan Didion most prominently—and film clips of the deceased Mary McCarthy and Susan Sontag, snapshots of Edmund Wilson, Robert Lowell, and W. H. Auden, and further interviews with its not very impressive current cast of scribblers. The film makes one realize two things: first, as David said upon the death of Saul, how the mighty have fallen; and, second, that they weren't all that mighty to begin with. Yet no paper attracted more attention, indeed reverence, than did *The New York Review* in the 1960's and '70s. At Northwestern University, where I taught, in the mailroom every second week each mailbox pigeonhole was filled with fresh copies of the paper. If academics go for some culture product in a big way, there is usually a reason—and behind the reason you are likely to find snobbery and political cowardice.

Robert Silvers is on camera a fair amount in the documentary, but never utters a sentence of the least interest. Silvers hasn't written anything I know about, and only now, hearing him speak at moderate length, it occurs to me that this is because he hasn't anything of great interest to say. In the documentary he is very self-satisfied and makes plain his feeling that the *New York Review* has fought the good fight, has always been on the right side of things, which of course it often wasn't and still isn't.

Of course many of the best editors never wrote, or wrote very little. I think here of Lord Jeffrey, Harold Ross, William Shawn, and others. I was myself an editor who wrote a great deal, and the truth is that I cared more about my own writing than I did about what went into the magazine I edited, though concern for one did not have to exclude concern for the other. As a writer, I have tended to prefer writing for editors who themselves do not write, if only because it eliminates any sense of subterranean competition between writer and editor and such editors, without any writing of their own on their minds, tend to pay more attention to their contributors' writing.

Over the years, I've had some excellent editing, though I've never built up the kind of dependence on an editor that so many of Maxwell Perkins's writers—Dreiser, Fitzgerald, Hemingway—did. At the moment I'm rather bogged down in my book on Charm, and I suppose a strong editor, a man or woman who can see both forest and trees would help. But thus far I haven't come upon such a person, nor do I expect to do so.

When I write for magazines and newspapers, I tend to write to please editors, though always taking care to please myself first. Some editors I know to be tougher than others, and these can sometimes bring one up a notch or two to a higher mark. After all these years, when I send a piece off to a magazine or paper, I am still nervous about the response it will bring from editors. The best editor, because of this, is the punctual editor. A few editors I work with, owing to e-mail, get back to me less than an hour after I send a piece off to them. If there is a heaven, may they find a place in it.

Most of what I send to magazines and papers requires—or at least gets—little editing, which is fine with me. The one place where I have found editing a bit troublesome is the *Atlantic*, and this because they do what I suppose must be called computer-editing. My Kafka piece appeared there. (I'm currently reading a biography of Philip Larkin in which Larkin calls *The Trial* "that gloomy convincing piece of bullshit," which is amusing and, by my lights, fairly accurate.) When I received it in its edited version, the text was marked by queries in three different colors: one color from the editor, one from the copy editor, and one from the fact-checker. The rainbow array quite flummoxed me, and I had to telephone the editor to walk me through it.

At the moment I have another piece at the *Atlantic*, this a 1,500-word scribble suggesting that, given the likely duration of the United States war with the Islamists, the nation ought to think about reinstituting the draft and not let this war be fought, as now, by a volunteer army that is chiefly composed of members of the underclass. I await another bit of multi-colored editing, with mild but genuine trepidation.

The history of this piece comes under the old Jewish rubric of "Shouldn't Be A Total Loss." I originally wrote it at 850 words for an Op-ed for the *Wall Street Journal*, where a gracious—and highly punctual—editor named Mark Laswell invites me from time to time to fire off my opinions. He couldn't use this piece, he told me, because there was too much sentiment against the notion of returning to a draft, and besides warfare had become too highly technological to be fought by two-year inductees. Undaunted, I added 700 words to the piece and sent it off to *The Weekly Standard*, where it met with the much the same objection. *The Atlantic,* which has less of a political line than either of the two earlier places I sent the piece, was pleased to have it.

My argument in the piece is first that it is unfair to have wars fought by an underclass and second that nations only get behind wars in which most families have members fighting in them. Such was the case with World War Two, the last American war that had true national support, less, I would argue, out of hatred for Hitler or wanting to save the Jews, than because everyone had a son, uncle, brother, father in it.

Now, you might ask—though as a good friend I trust you never would—where do I, a man of wide ignorance, come off putting forth such ideas in, of all places, the public prints. My answer is that my authority derives from my effrontery, or to use what is now the good English word, my *chutzpah*. The best weapon in a democracy, I would argue, is a fluent prose style. With it, and a few journalistic connections, one can attempt to make the case for cannibalism. (You know the joke, surely, about two cannibals sitting round the fire, bowls in hand, and one says to the other, "You don't like my brother, at least eat the noodles.") Theseadays, who knows, not to make that case, or at least give it a serious hearing, might result on a knock on the door from the political correctness police. "Cannibalism? I'm personally not for it— not that there's anything wrong with it, mind you, still . . ."

I recently read a remarkable novel that, until a month or so ago, I had not known about, *A Driven Leaf*—a phrase from the "Book of Job"—it was written by Milton Steinberg, a popular American rabbi of his day who died, at the age of 46, in 1950. This is the only novel Steinberg completed, though he is said to have been at work on another before his death. The book is in that always-suspect genre, the historical novel; suspect though it remains, some splendid novels have been written in it, among them Marguerite Yourcenar's *Hadrian* and, though I haven't read it in fifty years, Robert Grave's *I, Claudius*; John Williams's *Augustus,* and Steven Pressfield's *Hot Gates*, about the Spartans at Thermopylae aren't bad, either. These examples suggest that if one wants to write an historical novel, one does best to set it in the world of the Greeks or Romans.

. *A Driven Leaf* is set in the second century A. D., before and during the time of the Third Roman-Jewish War. The novel is about the ostensibly un-promising subject of the conflict, in the mind of a Jewish apostate named Elisha ben Abuyah, between faith and reason. A Jewish scholar of such prominence as to have attained to a seat on the Sanhedrin, Elisha encounters the work of Euclid and can never again settle for proofs that are not ax-iomatic and based on pure reason. Sounds rather dull, set out here so bla-tantly, but it isn't, not in the least. Steinberg's learning was genuine; he was also said to have been, from his pulpit at the Park Avenue Synagogue in New York, one of the great preachers of his day. The historical detail feels right. The subsidiary characters have a believable consistency. The book ends leaving its main character adrift, an old man knowing what he lost when his faith fell away, but unable to depart the path upon which the search for absolute reason has set him.

Historical though the treatment of the subject in *A Driven Leaf* is, its theme is very much alive, and remains, to my mind, the ultimate subject for all sentient people, except those who have already found the quest for faith preposterous. I, who have no confident religious faith, am not among the latter. Too many great figures, from Pascal to T. S. Eliot, found they couldn't live without faith; too many dopes—from Voltaire to Richard Dawkins— thought the mere notion of faith ridiculous. If I had to choose sides between them, I know in whose company I should prefer to find myself.

Your story about the violin teacher's put-down of his wretched student's playing reminds me that when he was a boy the older son of my friend Loie

Rosenfield—wife of Maury Rosenfield, of whom I've written to you earlier—came to her to announce that, after three years of trying, he was giving up playing violin. Loie began to cry. "Mother," the boy said, "if it means so much to you I'll continue, I'll try harder." Loie, dabbing at her eyes with her handkerchief, answered, "Not at all. I'm crying with relief, I couldn't have stood another year of your ghastly practicing." The story was told me by Andy Rosenfield, the son in question, which speaks well for him.

Keep on truckin'.

Best, Joe

LONDONSW7 5RF. 31.10.14.
Dear Joe,

The clocks have gone back (do we not wish that we had?) and winter's pall has been lowered, summarily, like a blanket over a garrulous parrot's cage. British masochism agrees to shorter days as it hopes, supposedly, for a return to isolation from the Continent where people speak all those bloody foreign languages. Time was that they could be derided for talking with their hands, but now every TV presenter has a make-me-an-offer gestural repertoire. Some—when seen in wide shot—add little dance steps, like graceless Astaires, as they seek to twinkle into popularity with Joe and Josephine Public. To be instantly recognizable requires frequency rather than charm or eloquence. The common ambition is to join the band of those you can set your clock by.

The political drive to detach England from what begins at Calais ("wogs" is the now banned term) is accelerated by the leader of the U.K.Independence Party, an elastic-faced man called Nigel Farage. His unlikely, not to say unBritish, name is pronounced not as if it chimed with "forage" which, in his many photo-ops papers, comes in a raised glass, but with "garage," in the somewhat froggy pronunciation, as against "garridge," as said by the sub-classy salts of the earth. Farage and his party may yet divide the electorate, but will never rule it. Patriotically void of culture, he sports a long, loud haw-haw-haw to dress his threadbare parish-pumposity. Neither short nor tall, neither fat nor thin, neither young nor old, he stands at the lusterless meeting point of Everyman and Mr. Pooter, who penned the *Diary of a Nobody*. Farage goes one better: he is *the* Nobody. Harmlessly dangerous, malevolently benign, he never says the same thing twice if it can be said three times. Like your Palin lady, he is the Booboisie's idea of someone who speaks his mind. If only he had one.

We are lucky that Anglo-Saxon reactionaries tend to take comic form. Meanwhile, the only slightly sinister, dexterous Marine le Pen moves, with plausible cunning, towards becoming a likely candidate, if not favorite, for the post of Madame le Président de la France after the unloved François Hollande comes to term. The whole world being in a state of chassis is nothing new, but—to say the least, and why not?—not all the music that goes round and round is playing our tune. Increasing deafness lends me a measure of insulation from the media's cacophonous commentators, though not, alas, from the long-into-Saturday-night thump-thump-thump of what our young London downstairs neighbors call music. Love them as myself? I confess, my dear Joseph, I have not felt the vocation. Tolerance and gritted teeth are constant companions in modern life.

In our London apartment, when there is silence below, there is thunder above as an Italian female and her frantic small son beat the uncarpeted floor above our heads, she with her flat feet, he with his understandable sprints to evade her. They have driven us first to distraction and now to something worse: the law, that bourne from which there are so few happy returns. Luckily, our son Stephen—he of the mighty forehand—has the calm nerve and the chums to do this without the conniptions (is that term now obsolete, even among Certain People?) to which age drives me like a crazy chauffeur, faster than one would wish and to no good end. The answer to such bad neighborliness ought, of course, be to hit back with Verdi, Donizetti and Rossini played *fff*, but I can no longer work to music unless it is Mozart on a piano and in the other room.

As you remarked in your last innings, it's curious how opera attracts the fur-lapped *gratin*. Last week, while scavenging where three paperbacks are offered for the price of two, I saw a fat biography of Jonathan Miller, to whom the world's opera houses have offered the ormolu frame in which he has always been happy to be pictured, even though, I am told, he isn't all that hot at staying in tune. He satisfies himself by having us listen to the staging and décor. His hedgehoggish trick is indeed a beauty: imaginative transposition; most memorably, for those who remember it, that *Rigoletto* set in Mafialand and Sicilianized witha de sunglasses anda de two-tone shoes. Does it matter that, if I remember rightly, the original story took place in foggy Mantova, Virgil's under-rated home town? Revamping settings and cozzies is the modish modern art of packaging; not negligible (by any means) but hardly capital. It dresses nostalgia in innovatory stylishness, the disposable form of style.

Jonathan has one indisputable claim to fame: when challenged, in *Beyond the Fringe,* by the Gentile, brilliant and personally quite nasty Peter Cook about the rumor that he was a J**, Jonathan replied, "I'm Jew*ish*. I don't go the whole hog." That was the moment when one should have sold his stock. Now, the zealots says, he has gone a little further in his detachment: he is merely *–ish.*

Back in the bookshop, despite the difficulty of finding a third Award-winning, overpraised volume, I limited my homage to Jonathan to checking whether I appeared in his index. I did, quite a few times; but I do not suspect him of any sentimental reminiscence of our co-habitation in St John's College, Cambridge. Dr. Sir Jonathan, as he now is, has a capacity for resentment which would leave him hard-done-by even while riding in triumph through Persepolis. There was, I am sure, no mention at all of his and his lady's having failed to show up for a dinner date at our house, in the 1960s, and then having his secretary call to apologize to Beetle, who was not appeased. When he deigned to phone himself, he craved her sympathy for the stammer which has never hindered him from public declarations. Now, I am sure, it has all become our fault for asking them at all. He and that other Miller, the *feu* Karl, married two rather beautiful sisters. I am not sure which of them was the luckier.

Whatever his gospel may say, Jonathan and I were once friends of a kind; there is an unmocking tribute to his youthful bounce in my early novel *The Earlsdon Way* and another, more vestigial and less larky, in *Lindmann.* There are/can be certain characters in my life who serve, sometimes repeatedly, as maquettes for fictional personae. Critics, clever or malign (or both), might divine that these lay and relaid figures have left some deep trace, whereas the truth is that they were/are composed of the elasticized stuff in which fancy can be comfortably gloved.

My memory is staffed with people I can again and again enjoy impersonating, nicely or nastily, but for whom, in person, I have no great appetite. My one-time publisher Tom Maschler is another. He is the only person with whom I have ever collaborated on a book (other than a translation). It was his idea, in 1959, to write a text-book, tongue-in-chic, about how to be a success. Elizabeth Jane Howard, the one-time mistress of Arthur Koestler and second-time wife of Kingsley Amis, compared the book to Laclos's *Les Liaisons Dangereuses*, but they have yet to stage and film it. Odd, isn't it, that no one I know of has thought to make the Laclos into a musical? Ditto

La Ronde. What can have kept Lord Lloyd Webber's appropriating hands off such eminently recyclable merchandise?

Re *The S-Man,* of which I wrote the half which amounts to ninety percent, I needed the money and it made quite a bit, thanks to Tom's energetic hustling. One Ian Hamilton, who ran Hutchinsons, our U.K. publishers, accused Tom of "bargaining like an Armenian," now—no doubt—an indictable racist slur, then a backhanded compliment. My Hollywood agent was for a long time one Ron Mardigian, one of the nicest hardbargainers a man could hope to be repped by, and an Armenian who taught me to count the stitches when bargaining for Persian/Turkish carpets. *The S-Man,* published under the pseudonym Mark Caine, has never figured in my "By The same Author" list, although it does contain some nice nasty lines, but Tom lays proud claim to it in *Who's Who.*

He recently published an autobiography, in which, I am told, he speaks of me from both sides of his often loud mouth (in *Lindmann,* the character based on Tom speaks frequently in CAPITAL LETTERS). When he asked me if I had read his auto number, I said ,"Did you send me a copy?" I recall a man at Cambridge who said of another of our friends "He lashes out his cigarettes like a man with no arms." That too would now be indictable offence, whether or not the chap was an Armenian. Tom Maschler had many, too obvious faults, but he was the greatest publisher of his time (he fostered John Fowles, Martin und Kingsley Amis, Ian McEwan, and who all else) and it is a smudging reflection on modern Britain that he has not received the smallest of the baubles which its society distributes to Sir Dribs and Lady Drabs of all sorts of ugly stripes.

I had/have a smartass line in *The Glittering Prizes,* "The friends you make at Cambridge will last you all your life, if you're very unlucky." While J. Miller and I were in the cast of the Footlights 1954 show which transferred with great success (much of it Jonathan's) to London's West End, he warned Beetle if I continued to express myself with the same asperity (I thought it wit), I should lose all my friends and make no new ones. It's true that I have very few still alive from my Cambridge days, but I have been very lucky, especially in recent years, in making new and better ones. Philip Roth, you may remember, divided his friends into those (Gentiles, presumably) who would and would not hide him if he was on the run from the Gestapo. How can one have the least idea of what anyone else would do in such a case or—if honest—what one would do oneself if called on to risk one's neck to save another's?

In one of his recent many books, a Frenchman called Alain Minc wrote (some say, plagiarized) a comparison between René Bousquet, a French functionary who eventually collaborated wholeheartedly with the Nazis, and his contemporary Jean Moulin, a pre-war *préfet* (departmental governor). As Bousquet turned Naziphile, Moulin forked left and became the head of the Gaullist Resistance. He was betrayed and tortured to death in Lyons in 1943. Bousquet survived the war and, as banker and socialite, did himself extremely well (he became an *ami intime* of President François Mitterrand) until someone rang his bell and shot him, fifty years after Moulin's death.

Alain Minc makes succinct play—trust a practiced larcenist not to hang about—with the head-and-tail of much the same coin aspect of the traitor and of the patriot for whose interment, in the Panthéon, André Malraux composed an encomium regularly regarded as a rhetorical masterpiece. I happen to have seen and heard the *noir et blanc* newsreel on which we hear Malraux's tremulous vibrato as, in a very high wind indeed, he delivers his protracted magniloquence. Alongside him in the presidential box is the silent, not to say silenced, General de Gaulle, stiff as an examiner can be, aching stoically for the climactic *clausula*. Malraux has something in common with what Isaiah Berlin said of George Steiner, that he was a "genuine phony." Both men have much to be said for them, and they have said a lot of it. Yet the world of letters and art, as well as that of pretentious imposture, owes something to them. Malraux was never quite the war hero he made himself out to be (he seems literally to have given himself the rank of Colonel and then enrolled, quite late, as one of the historic *chefs* of the Resistance) but his books on art, however much bluff they may contain, were more stimulating to my adolescent self than anything by Kenneth Clark or Willenski or even Gombrich, who was later very nice to Beetle at dinner. Malraux was a Monsieur Partout whose achievements, both real and supposititious, remain enviable.

As for Steiner, on his 1960s arrival he was a blast of cosmopolitan polyvalence in provincial Cambridge, which goes some of the way to explain why he was given the illustrious bum's rush of an "Extraordinary Fellowship" in Churchill College and had his way immutably blocked to any Faculty office. He had to settle for a professorship in Geneva where, if what his erotic memoir claims is at all true, his *garçonnière* doubled as a *fillière*. I see from Wikipedia that he was recently honored with "The Truman Capote Lifetime Achievement Award." How sad that the actor's sad demise denied G.S. the—as he would certainly call it—*sacre* of being impersonated on celluloid by Philip Seymour Hoffman!

So it goes, and so must I.

Tout à toi, Freddie.

November 12, 2014
Dear Freddie,

The fairly recent gimmick of opera directors dressing their characters, so to say, out of character has been going on a long time, as you know, in Shakespeare productions. Years ago I saw *Julius Caesar* done, as was done with the *Rigoletto* you mention, in Mafia costume. A week or so ago two people told me about a local production of *King Lear* that begins with recordings of Frank Sinatra songs, which are also played at various points in the play. (I'd always heard that Tony Bennett was Shakespeare's favorite Italian crooner, but what do I know?) Quick quiz: What Shakespeare play was most favored by the Yiddish theatre? The answer is *King Lear*. The reason of course is that it's a play about the ingratitude of children. Rather obvious, when one comes to think about it.

Stephen Potter mentions that a brilliant bit of one-upmanship is to be had by going to medical school and then not practicing. Jonathan Miller adroitly made this move, a move that suggests, somehow, genius. His stammer also helps; it implies a racing mind, crowded with penetrating thoughts, all struggling in the heavy traffic of dazzling brilliance, to get out. Miller has, I guess, had a good run, though I don't think he will leave much behind. He's not a talented writer; years ago I read his involuted little book on Marshal McCluhan, in the Frank Kermode Modern Masters series, which shed no light, nor cast any heat. Miller's American analogue is Mike Nichols, who also went from charming comedian to theatrical genius. Nichols has turned his directing prowess into lots more money than Jonathan Miller has done with his. One of the small but genuine pleasures in reaching our age is that one can see careers in full trajectory. Oscar Levant said that he knew Doris Day before she became a virgin. As I've mentioned earlier, I preferred Woody Allen before he became a genius, and I can remember, if I strain, Jonathan Miller when he was amusing.

American mid-term elections ended a week ago, with a galumphing victory for the Republicans and a defeat ("repudiation" is the word of choice) for President Obama and his bedraggled party. When it comes to political elections, I generally find my antipathies divided, and end up voting for the not all that much lesser evil. My first instinct is to vote, with a few exceptions, against all incumbents. "They're all thieves, you know," my mother used to say, raising her coffee cup to her lips, little finger bent. One of the not very urgent, nor ever likely to pass, bits of political business in American politics is the notion of setting term limits for members of Congress and of the Senate; the quite safe assumption behind this is that the longer they are in office the more corrupt they become. I am very much for this, feeling that none of them should be allowed in office for more than thirty-five minutes.

The dislike of Barack Obama runs high just now in America. People on the right loathe him, those in the left are gravely disappointed in him. I am in neither camp, perhaps because I didn't expect all that much from him to begin with. His main function, I thought, was, to be elected and thereby to help raise the cross of race from the backs of Americans, if only a little. How racist can the country be if it elects a black (all right, half-black) president, I thought. I have come to think him a dull man, and a less than highly energetic one. His standard left-wings views are dated, and his lethargy in foreign policy is no doubt dangerous. He ain't no pal to Israel, laboring as he does under the notion that the Arabs are amenable to reason. This much must be said for Obama: he is not corrupt, nor, sexually, a player, which, given the fairly recent history of the American presidency, are not minor items. When Obama was elected to the presidency, an American satirical paper called *The Onion* ran the headline, "Black Man Given Worst Job in America." Something to it. Obama will be fifty-six when he leaves office, which, with a bit of luck, will give him thirty or so years to gambol about as an ex-president. Better by far to be an ex- than current president, no? A finer resume entry is difficult to imagine: 2009–2017, Leader of the Free World.

As I've mentioned before, my one little contribution to the English language, is the word "virtucrat." A virtucrat is someone whose politics and life in general are propelled by his sense of his own grand virtue. The virtucrat is always positioning himself above the next person. I dine with Raphaels, and I return home to say how pleasant and amusing Freddie and Beetle are, but, you know Barbara, they don't quite seem to care as much about the fate of the planet as we. They seem to have left their toaster and other minor appliances plugged in, and don't compost their garbage, and generally do little to reduce their carbon footprint. Nice people, the Raphaels, charming even, but a touch wanting in their concern for the planet.

Last week I wrote and sent off to the *Wall Street Journal* and had accepted an Op-ed on the subject of the Virtucrat in politics, which I sent along to you in a separate e-mail. My main point is that he, the virtucrat, isn't fit

}316{

for politics, which is chiefly about compromise and deal-making and has little to do with virtue, Aristotle to the contrary notwithstanding. The Op-ed is a dopey form, an eight- or nine-hundred-word opinionation, which allows those of us who strike one off occasionally to play columnist for a day. Years ago I used to be asked to write them by the *New York Times*, more recently by the *Wall Street Journal*. I am paid $800 for my *WSJ* Op-eds plus the illusion that my voice is being heard, my influence felt. My own motive for writing an Op-ed from time to time is, apart from the money, the shucking off of minor obsessions into the form of opinions. I can generally write them in under two hours, which also allows me to think of myself as, you should pardon the expression, "Working Press."

Your mention of your former agent Ron Mardigian, "an Armenian," reminds me that I have never met an Armenian I haven't liked. Like Jews, they have been victims of genocide. I suppose the reputation of Armenians for bargaining comes from so many being in the rug business. Or so I think of them. I walked into a restaurant frequented by older Jews not long ago, many of them wearing toupees, and found myself remarking to my lunch companions, "There are more rugs in this joint than are to be found in an extended Armenian family."

I have a taste for, though insufficient experience to formulate my own, generalizations about nationality. My friend Edward Shils had both the taste and the experience. He had spent a vast amount of time in India; he taught half the year in England, first at the LSE, then at Cambridge (Kings, then Peterhouse); he knew German culture in great depth. Once I joined Edward for lunch with François Furet, the man who took the major interpretation of the French Revolution as class struggle away from the Marxists. The lunch was pleasing enough, and when it was over, and Edward and I were alone, he asked me what I thought about Furet. "A most impressive man," I answered, "though I sensed something slightly furtive about him." Edward paused, then said, "What do you expect? He is, after all, a Corsican."

Why is there something mildly absurd about George Steiner receiving the Truman Capote Lifetime Achievement Award? The thought of the two of them, Truman and George, at lunch together is a subject for a lovely comedy skit. Perhaps George could fill Truman in on with whom Aeschylus slept. What George would ask of Truman is harder to imagine. I just now looked up the former winners of the Capote Lifetime Achievement Award, and there is not one among them, from Helen Vendler to Seamus Heaney to Elaine Showalter, with whom Capote could have borne to have spent fifteen minutes.

Which goes to show that one never should leave money for a literary or academic prize in one's name. Reverting back to Edward Shils, not long after he died a few of his friends, I among them, raised $25,000 to have the University of Chicago designate the room he frequently taught in The Edward Shils room. A plaque on the door so denotes it, and on one of the walls in the room there is a portrait of Edward. A year or so after this, the university returned to ask me if I would like to help raise money to establish an annual Edward Shils Lecture. I didn't need more than ten seconds to say I wasn't interested. What I imagined is all sorts of social scientists—Jurgen Habermas, Richard Sennett, and others—giving these lectures and setting out ideas Edward would have found ridiculous when not outright pernicious. George Steiner, whom Edward found a highly comic figure, would doubtless by now have been among the Edward Shils Lecture lecturers.

Andrew Lloyd Webber's musical version of *Liaisons Dangereuses* would be a natural. I'm sure that he could find an engagingly happy ending for it. Hope you don't know the joke about the man who slips and falls off the balcony of his eighty-fourth-story penthouse in Manhattan. After a free fall of twenty stories, he hits a rubber mat hanging over one of the balconies on the sixty-third floor, which propels him back into the air. On the twenty-seconded floor, a series of thick towels set out to dry in the sun helps further to break his fall, sending him a bit out front of the building, where he lands onto the extended awning. From this awning he bounces off, trampoline-like, and happens to land atop an open moving van piled high with mattresses parked in front of the building. As he climbs down from truck, uninjured, the doorman from the building rushes up to him. "Sir," he exclaims, "I saw your fall, all of it. Sir, you are the luckiest man in New York." The man, re-establishing the crease in his trousers, answers, "No I'm not. The luckiest man in New York is Andrew Lloyd Webber."

At the opposite extreme from the glow left by Andrew Lloyd Webber productions, Barbara and I recently sat through, in two separate sessions, a four-hour HBO show called *Olive Kittredge*, an adaption from a novel by that title by Elizabeth Strout that won a Pulitzer Prize in 2009. I've not read the book, and have no plan to do so, but was attracted to the television adaptation by the appearance in the lead role in it of Frances McDormand, one of those actors—William H. Macy is another—who are capable of turning in surprising performances, sometimes turning dreck into gold; well, maybe bronze.

Olive Kittredge turned out to be sheer depression, unmitigated, unrelieved. The opening scene adumbrates a suicide on the part of the leading character, Olive Kittredge. Throughout the four hours, this character, whose mental condition, she herself informs us, comes from her father's having committed suicide, spreads her depression to her husband and only child and everyone else she encounters, on whom she bangs away with her dampening version of truth-telling and high standards. The show is punctuated by strokes, suicide attempts, hunting accidents, and a closing cameo appearance by Bill Murray, who hasn't talked to his only child for two years because she is living in a lesbian relationship. The Murray character and Olive, the last scene suggests, will carry on as a baggy-eyed couple, somehow finding comfort in one another's dreariness.

Frances McDormand is entirely believable, which is to say sad and terrifying at once, as Olive Kittredge, the shrewish wife and mother. The other characters are all well acted. But is acting enough to supplant the want of a genuine story? Apparently for lots of people it is, for the reviews of the HBO *Olive Kittredge* have been enthusiastic. When our four-hour stint was over, I felt I could not have withstood a moment more. Not catharsis but relief to be done with it was my reigning emotion. I don't understand, in theater, television, novels, depression that doesn't earn its way—that is, by ultimately being about something more than depression merely. In his essay on Turgenev, Henry James remarks that in the end we want to know what a writer feels about life. For the depression squad, the answer is that it is a rotten deal, not much more.

From the feeling distinctly older department, I recently read a review of an Israeli novel written by a writer named Asaf Gavron. Gavron, I learned from the reviewer, was born in 1968, which isn't shocking, some people after all having to be born every year. But the reviewer goes on to note that the author is a former rock musician (I'm still there, as long as I don't have to listen to his music) and—this is what got to me—a video-game designer. Would you read a novel by a video-game designer? I'm not sure I could.

They keep erecting, as you will have noticed, new ways of pushing one into old foggydom. Years ago I wrote to you that I thought one of the great dividers between generations was rock 'n' roll—those of us on our side of the divide were unable to take Elvis and much that followed seriously. New divides, though, are regularly being erected: the need never to be away from one's smart phone, a youth spent playing video games, the ability to view transgendering operations as a fairly normal procedure. I'm confident there's lots more to come. You, senor, qualify as a literary man of all work, working in all genres, doing translations, publishing novels and diaries and scholarly books and writing movies and television dramas and much else, but my best guess is that you'll not soon be designing video games. Please, I beseech you, do not tell me that you have just signed on for a vast advance to turn out twenty video games about the Peloponnesian War for PlayStation Network.

Best, Joe

LONDON SW7 5RF. 13.11.14.
Dear Joe,

Asked to select the period in Roman history in which he would choose to live, Edward Gibbon opted "without hesitation" for the Age of the Antonines, during which, he claimed, enlightened emperors sustained the happiness and prosperity of the human race (i.e., the Mediterranean world). This *sans pareille* period was bracketed between the death of the sadistic Domitian and the accession of Marcus Aurelius's son Commodus, the spendthrift playboy who played a dirty trick on Russell Crowe, in Ridley Scott's *Gladiator*, of a kind of which not a few of Master Crowe's acquaintances might not wholly have disapproved.

Crowe's seduction (I think the word is properly used here) of Meg Ryan, during the shooting of some non-hit, struck me an incidental *coup de Jarnac,* since she had been "set" to star in a script of mine before running off with the loutish Aussie. *Coup de Jarnac?* A term still allegedly current in classy French circles, it describes how a duelist, overmatched against the most redoubtable blade in chivalry's rankings, did not come out with his blade high, in the standard manner, but slashed the champion's hamstring, laying him instantly low. As he bled to death, the decked doyen had the grace to allow the wit of the stroke. But then, as John McEnroe said, "Show me a good loser and I'll show you a loser."

The second C.E.—as the politically corrected will call it—did not lose its charm for Gibbon, although it included Trajan's repression of one Jewish revolt and Hadrian's even more draconian response to Bar Kochba's ill-fated uprising. The dispersal of the Judaean Jews is always said to have followed. Does this make Trajan and Hadrian into antique Nazis or prove that "the Jews" have always been the bone in Europe's omelet? (Yes, delvers, there is a how-to-lose-the-public allusion here to a book by Peter de Vries—a Dutch humorist already—in which a diner sends back his omelet for the indicated reason.) I pretty much accept what you say re Kristol's refusal to accept that "we" can be, say, reasonable—in the Tony Judt manner—about Israel and "the Palestinians," but it makes small sense to talk about Roman anti-Semitism. To do so lends that sentiment deeper roots than it ever struck. The Romans had a zero-sum policy with regard to any rebellion. No one ever called J. Caesar anti-French, even though he slaughtered a million or more Gauls in order to reflate his treasure-chest and arm himself for the Big One, against other Romans, including his old son-in-law Pompey, the most victorious loser in ancient history.

The efficient, unloved Hadrian rated Greek kulchur (and what the cant calls Greek love) above all competitors, but he had no need of *theory* in order to bloody the bloody Judeans. I remain convinced that anti-Semitism springs, essentially, from Christian ideology. Its flaring recurrence no doubt has other sources, but even now I suspect that its latest recrudescence is fostered by a new(ish), post-Holocaust resentment: the dread that "the Jews" were right about Jesus and that, whatever the genius of *Christianisme,* the Church and adjacent institutions have been peddling a false prospectus for two thousand years. There ain't gonna be no Second Coming. (When a friend told Bernard Berenson that he had dreamed of that long-awaited event, B.B. said, "How interesting! In what *style*?") If "the Jews" were right all along not to buy in to Christian ideology, it is tempting, very, to blame them (as they have often been blamed) for the collapse of what they never subscribed to. By *wanting* it to be untrue, they contributed to its demise. As Peter Panickers will know, Tinkerbell can stay alive only if we all *believe* in fairies.

Why am I telling you all this? It comes partly from having been enough of a *bénévole* (some read "patsy") to undertake to scan a "proposal" by a Harvard professor (Martin Puchner by name) entitled *The Written Word.* The world is full of scribes rattling collecting boxes, so why should a tenured Prof, whose remit covers literature and much, much more, not fatten his funds? My fee-free opinion was, *grosso modo,* that the professor has something in common with Emil Jannings in *The Blue Angel* in which—you may remember, but how many do?—a pompous Herr Prof (played by Jannings) consents to sit on stage and have eggs broken on his infatuated head by Marlene "Can't 'Elp 'Eet" Dietrich, about whose flame mothy men are said, understandably indeed, to hover.

You *might* have hoped, I *did* hope, that Puchner, having achieved what lesser breeds might take to be eminence, would be soliciting backing, from Yale U.P. already, for a *magnum opus*, however inaccessible to the *profanum vulgus.* (It is said that *Principia Mathematica,* on which Russell and White-head, unprimed by gold, spent many a summer and as many damp Cambridge winters, is unlikely ever to have been read from alpha to omega by more than two other persons.) Puchner did not choose to take the high road. Instead, he came bearing clichés and glibnesses (glibbets?) in a scholarly stewpot. Oh the determination to be reader-friendly and innovative all at once! Early on, he tells us ". . . the advent of writing constitutes a quantum leap." Does no one in Harvard own a red pencil, or a blue? Who reads on after meeting "quantum leap" in any text?

Those who stick with Puchner are soon informed that Jesus had "students," but that he "refused" to write. Some oldsters will recognize a covert allusion to the chestnutty account of why Socrates and Jesus came to their cruel ends: "They didn't publish." I suspect that J. Christ esq., as my bygone mentor Guy Ramsey used to call him, was more like an Ayatollah, solemn and smiling, mild and menacing, all at once, than any podium-pacer of Puchner's stripe. I also suspect that some *echt*-orthodox rabbi has claimed that Christianity itself was nothing but the ur- and schismatic form of "liberal" Judaism, which just may be a little bit true; therefore not to be uttered *fff.* Personally, I regard orthodoxy as a block from which I am more than glad to have been chipped. (Welsh ex-prime minister Lloyd-George said of his quondam colleague, Herbert Samuel: "When they circumcised him, they threw away the wrong bit.")

Pressing on, Prof. P. tells the shekel-dispensers that the Greek phalanx consisted of "stacked soldiers." Should I be ashamed of myself for visualizing female recruits with big breasts? Turn a page or two and we are informed, *ex cathedra Harvardensi,* that the Socratic dialogues "began the tradition of Western philosophy." Please sir, I found myself waving from the back of the class, were there not several philosophers of renown and durable influence before Plato and more than a few—hang it all, professor P.!—who put their ideas in writing, not least Heraclitus, Parmenides, Pythagoras, Empedocles? As G. Steiner would leap, with no trace of a quantum, to mention, if not *assert,* in three loud languages, Martin Heidegger's notion of *existenz*-philo came from the pre-Socratics (even if they might not recognize his rendition).

Should I care that the Harvard man's stuff about Wittgenstein is mild and woolly? W.—about whom I dreamed as recently as last night, when we had a good discussion (i.e., he talked a lot, in front of a very hot fire)—did in fact write a good deal, although much of it was not published till after his death. The "anecdotal" nature of *Philosophical Investigations* is not evidence that he lacked coherence: its form reflected W.'s mature view that, as against that expressed in the intractable *Tractatus-Logico-Philosophicus*, which was theoretically unified, philosophy could not/ should not affect to parade a complete world-picture. Bits and pieces of accurate observation are the best we can do; thus did the deutero-L.W. (in Anglo-Saxon strip) argue against "ideology" without even mentioning it. P.'s popularizing spit-balling should do his reputation no good at all; but then again, today, who knows? And tomorrow, who will care? W., I am told by One Who Knows, is now pretty much non-curricular. *Sic transit . . .*

As Woodrow Wyatt might ask, Do I feel better after this excursion? A bit. Poor Puchner, however rich he may be in honors and, no doubt, will be in advances, is a victim of the plague sweeping the scribal community. Its regular symptom is that writers come out in hot and swollen *proposals*. I am presently a quarantined victim myself, since Steve Wasserman promises that with one more heave I may be thumbed upwards into election to pen or process a little number on *Why Antiquity Matters*. This, I suspect, is a title calculated to chime with other volumes in an open-ended series, of which one, so the net suggested recently, may well include a scholarly number on *Why Butt-fucking Matters*; or perhaps why it doesn't, whichever shall sell better among porn-again Christians.

My solitary boat against the current will need a stronger motor if I am not to be swept down the swift neo-Hebrus to the Lesbian shore; a metaphor, comrades, for the feeling that "the writer," as independent voice, saying what he or she will and to hell with the editors and sales managers, is a threatened species. The good news is, however, that my second volume of autobio has a publisher. My advance, as fat as meager funds allow, I am promised, will mean that I shall have (ah the future perfect tense, where should we classicists be without a chance to use it?) made something under $100 a week during the months of composition, as the fancy panters say. In other words, I get less, *pro rata, per diem, sub specie aeternitatis,* than the intern who slots the toner in my publisher's meanest printer. Yet the lure of print on the page, not the Kindle, keeps my home fire from going out. Mean-while, I have hopes that any minute now my loyal Hollywood producer (there are such people) will fit the last "element" into the production of the script, *This Man, This Woman*, which Meg's fugue with Russell aborted a dozen years ago. You will divine that there is no fool like an old screenwriter who thinks that that argosy may yet come in, laden with emancipating treas-ure from the New World.

I was all set to describe to you, at length, stroke by stroke, how we went, last night, across town to see the Match of the Century between Roger

Federer, your little pagod, and—in the red corner—Andy Murray, the Highland *flingueur*. But? No, worse: *and,* as in . . . and we did indeed make the trip to the end of the East End, there to witness "our" Andy horizontalized 6-0, 5-0 (at which point we quit the field where there had been no battle); we heard later that he avoided a double bagel by winning a single game. Our son Stephen, who presented us with the evening, thought Murray was injured, and he had better have been. Fortunately there was an excellent warm-up doubles, and some good snacks, so we had a fine time. If Murray were a prize-fighter, they would have withheld his purse for not trying. So, Raphael F. has no fine prose encapsulation to enter for the Ring Lardner award and must slink away, as did Murray, I trust, *sans* further *parole.*

Tout à toi, Freddie.

November 23, 2014
Dear Freddie,

You have a tough guy, fellow name of Edward Gibbon, on your side on the question of Roman anti-Semitism. The Romans, Gibbon claimed, were notably tolerant of the religious practices of their conquered subjects. They were, as he writes, "scarcely inclined to wrangle about their respective modes of faith or worship. It was indifferent to them what shape the folly of the multitude might choose to assume; and they approached, with the same inward contempt and the same external reverence, the altars of the Libyan, the Olympian, or the Capitoline Jupiter." The Romans could tolerate every kind of religious difference; what they couldn't tolerate was revolt, which was why they so brutally crushed the Bar Kochba uprising in Judea.

As for your assertion that true anti-Semitism started with Christianity, no argument from your correspondent in Chicago. I've just finished reading a most interesting little book by Milton Steinberg, whose novel *A Driven Leaf* I mentioned to you earlier, a book called *Basic Judaism.* In it Steinberg, who claims that the likenesses between Judaism and Christianity are greater than the differences, nonetheless sets out the differences, and to devastating effect. These differences, most originally set in motion by Paul, the amiable wed-or-burn man, listed seriatim are impressive.

Foremost, the Jews cannot believe in the feats of the Jesus of the Gospels: that he walked on water, that he raised the dead, that he exorcised demons who had inhabited a herd of swine, that he was born of a virgin, that he was resurrected, that finally he was the son of God. Jews cannot believe in his perfection as a man, and neither are they impressed by his want of interest in the life of reason, in philosophy, in science, in anything, really, but the after-life.

Steinberg tosses in these additional objections to the Pauline version of Christianity : "the insistence that the flesh is evil and to be suppressed; the notion of original sin and damnation from before the birth of all human beings; the conception of Jesus not as a man but as God made flesh; the conviction that men can be saved vicariously . . . ; the abrogation of the authority of Scripture and the Tradition, and the nullification of the commandments of the Torah; the faith that Jesus, having been resurrected from the dead, bides his time in Heaven until the hour is come for him to return to earth to judge mankind and establish God's Kingdom; the final and climactic doctrine that he who earnestly believes these things is automatically saved, but that he who denies them, no matter how virtuous otherwise, is lost to eternal perdition." Toss in the Jewish disbelief in "the Trinity, the miracle of the mass, the cult of saints, the intercessive power of Mary, and the doctrinal infallibility of the Popes," and you've got a hell of a lot of differences, I'd say, all of them crucial, none of which is easily made up during the course of a Jewish-Christian Brotherhood Week barbeque.

Only the Jesus who is "a great man, a gifted and exalted teacher" is palatable to Jewish belief, Jesus the teacher of compassion and forgiveness. These lessons of Jesus have of course been completely obliterated during the various inquisitions, pogroms, attempts at genocide, and other events many underwritten, others not in the least disapproved, by various Christian churches. Christian attitudes toward Jews over history are enough to make one doubt that the day when the yid will lie down with the goy is just round the corner.

Professor Puchner's poor performance on *The Written Word* is merely further evidence that the rot in academic life appears to have spread to the falsely sacred precincts of Harvard. For some while now this rot has corroded American English and History departments across the land, and attacked the social sciences like the locusts and frogs attacked Egypt, which leaves five other plagues to come. The motto of psychology, Auden once suggested, ought to be, "Have you heard this one?" That motto could now nicely apply to American higher education, excluding, let us hope, the hard—as opposed to the easy social—sciences. Here's one I not long ago heard: some genius at a southern university is teaching a course in vampire literature. Don't rub your eyes; you read it aright: vampire literature, Bela and doubtless other lugoses.

That Martin Puchner is a Harvard man is less than shocking, though Harvard was once *primus inter pares* in American education. Harvard on a Jewish boy's resume, to cite a commercial from radio days, was like sterling on silver—the McCoy, the real thing, passing Go with a lot more than $200. The school has taken quantum leaps down slippery slopes, you might say, though neither of us would. Murray Kempton once noted that intellectual contentment in America consists in not giving a damn about Harvard. And now Harvard, in the person of Professor Puchner and a cast of hundreds, has made it oh so much easier not to give that damn.

I almost wrote "the journalist Murray Kempton," on the assumption that Kempton's is a name you might not recognize. (You must tell me if you do or do not know it.) Would it have been a courtesy or a condescension to have used the tag "the journalist" before his name? This is not normally a problem between you and me; we know the same names, though I suspect you know a number of additional names that I do not. But in writing for a wider public, who can say what other people know?

I recently indited the following sentence: "Falstaff, Shakespeare's wittiest character, was himself an artist of verbal wit, the Falstaff who said, 'I am not only witty in myself, but the cause that wit is in other men.'" I did so for an essay on Wit that is to appear in *Commentary*. Did I need to bring in the name of the guy with the receding hairline? Was I condescending in doing so? Or was I worried that not all my readers would know who this Falstaff fellow is? Given I was writing for a Jewish magazine, might they have confused him with Falstaff Ginsburg? Seems unlikely, but I decided to take no chances.

I long ago discovered that one cannot know what others know when teaching undergraduates. If I used the name of an historical figure, even a relatively recent one, I found myself acquiring the tic of providing a brief bio of him in apposition: ". . . Mussolini, the fascist leader of Italy during World War Two . . . " Later in my teaching days, when I used to teach a course in prose composition to would-be writers, I would pass out a list of names and events—Diaghilev, Trotsky, Erik Satie, the Spanish Civil War, the 1913 Armory Show . . .—and ask who in the room could identify these items. Not many were able to do so. I ended this little exercise with a brief sermon instructing these students that, if they wished to pass themselves off as even mildly cultivated men and women, they were responsible for learning such things. Whether the exercise and sermon took, I have no way of knowing.

I myself at eighteen or twenty, not having come from a bookish home, was not at all knowledgeable. But the difference between these students and me at their age is that I was embarrassed by my ignorance. I'm not sure they were, or that the young today generally are. My youth of course was a time before laptops, Ipads, smart phones and the rest had become common equipage—before, that is to say, Google, that great student crib, which allows one to look up everything in a jiffy. Today it may be that, with information literally at their fingertips through these devices, the embarrassment at ignorance may be even less. Shame and fear, two important goads to education, or so when young I found, have been taken out of the game, but not necessarily, I suspect, to good effect.

Good to be reminded of the old use of "stacked" to mean amply bosomed. I haven't heard the phrase in a decade or two. A rough phrase of my Chicago boyhood was "she's built like a brick shit-house," the edifice in question being, I take it, an outhouse, or outdoor toilet. Strikes me today as a highly faulty simile. A similar criticism can be made of the word "jugs"—as in "nice jugs"—to describe admirable female breasts. "Boobs" also wants precision. Of the T-word, let us not speak. I not long ago met up with a woman whom I knew from high-school days, whom I told I thought her, in those days, a Jewish Audrey Hepburn—slender, elegant, something sad in her eyes—in an age when all the boys were interested in girls on the Elizabeth Taylor model: short, bosomy, not overly heavy on spiritual qualities.

I've been slogging away at various journalism assignments, among them a 2,000-word piece for Robert Messenger on a new biography of Philip Larkin, who has won his way through as the last poet admired by intelligent, non-intramural—which is to say people not in poetry biz—readers of the past fifty or so years. As you know, Larkin said that deprivation was for him what daffodils were for Wordsworth, and he had a way of making mild depression, even tinged with sourness, somehow attractive in poetry.

Larkin was for a while done in by an earlier biographer, a poet of tertiary interest named Andrew Motion—he was for a term your poet laureate—a supposed friend, who nailed him to the cross of political incorrectness. Larkin played political incorrectness for laughs, but Motion seems to have missed the joke. He was also anti-left in his politics, which caused him to be taken, by Motion, Tom Paulin, and others, as a vicious right-winger. In short, a bad guy, and bad guys, as we all know, don't write good poems. Was that Charlie Baudelaire who just left the room?

The new Larkin biography, written by a man named James Booth, who knew Larkin at Hull, sets the record straight. Among other things, he shows that, after their twenties, Larkin and Kingsley Amis were not such close friends as one might have thought. "I sometimes wonder if I really knew him," Kingsley A. said at Larkin's funeral. Truth is, he didn't. The pretense in this relationship was largely on Larkin's side. He pretended, in his letters to him, to be as hard-hearted and Tory-closed-minded as Amis, but it turns out that in so-called real life, Larkin was a tender-hearted character, kindly, liked by just about everyone who ever met or had to do with him, including his hundred or so employees at the Hull library, adored by the women he loved but could not bring himself to marry, in short a nice guy, a pussy cat.

Given a choice, I much prefer the writers I admire not to be pricks. (You know of course the difference between a prick and a schmuck? A schmuck just lies there.) I prefer not to think of Henry James, as the gay novelist Colm Toibin has him, ogling handsome young servants; I'd like to think T. S. Eliot in later life came to regret those wretched anti-Semitic references in "Gerontian" and in *After Strange Gods*. Some great writers, if not straight-out pricks, were what used to be called difficult personalities: Exhibit A. here would be Countess Tolstoy's husband. But if you are going to be an artist who is a difficult person, my feeling is that you ought to be a damn fine artist, up there at the Michelangelo, Tolstoy, Dostoyevsky, Beethoven level of operation. I have a story called "My Brother Eli," in which a novelist justifies his wretched behavior by declaring that his art has always come first. "Look," the novelist says to his philistine older brother, in expiation of his being a rotten father, "I don't expect you to understand this, but all the energy I have goes into my books—all of it. There isn't anything left for anything else." "Whaddya writing, the Bible?" the brother answers. "They're only novels, Eli. We're talking about human beings here, a son and grandchildren." I side of course with the philistine brother.

Your estimate of work on your latest volume of autobiography bringing in somewhere under $100 a week sounds about right to me. But as you go on to say it ain't the dough but something closer to the show that matters; here's a hint, to make a rhyme, you're hooked on print. I know because I, too, like you, have the writer's disease, and have it in full flower. The chief symptom of this disease shows up in the need to write nearly every day. Like all the most interesting diseases, writer's disease has no known cause and no known cure. Once the bug attacks, no antibiotic can drive it out. Unlike alcoholism and drug addiction, there is no place to confess and console with fellow sufferers. Live with it, the highest paid men in the head trades will tell you, just live with it, it ain't going away. To which I say, and thank God, too.

Best, Joe

LONDON S.W.7. 5RF. 25.11.14.
Dear Joe,

I have had a Hellenic week. It began with granddaughter Anna taking us to see Kristin Scott-Thomas, a big star, enlarged not only by patrician-seeming elegance (the fine nose and the slim wardrobe) but also by being bilingual in French. She has disposed of the frog father of her children, amiably I think, but kept his tongue. She was playing the part of Euripides' Elektra at the Old Vic, a theatre south of the river (like Shakespeare's Globe). On the walls hung pictures of the stars *d'antan*: Ralph Richardson and Larry Olivier, always wearing too much slap. Later, Richard Burton and John Neville had a season, or was it three?, of *mano-a-mano* alternations in the parts of Iago and Othello, and who all else. The pale Neville did not last the course to superstardom and went to Canada and had a nice life; burlier Burton became the emperor of Big Disappointments, as rich as anyone might wish, tupping where he would, luminously donged, one hears, and forever scowling at the publicity that glorified him. Finally, he leaped into the sauce as Empedocles did into the crater of Etna, procuring immortal renown. His picture hangs in the Edwardian townhouse-like Old Vic building, along with other ex-emperors of the boards and, when it was their taste, the bawds.

Kristin S.-T. abandoned her couturier to put on Elektra's timeless smock and there we were in the square in Old Argos, listening to recapitulatory lamentations about her mother Clytemnestra's doing in of the victorious Agamemnon. Woe on woe being the routine tragic style, she soon learns that her brother Orestes, in whom all her vengeful hopes are vested, is dead, but—ah those twisty Greeks—she hears it from his chum, Pylades, while shadow-lurking Orestes himself sharpens his dagger. I suspect you may have heard something of the matter. The lady S.-T. shouted it all at us, between spasms of gymnastics on the ashy floor, and then Orestes declared himself to her and Clytemnestra got the steely shaft, off stage. Normally, there are not many laughs there, dear, as John Schlesinger used to say; but S.-T. or her director contrived one or two. For instance, when she pulls out some of her hair to put on her father's tomb (a tonsorial habit of them old Hellenes) she goes "Ow!," not a line to be found in Our Author, but who's counting?

We did want it to be very good; it was not. The words were not allowed to do the work, so we had writhing on the floor and wringing of the cotton smock. Orestes stood while his sis went through a litany of mourning for him and looked as if he wished his bus for Corinth would turn up and spare him the embarrassment of sharing space with a nutty lady. Neither the director nor anyone else had considered what kind of expression—straight-faced amusement?—a man might wear while hearing his own death lamented. At length, there were huggies between sis and bro and in he went to stick it, literally, to his mama. That done, he returned to wait for Aegisthus to get home from the office. When the said usurper comes in, wearing an ancient Greekish skirt, quite as if he was on lease from another production, he is—in honor of multi-culturalism, racial integration and any of the numbers you first thought of—a . . . big black guy. Why not? Didn't Larry black up and roll his eyes when doing the state some service? Was R. Burton an authentic antique Roman when he did the business with Cleo, the all-American, impressively stacked queen of Egypt? Is Denzel Washington not an actor for all seasons? I take your point but . . . when Aegisthus opened his mouth, he announced himself as . . . how about an equal-opportunity player? Result: a dying fall that was close to a trip.

If the guy had been playing center-half for Arsenal Football Club, he might well have strengthened their shaky defense and earned honest applause. His presence on the stage was absurd, because incompetent. It is *almost* as if that inharmonious costume was wished upon him by those whose only means it was to question his merits. In *Pauvre Bitos,* a play by Jean Anouilh, the name character, who—if memory serves—is pilloried as an unsmiling deutero-Robespierre, turns up for dinner fancily dressed (I really should check, but what the hell?) in the Jacobin hat of a *pur et dur* and so becomes the butt of the company. So Aegisthus, our Mr. Big allows himself, for no evident reason, to be shunted into the off-stage abattoir and la Scott-Thomas is happy ever after.

I can imagine a director as naughty as John Schlesinger hinting, with some clarity, that it might be a modernizing *coup de théâtre,* if she felt like perpetrating one, for the lady to—as the gay jargon used to put it, under wraps—"cream herself" as her bro's offstage blow was struck. This occurs to me only now and is perhaps unworthy. Better than "ow!" though, because truer, involuntary; rather good actually, if subtly done. Our grand-daughterly host, being Sarah's honest daughter, was quick to announce her disappointment and we went and had Italian food, which is always OK, even when served by a Rumanian waitress who doesn't get *"olio e aceta,"* so I have to get it myself.

Two days later, I put on my mature scholar-type kit and go to the British Museum to meet and have lunch with Richard Seaford, a recently retired, boyish-looking professor of Greek, before a long afternoon of lectures on Hellenism and Judaism. He first leads me to the Parthenon frieze so wisely appropriated by Lord Elgin (who received nothing but stick for his premature curatorship) and indicates a vestigially draped young person offering a folded garment to a bearded gent. Is said figure, Richard would like to know, male or female? The visible left buttock is nicely shaped, the slightly averted head at a coquettish angle, the hair bunchy, one heel lifted . . . *Bref,* I think it's a girl, but with them Greeks, who can be sure? We go and eat Vitality salad and then repair to a lecture room without a view in V. Woolf's Bloomsbury where assorted Hellenists and Hebraists go to the podium, if never to the mat. Politeness rules, and why not? But only one Simon Goldhill, a cute Cambridge classicist with brave hi-there! titles to his credit—*Love, Sex and Tragedy* gives the flavor— has any capacity to communicate. And what does Raphael have to say about him later? "You can't make a Montaigne out of a Goldhill."

You have, I am sure, long, somnolent experience of professors who whisper their own words from their laptops with all of the communication skills of an airport announcer who has lost his voice. I listened, from the front of the room, with elderly frustration as all sorts of carefully bold opinions and footnoteworthy validations were paraded. Responders responded and my friend Seaford offered a few clear words of agreeable rebuttal and so went the day long into the dark evening.

At the bottom of the professorial eighth inning, some pundit cited Hegel—back from suspension—as saying that Jews were incapable of *haute couture* philosophizing because their texts were, let's say, unworldly, dependent on Him and His law. Nods were nodded and then I dared to ask if anyone had read Bettina Stangneth's new, well-publicized *Eichmann Before Jerusalem.* This announced that I had, and embarrassed them, since none had. Well, said I, in it that voluble German philosopher Adolf E., ex-*Obersturmbannfuhrer,* an anti-Semite *pur et dur* indeed, suddenly comes out, just once, with the assertion that the Jews are the most intelligent people on the planet, having erupted from the start-gate with premature, enviable, if typically sharp-practical, alacrity. Might it be, I asked the *gratin* that I saw before me, that Hegel's seemingly solemn disqualification of Hebrew "thought" was a displacement sideways of the dark, angry suspicion that they, the *Juden,* had known a thing or two rather sooner, and expressed it more tellingly, than Teutonic myth found comfortable? Philosophers too can lie, big-time. Did the panel give me best? Or even the shadow of a smile? Did anyone wonder how come this senile designer cardigan-wearer affected to be numbered among the prophets? I crept off, the nth Steppenwolf from the left, and walked the nocturnal streets back to S.W.7.

The next night came the capper. Some young ex-Cambridge people, co-led by the daughter of my famous contemporary, the stage-director *du jour après jour*, Peter Hall, who has mounted many productions and almost as many wives, had formed a company and were putting on their first production of . . . yes, folks, *Hippolytus* by Euripides (on a much better day than when he did the aforeseen *Elektra*). The kids had chosen the translation which I did, a few decades back, with my friend the late Kenneth McLeish. The show was staged literally in a white-tiled tunnel under the Victoria and Albert Museum, an arched space, perhaps thirty yards long, with a single row of chairs along each side. The audience of fifty or sixty was pitched right into the action.

We went in to find a roped Dionysos figure sitting on an oil drum, masked and horned, and—somehow—the thing was immediately both now and definitely then. On came the goddess Aphrodite, Peter Hall's daughter Emma, who would soon be playing Aphrodite's tragic dupe, Queen Phaedra, and—believe me, if you can—the play held us for over an hour of low-budget, high-energy, articulate freshness. What a *relief* to be able to tell the kids, and two older actors, how really, really good they were!

While I waited to deliver my applause, Beetle went discreetly home, three blocks away. This left me accessible to the approaches of one John Peter, a short, grey, wide ex-Hungarian person whom I knew when we were colleagues, of a distant kind, on the *Sunday Times,* and I was offered the job of drama critic, the only salaried employment which ever tempted me. But then—God help me, it was almost forty years ago!—our son Stephen said, "Does that mean I'll never see you in the evening?" So I relinquished the job to this recentish pupil of George Steiner who later described a book by aforesaid J.P. as "*Almost* major!"

My substitute's chance to express gratitude came many years later when, soon after Sarah's death, Stephen and I translated Jean Anouilh's *Becket.* It was put on at a fancy London theatre with the *Homeland* guy, was it?, as Becket, badly directed by one John Caird, whose father was a theologian whom I happened to have read on St. Paul. John Peter did not come himself, but sent a certain Victoria Segal (aha? Quite possibly!) to second-string us up, Stephen and me. The play closed quite soon, through no fault of the text, and *ça* was *ça*. So, the other evening, in the bowels of the V. and A., I asked Mr. Peter, whom I described somewhere as looking like a "disused violinist," whether the Segal bitch was a fluent French speaker. He couldn't imagine why I wanted to know. I didn't; I wanted him to know why I was not about to do hugs and kisses. He kept me talking for a long time, as those people do. Then he and his lady asked us to dinner. I said we didn't go out to dinner, except with family or close friends. Would we visit them anyway? "All the way to Bryanston Square and nothing to eat?" I said. Poor little guy!

Tout à toi, Freddie.

December 4, 2014
Dear Freddie,

Your words on the performance of Kristin Scott-Thomas remind me that we gringos have no actresses who can convincingly do aristocrats or even upper-class women on stage or in the movies. You also had Deborah Kerr. My guess is that Emma Thompson could in a pinch do one of the awful Mitford sisters. The Hepburn non-sisters, Audrey and Katherine, only one of whom was American, could do high born rather nicely. So far as I know Meryl Streep, the best contemporary American actor, has never been called on to do upper-class; her performance as that most eminently confident of bourgeoisie, Mrs. Thatcher, is as close as she has come. I suspect that Glenn Close would not to be up to the job. Do you suppose this is owing to America, for better or worse, never having had an aristocracy or even a legitimate upper—as opposed to a plutocratic—class?

Good to see that you have a strong review—not that you've ever written any other kind—of the Bettina Stangneth book on the monstrous Adolf Eichmann in the current issue of *Standpoint*. I'm pleased for various reasons, not least because I think it a good magazine, on the right side of things, and one that it took courage to begin in this the so-called digital age, and your contributions to it will make it all the better.

We've discussed before the great mixed blessing that is the Internet. I am myself in thrall to the damn thing, and could scarcely live without its many benefits: e-mail, Google, Wikipedia, and the rest. But I don't think that the Internet has much good in store for writers of our kind. By our kind I mean those for whom the style is a good part of the message. When I am confronted with a piece of writing on the Internet that runs to more than twenty-five or so paragraphs, an impatience gnaws at me. I find I want to scroll down. "O.K., pal," I mumble to its author, "what's your point anyhow?" My right hand clutches for the mouse, which will get me, literally, to the bottom line. I rarely feel this way about books or serious magazines. I am someone who considers skimming a literary sin, and in most of what I read—admittedly, in my reading I try to steer clear of *dreck*—I am not in the least tempted to do so. Only on the Internet does this skimming impulse kick in.

The reason, as I have said earlier, is that the Internet is not about serious writing, but instead is mainly about information.. Is there something about reading on a screen rather than on paper that causes one to all but pass over style? Has it to do with the mystery of pixels? Is solving this mystery a job for the quasi-fake science of brain studies? The Internet, in any case, needs a Marshall McCluhan, one a good bit smarter and more lucid than the original.

The problem for literature is that it is about all that is beyond mere information—beyond all this fiddle, to glom a title from one of the books of A. Alvarez, whom Philip Larkin used to refer to as El Al. But will we soon have a readership trained only to read for the facts, allowing thoughtfulness, penetration, style to pass unnoticed? Will they, before too much longer, fail to grasp what the real thing, literature, looks like?

I had better stop before I once again shift here into crank? You, I note, do not do crank, or at least you have never done so with me. By crank I mean older gents crankiness. Crank, I would remind you, is the expression of that host of complaints about today's culture and life in general, which are held up against, and found terribly wanting in comparison with, the golden days of one's youth and young manhood. When I was young, the crank rants, there was little crime, people left their doors unlocked, divorce was a rarity, writers were not (like today) crappers, publishers were honorable, politicians cared for the country and were not all in business for themselves, nobody wore goofy beards, people dressed with an eye toward elegance not with the schlepperosity of today, the water in showers was hotter and rained down with greater intensity, hamburgers tasted better. I have a friend, a man a few years older than I, with whom I meet for lunch once a month, and crank is our chief mode of expression. I enjoy these lunches hugely. They clear the sinuses of complaint.

Crank should of course only be spoken with contemporaries. What one must never do is shift into crank with people younger than oneself, who will quickly—and perhaps rightly—score one off as a bore. I had a friend named John Frederick Nims, who was a poet and teacher and for a too-brief spell editor of *Poetry Magazine*. John knew all the languages, and in conversation specialized in whimsy, at which he could be delightful. I knew he was older than I, but how much older I was never sure. He had thick black hair, which never turned grey. He had no physical complaints, or if he did, kept them to himself. Occasionally I would note a date would arise in connection with his career; he published a book of poems, for example, in the 1940s in a series of younger poets—Tennessee Williams was also in the series—for the publisher New Directions. Only when he died in 1999 did I learn, from his *New York Times* obituary, that John was born in 1913, and hence was twenty-four years older than I. Not long after his death I asked his wife Bonnie, who called him Nimsy, how John managed always to seem so ageless. "Nimsy had a little secret," she said. "He never talked about the past." Without the past to talk about, the crank is of course out of business.

Returning to *Standpoint*, that magazine's editors, in particular a nice man named Bob Low, have been most hospitable to my scribbles. I've never asked them to do anything, but over the past four or five years, they have come to me for contributions. It is the only magazine in my experience that has asked me for fiction. (I have a short story in its next issue.) My last lingering shreds of Anglophilia cause me to be pleased to appear, as the old expression had it, in its pages.

Beyond a certain age writers are often left on the sidelines, heart-broken wallflowers. In America this is especially true of novelists, sometimes quite good novelists, who have not hit the commercial success gong, and even to some who have sounded it. I had a friend named Albert Halper who was a Book-of-the-Month Club author in the 1930s and couldn't find a publisher for his novels in the 1970s. A novelist with the unfortunate name of George P. Elliott, who was also a savvy literary critic, found himself toward the end of his life in the same sad condition, publisherless. Some writers, as used to be said of old soldiers, just fade away. Not thus far true of you and me. May our luck hold out a good bit longer.

An editor who has always been receptive to my writing not long ago sent me a new biography of Bob Hope to review. On the principle of never running away from business, I agreed to do it, though I have no great interest in Bob Hope. I began reading the rather hum-drum biography a week or so ago, and did not make much progress, when, online, I noted that someone else had reviewed it for this same editor. When I apprised him of this, he was properly appalled at his memory lapse and apologetic. He said that he would in any case pay me my fee for the review. I wonder if he will remember to do so. If he assigned the same book to two reviewers, does he figure to remember to order a check for my fee, especially since I have no notion what the fee might be, for this is a magazine that pays me by the word. Truth is, I have no great interest in Bob Hope and the biography weighed in at 565 pages. A dullish book on a subject of secondary interest—distinctly, this, not my notion of a good time, and I am more pleased than not to be shut of it.

I have instead agreed to write for the same editor on the *Notebooks, 1922–1985* of Michael Oakeshott, a much richer and more congenial subject. Was Oakeshott a name you encountered during your analytical philosophy days at Cambridge? I should have thought not. He seems to have been his own man, Oakeshott, belonging to no schools, leaving no disciples. He is thought—he called himself—a conservative, but one coolly uninterested in turning back any clocks, or starting or aiding any political movement, or pushing any line. He was a conservative, I gather, less by politics than by temperament. I write, "I gather" because I've not really read Oakeshott, except in the most desultory way. This desultory reading suggests to me that he may be in the line of artist-philosophers, who aren't really philosophers at all. You may recall this snippet from the young T. S. Eliot, who began his intellectual life doing a Harvard doctoral dissertation on F. H. Bradley, in a letter to Norbert Weiner: "For *me*, as for Santayana, philosophy is chiefly literary criticism and conversation about life . . . The only reason why relativism does not do away with philosophy altogether, after all, is that there is no such thing to abolish. There is art, and there is science."

Earlier today I brought in some books to a local used bookseller, a nice young man in an old and regrettably dying business, who gives me credit in trade for them. I generally use this credit to buy art books for my granddaughter, or CDs for myself. Today I acquired a lovely CD called "Ella and Louis Sing Gershwin." Among the books I brought in were a few sent to me by publishers in the hope that I should find them worth writing about and a few others that I have read and have no desire to read again, and yet a few more that I now know that I shall never read because I've lost interest in the subject.

Two books in this last category that I sold this morning are *Selected Letters of Vanessa Bell* and *Letters of Katherine Mansfield*. The Mansfield-Middleton-Murray story has never much interested me; and as for Vanessa Bell, I find I can no longer bring myself to care in the least about the entire Bloomsbury crowd and their intramural fornications and relentless snobberies. Whom Vanessa bonked, the marital betrayals of Vita and Harold, the bisexuality of Lytton and Maynard, what pathetic Morgan did with his organ, no longer hold my interest. The entire subject of Bloomsbury now seems trivial to me.

Last week—November 30, to be more precise—marked the birthday one hundred and forty years ago of Winston Churchill, whose views of Bloomsbury, if he deigned to have any, would have been worth having. At Churchill's death in 1965, Leo Strauss wrote a brief eulogy, a portion of which I quote here: "The death of Churchill reminds us of the limitations of our craft, and therewith of our duty. We have no higher duty, and no more pressing duty, than to remind ourselves and our students, of political greatness, human greatness, of the peaks of human excellence. For we are supposed to train ourselves and others in seeing things as they are, and this means above all in seeing their greatness and their misery, their excellence and their vileness, their nobility and their triumphs, and therefore never to mistake mediocrity, however brilliant, for true greatness."

To shift abruptly into crank, isn't one of the saddest things about growing older witnessing mediocrity so often pumped up into greatness by people who don't know better. Doubtless this went on with the same frequency when we were younger, but now, at an age when I believe I have a surer purchase on what constitutes genuine greatness, it seems especially irritating, if not infuriating. Knowledge that it was probably ever thus is no consolation.

Crankily, Joe

P.S.: In your last you neglected to mention if Murray Kempton was a name known in England.

LONDON S.W.7. 5RF. 7.12.14.
Dear Joe,

You asked whether Murray Kempton meant anything to me. Might I have read him in the *New York Review of Books*? Or in its English subsidiary? Or both? Was Mr. K. (strangely recurrent, slightly sinister initial!) an Australian perhaps? A journalistic Ozziemandias then, his byline now stands among lone and level sands. Whether he was left or right, I cannot tell you, nor what his usual beef was. I remember Henry Fairlie because, back in the 1950s, he was the first (some say) to coin and regularly use the expression "The Establishment," to describe the old oligarchs/toffs who, whatever the stripe of the government, were the happy breed that really dominated English society.

It was, and remains, a comforting scandal that such people, despite all the mud and taxes thrown at them, despite no longer being allowed to ride from a view to a kill, are somehow still there, protection and menace, buckler and butt. The Establishment is even now being accused of a cover-up, this time not about Red Spies, but about squalid, perhaps murderous things done to children, from Care Homes, by a Certain Circle (including Tory M.P.s) during the early years of the Thatcher government. The whole bolus has yet to hit (and thrill/shock) the fans, but watch them spaces.

Although he died, with alcoholic assistance, in the U.S., twenty-five years or so ago, Fairlie lives on in that single phrase which he may have culled from Ralph Waldo Emerson, whose own quasi-rebellion against the New England establishment secured his entry into it. "Knock, knock" is a very old way of gaining entrance. Bernard Levin, of whom you may not have heard, was another London columnist who made his name by yahboo-sucking up to the politicos whom he satirized, in a right-wing mag, under the caper-and-bells pseudonym of Taper, before revealing his North London provenance. Bernard fought some good fights and was alone, Yeshiva-pale but never loitering, in denouncing the Soviet Union in the days when right-thinking men (and Doris Lessing) were all on the left. He was accused of hyperbolic absurdity when, in the 1970s, he went so far as to forecast the collapse of the Communist behemoth (he liked fancy locutions and saw himself, I daresay, as the Junius *de nos jours*) because of its humbug and oppressiveness.

The only other person to make the same forecast was Vladimir Nabokov, who was crankily precise in finding a reason which had nothing to do with Human Rights or the fallacies in Marxism/ Leninism: Volodya maintained that the Soviets' torture of the great Russian language would not go unavenged. Their Babel would collapse under the weight of its own misshapen verbiage. Those of us (you and me and who else?) who like to think that there is a need, by the use of neat and pointed speech, to puncture those who say "very unique" or "bored of," may not save the sum of things, and the pay ain't great, but—back to *Manhunt*—someone has to do it, ma'am.

When it comes to journalism, I am happy to give no more than a sliver of my time to it. The fate of workaday hacks (now all but outnumbered by hackettes) is so regularly down the swift Hebrus to the oubliette that some psychic tic must impel people on careers so perilous. The Editor and Mac the Knife have a common grin. A very good and able patron of mine, who for two decades commissioned me regularly to go *ici et là*, to destinations as far apart as the Black Sea and Oaxaca (where we witnessed a wet *Dia de los Muertos*, the locals sharing cheerful bake-meats with family ghosts in the candle-lit local cemetery), was recently summoned to a conference which, she began to realize, was not about beefing up her pages but about consenting to her own demise.

Our Readers, she was told, didn't have time for any more locally color-ful pieces about the glory that was Greece. They wanted to spool down and click for cheapo *sol y mar*. Christine had been with *The Sunday Times* for over twenty-five years. But, as my friend Brian Glanville puts it, in journal-ism fidelity is what they fuck you with. Someone somewhere up there had pricked the excellent Christine for proscription. Was it personal? I doubt it, just as I doubt whether the next great cull of millions of human beings will require religious or rhetorical justification or the recruitment of murderous louts to do the dirty work. If Stephen Hawking is right, the Almighty Com-puter will make terminal decisions without having, as was required of yes-teryear's scholarship candidate, to "give reasons." Even Hitler supposed that he was involved in some great crusade. Next time, folks, there will be no call for a Big Lie, however cracked. The dispassionate macro-descendant of Mr. Kubrick's Hal (in that stupendously tedious masterwork, *2001, Space Odyssey*) will rule selected tranches of human life insupportable. The deci-sion to eliminate will be statistical and no sooner clicked upon than exe-cuted. Nothing personal.

The irony of which we must not speak is that the voice in which Stephen Hawking broadcasts this chilling prediction is, on account of his cruel phys-ical affliction, a simulation. He has become the ghost in his own machinery. I met him once, when I was in favor at the London *Sunday Times* and was asked to present the professor with a thick gold pen for his best-selling *A Brief History of Time* at a many-tabled black-tie dinner. Why undertake such an unpaid, nerve-shredding task? For the same reason that the Parisian pros-titute gave as consolation for stomaching an unattractive client: *"Il m'a choisi."* To be selected exerts a certain traction, even to perform tasks with-out reward in cash or kudos. I was warned that Hawking's book was diffi-cult. Is it? It seemed to me that its brevity did more to account for its sales than its wit. The whole apocalyptic concatenation derived from the axiom that nothing could travel faster than light.

I took my anxious place at table, next to the mobile apparatus in which the genius was ensconced and tried to make appropriate conversation.

Unsurprisingly, the oracle was not prompt with repartee or with any kind of recognition of, or interest in, his imminent eulogist. As I waited for my tepid chicken and my cue, I swore never again; again. I recall only one carefully prepared off-the-cuff observation: Hawking had refuted his own axiom by proving that the human mind was capable of moving much faster than light. This did not get a standing ovation or even a facsimile thank you from my neighbor (whose use of a gold pen was likely to tend to zero). That dinner was the last occasion on which I saw Ken Tynan's beautiful wife Kathleen. Having refused to meet his sado-masochistic requirements, she was not quite ditched, more hedged by Ken's subsidiary attachment to a lady who shared his painful idea of pleasure. Oh, I also saw someone else for the last time that evening, an *intello* who had taken offense at my review of his new novel. I was glad to tell him that I had just been asked to write the screenplay. Did he smile? What was his then very well-known name? He too hopped it (on his left leg) to the U.S. Got it: Jonathan Raban.

Why do we do things, "pieces" not least? I learned from Michael Schmidt's very large and very enjoyable family history of The Novel (yes, I'm *ben citato*) that—until beatified as Our Lady of Bloomsbury—Virginia Woolf was a compulsive accepter of commissions to review books. She may have enjoyed the guineas, despite her contempt for Mr. Maugham, for being a literary tradesman, but I suspect that her instant availability also fell under the rubric "*Il m'a choisi.*" The Colonel's Lady (the title of one of Maugham's better stories, isn't it?) and Molly O'Grady often walk the same *trottoir.* I still do as much literary journalism as pretty well anyone asks, with pleasure and, I like to think, conscientiousness: I must read three or four books "around" every one I review. Motive? Vanity more than moolah. Why else would I undertake to write about Michael Schmidt's little 1,200-page number? Oaxaca-born Michael S. has for many years edited a little mag, *Poetry Nation Review,* now abbreviated to PNR and in its two-hundred and something-thingth edition. Donald Davie and one C. H. Cisson used to be part of the Right-minded editorial troika, but the mortal coil has shuffled them out of the pack.

Cisson was a solemn cove, deep blue, narrow with very steep sides, whose translation of Lucretius I reviewed with small enthusiasm. I never met him in the flesh but Michael persuaded me—why me?—to call him while he was sick unto death.In truth, which was the last cordial he needed, the only poem I recalled, by its title, was *In A Trojan Ditch.* I simulated belief in the lasting value of his *oeuvre* in which, at the last, he found small consolation. Racine, when told that he was dying, threw the unfinished, now unfinishable, manuscript of a new play into the fire. I hope my "terminal cocktail," as the medics call it, lulled C.H.S. as the shadows deepened. Norman Douglas, visited on his deathbed by ministering sisters, said, "Get those fucking nuns away from me." Way to go, as they say.

As for Donald Davie, he was, it seems, a ranking poet (I never read him), a pounder for Pound (aka Ole Ez) and a critical force for some good or other, somewhat to the left, unless it was to the right, of the other immensely influential Williams, the one who wasn't Bernard and advocated socialism *pur et dur* with all the *hwyl* and vinegar to be expected from the Welsh hills: Raymond, a pontificator whose bridge I never crossed. So Cisson died, Davie followed the yellow-brick road to campusville, U.S.A., and Michael S. was left in sole charge of the elegant little mag in which I have been able to speak my mind, at length, for instance about Ian McEwan's much lauded *On Chesil Beach*.

On the crank front, I don't think I am disposed to undue praise for things past. I did, however, go up to my old college in Cambridge two weeks ago, to see Michael Schmidt who happens to have alighted happily at St. John's and has, until the end of the academic year, very nice rooms on the same staircase where, in my time, a very good Hellenist called John Crook did his stuff. I am ashamed to say that I took against him very early on and never profited from his knowledge. A sense of missed scholarliness sat on me as Michael and I walked to lunch in the Senior Combination Room across mellow, red brick Second Court, in a corner of which, I think, William Wordsworth had his rooms. We happened to meet an undergraduate who stopped to salute Michael and shook my hand. I noticed on the top of his clutch of books one with the name Roland Barthes on it. Having discovered that the young man was reading English, I said, "You're reading Roland Barthes, I see." There was a crank's poise and then I slipped in the blade: "In French, I hope." He shook his head and showed me the text. I said, "If you're going to read English, which involves culling the kind of opinions which, this year, sit well with your examiners, I'd strongly advise you to learn at least one foreign language before you find yourself out in the world with nothing but modish ideas in your mind."

It was a deliberate out of character performance. I remembered a Nabokov story in which the narrator and his wife, I think she was, are having an angry quarrel in the Bois de Boulogne. As they yell and gesticulate, the man looks down the alley of chestnut trees and sees a young boy (I think) looking with dismay at their display. He stops himself and says, *grosso modo,* to the woman. "We must stop this. We're putting ugly furniture in that young person's memory." Of course Volodya put it better and more sweetly than his admirer, but the lesson is a good one and has stayed with me. It doesn't stop me behaving in an undignified or crude fashion, but it does make me feel bad about it. If the young guy learns to read Barthes in French (which ain't that difficult) the crackpot Old Johnian writer he met just that one time will have done him an invaluable service, *n'est-ce pas?*

Tout à toi, Freddie.

December 14, 2014
Dear Freddie,

Yes, Murray Kempton was in the stable of the *New York Review*, though he was probably more famous as an about-town columnist for various New York newspapers. He commanded an ornate style, highly exotic for newspaper journalism. He had eccentric and often interesting opinions, and sometimes took up the cause of unpopular underdogs, among them the Black Panthers. Born in 1917, he wrote a book about the 1930s, which I've not read but which I shouldn't doubt is interesting.

Another ten years, my guess is, and no one will know who Murray Kempton was. The same is probably true, without the ten-year wait, of Bernard Levin, who was in his way a Kemptonesque figure, with humor added. I read the *Spectator* in the days when he wrote as Taper, though I didn't then know who Taper was. I remember Bernard Levin best during his *That Was the Week That Was* and, later, *My Music,* days, which must have been the great high point in his career. I recall his thickish black-framed glasses, low hairline, and a vast quantity of hair piled high above an unmistakably Jewish *punim*. I just now checked his name on *Wikipedia* and discovered that the London *Times* called him "the most famous journalist of his day." That I fear is the epitaph of many a smart journalist, English and American. Alzheimer's brought down the curtain on his last act, forcing his retirement seven years before his death at the age of 76 in 2004.

To remain in threnodic mode a bit longer, the names Donald Davie and Raymond Williams are by now, too, pretty much wiped off the books of contemporary memory. I think we can probably toss in those of William Empson, who required so many differing kinds of ambiguity, and the now sadly dated Richard Hoggart, whose *Uses of Literacy*, though accurate in its prophesy, is no longer on anyone's screen. I know fame is advertised as fleeting, but they neglected to mention the speed with which it departs.

I don't suppose Henry Fairlie ever achieved the fame of the figures mentioned above. As you rightly say, the reinvention of the word Establishment, to describe any circle of secular power, is what remains of his reputation, if anyone remembers even that. I knew Fairlie, though not well, after he had left England to live in Washington, D.C. He was, I believe, an authentic bounder, unable to return to England owing to debt. I once invited him to an *American Scholar* dinner after one of the magazine's editorial meetings, and he turned up three sheets to the wind, schnockered, nicely crocked. At the dinner, he proposed the toast, "Fuck the Queen." It failed to charm.

In his early days, Fairlie was a contributor to *Encounter*, which for ten or so years was an immensely impressive magazine. In America, he signed on as a contributing editor of *The New Republic*. Here he attempted to do a Tocqueville turn, explaining America to Americans, but it didn't really come off. I remember hearing that, having insufficient funds to afford an apartment, he slept on a couch in the *New Republic* office. He died at sixty-six, his heart worn out, my guess is, from boozing and fighting off his self-induced poverty. No shortage of such sad stories in the world, as you will have noted.

The same *New Republic* that provided Henry Fairlie with a couch was the big story last week in what remains of the intellectual life in the United States. Over its hundred-year history the magazine was owned by various wealthy men with intellectual pretensions. Most infamous among these was Michael Straight, who fell in with Mcclean, Burgess & Co. at Cambridge in the 1930s, and later confessed to spying for the KGB, which helped to expose Anthony Blunt. The most recent owner of the magazine was a man named Martin Peretz, whose specialty seems to have been marrying wealthy women. Peretz was a standard liberal, but with an uncharacteristically, for a contemporary liberal, fierce devotion to the state of Israel.

The New Republic's literary editor Robert (Bobby, as he was called) Evett was generous to me. He let me, then in my mid-twenties, review just about anything I asked to review, and made good suggestions for other books I might review. He was a composer of modern music—never an easy life—a homosexual who was driven nearly nuts by a demon partner, a neurotic, a vicious gossip, and withal a very sweet character. He moved on to work at *The Atlantic* in Boston, where he asked me to do a few things, and we eventually lost touch. I owed him a good deal, and never properly repaid the debt.

A few years ago the *New Republic* was bought by a young man named Chris Hughes, who had the good fortune to have been the roommate, at Harvard, of Steven Zuckerberg, the founder of Facebook. Zuckerberg cut Hughes in, with the consequence that he is now said to be worth roughly half a billion dollars. When I wrote for it, the *New Republic* was a weekly; it has since been reduced to coming out twenty times a year. Hughes wants to make the magazine "a vertically integrated digital company," whatever that is. What it isn't, evidently, is a magazine in the sense you and I understand and have long revered superior magazines. For one thing, the young Chris Hughes and his new manager, a fellow who worked at Yahoo, are planning to reduce the number of issues annually of the magazine from twenty to twelve. For another he forced the resignation of the current editor and literary editor, which resulted in the resignation of two-thirds of the people on its over-crowded masthead. He, Hughes, has been claiming he didn't really want to change the magazine; nevertheless he insists that it needed to do more videos and interactive graphics and make better use of social media—the whole online cocktail, which I gather is what a "vertically integrated digital company" must do.

Walter Lippmann was an early editor of *The New Republic*. Edmund Wilson, *El Coñejito* himself, was one of the magazine's early literary editors, later replaced by Malcolm Cowley. Irving Howe, Alfred Kazin, and other literary critics who later came to modest fame got their start reviewing for the magazine. The magazine has been going slowly downhill over the years, but until recently it did at least attempt to do an imitation, however feeble, of its old eminent self. I dropped away from reading it for roughly a decade, and then two years ago resubscribed. I didn't find all that much to read in it. Under Chris Hughes and his Internet myrmidons, I assume that the downhill slide will now be more precipitate. The standard formula here is shorter articles on more ephemeral subjects accompanied by lots of empty photography, and chances for what the kids call "interactive participation." A product—if I were a Marxist, I would say "a commodity"—carrying the title of the old magazine will continue to be released out into in the world, but the machine will be devoid of any ghost. The English parallel to the *New Republic* would, I suppose, be *The New Statesman*. I once took great pleasure from that paper, and though I haven't held one in hand for years, whenever I read something from it online I find myself disappointed at its callow quality. The gradual disappearance of the *New Republic* is equivalent to the regular diminishment of the *New Statesman*. I suppose I could, in empty protest, cancel what is left of my subscription to the former, but whenever I think of writing a high dudgeon letter under the rubric Cancel My Subscription, I am reminded that William F. Buckley, Jr., at the *National Review*, when sent such a letter, used to reply with a postcard reading "Cancel it yourself."

The real import of the decline and fall of the *New Republic* is that it represents yet another victory for online over print culture, which means a triumph for the ephemeral over the perennial, the trivial over the serious, the low (make that "the no") brow over the high. Not a good thing, me not thinks but knows.

Yesterday afternoon I spent an hour and forty-five minutes watching an HBO documentary called *Regarding Susan Sontag* put together by a San Francisco woman named Nancy Kates interested in protest politics and the gay life. The only new thing I seemed to learn from it is that lesbians don't appear to age well, at least not those who had had love affairs with Susan Sontag. What the documentary reminded me of was Ms. Sontag's deep self-ishness. She never really did anything but exactly what she wanted to do. Her great regret, it turns out from this documentary, is not having written more fiction. All her fiction, or at least the too-ample portion of it I have read, arrived D.O.P., or dead on the page. How could it be otherwise? She never bothered to consult any desires but her own, or to learn anything about anyone other than herself. Although this documentary is meant to be admir-ing, not one of the many people interviewed for it speaks with convincing affection about its subject.

Part of Susan Sontag's problem may have been too early success on too flimsy grounds. The watershed moment for her fame was 1964, when in *Partisan Review*, at the age of thirty-one, she published her essay "Notes on Camp." Presto! Bango! she immediately became fodder for *Time Maga-zine* and *Vogue*. The documentary shows a bit from the movie *Bull Durham* in which the Kevin Kostner character calls Susan Sontag's novels "preten-tious crap" and the Susan Sarandon character replies that she admires them a lot. Susan Sontag became a household name, true chiefly in the households of the *kulturny*, where her name was a synecdoche for all that the putatively better educated who really didn't know any better thought of as intellectual. Hard to imagine that this kind of fame didn't go to her signature skunk-streaked head. At several points during the documentary Susan S. avers that the writer's true need is to confront reality. She goes off to wars—in Hanoi, in Sarajevo—because war is reality at its most vivid. Of course reality never laid a glove on her, nor she on it, poor girl.

I've earlier written that Susan Sontag, as Leavis said about the Sitwells, belongs to the history of publicity. That's true, I think; certainly there is no need to reread anything she wrote, for she reversed her major opinions—on Communism, on the uselessness of critical interpretation, etc.—and her humorless writing gives little pleasure; much of it, as has been said, reads like a poor translation from the French.

Yet I suspect that even a career like Susan Sontag's is no longer possible today. No figure of intellectual pretensions is likely for the foreseeable future to capture the attention that she did, if only because the new, the online, world is no longer in the least interested in the life of the mind. That world is too diffuse, too impatient, too self-regarding to care about mere intellectuals, even beautiful and exotic ones. The action is elsewhere.

I signed off my last e-mail to you as Crankily. This time I'll change salutation and end,

Gloomily, Joe

LONDON S.W.7 5RF. 16.12.14.
Dear Joe,

I am not sure whether or not I envy you your long slalom, zipping back and forth between the academy and literary journalism and then schussing sweetly through the short story gate. The people you met along the way are retrieved with such pitiless good humor that they almost certainly sound more fun and more feckless than they were. Your stories of editorial sessions and of rubbing shoulders with the intellectual *gratin* of New York and Chicago make me wonder where, as Mel Brooks has it, I went right. In 1950s London, I was reluctant to knock on doors unless I was sure that they would open. What savvy *arriviste* makes any such stipulation? As Simone de Beauvoir never said, One is not born an Englishman but, if educated in the right places, there's a risk you can become one.

My long, forked life began at Cambridge, where all good snakes felt their way onto the lower rungs of the ladder which, as a good metaphorical mixer would say, taken at the flood led on to fortune and the public prints. There was no degree like an Oxbridge degree in the good old, bad old days when no more than two percent of the U.K. population sported such honors. Good, steady jobs were not hard to find. I set my face against any kind of career at all. I didn't want to be at the mercy of, as I would never have said, even to myself, the *goyim*. The only way I knew to avoid subservience, of the kind which reduced my father to cypherdom, was to be a writer.

Had it not been for showbiz, I might have knocked harder in Fleet Street and classier locations. I wanted, very much, to be a great, glum novelist, a literary Van Gogh, huddled (and cuddled, if possible) in a garret, coughing out posthumous best-sellers; but before I left Cambridge I discovered, by chance, that I also liked to, and could, make people laugh. The small smiles of editors, when they can be elicited, are all very well, but once you have heard a full house laughing at your jokes, you are lost to single-mindedness. Duplicity is good for the dialogue.

As my forthcoming fatso autobio *Going Up* will reveal, I was lured into the lucrative cult of the bitch-goddess by one Leslie Bricusse, a student songwriter in need of someone to write dialogue for the musical comedy which he had the energy and shamelessness to put on while others cracked the secret of DNA or joined Dr. Leavis in the Common Pursuit (of first class degrees in English). Leslie was supposed to be reading French, but he preferred Cole Porter. After we came down, he took to showbiz with American zest (he had spent the war in Canada) and did not need to pull very hard to get me to follow. When I came to where the high and low roads branched, one up to Art, one down to The Biz, I did not hesitate before taking them both.

Leslie and I wrote a movie or two, but quite soon I detached myself. I wanted to make it new, and also to make it alone; but I was persuaded, in 1959, to write a little handbook, entitled *The S-Man*. The pseudonymous Mark Caine itemized the tactics by which an unscrupulous charmer might play Tarzan in the urban jungle and swing himself to the top branches. Although no one noticed, the discrete sections of the book were set out in a parody of the *Tractatus-Logico-Philosophicus*. To write under a pseudonym is a liberty which everyone should try at least once. I will not embarrass you with a volley of smartass quotations, not least because I don't have a copy handy and also because they may not be all that smart. I do recall, "When you are in bed with your boss's wife, never fail to leave your school-cap hanging in the hall." It was, as they say, that sort of a show, folks. Oh, one more: "Roughly speaking success and money are synonymous." That passed for telling it how it wasn't in the humbugging 1950s. Who cared, or guessed, that it parodied Wittgenstein's casual assertion "Ethics equals aesthetics." Or was it the other way round?

Elizabeth Jane Howard's review put *The S-Man* in the same class as—of all classmates—Laclos's *Les Liaisons Dangereuses. Par contre,* in the

New Statesman, my friend and patron Peter Green, who will be ninety years old in a week's time, although no kind of prig or prude, was scandalized by the cynicism of someone who, of course, he never suspected was honest Fred. Peter was the first editor, of a serious publication (i.e., one that paid its contributors), to accept a story of mine, while I was still an undergraduate. It was not his fault that the publisher went bust before I wowed them with my precociousness, but I have so often been grateful to him, for editorial acumen and sound advice, that I could wish that he was living his *très verte vieillesse* in somewhere more accessible than Iowa City. There are friends and friends and Peter, with whom I have never trekked in Arcadia or spent much time with in the flesh, is one of my closest. He has said many kind things about me, not least, quite recently, about my notebooks in the late, lamented *New Republic.* He thinks me a Man of Letters.

Crank as we may, the existence of the Net does have its sweet side: to exchange letters so freely and so quickly with you is the best evidence of that, as is the ability to stay in touch with Peter, who has just finished translating the *Iliad,* a job which he dares to say has never been done *accurately* before. Coming from P.M.G. this does not sound like a boast but what the frogs call a "*constatation,*" a statement of fact. He is now drawing breath before tackling the *Odyssey* which, interestingly and a little surprisingly, he thinks a much more grown-up piece of work.

Peter is a rare and fearless man for all seasons, and most literatures. Although *the* classical scholar of his generation, he made some bad career moves at Cambridge and, by his precocious genius (and piercing criticism of them), rendered himself disagreeable to the makers and breakers of academic progress. What seemed to ruin his prospects had the Nietzschean effect of making him stronger. He found a world elsewhere, first in Greece, then in the U.S., and has, I hope, never spared a thought for what might have been. Old Willie Maugham wrote a neat story, as you may recall, about a man who was a verger in some posh church and was fired because it was discovered that he couldn't read or write. He then went out and started a tobacconist shop which prospered into a chain and made him a rich man. The obvious (if you can think of it) twist came when someone said to him "Imagine what you might be today if only you'd learned how to read and write." Yes, fans, the answer is, he would still have been the verger of St Something's, Somewhere Square.

I was driven to become a writer not least because, with suburban naïveté, I imagined that being alone, and probably poor, would render me immune to the treachery of supposed friends, of the kind I had been at school with. Writing well would be the best revenge. I have never entirely lost the urge to get my own back, beautifully if possible. I try to use the English language with as much sharpness as I can contrive. O. Wilde was right: whether something is written with good motives or unworthy ones, the result can be judged, should be judged, by its quality alone. Jean-Paul Sartre knew this very well, or why would he have tried to convince us that there could be no "good" right-wing literature? What sane person can claim that the A-list of world literature does not contain a regiment of conservatives and reactionaries?

I do not wish to wear their uniform nor any other. It has always been part of the fun of reviewing to take an unexpected line. If my enemy has written a good book (it happens), I take more pleasure in praising him or her than I should in putting the shaft in. I do, however, have what you might call Herzog moments, in which I compose more or less indignant letters to strangers. May I unveil a corner of my paranoia? In my private self, I suspect Bellow of having based his closet correspondent on my *Lindmann,* who did the same thing two years before Bellow's little number came up. But then, as the old punch-line has it, "Lady, who cares?"

I am trying to cut down on fulmination but I do froth, at times, not least at presenters on the TV, especially the grander ones who, by their tone and controlled manual gestures, play the magisterial register. One such on the BBC is a certain Andrew Marr whom I caught the other day prancing through yet another montage of the Last War (the secular equivalent, in diminished England, of the Last Supper, and consumed as regularly). He was lamenting the fire-bombing of Dresden, an antique city reduced to ash by vindictive Anglo-Americans. We must, it seems, be sorry for the German "men, women and children" whose "innocence" he implied. The Germans were said to have fought bravely despite all that we threw at them. My Herzoggy (unsent) letter to Master Marr mentioned that I am faced, each morning, by the photograph of my mother's twenty-one-year-old "kid cousin," Irvin Weintraub. He is in the U.S.A.A.F. uniform which he wore as a glider pilot in the 1944 campaign in Holland. As he hit the ground, his glider was surrounded by S.S. men. The crew and the soldiers on board had no choice but to put their hands up. They were led away and, not long afterwards, murdered. Ah the brave, badly used Krauts!

As for the Dresden bombing and its "unnecessary" status, you may know that Victor Klemperer (cousin of the great Otto) was due to report to the railway station for deportation to, though he did not know it, Auschwitz on the following morning. The raid wrecked the city, destroyed Gestapo headquarters and burned its records. Victor Klemperer (and others, no doubt) were spared becoming ash themselves. Does that make it right that . . .? No, it makes it what it is and, as Bishop Berkeley would not have allowed, also another thing. God is no hands-on moralist, but He can do irony like a bastard. I ended my unsent letter, "Chuck it, Marr!" Do you think he would have taken the allusion?

Tout à toi, Freddie.

December 23, 2014
Dear Freddie,

At ninety, still churning out impressive work, Peter Green has attained the status of a phenomenon. I not long read him on Herodotus in *the London KilltheJews of Books* on Herodotus, on which he was first-class. His biography *Alexander of Macedon* is my current bedside book, and it is a superior work in the Gibbonian tradition of the philosophic historian. In it Peter G. sorts out the various myths and legends about Alexander, everywhere making judgments based on persuasive cause and effect, while keeping up a well-paced narrative flow, the whole informed by an impressive understanding of human nature. The prose isn't as rich as Gibbon's, but then no one's is or could be, yet is nonetheless filled with quiet delights and to me lots of new information.

Who knew that Alexander's great teacher Aristotle's appearance was, in Peter Green's words, "foppish, not to say eccentric. He was balding, spindle-shanked, and had small eyes. Perhaps in an effort to compensate for these disadvantages, he wore dandified clothes, cut and curled his hair in an affected manner, and spoke with a lisp. Numerous rings sparkled on his fingers: the overall effect must have been like the young Disraeli at his worst." Aristotle—who'd've thunk?

Three days ago we happened to watch, via Turner Classic Movies, the Robert Rossen film *Alexander the Great*, in which Aristotle appears in plain white toga with a full head of white hair and an ordinary beard. The reigning impression the movie leaves, though, is of the preposterous blond wig they plopped onto the still youthful skull of Richard Burton playing Alexander. Lots of fiddling with history in the movie, of course; Rossen's Darius is killed after his defeat at Issus, whereas we know he lived on to fight another day. The most egregious thing about the movie is the dialogue, which is ninety-seven percent declamation. No one merely speaks; everyone declaims, not least Philip, played well over the top by Frederick March in a way that makes one think those philippics of Demosthenes measured and more than reasonable. Not bad battle scenes, though, and I have an unconquerable *faiblesse* for guys got up in classical duds. Do you suppose there is any chance that in the next life we shall be allowed to walk around in tunics and togas?

The biographical note for Peter Green on my paperback edition of Alexander of Macedon has him as Dougherty Centennial Professor Emeritus of Classics at the University of Texas. Peter G. must have been part of the English classics drain that occurred sometime in the 1960s, when the University of Texas, backed by its wealthy alumni, acquired the services of D. S. Carne-Ross, William Arrowsmith (formerly of Yale), Peter Green, and others. How did Peter G. wind up in Iowa, I wonder? Sounds a bit like Ovid being sent into hopeless exile on the cold banks of the Danube, though Iowa City is said to be more sightly than it sounds.

I wonder, too, what Peter Green did to alienate the classicist powers that were at Oxbridge. I knew two of these powers, Arnaldo Momigliano and Hugh Lloyd-Jones; the latter of course ended his days as Regius Professor. Neither struck me as intolerant, nor likely to be put off by heterodox opinion of the kind Peter Green might harbor and broadcast. Hugh was most unpretentious, with a good laugh and witty in a way that his published work does not generally display. Like many men whose entire lives were spent at Oxford or Cambridge, there was something irretrievably boyish about him, despite his ample white hair.

I knew Hugh through his wife, Mary Lefkowitz, a professor of classics at Wellesley College, who was a member of the editorial board of *The American Scholar*. Mary was smart and courageous both; you may recall that she took on Martin Bernal's dopey thesis in *Black Athena: The Afro-asiatic Roots of Classical Civilization* that classical civilization really began in Africa, which wasn't an easy thing to do once the tyranny of political correctness was well underway, which by then it was. Mary, I believe, was Hugh's second wife, he her first husband. They were charmingly nuts about each other. I had a single—and singular—glimpse into their marriage when Hugh told me that, while Mary ironed his shirts, he read James or Proust to her. A touching picture of the domestic life of an immitigably high-brow marriage.

I've not read *Lindmann*, so cannot comment on the notion of Bellow's possible plagiary of your use of a narrator who writes amusing letters to famous people. Since Bellow painted from life, which is to say invented nothing, there is every chance that your charge would hold up in a high if alas non-existent literary court. Bellow's letters, to Nietzsche, Adlai Stevenson, and others are easily the most memorable thing in *Herzog*, which is otherwise a dullish novel about a guy complaining about his own naiveté at having been cuckolded by a friend and colleague.

Herzog, published in 1964, is more important for another reason. Along with Mary McCarthy's *The Group* (1963), it represents the first time the work of members of the once coterie-like New York intellectuals got, as they say on Wall Street, on the Big Board. Both novels were bestsellers. From this point forward, intellectuals in America were welcomed into a wider world. *The New Yorker*, once thought headquarters of the middlebrow enemy and a place where one should be ashamed to have one's writing appear, hired Dwight Macdonald and installed Harold Rosenberg, the most abstruse of the New York intellectuals, as its regular art critic. Many of these same New York intellectuals began to publish in *Esquire* and Huntington Hartford's short-lived but well-paying magazine *Show*. The *New York Times* hired Stanley Kauffmann, *The New Republic's* film critic, as its drama critic (a hire, as it used to be called, that didn't work out) and my friend Hilton Kramer as its principal art critic. The lines between highbrow and middlebrow culture began to become blurred, at least to the extent that writers, once content to be what Arnold Bennett called "small-public" writers, were now fishing in larger, if somewhat more polluted waters.

One might think this a good thing for the culture. By bringing the top down the effect would surely be to help bring the bottom up. Unlike British television, which was hospitable to such English intellectual figures as A. J. P. Taylor, Malcolm Muggeridge, Evelyn Waugh, and Trevor-Roper—the best American television and radio could do were the indefatigable middlebrows Clifton Fadiman and Bergen Evans. Something artificial there was about once small-public writers going big public.

I would add that to have a small number of readers really care about what one writes is no small gift. But if they are truly devoted readers that's all that matters, is it not? Do I see your lips forming around the word "Not?" Writers, being fantasts, want it both ways, or, if possible, three or four ways: devoted readers, the widest possible audience, big money, fame, and, thrown in at no extra charge, the love of beautiful women. Certainly I want all those things, except the fame and the love of beautiful women. I've already had the latter, and the small doses of the former that have come my way merely embarrass me.

The great good luck in being an even moderately successful writer is of course the freedom it allows from enslavement by a regular job. When you say that as a young man you set your "face against any kind of career at all," and that "the only way I knew how to avoid subservience, of the kind that reduced my father to cypherdom, was to become a writer," you are enunciating and obeying the eleventh Jewish commandment. This is the commandment, though not put in the imperative, that reads: Only a schmuck works for someone else.

If you work for someone else, the impeccable reasoning here runs, your destiny is not your own. At the whim of strangers you can be demoted, transferred to Houston, fired. Your plans can go up in flames owing to the incompetence of your employer or co-workers; you can fall under the sway of a petty tyrant; innumerable reversals of fortune can occur, none of your own making. Better always to be one's own boss, despite the headaches, also known as *tsuris*, than to fall among the great unwashed multitude known as employees. Such is the wisdom behind the eleventh commandment, and it strikes me as incontestable.

Did your father, I wonder, complain about his days at Shell? I rather doubt that he could as easily have been hired by Shell in America, even with his Oxford degree, because the great American corporations did not in those days hire many Jews. That they didn't has long remained among the historical gripes of American Jews. In good part this is behind the difficulty many American Jews, even unto this day, with Jewish CEOs now more common than streetwalkers, have in voting for candidates of the Republican Party. Republicanism means for them, or at least it did for their parents and grandparents, no matter how conservative their own views may be, anti-Semitism: restricted neighborhoods, a lock-out on corporate jobs, university quotas, and the rest. Thus the twelfth Jewish commandment: Only a *mishuganer* votes Republican.

I have recently had another Jamesian *donnée* dropped into my lap. A friend, who in his first and wretched marriage was a player, a chaser of skirts, mentioned in passing a week or so ago that he was one day in a restaurant with a woman not his wife when his father walked in with a woman also not his, his father's, wife. After a decent interval, his father sent him a note suggesting it was unseemly for both of them to be in the same restaurant while playing at the same game, and asked if he, my friend, might not be willing to leave. Seniority, his reasoning must have run, is owed its benefits. Sensible fellow, Dad. I'm now attempting to turn this incident into a tale I hope will be amusing if not necessarily edifying.

Your suggestion to write at least one book under a pseudonym is, I fear, a suggestion lost on me, whose vanity is too great to even contemplate taking on—apologies here to Joseph Conrad—a secret sharer. That you could do so at so early an age shows what a pro you were from the outset. I'm told that the too prolific novelist Joyce Carol Oates publishes even more novels under a pseudonym. Didn't Simenon also do so? Other detective-story writers publish under two or three different names. Then there is that popular author Anonymous. The last anonymously published book that made a splash in America was the roman with a skeleton *clef* called *Primary Colors*, a novel about Bill Clinton's first presidential campaign, written by a *Time Magazine* journalist named Joe Klein. I never read it, politics, even with fancy fornication added, not being the kind of bait at which this fish bites.

Nor could I work as a ghostwriter, though once, if the price were grand enough, I thought I might. My ego has by now swelled too greatly for that. I have a friend who wrote the memoirs of Abba Eban, and an acquaintance who does a fair amount of this kind of work. The latter ghost-wrote a bestseller under the name of an American auto mogul named Iacocca, after having flown around with him in private jets and listening to war stories about the Ford and Chrysler motor companies. Among other books, he did, simultaneously, the memoirs of a politician named Tip O'Neill and a Washington D.C. escort-service owner who called herself the Mayflower Madame. If he had got the galleys from these two books mixed up, I wonder if anyone would have noticed?

I note that the *TLS*, on which I am currently behind no fewer than fourteen numbers—I blame the editors, they provide too much of interest—has raised its American price to $185. Not an easy check to write, though with Christmas now at our throats, I shall give myself the present of another year's subscription. By next year at this time, I should be behind twenty-eight copies. Eventually—*kayna hora*, or may the evil eye not intercede—I'll be behind a full fifty-two issues and thus will be able to save $185. Smart, that Epstein, like a lox.

Merry Crotsmere, Joe

LONDON S.W.7 5RF 28.12.14.
Dear Joe,

So much for the holly and the oy vey! The celebration of Christmas becomes less Christian and less celebratory every year (we even forgot to put out the crackers and the "children" are now too old, or were too hungry, to notice). We sent fewer cards this year, favoring the solitary and those who might feel "dropped." As for presents, we did our best for the family, though I left the clever stuff, requiring literal shopping, to Beetle and limited myself to selecting suitable (I hope) books, very few of them from the *TLS* list, though I did give the twice-lauded book on Italy and citrus fruit to a couple of, I hope, lucky people.

I gave our screenwriter son Stephen, a sometime trader of quiet skill and steady nerve, *Flash Boys,* about the stock exchange jocks and jerks on whom the future of the West seems to depend. They just may, whether on purpose or by chance, bring it all crashing down, almost certainly with no moral or revolutionary intent but just "because" (an e-correspondent tells me this morning that the free-standing, all purpose excuse "because" is cited as the American Dialect Society's word of the year). The movie Because Without a Cause will never star some new James Dean, but there it is, a one-word confession of never-mindlessness in a society without the dutiful hurdles we used to clear or stumble through.

I tried to find Beetle some new novels to amuse her but contrived to thicken the stack (which included several inches of the latest Donna Tartt) with two that I had given her before, Penelope Fitzgerald's *The Beginning of Spring* and William Maxwell's *The Château,* both of which she had enjoyed and which I had not so much as sipped. A random tasting of Maxwell's clear prose failed to hook me: "As he and Barbara were undressing for bed, they remarked upon a curious fact" (p.137). I'm sorry, but surely either one or the other of the married duo said something first about this curiosity or else—also possible but not suggested—they both came out simultaneously with "You know something funny . . ." or words to that effect.

Later in the same paragraph I see, "Neither of them mentioned their reluctance to leave Paris, that afternoon, or the fact that their room, after the comforts of the hotel, seemed cold and cheerless." Without getting silly, of the things neither of them mentioned there is, surely, no end. The particular instance alluded to may be pertinent to their condition, but the room (in the eponymous château) either was "cold and cheerless" or it wasn't. If we are to take our trade seriously, "seeming" should be used to contrast with a real state of affairs. Can it be that the château room was really "warm and cheerful," but not to the aforesaid couple? Surely not; in which case Mr. Maxwell, a revered *New Yorker* editor, has got it slightly, but damagingly, wrong. Published just before the deluge which swept away coherence, plausibility and credible dialogue from the routine ambition of fictioneers, *The Château,* which I bet you have read, comes towards the end of the great tradition, inaugurated by *Daisy Miller,* of stories about Americans of various kinds coming to Europe. I am sure it is a worthy work, but the lack of specific focus dismays me, slightly but abruptly. However many famous persons may line up to testify to his perfect sense of pitch, Maxwell writes nicely, but not as a master should.

The best bookshop in our part of London still bears the name of its founder John Sandoe, a gentleman tradesman whose young red face suggested that stress might carry him off, as it did. The shop is in a one-way street off the King's Road, Chelsea, and has prospered not least because it is situated where affluence and Bohemian history coalesce. S.W.3 used to be a district of studios, pubs and arty wantonness of the kind which Joyce Cary framed in his trilogy devoted to Gulley Jimson. I suggested in my last innings that pseudonymity could be a liberation and, although preaching to the unconverted, I'll persist here by mentioning that, in an otherwise forgotten movie of *The Horse's Mouth,* John Bratby "ghosted" Gully's paintings and, liberated from the need to be his own slap-it-on Van Go come again, created some memorable images, not least of gnarled feet.

In the late 1980s, our daughter Sarah did a superb series of paintings, including several crucifixions, while impersonating my fictional TV character Guy Falcon. We have her study of a Roman soldier about to hammer in a nail. There is no sign of the crucifix or of the hand or foot which is about to be pierced, but one can hardly look at the image without wincing. Doris Lessing once wrote a novel under a false name and then did a "gotcha" when publishers didn't like it. I never liked the other ones either, apart from *The Golden Notebook.*

Back to Sandoe. The shop is one of the few left in London where, in a cottagey space, one can almost always find what one wants, even things one didn't know one wanted. Only rarely does anything have to be ordered. Hence I was surprised to be told last week, when I went to pay for the stack I had compiled, that they had a book for me which I had ordered back in March: *The Gallery* by John Horne Burns. On first sight of it, I could not believe that it was for me. That it had a (brief) introduction by Paul Fussell made it more likely. I opened it and saw that the Gallery in question was the Galeria Umberto Primo just off the Piazza della Republica in Naples. Then I remembered that my friend Brian Glanville had recommended the novel and knew the author.

Fussell tells me that Burns was educated at Andover and Harvard, but as Burns puts it "In the 19 days of crossing the Atlantic . . . I think I died as an American." His metaphorical death was precipitated by observing G.I.s stealing from each other, but before it killed him (at the age of thirty-seven), he was a merciless annotator of the horrors of war and of backstage hangers-on like the society lady turned Red Cross volunteer who saw some G.I.s in a jeep named "Wet Dream" and concluded that they had "frightful manners," thus justifying her recourse to the comforts which officers supplied.

Glanville knew Burns in Florence in the early 1950s (they had to be early: B. died in 1953). By that time, Burns had had only a serious *succès d'estime* with *The Gallery* and a disaster with his second novel. The third was generated with the help of more sauce than was good for it and found no takers. Brian recalls Burns drinking himself urgently to death and talking, at length, only to the *barista* who served him his poison. *The Gallery* belongs with Norman Lewis's *Naples '44* and Curzio Malaparte's *La Pelle* as masterpieces of wartime *verismo*, even though they no doubt contain passages of invention. *A proposito,* Malaparte claims that the whores of Naples (many very young girls driven onto the streets by starvation) sometimes wore blond pubic hairpieces to pique the appetites of black American soldiers. Do we disbelieve this? Or does political propriety require us to do so?

Malaparte (the anti-Buonaparte pseudonym of Kurt Erich Suckert) was a homegrown literary scapegrace to match ole Ez (Pound), the rat/*miglior fabbro* holed up in Rapallo. Unlike the latter, M. did actually go to war, as a reporter on the Russian front, and could not resist composing *Kaputt,* a cold-eyed account of the Wehrmacht's progress to catastrophe. Did he fabricate the magnificent image of a literally arrested horse-drawn German artillery unit, frozen in a lake in front of Leningrad, the horses marbled in ice as they lifted their forelegs and threw back their heads in a last gasp? True now, it remains *indimenticabile.*

Having been frequently in trouble with the Fascisti on account of his scornful attitude to just about everything and everyone, Malaparte was as adroit as Casanova in getting out of terminal trouble. He escaped punitive censure after the war and was not, I think, so much as docked of the cinema-sized, caramel-colored villa which his butt and admirer, the Duce, had allowed him to construct, against insular regulations, on Capri. M. played right-wing to Alberto Moravia on the left; both were outspoken observers of human folly; both wrote the clear Italian which persuades you that you're fluent in the language.

Burns was, as they used to say, "gay as a bird," but his memoir-novel gains, as Proust's did, from the absence of self-pity or self-advertisement. The author is at once omnipresent in his tone of voice and invisible in person. I have no prescriptive rules for how to deal with being Jew, gay, black or anything else in particular, but I prefer writers who bury special-case prides or grievances in a stylish or ironic way. If, as tendentious gays insist, "we are all really queer/bisexual/up for grabbing," then we can, as Wittgenstein put it, "divide through" by what we have in common and get on with writing as well as possible.

Italy seems more congenial, even in its degradation, to American writers than France. Maxwell, albeit as cool *avant la lettre* as Mr. Shawn would wish, treats the French with nervous circumspection and pretty well confesses to being uneasy with the nuances of their language. Julien Green is the only American transplant whose mastery of French was undeniable enough for him, alone among foreigners, to be elected to the *Académie française*. In very old age (he was ninety-eight when he died), he resigned from the *Académie* for reasons not itemized by the usual potted biographies. Green too was gay, but in the discreet tradition of French writers which has many illustrious instances, not least, I learned recently, François Mauriac who succeeded to Green's chair in the Academy, on the latter's death. Mauriac, *en bon Catholique,* was married with a family, but was known (so the dirt-diggers tell us) also to have, as the English used to put it, "batted for the other side." It would be a nice irony if Green had quit his seat in the Academy because some old *littérateur homophobe* called him "*Tante Julien,*" and another "auntie" had then taken his place.

George Steiner once told me an elaborate literary joke, of the unfunny kind, in which someone was alleged to have come up to Proust's friend Montesquiou at his dead chauffeur Iturri's funeral and said, "*Mort, Iturri te salue, tante*" ("Dead, Iturri salutes you, faggot"). This required Steiner's audience to spot the trans-linguistic pun on the Roman gladiators' refrain "*Morituri te salutant*" (those who are about to die salute you) regularly delivered to the presiding Caesar. We can be sure that Sid of all Caesars would give the thumbs down to that one. Incidentally, recent revisionists tell us that fewer gladiators died in the arena than used to be assumed. They were, like the children of slaves, valuable commodities and, like boxers run by the mob, worth saving for another time.

Which brings us, by a longish route, back to Rome and another American writer, of some quality, Alfred Hayes, whose wartime experiences in Italy generated a small masterpiece *The Girl on the Via Flaminia*. My introduction to Hayes's novella *In Love* is the only work of mine to appear in, or even to be noticed by, the *New York Review of Books* punditocracy. Hayes became fluent enough in Italian to help Roberto Rossellini with the screenplay of

Paisà before repairing to Hollywood where he had a career which resembled that of Daniel Fuchs, but with no Oscar at the end of its rainbow.

Tout à toi, Freddie.

January 2, 2015
Dear Freddie,

Our Christmas, Hanukkah, Kwanzaa, what have you, has been slimmed down nicely. In past years, Barbara would send out cards and chose elegant gifts for family and a few friends. She did all the work and I all the complaining—a nice division of labor, or so I always felt. Now we have cut out the middlemen—which is to say, the retailers—and I hand out cash to a few family members who can use it and to those people who have done work for us over the past year, and Barbara sends out cards only to those who send them to us. Only slightly contrary to the cliché that has Jews eating Chinese food—the food of our people, as I think of it—this year we were taken out to a sumptuous Christmas dinner at a suburban steak house called Ruth's Chris Restaurant by our son Mark and our two west coast grandchildren, Nick and Lily. In sum, we got through another holiday season unscathed.

Best perhaps at this time of the year to set aside the chilling fact that the adherents of the gentle Jesus have cost us Hebes more *tsuris* than all the world's pagans combined. Our only defense is jokes, preferably tasteless jokes. What, after all, can possibly be the point of a joke in good taste? Here is a seasonal joke that I believe qualifies.

The nail manufacturer Sidney Schwartz's thirty-nine-year-old, none-too-bright son Irwin beseeches his father to give him more responsibility in the business. Against his better judgment, Sidney allows him to handle the firm's Christmas advertising. Three days later, driving to work on the expressway, Sidney sees a large billboard of the crucifixion, with the caption beneath it reading, in bold red letters, "They Used Schwartz Nails." The moment he arrives at his desk Sidney calls in his son, and yells, "You idiot, you moron, you maniac, you'll cause riots, pogroms, God knows what! Change that goddamn billboard immediately!" The next day Sidney, driving to work, notes the same billboard, with Jesus still on the cross, but now with one arm hanging loose, a leg dangling, his head fallen onto his chest, with the caption reading, "They Didn't Use Schwartz Nails." At the conclusion of this joke it seems only appropriate to add, Merry Christmas to all and to all a good night.

William Maxwell's novel *The Chateau* is the only one of his few novels I found unreadable. I recall struggling through it, and it left no residue, none whatsoever. As for the two leading characters not doing a lot of "mentioning" to each other, I should attribute this to the ethos of the finer *goyim* in America, at least of Maxwell's generation—he was born in 1908—who weren't big either on complaining or on self-revelation. The chief problem with *The Chateau*, I suspect, is that it is about adults. Maxwell wrote best about children and the young. He was a man with one story to tell: the story of his own life, which was blasted by his losing his mother, when he was ten years old, to the 1918 flu epidemic. He wrote a quite good novel about this called *So Long, See You Tomorrow*, set in small-town Illinois, where he spent his early boyhood. My favorite of his novels is *The Folded Leaf,* which is partly set in my high school in Chicago, which Maxwell attended; the novel is about the friendship between two very different kind of boys: a likeable hardy and a recessive bookworm. (I'll let you guess which is Maxwell.) A few of our critical geniuses claim the novel is homosexual in its inspiration, to which I can only say, we sleep tonight, criticism stands guard. I read a slender memoir about Maxwell written by a then younger *New Yorker* writer named Alec Wilkson, which was most respectful, but all I can remember of it is that Maxwell, on his deathbed, at one point opened his eyes to exclaim, "Fuck their prizes!" I like that, a lot.

I know of John Horne Burns, but have never read him, nor am I likely to this side of the grave. (I assume, if somewhat shakily, that there will be plenty of time for reading on the other side of the grave and a library that will allow one to take out books for eternity.) Self-tortured homosexuals, as I gather Burns was, are not my cup of cocoa. I prefer those homosexuals who have come to terms with what must now be termed their gaiety, and make no bones about it. I'm thinking here of Somerset Maugham, W. H. Auden, Truman Capote, Noel Coward, and let us not neglect little Marcel. Maugham and Auden, true enough, had wretched taste in lovers, but that's another matter.

I believe the word you want to describe the blonde wigs worn by Neapolitan prostitutes after the Allied invasion is the good King Jamesian one of *merkin*, which is a pubic wig. The *OED* dates the first use of the word to 1617. A wealthy Jewish family currently residing in America carries the less than noble surname name of Merkin. They donated the money for

Merkin Hall in Lincoln Center. One of its scions, a boychik named Ezra, was heavily mixed up in the Madoff affair of recent years. Another is a writer named Daphne Merkin, who consistently fails to grasp that the confessional mode should stop before it lapses into the highly embarrassing. This Ms. Merkin published a piece in the *New Yorker* about her penchant, a penchant she recounts acting upon, for being spanked by men; another in which she wrote about her thirteen or so psychotherapists; and I seem to recall a piece in the *New York Times Magazine* about her going to her mother and asking for a substantial part of her likely inheritance now, goddammit. She is currently at work on a big book on her depression. As Max Beerbohm, in "Kolniyatsch," his parody of the reception accorded in England to a Dostoyevsky-like Russian writer, wrote: The "promised biography of the murdered grandmother is eagerly awaited by all . . ."

Over the past few weeks we have watched—or, rather, re-watched—the thirteen episodes of the 1976 BBC version of *I, Claudius*. I don't know how many decades ago I read—and recall rather liking—the Robert Graves novel from which it of course derives. The television version holds up pretty well. An actor named John Hurt goes well over the top as Caligula, so far over in the direction of malicious effeminacy that it is difficult to believe him actually guilty of incest with his sister. Historical mistakes creep in: That Julia's two sons, Lucius and Gaius, die in the wrong order is only one such error. In the television version, and I suspect in the Graves novel, ambiguity over key events is eliminated to make for clearer plot lines. The series ends with Agrappina, mother of that malicious fatboy who is said to have fiddled while a certain Italian capitol burned, poisoning Claudius to make certain that the aforementioned fatboy becomes emperor. Suetonius, who I gather is himself thought too often to indulge in gossip, on this point writes: "Most people think that Claudius was poisoned; but when, and by whom, is disputed."

What is winning about the show is, John Hurt apart, the acting, good solid English acting, and in all the parts, major and minor. Siobhan Philips as the wicked Livia is especially fine. Derek Jacoby, hobbling, stammering, painfully twitching away, ain't bad either. Jacoby is for me one of those actors—Ralph Richardson is another—whom one admires and also likes, while Laurence Olivier and John Gielgud will have to settle, in my book at least, for mere admiration alone. The script of *I, Claudius* is by a man named Jack Pulman, whom you may well have known and who made his living adapting various great works for British television and pegged out with a heart attack in his middle fifties.

The reason I bring all this up is that, on the DVD version of *I, Claudius* is attached a final track called "The Epic That Never Was." An hour or so long documentary made in 1965 and narrated by Dirk Bogarde, it is about a very expensive—extravagant Roman sets, a few of which are shown in the documentary, must have jacked up the cost—Josef von Sternberg film version of *I, Claudius*. This version was begun in 1937 and at mid-completion had to be scrapped because Merle Oberon, who played Messalina, was in a serious car accident. The producer, and the man whose idea it was—no surprise here—was the quite properly ambitious Alexander Korda. The documentary includes interviews with von Sternberg, Miss Oberon, Emlyn Williams (who then a young man plays Caligula with much greater restraint than John Hurt), Flora Robson (who was to play Livia), Robert Graves, the script girl, the costume designer, and a few others. Graves, who comes across as most unpretentious, allows that he agreed to sell the rights to his novels and to do the screenplay because he needed 4,000 pounds to retain his house (he got 8,000 for film rights and his work on the script).

But the great thing about this sadly aborted film—von Sternberg's ennobling prefix will not allow the plebian word "movie"—is the performance of Charles Laughton as Claudius. Once one has watched the ten or so minutes that the documentary shows of Laughton as Claudius, Derek Jacoby's performance in the same role comes to seem as if done by Stan Laurel. Although Laughton was pre-Method Actors Studio, he apparently made a great fuss about "getting into" his roles. Once you watch him play Claudius, though, you feel all the trouble he caused in delays, for von Sternberg and others on the set, would have been worth it. You are doubtless a much more sensitive judge of acting than I, who am not usually all that alive to acting to begin with, but Laughton doing Claudius really knocked off my socks (also shoes, shirt, and trousers). Balzac called "enchanted cigarettes" those books authors intended but never got round to writing. The great movies that never got made ought perhaps, in honor of the Jewish moguls who dominated Hollywood in the old days, to be called enchanted cigars. Von Sternberg's *I, Claudius* qualifies here as a Perfecto Supremo.

If I were editing a magazine or paper today, I would institute an end-of-the-year feature, contra the *TLS*, in which moderately distinguished writers were asked to list the books they hadn't read during the previous year and could promise not to read during the remainder of the millennium. Asked to contribute to such a feature, atop my list would be two volumes, totaling 1,844 pages, that constitute a new biography of Norman Mailer by a man named J. Michael Lennon and a collection of Mailer's letters edited by the same all-too-energetic fellow. When presented with some new *avant-garde* irrelevancy, as I mentioned earlier, Stravinsky used to ask (supply your own Russian accent here): "Who needs dis?" That's always a good question, but in the case of these two Mailer tomes it's almost a most pressing one.

Norman Mailer is by now surely, like the Sitwells and Ms. Sontag, part of the history not of literature but of publicity. He is to be read only by those interested in piecing together how the world went wacko in the late 1960s and '70s. During those years, able to garner vast amounts of attention for himself, he was what passed for the Great American Novelist. He thought himself a novelist of ideas. At one point he accused Saul Bellow of taking his ideas from books, while his were of his own making. No one ever disputed this; no one else, surely, could have, or would have wished to have, made them. One of his ideas was that modern architecture caused cancer. Another, set out in an essays called "The White Negro: Superficial Reflections on the Hipster," was that it made perfect sense, given the apocalyptic nature of contemporary life—fear of nuclear disaster and all that—to become a psychopath and murderer if only to exhibit one's existential authenticity. Mailer always pushed the pedal down hard on that word *existential*.

Foolish, stupid, close to criminal though his ideas were, Mailer was published in all the O.K. magazines. *Harper's*, then a so-called "hot book," gave up an entire issue to his *Armies of the Night*, an account of his joining the protesters against the Vietnam War on a march on the Pentagon. Along with a great novelist, Mailer fancied himself a sexual outlaw, always a mistake if one plans a long life, and he lived to eighty-four. I recall seeing him not long before his death on television, wearing hearing aids that clearly didn't do the job and walking on two iron canes, and wondering if he mightn't like to retract almost everything he wrote as a younger man.

If Evelyn Waugh were writing *A Handful of Dust* today, I would strenuously recommend that he change, and thereby much improve, the novel's ending, so that his sad protagonist, Tony Last, imprisoned by a madman in the fastness of the South American interior, be forced to read not Dickens but only Norman Mailer till the end of his days.

To the cliché 900-pound gorilla in the room, let us add that 900-odd-page biography and that 800-odd-page collection of letters on the same room's bookshelves. Ah, me, I just looked out my window and discovered it is yet another rainy day in the old Republic of Letters.

Best, Joe

LONDON S.W.7. 5RF. 6.1.2015.
Dear Joe,

I have no wish to preach to the unconverted but I have to say that what makes John Horne Burns' novel *The Gallery* so extraordinarily good, in my eyes, is that, although he was indeed a tortured homosexual, his novel is brilliant with observation, for instance of a long scene I have just read in which two U.S. army chaplains, one a Roman Catholic, the decorated Father Donovan, the other, Chaplain Bascom, a South Carolina Baptist, walk, talk and have a drink together (against Baptist principles, but what the heck) in war-torn 1944 Naples. The long scene ends rather melodramatically with their twin deaths, after they have run to try and save a Neapolitan waif from being crushed by an army truck, the only contrived note in a chapter of eighteen pages. It reminds me that Angus Wilson gave the manuscript, I think, of *Hemlock and After* to Evelyn Waugh, whose assessment of it was largely laudatory. He did, however, find the character of a village lady who lent out her rooms for amatory assignations to be an implausible misfit. "Hence," he said, *grosso modo,* "I presume she is drawn from life." And so she was.

Burns may well have seen such an accident in Naples, but it still don't seem *right,* perhaps because of the last sentences, from the point of view of the little girl, who has survived: "She put her gum into her mouth, Americani. For it wasn't the first time she'd seen the dead lying in the streets of Naples." I don't think that the dangling "Americani" reads well; and "For" at the beginning of the terminal sentence seems prissy, to a modern ear. Nevertheless, I defy any but a very good writer to make theological, never tendentious, banter read with unskippable vividness. Burns shows up Graham Greene's *Monsignor Quixote* for the dues-paying pamphlet it is. Greene's later work is, in general, perverted by what is supposed to validate it; fidelity serves to excuse false readings of the world, as it does with Sartre and other victims of ideology.

Infiltrating "real" events or personalities is prone to distort a fictional text and is rarely, even with Tolstoy, convincing. *The Fox In The Attic* by Richard (*High Wind in Jamaica*) Hughes began brilliantly with a dead man being brought in from, if I remember rightly from fifty years ago, a shoot on the marshes somewhere in England. I was all set to admire a *tour de force* when the next chapter introduced the real life character of Sir John Simon, the Home Secretary, at which point the tower lost its forcefulness. The only novelist I know who portrayed historical personages in such a way as to illuminate them, in a way no historian could manage, was Vassily Grossman in *Life and Fate.* The image of Adolf Hitler, having just heard of the catastrophe at Stalingrad, coming out of the Wolf's Lair in the gaunt forest of East Prussia and walking alone among the trees, knowing and at the same time denying that his great gamble was irretrievably lost, is one for the ages. Grossman can "see" the Fuhrer's lurching tread as he tries to keep his balance in the world that has overturned him. You mentioned how brilliant Charles Laughton was in the aborted movie version of *I, Claudius.* I recall Laughton saying in an interview that he could never inhabit a character until he had got his *walk* right. That's a true actor. Nuts to the sub-text and the psycho-truth: get the words and the walk right, and easy on the hand signals, and you impersonate the truth, with all its ambiguities intact.

Grossman is just as good, earlier in *Life and Fate,* when he depicts senior members of the Politburo going to tell Stalin in his *dacha* that Hitler has double-crossed him and invaded the U.S.S.R. Here Grossman catches the moment when, as Molotov and co. wake him, Stalin's eyes are full of fear: he assumes that they are there to kill him, as he had so many people whose "line" deviated from his own. Then Joseph Vissarionovich and his fellow felons realize that it is better that he be preserved, to take the flak if he couldn't get them out of the hole he has had them dig for the Russian people. Grossman's text was, of course, regarded as treasonous and survived in only one copy, I think, as did the poems of Catullus until the 13th century or so.

I have undertaken to do a book about the ancient world for the patrons of our last collection, Yale U.P. I have never been able to write a commissioned novel (it grew no bigger than its title, *The Electric Jew*), but no more have I felt the vocation to write non-fiction on spec. This little number has scarcely been subsidized by Maecenas, but being given time to take another look at the classical world has its lure. The original idea was that my book should add to a series on "Why X Matters," but that seemed likely, in the case of Antiquity, to give rise to a heap of what the Romans called "*crambe repetita*": cabbage served twice, of which I had no shortage at boarding school. So I have been permitted to vary the brief and write a number called *For Gold, For Praise, For Glory.* The swagger in the phrase is typical of its author, Sir Walter Ralegh, whose ambitions for all three led to his famous rise and fall. My theme is the competitive urge in Western civilization, beginning with Homer's Achilles and his rage to be the best.

The story, which Ralegh must have told himself, of his courtship (to put it nicely) of Elizabeth Throckmorton, is one of the most vivid, yet nicest, in the long story of what our friend Norman Mailer called, I seem to remember from my 1949 reading of *The Naked and the Dead,* "the old in-and-out" (I agree about Mailer's inflated self-regard, but *The Executioner's Song* is a masterpiece of American lower class life, isn't it?).

There are/can be, no absolute rules, but the licensing of the word "fuck" for almost all occasions has been an aesthetic catastrophe. It can be dated, with some accuracy, to the *Lady Chatterley* trial in 1960, as a result of which the book was deemed not to be obscene and all fucks broke loose, since when they have gone viral and then some. The trial's outcome depended largely on the "character witnesses," Morgan Forster and Richard Hoggart *en tête* (and didn't they preen themselves on their eminence?), though Lawrence's vindication, if that's what it was, owed something to the absurdity of the prosecuting counsel, Mervyn Griffiths-Jones, who asked the jury if *Lady C.* was the sort of book they would wish their servants to read.

Then modish Angus Wilson was one of the first to take advantage of the license granted to "fucking" by using it, in his 1961 novel, *The Old Men at the Zoo,* but only in the usual English way, not literally but to reinforce some fucking remark or other. I was bold enough to wonder, when reviewing the book, whether it was for this cant usage that D.H.L. had hung and suffered, so to say (his deification was part of the Leavisite gospel). Angus, who did many people good turns and on whom the literary world turned its back when, in old age, he fell suddenly from public favor, did not take offense at my snappy young review, nor was my point not without sharpness.

Lawrence hoped, we were promised, that the liberation of its vocabulary would give sex a new candid centrality in human life. The mixture of wishful fatuousness and social spite which animated *Lady Chatterley's Lover*, together with its literally flowery advertisements for Mary Janery, was soon exceeded in a slew of novels which confused obscenity with honesty and the collapse of art with the coming revolution that, with any luck, might turn the woeful, misery-ridden West into something much more like the blissful Soviet Union or Mao's floral China.

I still think that Lawrence's novels have some fine things in them, not least the scene (in *Women in Love,* is it?) where Gudrun throws stones at the image of the moon reflected on a nocturnal lake. (The scene may be in what the overquoted Martin Amis calls "*The Rainbore*"—a smartassery which earns no more than one ho in a possible ho-ho). The only long lesson I learned from D.H.L. was/is that there is nothing unmanly about helping with the washing up and other domestic banalities. As the Anglican hymn has it: "Who sweeps a room as for thy laws/Makes that and th'action fine."

It turns out, not very surprisingly, that Proust was as near absolutely right as makes no never mind in his argument with Gide over whether or not he should "come out" as a homosexual. Gide wanted fiction to be agit-prop, of whatever lofty order, and to have it proclaim, as he did, again *und* again, that there was nothing to be ashamed of, and much to enjoy, in pederasty. The indictment is properly leveled in André's case since, in *The Immoralist* for flagrant instance, his version of Tracy Tupman goes to what was then French North Africa in order to indulge his appetite for Arab boys who, there is small doubt, needed the money more than they craved penetration. The benefits, in aesthetic terms, of this particular candor are not obvious. Does anyone now read Gide, as we do Proust, to recapture the flavors, beauties and scandals of the past? I have enjoyed Gide's journals more than his fiction, but I'm not likely to revisit them. As for the novels, *au pannier!* But then again, what books of any kind is either of us—in the time left— likely to re-read?

The age of the canon has, no doubt, gone forever. I remember being surprised when, two or three decades ago, your old friend Hugh Lloyd-Jones became quite testy (no, *that* didn't surprise me) at the accusation that Classicists spent all their time rehearsing the same old texts and blowing off the same old dust. L.-J. claimed that, in fact, the library of the ancient world was constantly expanding, not least as a result of manuscripts discovered, like the Dead Sea Scrolls, in desert places where neither moth nor rust corrupted. Trying to refresh my thoughts about antiquity has led me, very late in my day, to rummage in other than the usual boxes. The old "imperialist" classicists had no time for anything but the Golden Ages of Greece and Rome, which coincided pretty well with the pursuit of Sir Walter's trio. The tenured professoriate viewed almost all post-fourth century Greek writers with the same suspicion that Romans of the same period did: "too clever by half" was the condemnatory rubric that branded them all. During my decade-plus of being some kind of a classicist, no one ever mentioned the name of Lucian, a Syrian of the second-century post J.C., who had the *cacoethes scribendi* which makes him the prototype of the working hack.

A free-lance journalist *avant la lettre,* living on his wits and his wit, he wrote in a rescripted version of Attic Greek, of the kind written half a millennium earlier, but did so in a way that was both amusing, since antiquarian, and also supremely, derisively lucid. Bernard Levin and Ambrose Bierce and H. L. Mencken played a similar game. The self-conscious resuscitation of lost elegance implied disdain for modern platitudinarians. (The ex-Romanian fascist E. M. Cioran aped eighteenth-century French epigrammatists, such as my Perigordine *chouchou* Joseph Joubert). In Cambridge recently, I found a nice *en regard* paperback of Lucian. His essay on Historians is a proleptic master-stroke: he might be talking about the whole gamut of modern historians who decorate their worn subjects with false vividness and trendy, distortionate locutions (Tom Holland's *Herodotus* is so heavy that Dorothy Parker would have difficulty in hurling it with the required force).

Lucian's smart scorn could be applied, with small cosmetic attention, to the whole panoply of overwriters, unduly insightful analysts and opportunist re-hashers who allow the *N.Y.R.B.* crowd to heap their Ossa on Pelion by glossing the glossy and tending the tendentious. Lucian is what Isaiah Berlin accused George Steiner of being, "a genuine phony." The long tradition of marginal men, Greeks and Semites, runs alongside Western culture, a kind of piquant parasitism which undermines and celebrates at the same time. To a great, often unacknowledged degree, such men depend on the good offices of the societies they anatomize (where would Karl Marx have been without the facilities of the British Museum reading room or Lenin without his asylum in Switzerland?). Bitch, bitch, bitch as we may, how lucky we are to live where we do, when we do, as we do! I take the opportunity to wish you, as Lucian might, *chronia polla,* many more years to celebrate on January 9.

Tout à toi, Freddie.

January 11, 2015
Dear Freddie,

I came across an interesting sentence in the *Notebooks of Michael Oakeshott*, a sentence that runs: "But culture is to know that there is much that one does not want to know." Long before I read this I had heard that, after a lecture in London, someone in the audience asked Oakeshott what his view was of the European Union, to which he answered (I don't have wording exactly) something like, "I don't see why I am required to have an opinion about that." I much like the sentiment behind both remarks. They are, implicitly, attacks on the aspiration toward omniscience on the part of contemporary intellectuals. What a relief it is not to know everything or feel obligated to have an opinion about things that are stirring up the rest of the world. In the United States just now the movie *Selma*, about Martin Luther King, Jr., is causing a great stir. How pleasing neither to see it nor have an opinion about it!

What a lengthy list mine would be of those things that I do not want to know! Near the top would the intricacies of contemporary politics and finance. (Oakeshott also writes: "A general interest & preoccupation with politics is the surest sign of a general decay in society," and "Politics are an inferior form of human activity.") I find I read less and less political news of a detailed kind, and am perfectly content to leave off my knowledge of this subject at the headline or television news level. No one, not even the experts, seems to know the intricacies of the American health-care system or is able properly to construe the statistics of unemployment. So why should I waste my time attempting to acquire what at best would be a distantly dilettantish knowledge of such things, especially when I can spend the same time reading, in Gibbon, that "Julian was convinced that he had seen the menacing countenance of the god of war; the council which he summoned of Tuscan Haruspices, unanimously pronounced that he should abstain from action; but on this occasion, necessity and reason were more prevalent than superstition; and the trumpets sounded at the break of day."

I'm reading Gibbon in the morning, in which Julian continues his attack on Sapor the Great King of Persia. In my bedside book just now, Peter Green's *Alexander of Macedon*, Alexander, some six hundred years earlier, is still in pursuit of Darius. Julian dies at thirty-two, Alexander at thirty-three, which suggests that the life of action, and no one saw more action than these two boyos, doesn't always pay off, except in the coin of fame. I'm more pleased to be in possession of what facts I know about the lives of Alexander and Julian than I would be to know the full details of Obamacare or the constitution of NATO. I haven't the least desire to be what is currently—and mistakenly—called a public intellectual. I am quite satisfied with being a private intellectual.

Returning to Oakeshott's *mot* about culture being able to discern what one doesn't need to know, a trickier matter is what does one need to know to consider oneself cultured. A lot less now that a century ago, I suspect, when the knowledge of several foreign languages was part of the admittance fee. Of course the knowledge of foreign languages alone is not enough to qualify one as cultured. Wide reading would be included, but how wide, exactly? Need Chinese and Indian literatures be included? Having thoughtfully listened to much music would be part of being cultured, and, I suppose, lots of opera (I drop out here). Experience of visual art, including film, would be another item on the checklist, yet the visual art of how many different cultures? How many historical narratives must the cultured person have mastered? Set out quantitatively like this, the culture game, I fear, looks distinctly like a mug's game. Scarcely anyone qualifies; nobody wins.

One cannot begin to consider oneself cultured without having imbibed a fair amount of what the world has decided to call cap-C culture, which may come down to Matthew Arnold's the best that has been thought and written, also painted, sculpted, composed, played, filmed, and staged. One of the nice things about cap-C culture is that one is forever filling in gaps in one's own (pretensions to) culture. Only this past week, for example, did I see for the first time Charlie Chaplin's *The Great Dictator*, which is culture without pain. I shouldn't mind replaying every morning Chaplin's *führer* Hynkel doing his dance with the balloon representing the globe of the world, a world soon, presumably, to be his. There must be seventy or eighty such cultural monuments, if not more, that I have missed out on, and, the clock running rather fast these days, shall never get round to possessing.

Then there is the question of all of putative culture that one has ingested yet forgotten. A personal case in point here is Dostoyevsky's *The Idiot*, which I've read twice and whose plot I have now twice forgot. All I can remember is the book's main character, Prince Myshkin, an epileptic (like Fyodor Mikhailovich, his creator) who was idiotic only in the way of naif moral geniuses. I have known a few people, all of them serious scholars who forgot nothing they ever read; maybe the difference between great scholars and the rest of us is that they have superior mental filing systems. But one of the fascinations of culture is that one doesn't have to remember great books, plays, music, and the rest to have it nonetheless leave a significant residue.

One can recognize a cultured person when one sees him. He is, or ought to be, a person with a point of view informed by knowledge, however glancing, of the travails and glories of past cultures. This gives him a feeling of his own towering insignificance and the confident sense that he is here on earth on a visitor's permit, revocable at any moment and never renewable. These two facts alone ought to confer upon him not depression but an abiding sense of humor. For surely one of the main lessons of culture is that, apart from an occasional flare-up of greatness and grandeur, human beings are essentially comic characters. Lots of people in possession of wide culture, in the quantifiable sense, do not, on these grounds, qualify as in the least cultured. Culture is also a matter of temperament and of spirit. Culture is, then, not what one knows, or even what one has known, but, like style, a way of looking at the world. End of lecture on the possession of culture. Tomorrow, class, we'll take up the jollier subject of the Happy Barbarian.

I regret to report my agreement with your point about fact often intruding upon and spoiling fiction. I say "regret" because I am just now undergoing difficulty in attempting to compose a story whose principal character is probably too firmly based on an actual person. I mentioned this fellow to you in *Distant Intimacy*: a man named William Lichtman, a World War Two veteran who claimed also to have flown in the Israeli War of Independence. He was a strong though, in E. M. Forster's term, a flat character. He may have been too strong and too flat to be believable in fiction. I need in my story to round him out in a way that he wasn't in reality in the least rounded—that is, capable of behavior that surprises—in life.

I met Bill Lichtman in the middle 1970s through Saul Bellow who sent him to me for help with a novel that he, Lichtman, was writing. In those days, ever in need of money, I did bits of free-lance editing when the fee was decent. The manuscript he sent to me was in such a shabby state that it didn't even qualify as a mess. I met him not long after to return his ragtag manuscript to him and he told me that the week before his wife had killed herself by overdosing on pills of various sorts. This wife, it turns out, was much younger than he, and he knew about her drug problem when he married her, only a few years before her death. In his apartment one day, I noted a photograph of her. She was in every wise much more attractive than he. When there is too great a physical discrepancy between a husband and a wife, I always assume there is something other than a conventional love story behind the marriage. Without the problem, my guess is, she may never have married him.

I never edited Bill Lichtman's novel, which as far as I know was not published, either through a commercial publisher or a vanity press. He would from time to time call to invite me to meet him for lunch or coffee. I sometimes went because he seemed to me so a lonely man. He was small and bald and walked with a limp. He was aggressive and obsessive in his view that the world was out to get the Jews. (Not an entirely foolish notion, I need scarcely add.) He had an impressive absence of liberal sentiment. He had been a cop, and spoke as if violence were something he had lived with on easy terms. If he had a motto, it would have been: "I take no shit from anyone."

I haven't heard from Bill Lichtman in more than fifteen years. If he is still alive, he would be ninety-six, and doubtless by now nicely pickled in dementia. I inserted a character resembling him in a cameo role in a story of mine called "Freddy Duchamp in Action." I hope I have limned in enough details for you to grasp why he seems so tempting to write about in fiction. But he may well be, as you suggest, too real to me to make him a convincing character in fiction. My problem at the moment is that I can't seem to find a plot in which to insert him. By a plot I mean a conflict, for conflict, I feel, remains at the center of good story telling, even though in our day epiphany, the quiet sly ending of a story on a minor insight, has moved in to occupy the center from its old and proper place out on the periphery. Epiphany, periphery, oedipus, schmoedipus, the main thing, I continue to believe, is a writer should have a story just as a boy should love his mother.

Today's *New York Times* carries an obituary of an American writer named Robert Stone, who was my exact contemporary. As a novelist he was a coming man who, as Maurice Bowra said of Cyril Connolly, never arrived. One of his early novels (he wrote eight) won a National Book Award, and this in the day when the National Book Award carried the *réclame* of the Booker Prize today. The same novel—called *Dog Soldiers*—was made into a movie called *Who'll Stop the Rain* with Nick Nolte. Other prizes, fellowships, grants followed. Stone was talented. He did action well, and is the only writer I've ever read who could convincingly describe characters viewing the world while high on drugs. He was also an old-fashioned novelist in the sense of writing about subjects that entailed first-hand knowledge of the exotic places in which he set his novels; in his case these places included Vietnam, Central America, New Orleans, and others. He hung out with Ken Kesey and his merry dopers. He was, he led one to believe, a fairly heavy doper himself.

Robert Stone's problem was politics. His theme, carried over from novel to novel—or at least over the first four of his novels that I read before I deserted him—was the crushing effects upon the world of American innocence. This quickly turned into standard left-wing anti-Americanism, which, mixed not very gently with an apocalyptic mysticism, did not make for an enticing literary cocktail. In later years Stone, whom one once thought admirable in his independence, joined the gang of *bien pensants*. He was a pal of Salmagundi (as Philip Larkin called him) Rushdie. Such following as he had as a novelist fell away; at least his name was no longer much bruited about in all the presumably right places. In his later years, he sported a white beard, a comb-over, and a Tolstoyan potato nose. Poor guy, he seems to have lived F. Scott Fitzgerald's apothegm holding that "there are no second acts in American lives." He died of emphysema, not the pleasantest of exits.

I wish before closing to award another highly uncoveted Racso. The envelope, please . . . and the winner is: *California Suite* (1978), directed by Herbert Ross, produced by Ray Stark, starring just about everyone you can think of, and ill-written by Neil Simon. This is a movie converted from a stage play and meant to float on its dazzling dialogue. This dialogue, relentlessly but not truly clever, is what sinks the movie. The movie is meant to demonstrate Neil Simon's easy brilliance, but it isn't easy (on its viewers) and not in the least brilliant.

In his day, Neil Simon must have been the most cashable writer going. Like your man Willie Maugham, he sometimes had two or three plays on Broadway and several more in production touring on the road. Near as I can tell, he had one entertaining idea in his long and successful career: that for *The Odd Couple*. He must have written *California Suite* in the blinding light of overconfidence, for nothing in any one of its four different separate-stories (none worthy of summarizing) works; much is plain stupid. The movie gives repartee a bad name; it also makes one feel foolish for having spent time watching it. I hope Neil Simon has room for this Racso on his mantel alongside all his other awards. I hope, too, he had an uproarious laugh all the way to the bank.

Best, Joe

LONDON S.W.7. 5RF. 19.1.2015.
Dear Joe,

Soon after the events of last week, in which the cartoonists and journalists of *Charlie Hebdo* were shot at their desks and then—in another part of Paris—four Jews were murdered in a Kosher supermarket, I had a letter from my Cleveland-based friend Neal Sokol. Crediting me with more knowledge of "things French" than I should be wise to claim, he asked for any views he and his Rabbi wife could share with the readers of the "upcoming Jewish Federation bulletin." Oh God, must I? Sokol, a very generous person, recently sent me a refurbished copy of Michelangelo Antonioni's *L'Avventura*, for which my admiration remains undimmed, despite having learnt of the fortuitous reasons for its jagged, seemingly innovative form. Courtesy demanded some kind of an answer. What could I say, with any honesty, about the two French-born brothers, their savage double act and about the killings in a kosher supermarket that redoubled it?

Quite a few things which are unlikely to be acceptable by editors. For prime instance, that more such incidents are likely, just as a second, third and fourth volley often follows any TV series that gains wide attention. The cross-fertilization of media and terrorism leads them to feed off each other. It remains doubtful whether French society is in imminent danger from some Islamic avalanche or that some kind of race war (against Muslims) will take place; but more ugly things almost certainly will, because they have, in the Middle East and Nigeria, and because what happened in Paris was, in more than one sense, a "hit." Whatever works ratings-wise will have a sequel.

There is an old story about Hitler, in hiding in South America, telling someone that "next time," he will finish off the Jews and also two ballet-dancers. "Why two ballet-dancers?" says the other man. "There you are," says Adolf, "no one cares what happens to Jews." A grand op-ed article by historian Robert Tombs (Fellow of my old college) in the *Sunday Times* of January 25th never mentions the killing of four Jews in a kosher supermarket. The omission implies, intentionally or not—the latter alternative both more innocent and more sinister—that the *Charlie Hebdo* murders were significant, while those of the Jews were a mere *fait divers*. Professor Tombs gives the impression that killing cartoonists is an outrage, but killing Jews of small importance. This is in line with the views of the U.K. academics who congratulate themselves on placing an embargo on Israeli scholars. Time was that French left-wing *intellos* marched under the banner "*Nous sommes tous des Juifs allemands.*" That parade primed Alain Finkielkraut's secession from *soixante-huitard* altogether-boyishness: the marchers were not German Jews and they were just showing off. Today's students are disposed to say "*Nous sommes tous des Palestiniens*"; and think that that licenses them to intimidate Jews and abuse Israel for defending its citizens. How many left-wingers make any noise about the thousands of Palestinians murdered by their "brothers" in Syria and elsewhere?

Tombs writes:

> "To identify with Charlie Hebdo as the torchbearer of freedom is . . . to identify with this republican vision [of 'republican values' mentioned earlier]. The murder of the cartoonists has been alarmingly successful in terms of the terrorists' presumed aims of deepening and dramatizing existing divisions. Charlie Hebdo's secularism, extraordinarily brave in the light of threats of arson and murder, nevertheless seems part of France's problem rather than its solution. Rather than forcing fundamentalists to be free, it has furnished them with further grievances."

This ignores the killers' loudly announced reason for the outrage: to "avenge the prophet." Tombs makes it seem that *Charlie Hebdo's* outrageousness—its *raison d'être*—provoked the murder of its staff and was, for that reason, somewhat deplorable, since it added to France's "problem." Secularism (here attached to *Charlie Hebdo* but, I suppose, meant as a general idea) is first accused of coercion and then declared to be the generator of grievances. Is there any evidence that terrorism would not exist if believers in an Open Society, but not necessarily enemies of God or religion, were to abate their unwise enthusiasm for freedom?

Tombs's failure even to mention the killing of the Jews is not, as old-style Marxists used to say, an accident. Any allusion to that minor incident would require a different "logic" of explanation, though we need not doubt that, in the same generous spirit, Tombs would have it that the victims were somehow responsible for their own murder, since the existence of Jews is itself upsetting to Muslims of a certain quite wide stripe. Tombs seems to be arguing that liberal culture, which allows religious views but seeks, or sought, to propagate "humane values," is an affront to bigots and should abate its fervor. The disaster of the spread and subsidy of "faith schools," under Tony Blair's aegis, is turned into an example of good old British shrewdness in averting wrath.

The condition of the French republic is unhappy for a slew of reasons. The post-*Charlie* presidential performance of François Hollande, while being as close as possible to what is required of him, has been more useful to him, since he is very unpopular, than it is evidence of a sudden new crisis. Hollande may well become the beneficiary of what he deplores. "Socialism," which has fostered his political ascent (as the Church might have three or four centuries ago), is now a career, not a creed. Hollande has the lineaments of Stendhal's signature opportunist Julien Sorel, seducer *de tout bord*. As for the socialism he affects to stand for, it is now less a blueprint than a brand of bottled snake-oil, profitably hustled only by those who live above the talking shop that the *bon* François managed for some years.

What really, really matters to the French, as to all democratic citizens, is that the economy should prosper; and it doesn't. As prosperity recedes, the rocks of division come up and gash the solidarity on which the *citoyens* like to pride themselves, not least because they dread its fragility. Both on the street and in the Chamber of Deputies, the singing of the Marseillaise (great number!) brought tears to the eyes. Who cares to notice that the words of the Marseillaise are belligerent and bloodthirsty almost to the same degree as the *Horst Wessel Lied*, which also had a tune to march to? Whisper it quietly: the blood that the citizens of vintage 1789 were tramping out tunefully to spill was that of other French people, the reactionary Baddies. Did resentment at the destruction of Provençal culture help to sharpen the southerners' scythes? Revolutionary enthusiasm thrives on the fantasy of a happy future and also, very often, accelerates on adrenalin supplied by the "return of the repressed." Brave new causes often have antique roots.

Obama's unpopularity, however great it is, may be due to his manifest want of diplomatic finesse, but has at least a little something to do with— to put it carefully—some electors' regret at what they were obliged to applaud, their own applause not least, at the election of a somewhat black man as President. Obama may or may not have "failed"; but it would suit a certain contingent to have their original misgivings confirmed, although they must never say so. This double-bind (in various period styles and forms) keeps the world together, and divided. Ashamed of losing their empire, the French did not welcome the advent, after 1962, of hundreds of thousands, now descended into millions, of North African Muslims who fled from their native land.

The first wave consisted largely of "Harkis" who had served in the French army and feared the revenge of their "brothers" (those who stayed behind were, it is said, made literally to swallow the medals which the French had awarded them). Substantial numbers of immigrants settled in virtual "camps" in the South and in ghetto districts around Paris. Since their presence was a reminder of the national humiliation of a lost empire, most of the "Arabs" remained unassimilated. They now constitute the French "Palestinians," *mais il faut pas le dire.* Their religion both bonds and brands them; but they are, in the imperial tradition, French citizens and they and their progeny have the vote. Now about ten percent of the population, they could be determinant in a future election.

That, rather than fear of "outrages," is what keeps Frenchmen awake at night. It is at least slightly relevant to note that not a few of those on the Left in pre-1914 France were opposed to the enfranchisement of women because, not without reason, they feared that French females would be manipulated by the clergy into voting for reactionary politicians. Who can be confident that, when Muslims amount to a determinant electoral force, they will not ally themselves with the extreme Right and put into operation the latent (?) anti-Semitism of a wide *tranche* of the electorate? Nostalgia for Pétain supplies compost for the Right just as righteous denunciation of Israel is almost all that is left of the "anti-colonialism" of the Left. There is a very old, recurrently effective way of reconciling a society by implicating all its members in common acts of ritual/ murderous violence. *Kristallnacht* is an obvious instance, but the left-wing guru Michel Foucault's prompt applause, in 1979, for the "people's justice" of the Ayatollahs in Iran indicates the abiding charm of the scapegoat mechanism. Indifference to the murders in the kosher supermarket is a straw in a nasty breeze.

Many French Muslims have a grudge, in whatever practical or nostalgic form, against France: hence, *grosso modo,* the charm of fundamentalism. It speaks for the folly of the Harkis' fathers and grandfathers in trusting the French to take care of them; it throws back the grant of citizenship and its small rewards; it supplies a new, pure, ungrateful identity. Outcasts, even those who were never entirely out, enjoy dramatic, action-man casting. Being ruthless becomes a pious duty. The fact that the two gunmen who killed the *Charlie Hebdo* cartoonists were French-born is a very small paradox. It is no wild speculation to guess that the notion that they should be grateful struck them as a kind of Uncle Tommery. Poison is a common home-grown crop. Jean-Paul Sartre's notion, expressed in his introduction to Franz Fanon's *Les Damnés de la Terre*, that a man liberates himself into true manhood by killing a (colonialist) oppressor, has come home to roost.

If the majority of Muslim immigrants failed to prosper, they have certainly proliferated: the under-class—which Karl Marx regarded with such anxious ambivalence, hence his wish to lead it—threatens to swamp the ballot-boxes of, say, 2022. Michel Houellebecq's new dystopic novel, *Soumission* (which *Charlie Hebdo* was about to fanfare) is set in that year. It posits a nice Muslim, brought to presidential power with the helpless help of the Left, what's left of it. The realization of Houellebecq's accurate exaggerations (he foresaw gunshots in Paris) makes it more likely that Marine Le Pen, the all too plausible and articulate leaderene of the quasi-fascist Front National, will have a good chance of being a finalist in 2017.

President Hollande has said that he will not stand unless unemployment recedes. If he limps away, *la* Le Pen may be the only nationally known face in the ballot. If not, what chance will there be of the re-election of Mr. Wobbly (as the *citoyens* depict him)? In today's circumstances, the French look around, as they often do, for a Strong Man. The trouble is, there is no de Gaulle, nor even a Mitterrand, in sight. Nicholas Sarkozy is girding his loins, but they are, it may be, too well known to the French electorate to carry him to victory. The New (tottering) Europe distrusts Great Men. Comes the hour, comes the woman, *hélas*!

Whatever the dread of the West with regard to Islam, it is shadowed by something one could typify, nicely, as resentment of "the Jews." They have persisted despite the "truth" of Christianity and, in the present state of that faith, can be said perhaps to have been right (a Nazi Jesuit feared as much towards the end of WW 2): what if there is no salvation and the notion of love superseding the law always was a piety too far? Man cannot function by emotions and fine feelings; the state of law must come first; but impatient, self-confident young men rarely think so. Shame about the Holocaust is very nice; not so nice is the repressed wish that the extermination of the Jews had been *justified,* in which case no one would have had to feel guilty. The conduct of the state of Israel has been welcomed, and its "racism" exaggerated, because it furnishes a retroactive sentiment that "we" (Europeans) need not feel bad about Auschwitz. The award-winning playwright Caryl Churchill made out in one of her tractarian plays that Jews/Israelis are taught to hate Arabs, quite as if the reverse were not the truth.

This echoes a long strand in Christian theology which would have it that the conversion of the Jews is the one impediment to salvation and, in some people's opinions, to the return of the Messiah. For such people, the obstinate persistence of "the Jews" is a multi-purpose threat to peace on earth. In a time of manifold uncertainty, in which most Europeans not only do not know what is wanted of them but also wonder what they should want for themselves, idealists (Greens, anti-capitalists and the rest) and fanatics converge, somewhat, on One Solutionism of the kind which wants the dispossession of "the Jews" to be the answer to all the world's ills.

The European Union has reduced mankind to *homo economicus* in all practical accountability. Values have yielded to prices. Statistics are the sole reliable, public measure of well-being. If the sums start not to add up and the financial contracts snap (with the collapse of the Euro), there is likely to be reversion to strident nationalism and to anti-Semitism, the universal *sauce piquante*, beloved left and right and not unpalatable to the soggy center as represented in England by the United (not to say "untied") Kingdom Independence Party. A broad band of Islamic doctrine teaches that it is right to kill Jews and, thanks to Tony Blair, preachers of that opinion are paid by the British taxpayer, in "Faith Schools," to deliver murderous sermons as a curricular habit. Am I sure? No. Will I bet? Yes. Will I find many takers?

There is, in Muslim and "Christian" thinking, and practice, a long habit of finding nothing wrong in slaughtering Jews: for example, some six thousand or so were massacred by Muslims in the Kingdom of Granada in 1066. Why else than under Muslim "license" does "Kill Jews" get written on bus stops in northern England? It's also fun to do, but then so was the righteous theft of whatever belonged to Europe's Jews and, in many cases, never returned to them. More, much more, can be said about what Marine Le Pen's father called a "*point de détail*": the Holocaust and its irksome shadow.

Robert Tombs's fanciful notion that *Liberté* should be abandoned but that it can be survived by *Egalité* (an economic and social impossibility) is an advertisement for demo-fascism, all the more enticing for its anodyne formulation. Some crackpot will soon be arguing that the existence of kosher supermarkets is also a "provocation"; Jews would be well-advised to keep their heads down, a convenient posture in which, eventually, to cut them off, in the interests, no doubt, of *égalité*. The omission from Tombs's article of the murders in the unfashionable *rue quoique ce soit* is indeed significant, precisely because we are led to think that they are of no importance.

Not many laughs here. That is the doleful measure of How We Live Now. What else can I tell you? This morning Beetle and I received a letter from Queen Elizabeth II, congratulating us on our Diamond Wedding Anniversary, which took place two days ago. How lucky we have been; *I* have been!

Tout à toi, Freddie.

January 24, 2015
Dear Freddie,

We have been at our second go at e-mail correspondence for a bit more than a year now, and I hear the friendly pub-keeper call out, "Time, gentlemen, time." If he were a movie director he would of course instead say, "That's a wrap," which, for this book, it now nearly is.

The past year was no *annus mirabilis*, not for politics, literature, the movies, athletics, or, best as I can make out, much of anything else. I've been reading a biography of the now nearly forgotten George Meredith, who published *The Ordeal of Richard Feverel* in 1859. That same year, Lionel Stevenson, Meredith's biographer, points out, Carlyle finished the first volume of his *Frederick the Great*, J. S. Mill published *On Liberty*, Dickens A *Tale of Two Cities*, and Thackeray *The Virginian*. Tennyson brought out the major part of *Idylls of the King* and Edward Fitzgerald his translation of Omar Khayyam and Ruskin the final volumes of his *Modern Painters*. George Eliot gave up reviewing books on philosophy and turned out *Adam*

Bede, her first novel. Charles Darwin, to round off the extraordinary year nicely, contributed a little item called *Origin of the Species*.

Most unlikely that a hundred or so years from now a similar list of achievement will be up for mention for the year 2014. Instead historians will note that the Islamo-thugs got underway in earnest, adding beheadings and burnings of the innocent to their repertoire of barbarisms. Print culture took several punches in the bread basket from that fast and slippery welterweight called the Internet. Politics was business as usual, empty suits emitting empty utterances. Few memorable novels, movies, or other new works of art were brought out. 2014—the year, let us call it, of the Smart Phone.

Yet, by me, as the old Jews used to say, and as an old Jew I am now myself entitled to say, things could have been worse. Every year on my birthday I used to ask to get a little smarter in the year ahead; since turning seventy, I ask not to get much dumber. I like to believe I haven't, at least not precipitously, at least not yet, got too much dumber. Although it is perhaps not for me to say, I don't sense my small talent has diminished. (I invoke the Knock-Wood Insurance Company here.) Four or five magazine editors continue to ask me to do my little prose dances. This past year I have published a book of essays to for the most part respectful reviews. Ideas for stories still come to me. I continue to receive a slow but steady flow of appreciative letters and e-mails from readers. I hope this next year to publish a book of short stories. My health seems to be holding up. (Knocking wood again here, disregarding entirely the possibility of cancer of the knuckles.) I am quite as far from complaint as a man with a naturally complaining nature can be. I have, in short, lots of reasons to let all my thinks, as Auden says in one of his poems, be thanks.

One of the things I am thankful for is your continuing friendship. Not only am I able to speak (through writing) to you with an easy candor, but I am able to do so with a happy confidence that you always take my meanings, get my jokes, pick up my little tricks (or are they tics?) of style. We share a strong, some might say overpowering, sense of whimsy about the world and the low and goofy motives floating about in it. This has been no small comfort. I have in the past written for myself, and anyone who cared to eavesdrop, but you, though I realize you didn't sign up for the job, turn out to be my ideal reader. We have a strong sense of rapport, or rappaport, as I prefer to think of it. So I have long felt; so I continue to feel.

What others who have read the now more than 300,000 combined words that comprise our two volumes of e-mail correspondence will make of these words I cannot easily imagine. What I hope is that a few among them will be able to grasp how much fun it has been to rally back and forth our views, opinions, observations, and insights. Never once did I look upon responding to your missives as burdensome. Nor did I ever feel in the least pressed to arrive at the two thousand or so words of my end of each of our exchanges. I felt as if I could ramble on for another thousand or so words without, unlike the tennis players of the current era, having to towel off.

In the mode of Max Beerbohm's Enoch Soames, I wonder, fifty or sixty years from now, if there remains a library housing not just screens but books, or a last used-bookstore in a low-rent district of London or New York, where one or the other or both of our two volumes finds a home, what will that oddly curious person who picks them up make of our correspondence? Will he learn something about the literary life in the early decades of the twenty-first century? Will he find us trustworthy cicerones to the culture of our time? I would settle for his thinking that we were two mildly amusing fellows who seemed to be enjoying themselves in each other's company.

Assuming we are both still in the game, I propose we look both ways when crossing the road, not take up sky diving, or choose to undergo transgender surgery, and two or three years from now turn out yet another of these books of our correspondence. It's been a kick, Freddie, a very great kick, and I shall always be grateful to you for proposing this collaboration in the first place.

Affectionately, Joe

London S.W.7. 5RF. 29.1.15.
Dear Joe,

My old friend John Patrick Sullivan used rather frequently to observe, in an exaggerated version of his native Liverpudlian accent, "Parting is such sweet sorrow." He did quite a bit of it, with wives and places of employment, as he proceeded from the Liverpool docker's back-to-back place of his birth to Santa Barbara, California, where he died, twenty years ago, as a "professor seven" *(le top du top*, as the frogs say). The other day, I had an e-mail from his brother Denis, who says that I and the Latinist Anthony Boyle, of U.S.C., are his only "living links" with John. He refers to Sullivan's thesis on A. E. Housman, which I knew nothing about. In truth, I seem to have known very little about J.P.S.'s later life (after Cambridge). Denis, whom I met a couple of times at Cambridge, has clearly been somewhat under his older brother's shadow, but seems to have quite a sunny temper for all that. John's sex life appears to have swung in various directions, giving a salty meaning to the phrase "state of affairs" and—if you like—"comings and goings."

I have written a good deal about John in my mostly-Cambridge autobiography *Going Up*, due in June. Its publisher trades under the aegis of an outfit called Backbite and I shall, I suppose, be accused of a measure of that typically authorial activity of dumping on other people, not a few of them dead. I hope that Denis Sullivan will not think that I have soiled his brother's memory. I recall John with more affection that my cool prose declares. All the same, it would be nice to think that I have rendered John some service by commemorating his youthful enthusiasms, scholarship among them, as I have. Somewhat like my daughter Sarah, who saw even those she loved with steady acumen, I paint people as I see them in the mind's partial, but unblinking, eye. We must take our chances with each other, must we not?

In truth, we do indeed all go into the dark and once the witnesses are silenced, what is left? I have said all kinds of things, not all of them kind, about all sorts of people, in our correspondence not least. I should like to think that, if I have been *parti pris*, I have not told deliberate lies. The Kubrick family, for instance, has been sedulous in seeking to efface any contribution I made to *Eyes Wide Shut* (never a "credit" that I should wish to parade at the last judgment) and they even managed to have it put in my Wikipedia entry that my little book about Maestro Stan had been "discredited." The discreditors were not only the Harlans (aka S.K.'s widow and brother), but also Michael Herr, who was getting his own back for a review of his crappy "novel" about Walter Winchell. In fact, apart from cosmetic generosities, *Eyes Wide Open* was nothing if not truthful. Beetle thought I portrayed myself with undue modesty. Now, I see (not that I look in that mirror a lot), that the discreditation has been removed, by whose hand I shall never know. I allude to this petty matter only because it reminds me of how tenuously our reputations dangle, if they do, on the "written evidence" that hangs on history's dirty-washing line.

People may not like what is written about them or their attachments but it is almost always better than nothing. What do we know of Agag other than that he walked "delicately," a superb choice of adverb by one of King James's biblical team? I saw the same adverb applied to King Ahab's pedestrianism the other day, a typical I-think-I'm-right piece of internet journalism. How many brave acts have passed unhymned since Leonidas and his

Spartans held the pass at Thermopylae? Does it matter that the Three Hundred, who are now assumed to have been the king's full force, were supplemented, during the days when they did indeed stall the Persian advance, by several thousand allied troops, of whatever second-rank quality, and who were allowed to drift away when it was clear that Ephialtes had led the Persians round the mountain to outflank the Greeks? A recent *coupure* tells me that Thermopylae was the "victory" that led to us having Socrates and allied tradesmen as our intellectual ancestors.

Film now furnishes any number of false histories which are assumed into "evidence" for what happened in the irretrievable past. I am promised, and believe, that the hit-movie *Selma* has effaced the part played, in the actual march from Montgomery, by Rabbi Abraham Heschel, presumably (make that "undoubtedly") because the black sales department felt that its audience would feel demeaned, to put it nicely, by being told that Heschel walked arm-in-arm with the sanitized Martin Luther King played, very well indeed, by an English actor, David Oyelowo. In Heschel's place, the producers have promoted a Greek Orthodox priest who, sources close to the truth tell me, played a negligible part, if any at all, in the actual proceedings. There is a very, very brief glimpse of a head wearing a *yarmulke,* but that's all you get, folks. We live in an age of glorified cant and there ain't a thing to do about it except shine a nervous light, with style, if possible.

Beetle has been right through my contributions to our tango to the music of time and fears that I too often indulged my habit of running myself down. Why do that when there are so many people who can do it for fun or, perhaps, for a living? Taking oneself seriously is, of course, a necessary preliminary to have other people do the same; but Montaigne was right, however grand our perch, we can sit on it only on that one pair of buttocks. Willie Maugham, who especially detested his brother, Frederick, a successful barrister and, at his peak, the Lord Chancellor of Great Britain, suggested that judges, however wigged and gowned to garnish their impersonation of Justice, should have a toilet roll on the desk in front of them, as if to remind them of Micheau's *nihil humanum* slogan. Did it occur to Willie that the number two judge in England carries the official title of "Lord of the Rolls"? If so, he resisted the temptation which this Frederic would not, has not.

I am, you may guess, putting off the moment when my ship, frail barque as it may be, detaches itself from the quay and begins to slip away. I can remember how, in 1938, my parents waved and waved from the Cabin Class deck of the M.V. *Britannic* to their New York friends on the dock as—in a flurry of flung colored tapes—we were towed out of Dock 14 (in truth, I am not sure of the number) and left the U.S., as it turned out, forever. I watched and did not weep, as Irene may have, and Cedric would make sure he did not, and—perhaps creeps in—it was then that I became more an observer of the outside world and its inhabitants than an integral part of it. Beetle thinks that my new volume of autobio also gives the impression that I did not much like anybody that I knew in the years it covers. She is too modest to say, out loud, that she is the great, luminous exception. When my agent first read the text, she said that it was a love story; and I suppose it is, and why not? You may have smiled to yourself at the frequency of my allusions to Beetle.

If I give the impression that we have never had cross words, cross patches even, well, no one is obliged to tell the whole truth, least of all about one's marriage, especially if it is, and one wishes it to be, "on-going." I recall an old black male hooker, in a 1960s documentary, whose response to certain questions was "Don't Never Tell," delivered with a smile. It may be— such is age—that I have mentioned this character before. Very well, I have done it again. Another quotation comes to mind, from Arthur Miller's *A View from the Bridge*, in which the leading character (something of an incestuous paedophile, if I remember rightly) is eulogized, I think by some stand-in version of a Greek chorus-man, as someone who "allowed himself to be fully known." Am I out of line (my favorite pose) when I wonder how welcome one would be, regardless of any unusual proclivities in the *meum-tuum* line, if one spilled all one's beans and honored the Miller notion of a certain kind of, say, generosity? Once again, the deli joke with the pay-off "Lady, who cares?" limps into view. I do not presume to think that you have made yourself fully known, and I hope I have not. There is some tact in not wishing people to take a personal interest in what is/has been wrapped in, so to say, *all* one's mental Kleenex.

You have presented a certain J.E. to me, the one I am very pleased to hear from, laugh at, and learn from and, yes, I hope I have done something similar. There is a courtesy in reticence, and candor of a kind that can be taken or left. The modern arts just may have made too much of a point in letting it all hang out. I would sooner look at Cézanne, who asked his sitters, especially his patient wife, to stay as still as "an apple" (which recalls the menace with which Jean Gabin, playing the usual underworld curmudgeon, delivered the apostrophe "*Ma pomme*" to some quaking sidekick) than gaze, with a show of amazement, at the late Lucien Freud's muddily "honest" depictions of sagging male and female parts. Who, as they used to say, needs it?

So, I can imagine you reading this and knowing that I want to say more and will not, to avoid embarrassing myself or you. As I fling my paper ribbon towards your shore, am I wondering if we shall ever meet in person and what kind of a show that will be, folks? Yes. Can I imagine what comedy might follow? So can you. But your stories promise that, against sullen expectation, we might indeed warm to each other in the flesh as we have on the page. Let's leave it like that, *mon* not so *vieux*! The false folk on TV make fun of the phrase "It's been . . . emotional!" But it is, and had better be, if we are really friends; and I think we are.

Un de ces jours, my dear Joe. *Con gran affetto* (yes, it's easier in foreign!) And, as those on the deck call down, "Don't forget to write!" As if either of us could, one way or another.

Tout a toi, Freddie.

Index

Abernathy, Ralph, 242
About Last Night (movie), 87
Academic Questions (journal), 103
Achilles, 141
Ackerley, J.R., 2, 46, 48–49
Ackroyd, Peter, 298–99
Ackroyd, Roger, 14
Adam Bede (Eliot), 379–80
Adler, Renata, 297
Aeschylus, 208, 275
After Julius (Howard), 70
After Strange Gods (Eliot), 328
Agee, James, 212
Albee, Edward, 3, 300
Aleichem, Sholem, 13, 82
Alexander of Macedon (Green), 350–
  51, 369
Alexander the Great (movie), 350–51
Algonquin Round Table, 253
Algren, Nelson, 170–71
Alighieri, Dante, 3, 32, 119, 149, 215,
  230, 254
All Souls' College, 27
Allen, Woody, 63, 66–67, 315
Alms for Oblivion (Raven), 80
Althusser, Louis, 158
Alvarez, A., 334
Ambition (Epstein), 290
American Colony (Brackett), 292
American Institute of Arts and Letters,
  73–74
American PEN, 74
The American Scholar, 31, 212, 262,
  268–80, 343, 351
Amis, Kingsley, 72, 83, 201, 241, 260,
  312–13, 327–28

Amis, Martin, 313, 366
Amos 'n Andy (radio show), 137
An Affair to Remember (movie), 61, 62
Anatomy of Melancholy (Burton), 68–
  69
Ancient Evening (Mailer), 259
Anderson, Jon, 23
Anna Karenina (Tolstoy), 26, 98, 156–
  57, 174
Annan, Noel, 186, 297
Anouilh, Jean, 330, 333
The Anti-Death League (Kingsley
  Amis), 72
Antonioni, Michelangelo, 373
Appel, Alfred, 182
Appleyard, Bryan, 84, 88
Appointment in Samarra (O'Hara), 55,
  58, 190, 204
Arafat, Yasser, 237
Archer, Isabel, 179, 181
Arendt, Hannah, 170, 231, 276
Areté (magazine), 100–101
Aristodemus, 145
The Aristos (Fowles), 228
Aristotle, 90, 118, 317, 350
Arkansas Gazette, 165
Armies of the Night (Mailer), 363
Arnold, Matthew, 370
Arrowsmith, William, 351
Arsenal, 92–94
The Aspern Papers (James), 153
Associated Television, 254
Astaire, Fred, 114
At Freddie's (Fitzgerald), 89
Atiyah, Michael, 69
The Atlantic, 123, 140, 307–8, 343

Aubrey, James T., 217–18
Aubrey, John, 247
Auden, W.H., 15, 101, 294, 297, 305–6, 325, 360
Auerbach, Erich, 3, 40–41, 45
"August: Osage County" (movie), 22
Augustus (Williams), 309
Austen, Jane, 58
Austin, J.L., 84
Away from Her (movie), 65
Axelrod, George, 161
Axios Press, 120
Ayer, A.J., 283
Ayrton, Michael, 71, 78, 257

Babel, Isaac, 234
Babington, Thomas, 28
Bacall, Lauren, 162, 252, 253
Badian, E., 297
Bagnold, Enid, 46
Balanchine, George, 189
Baldock, Robert, 191
Balfour, A. J., 238
Balzac, Honoré, 16, 362
Bang the Drum Slowly (movie), 281
The Bankrupts (Glanville), 285
Bannen, Ian, 254
Bannett, Alan, 195
Barnes, Julian, 110–11, 115
Barrett, William, 220
Barth, John, 248, 259–60
Barthes, Roland, 341–42
"Bartlestein's First Fling" (Epstein), 59
Barzun, Jacques, 212, 220, 222
Baudelaire, Charles, 38, 327
Bayley, John, 161
Bea Lillie Show, 13–14
Beatty, Warren, 61–62, 67
Beaumont, Binkie, 13, 15
Because I Was Flesh (Dahlberg), 40
Becher, Tony, 7
Becket (Anouilh), 333
Beerbohm, Max, 15, 38, 39, 75–76, 106, 213, 223, 253, 290, 361, 381

Beethoven, Ludwig, 149
The Beginning of Spring (Fitzgerald), 355
Behrman, S. N., 253–54, 261
Behrman, S.N., 75
Belafonte, Harry, 63
The Bell Jar (Plath), 259
Bellow, Saul, 60, 76, 170, 181, 194, 261, 300, 306, 351–52, 363, 371
Benchley, Robert, 54
Benedict, Clare, 139
Benedict XIII (pope), 158
Ben-Gurion, David, 210
Benigni, Roberto, 232
Benn, Gottfried, 155
Bennett, Arnold, 60, 352
Bennett, Tony, 315
Benning, Annette, 62
Berenson, Bernard, 32, 270–72, 290, 321
Bergman, Ingmar, 194
Bergonzi, Bernard, 236
Bergson, Henri, 163
Berlin, Irving, 253–54
Berlin, Isaiah, 31, 174, 200, 215, 236, 314, 368
Bernal, Martin, 351
Bernhard, Thomas, 17
Bernsetin, Carl, 57
Bernstein, Jeremy, 69
Bernstein, Leonard, 8, 236
Beyond The Fringe (theatre), 199, 312
BHL, 6
Bierce, Ambrose, 367
Big D, 3
The Big Sleep (movie), 161–62, 252
Billington, Kevin, 286
Bina Gardens, 86
Binyon, Laurence, 3
Birkerts, Sven, 220
Black, Conrad, 23
Black Athena: The Afro-asiatic Roots of Classical Civilization (Bernal), 351

Black Lamb and Grey Falcon (West), 47

Blair, Eric, 283

Blair, Tony, 375, 378

Blanchett, Cate, 63, 64

Bloom, Claire, 175, 180–81

Bloom, Harold, 132

Bloomsbury, 331, 336–37, 340

Blue Flower (Fitzgerald), 89

Blue is the Warmest Color (movie), 38

Blue Jasmine (movie), 63–64, 66

The Blue Angel (movie), 321

Blunt, Anthony, 343

Boardwalk Empire (TV show), 34, 108, 112

Boasts (Fitzgerald), 18

Bodkin, Maud, 169

Bogarde, Dirk, 274, 362

Bogart, Humphrey, 162, 252–53

Booker Prize, 89

Books and Beginnings (bookstore), 203–4

The Bookshop (Fitzgerald), 89

Booth, James, 327

Bor, Mr., 254, 256

Borge, Victor, 67–68

Borges, Jorge Luis, 288, 291

Bottrall, Ronald, 294

Bousquet, René, 313–14

Bowersock, Glen, 90

Bowra, Maurice, 49, 295, 372

Boyd, Will, 258

Boyle, Anthony, 381

Brackett, Charlie, 292–93

Bradbury, Malcom, 33

Bradley, F. H., 336

Braine, John, 263

Branagh, Kenneth, 66

Bratby, John, 356

Breaking Bad (TV series), 34

The Breast (Roth), 259, 267

Bricusse, Leslie, 6–7, 12–14, 347

A Brief History of Time (Hawking), 339

Broderick, Matthew, 98

Brody, Adrien, 232

Brokaw, Tom, 49, 124, 230

Brombert, Victor, 3

Brook, Peter, 161

Brooks, Mel, 63, 346

Brown, Craig, 35

Brown, David, 247–48

Brown, Gordon, 14

Brown, Peter, 90, 213

Bruce, Lenny, 196

Buchanan, Tom, 51–52

Buckley, William F., Jr., 345

Buddenbrooks (Mann), 17

Bull Durham (movie), 345

A Bullet in the Ballet (Brahms and Simon), 19

Bullock, Sandra, 63

Burgess, Anthony, 273

Burke, Kenneth, 5

Burns, George, 250

Burns, John Horne, 356–57, 360, 364

Burton, Richard, 329, 350

Burton, Robert, 68–69

Buruma, Ian, 159

Butler, Samuel, 128

Butterfield 8 (O'Hara), 204

Byatt, Antonia, 95

Byron, George Gordon, 48, 143, 149, 187

A Cab at the Door (Pritchett), 146

Caesar, Sid, 67

Cagney, Jimmy, 154, 157

Caine, Mark (pseudonym), 313, 347

The Caine Mutiny (Wouk), 55, 209

Caird, John, 333

Cakes and Ale (Maugham), 153, 286

California Suite (movie), 373

Calvino, Italo, 155

Cambridge University, 6

Cambridge University Footlights, 6

Camus, Albert, 158, 171, 241

Capa, Robert, 20–21

Capote, Truman, 317, 360
Carey, John, 84–85, 88, 102
Carlyle, Jane, 128
Carlyle, Thomas, 128
Carne-Ross, D. S., 351
Carr, E.H., 31–32
Carter, William C., 162–63
Cartledge, Paul, 30, 140, 145
Cary, Joyce, 356
Casati, Luisa, 185
Catch-22 (Heller), 172
Catcher in the Rye (Salinger), 42–43
Cather, Willa, 300
Catherine the Great, 245–47, 250
Catholic Church, 23
Catullus, 365
Caulfield, Holden, 11
Cavafy, Constantine P., 137, 173, 177,
    191–93, 204, 216–17, 226, 295
Cavalcade (movie), 12
Cavendish Hotel, 80
Cecil, Robert, 248
Celebrity (movie), 66
Celiac Disease, 17–18
Cellini, Benvenuto, 146
Centaur (Updike), 55
Cercas, Javier, 134
Cerf, Bennett, 121
Cervantes, 129
Cézanne, Paul, 54, 384
Chamberlain, Neville, 54
Chandler, Raymond, 14, 162
Chaplin, Charlie, 124, 256, 276, 370
Charles II, King of England, 37
Charlie Hebdo, 373–75, 377
Charnwood, Lord, 291
Charterhouse, 47
Chase, David, 34
The Château (Maxwell), 355, 360
Chekhov, Anton, 16, 52, 100, 175
Chelsea, 92–94
Chesterton, G. K., 284
Chicago Reader, 278
Chicago Tribune, 24, 173, 289

Chomsky, Noam, 158
Chopin, Frédéric, 87
Christ Church, 28
Christian, Fletcher, 55
Christian Science, 140, 146
Christie, Julie, 65, 184, 274
Christine, 339
Chronicles of Wasted Time (Mug-
    geridge), 265
Churchill, Caryl, 378
Churchill, Winston, 15, 228, 337
*Churchill's Black Dog, Kafka's Mice
    and other essays* (Storr), 9
CIA, 32
Cicero, 90
Cinna, 206–7
Cioran, E. M., 137, 368
Cisson, C. H., 340, 341
City Slickers (movie), 281
Civil Rights Movement, 242
Civilization (TV series), 164
Clark, Alan, 30
Clark, Jim, 258
Clark, Kenneth, 164, 314
Cleopatra (movie), 186
Clinton, Hillary, 243
Clinton, William Jefferson, 250, 354
Clooney, George, 63–64, 172
Close, Glenn, 84, 333
Cockburn, 159
Cocks, Geoffrey, 169
Cohen, Nat, 184
Coleridge, Samuel Taylor, 19–20
Commentary, 32, 179–80, 234, 279,
    281, 285, 289, 298–99, 326
Commentary Online, 291
Complete Cavafy (Mendelsohn), 191–
    92
Concept of Mind (Ryle), 117
Conclusive Evidence (Nabokov), 146
Confessions of Felix Krull (Mann), 16–
    17
Connolly, Cyril, 32, 35, 46, 100–101,
    286, 294, 295, 372

Connolly, John, 181–82
The Conquest of Mexico (Prescott), 28
Conrad, Joseph, 354
Conti, Tom, 178
Cook, Peter, 312
Cooke, Alistair, 68
Cooper, Duff, 14
Cooper, Gary, 154, 183
Cooper, William (pseudonym of Harry Hoff), 273
Coppola, Francis Ford, 62
Cosi fan tutti (opera), 305
Cotton Club, 62
"The Count and the Prince" (Epstein), 59
The Coup (Updike), 150
Coward, Noel, 3–4, 12–13, 15, 85, 98, 121, 360
Cowell, Simon, 68
Cowley, Malcolm, 344
Cowling, Maurice, 31
Cozzens, James Gould, 132
Cromwell, Oliver, 37
Cronkite, Walter, 230
Crook, John, 341
Crowe, Cameron, 252–53
Crowe, Russell, 320
Cruz, Penelope, 152
Crystal, Billy, 281
Cuddihy, 276
Curtius, E.R., 41

Dahlberg, Edward, 40
The Daily Beast, 291
Daily Mail, 35
Daily Telegraph, 15–16, 76
Daisy Miller (James), 149, 356
A Dance in the Sun (Jacobson), 186
D'Annunzio, Gabriele, 134, 138
Darling (movie), 184, 258, 274
Darwin, Charles, 380
Davenport-Hines, Richard, 1, 27, 79
Davidson, Max, 76
Davie, Donald, 340–42

Dawkins, Richard, 309
Day, Doris, 154, 315
de Beauvoir, Simone, 170–71, 346
de Caprio, Leonardo, 63
de Charlus, Baron (fictional character), 295
de Gaulle, Charles, 236–37, 240, 314, 377
de Montherlant, Henry, 56
De Niro, Robert, 281
De Quincey, Thomas, 196
de Vries, Peter, 320
The Dead Poets Society (movie), 252
Deadwood (TV series), 34
Death of the Fox (movie), 186, 247–48
The Decline and Fall of the Roman Empire (Gibbon), 28
Decter, Midge, 289
The Defense (Nabokov), 182
A Delicate Truth (Le Carre), 35
Demaratus, 140
Denaxas, Artemis, 302
Dennehy, Brian, 88
Depardieu, Gérard, 128
Dern, Bruce, 202–3, 281
Derrida, Jacques, 241
Design for Living (movie), 12
The Destruction of The European Jews (Hilberg), 231
Deutsch, David, 286
DeVito, Danny, 183
Diamond, I. A. L. (Izzy), 63, 292
"A Diamond as Big as The Ritz" (Fitzgerald), 281
Diaries (Kennan), 243
The Diary of a Nobody (Grossmith and Grossmith), 264, 310
The Diary of Noel Coward (Coward), 3
Dickens, Charles, 85, 379
Didion, Joan, 297–98, 306
Dietrich, Marlene, 321
Dimoula, Kiki, 190–91
Discourses of Epictetus (Hughes), 282
Diski, Jenny, 298

Disney, 87
Dispatches (Herr), 171–72
Disraeli, Benjamin, 137, 243, 350
Distant Intimacy (Raphael and Epstein), 1, 35, 131, 155, 278–79, 371
Djokovic, Novak, 18
Doctorow, E.L., 87–88
Dodd, E.R., 30
Dog Soldiers (Stone), 372
Don Fernando (Maugham), 294
Don Juan (fictional character), 143
Donen, Stanley, 62, 70, 185
Donne, John, 85
The Doors, 197–98
Dos Passos, John, 252
Dostoyevsky, Fyodor, 38, 90, 144, 174–75, 370
Double Indemnity (movie), 162
Douglas, Michael, 84, 295
Douglas, Norman, 30, 265
Downing, Ben, 191
Doyle, Conan, 218
Dreiser, Theodore, 58, 307
The Driven Leaf (Steinberg), 309, 324–25
Dubos, René, 212
Dunn, John Gregory, 297
Dunne, Irene, 61–62
Dupee, F. W., 222
Durante, Jimmy, 60
Duveen, Lord, 253

The Earlsdon Way (Raphael), 78, 312
Easy Aces (radio show), 68
Eban, Abba, 354
Eckermann, Johann Peter, 298
Edel, Leon, 90, 142, 147–49, 215
Eden, Anthony, 228, 257
The Ed Sullivan Show (TV show), 67–68
Edward Lewis Wallant Prize, 173
Eggar, Samantha, 254
Eichmann, Adolf, 276, 333

Eichmann Before Jerusalem (Stangneth), 330
Eichmann in Jerusalem (Arendt), 231
Einstein, Albert, 183
Eisenstein, Sergei, 245–46
Ejiofar, Chiwete, 63
The Electric Jew (Raphael), 365
Elektra (play), 329–31
Eliot, George, 379
Eliot, T.S., 28, 85, 86, 100, 241, 293, 309, 328, 336
Eliot, Valerie, 85
Elizabeth I (queen), 247
Elizabeth II (queen), 379
Elkins, Hilly, 176
Elliott, George P., 335, 379
Emerson, Ralph Waldo, 99
Emotional Support Dogs, 48
Empedocles, 208, 322
Encounter, 27, 32, 105–6, 343
The End of the Affair (Greene), 268
The End of the Road (Barth), 248
England Made Me (Greene), 264
Envy (Epstein), 129–30, 240
Ephron, Nora, 57, 105
Epictetus, 282
Esquire (magazine), 67, 105–6, 148, 172, 289, 352
Esquire, A.H., 30
Essays in Biography (Epstein), 120–21
Ettedjui, Joseph, 229
Ettedjui, Paul, 229
Euripides, 208, 331
Evans, Bergen, 352
Evans, Bob, 62, 200
Evett, Bob, 106
Evett, Robert (Bobby), 343
Ewer, William Norman, 240
The Ewings (O'Hara), 204
The Executioner's Song (Mailer), 366
Eyes Wide Shut (movie), 168–69, 382

Fabulous Small Jews (Epstein), 244
Fadiman, Clifton, 352

Fairbanks, Douglas, Jr., 190
Fairfield, Cecily, 95
Fairlie, Henry, 337–38, 343
Falcon, Guy (fictional character), 356
Fallen Angels (Coward), 12–13
Fanon, Franz, 377
Fantasia of the Unconscious
    (Lawrence), 227
Far From the Madding Crowd (movie),
    184, 258
Farage, Nigel, 310
Fatal Attraction (play), 83–84, 87
Fatherland (Harris), 6
Fathers and Sons (Turgenev), 174, 178
Faulkner, William, 161
Federer, Roger, 23, 323–24
Feinstein, Elaine, 209, 210
Fellini, Federico, 44
Ferguson, Alex, 93
Ferguson, Niall, 28, 159, 210
Ferman, James (Jim), 254–56, 262
Ferrer, Mel, 157
A Few Good Men (movie), 55
Fichte, Johann Göttlieb, 42
Fiction and the Reading Public
    (Leavis), 294
Fields, W. C., 220
The Fifty Year Argument (documen-
    tary), 306
Figes, Orlando, 28
Finkielkraut, Alain, 374
Finnegan's Wake (Joyce), 129
Finney, Albert, 184
Firbank, Ronald, 293
Firth, Colin, 152
Fitzgerald, Edward, 379
Fitzgerald, F. Scott, 18, 51–52, 57, 126,
    129, 204, 212, 281, 293, 307, 372
Fitzgerald, Penelope, 79, 89, 134, 355
The Five (Jabotinsky), 234, 243–44
Flaccus, Q. Horatius, 53
Flash Boys (Lewis), 355
Flaubert, Gustave, 38
Flight Into Camden (Storey), 255

The Floating Opera (Barth), 259
Flynn, Errol, 190
The Folded Leaf (Maxwell), 360
"The Folly and the Ivy" (Epstein), 91
Fonda, Henry, 157
For Gold, For Praise, For Glory
    (Raphael), 365
Ford, Ford Madox, 241
Ford, Henry, 40
Forster, E.M., 43, 137, 143, 371
Forster, Morgan, 366
The Forsyte Saga, 98
Forte, Will, 202
Foster, Jodie, 139
Foster, John, 144
Foucault, Michel, 241, 377
Fowler, H. W., 269
Fowles, John, 228, 313
The Fox In The Attic (Hughes), 364
Franck, Cesar, 163
Franco's Crypt (Treglown), 134
Franklin, Ben, 128, 146
Frederick the Great (Churchill), 379
Freedland, Jonathan, 226–27
Freud, Lucien, 45, 384
Freud, Sigmund, 147–48
Freund, Paul, 212
Friedlander, Paul, 69
From the Terrace (O'Hara), 55, 204
Fromm, Erich, 186
Frost, David, 266, 268
Fuchs, Daniel, 154, 359
"fuck you up" (Larkin), 17–18
Fuller, Roy, 5
Furbank, P. N., 143
Furet, François, 317
Fussell, Paul, 356

Gabin, Jean, 384
Galba, Emperor, 29
The Gallery (Burns), 356–57, 364
Garbo, Greta, 26, 156, 253
Garfield, John, 50
Garland, Judy, 185

Garnett, Constance, 115
Garnett, David, 143
Garrett, George, 186, 247
Gavron, Asaf, 319
Geary, Father, 218
Gelbart, Larry, 67
George VI (king), 133
Gerber, Merill Joan, 205
Gere, Richard, 152
Gershwin, George, 144
Gershwin, Ira, 41, 162
Gibbon, Edward, 28, 320, 324, 369
Gibbs, Wolcott, 33
Gide, André, 367
Gielgud, John, 71, 361
Gifford Lectures, 148
Gilbert, W. S., 305
Giles Goat Boy (Barth), 259
Gilliatt, Penelope, 89
Gingold, Hermione, 6, 7–8, 11–12
Ginsberg, Allen, 85
Girard, René, 5, 45, 84, 219, 229, 239
Girardi, William, 131
The Girl on the Via Flaminia (Hayes),
    358
Gladiator (movie), 320
Gladstone, William, 37–38
Glanville, Brian, 47, 99, 285–86, 339,
    356–57
Glanville, Mark, 29–30
Glass, Philip, 87
Glatt, Hyman, 245
The Glittering Prizes (TV series), 119–
    20, 256, 267, 313
Godard, Jean-Luc, 168
Godfather movies, 281
Goethe, Johann Wolfgang von, 17,
    271, 298
Going Up (Raphael), 186, 347, 382
Goldberg, Jeffrey, 140
Goldberg, Whoopi, 183
The Golden Notebook (Lessing), 356
Goldman, Albert, 196–98
Gombrich, Ernst, 314

The Good Soldier (Ford), 241
Good Will Hunting (movie), 252
Goodfellas (movie), 62
Goodman, Allegra, 179
Goodman, Len, 114
Goodman, Martin, 273–75
The Good Soldier (Ford), 129
Goodwin, Doris Kearns, 106
Gordon, George, 143
Gordon, Harry, 255
Goya, Francisco, 209
Grammys, 8
Grant, Cary, 61, 64, 154
Graves, Robert, 133, 309, 361–62
Gravity, 38, 63–65
The Great Dictator (movie), 370
The Great Gatsby (Fitzgerald), 126,
    129
The Great Philosophers, 117
The Greeks and the Irrational (Dodd),
    30
The Greek Interpreter (Doyle), 218
Green, Julien, 358
Green, Peter, 30, 302, 348, 350–51
Greenberg, Seymour, 130
Greene, Graham, 109, 153, 264, 268,
    364, 369
Gregh, Fernand, 210
Grey, Edward, 53–54
Griffiths-Jones, Mervyn, 366
Gross, John, 97–98, 156, 186
Gross, Miriam, 118
Grossman, Lev, 231
Grossman, Vasily, 365
The Group (McCarthy), 60, 352
Guide for the Perplexed (Maimonides),
    195
Guizot, François, 235
Gwynne, N. M., 244, 269, 270
Gwynne's Grammar (Gwynne), 244
Gypsy (musical), 8

Habermas, Jurgen, 318
Hadrian (Yourcenar), 309

Haig, Douglas, 31
Halevi, Yehuda, 234
Halkin, Hillel, 234
Hall, Peter, 69, 331
Halper, Albert, 335
Hamilton, Ian, 313
Hamlet (movie), 183
A Handful of Dust (Waugh), 363
"A Hanging" (Orwell), 146
Hanks, Tom, 183
Hannah and her Sisters (movie), 65
Hardcastle, Fiona, 15, 76
Harkis, 376–77
Harley, Jane, 48
Harlot's Ghost (Mailer), 259
Harold, Childe, 143
Harold Washington Literary Award,
    173
Harper's, 363
Harper's Magazine, 96
Harrelson, Woody, 266
Harris, Frank, 21, 35, 37, 39
Harris, Jed, 62
Harris, Robert, 6
Hartford, Huntington, 352
Harvard Hates America (LeBoutillier),
    265
Hastings, Selena, 153
The Hat on the Bed (O'Hara), 54
Hawking, Stephen, 339–40
Hawthorne, Nathaniel, 149
Haydn, Joseph, 298
Haydon, Hiram, 212
Hayes, Alfred, 358
Hayes, Harold T.P., 105
Hazlitt, William, 131, 220
Hazzard, Shirley, 254
Heaney, Seamus, 317
The Heart of the Matter (Greene), 268
Heartburn (Ephron), 57
The Heartland Prize, 173
Hecht, Anthony, 205
Hecht, Ben, 162, 281
Hefferman, Seymour, 251

Hefner, Hugh, 181–82
Hegel, Georg Wilhelm Friedrich, 42,
    330
Heidegger, Martin, 322
Heller, Erich, 215, 223
Heller, Joseph, 172
Hellman, Lillian, 212
Hemingway, Ernest, 54, 58, 212, 307
Hemlock and After (Wilson), 364
Henry IV (king), 28
Henry James (Edel), 147
Hensher, Philip, 102
Hepburn, Audrey, 128, 136, 152, 157,
    180, 247, 327, 333
Hepburn, Katherine, 333
Hepner, Gershon, 110
Heraclitus, 322
Herman, David, 195
Herodotus, 90, 115, 140, 145, 301, 350
Herodotus (Holland), 368
Herr, Michael, 168, 171–72, 382
Herzog (Bellow), 60, 352
Heschel, Abraham, 383
High Noon (movie), 183
Hilberg, Raul, 228, 231
Hills Like White Elephants (Heming-
    way), 54
Hippolytus (play), 331
Hirsch, Edward, 232–33, 298
History of Ferdinand and Isabella
    (Prescott), 28
*History of the Reign of the Emperor
    Charles the Fifth* (Prescott), 28
History of the World (Ralegh), 247
The History Man (Bradbury), 33
Hitchens, Christopher, 24, 30, 159,
    172, 298
Hitler, Adolf, 16, 28, 201, 228, 242,
    276, 308, 339, 365, 374
Hitler Diaries, 27
Hockney, David, 45
Hoff, Harry, 273
Hoffman, Dustin, 62, 154
Hoffman, Philip Seymour, 314

Hogg, Quintin, 283
Hoggart, Richard, 342, 366
Holland, Tom, 90, 115, 140, 145, 368
Hollande, François, 235, 311, 375
Homage to Catalonia (Orwell), 146
Homer, 365
Hood, Ann, 151
Hook, Sidney, 114, 220
Hope, Bob, 335–36
Horace, 53, 150
Horizon, 294
Horizon (Connolly), 32, 100–101
The Horse Knows the Way (O'Hara), 51–52, 204
The Horse's Mouth (Bratby), 356
Hot Gates (Pressfield), 309
Houellecbecq, Michel, 377
House of Lords, 23
Housman, A. E., 381
How Literature Saved My Life (Shields), 9–10
Howard, Elizabeth Jane, 70, 72–73, 312, 347
Howe, Irving, 344
Howells, William Dean, 205
Hudson Review, 131
Hughes, Chris, 344
Hughes, Richard, 364
Hughes, William, 282
Hughes-Hallett, Lucy, 134
Hulme, T.E., 45
The Human Factor (Greene), 264
Hurt, John, 361
Huxley, Aldous, 227
The Hysterectomy Waltz (Gerber), 205

I, Claudius (Graves), 309, 361–62, 365
The Idiot (Dostoyevsky), 370
Idylls of the King (Tennyson), 379
Il Lungo Viaggio di Primo Levi, 86
Iliad (Homer), 348
The Immoralist (Gide), 367
Impromptu (movie), 87
In A Trojan Ditch (Sisson), 340

In Love (Hayes), 358
Inferno (Dante), 254
Interlude (movie), 281, 286–87
Irving, John, 299
"Isn't It a Pity" (song), 162
Israel, Jonathan, 159

Jabotinsky, Vladimir, 234, 243
Jacboson, Dan, 179–80, 186–87
Jackson, Jesse, 242
Jacobosh, Siegfried, 88
Jacobsohn, Peter, 88
Jacoby, Derek, 361, 362
Jagger, Mick, 157
James, Clive, 24, 119, 298
James, Henry, 16, 74, 77, 98, 129, 131–32, 139–40, 142, 147, 149, 153, 170, 179, 181, 215–16, 261–62, 280, 293, 319, 328
James, P.D., 14
James, William, 148, 215–16, 261, 301
Janeway, Eliot, 123
Janeway, Michael, 123
Jannings, Emil, 321
Jarrell, Randall, 244
Jason, David, 33
Jeffrey, Lord, 307
Jenkins, Alan, 191
Jenkins, Roy, 37–38
Jimson, Gulley, 356
Job (Girard), 229
Johnson, Daniel, 101–2
Johnson, Don, 189
Johnson, Samuel, 271
Jordan, Robin, 28
Joseph and His Brothers (Mann), 17
Josephus, Flavius, 143, 164, 211, 273, 275
Joubert, Joseph, 170, 368
Jourdan, Louis, 154
Joyce, James, 94, 100, 129, 254
Judt, Tony, 321
Jules et Jim (movie), 287
Julius Caesar (play), 315

Kafka, Franz, 16–17, 116, 177, 267, 308
Kant, Immanuel, 42, 267
"Kaplan's Big Deal" (Epstein), 59
Kasdan, Lawrence, 182–83
Kates, Nancy, 345
Kauffmann, Stanley, 352
Kaufman, George S., 253
Kaye, Danny, 199–200
Kazan, Elia, 124
Kazan, Gadge, 116
Kazin, Alfred, 156, 223, 344
Kear, Alroy, 153, 286
Keaton, Buster, 75
Keaton, Diane, 91
Keats, John, 212, 302
Kedourie, Elie, 238
Kelly, Grace, 183
Kempton, Murray, 326–37, 342
Kennan, George F., 3, 65, 75, 243
The Kennan Diaries (Kennan), 76–77
Kennedy, Joe, 204
Kennedy, John F., 27, 105, 221
Kermode, Frank, 32, 200
Kerouac, Jack, 85
Kerr, Deborah, 61, 333
Kerry, John, 136
Kesey, Ken, 372
Key Largo (movie), 252
Khruschhev, Nikita, 239
King, Martin Luther, Jr., 242, 369, 383
King Lear (play), 44, 315
Kingsmill, Hugh, 189
Kirk, Geoffrey, 219
"Kizerman and Feigenbaum" (Epstein), 300
Klein, Joe, 354
Klemperer, Victor, 349–50
Knightley, Keira, 26
Knopf, Alfred A., 75–76, 121
Knox, Ronald, 89
Koestler, Arthur, 70, 178, 271, 294, 312
Korda, Alexander, 362

Kossoff, David, 285–86
Kostner, Kevin, 345
Kramer, Esta, 66
Kramer, Hilton, 66, 82, 114, 182, 352
Kraus, Karl, 272
Kristeva, Julia, 150, 158
Kristol, 321
Kristol, Irving, 32, 105–6
Kubla Khan (Coleridge), 19–20
Kubrick, Christiane, 125
Kubrick, Stanley, 125, 128, 151, 160, 167–69, 172, 217–18, 273, 281, 339
Kushner, Harold, 224

La Boétie, Etienne de, 124–25, 131
La Pelle (Malaparte), 357
La Ronde (movie), 185, 313
Labro, Philippe, 248
Laclos, Pierre Choderlos de, 312, 347
Lacombe Lucien (movie), 275
Lady Chatterley's Lover (Lawrence), 366
Lambert, Michael, 71–72
L'Amérique au jour le jour (de Beauvoir), 170
Lampedusa, Giuseppe Di, 306
Lancelot (Percy), 224
Lane, Mark, 27, 31
Lardner, Ring, 58, 324
Larkin, Philip, 17–18, 97, 220, 308, 327–28, 334, 372
Lasky, Melvin, 32, 106
The Last Detective (TV series), 33
Laswell, Mark, 308
The Laughing Policeman (movie), 281
Laughton, Charles, 362, 365
Laura (Nabokov), 182
Laurel, Stan, 362
Laurence Olivier Award, 8
L'Avventura (movie), 373
Law, Jude, 26
Lawrence, D.H., 54, 138, 227, 255, 366
Lawrence, Frieda, 293

Lawrence, Gertie, 12
Lawrence, T.E., 133
Lawrence and Wishart, 218
Lawson, Nigella, 95
Lawton, Tommy, 93
Le Carre, John, 35
Le Pen, Marine, 311, 377, 379
Le Solstice de Juin, 56
Leavis, Frank, 227, 293–45, 347
Leavises, F.R., 26
Lebowitz, Fran, 306
Lee, Hermione, 134
Lefkowitz, Mary, 351
Leibowitz, Herb, 191
Leigh, Vivien, 26, 156
Lenin, Vladimir Ilych, 171, 189
Lennon, J. Michael, 362
Leonidas, 382
Leopardi, Giacomo, 53, 94, 150
The Leopard (Lampedusa), 306
Les Damnés de la Terre (Fanon), 377
Les Liaisons Dangereuses (Laclos), 312, 318, 347
Les Mandarins (de Beauvoir), 170
Les Mots (Sartre), 144
Leslie, Cole, 15
Lessing, Doris, 45, 177, 338, 355
Letters of Katherine Mansfield, 336
Levant, Oscar, 144, 315
Levegnini, Renata, 191
Levi, Primo, 231, 241
Levin, Bernard, 338, 342, 367
Lévi-Strauss, Claude, 158
Levitas, S.M., 114
Levy, Bernard-Henri, 241
Levy, Stuart, 184
Lewis, Norman, 357
Lewis, Sinclair, 108, 261
Lichtman, William (Bill), 371–72
Lie Down in Darkness (Styron), 212
Liebowitz, Jake, 91
Life and Fate (Grossman), 231, 365
Life and Loves (Harris), 21
Life is Beautiful (movie), 232

Like Men Betrayed (Raphael), 302
Lillie, Beatrice, 7, 12, 14, 117, 257
Lincoln, Abraham, 3, 137, 291
Lindmann (Raphael), 255, 302, 312, 351
Linney, Laura, 98
The Lion King (movie and play), 87
Lipman, Sam, 87
Lippmann, Walter, 344
A Literary Education and Other Essays (Epstein), 220, 261
Literary Review, 109, 273
"The Literary Worker's Polonius" (Wilson), 299
A Little Night Music (musical), 7–8
Lloyd-George, David, 322
Lloyd-Jones, Hugh, 90, 297, 351, 367
Lobell, Mike, 151–54
Lolita (Nabokov), 177, 182
London Review of Books, 156, 298
London West End theatre, 13
Lonergan, Kenneth, 98
Long, George, 282
The Long March (Styron), 209
Los Angeles Review of Books, 220
Los Angeles Times Book Review, 155
"A Loss for Words" (Epstein), 130
Lost in Austen (movie and TV mini-series), 272
Lost in the Fun House (Barth), 259
Lost Weekend (movie), 292
Louis, Joe, 94, 97
Love Me or Leave Me (movie), 154
Love Story (movie), 62
Lovell, Bernard, 69
Lovey Childs (O'Hara), 54
Low, Robert, 1, 335
Lowell, Katya, 73
Lowell, Robert, 205, 306
Lucian, 367, 368
Lumet, Sidney, 91
Luther, Martin, 228
Luttwak, Ed, 227
Lynch, Bohun, 290

Macbeth (play), 71

Macdonald, Dwight, 103–4, 105, 243, 352

Macy, William H., 318

Mad Men (TV series), 266

Madame Bovary (movie), 115

Madoff, Bernie, 296–97

The Magic Mountain (Mann), 17

Magris, Claudio, 30

Mailer, Norman, 105, 181, 212, 259, 299, 362–63, 366

Maimonides, 195

Making It (Podhoretz), 279, 284, 289–90

Malaparte, Curzio (pseudonym), 357

Malle, Louis, 275

Malraux, André, 314

The Maltese Falcon (movie), 5

Mamet, David, 87, 173

Manckiewicz, Joe, 186

Manent, Pierre, 209, 210, 219

Mankiewicz, Herman, 162

Mankowitz, Wolf, 294

Mann, Thomas, 16–17, 131, 214, 267, 275

Mao Zedong, 158

Marathon Man (movie), 62

Marcel Proust, A Life (Tadie), 162

March, Frederick, 351

Marchand, Leslie A., 143, 149

Marciano, Rocky, 97

Mardigian, Ron, 313, 317

Margolis, Ralph, 154

Marr, Andrew, 349

"Marshal Wexler's Brilliant Career" (Epstein), 194

A Martian Writes Home (Raine), 100

Marx, Groucho, 74

Marx, Harpo, 138

Marx, Karl, 368, 377

Maschler, Tom, 72, 303, 312–13

Maschwitz, Eric, 7

Mason, Jackie, 67–68

Masters of the Game (Epstein), 120

Mattathias, Joseph ben, 143

A Matter of Time (movie), 185

Matthau, Walter, 21, 281

Matthews, Stanley, 93

Maugham, Somerset, 15, 49, 80, 153, 261, 265, 293–94, 340, 348, 360, 373

Maugham, Willie, 12, 38–39, 126–27

Maurice (Forster), 137

Maurras, Charles, 237

Maxwell, William, 355–56, 358, 360

Mayer, Louis B., 4, 6, 154

McCarthy, Mary, 60, 101, 169, 170, 306, 352

McDormand, Frances, 318–19

McEnroe, John, 320

McEwan, Ian, 19, 53, 241, 313

McGraw, Ali, 62

McLeish, Kenneth, 78, 219, 330

McLuhan, Marshall, 200–201, 315, 334

McQueen, Steve, 62

Mean Streets (movie), 62

Meir, Golda, 239

Memoirs of a Shy Pornographer (Patchen), 59

Menaker, Daniel, 24

Mencken, H. L., 221, 251, 257, 367

Mendelsohn, Daniel, 29, 81, 191–93, 204–5, 216–17, 220, 226, 295, 297

Mendes, Sam, 44, 84

Mengers, Sue, 232

Meredith, George, 379

Merkin, Daphne, 361

Messadié, Gerald, 192, 216–17, 264

Messenger, Robert, 4–6, 32, 244, 292–93, 299, 327

Metamorphosis (Kafka), 267

Meyer, Michael, 78

Meyers, Jeffrey, 70, 95, 298–99

MGM, 185, 217, 253

Miami Vice (TV show), 189

Michael Oakeshott: Notebooks, 1922–1986, 336, 368

Micheau, 209, 219, 383
Midler, Bette, 183, 301
Midnight in Paris (movie), 66
Mighty Aphrodite (movie), 65
The Mikado (operetta), 305
Milch (German field-marshal), 226
Milch, David, 34
Mill, John Stuart, 146, 379
Miller, Arthur, 3, 262, 384
Miller, Jonathan, 6, 37, 69, 134, 181,
    195–96, 198–202, 306, 311–13,
    315
Miller, Karl, 186, 286, 294, 304–5, 312
Miller, Manny, 201
Milton, John, 293
Mimesis (Auerbach), 3, 40–41, 45
Minc, Alain, 313
Minnelli, Liza, 185
Minnelli, Vincent, 185
Mitchell, Adrian, 281
Mitchell, Joseph, 260
Mitterrand, François, 314, 377
Modern Painters (Ruskin), 379
Modiano, Patrick, 275
Molière, 6
Momigliano, Arnaldo, 31, 89–91, 94–
    95, 156, 212, 291, 297, 351
Mon Amitié avec Marcel Proust
    (Gregh), 210
Monestquiou, Robert de, 358
Monk, Ray, 19, 117–19
Monnet, Jean, 235, 239
Monsignor Quixote (Greene), 364
Montaigne, Michel de, 50, 129, 131,
    145
Montesquieu, Charles-Louis, 74
Moonlighting (TV show), 80
Moore, Demi, 151
Moore, Henry, 271
Moore, Tom, 143
Moravia, Alberto, 274, 357
Morgan, Piers, 68, 76
Morrow, Dwight, 138
Morson, Gary Saul, 224

Mortimer, Raymond, 286
Mosley, Oswald, 19
Mostel, Zero, 183
Motion, Andrew, 327
Moulin, Jean, 314
Mourinho, José, 93
Muggeridge, Kitty, 266, 268
Muggeridge, Malcolm, 105, 257, 260–
    61, 263–64, 265–66, 352
Muir, Frank, 61, 68
Mumford (movie), 182
Munro, Alice, 59–60, 84
Murdoch, Iris, 161
Murphy, Gerald, 126
Murphy, Sarah, 126
Murray, Andy, 324
Murray, Bill, 319
Murray, John, 143
Murrow, Edward R., 230
Musil, Robert, 17
Musing on Mortality (Brombert), 3
Mussolini, Benito, 69–70
Mutiny on the Bounty (Christian), 55
My Dog Tulip (Ackerley), 2
My Life and Loves (Harris), 35, 37
My Music (TV show), 342
My Thoughts (Montesquiei), 74
My Word (radio show), 68

Nabokov, Dimitri, 182
Nabokov, Sergey, 147
Nabokov, Vladimir, 68, 84, 122, 124,
    146–48, 177–78, 182, 224, 266,
    338, 341
Naipul, V.S., 60, 165
The Naked and the Dead (Mailer), 366
Namier, Lewis, 31–32
Naples '44 (Lewis), 357
Nasser, Gamal Abdel, 252
"Natalie Jackson," 55
National Review, 345
Nebraska (movie), 65, 202–3
"The Necessity of Anti-Semitism"
    (Raphael), 240

Neil, Jerry, 165–66
Nelson, Bob, 203
Nero, 136
Neville, John, 329
The New Leader, 103, 114, 123, 197
The New Republic, 106, 295, 343–45, 352
The New Republic Daily, 291
The New Statesman, 344, 348
New York Review of Books (NYRB), 1, 156, 236–37, 295–96, 306, 342, 358, 368
The New York Review, 307
New York Times, 1, 114, 123, 137, 289, 291, 317, 352, 361, 372
The New Yorker, 32–34, 232–33, 253, 298, 352, 355, 360
A New Wife (movie), 91
Newman, Paul, 152
The New Criterion (magazine), 131–32
Newton, Isaac, 178
Nichols, Mike, 89, 230, 315
Nicholson, Jack, 55, 57, 66
Nicolson, Harold, 27, 133–34, 138–39, 286
Nietzsche, Friedrich, 42
Nightingale, Benedict, 89
Nimmo, Dorothy, 190–91
Nims, John Frederick, 137, 334–35
Nisberg, Jack, 183
Nobel Prize, 51, 59–60
The Noel Coward Diaries (Coward), 15
Nolte, Nick, 372
Norden, Dennis, 61, 68
Northwestern University, 137, 163, 278, 289, 307
"Notes on Camp" (Sontag), 345
Nothing But the Best (movie), 286
The Nude (Read), 223
Nunn, Trevor, 83–84

Oakeshott, Michael, 336, 368–69
Oates, Joyce Carol, 297–98, 299, 354

Obama, Barack, 139, 188, 243, 315–16, 376
Oberon, Merle, 362
The Odd Couple (movie), 373
Odyssey (Homer), 30, 348
Of Human Bondage (Maugham), 49
Of The Farm (Updike), 150
Offshore (Fitzgerald), 89
Ogden, C.K., 125
O'Grady, Molly, 340
O'Hara, John, 51–52, 54–55, 58, 190, 204, 261
Oken, Stuart, 86–87
Old Calabria, 30
The Old Men at the Zoo (Wilson), 366
Olive Kittredge (Strout), 318–19
Olivier, Laurence, 62, 201, 329, 361
On Chesil Beach (McEwan), 53
"On Joseph Epstein" (Giraldi), 131
On Liberty (Mill), 379
One Hundred Letters from Hugh Trevor-Roper (Trevor-Roper), 31
O'Neill, Eugene, 262
O'Neill, Tip, 354
The Onion, 316
Open Society, 229
Ophul, Max, 185
Oppenheimer, J. Robert, 118
The Ordeal of Civility (Cuddihy), 276
The Ordeal of Richard Feverel (Meredith), 379
Origin of the Species (Darwin), 380
Orwell, George, 131, 145–46, 211, 241, 257, 262–63, 280, 283
Orwell, Sonia, 260
Osborne, John, 3, 89, 263
Oscars, 8, 22, 63, 65, 77
Osmond, Gilbert, 181
Our Gang (Roth), 259
Out of the Blue (movie), 6
Ovid, 275
Oxford University Press, 31
Oyelowo, David, 383

Pacino, Al, 66, 91
Paget, Nicola, 156
Painter, George, 150, 162
Paisà (movie), 358–59
Pal Joey (musical), 261
Palance, Jack, 281
Pale Fire (Nabokov), 84
Panama, Norman, 70
Paramount Studios, 200, 203
The Parched Parrot (Epstein), 124
Parker, Dorothy, 236, 368
Parmenides, 322
Parnassus (Leibowitz, editor), 191
Partisan Review, 345
Pascal, Blaise, 131, 209, 213, 219,
    266, 309
Pask, Gordon, 116
Patchen, Kenneth, 59
Paulin, Tom, 327
Pauvre Bitos (play), 330
Payn, Graham, 15
Payne, Alexander, 203
Peirce, C.S., 107
Penn, Sean, 151
People in a Diary (Behrman), 253
Percy, Walker, 224
Peretz, Martin, 343
Perkins, Maxwell, 121, 307
Perl, Jed, 295
Perlasca, Giorgio, 275
*The Persecution and Assassination of
    Jean-Paul Marat as Performed by
    the Inmates of the Asylum of Char-
    enton Under the Direction of the
    Marquis de Sade* (play), 161
Pesci, Joe, 183
Pétain, Marshal, 150
Peters, Roberta, 67–68
Pfeiffer, Michelle, 66
Philips, Siobhan, 361
Philosophical Investigations (Wittgen-
    stein), 322
The Pianist (movie), 232
Picasso, Pablo, 149, 298

Pinker, Steven, 244, 269–70
Pinter, Harold, 3, 19, 78, 92, 118, 210
Pitt, Brad, 172, 301
Pizarro, Francisco, 28
Plath, Sylvia, 259
Play Parade (Coward), 12
The Plot Against America (Roth), 6
Plutarch, 90
Pnin (Nabokov), 182
Podhoretz, John, 284
Podhoretz, Norman, 106, 279, 284,
    285, 289
Poetry Magazine, 335
Poetry Nation Review (PNR), 340
Poitier, Sidney, 63
Pollitt, Harry, 258
Pooter (fictional character), 264, 310
Popper, Karl, 117, 229
Porter, Cole, 214, 347
Porter, Fairfield, 22
4Porter, Katie, 224
Portrait of Max (Behrman), 75, 253
The Portrait of a Lady (James), 179,
    250, 280
The Possessed (Dostoyevsky), 174
"Postcards" (Epstein), 251
Potemkin, Grigori, 245
Potter, Stephen, 196, 315
Poulet, Gaston, 163
Poulet Quartet, 163
Pound, Ezra, 216, 341, 357
Powell, Anthony, 5
Prentice, Abra, 23
Prescott, William Hickling, 28, 30
Presidential Medal for the Humanities,
    173
Pressfield, Steven, 309
Prévert, Jacques, 295
Pride and Prejudice (Austen), 58
Priestley, Jack, 95
Primary Colors (Klein), 354
Prince of Tides (movie), 304
Principia Mathematica (Russell and
    Whitehead), 322

The Prisoner (Tilsley), 168
Pritchett, V. S., 146
Private Lives (movie), 12
Private Views (Raphael), 70, 73
Prix Simonnet, 169
The Producers (movie), 183
Proffitt, Stuart, 118
Proust, Marcel, 6, 55, 98, 129, 149,
    162–63, 166, 265, 357–58, 360,
    367
Pryce-Jones, David, 210
Puchner, Martin, 321–22, 323, 325–26
Pulitzers, 8
Pulman, Jack, 361
Punch, 89
Putin, Vladimir, 82–83, 246
Pythagoras, 322

Quadrangle Club, 90
Quai d'Orsay, 30
Quarto (magazine), 100
Quito, 40

Raban, Jonathan, 340
Racine, Jean, 44
Racso, 272, 275, 297, 373
Raft, George, 157
A Rage to Live (O'Hara), 204
Ragtime (Doctorow), 87–88
Raine, Craig, 86, 99–103, 109, 116,
    191, 217, 220
Ralegh, Walter, 22, 186–87, 247–48,
    365–67
Ramsey, Guy, 35, 78, 107–8, 322
Random House, 24
Ransoms, John Crowe, 26
The Rape of Tamar (Jacobson), 180
Raphael, Paul, 276
Raphael, Sarah, 4, 72, 120, 187, 333,
    356, 382
Raphael, Stephen, 44, 83, 151–53, 169,
    217, 311, 333, 355
Raven, Simon, 80, 143
Read, Herbert, 223

The Reader (Schlink), 5
Reality Hunger (Shields), 9
Reed, Henry, 59
Reed, Rex, 67
Regarding Susan Sontag (documen-
    tary), 345
Rego, Paula, 69
Reiner, Carl, 67
Revolutionary Road (movie), 44
Richardson, Ralph, 329, 361
Richler, Mordecai, 168
Richman, Stella, 254
Richmond, Bruce, 16
Rickman, Alan, 12
Ricks, C., 86
Rigoletto (opera), 311, 315
Rinehart, Rick, 120
Ringleblum, Emmanuel, 231
Rivers, Joan, 195
The Road to the Open (Schnitzler), 245
The Road to Wigar Pier (Orwell), 146
Robards, Jason, 253
Roberts, Andrew, 79–80
Roberts, Julia, 66, 172, 183
Robeson, Paul, 236
Robson, Flora, 362
Roché, Henri-Pierre, 287
Rockefeller, John D., 23
Rome and Jerusalem (Goodman), 273
A Room of One's Own (Woolf), 300
Roosevelt, Franklin D., 228
Rose, Jacqueline, 211, 225
Rosenberg, Harold, 352
Rosenfield, Andy, 282, 310
Rosenfield, Loie, 281–82, 309–10
Rosenfield, Maury, 281–82, 310
Rosenheim, Ned, 280
Ross, Harold, 253, 307
Ross, Herbert, 267, 373
Rossellini, Roberto, 358
Rossen, Robert, 350
Roth, Philip, 6, 69, 175, 180–81, 251,
    259, 267, 285, 313
Rousseau, Jean-Jacques, 146

Rowman & Littlefield Publishing Group, 120
Rowse, A.L., 27
Royal East Kent Regiment (The Buffs), 141
Royal Society of Literature, 70, 73, 95
Rudy, Joe, 111–12
Ruffalo, Mark, 98
Rush to Judgment (Lane), 27
Rushdie, Salman, 241, 259, 372
Ruskin, John, 379
Russell, Bertrand, 114, 127, 138, 167, 184, 256, 270–71, 322
Rustin, Bayard, 242
Ryan, Alan, 100
Ryan, Meg, 66, 151, 320
Ryle, Gilbert, 117

Sackville-West, Vita, 139
Said, Edward, 237
Sainte-Beuve, Charles Augustin, 6, 246–47
Salinger, J.D., 42–43, 98
Sallis, Peter, 127
Sallust (Syme), 206
Samuel, Herbert, 322
Sand, George, 87, 138
Sandoe, John, 356
Santayana, George, 42, 262, 271, 336
Sarandon, Susan, 345
Sarkozy, Nicholas, 377
Sartre, Jean-Paul, 144, 158, 166, 170–71, 349, 377
Satterfield, Bob, 40
Satterfield, Iona, 40
Savile, Jimmy, 21–22, 36–37, 177
Sawyer, Diane, 230
Scargill, Arthur, 133, 137
Schama, Simon, 159, 163–65
Scheider, Rob, 62
Schelling, Friedrich Wilhelm Joseph, 42
Schindler's List (movie), 232
Schlesinger, John, 62, 100, 184–85, 329, 330

Schlink, Bernhard, 5
Schmidt, Michael, 53, 340, 341
Schnitzler, Arthur, 169, 245, 246
Schopenhauer, Arthur, 41–42, 60, 162, 267
Schumann, Robert, 235, 239
Scorsese, Martin, 63, 297, 306
Scott, Ridley, 320
Scott-Thomas, Kristin, 329, 330, 333
Scrutiny, 294
Scruton, Roger, 117
Seaford, Richard, 330–31
Sebald, W.G., 17
Segal, Victoria, 333
Selected Letters of Vanessa Bell, 336
Selma (movie), 383
Selznick, David, 253
Seneca, 136
Sennett, Richard, 318
The Sense of Style (Pinker), 244
The Serious Man (Storey), 255
Service Dogs, 48
Sessi, Frediano, 86
Sewanee Review, 205
Seymour, Miranda, 70
Shakespeare, William, 149, 315
Sharpton, Al, 242
Shaw, George Bernard, 189
Shawn, William, 307
Sheed, Wilfrid, 279, 284–85
Sheehan, Winfield, 254
Shelley, Percy Bysshe, 265
Shephers, Cybill, 80
Shields, David, 9–10
Shils, Edward, 31, 50, 57–58, 77, 82, 89–90, 156, 189, 203, 212, 280, 291, 317, 318
The Shining (King), 169
"Shooting an Elephant" (Orwell), 146
Shores of Light (Wilson), 299
Short, Martin, 182
Show, 352
Showalter, Elaine, 317
Silvers, Robert, 156, 217, 236, 295,

296–97, 307

Simenon, Georges, 354

Simmons, Jean, 7–8, 180

Simon, John, 155–56, 158–59, 170, 185, 365

Simon, Neil, 13, 67, 373

Simon, Paul, 140

Sinatra, Frank, 105, 253, 315

Singer, Isaac Bashevis, 206, 232

Sisman, Adam, 27, 31

Sister Carrie (Dreiser), 58

Sitwells, 345, 363

Skidelsky, Robert, 19

Skidelsky, William, 23

Skyfall (movie), 44

Sladek, Nancy, 273

The S-Man (Caine), 313, 347

Smith, F.E., 84

Smith, Frank, 35

Smith, Logan Pearsall, 270

Smith, Sidney, 136

Snobbery (Epstein), 75, 155

Snow, Charles, 273

So Long, See You Tomorrow (Maxwell), 360

Socrates, 208, 211

Sokol, Neal, 373

Soldados de Salamina (Cercas), 134

Sollers, Philippe, 158

Some People (Nicolson), 138

Some Talk of Alexander (Raphael), 204, 210

Somewhere Off The Coast of Maine (Hood), 151

Somme, Battle of the, 20

Sondheim, Stephen, 8–9

Sons and Lovers (Lawrence), 98

Sontag, Susan, 158, 170, 306, 345–46, 363

Sophie's Choice (Styron), 209

The Sopranos (TV show), 34

Sorel, Julien, 375

Sorensen, Ted, 132–33, 137

The Sot-Weed Factor (Barth), 248, 259

Soumission (Houellebecq), 377

Sowell, Thomas, 243

Sparrow, Warden, 27

Speak, Memory (Nabokov), 68, 146, 147, 182

Spectator, 342

Speer, Albert, 225

Spender, Koestler and Co., 27

Spender, Stephen, 32, 86, 105–6, 257–58, 262–63

Spielberg, Steven, 232, 276

Spinoza, Baruch, 83

A Spoilt Boy (Raphael), 118

St. Gertrude's, 23

Stalin, Joseph, 158, 239

Standpoint, 195, 300, 333

Stangneth, Bettina, 330, 333

Stark, Ray, 373

Steele, Shelby, 243

Steiger, Rod, 180

Stein, Gertrude, 88

Stein, Leo, 88

Steinberg, Milton, 309, 324–25

Steiner, George, 71–72, 100, 201, 209, 219, 223, 232, 295, 314, 317–18, 322, 333, 358, 368

Steiner, Zara, 71

Stendhal, 127, 375

Stephen Ward (musical), 36

Stern, Jonathan, 280

Stevenson, Lionel, 379

Stiller, Ben, 66

Stone, Lawrence, 27, 32

Stone, Oliver, 62

Stone, Phil, 96

Stone, Robert, 299, 372

Stoner (Williams), 53

Stoppard, Tom, 26

Storey, David, 255–56, 263

Storr, Anthony, 9, 14

The Story of the Jews (TV series), 163

Strachey, Lytton, 141

Straight, Michael, 343

Strauss, Leo, 337

Stravinsky, Igor, 87, 363
Streep, Meryl, 98, 333
Streisand, Barbra, 304
Striptease (movie), 151
Strout, Elizabeth, 318
Strozzi, Bernardo, 144
Studies in Historiography
   (Momigliano), 90–91
Study of History (Toynbee), 27
Styne, Jule, 8
Styron, William, 181, 208, 209, 212–
   13, 218
"Such, Such Were the Joys" (Orwell),
   146
Suckert, Kurt Erich, 357
Sullivan, Denis, 381–82
Sullivan, John Patrick, 381, 382
Sunday in the Park with George (musi-
   cal), 8
Sunday Telegraph, 118
Sunday Times (newspaper), 27–28, 71,
   84, 99–100, 102
Sunset and Twilight (Berenson), 270–
   71
Sunset Boulevard (movie), 292
The Sunshine Boys (Simon), 13
Sutro, John, 153
Swann, Charles, 59
Swift, Jonathan, 187
Sykes, Christopher, 69, 73–74, 94–95
Syme, Ronald, 206

Tacitus, 29
Tadie, Jean-Yves, 162
Taft, Gene, 61, 200
A Tale of Two Cities (Dickens), 379
Talese, Gay, 105
Taper (pseudonym), 338, 342
Tartt, Donna, 355
Taylor, A.J.P., 29, 31–32, 280, 352
Taylor, D.J., 4, 101, 119
Taylor, Elizabeth, 327
Taylor, Frederick, 40
Taylor Trade Publishers, 120

Teller, Edward, 69
Ten North Frederick (O'Hara), 204
1066 And All That (Yeatman and Sel-
   lar), 211
"Tennants," 13
Tennyson, Alfred Lord, 379
Terkel, Studs, 205
Thackeray, William Makepeace, 17,
   379
That Was the Week That Was (TV
   show), 342
Thatcher, Margaret, 333
Theatre Royal, 83
"These Foolish Things" (Maschwitz), 7
Thieves in the Night (Koestler), 294
Things Past (Muggeridge), 268
The Third Man (Greene), 268
"This Little Light of Mine" (song), 24
This Man, This Woman (movie), 151–
   52, 323
This Sporting Life (Storey), 255
Thomas, Dylan, 24, 294
Thomas, Hugh, 80
Thomas Mann's Diaries, 1918–1939
   (Mann), 16–17
Thompson, Emma, 333
Three Penny Review, 292
Throckmorton, Elizabeth, 247, 366
Thucydides, 90
Ticks and Crosses (Raphael), 1
Tilsley, Vincent, 168
Time, History, and Literature (Auer-
   bach), 40
Time magazine, 23, 345, 354
Times Literary Supplement, 177, 190–
   93, 204, 216, 223, 295, 354, 355,
   362
Titanic (movie, 1953), 292
TLS, 32–33, 79, 82, 85, 102, 108
To Have and Have Not (movie), 252
"To Philosophize Is to Know How to
   Die" (Montaigne), 50
To The Lighthouse (Woolf), 293,
   300

Toibin, Colm, 328
Tolstoy (Troyat), 174, 178
Tolstoy, Leo, 16, 174–75, 364
Tombs, Robert, 374–75, 379
Tommies, 20
Tonys, 8
Top of the Pops, 21–22
Tornatore, Giuseppe, 169
Touchette, Ralph, 179
Town & Country (magazine), 104
Toynbee, Arnold, 27, 32
Tractatus-Logico-Philosophicus
    (Wittgenstein), 323, 347
Transatlantic Blues (Sheed), 284
The Transit of Venus (Hazzard), 254
Transparent Things (Nabokov), 224
Traumnovelle (Schnitzler), 169
Tree, Herbert Beerbohm, 213
Treglown, Jeremy, 134
Trevor-Roper, Hugh, 27, 30–32, 46,
    79, 220, 236, 297, 352
The Trial (Kafka), 308
Trilling, Diana, 197, 212
Trilling, Lionel, 114, 222
Trollope, Anthony, 299
The Trouble With England (Raphael),
    254–55
Troyat, Henri, 173–74, 175, 178
True Detective (TV mini-series), 266
Truffaut, François, 287
Truman, Harry, 271
Tupman, Tracy, 367
Turgenev (Troyat), 174
Turgenev, Ivan, 173–75, 178
Turner, Nat, 208
Turner, Reggie, 35, 36
Turner Classic Movies, 350
Tutin, Dorothy, 12
12 Years a Slave (movie), 62–63, 65
20th Century Fox, 247, 254
Two for the Road (movie), 62, 70, 132–
    33, 152, 247
2001, A Space Odyssey (movie), 217,
    339

Tyldesley-Jones, 226
Tynan, Ken, 6–7, 14, 70, 183, 340
Tyson, Mike, 183

University of Edinburgh, 148
The Untouchables (movie), 173
Updike, John, 55, 138, 149–50, 175,
    181, 194, 259, 299
The Uses of Division (Bayley), 161
Uses of Literacy (Hoggart), 342

Vachaud, Laurent, 168, 169
Valéry, Paul, 295
Vanity Fair (magazine), 105, 167,
    172
"The Vanity of Existence," 41
Varieties of Religious Experience
    (James), 148, 215
Vendler, Helen, 317
Venus, Rokeby, 21
Vermès, Géza, 135
Viardot, Pauline, 174
The View from the Bridge (Miller),
    384
The Virginian (Thackeray), 379
Vogue, 345
Voltaire, 275, 309
von Sternberg, Josef, 362

Wall Street (movie), 62
Wall Street Journal, 4, 25, 165, 188,
    244, 269, 308, 316–17
Walpole, Robert, 235
Waltser, Robert, 17
War and Peace (movie), 224
War and Peace (Tolstoy), 157, 175
Warner, Sylvia Townsend, 258
Warner Bros., 86–87
Warren, Kenneth J., 127
Warren Report, 27
Washington, Denzel, 63
WASPs, 18
Wasserman, Steve, 70, 323
Watson, James, 69

Waugh, Evelyn, 31, 69, 73, 109, 241, 268, 285, 352, 363–64
Webb, Beatrice, 268
Webber, Andrew Lloyd, 313, 318
Webster, Daniel, 187
Wedgwood, C.V., 31
The Weekly Standard, 40, 155, 308
Weiner, Norbert, 336
Weissbord, Burt, 91
A Well-Dressed Man (Raphael), 127
Welles, Orson, 183
Wells, H.G., 39, 46
Weltbuhne (journal), 88
Wenger, Arsène, 93
Werner, Oskar, 281, 286–87
Wesker, Arnold, 3
West, Anthony, 39, 47
West, Nathaniel, 212
West, Rebecca, 39, 47, 95, 265
West Side Story (musical), 8
Wharton, Edith, 300
What Makes Tommy Run (movie), 70
Wheel of Fortune (TV show), 155
Wheeler, John, 212
When Bad Things Happen to Good People (Kushner), 224
The Whisperers (Figes), 28
White, Vanna, 155
"The White Negro: Superficial Reflections on the Hipster" (Bellow), 363
Whitehead, Alfred North, 322
Who'll Stop the Rain (movie), 372
Wiesel, Elie, 231
Wilde, Oscar, 35–36, 98, 113, 349
Wilder, Billy, 252–53, 292, 304
Wilkins, Roy, 242
Wilkson, Alec, 360
Will, George, 76
Willenski, 314
William Morris Agency, 79
Williams, Bernard, 142
Williams, Emlyn, 362
Williams, John, 53, 309

Williams, Raymond, 342
Williams, Robin, 252
Williams, Tennessee, 262, 335
The Williamsburg Trilogy (Fuchs), 154
Williamson, Henry, 228
Willis, Bruce, 80
Wilson, A.N., 79–80, 82
Wilson, Angus, 364, 366
Wilson, Colin, 223
Wilson, Donald, 157
Wilson, Edmund, 14, 89, 158, 259, 299, 306, 344
Wilson, Robert, 280
Wilson, Woodrow, 238, 243
Winchell, Walter, 172, 382
Wineapple, Brenda, 88
Wired (TV show), 34
"Wise, Foolish, Enchanting Lady Mary" (Epstein), 282
Wisse, Ruth, 250
Wittgenstein, Ludwig, 42, 200, 218–19, 294, 322, 358
Wolf, Dick, 34
Wolf on Wall Street (movie), 62–63
Wolfe, Tom, 105, 236
Wolfson, Harry, 224
Wolpe, David, 140
Women in Love (Lawrence), 366
Wood, James, 150
Wood, Natalie, 55
Woods, 159
Woolf, Leonard, 283
Woolf, Virginia, 109, 293, 300, 340
Wordsworth, William, 327, 341
World War II, 42
World Within World (Spender), 258
Wouk, Herman, 55, 209
Wright, Joe, 26
Wrigley Field, 91
The Written Word (Puchner), 321, 325
Wurtzel, Sol, 254
Wyatt, Woodrow, 183–86, 194, 257, 259, 323

Xerxes, 140

Yates, Richard, 44
The Year of Magical Thinking (Didion), 297
Yeats, William Butler, 229
You Can Count on Me (movie), 98
Young, Vernon, 194
Young, Whitney, 242

Your Show of Shows (TV show), 67
Yourcenar, Marguerite, 309

Zangwill, Israel, 71
Zanuck, Darryl, 248
Zanuck, Dick, 247–48
Zibaldone (Leopardi), 53
Zola, Emile, 241, 295
Zuckerberg, Steven, 344